**W9-BBX-337**

Customer service analysis	Database design Database querying and reporting	Chapter 8
Sales lead and customer analysis	Database design Database querying and reporting	Chapter 11
Blog creation and design	Blog creation tool	Chapter 12

Internet Skills

Using online software tools for job hunting and career development	Chapter 1
Using online interactive mapping software to plan efficient transportation routes	Chapter 2
Researching product information Evaluating Web sites for auto sales	Chapter 3
Researching travel costs using online travel sites	Chapter 4
Searching online databases for products and services	Chapter 5
Using Web search engines for business research	Chapter 6
Researching and evaluating business outsourcing services	Chapter 7
Researching and evaluating supply chain management services	Chapter 8
Evaluating e-commerce hosting services	Chapter 9
Using shopping bots to compare product price, features, and availability	Chapter 10
Analyzing Web site design	Chapter 11
Using Internet newsgroups for marketing	Chapter 12

Analytical, Writing, and Presentation Skills *

Business Problem	Chapter
Management analysis of a business	Chapter 1
Value chain and competitive forces analysis Business strategy formulation	Chapter 3
Employee productivity analysis	Chapter 6
Disaster recovery planning	Chapter 7
Locating and evaluating suppliers	Chapter 8
Developing an e-commerce strategy	Chapter 9
Formulating a corporate privacy policy	Chapter 12

Essentials of Management Information Systems

Ninth Edition

Kenneth C. Laudon
New York University

Jane P. Laudon
Azimuth Information Systems

Prentice Hall

Boston   Columbus   Indianapolis   New York   San Francisco   Upper Saddle River
Amsterdam   Cape Town   Dubai   London   Madrid   Milan   Munich   Paris   Montreal   Toronto
Delhi   Mexico City   Sao Paulo   Sydney   Hong Kong   Seoul   Singapore   Taipei   Tokyo

Editorial Director: Sally Yagan
Editor in Chief: Eric Svendsen
Executive Editor: Bob Horan
Editorial Project Manager: Kelly Loftus
Editorial Assistant: Jason Calcano
Director of Marketing: Patrice Lumumba Jones
Senior Marketing Manager: Anne Fahlgren
Marketing Assistant: Melinda Jensen
Senior Managing Editor: Judy Leale
Senior Production Project Manager: Karalyn Holland
Senior Operations Supervisor: Arnold Vila
Operations Specialist: Ilene Kahn
Senior Art Director: Janet Slowik

Art Director: Steve Frim
Cover Illustrator and Designer: Bobby Starnes
Manager, Visual Research: Beth Brenzel
Manager, Rights and Permissions: Shannon Barbe
Manager, Cover Visual Research & Permissions: Karen Sanatar
Media Editor: Denise Vaughn
Media Project Manager: Lisa Rinaldi
Full Service Project Management: Azimuth Interactive, Inc.
Composition: Azimuth Interactive, Inc.
Printer/Binder: Courier/Kendallville
Cover Printer: Lehigh-Phoenix Color/Hagarstown
Text Font: 10.5/12.5 Times LT Std, 9.5pt

Credits and acknowledgements borrowed from other sources and reproduced, with permission, in this textbook appear on page C-1.

Microsoft® and Windows® are registered trademarks of the Microsoft Corporation in the U.S.A. and other countries. Screen shots and icons reprinted with permission from the Microsoft Corporation. This book is not sponsored or endorsed by or affiliated with the Microsoft Corporation.

Library of Congress Cataloging-in-Publication Information is Available

10 9 8 7 6 5 4 3 2 1

Prentice Hall
is an imprint of

www.pearsonhighered.com

ISBN 10: 0-13-611099-1
ISBN 13: 978-0-13-611099-6

About the Authors

Kenneth C. Laudon is a Professor of Information Systems at New York University's Stern School of Business. He holds a B.A. in Economics from Stanford and a Ph.D. from Columbia University. He has authored twelve books dealing with electronic commerce, information systems, organizations, and society. Professor Laudon has also written over forty articles concerned with the social, organizational, and management impacts of information systems, privacy, ethics, and multimedia technology.

Professor Laudon's current research is on the planning and management of large-scale information systems and multimedia information technology. He has received grants from the National Science Foundation to study the evolution of national information systems at the Social Security Administration, the IRS, and the FBI. Ken's research focuses on enterprise system implementation, computer-related organizational and occupational changes in large organizations, changes in management ideology, changes in public policy, and understanding productivity change in the knowledge sector.

Ken Laudon has testified as an expert before the United States Congress. He has been a researcher and consultant to the Office of Technology Assessment (United States Congress), Department of Homeland Security, and to the Office of the President, several executive branch agencies, and Congressional Committees. Professor Laudon also acts as an in-house educator for several consulting firms and as a consultant on systems planning and strategy to several Fortune 500 firms.

At NYU's Stern School of Business, Ken Laudon teaches courses on Managing the Digital Firm, Information Technology and Corporate Strategy, Professional Responsibility (Ethics), and Electronic Commerce and Digital Markets. Ken Laudon's hobby is sailing.

Jane Price Laudon is a management consultant in the information systems area and the author of seven books. Her special interests include systems analysis, data management, MIS auditing, software evaluation, and teaching business professionals how to design and use information systems.

Jane received her Ph.D. from Columbia University, her M.A. from Harvard University, and her B.A. from Barnard College. She has taught at Columbia University and the New York University Stern School of Business. She maintains a lifelong interest in Oriental languages and civilizations.

The Laudons have two daughters, Erica and Elisabeth, to whom this book is dedicated.

Brief Contents

Complete Contents

II Information Technology Infrastructure 113

III Key System Applications for the Digital Age 269

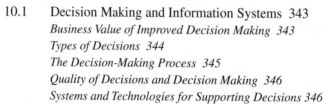

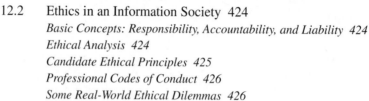

Preface

We wrote this book for business school students who wanted an in-depth look at how today's business firms use information technologies and systems to achieve corporate objectives in 2010. Information systems are one of the major tools available to business managers for achieving operational excellence, developing new products and services, improving decision making, and achieving competitive advantage. Students will find here the most up-to-date and comprehensive overview of information systems used by business firms today.

When interviewing potential employees, business firms often look for new hires who know how to use information systems and technologies for achieving bottom-line business results. Regardless of whether you are an accounting, finance, management, operations management, marketing, or information systems major, the knowledge and information you find in this book will be valuable throughout your business career.

What's New in This Edition

CURRENCY

The 9th edition features all new opening, closing and "Interactive Session" cases. The text, figures, tables, and cases have been updated through October 2009 with the latest sources from industry and MIS research.

NEW FEATURES

- 2 new Management Decision Problems per chapter
- New Video Cases Package: 26 video case studies (2 or more per chapter) and 12 instructional videos
- New Collaboration and Teamwork Projects in each chapter using open-source collaboration tools
- New online Learning Tracks extend learning beyond the book

NEW TOPICS

- Emerging mobile digital platform
- Collaboration systems and tools
- Cloud computing
- Cloud-based software services and tools
- Windows 7 and mobile operating systems
- Office 2010 and Google Apps
- Green computing
- 4G networks
- Unified communications
- Network neutrality
- Search engine optimization (SEO)
- Free/Freemium e-commerce business models

- The 'wisdom of crowds' and crowdsourcing
- E-Commerce revenue models
- Building an e-commerce Web site
- Business process management
- Web mining and text mining
- Unified threat management
- Security issues for cloud and mobile platforms
- Next-generation enterprise applications

What's New in MIS?

Plenty. In fact, there's a whole new world of doing business using new technologies for managing and organizing. What makes the MIS field the most exciting area of study in schools of business is the continuous change in technology, management, and business processes. (Chapter 1 describes these changes in more detail.)

A continuing stream of information technology innovations is transforming the traditional business world. Examples include the emergence of cloud computing, the growth of a mobile digital business platform based on smartphones and netbook computers, and not least, the use of social networks by managers to achieve business objectives. Most of these changes have occurred in the last few years. These innovations are enabling entrepreneurs and innovative traditional firms to create new products and services, develop new business models, and transform the day-to-day conduct of business. In the process, some old businesses, even industries, are being destroyed while new businesses are springing up.

For instance, the emergence of online music stores—driven by millions of consumers who prefer iPods and MP3 players—has forever changed the older business model of music on physical devices, such as records and CDs. Online video rentals are similarly transforming the old model of distributing films through theaters and then through DVD rentals at physical stores. New high-speed broadband connections to the home have supported these two business changes.

E-commerce is back, generating over $230 billion in revenues in 2009, and estimated to grow to over $330 billion in 2014. Amazon's revenues grew 19% annually in 2009 despite the recession, while offline retail declined 14%. E-commerce is changing how firms design, produce and deliver their products and services. E-commerce has reinvented itself again, disrupting the traditional marketing and advertising industry and putting major media and content firms in jeopardy. Facebook and other social networking sites such as YouTube, Twitter, and Second Life, exemplify the new face of e-commerce in the 21st Century. They provide services and sell ad space. When we think of e-commerce we tend to think of a selling physical products. While this iconic vision of e-commerce is still very powerful, and the fastest growing form of retail in the U.S., growing up alongside is a whole new value stream based on selling services, not goods. It's a services model of e-commerce. Information systems and technologies are the foundation of this new services-based e-commerce.

Likewise, the management of business firms has changed: With new mobile smartphones, high-speed wireless Wi-Fi networks, and wireless laptop computers, remote salespeople on the road are only seconds away from their managers' questions and oversight. Managers on the move are in direct, continuous contact with their employees. The growth of enterprise-wide information systems with extraordinarily rich data means that managers no longer operate in a fog of confusion, but instead have online, nearly instant, access to the really important information they need for accurate and timely decisions. In addition to their public uses on the Web, wikis and blogs are becoming important corporate tools for communication, collaboration, and information sharing.

The Ninth Edition: The Comprehensive Solution for the MIS Curriculum

Since its inception, this text has helped to define the MIS course around the globe. This edition continues to be authoritative, but is also more customizable, flexible, and geared to meeting the needs of different colleges, universities, and individual instructors. This book is now part of a complete learning package that includes the core text and an extensive offering of supplemental materials on the Web.

The core text consists of 12 chapters with hands-on projects covering the most essential topics in MIS. New to the core text this year is the Video Case Study and Instructional Video Package: 26 video case studies plus 12 instructional videos that illustrate business uses of information systems, explain new technologies, and explore concepts. Videos are keyed to the topics of each chapter. In addition, for students and instructors who want to go deeper into selected topics, there are forty-seven online Learning Tracks that cover a variety of MIS topics in greater depth.

MyMISLab provides more in-depth coverage of chapter topics, career resources, additional case studies, supplementary chapter material, and data files for hands-on projects.

THE CORE TEXT

The core text provides an overview of fundamental MIS concepts using an integrated framework for describing and analyzing information systems. This framework shows information systems composed of people, organization, and technology elements and is reinforced in student projects and case studies.

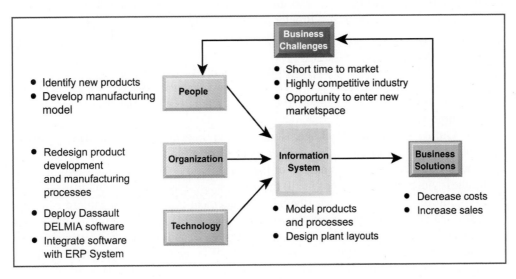

A diagram accompanying each chapter-opening case graphically illustrates how people, organization, and technology elements work together to create an information system solution to the business challenges discussed in the case.

Chapter Organization
Each chapter contains the following elements:
- A chapter-opening case describing a real-world organization to establish the theme and importance of the chapter
- A diagram analyzing the opening case in terms of the management, organization, and technology model used throughout the text
- A series of Learning Objectives
- Two Interactive Sessions with Case Study Questions and MIS in Action projects
- A Hands-on MIS Projects section featuring two Management Decision Problems, a hands-on application software project, and a project to develop Internet skills
- A Learning Tracks section identifying supplementary material on MyMISLab

- A chapter Review Summary keyed to the Student Learning Objectives
- A list of Key Terms that students can use to review concepts
- Review Questions for students to test their comprehension of chapter material
- Discussion Questions raised by the broader themes of the chapter
- Video Cases. Instructors can download step-by-step instructions for accessing the video cases from the Instructor Resources page at www.pearsonhighered.com/laudon.
- A Collaboration and Teamwork project to develop teamwork and presentation skills, with options for using open-source collaboration tools
- A chapter-ending case study for students to apply chapter concepts

KEY FEATURES

We have enhanced the text to make it more interactive, leading-edge, and appealing to both students and instructors. The ninth edition includes the following features and learning tools:

Business-Driven with Real-World Business Cases and Examples

The text helps students see the direct connection between information systems and business performance. It describes the main business objectives driving the use of information systems and technologies in corporations all over the world: operational excellence; new products and services; customer and supplier intimacy; improved decision making; competitive advantage; and survival. In-text examples and case studies show students how specific companies use information systems to achieve these objectives.

We use current (2010) examples from business and public organizations throughout the text to illustrate the important concepts in each chapter. All the case studies describe companies or organizations that are familiar to students, such as Google, Facebook, Twitter, Coca-Cola, eBay, the New York Yankees, Procter & Gamble, and the Boston Celtics.

Interactivity

There's no better way to learn about MIS than by doing MIS! We provide different kinds of hands-on projects where students can work with real-world business scenarios and data, and learn first hand what MIS is all about. These projects heighten student involvement in this exciting subject.

- **New Online Video Case Package.** Heighten your students' interest in MIS by having them watch short videos online, either in-class or at home or work, then apply the concepts of the book to the analysis of the video. Every chapter contains two or more business video cases (26 videos in all) that explain how business firms and managers are using information systems, describe new management practices, and explore concepts discussed in the chapter. Each video case consists of a video about a real-world company, or a concept in MIS, a background text case, and case study questions. These video cases enhance students' understanding of MIS topics and the relevance of MIS to the business world. In addition, there are 12 Instructional Videos that describe developments and concepts in MIS, keyed to respective chapters.
- **New Management Decision Problems.** 2 new Management Decision Problems per chapter teach students how to apply chapter concepts to real-world business scenarios requiring analysis and decision making.
- **New Collaboration and Teamwork Projects.** Each chapter features a collaborative project that encourages students working in teams to use Google sites, Google Docs, and other open-source collaboration tools. The first team project in Chapter 1 asks students to build a collaborative Google site.
- **Hands-on MIS Projects.** Every chapter concludes with a Hands-on MIS Projects section containing three types of projects: two Management Decision Problems, a hands-on application software exercise using Microsoft Excel, Access, or Web page and blog creation tools, and a project that develops Internet business skills. A Dirt Bikes

MANAGEMENT DECISION PROBLEMS

1. U.S. Pharma Corporation is headquartered in New Jersey but has research sites Germany, France, the United Kingdom, Switzerland, and Australia. Research and development of new pharmaceuticals is the key to ongoing profits, and U.S. Pharma researches and tests thousands of possible drugs. The company's researchers need to share information with others within and outside the company, including the U.S. Food and Drug Administration, the World Health Organization, and the International Federation of Pharmaceutical Manufacturers & Associations. Also critical is access to health information sites, such as the U.S. National Library of Medicine and to industry conferences and professional journals. Design a knowledge portal for U.S. Pharma's researchers. Include in your design specifications relevant internal systems and databases, external sources of information, and internal and external communication and collaboration tools. Design a home page for your portal.

Two real-world business scenarios per chapter provide opportunities for students to apply chapter concepts and practice management decision making.

The database includes fields for store identification number, sales region number, item number, item description, unit price, units sold, and the weekly sales period when the sales were made.

ID	Store No	Sales Region	Item No	Item Description	Unit Price	Units Sold	Week Ending
1	1	South	2005	17" monitor	$229.00	28	8/28/2009
2	1	South	2005	17" monitor	$229.00	30	9/25/2009
3	1	South	2005	17" monitor	$229.00	9	10/30/2009
4	1	South	3006	101 Keyboard	$19.95	30	8/28/2009
5	1	South	3006	101 Keyboard	$19.95	35	9/25/2009
6	1	South	3006	101 Keyboard	$19.95	39	10/30/2009
7	1	South	6050	PC Mouse	$8.95	28	8/28/2009
8	1	South	6050	PC Mouse	$8.95	3	9/25/2009
9	1	South	6050	PC Mouse	$8.95	38	10/30/2009
10	1	South	8500	Desktop CPU	$849.95	25	8/28/2009

Record: 1 of 10   No Filter   Search

Develop some reports and queries to make this information more useful for running the business. Sales and production managers want answers to the following questions:
- Which products should be restocked?
- Which stores and sales regions would benefit from a promotional campaign and additional marketing?
- When (what time of year) should products be offered at full price, and when should discounts be used?

You can easily modify the database table to find and report your answers. Print your

Students practice using software in real-world settings for achieving operational excellence and enhancing decision making.

IMPROVING DECISION MAKING: USING INTELLIGENT AGENTS FOR COMPARISON SHOPPING

Software skills: Web browser and shopping bot software
Business skills: Product evaluation and selection

This project will give you experience using shopping bots to search online for products, find product information, and find the best prices and vendors.

You have decided to purchase a new digital camera. Select a digital camera you might want to purchase, such as the Canon PowerShot SX120 or the Olympus Stylus-7010. To purchase the camera as inexpensively as possible, try several of the shopping bot sites, which do the price comparisons for you. Visit MySimon (www.mysimon.com), BizRate.com (www.bizrate.com), and Google Product Search. Compare these shopping sites in terms of their ease of use, number of offerings, speed in obtaining information, thoroughness of information offered about the product and seller, and price selection. Which site or sites would you use and why? Which camera would you select and why? How helpful were these sites for making your decision?

Each chapter features a project to develop Internet skills for accessing information, conducting research, and performing online calculations and analysis.

USA Running Case in MyMISLab provides additional hands-on projects for each chapter.

- **Interactive Sessions.** Two short cases in each chapter have been redesigned as Interactive Sessions to be used in the classroom (or on Internet discussion boards) to stimulate student interest and active learning. Each case concludes with two types of activities: *Case Study Questions* and *MIS in Action*. The *Case Study Questions* provide topics for class discussion, Internet discussion, or written assignments. *MIS in Action* features hands-on Web activities for exploring issues discussed in the case more deeply.

Each chapter contains two Interactive Sessions on People, Organizations, or Technology using real-world companies to illustrate chapter concepts and issues.

INTERACTIVE SESSION: PEOPLE   Credit Bureau Errors—Big People Problems

You've found the car of your dreams, you have a good job and enough money for a down payment. All you need is an auto loan for $14,000. You have a few credit card bills, which you diligently pay off each month. But when you apply for the loan you're turned down. When you ask why, you're told you have an overdue loan from a bank you've never heard of. You've just become one of the millions of people who have been victimized by inaccurate or outdated data in credit bureaus' information systems.

Most data on U.S. consumers' credit histories are collected and maintained by three national credit reporting agencies: Experian, Equifax, and TransUnion. These organizations collect data from various sources to create a detailed dossier of an individual's borrowing and bill paying habits. This information helps lenders assess a person's credit worthiness, the ability to pay back a loan, and can affect the interest rate and other terms of a loan, including whether a loan will be granted in the first place. It can even affect the chances of finding a job, since employers increasingly check credit reports before hiring new employees.

U.S. credit bureaus collect personal information and financial data from a variety of sources, including creditors, lenders, utilities, debt collection agencies, and the courts. These data are aggregated and stored in massive databases maintained by the credit bureaus. The credit bureaus then sell this information to other companies to use for credit assessment.

The credit bureaus claim they know which credit cards are in each consumer's wallet, how much is due on the mortgage, and whether the electric bill is paid on time. But if the wrong information gets into their systems, whether through identity theft or errors transmitted by creditors, watch out! Untangling the mess can be almost impossible.

The bureaus understand the importance of providing accurate information to both lenders and con-

Identifying personal information includes items such as first name, last name and middle initial, full current address and zip code, full previous address and zip code, and social security number. The new credit information goes into the consumer credit file that it best matches.

The credit bureaus rarely obtain all the information matching in all the fields, so they have to determine how much variation to allow and still call it a match. Imperfect data lead to imperfect matches. A consumer might provide incomplete or inaccurate information on a credit application. A creditor might submit incomplete or inaccurate information to the credit bureaus. If the wrong person matches better than anyone else, the data could unfortunately go into the wrong account.

Perhaps the consumer didn't write clearly on the account application. Name variations on different credit accounts can also result in less- than-perfect matches. Take the name Edward Jeffrey Johnson. One account may say Edward Johnson. Another may say Ed Johnson. Another might say Edward J. Johnson. Suppose the last two digits of Edward's social security number get transposed—more chance for mismatches.

If the name or social security number on another person's account partially matches the data in your file, the computer might attach that person's data to your record. Your record might likewise be corrupted if workers in companies supplying tax and bankruptcy data from court and government records accidentally transpose a digit or misread a document.

The credit bureaus claim it is impossible for them to monitor the accuracy of the 3.5 billion pieces of credit account information they receive each month. They must continually contend with bogus claims from consumers who falsify lender information or use shady credit-repair companies that challenge all the negative information on a credit report regardless of its validity. To separate the good from the bad, the credit

MIS in Action projects encourage students to learn more about the companies and issues discussed in the case studies.

CASE STUDY QUESTIONS   MIS IN ACTION

1. Assess the business impact of credit bureaus' data quality problems (for the credit bureaus, for lenders, for individuals).

2. Are any ethical issues raised by credit bureaus' data quality problems? Explain your answer.

3. Analyze the people, organization, and technology factors responsible for credit bureaus' data quality problems.

4. What can be done to solve these problems?

Go to the Experian Web site (www.experian.com) and explore the site, with special attention to its services for businesses and small businesses. Then answer the following questions:

1. List and describe five services for businesses and explain how each uses consumer data. Describe the kinds of businesses that would use these services.

2. Explain how each of these services is affected by inaccurate consumer data.

ASSESSMENT AND AACSB ASSESSMENT GUIDELINES

The Association to Advance Collegiate Schools of Business (AACSB) is a not-for-profit corporation of educational institutions, corporations and other organizations that seeks to improve business education primarily by accrediting university business programs. As a part of its accreditation activities, the AACSB has developed an Assurance of Learning Program designed to ensure that schools do in fact teach students what they promise. Schools are required to state a clear mission, develop a coherent business program, identify student learning objectives, and then prove that students do in fact achieve the objectives.

We have attempted in this book to support AACSB efforts to encourage assessment-based education. The front end papers of this edition identify student learning objectives and anticipated outcomes for our Hands-on MIS projects. In the Instructor Resource Center and MyMISLab is a more inclusive and detailed *assessment matrix* that identifies the learning objectives of each chapter and points to all the available assessment tools for ensuring students in fact do achieve the learning objectives. Because each school is different and may have different missions and learning objectives, no single document can satisfy all situations. The authors will provide custom advice on how to use this text in their colleges with different missions and assessment needs. Please e-mail the authors or contact your local Pearson Prentice Hall representative for contact information.

For more information on the AACSB Assurance of Learning Program, and how this text supports assessment-based learning, please visit the Instructor Resource Center and MyMISLab.

Customization and Flexibility: New Learning Track Modules:

Our **Learning Tracks** feature gives instructors the flexibility to provide in-depth coverage of the topics they choose. There are over forty Learning Tracks available to instructors and students. A Learning Tracks section at the end of each chapter directs students to short essays or additional chapters in MyMISLab. This supplementary content takes students deeper into MIS topics, concepts and debates; reviews basic technology concepts in hardware, software, database design, telecommunications, and other areas; and provide additional hands-on software instruction. The Ninth Edition includes new Learning Tracks on Cloud Computing, Managing Knowledge and Collaboration, Web 2.0, The Mobile Digital Platform, and A Primer on Business Process Management, plus additional coverage of Computer Hardware and Software technology.

Author-Certified Test bank and Supplements

- **Author-Certified Test Bank.** The authors have worked closely with skilled test item writers to ensure that higher level cognitive skills are tested. Test bank multiple choice questions include questions on content, but also include many questions that require analysis, synthesis, and evaluation skills.
- **Annotated Slides.** The authors have prepared a comprehensive collection of fifty PowerPoint slides to be used in your lectures. Many of these slides are the same as used by Ken Laudon in his MIS classes and executive education presentations. Each of the slides is annotated with teaching suggestions for asking students questions, developing in-class lists that illustrate key concepts, and recommending other firms as examples in addition to those provided in the text. The annotations are like an Instructor's Manual built into the slides and make it easier to teach the course effectively.

Globalization

This edition has even more global emphasis than previous editions. New material on globalization (Chapter 1), global workgroup collaboration (Chapter 2), software localization (Chapter 4), global security threats (Chapter 7), global supply chains (Chapter 8), global marketplaces (Chapter 9), and offshore outsourcing (Chapter 11), accompanied by numerous examples of multinational and non-U.S. companies, show how to use IS in a global business environment.

Student Learning-Focused

Student Learning Objectives are organized around a set of study questions to focus student attention. Each chapter concludes with a Review Summary and Review Questions organized around these study questions.

MyMISLab

MyMISLab is a Web-based assessment and tutorial tool that provides practice and testing while personalizing course content and providing student and class assessment and reporting. Your course is not the same as the course taught down the hall. Now, all the resources both you and your students need for course success are in one place—flexible and easily organized and adapted for your individual course experience. Visit www.mymislab.com to see how you can Teach. Learn. Experience. MIS.

Career Resources

MyMISLab also provides extensive Career Resources, including job-hunting guides and instructions on how to build a Digital Portfolio demonstrating the business knowledge, application software proficiency, and Internet skills acquired from using the text. The portfolio can be included in a resume or job application or used as a learning assessment tool for instructors.

Instructional Support Materials

Instructor's Resource CD-ROM

Most of the support materials described in the following sections are conveniently available for adopters on the Instructor's Resource CD-ROM. The CD includes the Instructor's Manual, Lecture Notes, Test Item File, PowerPoint slides, and the helpful lecture tool "Image Library."

Image Library (on Web and Instructor's Resource CD-ROM)

The Image Library is an impressive resource to help instructors create vibrant lecture presentations. Almost every figure and photo in the text is provided and organized by chapter for convenience. These images and lecture notes can be imported easily into Microsoft PowerPoint to create new presentations or to add to existing ones.

Instructor's Manual (on Web and Instructor's Resource CD-ROM)

The Instructor's Manual features not only answers to review, discussion, case study, and group project questions but also an in-depth lecture outline, teaching objectives, key terms, teaching suggestions, and Internet resources.

Test Item File (on Web and Instructor's Resource CD-ROM)

The Test Item File is a comprehensive collection of true—false, multiple-choice, fill-in-the-blank, and essay questions. The questions are rated by difficulty level and the answers are referenced by section. The test item file also contains questions tagged to the AACSB learning standards. An electronic version of the Test Item File is available in TestGen and TestGen conversions are available for BlackBoard or WebCT course management systems. All TestGen files are available for download at the Instructor Resource Center.

PowerPoint Slides (on Web and Instructor's Resource CD-ROM)

Electronic color slides created by Azimuth Interactive Corporation, Inc., are available in Microsoft PowerPoint. The slides illuminate and build on key concepts in the text.

Video Cases and Instructional Videos

Instructors can download step-by-step instructions for accessing the video cases from the Instructor Resources page at www.pearsonhighered.com/laudon.

The following is a list of video cases and instructional videos:

Chapter	Video
Chapter 1: Business Information Systems in Your Career	Case 1: UPS Global Operations with the DIAD IV Case 2: IBM, Cisco, Google: Global Warming by Computer
Chapter 2: Global E-Business: and Collaboration	Case 1: How FedEx Works: Enterprise Systems Case 2: Oracle's Austin Data Center Instructional Video 1: FedEx Improves Customer Experience with Integrated Mapping & Location Data
Chapter 3: Achieving Competitive Advantage with Information Systems	Case 1: National Basketball Association: Competing on Global Delivery With Akamai OS Streaming Case 2: Customer Relationship Management for San Francisco's City Government
Chapter 4: IT Infrastructure: Hardware and Software	Case 1: Hudson's Bay Company and IBM: Virtual Blade Platform Case 2: Salesforce.com: SFA on the iPhone and iPod Touch Instructional Video 1: Google and IBM Produce Cloud Computing Instructional Video 2: IBM Blue Cloud is Ready-to-Use Computing Instructional Video 3: What the Hell is Cloud Computing? Instructional Video 4: What is AJAX and How Does it Work? Instructional Video 5: Yahoo's FireEagle Geolocation Service
Chapter 5: Foundations of Business Intelligence: Databases and Information Management	Case 1: Maruti Suzuki Business Intelligence and Enterprise Databases Case 2: Data Warehousing at REI: Understanding the Customer
Chapter 6: Telecommunications, the Internet, and Wireless Technology	Case 1: Cisco Telepresence: Meeting Without Traveling Case 2: Unified Communications Systems With Virtual Collaboration: IBM and Forterra Instructional Video 1: AT&T Launches Managed Cisco Telepresence Solution Instructional Video 2: CNN Telepresence Instructional Video 3: Microsoft: Unified Communications and Pos MalaysiaManagement
Chapter 7: Securing Information Systems	Case 1: IBM Zone Trusted Information Channel (ZTIC) Case 2: Open ID and Web Security Instructional Video 1: The Quest for Identity 2.0 Instructional Video 2: Identity 2.0
Chapter 8: Achieving Operational Excellence and Customer Intimacy: Enterprise Applications	Case 1: Sinosteel Strengthens Business Management with ERP Applications Case 2: Ingram Micro and H&R Block Get Close to Their Customers
Chapter 9: E-Commerce: Digital Markets, Digital Goods	Case 1: M-Commerce: The Past, Present, and Future Case 2: Ford AutoXchange B2B Marketplace
Chapter 10: Improving Decision Making and Managing Knowledge	Case 1: L'Oréal: Knowledge Management Using Microsoft SharePoint Case 2: IdeaScale Crowdsourcing: Where Ideas Come to Life Case 3: Antivia: Community-based Collaborative Business Intelligence Case 4: IBM and Cognos: Business Intelligence and Analytics for Improved Decision Making
Chapter 11: Building Information Systems and Managing Projects	Case 1: IBM: Business Process Management in a Service-Oriented Architecture Case 2: Startup Appcelerator For Rapid Rich App Development Instructional Video 1: Salesforce and Google: Developing Sales Support Systems with Online Apps
Chapter 12: Ethical and Social Issues in Information Systems	Case 1: Net Neutrality: Neutral Networks Work Case 2: Data Mining for Terrorists and Innocents

Acknowledgments

The production of any book involves valued contributions from a number of persons. We would like to thank all of our editors for encouragement, insight, and strong support for many years. We thank Bob Horan for guiding the development of this edition and Kelly Loftus for her role in managing the project.

We praise Karalyn Holland for overseeing production for this project. Our special thanks go to our supplement authors for their work. We are indebted to William Anderson for his assistance in the writing and production of the text and to Megan Miller for her help during production. We thank Diana R. Craig for her assistance with database topics.

Special thanks to colleagues at the Stern School of Business at New York University; to Professor Edward Stohr of Stevens Institute of Technology; to Professors Al Croker and Michael Palley of Baruch College and New York University; to Professor Lawrence Andrew of Western Illinois University; to Professor Detlef Schoder of the University of Cologne; to Professor Walter Brenner of the University of St. Gallen; to Professor Lutz Kolbe of the University of Gottingen; to Professor Donald Marchand of the International Institute for Management Development; and to Professor Daniel Botha of Stellenbosch University who provided additional suggestions for improvement. Thank you to Professor Ken Kraemer, University of California at Irvine, and Professor John King, University of Michigan, for more than a decade's long discussion of information systems and organizations. And a special remembrance and dedication to Professor Rob Kling, University of Indiana, for being my friend and colleague over so many years.

We also want to especially thank all our reviewers whose suggestions helped improve our texts. Reviewers for this edition include the following:

Sherry L. Fowler, *North Carolina State University*
Richard Grenci, *John Carroll University*
Shohreh Hashemi, *University of Houston—Downtown*
Duke Hutchings, *Elon University*
Jeffrey Livermore, *Walsh College*
Michelle Parker, *Indiana University—Purdue University Fort Wayne*
Peter A. Rosen, *University of Evansville*
Donna M. Schaeffer, *Marymount University*
Werner Schenk, *University of Rochester*
Marie A. Wright, *Western Connecticut State University*
James H. Yu, *Santa Clara University*
Fan Zhao, *Florida Gulf Coast University*

Information Systems in the Digital Age

PART I

1 **Business Information Systems in Your Career**

2 **Global E-Business and Collaboration**

3 **Achieving Competitive Advantage with Information Systems**

Part I introduces the major themes and the problem-solving approaches that are used throughout the book. While surveying the role of information systems in today's businesses, this part raises several major questions: What is an information system? Why are information systems so essential in businesses today? How can information systems help businesses become more competitive? What do I need to know about information systems to succeed in my business career?

Business Information Systems in Your Career

CHAPTER 1

STUDENT LEARNING OBJECTIVES

After completing this chapter, you will be able to answer the following questions:

1. How are information systems transforming business, and what is their relationship to globalization?

2. Why are information systems so essential for running and managing a business today?

3. What exactly is an information system? How does it work? What are its people, organization, and technology components?

4. How will a four-step method for business problem solving help you solve information system-related problems?

5. How will information systems affect business careers, and what information systems skills and knowledge are essential?

CHAPTER OUTLINE

THE NEW YANKEE STADIUM LOOKS TO THE FUTURE

Although baseball is a sport, it's also big business, requiring revenue from tickets to games, television broadcasts, and other sources to pay for teams. Salaries for top players have ballooned, as have ticket prices. Many fans now watch games on television rather than attending them in person or choose other forms of entertainment, such as electronic games. One way to keep stadiums full of fans, and to keep fans at home happy as well, is to enrich the fan experience by offering more video and services based on technology. When the New York Yankees built a new Yankee Stadium, they did just that.

The new Yankee Stadium, which opened on April 2, 2009, isn't just another ballpark: It's the stadium of the future. It is the most wired, connected, and video-enabled stadium in all of baseball. Although the new stadium is similar in design to the original Yankee Stadium, built in 1923, the interior has more space and amenities, including more intensive use of video and computer technology. Baseball fans love video. According to Ron Ricci, co-chairman of Cisco Systems' sports and entertainment divi-

sion, "It's what fans want to see, to see more angles and do it on their terms." Cisco Systems supplied the computer and networking technology for the new stadium.

Throughout the stadium, including the Great Hall, the Yankees Museum, and in-stadium restaurants and concession areas, 1,100 flat-panel high-definition TV monitors display live game coverage, up-to-date sports scores, archival and highlight video, promotional messages, news, weather, and traffic updates. There is also a huge monitor in center field that is 100 feet wide and 59 feet high. At the conclusion of games, the monitors provide up-to-the-moment traffic information and directions to the nearest stadium exits.

The monitors are designed to surround fans visually from the moment they enter the stadium, especially when they stray from a direct view of the ball field. The pervasiveness of this technology ensures that while fans are buying a hamburger or a soda, they will never miss a play. The Yankees team controls all the monitors centrally and is able to offer different content on each one. Monitors are located at concession stands, around restaurants and bars, in restrooms, and inside 59 luxury and party suites. If a Yankee player wants to review a game to see how he played, monitors in the team's video room will display what he did from any angle. Each Yankee also has a computer at his locker.

The luxury suites have special touch-screen phones for well-heeled fans to use when ordering food and merchandise. At the stadium business center, Cisco interactive videoconferencing technology will link to a library in the Bronx and to other New York City locations, such as hospitals. Players and executives will be able to videoconference and talk to fans before or after the games. Eventually, data and video from the Stadium will be delivered to fans' home televisions and mobile devices. And inside the stadium, fans in each seat will be able to use their mobile phones to order from the concessions or view instant replays.

The Yankees also have their own Web site, Yankees.com, where fans can watch in-market Yankees games live online, check game scores, find out more about their favorite players, purchase tickets to games, and shop for caps, baseball cards and memorabilia. The site also features fantasy baseball games, where fans compete with each other by managing "fantasy teams" based on real players' statistics.

Sources: Dean Meminger, "Yankees' New Stadium Is More than a Ballpark," NY2.com, April 2, 2009; Richard Sandomir, "Boldly Going Where No Stadium Has Gone Before," *The New York Times*, November 12, 2008; and "Cisco Systems, "Cisco Brings High-Definition Video and Advanced Communications Technology to the New Yankee Stadium, Creating the Ultimate Fan Experience," Cisco.com, November 11, 2008.

The challenges facing the New York Yankees and other baseball teams show why information systems are so essential today. Major league baseball is a business as well as a sport, and teams such as the Yankees need to take in revenue from games in order to stay in business. Ticket prices have risen, stadium attendance is dwindling for some teams, and the sport must also compete with other forms of entertainment, including electronic games and the Internet.

The chapter-opening diagram calls attention to important points raised by this case and this chapter. To increase stadium attendance and revenue, the New York Yankees chose to modernize Yankee Stadium and rely on information technology to provide new interactive services to fans inside and outside the Stadium. These services include high-definition television monitors displaying live game coverage, up-to-date sports scores, video, promotional messages, news, weather, and traffic information; touch screens for ordering food and merchandise; interactive videoconferencing technology for connecting to fans and the community; and, eventually, data and video broadcast to fans' home television sets and mobile handhelds. The Yankees' Web site provides a new channel for interacting with fans, selling tickets to games, and selling other team-related products.

It is also important to note that these technologies changed the way the Yankees run their business. Yankee Stadium's systems for delivering game coverage, information, and interactive services changed the flow of work for ticketing, seating, crowd management, and ordering food and other items from concessions. These changes had to be carefully planned to make sure they enhanced service, efficiency, and profitability.

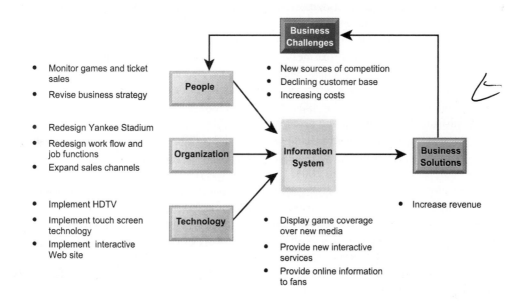

1.1 The Role of Information Systems in Business Today

It's not business as usual in America any more, or the rest of the global economy. In 2009, American businesses will invest nearly $1 trillion in information systems hardware, software, and telecommunications equipment—more than half of all capital investment in the United States. In addition, they will spend another $275 billion on business and management consulting and services-much of which involves redesigning firms' business operations to take advantage of these new technologies. More than half of all business investment in the United States each year involves information systems and technologies.

HOW INFORMATION SYSTEMS ARE TRANSFORMING BUSINESS

You can see the results of this massive spending around you every day by observing how people conduct business. More wireless cell phone accounts were opened in 2008 than telephone landlines installed. Cell phones, BlackBerrys, wireless handhelds, e-mail, and online conferencing over the Internet have all become essential tools of business. In 2008, more than 75 million businesses had dot-com Internet sites registered. Approximately 199 million Americans are online, 14 million purchase something every day on the Internet, 40 million research a product, and 100 million use a search engine. What this means is that if you and your business aren't connected to the Internet and wireless networks, chances are you are not being as effective as you could be (Pew Internet and American Life, 2009).

Despite the economic downturn in 2008, FedEx moved over 200 million packages in the United States, mostly overnight, and United Parcel Service (UPS) moved more than 600 million packages, as businesses sought to sense and respond to rapidly changing customer demand, reduce inventories to the lowest possible levels, and achieve higher levels of operational efficiency. Supply chains have become more fast paced, with companies of all sizes depending on the delivery of just-in-time inventory to help them compete. Companies today manage their inventories in near real time in order to reduce their overhead costs and get to market faster. If you are not a part of this new supply chain management economy, chances are your business is not as efficient as it could be.

As newspaper readership continues to decline, 106 million people read at least some of their news online, 70 million read actual newspapers online, and 88 million use a social networking site like Facebook or MySpace. Sixty million bank online, and 55 million now read blogs, creating an explosion of new writers, readers, and new forms of customer feedback that did not exist before. Adding to this mix of new social media, about 8 million people use Twitter, the online and cellular text messaging service, including many Fortune 1000 firms communicating with their customers. This means your customers are empowered and able to talk to each other about your business products and services. Do you have a solid online customer relationship program in place? Do you know what your customers are saying about your firm? Is your marketing department listening?

E-commerce and Internet advertising are growing in 2009 despite an economic recession at a time when traditional advertising and commerce are shrinking. Google's online ad revenues surpassed $22 billion in 2008. E-commerce revenues expanded over 5 percent in 2008, and showed no decline in 2009 (while traditional retail fell 5 percent). Is your advertising department reaching this new Web-based customer?

New federal security and accounting laws require many businesses to keep e-mail messages for five years. Coupled with existing occupational and health laws requiring firms to store employee chemical exposure data for up to 60 years, these laws are spurring the growth of digital information now estimated to be 5 exabytes, equivalent to 37,000 Libraries of Congress. Does your compliance department meet the minimal requirements for storing financial, health, and occupational information? If they don't, your entire business may be at risk.

Briefly, it's a new world of doing business, one that will greatly affect your future business career. Along with the changes in business come changes in jobs and careers. No matter whether you are a finance, accounting, management, marketing, operations management, or information systems major, how you work, where you work, and how well you are compensated will all be affected by business information systems. The purpose of this book is to help you understand and benefit from these new business realities and opportunities.

WHAT'S NEW IN MANAGEMENT INFORMATION SYSTEMS?

Lots! What makes management information systems the most exciting topic in business is the continual change in technology, management use of the technology, and the impact on business success. New businesses and industries appear, old ones decline, and successful firms are those that learn how to use the new technologies. Table 1.1 summarizes the major new themes in business uses of information systems. These themes will appear throughout the book in all the chapters, so it might be a good idea to take some time now and discuss these with your professor and other students.

In the technology area there are three interrelated changes: (1) the emerging mobile digital platform, (2) the growth of online software as a service, and (3) the growth in "cloud computing" where more and more business software runs over the Internet.

IPhones, BlackBerrys, and tiny Web-surfing netbooks are not just gadgets or entertainment outlets. They represent new emerging computing platforms based on an array of new hardware and software technologies. More and more business computing is moving from PCs and desktop machines to these mobile devices. Managers are increasingly using these devices to coordinate work, communicate with employees, and provide information for decision making. We call these developments the "emerging mobile platform."

Managers routinely use so-called "Web 2.0" technologies like social networking, collaboration tools, and wikis in order to make better, faster decisions. As management behavior changes, how work gets organized, coordinated, and measured also changes. By connecting employees working on teams and projects, the social network is where works gets done, where plans are executed, and where managers manage. Collaboration spaces are where employees meet one another, even when they are separated by continents and time zones.

The strength of cloud computing, and the growth of the mobile digital platform, mean that organizations can rely more on telework, remote work, and distributed decision making. This same platform means firms can outsource more work, and rely on markets (rather than employees) to build value. It also means that firms can collaborate with suppliers and customers to create new products, or make existing products more efficiently.

TABLE 1.1

What's New in MIS

Change	Business Impact
TECHNOLOGY	
Cloud computing platform emerges as a major business area of innovation	A flexible collection of computers on the Internet begins to perform tasks traditionally performed on corporate computers.
Growth in software as a service (SaaS)	Major business applications are now delivered online as an Internet service rather than as boxed software or custom systems.
A mobile digital platform emerges to compete with the PC as a business system	Apple opens its iPhone software to developers, and then opens an Applications Store on iTunes where business users can download thousands of applications to support collaboration, location-based services, and communication with colleagues. Small portable lightweight, low-cost, net-centric subnotebook computers become a major segment of the laptop marketplace.
PEOPLE	
Managers adopt online collaboration and social networking software to improve coordination, collaboration, and knowledge sharing	Google Apps, Google Sites, Microsoft's Windows SharePoint Services, and IBM's Lotus Connections are used by over 100 million business professionals worldwide to support blogs, project management, online meetings, personal profiles, social bookmarks, and online communities.
Business intelligence applications accelerate	More powerful data analytics and interactive dashboards provide real-time performance information to managers to enhance management control and decision making.
Virtual meetings proliferate	Managers adopt telepresence video conferencing and Web conferencing technologies to reduce travel time, and cost, while improving collaboration and decision making.
ORGANIZATIONS	
Web 2.0 applications are widely adopted by firms	Web-based services enable employees to interact as online communities using blogs, Wikis, e-mail, and instant messaging services. Facebook and MySpace create new opportunities for business to collaborate with customers and vendors.
Telework gains momentum in the workplace	The Internet, wireless laptops, iPhones, and BlackBerrys make it possible for growing numbers of people to work away from the traditional office. Fifty-five percent of U.S. businesses have some form of remote work program.
Co-creation of business value	Sources of business value shift from products to solutions and experiences and from internal sources to networks of suppliers and collaboration with customers. Supply chains and product development become more global and collaborative; customer interactions help firms define new products and services.

You can see some of these trends at work in the Interactive Session on Organizations. Millions of managers rely heavily on the mobile digital platform to coordinate suppliers and shipments, satisfy customers, and manage their employees. A business day without these mobile devices or Internet access would be unthinkable. As you read this case, note how the emerging mobile platform greatly enhances the accuracy, speed, and richness of decision making.

Can you run your company out of your pocket? Perhaps not entirely, but there are many functions today that can be performed using an iPhone, BlackBerry, or other mobile handheld device. The smartphone has been called the "Swiss Army knife of the digital age." A flick of the finger turns it into a Web browser, a telephone, a camera, a music or video player, an e-mail and messaging machine, and for some, a gateway into corporate systems. New software applications for social networking and sales force management (CRM) make these devices even more versatile business tools.

The BlackBerry has been the favored mobile handheld for business because it was optimized for e-mail and messaging, with strong security and tools for accessing internal corporate systems. Now that's changing. Companies large and small are starting to deploy Apple's iPhone to conduct more of their work. For some, these handhelds have become necessities.

Doylestown Hospital, a community medical center near Philadelphia, has a mobile workforce of 360 independent physicians treating thousands of patients. The physicians use the iPhone 3G to stay connected around the clock to hospital staff, colleagues, and patient information. Doylestown doctors use iPhone features such as e-mail, calendar, and contacts from Microsoft Exchange ActiveSync. The iPhone allows them to receive time-sensitive e-mail alerts from the hospital. Voice communication is important as well, and the iPhone allows the doctors to be on call wherever they are.

Doylestown Hospital customized the iPhone to provide doctors with secure mobile access from any location in the world to the hospital's MEDITECH electronic medical records system. MEDITECH delivers information on vital signs, medications, lab results, allergies, nurses' notes, therapy results, and even patient diets to the iPhone screen. "Every radiographic image a patient has had, every dictated report from a specialist is available on the iPhone," notes Dr. Scott Levy, Doylestown Hospital's Vice President and Chief Medical Officer. Doylestown doctors also use the iPhone at the patient's bedside to access medical reference applications such as Epocrates Essentials to help them interpret lab results and obtain medication information.

Doylestown's information systems department was able to establish the same high level of security for authenticating users of the system and tracking user activity as it maintains with all the hospital's Web-based medical records applications. Information is stored securely on the hospital's own server computer.

D.W. Morgan, headquartered in Pleasanton, California, serves as a supply chain consultant and transportation and logistics service provider to companies such as AT&T, Apple Computer, Johnson & Johnson, Lockheed Martin, and Chevron. It has operations in more than 85 countries on four continents, moving critical inventory to factories that use a just-in-time (JIT) strategy. In JIT, retailers and manufacturers maintain almost no excess on-hand inventory, relying upon suppliers to deliver raw materials, components, or products shortly before they are needed.

In this type of production environment, it's absolutely critical to know the exact moment when delivery trucks will arrive. In the past, it took many phone calls and a great deal of manual effort to provide customers with such precise up-to-the-minute information. The company was able to develop a ChainLinq Mobile application for its 30 drivers that updates shipment information, collects signatures, and provides global positioning system (GPS) locations on each individual box it delivers.

As Morgan's drivers make their shipments, they use ChainLinq to record pickups and status updates. When they reach their destination, they collect a signature on the iPhone screen. Data collected at each point along the way, including a date-stamp and time-stamped GPS location pinpointed on a Google map, are uploaded to the company's servers. The servers make the data available to customers on the company's Web site. Morgan's competitors take about 20 minutes to half a day to provide proof of delivery; Morgan can do it immediately.

Aedas Sport is one of the world's foremost designers of multipurpose sports, entertainment, and exhibition facilities. Every employee is equipped with an iPhone. Designers and architects, who work in an almost continuous stream of communication, use their iPhone cameras to take pictures of designs, models, and construction sites. They send the photos along with e-mail, text messages, and documents around the office. And of course they use the iPhone for telephone calls. Productivity has jumped as much as 400 percent.

The iPhone has made it possible for Aedas Sport to build a large archive of visual assets without planning or extra effort. The firm sends a book with all the iPhone photos of its projects to every prospective client to demonstrate the talent and creativity of the firm.

Sources: Steve Lohr, "Smartphone Rises Fast from Gadget to Necessity," *The New York Times*, June 10, 2009; Sara Silver, "Consumers Drive Bulk of BlackBerry Growth," *The Wall Street Journal*, June 19, 2009; Matt Richtel and Laura M. Holdon, "Play Flute, Name a Tune (or Make a Call)," *The New York Times*, January 2, 2009; and Apple iPhone in Business Profiles, www.apple.com, accessed August 3, 2009.

CASE STUDY QUESTIONS

1. What kinds of applications are described here? What business functions do they support? How do they improve operational efficiency and decision making?

2. Identify the problems that businesses in this case study solved by using mobile digital devices.

3. What kinds of businesses are most likely to benefit from equipping their employees with mobile digital devices such as iPhones and BlackBerrys?

4. D.W. Morgan's CEO has stated, "The iPhone is not a game changer, it's an industry changer. It changes the way that you can interact with your customers (and) with your suppliers." Discuss the implications of this statement.

MIS IN ACTION

Explore the Web sites for the Apple iPhone 3G, the BlackBerry, and the Palm Pre, then answer the following questions:

1. List and describe the capabilities of each of these devices and give examples of how they could be used by businesses.

2. List and describe three downloadable business applications for each device and describe their business benefits.

GLOBALIZATION CHALLENGES AND OPPORTUNITIES: A FLATTENED WORLD

In 1492, Columbus reaffirmed what astronomers were long saying: the world was round and the seas could be safely sailed. As it turned out, the world was populated by peoples and languages living in near total isolation from one another, with great disparities in economic and scientific development. The world trade that ensued after Columbus's voyages has brought these peoples and cultures closer. The "industrial revolution" was really a worldwide phenomenon energized by expansion of trade among nations.

By 2005, journalist Thomas Friedman wrote an influential book declaring the world was now "flat," by which he meant that the Internet and global communications had greatly reduced the economic and cultural advantages of developed countries. U.S. and European countries were in a fight for their economic lives, competing for jobs, markets, resources, and even ideas with highly educated, motivated populations in low-wage areas in the less developed world (Friedman, 2007). This "globalization" presents you and your business with both challenges and opportunities.

A growing percentage of the economy of the United States and other advanced industrial countries in Europe and Asia depends on imports and exports. In 2009, more than 33 percent of the U.S. economy resulted from foreign trade, both imports and exports. In Europe and

Top iPhone Business Applications
1. *Job Search*
2. *QuickVoice Recorder*
3. *FedEx Mobile for iPhone*
4. *ZIPFinder Free Zip Code Locator*
5. *ITalk Recorder*
6. *WiFi HD Free (Wireless Hard Disk Drive)*
7. *Remote Desktop Lite*
8. *Quickoffice Mobile Office Suite*

Whether it's attending an online meeting, checking orders, working with files and documents, or obtaining business intelligence, Apple's iPhone offers many possibilities for business users. Its stunning multitouch display, full Internet browsing, digital camera, and capabilities for messaging, voice transmission, and document management, make it an all-purpose platform for mobile computing.

Asia, the number exceeds 50 percent. Many Fortune 500 U.S. firms derive half their revenues from foreign operations. For instance, more than half of Intel's revenues in 2008 came from overseas sales of its microprocessors. Toys for chips: 80 percent of the toys sold in the United States are manufactured in China, while about 90 percent of the PCs manufactured in China use American-made Intel or Advanced Micro Design (AMD) chips.

It's not just goods that move across borders. So too do jobs, some of them high-level jobs that pay well and require a college degree. In the past decade, the United States lost several million manufacturing jobs to offshore, low-wage producers. But manufacturing is now a very small part of U.S. employment (less than 12 percent). In a normal year, about 300,000 service jobs move offshore to lower-wage countries, many of them in less-skilled information system occupations, but also including "tradable service" jobs in architecture, financial services, customer call centers, consulting, engineering, and even radiology.

On the plus side, the U.S. economy creates over 3.5 million new jobs a year, and employment in information systems, and the other service occupations listed previously, has expanded in sheer numbers, wages, productivity, and quality of work. Outsourcing has actually accelerated the development of new systems in the United States and worldwide. In the midst of a recession in 2009, jobs in information systems are among the most in demand.

The challenge for you as a business student is to develop high-level skills through education and on-the-job experience that cannot be outsourced. The challenge for your business is to avoid markets for goods and services that can be produced offshore much less expensively. The opportunities are equally immense. You can learn how to profit from the lower costs available in world markets and the chance to serve a marketplace with billions of customers. You have the opportunity to develop higher-level and more profitable products and services. You will find throughout this book examples of companies and individuals who either failed or succeeded in using information systems to adapt to this new global environment.

What does globalization have to do with management information systems? That's simple: everything. The emergence of the Internet into a full-blown international communications system has drastically reduced the costs of operating and transacting on a global scale. Communication between a factory floor in Shanghai and a distribution center in Sioux Falls, South Dakota, is now instant and virtually free. Customers now can shop in a worldwide marketplace, obtaining price and quality information reliably 24 hours a day. Firms producing goods and services on a global scale achieve extraordinary cost reductions by finding low-cost suppliers and managing production facilities in other countries. Internet service firms, such as Google and eBay, are able to replicate their business models and services in multiple countries without having to redesign their expensive fixed-cost information systems infrastructure. Over half of eBay's revenues in 2009 originated outside the United States. Briefly, information systems enable globalization.

BUSINESS DRIVERS OF INFORMATION SYSTEMS

What makes information systems so essential today? Why are businesses investing so much in information systems and technologies? They do so to achieve six important business objectives: operational excellence; new products, services, and business models; customer and supplier intimacy; improved decision making; competitive advantage; and survival.

Operational Excellence

Businesses continuously seek to improve the efficiency of their operations in order to achieve higher profitability. Information systems and technologies are some of the most important tools available to managers for achieving higher levels of efficiency and productivity in business operations, especially when coupled with changes in business practices and management behavior.

Wal-Mart, the largest retailer on Earth, exemplifies the power of information systems coupled with brilliant business practices and supportive management to achieve world-class operational efficiency. In 2008, Wal-Mart achieved more than $400 billion in sales—nearly one-tenth of retail sales in the United States—in large part because of its Retail Link system, which digitally links its suppliers to every one of Wal-Mart's 7,873 stores worldwide. As soon as a customer purchases an item, the supplier monitoring the item knows to ship a replacement to the shelf. Wal-Mart is the most efficient retail store in the industry, achieving sales of more than $28 per square foot, compared to its closest competitor, Target, at $23 a square foot, with other retail firms producing less than $12 a square foot.

New Products, Services, and Business Models

Information systems and technologies are a major enabling tool for firms to create new products and services, as well as entirely new business models. A **business model** describes how a company produces, delivers, and sells a product or service to create wealth. Today's music industry is vastly different from the industry in 2000. Apple Inc. transformed an old business model of music distribution based on vinyl records, tapes, and CDs into an online, legal distribution model based on its own iPod technology platform. Apple has prospered from a continuing stream of innovations, including the original iPod, the iPod nano, the iTunes music service, the iPod video player, and the iPhone.

Customer and Supplier Intimacy

When a business really knows its customers and serves them well, the way they want to be served, the customers generally respond by returning and purchasing more. This raises revenues and profits. Likewise with suppliers: the more a business engages its suppliers, the better the suppliers can provide vital inputs. This lowers costs. How to really know your customers, or suppliers, is a central problem for businesses with millions of offline and online customers.

The Mandarin Oriental in Manhattan and other high-end hotels exemplify the use of information systems and technologies to achieve customer intimacy. These hotels use computers to keep track of guests' preferences, such as their preferred room temperature, check-in time, frequently dialed telephone numbers, and television programs, and store these data in a giant data repository. Individual rooms in the hotels are networked to a central network server computer so that they can be remotely monitored or controlled. When a customer arrives at one of these hotels, the system automatically changes the room conditions, such as dimming the lights, setting the room temperature, or selecting appropriate music, based on the customer's digital profile. The hotels also analyze their customer data to identify their best customers and to develop individualized marketing campaigns based on customers' preferences.

JCPenney exemplifies the benefits of information systems-enabled supplier intimacy. Every time a dress shirt is bought at a JCPenney store in the United States, the record of the sale appears immediately on computers in Hong Kong at TAL Apparel Ltd., a giant

Transpara's Mobile Dashboard delivers comprehensive and accurate information for decision making. The graphical overview of key performance indicators helps managers quickly spot areas that need attention.

contract manufacturer that produces one in eight dress shirts sold in the United States. TAL runs the numbers through a computer model it developed and decides how many replacement shirts to make, and in what styles, colors, and sizes. TAL then sends the shirts to each JCPenney store, completely bypassing the retailer's warehouses. In other words, JCPenney's surplus shirt inventory is near zero, as is the cost of storing it.

Improved Decision Making

Many business managers operate in an information fog bank, never really having the right information at the right time to make an informed decision. Instead, managers rely on forecasts, best guesses, and luck. The result is over- or underproduction of goods and services, misallocation of resources, and poor response times. These poor outcomes raise costs and lose customers. In the past 10 years, information systems and technologies have made it possible for managers to use real-time data from the marketplace when making decisions.

For instance, Verizon Corporation, one of the largest regional Bell operating companies in the United States, uses a Web-based digital dashboard to provide managers with precise real-time information on customer complaints, network performance for each locality served, and line outages or storm-damaged lines. Using this information, managers can immediately allocate repair resources to affected areas, inform consumers of repair efforts, and restore service fast.

Competitive Advantage

When firms achieve one or more of these business objectives—operational excellence; new products, services, and business models; customer/supplier intimacy; and improved decision making—chances are they have already achieved a competitive advantage. Doing things better than your competitors, charging less for superior products, and responding to customers and suppliers in real time all add up to higher sales and higher profits that your competitors cannot match.

Perhaps no other company exemplifies all of these attributes leading to competitive advantage more than Toyota Motor Company. Toyota has become the world's largest automaker because of its high level of efficiency and quality. Competitors struggle to keep up. Toyota's legendary Toyota Production System (TPS) focuses on organizing work to eliminate waste, making continuous improvements, and optimizing customer value. Information systems help Toyota implement the TPS and produce vehicles based on what customers have actually ordered.

Survival

Business firms also invest in information systems and technologies because they are necessities of doing business. Sometimes these necessities are driven by industry-level changes. For instance, after Citibank introduced the first automated teller machines (ATMs) in the New York region in 1977 to attract customers through higher service levels, its competitors rushed to provide ATMs to their customers to keep up with Citibank. Today, virtually all banks in the United States have regional ATMs and link to national and international ATM networks, such as CIRRUS. Providing ATM services to retail banking customers is simply a requirement of being in and surviving in the retail banking business.

Many federal and state statutes and regulations create a legal duty for companies and their employees to retain records, including digital records. For instance, the Toxic Substances Control Act (1976), which regulates the exposure of U.S. workers to more than 75,000 toxic chemicals, requires firms to retain records on employee exposure for 30 years. The Sarbanes-Oxley Act (2002), which was intended to improve the accountability of public firms and their auditors, requires public companies to retain audit working papers and records, including all e-mails, for five years. Firms turn to information systems and technologies to provide the capability to respond to these information retention and reporting requirements.

1.2 Perspectives on Information Systems and Information Technology

So far we've used *information systems* and *technologies* informally without defining the terms. **Information technology (IT)** consists of all the hardware and software that a firm needs to use in order to achieve its business objectives. This includes not only computer machines, disk drives, and mobile handheld devices but also software, such as the Windows or Linux operating systems, the Microsoft Office desktop productivity suite, and the many thousands of computer programs that can be found in a typical large firm. "Information systems" are more complex and can be best be understood by looking at them from both a technology and a business perspective.

WHAT IS AN INFORMATION SYSTEM?

An **information system (IS)** can be defined technically as a set of interrelated components that collect (or retrieve), process, store, and distribute information to support decision making, coordinating, and control in an organization. In addition, information systems may also help managers and workers analyze problems, visualize complex subjects, and create new products.

Information systems contain information about significant people, places, and things within the organization or in the environment surrounding it. By **information** we mean data that have been shaped into a form that is meaningful and useful to human beings. **Data**, in contrast, are streams of raw facts representing events occurring in organizations or the physical environment before they have been organized and arranged into a form that people can understand and use.

A brief example contrasting information and data may prove useful. Supermarket checkout counters scan millions of pieces of data, such as bar codes, that describe the product. Such pieces of data can be totaled and analyzed to provide meaningful information, such as the total number of bottles of dish detergent sold at a particular store, which brands of dish detergent were selling the most rapidly at that store or sales territory, or the total amount spent on that brand of dish detergent at that store or sales region (see Figure 1-1).

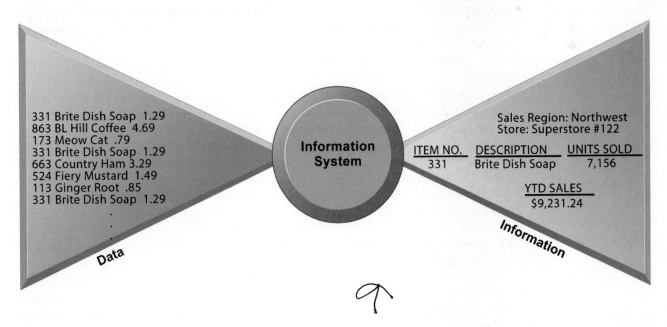

Figure 1-1
Data and Information
Raw data from a supermarket checkout counter can be processed and organized to produce meaningful information, such as the total unit sales of dish detergent or the total sales revenue from dish detergent for a specific store or sales territory.

Figure 1-2
Functions of an
Information System
*An information system
contains information
about an organization
and its surrounding
environment. Three basic
activities—input, pro-
cessing, and output—
produce the information
organizations need.
Feedback is output
returned to appropriate
people or activities in the
organization to evaluate
and refine the input.
Environmental actors,
such as customers,
suppliers, competitors,
stockholders, and regula-
tory agencies, interact
with the organization and
its information systems.*

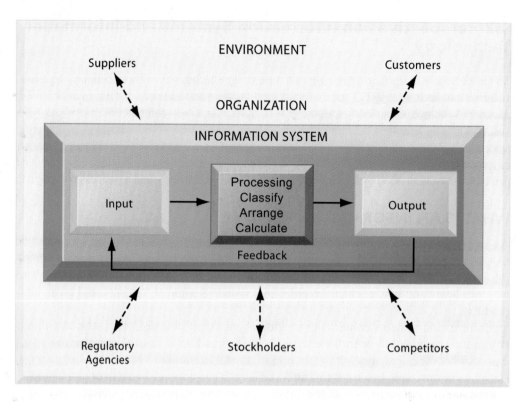

Three activities in an information system produce the information that organizations need to make decisions, control operations, analyze problems, and create new products or services. These activities are input, processing, and output (see Figure 1-2). **Input** captures or collects raw data from within the organization or from its external environment. **Processing** converts this raw input into a meaningful form. **Output** transfers the processed information to the people who will use it or to the activities for which it will be used. Information systems also require **feedback**, which is output that is returned to appropriate members of the organization to help them evaluate or correct the input stage.

In the Yankees' system for selling tickets through its Web site, the raw input consists of order data for tickets, such as the purchaser's name, address, credit card number, number of tickets ordered, and the date of the game for which the ticket is being purchased. Computers store these data and process them to calculate order totals, to track ticket purchases, and to send requests for payment to credit card companies. The output consists of tickets to print, receipts for orders, and reports on online ticket orders. The system provides meaningful information, such as the number of tickets sold for a particular game, the total number of tickets sold each year, and frequent customers.

Although computer-based information systems use computer technology to process raw data into meaningful information, there is a sharp distinction between a computer and a computer program and an information system. Electronic computers and related software programs are the technical foundation, the tools and materials, of modern information systems. Computers provide the equipment for storing and processing information. Computer programs, or software, are sets of operating instructions that direct and control computer processing. Knowing how computers and computer programs work is important in designing solutions to organizational problems, but computers are only part of an information system.

A house is an appropriate analogy. Houses are built with hammers, nails, and wood, but these alone do not make a house. The architecture, design, setting, landscaping, and all of the decisions that lead to the creation of these features are part of the house and are crucial for solving the problem of putting a roof over one's head. Computers and programs are the hammer, nails, and lumber of computer-based information systems, but alone they cannot produce the information a particular organization needs. To understand information systems, you must understand the problems they are designed to solve, their architectural and design elements, and the organizational processes that lead to these solutions.

IT ISN'T SIMPLY TECHNOLOGY: THE ROLE OF PEOPLE AND ORGANIZATIONS

To fully understand information systems, you will need to be aware of the broader organization, people, and information technology dimensions of systems (see Figure 1-3) and their power to provide solutions to challenges and problems in the business environment. We refer to this broader understanding of information systems, which encompasses an understanding of the people and organizational dimensions of systems as well as the technical dimensions of systems, as **information systems literacy**. Information systems literacy includes a behavioral as well as a technical approach to studying information systems. **Computer literacy**, in contrast, focuses primarily on knowledge of information technology.

The field of **management information systems (MIS)** tries to achieve this broader information systems literacy. MIS deals with behavioral issues as well as technical issues surrounding the development, use, and impact of information systems used by managers and employees in the firm.

DIMENSIONS OF INFORMATION SYSTEMS

Let's examine each of the dimensions of information systems—organizations, people, and information technology.

Organizations

Information systems are an integral part of organizations. And although we tend to think about information technology changing organizations and business firms, it is, in fact, a two-way street: The history and culture of business firms also affects how the technology is used and how it should be used. In order to understand how a specific business firm uses information systems, you need to know something about the structure, history, and culture of the company.

Organizations have a structure that is composed of different levels and specialties. Their structures reveal a clear-cut division of labor. A business firm is organized as a hierarchy, or a pyramid structure, of rising authority and responsibility. The upper levels of the hierarchy

Figure 1-3
Information Systems Are More Than Computers
Using information systems effectively requires an understanding of the organization, people, and information technology shaping the systems. An information system provides a solution to important business problems or challenges facing the firm.

consist of managerial, professional, and technical employees, whereas the lower levels consist of operational personnel. Experts are employed and trained for different business functions, such as sales and marketing, manufacturing and production, finance and accounting, and human resources. Information systems are built by the firm in order to serve these different specialties and different levels of the firm. Chapter 2 provides more detail on these business functions and organizational levels and the ways in which they are supported by information systems.

An organization accomplishes and coordinates work through this structured hierarchy and through its **business processes,** which are logically related tasks and behaviors for accomplishing work. Developing a new product, fulfilling an order, and hiring a new employee are examples of business processes.

Most organizations' business processes include formal rules that have been developed over a long time for accomplishing tasks. These rules guide employees in a variety of procedures, from writing an invoice to responding to customer complaints. Some of these business processes have been written down, but others are informal work practices, such as a requirement to return telephone calls from co-workers or customers, that are not formally documented. Information systems automate many business processes. For instance, how a customer receives credit or how a customer is billed is often determined by an information system that incorporates a set of formal business processes.

Each organization has a unique **culture,** or fundamental set of assumptions, values, and ways of doing things, that has been accepted by most of its members. Parts of an organization's culture can always be found embedded in its information systems. For instance, the United Parcel Service's concern with placing service to the customer first is an aspect of its organizational culture that can be found in the company's package tracking systems.

Different levels and specialties in an organization create different interests and points of view. These views often conflict. Conflict is the basis for organizational politics. Information systems come out of this cauldron of differing perspectives, conflicts, compromises, and agreements that are a natural part of all organizations.

People

A business is only as good as the people who work there and run it. Likewise with information systems—they are useless without skilled people to build and maintain them, and without people who can understand how to use the information in a system to achieve business objectives.

For instance, a call center that provides help to customers using an advanced customer relationship management system (described in later chapters) is useless if employees are not adequately trained to deal with customers, find solutions to their problems, and leave the customer feeling that the company cares for them. Likewise, employee attitudes about their jobs, employers, or technology can have a powerful effect on their abilities to use information systems productively.

Business firms require many different kinds of skills and people, including managers as well as rank-and-file employees. The job of managers is to make sense out of the many situations faced by organizations, make decisions, and formulate action plans to solve organizational problems. Managers perceive business challenges in the environment, they set the organizational strategy for responding to those challenges, and they allocate the human and financial resources to coordinate the work and achieve success. Throughout, they must exercise responsible leadership.

But managers must do more than manage what already exists. They must also create new products and services and even re-create the organization from time to time. A substantial part of management responsibility is creative work driven by new knowledge and information. Information technology can play a powerful role in helping managers develop novel solutions to a broad range of problems.

As you will learn throughout this text, technology is relatively inexpensive today, but people are very expensive. Because people are the only ones capable of business problem solving and converting information technology into useful business solutions, we spend considerable effort in this text looking at the people dimension of information systems.

Technology

Information technology is one of many tools managers use to cope with change and complexity. **Computer hardware** is the physical equipment used for input, processing, and output activities in an information system. It consists of the following: computers of various sizes and shapes; various input, output, and storage devices; and telecommunications devices that link computers together.

Computer software consists of the detailed, preprogrammed instructions that control and coordinate the computer hardware components in an information system. Chapter 4 describes the contemporary software and hardware platforms used by firms today in greater detail.

Data management technology consists of the software governing the organization of data on physical storage media. More detail on data organization and access methods can be found in Chapter 5.

Networking and telecommunications technology, consisting of both physical devices and software, links the various pieces of hardware and transfers data from one physical location to another. Computers and communications equipment can be connected in networks for sharing voice, data, images, sound, and video. A **network** links two or more computers to share data or resources, such as a printer.

The world's largest and most widely used network is the **Internet**. The Internet is a global "network of networks" that uses universal standards (described in Chapter 6) to connect millions of different networks in nearly 200 countries around the world.

The Internet has created a new "universal" technology platform on which to build new products, services, strategies, and business models. This same technology platform has internal uses, providing the connectivity to link different systems and networks within the firm. Internal corporate networks based on Internet technology are called **intranets**. Private intranets extended to authorized users outside the organization are called **extranets**, and firms use such networks to coordinate their activities with other firms for making purchases, collaborating on design, and performing other interorganizational work. For most business firms today, using Internet technology is a business necessity and a competitive advantage.

The **World Wide Web** is a service provided by the Internet that uses universally accepted standards for storing, retrieving, formatting, and displaying information in a page format on the Internet. Web pages contain text, graphics, animations, sound, and video and are linked to other Web pages. By clicking on highlighted words or buttons on a Web page, you can link to related pages to find additional information and links to other locations on the Web. The Web can serve as the foundation for new kinds of information systems such as UPS's Web-based package tracking system or the Yankees' online system for ordering tickets and playing "fantasy" baseball described in the chapter-opening case.

All of these technologies, along with the people required to run and manage them, represent resources that can be shared throughout the organization and constitute the firm's **information technology (IT) infrastructure**. The IT infrastructure provides the foundation, or *platform*, on which the firm can build its specific information systems. Each organization must carefully design and manage its information technology infrastructure so that it has the set of technology services it needs for the work it wants to accomplish with information systems. Chapters 4 through 7 of this text examine each major technology component of information technology infrastructure and show how they all work together to create the technology platform for the organization.

The Interactive Session on Technology describes some of the typical technologies used in computer-based information systems today. UPS invests heavily in information systems technology to make its business more efficient and customer oriented. It uses an array of information technologies including bar code scanning systems, wireless networks, large

United Parcel Service (UPS) started out in 1907 in a closet-sized basement office. Jim Casey and Claude Ryan—two teenagers from Seattle with two bicycles and one phone—promised the "best service and lowest rates." UPS has used this formula successfully for more than a century to become the world's largest ground and air package-distribution company. It is a global enterprise with more than 415,000 employees, 99,000 vehicles, and the world's eighth largest airline.

Today, UPS delivers more than 15 million parcels and documents each day in the United States and more than 200 other countries and territories. The firm has been able to maintain leadership in small-package delivery services despite stiff competition from FedEx and Airborne Express by investing heavily in advanced information technology. UPS spends more than $1 billion each year to maintain a high level of customer service while keeping costs low and streamlining its overall operations.

It all starts with the scannable bar-coded label attached to a package, which contains detailed information about the sender, the destination, and when the package should arrive. Customers can download and print their own labels using special software provided by UPS or by accessing the UPS Web site. Before the package is even picked up, information from the "smart" label is transmitted to one of UPS's computer centers in Mahwah, New Jersey, or Alpharetta, Georgia, and sent to the distribution center nearest its final destination. Dispatchers at this center download the label data and use special software to create the most efficient delivery route for each driver that considers traffic, weather conditions, and the location of each stop. UPS estimates its delivery trucks save 28 million miles and burn 3 million fewer gallons of fuel each year.

The first thing a UPS driver picks up each day is a handheld computer called a Delivery Information Acquisition Device (DIAD), which can access one of the wireless networks cell phones rely on. As soon as the driver logs on, his or her day's route is downloaded onto the handheld. The DIAD also automatically captures customers' signatures along with pickup and delivery information. Package tracking information is then transmitted to UPS's computer network for storage and processing. From there, the information can be accessed worldwide to provide proof of delivery to customers or to respond to customer queries. It usually takes less than 60 seconds from the time a driver presses "complete" on the DIAD for the new information to be available on the Web.

Through its automated package tracking system, UPS can monitor and even re-route packages throughout the delivery process. At various points along the route from sender to receiver, bar code devices scan shipping information on the package label and feed data about the progress of the package into the central computer. Customer service representatives are able to check the status of any package from desktop computers linked to the central computers and respond immediately to inquiries from customers. UPS customers can also access this information from the company's Web site using their own computers or wireless devices.

Anyone with a package to ship can access the UPS Web site to track packages, check delivery routes, calculate shipping rates, determine time in transit, print labels, and schedule a pickup. The data collected at the UPS Web site are transmitted to the UPS central computer and then back to the customer after processing. UPS also provides tools that enable customers, such Cisco Systems, to embed UPS functions, such as tracking and cost calculations, into their own Web sites so that they can track shipments without visiting the UPS site.

In June 2009, UPS launched a new Web-based Post-Sales Order Management System (OMS) that manages global service orders and inventory for critical parts fulfillment. The system enables high-tech electronics, aerospace, medical equipment, and other companies anywhere in the world that ship critical parts to quickly assess their critical parts inventory, determine the most optimal routing strategy to meet customer needs, place orders online, and track parts from the warehouse to the end user. An automated e-mail or fax feature keeps customers informed of each shipping milestone and can provide notification of any changes to flight schedules for commercial airlines carrying their parts. Once orders are complete, companies can print documents such as labels and bills of lading in multiple languages.

UPS is now leveraging its decades of expertise managing its own global delivery network to manage logistics and supply chain activities for other companies. It created a UPS Supply Chain Solutions division that provides a complete bundle of standardized services to subscribing companies at a fraction of what it would cost to build their own systems and infrastructure. These services include supply chain design and management, freight forwarding, customs brokerage, mail services, multimodal transportation, and financial services, in addition to logistics services.

Servalite, an East Moline, Illinois manufacturer of fasteners, sells 40,000 different products to hardware stores and larger home improvement stores. The company had used multiple warehouses to provide two-day delivery nationwide. UPS created a new logistics plan for the company that helped it reduce freight time in transit and consolidate inventory. Thanks to these improvements, Servalite has been able to keep its two-day delivery guarantee while lowering warehousing and inventory costs.

Sources: United Parcel Service, "In a Tighter Economy, a Manufacturer Fastens Down Its Logistics," *UPS Compass*, Winter 2009; Chris Murphy, "In for the Long Haul," *Information Week*, January 19, 2009; United Parcel Service, " UPS Unveils Global Technology for Critical Parts Fulfillment," June 16, 2009; and www.ups.com, accessed August 6, 2009.

CASE STUDY QUESTIONS

1. What are the inputs, processing, and outputs of UPS's package tracking system?

2. What technologies are used by UPS? How are these technologies related to UPS's business model and business objectives?

3. What problems do UPS's information systems solve? What would happen if these systems were not available?

MIS IN ACTION

Explore the UPS Web site (www.ups.com) and answer the following questions:

1. What kind of information and services does the Web site provide for individuals, small businesses, and large businesses? List these services.

2. Go to the Business Solutions portion of the UPS Web site. Browse the UPS Business Solutions by category (such as shipment delivery returns or international trade) and write a description of all the services UPS provides for one of these categories. Explain how a business would benefit from these services.

3. Explain how the Web site helps UPS achieve some or all of the strategic business objectives we described earlier in this chapter. What would be the impact on UPS's business if this Web site were not available?

Using a handheld computer called a Delivery Information Acquisition Device (DIAD), UPS drivers automatically capture customers' signatures along with pickup, delivery, and time card information. UPS information systems use these data to track packages while they are being transported.

mainframe computers, handheld computers, the Internet, and many different pieces of software for tracking packages, calculating fees, maintaining customer accounts, and managing logistics. As you read this case, try to identify the problem this company was facing, what alternative solutions were available to management, and how well the chosen solution worked.

Let's identify the organization, people, and technology elements in the UPS package tracking system we have just described. The organization element anchors the package tracking system in UPS's sales and production functions (the main product of UPS is a service—package delivery). It specifies the required procedures for identifying packages with both sender and recipient information, taking inventory, tracking the packages en route, and providing package status reports for UPS customers and customer service representatives.

The system must also provide information to satisfy the needs of managers and workers. UPS drivers need to be trained in both package pickup and delivery procedures and in how to use the package tracking system so that they can work efficiently and effectively. UPS customers may need some training to use UPS in-house package tracking software or the UPS Web site.

UPS's management is responsible for monitoring service levels and costs and for promoting the company's strategy of combining low cost and superior service. Management decided to use automation to increase the ease of sending a package using UPS and of checking its delivery status, thereby reducing delivery costs and increasing sales revenues.

The technology supporting this system consists of handheld computers, bar code scanners, wired and wireless communications networks, desktop computers, UPS's central computer, storage technology for the package delivery data, UPS in-house package tracking software, and software to access the World Wide Web. The result is an information system solution to the business challenge of providing a high level of service with low prices in the face of mounting competition.

1.3 Understanding Information Systems: A Business Problem-Solving Approach

Our approach to understanding information systems is to consider information systems and technologies as solutions to a variety of business challenges and problems. We refer to this as a "problem-solving approach." Businesses face many challenges and problems, and information systems are one major way of solving these problems. All of the cases in this book illustrate how a company used information systems to solve a specific problem.

The problem-solving approach has direct relevance to your future career. Your future employers will hire you because you are able to solve business problems and achieve business objectives. Your knowledge of how information systems contribute to problem solving will be very helpful to both you and your employers.

THE PROBLEM-SOLVING APPROACH

At first glance, problem solving in daily life seems to be perfectly straightforward: A machine breaks down, parts and oil spill all over the floor, and, obviously, somebody has to do something about it. So, of course, you find a tool around the shop and start repairing the machine. After a cleanup and proper inspection of other parts, you start the machine, and production resumes.

No doubt some problems in business are this straightforward. But few problems are this simple in the real world of business. In real-world business firms, a number of major factors are simultaneously involved in problems. These major factors can usefully be grouped into three categories: *organization, technology,* and *people.* In other words, a whole set of problems is usually involved.

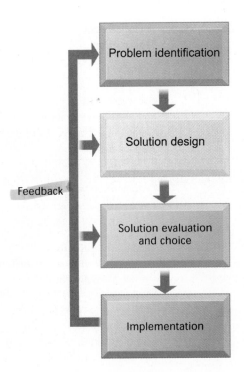

Figure 1-4
Problem Solving Is a Continuous Four-Step Process
During implementation and thereafter, the outcome must be continually measured and the information about how well the solution is working is fed back to the problem solvers. In this way, the identification of the problem can change over time, solutions can be changed, and new choices made, all based on experience.

A MODEL OF THE PROBLEM-SOLVING PROCESS

There is a simple model of problem solving that you can use to help you understand and solve business problems using information systems. You can think of business problem-solving as a four-step process (see Figure 1-4). Most problem solvers work through this model on their way to finding a solution. Let's take a brief look at each step.

Problem Identification

The first step in the problem-solving process is to understand what kind of problem exists. Contrary to popular beliefs, problems are not like basketballs on a court simply waiting to be picked up by some "objective" problem solver. Before problems can be solved, there must be agreement in a business that a problem exists, about what the problem is, about what its causes are, and about what can be done about the problem given the limited resources of the organization. Problems have to be properly defined by people in an organization before they can be solved.

For instance, what at first glance what might seem like a problem with employees not adequately responding to customers in a timely and accurate manner might in reality be a result of a older, out-of-date information system for keeping track of customers. Or it might be a combination of both poor employee incentives for treating customers well and an outdated system. Once you understand this critical fact, you can start to solve problems creatively. Finding answers to these questions will require fact gathering, interviews with people involved in the problem, and analysis of documents.

In this text, we emphasize three different and typical dimensions of business problems: organizations, technology, and people (see Table 1.2). Typical organizational problems include poor business processes (usually inherited from the past), unsupportive culture, political in-fighting, and changes in the organization's surrounding environment. Typical technology problems include insufficient or aging hardware, outdated software, inadequate database capacity, insufficient telecommunications capacity, and the incompatibility of old systems with new technology. Typical people problems include employee training, difficulties of evaluating performance, legal and regulatory compliance, ergonomics, poor or indecisive management, and employee support and participation. When you begin to

TABLE 1.2

**Dimensions of
Business Problems**

Dimension	Description
Organizational dimensions	Outdated business processes
	Unsupportive culture and attitudes
	Political conflict
	Turbulent business environment, change
	Complexity of task
	Inadequate resources
Technology dimensions	Insufficient or aging hardware
	Outdated software
	Inadequate database capacity
	Insufficient telecommunications capacity
	Incompatibility of old systems with new technology
	Rapid technological change
People dimensions	Lack of employee training
	Difficulties of evaluating performance
	Legal and regulatory compliance
	Work environment
	Lack of employee support and participation
	Indecisive management
	Poor management

analyze a business problem, you will find these dimensions are helpful guides to understanding the kind of problem with which you are working.

Solution Design
The second step is to design solutions to the problem(s) you have identified. As it turns out, there are usually a great many "solutions" to any given problem, and the choice of solution often reflects the differing perspectives of people in an organization. You should try to consider as many different solutions as possible so that you can understand the range of possible solutions. Some solutions emphasize technology; others focus on change in the organization and people aspects of the problem. As you will find throughout the text, most successful solutions result from an integrated approach in which new technologies are accompanied by changes in organization and people.

Solution Evaluation and Choice
Choosing the "best" solution for your business firm is the next step in the process. Some of the factors to consider when trying to find the "best" single solution are the cost of the solution, the feasibility of the solution for your business given existing resources and skills, and the length of time required to build and implement the solution. Also very important at this point are the attitudes and support of your employees and managers. A solution that does not have the support of all the major interests in the business can quickly turn into a disaster.

Implementation
The best solution is one that can be implemented. Implementation of an information system solution involves building the solution and introducing it into the organization. This includes purchasing or building the software and hardware—the technology part of the equation. The software must be tested in a realistic business setting; then employees need to be trained, and documentation about how to use the new system needs to be written.

You will definitely need to think about change management. **Change management** refers to the many techniques used to bring about successful change in a business. Nearly all information systems require changes in the firm's business processes and, therefore, changes in what hundreds or even thousands of employees do every day. You will have to design new, more efficient business processes, and then figure out how to encourage employees to adapt to these new ways of doing business. This may require meeting sessions to introduce the change to groups of employees, new training modules to bring employees quickly up to speed on the new information systems and processes, and finally some kind of rewards or incentives to encourage people to enthusiastically support the changes.

Implementation also includes the measurement of outcomes. After a solution has been implemented, it must be evaluated to determine how well it is working and whether any additional changes are required to meet the original objectives. This information is fed back to the problem solvers. In this way, the identification of the problem can change over time, solutions can be changed, and new choices made, all based on experience.

Problem Solving: A Process, Not an Event

It is often assumed that once a problem is "solved," it goes away and can be forgotten about. And it is easy to fall into the trap of thinking about problem solving as an event that is "over" at some point, like a relay race or a baseball game. Often in the real world this does not happen. Sometimes the chosen solution does not work, and new solutions are required.

For instance, the U.S. National Aeronautics and Space Administration (NASA) spent more than $1 billion to fix a problem with shedding foam on the space shuttle. Experience proved the initial solution did not work. More often, the chosen solution partially works but needs a lot of continuous changes to truly "fit" the situation. Initial solutions are often rough approximations at first of what ultimately "works." Sometimes, the nature of the problem changes in a way that makes the initial solution ineffective. For instance, hackers create new variations on computer viruses that require continually evolving antivirus programs to hold in check. For all these reasons, problem solving is a continuous process rather than a single event.

THE ROLE OF CRITICAL THINKING IN PROBLEM SOLVING

It is amazingly easy to accept someone else's definition of a problem or to adopt the opinions of some authoritative group that has "objectively" analyzed the problem and offers quick solutions. You should try to resist this tendency to accept existing definitions of any problem. Through the natural flow of decision making, it is essential that you try to maintain some distance from any specific solution until you are sure you have properly identified the problem, developed understanding, and analyzed alternatives. Otherwise, you may leap off in the wrong direction, solve the wrong problem, and waste resources. You will have to engage in some critical-thinking exercises.

Critical thinking can be briefly defined as the sustained suspension of judgment with an awareness of multiple perspectives and alternatives. It involves at least four elements:

- Maintaining doubt and suspending judgment
- Being aware of different perspectives
- Testing alternatives and letting experience guide
- Being aware of organizational and personal limitations

Simply following a rote pattern of decision making, or a model, does not guarantee a correct solution. The best protection against incorrect results is to engage in critical thinking throughout the problem-solving process.

First, maintain doubt and suspend judgment. Perhaps the most frequent error in problem solving is to arrive prematurely at a judgment about the nature of the problem. By doubting all solutions at first and refusing to rush to a judgment, you create the necessary mental conditions to take a fresh, creative look at problems, and you keep open the chance to make a creative contribution.

Second, recognize that all interesting business problems have many dimensions and that the same problem can be viewed from different perspectives. In this text, we have emphasized the usefulness of three perspectives on business problems: technology, organizations, and people. Within each of these very broad perspectives are many subperspectives, or views. The *technology perspective*, for instance, includes a consideration of all the components in the firm's IT infrastructure and the way they work together. The *organization perspective* includes a consideration of a firm's business processes, structure, culture, and politics. The *people perspective* includes consideration of the firm's management, as well as employees as individuals and their interrelationships in workgroups.

You will have to decide for yourself which major perspectives are useful for viewing a given problem. The ultimate criterion here is usefulness: Does adopting a certain perspective tell you something more about the problem that is useful for solving the problem? If not, reject that perspective as being not meaningful in this situation and look for other perspectives.

The third element of critical thinking involves testing alternatives, or modeling solutions to problems, letting experience be the guide. Not all contingencies can be known in advance, and much can be learned through experience. Therefore, experiment, gather data, and reassess the problem periodically.

THE CONNECTION BETWEEN BUSINESS OBJECTIVES, PROBLEMS, AND SOLUTIONS

Now let's make the connection between business information systems and the problem-solving approach. At the beginning of this chapter we talked about the six reasons business firms invest in information systems and technologies. We identified six business objectives of information systems: operational excellence; new products, services, and business models; customer/supplier intimacy; improved decision making; strategic advantage; and survival. When firms cannot achieve these objectives, they become "challenges" or "problems" that receive attention. Managers and employees who are aware of these challenges often turn to information systems as one of the solutions, or the entire solution.

Review the diagram at the beginning of this chapter. The diagram shows how the Yankees' systems solved the business problem presented by declining interest in baseball games and competition from television and other media. These systems provide a solution that takes advantage of new interactive digital technology and opportunities created by the Internet. They opened up new channels for selling tickets and interacting with customers that improved business performance. The diagram also illustrates how people, technology, and organizational elements work together to create the systems.

Each chapter of this text begins with a diagram similar to this one to help you analyze the chapter-opening case. You can use this diagram as a starting point for analyzing any information system or information system problem you encounter.

1.4 Information Systems and Your Career

Looking out to 2016, the U.S. economy will create 15.6 million new jobs and 30 million existing jobs will open up as their occupants retire. More than 95 percent of the new jobs will be created in the service sector. The vast majority of these new jobs and replacement jobs will require a college degree to perform (Statistical Abstract, 2008; U.S. Bureau of Labor Statistics, 2009).

What this means is that U.S. business firms are looking for candidates who have a broad range of problem-solving skills—the ability to read, write, and present ideas—as well as the technical skills required for specific tasks. Regardless of your business school major, or your future occupation, information systems and technologies will play a major and expanding role in your day-to-day work and your career. Your career opportunities, and your compensation, will in part depend on your ability to help business firms use information systems to achieve their objectives.

HOW INFORMATION SYSTEMS WILL AFFECT BUSINESS CAREERS

IIn the following sections, we describe how specific occupations will be affected by information systems and what skills you should be building in order to benefit from this emerging labor market. Let's look at the career opportunities for business school majors.

Accounting

There are about 1.8 million accountants in the U.S. labor force today, and the field is expected to expand by 18 percent by the year 2016, adding 300,000 new jobs, and a similar number of jobs to replace retirees. This above-average growth in accounting is in part driven by new accounting laws for public companies, greater scrutiny of public and private firms by government tax auditors, and a growing demand for management and operational advice.

Accountants can be broadly classified as public accountants, management accountants, government accountants, and internal auditors. Accountants provide a broad range of services to business firms including preparing, analyzing, and verifying financial documents; budget analysis; financial planning; information technology consulting; and limited legal services. A new specialty called "forensic accounting" investigates white-collar crimes, such as securities fraud and embezzlement, bankruptcies and contract disputes, and other possibly criminal financial transactions.

Accountants rely heavily on information systems to summarize transactions, create financial records, organize data, and perform financial analysis. As a result of new public laws, accountants are beginning to perform more technical duties, such as implementing, controlling, and auditing systems and networks, and developing technology plans and budgets.

What kinds of information system skills are really important for accounting majors given these changes in the accounting profession? Here is a short list:

- Knowledge of current and likely future changes in information technology, including hardware, software, and telecommunications, which will be used by public and private firms, government agencies, and financial advisors as they perform auditing and accounting functions. Accounting professionals also require knowledge of accounting and financial applications and design factors to ensure firms are able to maintain accounting records and perform auditing functions. An understanding of system and network security issues to protect the integrity of accounting systems is also essential.
- Because so many transactions are occurring over the Internet, accountants need to understand online transaction and reporting systems, and how systems are used to achieve management accounting functions in an online, wireless, and mobile business environment.

Finance

If you include financial analysts, stock analysts, insurance underwriters, and related financial service occupations, there are currently 2 million managers in finance. Financial managers develop financial reports, direct investment activities, and implement cash management strategies. There are about 1.1 million financial managers in the U.S. labor force and this occupation is expected to grow by about 20 percent by 2016, adding over 200,000 new jobs and replacing about 100,000 additional jobs.

Financial managers play important roles in planning, organizing, and implementing information system strategies for their firms. Financial managers work directly with a firm's board of directors and senior management to ensure investments in information systems help achieve corporate goals and achieve high returns. The relationship between information systems and the practice of modern financial management and services is so strong that many advise finance majors to also co-major in information systems (and vice versa).

What kinds of information system skills should finance majors develop? Following is a brief list:

- An understanding of likely future changes in information technology, including hardware, software, and telecommunications, that will be used by financial managers and financial service firms. This includes an understanding of financial applications and design factors to ensure firms are able to manage their investments, cash, and risks along with new mobile and wireless applications to manage financial reporting. As new trading systems emerge, financial service firms and managers will need to understand how these systems work and how they will change their firm's business.

- Knowledge of the new role played by enterprise-wide financial reporting systems on a global and national scale. As more and more transactions move online, finance majors need to understand online transaction reporting systems and management of online system investments.

Marketing

No field has undergone more technology-driven change in the past five years than marketing and advertising. The explosion in e-commerce activity described earlier means that eyeballs are moving rapidly to the Internet. As a result, Internet advertising is the fastest growing form of advertising, reaching $24 billion in 2009. Product branding and customer communication are moving online at a fast pace.

There are about 900,000 marketing, public relations, sales, and advertising managers in the U.S. labor force. This field is growing faster than average, and is expected to add more than 162,000 jobs by 2016 and replace an additional 100,000 employees who are retiring. There is a much larger group of 2.6 million nonmanagerial employees in marketing-related occupations (art, design, entertainment, sports, and media) and more than 15.9 million employees in sales. These occupations together are expected to create an additional 3.3 million jobs by 2016.

Here are some of the general information systems skills on which marketing majors should focus:

- An ability to understand Internet and marketing database systems, and how they impact traditional marketing activities, such as brand development, production promotion, and sales. This would include an understanding of design factors to ensure firms are able to market their products, develop reports on product performance, retrieve feedback from customers, and manage product development.

- An understanding of how enterprise wide-systems for product management, sales force management, and customer relationship management are used to develop products that consumers want, to manage the customer relationship, and to manage an increasingly mobile sales force.

Operations Management in Services and Manufacturing

The growing size and complexity of modern industrial production and the emergence of huge global service companies have created a growing demand for employees who can coordinate and optimize the resources required to produce goods and services. Operations management as a discipline is directly relevant to three occupational categories: industrial production managers, administrative service managers, and operations analysts.

Production managers, administrative service managers, and operations analysts will be employing information systems and technologies every day to accomplish their jobs, with extensive use of database and analytical software. Here are the general information systems skills on which operations management majors should focus:

- Knowledge of the changing hardware and software platforms that will be used in operations management. This would include an understanding of the role that databases, modeling tools, and business analytical software play in production and services management.
- An in-depth understanding of how enterprise-wide information systems for production management, supplier management, sales force management, and customer relationship management are used to achieve efficient operations and meet other firm objectives.

Management

Management is the largest single group in the U.S. business labor force with more than 15 million members, not including an additional 627,000 management consultants. Overall, the management corps in the United States is expected to expand faster than other occupational groups, adding about 3 million new jobs by 2016, with about 2 million openings in this period to replace retirements. There are more than 20 different types of managers tracked by the Bureau of Labor Statistics, all the way from chief executive officer, to human resource managers, production managers, project managers, lodging managers, medical managers, and community service managers.

The job of management has been transformed by information systems. Arguably, it would be impossible to manage business firms today, even very small firms, without the extensive use of information systems. Nearly all U.S. managers use information systems and technologies every day to accomplish their jobs, from desktop productivity tools to applications coordinating the entire enterprise. Here are the general information systems skills on which management majors should focus:

- Knowledge of new hardware and software that can make management more efficient and effective, enhance leadership and coordination capabilities, and improve the achievement of corporate business objectives in the broadest sense. This would include an understanding of the role that databases play in managing information resources of the firm, and the role of new communication and collaboration technologies, such as wikis, blogs, and wireless mobile computing.

The job of management requires extensive use of information systems to support decision making and to monitor the performance of the firm.

- An in-depth understanding of how enterprise-wide information systems for production management, supplier management, sales force management, and customer relationship management are used to achieve efficient operations and help managers make better decisions for improving firm performance.

Information Systems

The information systems field is arguably one of the most fast-changing and dynamic of all the business professions because information technologies are among the most important tools for achieving business firms' key objectives. The explosive growth of business information systems has generated a growing demand for information systems employees and managers who work with other business professionals to design and develop new hardware and software systems to serve the needs of business. Of the top 20 fastest growing occupations through 2016, five are information systems occupations.

There are about 467,000 information system managers in the United States, with an estimated growth rate of 36 percent through 2016, expanding the number of new jobs by more than 168,000 new positions, with an additional 80,000 new hires required for replacements. As businesses and government agencies increasingly rely on the Internet for communication and computing resources, system and network security management positions are growing very rapidly. The fastest growing U.S. occupational group is network systems and data communications analysts, with a projected growth rate of 50 percent.

Outsourcing and Offshoring The Internet has created new opportunities for outsourcing many information systems jobs, along with many other service sector and manufacturing jobs. There are two kinds of outsourcing: outsourcing to domestic U.S. firms and offshore outsourcing to low-wage countries, such as India and eastern European countries. Even this distinction blurs as domestic service providers, such as IBM, develop global outsourcing centers in India.

The impact of domestic outsourcing on the overall demand for information technology employment through 2016 is most likely quite small. Service provider firms, such as Hewlett-Packard and Accenture, add domestic IT employees as they expand their domestic IT services, while domestic companies' information systems departments lose some employees or do not hire new employees.

Offshore outsourcing to low-wage countries has been controversial because U.S. workers fear it will reduce demand for U.S. information systems employment. However, this fear is overblown given the huge demand for new information system hires in the United States through 2016. In fact, reducing the cost of providing information technology services to U.S. corporations by offshoring labor-intensive and lower-level jobs may increase the demand for U.S.-based information system workers as firms find the price of investing in information technology falls relative to other investments while its power to increase revenues and profits grows.

The most common and successful offshore outsourcing projects involve production programming and system maintenance programming work, along with call center work related to customer relationship management systems. However, inflation in Indian wages for technology work, coupled with the additional management costs incurred in outsourcing projects, is leading to a counter movement of jobs back to the United States. Moreover, although technical IS jobs can be outsourced easily, all those management and organizational tasks required in systems development—including business process design, customer interface, and supply chain management—often remain in the United States. The net result is that offshore outsourcing will increase demand in the United States for managerial IS positions.

Given all these factors in the IT labor market, on what kinds of skills should information system majors focus? Following is a list of general skills we believe will optimize employment opportunities:

- An in-depth knowledge of how new and emerging hardware and software can be used by business firms to make them more efficient and effective, enhance customer and supplier intimacy, improve decision making, achieve competitive advantage, and ensure firm sur-

vival. This includes an in-depth understanding of databases, database design, implementation, and management.
- An ability to take a leadership role in the design and implementation of new information systems, work with other business professionals to ensure systems meet business objectives, and work with software packages providing new system solutions.

INFORMATION SYSTEMS AND YOUR CAREER: WRAP-UP

Looking back at the information system skills required for specific majors, there are some common themes that affect all business majors. Following is a list of these common requirements for information system skills and knowledge:

- All business students, regardless of major, should understand how information systems and technologies can help firms achieve business objectives such as achieving operational efficiency, developing new products and services, and maintaining customer intimacy.
- Perhaps the most dominant theme that pervades this review of necessary job skills is the central role of databases in a modern firm. Each of the careers we have just described relies heavily in practice on databases.
- With the pervasive growth in databases comes inevitably an exponential growth in digital information and a resulting challenge to managers trying to understand all this information. Regardless of major, business students need to develop skills in analysis of information and helping firms understand and make sense out of their environments.
- All business majors need to be able to work with specialists and system designers who build and implement information systems. This is necessary to ensure that the systems that are built actually service business purposes and provide the information and understanding required by managers and employees.
- Each of the business majors will be impacted by changes in the ethical, social, and legal environment of business. Business school students need to understand how information systems can be used to meet business requirements for reporting to government regulators and the public and how information systems impact the ethical issues in their fields.

HOW THIS BOOK PREPARES YOU FOR THE FUTURE

This book is explicitly designed to prepare you for your future business career. It provides you with the necessary knowledge and foundation concepts for understanding the role of information systems in business organizations. You will be able to use this knowledge to identify opportunities for increasing the effectiveness of your business. You will learn how to use information systems to improve operations, create new products and services, improve decision making, increase customer intimacy, and promote competitive advantage.

Equally important, this book develops your ability to use information systems to solve problems that you will encounter on the job. You will learn how to analyze and define a business problem and how to design an appropriate information system solution. You will deepen your critical-thinking and problem-solving skills. The following features of the text and the accompanying learning package reinforce this problem-solving and career orientation.

A Framework for Describing and Analyzing Information Systems

The text provides you with a framework for analyzing and solving problems by examining the people, organizational, and technology components of information systems. This framework is used repeatedly throughout the text to help you understand information systems in business and analyze information systems problems.

A Four-Step Model for Problem Solving

The text provides you with a four-step method for solving business problems, which we introduced in this chapter. You will learn how to identify a business problem, design alternative solutions, choose the correct solution, and implement the solution. You will be asked to use this problem-solving method to solve the case studies in each chapter. Chapter 11 will show you how to use this approach to design and build new information systems.

Hands-On MIS Projects for Stimulating Critical Thinking and Problem Solving

Each chapter concludes with a series of hands-on MIS projects to sharpen your critical-thinking and problem-solving skills. These projects include two Management Decision Problems, hands-on application software problems, and projects for building Internet skills. For each of these projects, we identify both the business skills and the software skills required for the solution.

Career Resources

To make sure you know how the text is directly useful in your future business career, we've added a full set of Career Resources to help you with career development and job hunting.

Digital Portfolio MyMISLab includes a template for preparing a structured digital portfolio to demonstrate the business knowledge, application software skills, Internet skills, and analytical skills you have acquired in this course. You can include this portfolio in your resume or job applications. Your professors can also use the portfolio to assess the skills you have learned.

Career Resources A Career Resources section in MyMISLab shows you how to integrate what you have learned in this course in your resume, cover letter, and job interview to improve your chances for success in the job market.

1.5 Hands-On MIS Projects

The projects in this section give you hands-on experience in analyzing financial reporting and inventory management problems, using data management software to improve management decision making about increasing sales, and using Internet software for researching job requirements.

MANAGEMENT DECISION PROBLEMS

1. Snyders of Hanover, which sells about 80 million bags of pretzels, snack chips, and organic snack items each year, had its financial department use spreadsheets and manual processes for much of its data gathering and reporting. Hanover's financial analyst would spend the entire final week of every month collecting spreadsheets from the heads of more than 50 departments worldwide. She would then consolidate and re-enter all the data into another spreadsheet, which would serve as the company's monthly profit-and-loss statement. If a department needed to update its data after submitting the spreadsheet to the main office, the analyst had to return the original spreadsheet, then wait for the department to re-submit its data before finally submitting the updated data in the consolidated document. Assess the impact of this situation on business performance and management decision making.

2. Dollar General Corporation operates deep-discount stores offering housewares, cleaning supplies, clothing, health and beauty aids, and packaged food, with most items selling for $1. Its business model calls for keeping costs as low as possible. Although the company uses information systems (such as a point-of-sale system to track sales at the register), it deploys them very sparingly to keep expenditures to the minimum. The company has no automated method for keeping track of inventory at each store. Managers know approximately how many cases of a particular product the store is supposed to receive when a delivery truck arrives, but the stores lack technology for scanning the cases or verifying the item count inside the cases. Merchandise losses from theft or other mishaps have been rising and now represent over 3 percent of total sales. What decisions have to be made before investing in an information system solution?

IMPROVING DECISION MAKING: USING DATABASES TO ANALYZE SALES TRENDS

Software skills: Database querying and reporting
Business skills: Sales trend analysis

You can find out how information systems improve management decision making in this exercise. Rather than guessing or relying on estimates and experience, managers today rely on information stored in databases. In this project, you will start out with raw transactional sales data and use Microsoft Access database software to develop queries and reports that help managers make better decisions about product pricing, sales promotions, and inventory replenishment. A part of the database is shown in the following figure.

In MyMISLab, you can find a Store and Regional Sales Database developed in Microsoft Access. The database contains raw data on weekly store sales of computer equipment in various sales regions. You will use Access to manage the data and turn them into useful business information.

The database includes fields for store identification number, sales region, item number, item description, unit price, units sold, and the weekly sales period when the sales were made.

ID	Store No	Sales Region	Item No	Item Description	Unit Price	Units Sold	Week Ending
1	1	South	2005	17" monitor	$229.00	28	8/28/2009
2	1	South	2005	17" monitor	$229.00	30	9/25/2009
3	1	South	2005	17" monitor	$229.00	9	10/30/2009
4	1	South	3006	101 Keyboard	$19.95	30	8/28/2009
5	1	South	3006	101 Keyboard	$19.95	35	9/25/2009
6	1	South	3006	101 Keyboard	$19.95	39	10/30/2009
7	1	South	6050	PC Mouse	$8.95	28	8/28/2009
8	1	South	6050	PC Mouse	$8.95	3	9/25/2009
9	1	South	6050	PC Mouse	$8.95	38	10/30/2009
10	1	South	8500	Desktop CPU	$849.95	25	8/28/2009

Record: 1 of 10 No Filter Search

Develop some reports and queries to make this information more useful for running the business. Sales and production managers want answers to the following questions:

- Which products should be restocked?
- Which stores and sales regions would benefit from a promotional campaign and additional marketing?
- When (what time of year) should products be offered at full price, and when should discounts be used?

You can easily modify the database table to find and report your answers. Print your reports and results of queries.

IMPROVING DECISION MAKING: USING THE INTERNET TO LOCATE JOBS REQUIRING INFORMATION SYSTEMS KNOWLEDGE

Software skills: Internet-based software
Business skills: Job searching

Visit job-posting Web sites such as Monster.com or hotjobs.com. Spend some time at the sites examining jobs for accounting, finance, sales, marketing, and human resources. Find two or three descriptions of jobs that require some information systems knowledge. What information systems knowledge do these jobs require? What do you need to do to prepare for these jobs? Write a one- to two-page report summarizing your findings.

Review Summary

1 **How are information systems transforming business, and what is their relationship to globalization?** E-mail, online conferencing, and cell phones have become essential tools for conducting business. Information systems are the foundation of fast-paced supply chains. The Internet allows businesses to buy, sell, advertise, and solicit customer feedback online. The Internet has stimulated globalization by dramatically reducing the costs of producing, buying, and selling goods on a global scale.

2 **Why are information systems so essential for running and managing a business today?** Information systems are a foundation for conducting business today. In many industries, survival and even existence is difficult without extensive use of information technology. Businesses use information systems to achieve six major objectives: operational excellence; new products, services, and business models; customer/supplier intimacy; improved decision making; competitive advantage; and day-to-day survival.

3 **What exactly is an information system? How does it work? What are its people, organization, and technology components?** From a technical perspective, an information system collects, stores, and disseminates information from an organization's environment and internal operations to support organizational functions and decision making, communication, coordination, control, analysis, and visualization. Information systems transform raw data into useful information through three basic activities: input, processing, and output. From a business perspective, an information system provides a solution to a problem or challenge facing a firm and represents a combination of people, organization, and technology elements.

The people dimension of information systems involves issues such as training, job attitudes, and management behavior. The technology dimension consists of computer hardware, software, data management technology, and networking/telecommunications technology, including the Internet. The organization dimension of information systems involves issues such as the organization's hierarchy, functional specialties, business processes, culture, and political interest groups.

4 **How will a four-step method for business problem solving help you solve information system-related problems?** Problem identification involves understanding what kind of problem is being presented, and identifying people, organizational, and technology factors. Solution design involves designing several alternative solutions to the problem that has been identified. Evaluation and choice entails selecting the best solution, taking into account its cost and the available resources and skills in the business. Implementation of an information system solution entails purchasing or building hardware and software, testing the software, providing employees with training and documentation, managing change as the system is introduced into the organization, and measuring the outcome. Problem solving requires critical thinking in which one suspends judgment to consider multiple perspectives and alternatives.

5 **How will information systems affect business careers, and what information system skills and knowledge are essential?** Business careers in accounting, finance, marketing, operations management, management and human resources, and information systems all will need an understanding of how information systems help firms achieve major business objectives; an appreciation of the central role of databases; skills in information analysis and business intelligence; sensitivity to the ethical, social, and legal issues raised by systems; and the ability to work with technology specialists and other business professionals in designing and building systems.

Key Terms

Business model, 11
Business processes, 16
Change management, 23
Computer hardware, 17
Computer literacy, 15
Computer software, 17
Critical thinking, 23
Culture, 16
Data, 13
Data management technology, 17

Extranets, 17
Feedback, 14
Information, 13
Information system (IS), 13
Information systems literacy, 15
Information technology (IT), 13
Information technology (IT) infrastructure, 17
Input, 14

Internet, 17
Intranets, 17
Management information systems (MIS), 15
Network, 17
Networking and telecommunications technology, 17
Output, 14
Processing, 14
World Wide Web, 17

Review Questions

1. How are information systems transforming business, and what is their relationship to globalization?
• Describe how information systems have changed the way businesses operate and their products and services.
• Describe the challenges and opportunities of globalization in a "flattened" world.

2. Why are information systems so essential for running and managing a business today?
• List and describe the six reasons why information systems are so important for business today.

3. What exactly is an information system? How does it work? What are its people, organization, and technology components?
• List and describe the organizational, people, and technology dimensions of information systems.
• Define an information system and describe the activities it performs.
• Distinguish between data and information and between information systems literacy and computer literacy.
• Explain how the Internet and the World Wide Web are related to the other technology components of information systems.

4. How will a four-step method for business problem solving help you solve information system-related problems?
- List and describe each of the four steps for solving business problems.
- Give some examples of people, organizational, and technology problems found in businesses.
- Describe the relationship of critical thinking to problem solving.
- Describe the role of information systems in business problem solving.

5. How will information systems affect business careers, and what information system skills and knowledge are essential?
- Describe the role of information systems in careers in accounting, finance, marketing, management, and operations management, and explain how careers in information systems have been affected by new technologies and outsourcing.
- List and describe the information system skills and knowledge that are essential for all business careers.

Discussion Questions

1. What are the implications of globalization when you have to look for a job? What can you do to prepare yourself for competing in a globalized business environment? How would knowledge of information systems help you compete?

2. If you were setting up the Web site for another Major League Baseball team, what people, organization, and technology issues might you encounter?

Video Cases

Video Cases and Instructional Videos illustrating some of the concepts in this chapter are available. Contact your instructor to access these videos.

Collaborating and Teamwork

Creating a Web Site for Team Collaboration

Form a team with three or four classmates. Then use the tools at Google Sites to create a Web site for your team. You will need to a create Google account for the site and specify the collaborators (your team members) who are allowed to access the site and make contributions. Specify your professor as the viewer of the site so that person can evaluate your work. Assign a name to the site. Select a theme for the site and make any changes you wish to colors and fonts. Add features for project announcements and a repository for team documents, source materials, illustrations, electronic presentations, and Web pages of interest. You can add other features if you wish. Use Google to create a calendar for your team. After you complete this exercise, you can use this Web site and calendar for your other team projects.

BUSINESS PROBLEM-SOLVING CASE

What's the Buzz on Smart Grids?

The existing electricity infrastructure in the United States is outdated and inefficient. Energy companies provide power to consumers, but the grid provides no information about how the consumers are using that energy, making it difficult to develop more efficient approaches to distribution. Also, the current electricity grid offers few ways to handle power provided by alternative energy sources, which are critical components of most efforts to go "green". Enter the smart grid.

A smart grid delivers electricity from suppliers to consumers using digital technology to save energy, reduce cost, and increase reliability and transparency. The smart grid enables information to flow back and forth between electric power providers and consumers to allow both consumers and energy companies to make more intelligent decisions regarding energy consumption and production. Information from smart grids would show utilities when to raise prices when demand is high and lower them when demand lessens. Smart grids would also help consumers program high-use electrical appliances like heating and air conditioning systems to reduce consumption during times of peak usage. If implemented nationwide, proponents believe, smart grids would lead to a 5 to 15 percent decrease in energy consumption.

Managing the information flowing in these smart grids requires technology: networks and switches for power management, sensor and monitoring devices to track energy usage and distribution trends, systems to provide energy suppliers and consumers with usage data, communications systems to relay data along the entire energy supply system, and systems linked to programmable appliances to run them when energy is least costly.

If consumers had in-home displays showing how much energy they are consuming at any moment and the price of that energy, they are more likely to curb their consumption to cut costs. Home thermostats and appliances could adjust on their own automatically, depending on the cost of power, and even obtain that power from nontraditional sources, such as a neighbor's rooftop solar panel. Instead of power flowing from a small number of power plants, the smart grid will make it possible to have a distributed energy system. Electricity will flow from homes and businesses into the grid, and they will use power from local and faraway sources. Besides increasing energy efficiency, converting to smart grids along with other related energy initiatives could create up to 370,000 jobs.

That's why pioneering smart grid projects such as SmartGridCity in Boulder, Colorado, are attracting attention. SmartGridCity represents a collaboration by Xcel Energy Inc. and residents of Boulder to test the viability of smart grids on a smaller scale. Participants can check their power consumption levels and costs online, and will soon be able to program home appliances over the Web. Customers access this information and set goals and guidelines for their home's energy usage through a Web portal.

SmartGridCity is also attempting to turn homes into "miniature power plants" using solar-powered battery packs that "TiVo electricity", or stash it away to use at a later time. This serves as backup power for homes using the packs, but Xcel can also tap into that power during times of peak energy consumption to lessen the overall energy load. Xcel will be able to remotely adjust thermostats and water heaters and will have much better information about the power consumption of their consumers.

Bud Peterson, chancellor of the University of Colorado at Boulder, and his wife Val have worked with Xcel to turn their home into the prototype residence for the SmartGridCity project. Their house was supplied with a six-kilowatt photovoltaic system on two roofs, four thermostats controlled via the Web, a plug-in hybrid electric vehicle (PHEV) Ford Escape, and other high-tech, smart grid-compatible features. Xcel employees are able to monitor periods of high power consumption and how much energy the Escape is using on the road.

A digital dashboard in the Peterson's house displays power usage information in dozens of different ways—live household consumption and production, stored backup power, carbon emission reductions translated into gallons of gasoline, and acres of trees saved each year. The dashboard also allows the Petersons to program their home thermostats to adjust the temperature by room, time of day, and season. Since the project began in the spring of 2008, the Petersons have been able to reduce their electricity use by one-third.

Xcel is not alone. Hundreds of technology companies and almost every major electric utility company see smart grids as the wave of the future. Heightening interest is $4.5 billion in federal economic recovery money for smart grid technology.

Duke Energy spent $35 million on smart grid initiatives even before the economic stimulus plan was announced. It installed 80,000 smart meters as part of a pilot project in Charlotte, North Carolina, to provide business and residential customers with up-to-the-minute information on their energy use, as well as data on how much their appliances cost to operate. This helps them save money by curbing usage during peak times when rates are high or by replacing inefficient appliances. Duke now plans to spend $1 billion on sensors, intelligent meters, and other upgrades for a smart grid serving 700,000 customers in Cincinnati.

Florida Power and Light is budgeting $200 million for smart meters covering one million homes and businesses in the Miami area over the next two years. Center Point Energy, which services 2.2 million customers in the metropolitan Houston area, is planning to spend $1 billion over the next five years on a smart grid. Although residential customers will be charged an extra $3.24 per month, the company says this amount will be more than offset by energy savings.

Google has developed a free Web service called PowerMeter for tracking energy use in houses or businesses as power is consumed. It expects other companies to build the devices that will supply data to PowerMeter.

Wireless phone companies are also salivating over the opportunity to provide wireless communication links with the two-way meters being installed as part of the fledgling smart grids being developed in California, Texas, and sites like Boulder. AT&T, T-Mobile, Sprint Nextel, and Verizon Wireless are competing to team with utilities in providing a wireless communication link between their networks and smart meters. Users will be able to wirelessly receive alerts about outages, manage their service remotely, and sign up for a variety of rate plans.

There are a number of challenges facing the efforts to implement smart grids. Changing the infrastructure of our electricity grids is a daunting task. Two-way meters that allow information to flow both to and from homes need to be installed at any home or building that uses electric power—in other words, essentially everywhere. Some SmartGridCity participants reported that the dashboard they used to manage their appliances was too confusing and high-tech. Even Val Peterson admitted that at first, managing the information about her power usage supplied through the Xcel Web portal was an intimidating process.

The smart grid won't be cheap, with estimated costs running as high as $75 billion. Meters run $250 to $500 each when they are accompanied by new utility billing systems. Who is going to pay the bill? Is the average consumer willing to pay the upfront costs for a smart grid system and then respond appropriately to price signals? Will consumers get the promised payback if they buy into smart grid technology? Might "smart meters" be too intrusive? Would a highly computerized grid increase the risk of cyberattacks?

Jack Oliphant, a retiree living north of Houston in Spring, Texas, believes that the $444 he will pay Center Point for a smart meter won't justify the expense. "There's no mystery about how you save energy," he says. "You turn down the air conditioner and shut off some lights. I don't need an expensive meter to do that." Others have pointed out other less-expensive methods of energy consumption. Marcel Hawiger, an attorney for The Utility Reform Network, a San Francisco consumer advocacy group, favors expanding existing air conditioner-cycling programs, where utilities are able to control air conditioners so they take turns coming on and off, thereby reducing demands on the electric system. He believes air conditioner controllers, which control temperature settings and compressors to reduce overall energy costs, provide much of the benefit of smart meters at a fraction of their cost.

Consumer advocates have vowed to fight smart grids if they boost rates for customers who are unable or unwilling to use Web portals and allow energy companies to control aspects of their appliances. Advocates also argue that smart grids represent an Orwellian intrusion of people's right to use their appliances as they see fit without disclosing facts about their usage to others. A proposal by officials in California to require all new homes to have remotely adjustable thermostats was soundly defeated after critics worried about the privacy implications.

Energy companies stand to lose money as individuals conserve more electricity, creating a disincentive for them to cooperate with conservation efforts like smart grids. And, last but not least, in the short term, smart grid technologies will be expensive to implement. Patience will be critical as energy companies and local communities work to set up new technologies and pricing plans.

Sources: K.C. Jones, "Smart Grids to Get Jolt from IT," *Information Week*, March 23, 2009; H. Josef Hebert, "'Smart Grid'-Buzz of the Electric Power Industry," Associated Press, June 6, 2009; Rebecca Smith, "Smart Meter, Dumb Idea?" *The Wall Street Journal*, April 27, 2009; Stephanie Simon, "The More Your Know…" *The Wall Street Journal*, February 9, 2009; and Matthew Wald and Miguel Helft, "Google Taking a Step into Power Metering," *The New York Times*, February 10, 2009.

Case Study Questions

1. How do smart grids differ from the current electricity infrastructure in the United States?
2. What people, organization, and technology issues should be considered when developing a smart grid?
3. What challenge to the development of smart grids do you think is most likely to hamper their development?
4. What other areas of our infrastructure could benefit from "smart" technologies? Describe one example not listed in the case.
5. Would you like your home and your community to be part of a smart grid? Why or why not? Explain.

Global E-Business and Collaboration

CHAPTER 2

STUDENT LEARNING OBJECTIVES

After completing this chapter, you will be able to answer the following questions:

1. What are the major features of a business that are important for understanding the role of information systems?

2. How do systems serve the various levels of management in a business?

3. How do enterprise applications and intranets improve organizational performance?

4. Why are systems for collaboration and teamwork so important and what technologies do they use?

5. What is the role of the information systems function in a business?

CHAPTER OUTLINE

THE TATA NANO MAKES HISTORY USING DIGITAL MANUFACTURING

On March 23, 2009, India's Tata Motors rolled out its Nano car. It was an historic moment, because the Nano was the cheapest auto ever made at that time, with a price tag around US $2,500. The Nano joined Ford's Model T as a car within reach of millions of people who previously could not afford one. With a top speed of 105 kilometers (65 miles) per hour, the Nano has a two-cylinder engine; four-speed manual transmission; no air conditioning, electric windows, or power steering; and fuel efficiency of 50 miles per gallon.

Tata Motors started its Nano project in 2003, when a team was charged with creating a car that would cost no more than about US $2,500 without compromising on safety, aesthetics, or value to the customer. It was a Herculean task. Tata met the challenge by using digital manufacturing (DM) systems to dramatically shorten the time required to design the new product and bring it to market. The ability to develop and produce new products with many different variations within a very short time span is a key competitive advantage in the automotive industry.

Until a few years ago, it would have been impossible to design and produce the Nano at this price. Tata Motors had outdated manufacturing processes. Manual effort was required to create and maintain processes, plants, and product design, resulting in longer lead times to choose the appropriate tools for an operation. The company had to create programs manually for assembly line robots, a process that was error-prone and time-consuming. Such delays had a number of negative consequences: Data used to plan a vehicle became useless over time, and the company was unable to easily change its product mix, roll out a new product on an existing production line, or schedule the assembly of two different products on the same line.

All that changed in July 2005 when Tata Motors switched to digital manufacturing using Dassault Systemes' Digital Enterprise Lean Manufacturing Interactive Application (DELMIA). Digital manufacturing automates processes in product design and production engineering planning, enabling Tata to plan manufacturing processes, design plant layouts, and then simulate the repercussions of those plans, including the impact of new manufacturing techniques and changes of products on existing production lines. It provides data to Tata's SAP enterprise resource planning system, which costs out a product, an assembly, or a sub-assembly. Digital manufacturing also simulates the movements of people working on the shop floor so that planners can design more efficient work processes. Companies using digital manufacturing can model products and operations and make changes to them on the computer. This cuts down on the use of expensive physical prototypes, which must be rebuilt each time a design changes.

According to T. N. Umamaheshwaran, who headed Tata Motors' digital manufacturing program, "We can't imagine what would take place at a new plant, if we did not have DM Tools. Two years before the first stone of a plant is laid, we already start working on it. We don't even know where the site will be, but we know what it will take to make 750 cars a day."

As a result of adopting digital manufacturing, Tata Motors has reduced time-to-market for new passenger cars by at least six months. The company can now rapidly identify areas of "work overload" and constraints while quickly adapting assembly lines to accommodate multiple automobile variations. The ability to simulate facilities and processes has reduced the cost of physical rework. Manufacturing and facilities planning now take 30 percent less time, with a 20 percent reduction in the cost of the manufacturing planning process. For certain functions, the time to design an entire process end-to-end has been reduced by over 50 percent.

Sources: Salil Panchal, "India's Tata Rolls Out World's Cheapest Car," Agence-France Presse, March 23, 2009; Santanu Choudhury, "Tata Hopes Tiny Car Is a Big Hit," The Wall Street Journal, March 21, 2009; Jessie Scanlon, "What Can Tata's Nano Teach Detroit?" Business Week, March 18, 2009; and Gunjan Trivedi, "Driving Down Cost," CIO Asia, February 2008.

The experience of Tata Motors illustrates how much companies today rely on information systems to run their businesses and drive innovation, growth, and profitability. It also shows the importance of collaboration and teamwork in a company's ability to innovate, execute, and improve overall business performance.

The chapter-opening diagram calls attention to important points raised by this case and this chapter. Tata Motors was confronted with both a problem and an opportunity. The company operates in a highly competitive industry where the manufacturers are expected to bring new car models with many different variations to market very quickly, but it was slowed down by relying too much on manual processes. Tata management identified opportunities to use information systems to improve business performance and also to enter a new marketspace—specifically consumers in India and other developing countries who wanted cars but could not afford them.

Management decided to design and develop a car for this market and to switch to digital manufacturing for all of its auto production. Technology alone would not have provided a solution. The company had to revise many of its manufacturing processes to support digital

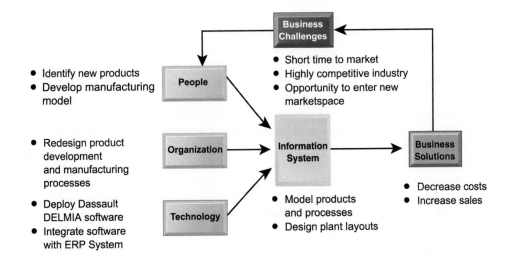

manufacturing. Once that was accomplished, Dassault's DELMIA software proved invaluable for modeling designs, factories, and production processes and for coordinating information between processes. Digital manufacturing systems increased flexibility and efficiency while decreasing production costs, and made it possible to pioneer in low-cost cars such as the Nano.

2.1 Components of a Business

A **business** is a formal organization whose aim is to produce products or provide services for a profit—that is, to sell products at a price greater than the costs of production. Customers are willing to pay this price because they believe they receive a value greater than or equal to the sale price. Business firms purchase inputs and resources from the larger environment (suppliers who are often other firms). Employees of the business firm transform these inputs by adding value to them in the production process.

There are of course nonprofit firms and government agencies that are complex formal organizations that produce services and products but do not operate in order to produce a profit. Nevertheless, even these kinds of organizations consume resources from their environments, add value to these inputs, and deliver their outputs to constituents and customers. In general, the information systems found in government and nonprofit organizations are remarkably similar to those found in private industry.

ORGANIZING A BUSINESS: BASIC BUSINESS FUNCTIONS

Imagine that you wanted to set up your own business. Simply deciding to go into business is the most important decision, but next is the question of what product or service to produce (and hopefully sell). The decision of what to produce is called a *strategic choice* because it determines your likely customers, the kinds of employees you will need, the production methods and facilities needed, the marketing themes, and many other choices.

Once you decide what to produce, what kind of organization do you need? First, you need to develop a production division—an arrangement of people, machines, and business processes (procedures) that will produce the product. Second, you need a sales and marketing group who will attract customers, sell the product, and keep track of after-sales issues, such as warranties and maintenance. Third, once you generate sales, you will need a finance and accounting group to keep track of financial transactions, such as orders, invoices, disbursements, and payroll. In addition, this group will seek out sources of credit and finance. Finally, you will need a group of people to focus on recruiting, hiring, training, and retaining employees. Figure 2-1 summarizes the four basic functions found in every business.

If you were an entrepreneur or your business was very small with only a few employees, you would not need, and probably could not afford, all these separate groups of people. Instead, in small firms, you would be performing all these functions yourself or with a few others. No wonder small firms have a high mortality rate! In any event, even in small firms, the four basic functions of a firm are required. Larger firms often will have separate departments for each function: production and manufacturing, sales and marketing, finance and accounting, and human resources.

Figure 2-1 is also useful for thinking about the basic entities that make up a business. The five basic entities in a business with which it must deal are: suppliers, customers, employees, invoices/payments, and, of course, products and services. There are many other entities that a business must manage and monitor, but these are the basic ones at the foundation of any business.

BUSINESS PROCESSES

Once you identify the basic business functions and entities for your business, your next job is to describe exactly how you want your employees to perform these functions. What specific tasks do you want your sales personnel to perform, in what order, and on what schedule? What steps do you want production employees to follow as they transform raw resources into finished products? How will customer orders be fulfilled? How will vendor bills be paid?

The actual steps and tasks that describe how work is organized in a business are called **business processes**. A business process is a logically related set of activities that define how specific business tasks are performed. Business processes also refer to the unique ways in which work, information, and knowledge are coordinated in a specific organization.

**Figure 2-1
The Four Major
Functions of a
Business**
Every business, regardless of its size, must perform four functions to succeed. It must produce the product or service; market and sell the product or service; keep track of accounting and financial transactions; and perform basic human resources tasks, such as hiring and retaining employees.

TABLE 2.1

Examples of Functional Business Processes

Functional Area	Business Process
Manufacturing and production	Assembling the product
	Checking for quality
	Producing bills of materials
Sales and marketing	Identifying customers
	Making customers aware of the product
	Selling the product
Finance and accounting	Paying creditors
	Creating financial statements
	Managing cash accounts
Human resources	Hiring employees
	Evaluating employees' job performance
	Enrolling employees in benefits plans

Every business can be seen as a collection of business processes. Some of these processes are part of larger encompassing processes. (In the chapter-opening case on Tata Motors, for instance, designing a new car model, manufacturing components, and assembling the finished car are all part of the overall production process.) Many business processes are tied to a specific functional area. For example, the sales and marketing function would be responsible for identifying customers, and the human resources function would be responsible for hiring employees. Table 2.1 describes some typical business processes for each of the functional areas of business.

Other business processes cross many different functional areas and require coordination across departments. Consider the seemingly simple business process of fulfilling a customer order (see Figure 2-2). Initially, the sales department receives a sales order. The order will pass first to accounting to ensure the customer can pay for the order either by a credit verification or request for immediate payment prior to shipping. Once the customer credit is established, the production department has to pull the product from inventory or produce the

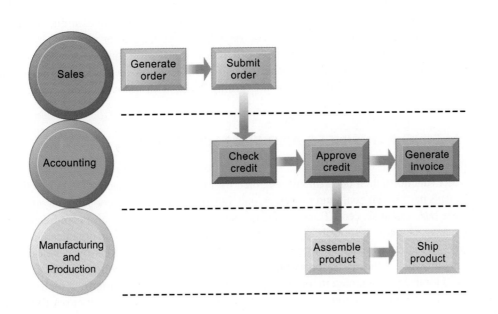

Figure 2-2
The Order Fulfillment Process
Fulfilling a customer order involves a complex set of steps that requires the close coordination of the sales, accounting, and manufacturing functions.

product. Then the product will need to be shipped (and this may require working with a logistics firm, such as UPS or FedEx). A bill or invoice will then have to be generated by the accounting department, and a notice will be sent to the customer indicating that the product has shipped. Sales will have to be notified of the shipment and prepare to support the customer by answering calls or fulfilling warranty claims.

What at first appears to be a simple process, fulfilling an order, turns out to be a very complicated series of business processes that require the close coordination of major functional groups in a firm. Moreover, to efficiently perform all these steps in the order fulfillment process requires a great deal of information and the rapid flow of information within the firm, with business partners such as delivery firms, and with the customer. The particular order fulfillment process we have just described is not only *cross-functional*, it is also *interorganizational* because it includes interactions with delivery firms and customers who are outside the boundaries of the organization. Ordering raw materials or components from suppliers would be another interorganizational business process.

To a large extent, the efficiency of a business firm depends on how well its internal and interorganizational business processes are designed and coordinated. A company's business processes can be a source of competitive strength if they enable the company to innovate or to execute better than its rivals. Business processes can also be liabilities if they are based on outdated ways of working that impede organizational responsiveness and efficiency. The chapter-opening case on Tata Motors product development and manufacturing processes clearly illustrates these points.

How Information Technology Enhances Business Processes

Exactly how do information systems enhance business processes? Information systems automate many steps in business processes that were formerly performed manually, such as checking a client's credit, or generating an invoice and shipping order. But today, information technology can do much more. New technology can actually change the flow of information, making it possible for many more people to access and share information, replacing sequential steps with tasks that can be performed simultaneously, and eliminating delays in decision making. It can even transform the way the business works and drive new business models. Ordering a book online from Amazon.com and downloading a music track from iTunes are entirely new business processes based on new business models that are inconceivable without information technology.

That's why it's so important to pay close attention to business processes, both in your information systems course and in your future career. By analyzing business processes, you can achieve a very clear understanding of how a business actually works. Moreover, by conducting a business process analysis, you will also begin to understand how to change the business to make it more efficient or effective. Throughout this book we examine business processes with a view to understanding how they might be changed, or replaced, by using information technology to achieve greater efficiency, innovation, and customer service. Chapter 3 discusses the business impact of using information technology to redesign business processes, and MyMISLab has a Learning Track with more detailed coverage of this topic.

MANAGING A BUSINESS AND FIRM HIERARCHIES

What is missing from Figures 2-1 and 2-2 is any notion of how to coordinate and control the four major functions, their departments, and their business processes. Each of these functional departments has its own goals and processes, and they obviously need to cooperate in order for the whole business to succeed. Business firms, like all organizations, achieve coordination by hiring managers whose responsibility is to ensure all the various parts of an organization work together. Firms coordinate the work of employees in various divisions by developing a hierarchy in which authority (responsibility and accountability) is concentrated at the top.

The hierarchy of management is composed of **senior management**, which makes long-range strategic decisions about products and services as well as ensures financial performance of the firm; **middle management**, which carries out the programs and plans of senior management; and **operational management**, which is responsible for monitoring the daily activities of the business. **Knowledge workers**, such as engineers, scientists, or architects, design products or services and create new knowledge for the firm, whereas **data workers**, such as secretaries or clerks, assist with administrative work at all levels of the firm. **Production or service workers** actually produce the product and deliver the service (Figure 2-3).

Each of these groups has different needs for information given their different responsibilities. Senior managers need summary information that can quickly inform them about the overall performance of the firm, such as gross sales revenues, sales by product group and region, and overall profitability. Middle managers need more specific information on the results of specific functional areas and departments of the firm, such as sales contacts by the sales force, production statistics for specific factories or product lines, employment levels and costs, and sales revenues for each month or even each day. Operational managers need transaction-level information, such as the number of parts in inventory each day or the number of hours logged on Tuesday by each employee. Knowledge workers may need access to external scientific databases or internal databases with organizational knowledge. Finally, production workers need access to information from production machines, and service workers need access to customer records in order to take orders and answer questions from customers.

THE BUSINESS ENVIRONMENT

So far we have talked about business as if it operated in a vacuum. Nothing could be further from the truth. In fact, business firms depend heavily on their environments to supply capital, labor, customers, new technology, services and products, stable markets and legal systems, and general educational resources. Even a pizza parlor cannot survive long without a supportive environment that delivers the cheese, tomato sauce, and flour!

Figure 2-4 summarizes the key actors in the environment of every business. To stay in business, a firm must monitor changes in its environment and share information with the key entities in that environment. For instance, a firm must respond to political shifts, respond to changes in the overall economy (such as changes in labor rates and price inflation), keep track of new technologies, and respond to changes in the global business environment (such as foreign exchange rates). In its immediate environment, firms need to track and share information with suppliers, customers, stockholders, regulators, and logistic partners (such as shipping firms).

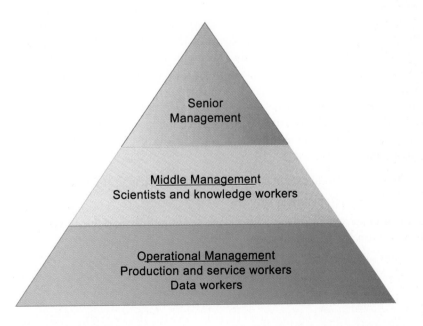

Figure 2-3
Levels in a Firm
Business organizations are hierarchies consisting of three principal levels: senior management, middle management, and operational management. Information systems serve each of these levels. Scientists and knowledge workers often work with middle management.

Figure 2-4
The Business
Environment
To be successful, an
organization must
constantly monitor and
respond to—or even
anticipate—develop-
ments in its environment.
A firm's environment
includes specific groups
with which the business
must deal directly, such
as customers, suppliers,
and competitors as well
as the broader general
environment, including
socioeconomic trends,
political conditions, tech-
nological innovations,
and global events.

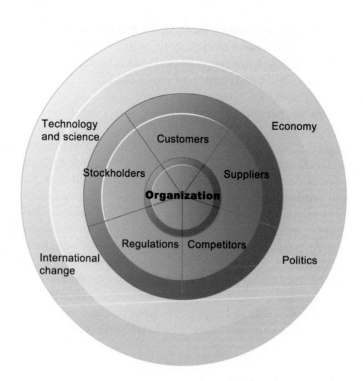

Business environments are constantly changing: New developments in technology, politics, customer preferences, and regulations happen all the time. In general, when businesses
fail, it is often because they failed to respond adequately to changes in their environments.

Changes in technology, such as the Internet, are forcing entire industries and leading
firms to change their business models or suffer failure. Apple's iTunes and other online
music download services are making the music industry's traditional business model based
on distributing music on CDs obsolete. Another example is the photography business.
Digital photography has forced Eastman Kodak to downsize and move into digital cameras
and Internet photography services because most of the consumer marketplace no longer
wants to use traditional cameras with film.

THE ROLE OF INFORMATION SYSTEMS IN A BUSINESS

Until now we have not mentioned information systems. But from the brief review of
business functions, entities, and environments, you can see the critical role that information
plays in the life of a business. Up until the mid 1950s, firms managed all this information
and information flow with paper records. During the past 50 years, more and more business
information and the flow of information among key business actors in the environment has
been computerized.

Businesses invest in information systems as a way to cope with and manage their
internal production functions and to cope with the demands of key actors in their environments. Specifically, as we noted in Chapter 1, firms invest in information systems for the
following business objectives:

- To achieve operational excellence (productivity, efficiency, agility)
- To develop new products and services
- To attain customer intimacy and service (continuous marketing, sales, and service;
  customization and personalization)
- To improve decision making (accuracy and speed)
- To achieve competitive advantage
- To ensure survival

2.2 Types of Business Information Systems

Now it is time to look more closely at how businesses use information systems to achieve these goals. Because there are different interests, specialties, and levels in an organization, there are different kinds of systems. No single system can provide all the information an organization needs.

A typical business organization will have systems supporting processes for each of the major business functions—systems for sales and marketing, manufacturing and production, finance and accounting, and human resources. You can find examples of systems for each of these business functions in the Learning Tracks for this chapter. Functional systems that operated independently of each other are becoming a thing of the past because they could not easily share information to support cross-functional business processes. They are being replaced with large-scale cross-functional systems that integrate the activities of related business processes and organizational units. We describe these integrated cross-functional applications later in this section.

A typical firm will also have different systems supporting the decision making needs of each of the main management groups we described earlier. Operational management, middle management, and senior management each use a specific type of system to support the decisions they must make to run the company. Let's look at these systems and the types of decisions they support.

SYSTEMS FOR DIFFERENT LEVELS OF MANAGEMENT

A business firm has systems to support decision making and activities at different levels of the organization. Each of the main management groups we described earlier uses a different type of system to deliver the information required to manage the company. These systems can be classified as transaction processing systems, management information systems, decision-support systems, and systems for executive support.

Transaction Processing Systems

Operational managers need systems that keep track of the elementary activities and transactions of the organization, such as sales, receipts, cash deposits, payroll, credit decisions, and the flow of materials in a factory. **Transaction processing systems (TPS)** provide this kind of information. A transaction processing system is a computerized system that performs and records the daily routine transactions necessary to conduct business, such as sales order entry, hotel reservations, payroll, employee record keeping, and shipping.

The principal purpose of systems at this level is to answer routine questions and to track the flow of transactions through the organization. How many parts are in inventory? What happened to Mr. Williams's payment? To answer these kinds of questions, information generally must be easily available, current, and accurate.

At the operational level, tasks, resources, and goals are predefined and highly structured. The decision to grant credit to a customer, for instance, is made by a lower-level supervisor according to predefined criteria. All that must be determined is whether the customer meets the criteria.

Figure 2-5 illustrates a TPS for payroll processing. A payroll system keeps track of money paid to employees. An employee time sheet with the employee's name, social security number, and number of hours worked per week represents a single transaction for this system. Once this transaction is input into the system, it updates the system's file (or database—see Chapter 5) that permanently maintains employee information for the organization. The data in the system are combined in different ways to create reports of interest to management and government agencies and to send paychecks to employees.

Figure 2-5
A Payroll TPS
A TPS for payroll processing captures employee payment transaction data (such as a timecard). System outputs include online and hard copy reports for management and employee paychecks.

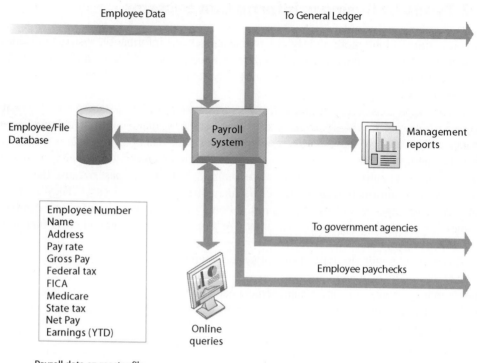

Managers need TPS to monitor the status of internal operations and the firm's relations with the external environment. TPS are also major producers of information for the other systems and business functions. For example, the payroll system illustrated in Figure 2-5, along with other accounting TPS, supplies data to the company's general ledger system, which is responsible for maintaining records of the firm's income and expenses and for producing reports such as income statements and balance sheets. It also supplies employee payment history data for insurance, pension, and other benefits calculations to the firm's human resources function and employee payment data to government agencies such as the U.S. Internal Revenue Service and Social Security Administration.

Transaction processing systems are often so central to a business that TPS failure for a few hours can lead to a firm's demise and perhaps that of other firms linked to it. Imagine what would happen to UPS if its package tracking system were not working! What would the airlines do without their computerized reservation systems?

Management Information Systems and Decision-Support Systems

Middle management needs systems to help with monitoring, controlling, decision-making, and administrative activities. The principal question addressed by such systems is this: Are things working well?

In Chapter 1, we define management information systems as the study of information systems in business and management. The term **management information systems (MIS)** also designates a specific category of information systems serving middle management. MIS provide middle managers with reports on the organization's current performance. This information is used to monitor and control the business and predict future performance.

MIS summarize and report on the company's basic operations using data supplied by transaction processing systems. The basic transaction data from TPS are compressed and usually presented in reports that are produced on a regular schedule. Today, many of these reports are delivered online. Figure 2-6 shows how a typical MIS transforms transaction-level data from inventory, production, and accounting into MIS files that are used to provide managers with reports. Figure 2-7 shows a sample report from this system.

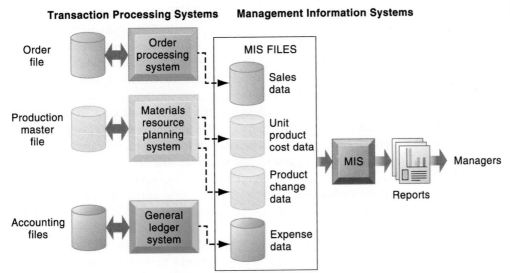

Transaction Processing Systems   Management Information Systems

Figure 2-6
How Management
Information Systems
Obtain Their Data
from the
Organization's TPS
In the system illustrated by this diagram, three TPS supply summarized transaction data to the MIS reporting system at the end of the time period. Managers gain access to the organizational data through the MIS, which provides them with the appropriate reports.

MIS serve managers primarily interested in weekly, monthly, and yearly results, although some MIS enable managers to drill down to see daily or hourly data if required. MIS generally provide answers to routine questions that have been specified in advance and have a predefined procedure for answering them. For instance, MIS reports might list the total pounds of lettuce used this quarter by a fast-food chain or, as illustrated in Figure 2-7, compare total annual sales figures for specific products to planned targets. These systems generally are not flexible and have little analytical capability. Most MIS use simple routines, such as summaries and comparisons, as opposed to sophisticated mathematical models or statistical techniques.

Decision-support systems (DSS) support nonroutine decision making for middle management. They focus on problems that are unique and rapidly changing, for which the procedure for arriving at a solution may not be fully predefined in advance. They try to answer questions such as these: What would be the impact on production schedules if we were to double sales in the month of December? What would happen to our return on investment if a factory schedule were delayed for six months?

Consolidated Consumer Products Corporation Sales by Product and Sales Region: 2010

PRODUCT CODE	PRODUCT DESCRIPTION	SALES REGION	ACTUAL SALES	PLANNED	ACTUAL versus PLANNED
4469	Carpet Cleaner	Northeast	4,066,700	4,800,000	0.85
		South	3,778,112	3,750,000	1.01
		Midwest	4,867,001	4,600,000	1.06
		West	4,003,440	4,400,000	0.91
	TOTAL		16,715,253	17,550,000	0.95
5674	Room Freshener	Northeast	3,676,700	3,900,000	0.94
		South	5,608,112	4,700,000	1.19
		Midwest	4,711,001	4,200,000	1.12
		West	4,563,440	4,900,000	0.93
	TOTAL		18,559,253	17,700,000	1.05

Figure 2-7
Sample MIS Report
This report, showing summarized annual sales data, was produced by the MIS in Figure 2-6.

Although DSS use internal information from TPS and MIS, they often bring in information from external sources, such as current stock prices or product prices of competitors. These systems use a variety of models to analyze data, or they condense large amounts of data into a form in which decision makers can analyze them. DSS are designed so that users can work with them directly; these systems explicitly include user-friendly software.

An interesting, small, but powerful, DSS is the voyage-estimating system of a subsidiary of a large American metals company that exists primarily to carry bulk cargoes of coal, oil, ores, and finished products for its parent company. The firm owns some vessels, charters others, and bids for shipping contracts in the open market to carry general cargo. A voyage-estimating system calculates financial and technical voyage details. Financial calculations include ship/time costs (fuel, labor, capital), freight rates for various types of cargo, and port expenses. Technical details include a myriad of factors, such as ship cargo capacity, speed, port distances, fuel and water consumption, and loading patterns (location of cargo for different ports).

The system can answer questions such as the following: Given a customer delivery schedule and an offered freight rate, which vessel should be assigned at what rate to maximize profits? What is the optimal speed at which a particular vessel can optimize its profit and still meet its delivery schedule? What is the optimal loading pattern for a ship bound for the U.S. West Coast from Malaysia? Figure 2-8 illustrates the DSS built for this company. The system operates on a powerful desktop personal computer, providing a system of menus that makes it easy for users to enter data or obtain information.

This voyage-estimating DSS draws heavily on analytical models. Other types of DSS are less model-driven, focusing instead on extracting useful information to support decision making from massive quantities of data. For example, Intrawest—the largest ski operator in North America—collects and stores large amounts of customer data from its Web site, call center, lodging reservations, ski schools, and ski equipment rental stores. It uses special software to analyze these data to determine the value, revenue potential, and loyalty of each customer so managers can make better decisions on how to target their marketing programs. The system segments customers into seven categories based on needs, attitudes, and behaviors, ranging from "passionate experts" to "value-minded family vacationers." The company then e-mails video clips that would appeal to each segment to encourage more visits to its resorts.

Sometimes you'll hear DSS referred to as *business intelligence systems* because they focus on helping users make better business decisions. You'll learn more about them in Chapters 5 and 10.

Figure 2-8
Voyage-Estimating Decision-Support System
This DSS operates on a powerful PC. It is used daily by managers who must develop bids on shipping contracts.

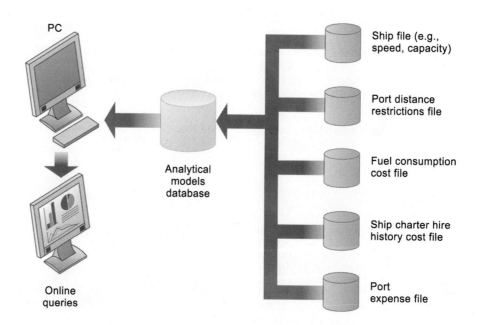

Executive Support Systems for Senior Management

Senior managers need systems that address strategic issues and long-term trends, both in the firm and in the external environment. They are concerned with questions such as these: What will employment levels be in five years? What are the long-term industry cost trends, and where does our firm fit in? What products should we be making in five years? What new acquisitions would protect us from cyclical business swings?

Executive support systems (ESS) help senior management make these decisions. ESS address nonroutine decisions requiring judgment, evaluation, and insight because there is no agreed-on procedure for arriving at a solution. ESS present graphs and data from many sources through an interface that is easy for senior managers to use. Often the information is delivered to senior executives through a **portal**, which uses a Web interface to present integrated personalized business content. You will learn more about other applications of portals in Chapters 9 and 10.

ESS are designed to incorporate data about external events, such as new tax laws or competitors, but they also draw summarized information from internal MIS and DSS. They filter, compress, and track critical data, displaying the data of greatest importance to senior managers. For example, the CEO of Leiner Health Products, the largest manufacturer of private-label vitamins and supplements in the United States, has an ESS that provides on his desktop a minute-to-minute view of the firm's financial performance as measured by working capital, accounts receivable, accounts payable, cash flow, and inventory. The information is presented in the form of a **digital dashboard**, which displays on a single screen graphs and charts of key performance indicators for managing a company. Digital dashboards are becoming an increasingly popular tool for management decision makers.

Figure 2-9 illustrates a model of an ESS. It consists of workstations with menus, interactive graphics, and communications capabilities that can be used to access historical and competitive data from internal corporate systems and external databases such as Dow Jones Factiva or the Gallup Poll. More details on leading-edge applications of DSS and ESS can be found in Chapter 10.

The Interactive Session on Organizations describes real-world examples of several of these types of systems used by a company that is attempting to grow from a successful local restaurant into a nationwide fast-food chain. Note the types of systems illustrated by this case and the role they play in improving both operations and decision making.

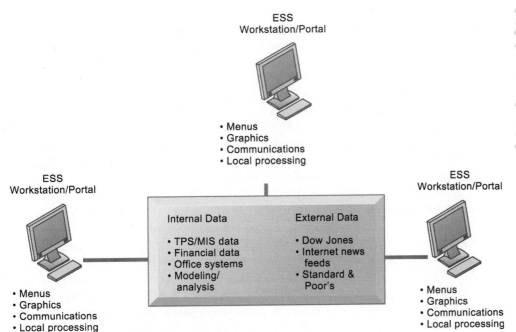

ESS
Workstation/Portal

• Menus
• Graphics
• Communications
• Local processing

ESS
Workstation/Portal

• Menus
• Graphics
• Communications
• Local processing

ESS
Workstation/Portal

Internal Data

• TPS/MIS data
• Financial data
• Office systems
• Modeling/
  analysis

External Data

• Dow Jones
• Internet news
  feeds
• Standard &
  Poor's

• Menus
• Graphics
• Communications
• Local processing

**Figure 2-9
Model of an
Executive Support
System**
This system pools data from diverse internal and external sources and makes them available to executives in an easy-to-use form.

INTERACTIVE SESSION: ORGANIZATIONS

'Fresh, Hot, Fast' —Can Information Systems Help Johnny's Lunch Go National?

In 1936, Johnny Colera began selling hot dogs at his lunch counter in Jamestown, New York. Thanks to his special chili sauce and savvy business management, his restaurant, named Johnny's Lunch, became a huge success and a local institution. Johnny's Lunch offers good food, low prices, top-notch service, and a unique store atmosphere, featuring Johnny's Hots hot dogs, burgers, fries, onion rings, and shakes, as well as less common options like homemade rice pudding.

The restaurant now wants to grow into a national QSR (quick-service restaurant, or fast food) leader similar to McDonald's. The company is currently led by two of Colera's grandchildren, Anthony and John Calamunci, and a newly assembled team of executives with experience in the QSR industry.

Growing the company from its humble origins into a national presence faces significant challenges. One will be to retain the restaurant's small-town, local flavor as franchises proliferate across the country. Accomplishing this goal will require a coordinated effort.

Another challenge for Johnny's Lunch will be to sustain growth despite the impact of a weak economy. Analysts predict that the slow economy will threaten growth potential for QSRs; it's estimated that the sector's annual growth will slow to 2% or 3%, down from much higher rates during more promising times. The company hopes that familiar and cheap food will translate to success even in an economic downturn during 2009 and beyond.

Management wanted to expand to 30-50 restaurants by the end of 2008, with a goal of as many as 3,000 locations nationwide in the following 5 years. There are only 3,300 hot dog restaurants in the country, and the most prominent chains like Nathan's Famous and Wienerschnitzel have only 180 and 250 outlets, respectively. Johnny's Lunch and industry analysts believe that there is room for the explosive growth the company is planning.

Johnny's Lunch hopes to overcome these challenges with the help of state-of-the-art technology, including sophisticated mapping technology to scout locations, state-of-the-art point-of-sale (POS) systems, and inventory management systems that ensure freshness and reduce costs.

Pitney Bowes MapInfo has allowed Johnny's to take a scientific approach to choosing spots for new restaurants. MapInfo's Predictive Analytics group interviewed 800 customers at the original Jamestown restaurant to identify the types of customers Johnny's Lunch attracted. Half were families; most were ages

16–24 or over 60 and had lower-middle to upper-middle class incomes. The interviews also determined the distribution of customers coming into the restaurant from work, home, shopping, or some other location.

MapInfo's Smart Site Solutions analytics technology helped Johnny's Lunch use this information to pinpoint potential markets and to identify the optimal number of sites within the market to maximize sales. Smart Site Solutions separated the country into many designated market areas (DMAs) showing the level of competition, demographics, and characteristics of prospective franchise locations. Pitney Bowes consultants determined which of 72 "clusters", or neighborhood types, best match the restaurant's optimal target areas from a variety of perspectives. Using this data within the Smart Site Solutions model allowed Johnny's Lunch to identify approximately 4,500 optimal trade areas across the country. The executive team believes that these areas possess the best opportunities for successful Johnny's Lunch franchises.

Using data such as trade area size, buffer distance between stores, customer profile, and more, Smart Site Solutions created a model that predicted the potential success of various sites. The processes allowed Johnny's Lunch to identify sites without a wealth of historical sales data. Target spots include strip malls in facilities ranging from 1,400–1,800 feet, as opposed to freestanding locations, which tend to cost more to set up. The company also hopes that its franchises will be placed alongside well-known national brands, which will give Johnny's Lunch immediate credibility among consumers.

Another area in which Johnny's Lunch is using advanced technology to spur growth is its POS system. A POS system captures sales transaction data at the actual physical location where goods or services are bought or sold through electronic cash registers or handheld scanners. Company executives have selected the MICROS 3700 POS system from MICROS Systems as the system all their franchises will use as Johnny's Lunch expands. A good POS system helps monitor inventory, control waste, and adhere to government regulations (for example, if food takes too long to prepare, if a cashier voids excessive transactions, or if any violations of labor laws occur, the system will alert employees). The MICROS system does all this and provides several other advantages. The system has impressed Johnny's Lunch with how easy it is to understand and use, and MICROS is a large company with national reach and vendor locations throughout the country. This means that as Johnny's

Lunch grows nationally, MICROS will continue to be able to meet the company's needs throughout the United States and should be simple for new franchises to master. The system also allows the company to track useful data about consumers' habits, such as how much food is eaten in the restaurant as opposed to how much is carried out.

Until recently, the company exclusively used laptop computers and two POS systems to run the business. Johnny's Lunch currently uses a single custom-made server from Dell Direct, but plans to add more new servers in the near future—one for marketing data, and one that will network all locations' POS systems—as part of an IT overhaul. Johnny's Lunch also plans to upgrade its Web site, incorporating a portal that will allow franchise operators to place orders and download pertinent information.

Sources: "Hot Dog: Franchising with Technology," Baselinemag.com, April 30, 2008; www.johnnyslunch.com, accessed June 15, 2009; and Karen E. Klein, "Finding the Perfect Location," *BusinessWeek*, March 2008.

CASE STUDY QUESTIONS

1. Describe Johnny's Lunch's business model and business strategy. What challenges does Johnny's Lunch face as it begins its expansion?

2. What systems has the company used or plans to use to overcome these challenges? What types of systems are they? What role will each play in helping Johnny's Lunch overcome these challenges?

3. What other kinds of systems described in this chapter might help Johnny's Lunch as it expands?

4. Do you believe Johnny's Lunch will be successful in its attempts to expand nationally? Why or why not?

MIS IN ACTION

Visit Johnny's Lunch Web site (www.johnnyslunch.com) and then answer the following questions:

1. What is the target audience for this Web site? What is the objective of the Web site? How easy is it to use? How useful is it in attracting customers? How well does this Web site support the company's business strategy?

2. How many franchise locations are described on the Web site? Where are they located? What does this tell you about the company's expansion strategy?

SYSTEMS THAT SPAN THE ENTERPRISE

Reviewing all the different types of systems we have just described, you might wonder how a business can manage all the information in these different systems. You might also wonder how costly it is to maintain so many different systems. And you might wonder how all these different systems can share information and how managers and employees are able to coordinate their work. In fact, these are all important questions for businesses today.

Enterprise Applications

Getting all the different kinds of systems in a company to work together has proven a major challenge. Typically, corporations are put together both through normal "organic" growth and through acquisition of smaller firms. Over a period of time, corporations end up with a collection of systems, most of them older, and face the challenge of getting them all to "talk" with one another and work together as one corporate system. There are several solutions to this problem.

One solution is to implement **enterprise applications**, which are systems that span functional areas, focus on executing business processes across the business firm, and include all levels of management. Enterprise applications help businesses become more flexible and productive by coordinating their business processes more closely and integrating groups of processes so they focus on efficient management of resources and customer service.

There are four major enterprise applications: enterprise systems, supply chain management systems, customer relationship management systems, and knowledge management systems. Each of these enterprise applications integrates a related set of functions and business processes to enhance the performance of the organization as a whole. Figure 2-10 shows that the architecture for these enterprise applications encompasses processes spanning the entire organization and, in some cases, extending beyond the organization to customers, suppliers, and other key business partners.

Enterprise Systems Firms use **enterprise systems**, also known as *enterprise resource planning (ERP) systems*, to integrate business processes in manufacturing and production, finance and accounting, sales and marketing, and human resources into a single software system. Information that was previously fragmented in many different systems is stored in a single comprehensive data repository where it can be used by many different parts of the business.

For example, when a customer places an order, the order data flow automatically to other parts of the company that are affected by them. The order transaction triggers the warehouse to pick the ordered products and schedule shipment. The warehouse informs the factory to replenish whatever has been depleted. The accounting department is notified to send the customer an invoice. Customer service representatives track the progress of the order through every step to inform customers about the status of their orders. Managers are able to use firm-wide information to make more precise and timely decisions about daily operations and longer-term planning.

Supply Chain Management Systems Firms use **supply chain management (SCM) systems** to help manage relationships with their suppliers. These systems help suppliers, purchasing firms, distributors, and logistics companies share information about orders, produc-

Figure 2-10
Enterprise Application Architecture
Enterprise applications automate processes that span multiple business functions and organizational levels and may extend outside the organization.

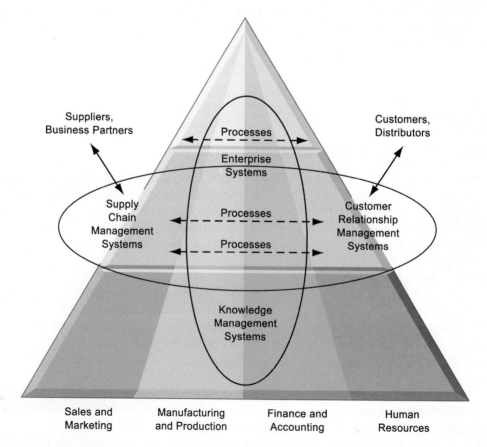

tion, inventory levels, and delivery of products and services so that they can source, produce, and deliver goods and services efficiently. The ultimate objective is to get the right amount of their products from their source to their point of consumption in the least amount of time and at the lowest cost. These systems increase firm profitability by lowering the costs of moving and making products and by enabling managers to make better decisions about how to organize and schedule sourcing, production, and distribution.

Supply chain management systems are one type of **interorganizational system** because they automate the flow of information across organizational boundaries. You will find examples of other types of interorganizational information systems throughout this text because such systems make it possible for firms to link electronically to customers and to outsource their work to other companies.

Customer Relationship Management Systems Firms use **customer relationship management (CRM) systems** to help manage their relationships with their customers. CRM systems provide information to coordinate all of the business processes that deal with customers in sales, marketing, and service to optimize revenue, customer satisfaction, and customer retention. This information helps firms identify, attract, and retain the most profitable customers; provide better service to existing customers; and increase sales.

Knowledge Management Systems Some firms perform better than others because they have better knowledge about how to create, produce, and deliver products and services. This firm knowledge is difficult to imitate, unique, and can be leveraged into long-term strategic benefits. **Knowledge management systems (KMS)** enable organizations to better manage processes for capturing and applying knowledge and expertise. These systems collect all relevant knowledge and experience in the firm, and make it available wherever and whenever it is needed to improve business processes and management decisions. They also link the firm to external sources of knowledge.

We examine enterprise systems and systems for supply chain management and customer relationship management in greater detail in Chapter 8. We discuss collaboration systems that support knowledge management in this chapter and cover other types of knowledge management applications in Chapter 10.

INTRANETS AND EXTRANETS

Enterprise applications create deep-seated changes in the way the firm conducts its business, and they offer many opportunities to integrate the important business data into a single system. They are also costly and difficult to implement. Companies also use intranets and extranets to integrate data, customers, vendors, and their own business processes.

Intranets are simply internal company Web sites that are accessible only by employees. The term 'intranet' is used to refer to the fact that it is an internal network, in contrast to the Internet which is a network between organizations and other networks. Intranets use the same technologies and techniques as the larger Internet, and they often are simply a private access area in a larger company Web site. Likewise with extranets. Extranets are company Web sites that are accessible usually only to vendors and suppliers, and used to coordinate the movement of supplies to the firm's production apparatus. Many universities use intranets to keep students informed, and to distribute class content and administrative messages to students taking a specific class. These intranets are accessible only to members of the university community, not the general public using the Internet.

Intranets and extranets deserve mention here as one of the tools firms use to increase integration and expedite the flow of information within the firm, and with customers and suppliers. We describe the technology for intranets and extranets in more detail in Chapter 6.

An intranet typically centers on a portal that provides a single point of access to information from several different systems and to documents using a Web interface. Such portals can be customized to suit the information needs of specific business groups and individual users if required. They usually feature e-mail, collaboration tools, and tools for searching for internal corporate systems and documents.

For example, SwissAir's corporate intranet for sales provides its salespeople with sales leads, fares, statistics, libraries of best practices, access to incentive programs, discussion groups, and collaborative workspaces. The intranet includes a Sales Ticket capability that displays bulletins about unfilled airplane seats around the world to help the sales staff work with colleagues and with travel agents who can help them fill those seats.

E-BUSINESS, E-COMMERCE, AND E-GOVERNMENT

The systems and technologies we have just described are transforming firms' relationships with customers, employees, suppliers, and logistic partners into digital relationships using networks and the Internet. So much business is now enabled by or based upon digital networks that we use the terms *electronic business* and *electronic commerce* frequently throughout this text.

Electronic business, or **e-business**, refers to the use of digital technology and the Internet to execute the major business processes in the enterprise. E-business includes activities for the internal management of the firm and for coordination with suppliers and other business partners. It also includes **electronic commerce**, or **e-commerce**. E-commerce is the part of e-business that deals with the buying and selling of goods and services over the Internet. It also encompasses activities supporting those market transactions, such as advertising, marketing, customer support, security, delivery, and payment.

The technologies associated with e-business have also brought about similar changes in the public sector. Governments on all levels are using Internet technology to deliver information and services to citizens, employees, and businesses with which they work. **E-government** refers to the application of the Internet and networking technologies to digitally enable government and public sector agencies' relationships with citizens, businesses, and other arms of government. In addition to improving delivery of government services, e-government can make government operations more efficient and also empower citizens by giving them easier access to information and the ability to network electronically with other citizens. For example, citizens in some states can renew their driver's licenses or apply for unemployment benefits online, and the Internet has become a powerful tool for instantly mobilizing interest groups for political action and fund-raising.

2.3 Systems for Collaboration and Teamwork

With all these systems and information, you might wonder how is it possible to make sense out of them? How do people working in firms pull it all together, work towards common goals, and coordinate plans and actions? Information systems can't make decisions, hire or fire people, sign contracts, agree on deals, or adjust the price of goods to the marketplace. In addition to the types of systems we have just described, businesses need special systems to support collaboration and teamwork.

WHAT IS COLLABORATION?

Collaboration is working with others to achieve shared and explicit goals. Collaboration focuses on task or mission accomplishment and usually takes place in a business, or other organization, and between businesses. You collaborate with a colleague in Tokyo having expertise on a topic about which you know nothing. You collaborate with many colleagues in publishing a company blog. If you're in a law firm, you collaborate with accountants in an accounting firm in servicing the needs of a client with tax problems. Collaboration can be short-lived, lasting a few minutes, or longer term, depending on the nature of the task and the relationship among participants. Collaboration can be one-to-one or many-to-many.

Employees may collaborate in informal groups that are not a formal part of the business firm's organizational structure or they may be organized into formal teams. **Teams** are part of the organization's business structure for getting things done. Teams have a specific mission that someone in the business assigned to them. They have a job to complete. The members of the team need to collaborate on the accomplishment of specific tasks and collectively achieve the team mission. The team mission might be to "win the game," or "increase online sales by 10%," or "prevent insulating foam from falling off a space shuttle." Teams are often short-lived, depending on the problems they tackle and the length of time needed to find a solution and accomplish the mission.

Collaboration and teamwork are more important today than ever for a variety of reasons.

- *Changing nature of work.* The nature of work has changed from factory manufacturing and pre-computer office work where each stage in the production process occurred independently of one another, and was coordinated by supervisors. Work was organized into silos. Within a silo, work passed from one machine tool station to another, from one desktop to another, until the finished product was completed. Today, the kinds of jobs we have require much closer coordination and interaction among the parties involved in producing the service or product. A recent report from the consulting firm McKinsey and Company argued that 41 percent of the U.S. labor force is now composed of jobs where interaction (talking, e-mailing, presenting, and persuading) is the primary value-adding activity. Moreover, "interaction" jobs are the fastest growing: 70 percent of all new jobs created since 1998 are "interaction" jobs. Even in factories, workers today often work in production groups, or pods.

- *Growth of professional work.* "Interaction" jobs tend to be professional jobs in the service sector that require close coordination, and collaboration. Professional jobs require substantial education, and the sharing of information and opinions to get work done. Each actor on the job brings specialized expertise to the problem, and all the actors need to take one another into account in order to accomplish the job.

- *Changing organization of the firm.* For most of the industrial age, managers organized work in a hierarchical fashion. Orders came down the hierarchy, and responses moved back up the hierarchy. Today, work is organized into groups and teams, who are expected to develop their own methods for accomplishing the task. Senior managers observe and measure results, but are much less likely to issue detailed orders or operating procedures. In part this is because expertise has been pushed down in the organization, as have decision making powers.

- *Changing scope of the firm.* The work of the firm has changed a single location to multiple locations—offices or factories throughout a region, a nation, or even around the globe. For instance, Henry Ford developed the first mass-production automobile plant at a single Dearborn, Michigan factory. In 2010, Ford will produce about 3 million automobiles and employ over 200,000 employees at 88 plants and facilities worldwide. With this kind of global presence, the need for close coordination of design, production, marketing, distribution, and service obviously takes on new importance and scale. Large global companies need to have teams working on a global basis.

- *Emphasis on innovation.* While we tend to think of innovations in business and science as coming from great individuals, but more common is that these great individuals are working with a team of brilliant colleagues, and all have been preceded by a long line of earlier innovators and innovations. Think of Bill Gates and Steve Jobs (founders of Microsoft and Apple), both of whom are highly regarded innovators, and both of whom built strong collaborative teams to nurture and support innovation in their firms. Their initial innovations derived from close collaboration with colleagues and partners. Innovation in other words is a group and social process, and most innovations derive from collaboration among individuals in a lab, a business, or government agencies. Strong collaborative practices and technologies are believed to increase the rate and quality of innovation.

- *Changing culture of work and business.* Most research on collaboration supports the notion that diverse teams produce better outputs, faster, than individuals working on their own. Popular notions of the crowd ("crowdsourcing," and the "wisdom of crowds") also provide cultural support for collaboration and teamwork.

BUSINESS BENEFITS OF COLLABORATION AND TEAMWORK

There are many articles and books that have been written about collaboration, some of them by business executives and consultants, and a great many by academic researchers in a variety of businesses. Nearly all of this research is anecdotal. Nevertheless, among both business and academic communities there is a general belief that the more a business firm is "collaborative," the more successful it will be, and that collaboration within and among firms is more essential than in the past. According to Jaclyn Kostner, Ph.D., an expert on high-performance virtual collaboration, "Collaboration can positively impact each of the gold standards of performance—profitability, profit growth, and sales growth—to determine a company's overall performance in the marketplace" (Frost and White, 2007). A rare study of the value of collaboration found that the overall economic benefit of collaboration was significant: for every word seen by an employee in e-mails from others, $70 of additional revenue was generated (Aral, Brynjolfsson, and Van Alstyne, 2007).

Table 2.2 summarizes some of the benefits of collaboration identified by previous writers and scholars.

Figure 2-11 graphically illustrates how collaboration is believed to impact business performance.

TABLE 2.2

Business Benefits of Collaboration

Benefit	Rationale
Productivity	People working together can complete a complex task faster than the same number of people working in isolation from one another. There will be fewer errors.
Quality	People working collaboratively can communicate errors, and corrective actions faster than if they work in isolation. There will be a reduction in buffers and time delay among production units.
Innovation	People working collaboratively in groups can come up with more innovative ideas for products, services, and administration than the same number working in isolation from one another. There are advantages in group diversity and "the wisdom of crowds."
Customer service	People working together in teams can solve customer complaints and issues faster and more effectively than if they were working in isolation from one another.
Financial performance (profitability, sales, and sales growth)	As a result of all of the above, collaborative firms have superior sales, sales growth, and financial performance.

Collaboration Capability

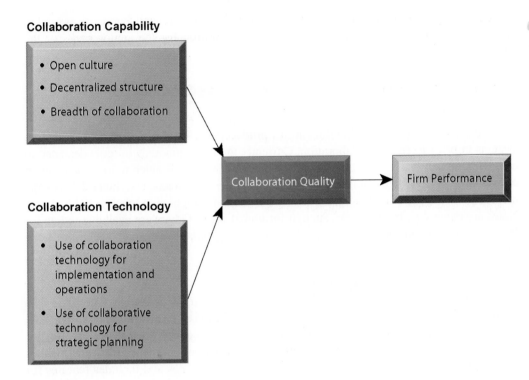

Figure 2-11
Requirements for
Collaboration
Successful collaboration requires an appropriate organizational structure and culture, along with appropriate collaboration technology.

While there are many presumed benefits to collaboration, you really need a supportive business firm culture and the right decentralized structure before you can achieve meaningful collaboration. You also need a healthy investment in collaborative technologies. We now examine these requirements.

BUILDING A COLLABORATIVE CULTURE

Collaboration won't take place spontaneously in a business firm, especially if there is no supportive culture. Business firms, especially large firms, had in the past a reputation for being "command and control" organizations where the top leaders thought up all the really important matters, and then ordered lower level employees to execute senior management plans. The job of middle management supposedly was to pass messages back and forth, up and down the hierarchy.

To some extent this is a caricature of how firms used to behave in the 1950s to 1990s, but caricatures often have some truth. Command and control firms required lower-level employees to carry out orders without asking too many questions, with no responsibility to improve processes, and with no rewards for teamwork or team performance. If your workgroup needed help from another work group, that was something for the bosses to figure out. You never communicated horizontally, always vertically, so management could control the process. As long as employees showed up for work, and performed the job satisfactorily, that's all that was required. Together, the expectations of management and employees formed a culture, a set of assumptions about common goals and how people should behave. It is surprising how many business firms still operate this way.

A collaborative business culture is very different. Senior managers are responsible for achieving results, but rely on teams of employees to achieve and implement the results. Policies, products, designs, processes, and systems are much more dependent on teams at all levels of the organization to devise, to create, and to build. Teams are rewarded for their performance, and individuals are rewarded for their performance in a team. You might be a brilliant star on a failed team and receive only half the rewards. The function of middle managers is to build the teams, coordinate their work, and monitor their performance. In a collaborative culture, senior management establishes collaboration and teamwork as vital to the organization, and it actually implements collaboration for the senior ranks of the business as well.

TOOLS AND TECHNOLOGIES FOR COLLABORATION AND TEAMWORK

A collaborative, team-oriented culture won't produce benefits if there are no information systems in place to enable collaboration. Currently there are hundreds of tools designed to deal with the fact that, in order to succeed in our jobs, we are all much more dependent on one another, our fellow employees, customers, suppliers and managers. Table 2.3 lists the most important types of collaboration software tools. Some high-end tools like IBM's Lotus Notes are expensive, but powerful enough for global firms. Others are available online for free (or with premium versions for a modest fee) and are suitable for small businesses. Let's look more closely at some of these tools.

E-mail and Instant Messaging (IM)

Worldwide, one in six people in the world, about 1.4 billion, use e-mail. There are also about 47 billion instant messages sent every day, 10 billion of which originate in business networks. E-mail and instant messaging have been embraced by corporations as a major communication and collaboration tool supporting interaction jobs. Their software operates on computers, cell phones, and other wireless handheld devices and includes features for sharing files as well as transmitting messages. Many instant messaging systems allow users to engage in real-time conversations with multiple participants simultaneously. Gartner technology consultants predict that with in a few years, instant messaging will be the "de facto tool" for voice, video, and text chat for 95 percent of employees in big companies.

Social Networking

We've all visited social networking sites such as MySpace, Facebook, and Friendster, which feature tools to help people share their interests and interact. Social networking tools are quickly becoming a corporate tool for sharing ideas and collaborating among interaction-based jobs in the firm. Social networking sites such as Linkedin.com provide networking services to business professionals, while other niche sites have sprung up to serve lawyers, doctors, engineers, and even dentists. IBM built a Community Tools component into its Lotus Notes collaboration software to add social networking features. Users are able to submit questions to others in the company and receive answers via instant messaging.

TABLE 2.3 Fifteen Categories of Collaborative Software Tools	E-mail and instant messaging White boarding

E-mail and instant messaging	White boarding
Collaborative writing	Web presenting
Collaborative reviewing/editing	Work scheduling
Event scheduling	Document sharing (including wikis)
File sharing	Mind mapping
Screen sharing	Large-audience Webinars
Audio conferencing	Co-browsing
Video conferencing	

Source: Mindmeister.com, 2009

Wikis

Wikis are a type of Web site that makes it easy for users to contribute and edit text content and graphics without any knowledge of Web page development or programming techniques. The most well-known wiki is Wikipedia, the largest collaboratively edited reference project in the world. It relies on volunteers, makes no money and accepts no advertising. Wikipedia is the ninth most visited site in the United States (Amazon is tenth), with over 64 million unique visitors each month. Wikipedia is the world's most successful online encyclopedia.

Wikis are ideal tools for storing and sharing company knowledge and insights. Enterprise software vendor SAP AG has a wiki that acts as a base of information for people outside the company, such as customers and software developers who build programs that interact with SAP software. In the past, those people asked and sometimes answered questions in an informal way on SAP online forums, but that was an inefficient system, with people asking and answering the same questions over and over.

At Intel Corporation, employees built their own internal wiki , and it has been edited over 100,000 times and viewed more than 27 million times by Intel employees. The most common search is for the meaning of Intel acronyms such as EASE for "employee access support environment" and POR for "plan of record." Other popular resources include a page about software engineering processes at the company. Wikis are destined to become the major repository for unstructured corporate knowledge in the next five years in part because they are so much less costly than formal knowledge management systems and they can be much more dynamic and current.

Virtual Worlds

Virtual worlds, such as Second Life, are online 3-D environments populated by "residents" who have built graphical representations of themselves known as avatars. Organizations such as IBM and Insead, an international business school with campuses in France and Singapore, are using this virtual world to house online meetings, training sessions, and "lounges." Real-world people represented by avatars meet, interact, and exchange ideas at these virtual locations. Communication takes place in the form of text messages similar to instant messages.

Internet-Based Collaboration Environments

There are now suites of software products providing multi-function platforms for workgroup collaboration among teams of employees who work together from many different locations. These include Internet-based audio conferencing and video conferencing systems, online software services such as Google Apps/Google Sites, and corporate collaboration systems such as Lotus Notes, Socialtext, and Microsoft SharePoint.

Virtual Meeting Systems For many businesses, including investment banking, accounting, law, technology services, and management consulting, extensive travel is a fact of life. The expenses incurred by business travel have been steadily rising in recent years, primarily due to increasing energy costs. In an effort to reduce travel expenses, many companies, both large and small, are adopting videoconferencing and Web conferencing technologies. Companies such as Heinz, General Electric, Pepsico, and Wachovia are using virtual meeting systems for product briefings, training course, strategy sessions, and even inspirational chats.

An important feature of leading-edge, high-end videoconferencing systems is **telepresence** technology, which allows a person to give the appearance of being present at a location other than his or her true physical location. The Interactive Session on Technology describes telepresence and other technologies for hosting these "virtual" meetings. You can also find video cases on this topic.

INTERACTIVE SESSION: TECHNOLOGY   Virtual Meetings: Smart Management

Instead of taking that 6:30 a.m. flight to make a round of meetings in Dallas, wouldn't it be great if you could attend these events without leaving your desktop? Today you can, thanks to technologies for videoconferencing and for hosting online meetings over the Web. A June 2008 report issued by the Global e-Sustainability Initiative and the Climate Group estimated that up to 20 percent of business travel could be replaced by virtual meeting technology.

A videoconference allows individuals at two or more locations to communicate through two-way video and audio transmissions at the same time. The critical feature of videoconferencing is the digital compression of audio and video streams by a device called a codec. Those streams are then divided into packets and transmitted over a network or the Internet. Until recently, the technology has been plagued by poor audio and video performance in the past, usually related to the speed at which the streams were transmitted, and its cost was prohibitively high for all but the largest and most powerful corporations. Most companies deemed videoconferencing as a poor substitute for face-to-face meetings.

However, vast improvements in videoconferencing and associated technologies have renewed interest in this way of working. Videoconferencing is now growing at an annual rate of 30 percent. Proponents of the technology claim that it does more than simply reduce costs. It allows for "better" meetings as well: It's easier to meet with partners, suppliers, subsidiaries, and colleagues from within the office or around the world on a more frequent basis, which in most cases simply cannot be reasonably accomplished through travel. You can also meet with contacts that you wouldn't be able to meet at all without videoconferencing technology.

For example, Rip Curl, a Costa Mesa, California producer of surfing equipment, uses videoconferencing to help its designers, marketers, and manufacturers collaborate on new products. Executive recruiting firm Korn/Ferry International uses video interviews to screen potential candidates before presenting them to clients.

Today's state-of-the-art videoconferencing systems display sharp high-definition TV images. The top-of-the-line videoconferencing technology is known as telepresence. Telepresence strives to make users feel as if they are actually present in a location different from their own. You can sit across a table from a large screen showing someone who looks quite real and life-size, but may be in Brussels or Hong Kong. Only the handshake and exchange of business

cards are missing. Telepresence products provide the highest-quality videoconferencing available on the market to date. Only a handful of companies, such as Cisco, HP, and Polycom, supply these products. Prices for fully equipped telepresence rooms can run to $500,000.

Companies able to afford this technology report large savings. For example, technology consulting firm Accenture reports that it eliminated expenditures for 240 international trips and 120 domestic flights in a single month. The ability to reach customers and partners is also dramatically increased. Other business travelers report tenfold increases in the number of customers and partners they are able to reach for a fraction of the previous price per person. Cisco has over 200 telepresence rooms and predicts that it saves $100 million in travel costs each year.

Videoconferencing products have not traditionally been feasible for small businesses, but another company, LifeSize, has introduced an affordable line of products for as low as $5,000. Reviews of the LifeSize product indicate that when a great deal of movement occurs in a frame, the screen blurs and distorts somewhat. But overall, the product is easy to use and will allow many smaller companies to use a high-quality videoconferencing product.

There are even some free Internet-based options like Skype videoconferencing and ooVoo. These products are of lower quality than traditional videoconferencing products, and they are proprietary, meaning they can only talk to others using that very same system. Most videoconferencing and telepresence products are able to interact with a variety of other devices. Higher-end systems include features like multiparty conferencing, video mail with unlimited storage, no long-distance fees, and a detailed call history.

Companies of all sizes are finding Web-based online meeting tools such as WebEx, Microsoft Office Live Meeting, and Adobe Acrobat Connect especially helpful for training and sales presentations. These products enable participants to share documents and presentations in conjunction with audio conferencing and live video via Webcam. Cornerstone Information systems, a Bloomington, Indiana business software company with 60 employees, cut its travel costs by 60 percent and the average time to close a new sale by 30 percent by performing many product demonstrations online.

Before setting up videoconferencing or telepresence, it's important for a company to make sure it really needs the technology to ensure that it will be a profitable venture. Companies should determine how their employees conduct meetings, how they communicate and with what technologies, how much travel they do, and their network's capabilities. There are still plenty of times when face-to-face interaction is more desirable, and often traveling to meet a client is essential for cultivating clients and closing sales.

Videoconferencing figures to have an impact on the business world in other ways, as well. More employees may be able to work closer to home and balance their work and personal lives more efficiently; traditional office environments and corporate head-

quarters may shrink or disappear; and freelancers, contractors, and workers from other countries will become a larger portion of the global economy.

Sources: Christopher Musico, "Web Conferencing: Calling Your Conference to Order," *Customer Relationship Management*, February 2009; Brian Nadel, "3 Videoconferencing Services Pick Up Where Your Travel Budget Leaves Off," *Computerworld*, January 6, 2009; Johna Till Johnson, "Videoconferencing Hits the Big Times.... For Real," *Computerworld*, May 28, 2009; Steve Lohr, "As Travel Costs Rise, More Meetings Go Virtual," *The New York Times*, July 22, 2008; Karen D. Schwartz, "Videoconferencing on a Budget," *eWeek*, May 29, 2008; and Mike Fratto, "High-Def Conferencing At a Low Price," *Information Week*, July 14, 2008.

CASE STUDY QUESTIONS

1. One consulting firm has predicted that video and Web conferencing will make business travel extinct. Do you agree? Why or why not?

2. What is the distinction between videoconferencing and telepresence?

3. What are the ways in which videoconferencing provides value to a business? Would you consider it smart management? Explain your answer.

4. If you were in charge of a small business, would you choose to implement videoconferencing? What factors would you consider in your decision?

MIS IN ACTION

Explore the WebEx Web site (www.webex.com) and note all of its capabilities for both small and large businesses.

1. List and describe its capabilities for small, medium and large businesses. How useful is WebEx? How can it help companies save time and money?

2. Compare WebEx video capabilities with the videoconferencing capabilities described in this case.

3. Describe the steps you would take to prepare for a Web conference as opposed to a face-to-face conference.

Google Apps/Google Sites One of the most widely used "free" online services for collaboration is Google Apps/Google Sites. Google Sites (formerly JotSpot) allows users to quickly create online group-editable Web sites. Google Sites is one part of the larger Google Apps suite of tools. Google Sites users can design and populate Web sites in minutes and can, without any advanced technical skills, post a variety of files including calendars, text, spreadsheets, and videos for private, group, or public viewing and editing.

Google Apps work with Google Sites and include the typical desktop productivity office software tools (word processing, spreadsheets, presentation, contact management, messaging, and mail). A Premier edition charging businesses $50 per year for each user offers 25 gigabytes of mail storage, a 99.9% percent uptime guarantee for e-mail, tools to integrate with the firm's existing infrastructure, and 24/7 phone support. Table 2.4 describes some of the capabilities of Google Apps/GoogleSites.

Google is in the process of finalizing an additional Web-based platform for collaboration and communication called Google Wave. Google Wave has strong real-time and collaborative features. "Waves" are "equal parts conversation and document," in which any participant of a wave can reply anywhere in the message, edit the content, and add or remove participants at any point in the process. Users are able to see responses from other participants on their "wave" while typing occurs. Thus, waves not only can function as e-mail and threaded discussions but also as an instant messaging service. (A threaded discussion consists of series of messages in response to an initial message or topic.) Google will let people run their own Wave servers.

Google Apps/Google Sites Capability	Description
Google Calendar	Private and shared calendars; multiple calendars.
Google Gmail	Google's free online e-mail service, with mobile access capabilities.
Google Talk	Instant messaging, text and voice chat
Google Docs	Online word processing, electronic presentation software, spreadsheets; online editing, sharing, publishing
Google Sites	Team collaboration sites for sharing of documents, schedules, calendars, searching documents; creation of group wikis
Google Video	Firm-wide video sharing and commenting capability

Microsoft SharePoint Microsoft SharePoint is the most widely adopted collaboration system for small and medium-sized firms that use Microsoft server and networking products. Several larger firms have adopted it as well. SharePoint is a browser-based collaboration and document management platform, combined with a powerful search engine that is installed on corporate servers.

SharePoint has a Web-based interface and close integration with everyday tools such as Microsoft Office desktop software products. Microsoft's strategy is to take advantage of its "ownership" of the desktop through its Microsoft Office and Windows products. For Microsoft, the path towards enterprise-wide collaboration starts with the Office desktop and Microsoft network servers. SharePoint software makes it possible for employees to share their Office documents and collaborate on projects using Office documents as the foundation.

SharePoint products and technologies provide a platform for Web-based collaboration at the enterprise level. SharePoint can be used to host Web sites that organize and store information in one central location to enable teams to coordinate work activities, collaborate on and publish documents, maintain task lists, implement workflows, and share information via wikis and blogs. Because SharePoint stores and organizes information in one place, users can find relevant information quickly and efficiently while working together closely on tasks, projects, and documents.

Here is a list of SharePoint's major capabilities:

- Provides a single workspace for teams to coordinate schedules, organize documents, and participate in discussions, within the organization or over an extranet.
- Facilitates creation and management of documents with the ability to control versions, view past revisions, and enforce document-specific security and maintain document libraries.
- Provides announcements, alerts, and discussion boards to inform users when actions are required or changes are made to existing documentation or information.
- Supports personalized content and both personal and public views of documents and applications
- Provides templates for blogs and wikis to help teams share information and brainstorm.
- Provides tools to manage document libraries, lists, calendars, tasks, and discussion boards offline, and to synchronize changes when reconnected to the network.
- Provides enterprise search tools for locating people, expertise, and content.

Ampacet, a specialty chemical manufacturer with global research and development (R&D) activities, adopted Microsoft Office SharePoint Server 2007 along with Microsoft Office 2007 to expedite, coordinate, and centralize its product development process. The company has 5 major R&D facilities and 17 manufacturing sites in multiple locations worldwide that had operated somewhat independently—and inefficiently—in developing new products. The SharePoint server provided community Web sites for team collaboration where R&D staff could easily collect, share, and manage product development information with other facilities around the world. SharePoint features for automated workflows enabled Ampacet to create a consistent process across the company for organizing new product development data and a central repository for Microsoft Excel spreadsheets, dashboards, and other R&D project documents (Microsoft, 2009).

Lotus Notes For very large firms (Fortune 1000 and Russell 2000 firms) the most widely used collaboration tool is IBM's Lotus Notes. Lotus Notes was an early example of *groupware*, a collaborative software system with capabilities for sharing calendars, collective writing and editing, shared database access, and electronic meetings, with each participant able to see and display information from others and other activities. Notes is now Web-enabled with enhancements for social networking (Lotus Connections) and a scripting and application development environment so that users can build custom applications to suit their unique needs.

IBM Software Group defines Lotus Notes as an "integrated desktop client option for accessing business e-mail, calendars, and applications on an IBM Lotus Domino server." The Notes software installed on the user's client computer allows the machine to be used as a platform for e-mail, instant messaging (working with Lotus Sametime), Web browsing, and calendar/resource reservation work, as well as for interacting with collaborative applications. Today, Notes also provides blogs, wikis, RSS aggregators, CRM, and help desk systems.

Thousands of employees at hundreds of large firms such as the Toshiba, Air France, and Global Hyatt Corporation use IBM Lotus Notes as their primary collaboration and teamwork tools. Firmwide installations of Lotus Notes can cost millions of dollars a year for a large Fortune 1000 firm, whereas Google Apps/Google Sites comes in a limited free version or a more sophisticated premium version for $50 per user/per year. A client-server product like Lotus Notes inherently involves the central IS department, and it is a major implementation effort. Online software services are therefore attractive because they do not require any installation on corporate servers, or even the IS department to be involved. Nevertheless, existing online tools like the Google collaboration services are not as powerful as those found in Lotus Notes, and it is unclear whether they could scale to the size of a global firm (at least for now).

Very large firms adopt IBM Lotus Notes because it promises higher levels of security and reliability, and the sense that the firm retains control over sensitive information. For example, EuroChem, the largest agrochemical company in Russia and one of Europe's top three fertilizer producers, uses Lotus Notes to create a single standard platform for collaboration and document management. The software facilitates cooperation and collaboration among geographically dispersed regional production centers and provides a secure automated platform for document exchange. With Lotus Notes, EuroChem is able to register and control all documents, to establish routing paths for document approval, and to maintain a full history of all movements and changes. Security features allow the company to create a personalized work environment for each user and to prevent unauthorized users from accessing sensitive information (IBM, 2009).

Large firms in general do not feel secure using popular online software services for "strategic" applications because of the implicit security concerns, and the dependency on external vendor's computing resources. Most experts agree, however, that these concerns will diminish as experience with online tools grows, and the sophistication of online software service suppliers increases to protect security and reduce vulnerability. Table 2.5 describes additional popular online collaboration tools.

TABLE 2.5

Other Popular Online Collaboration Tools

Tool	Description
Socialtext	An enterprise server-based collaboration environment which provides social networking, Twitter-like micro-blogging , wiki workspaces, with integrated weblogs, distributed spreadsheets, and a personal home page for every user. Connectors to Microsoft SharePoint and Lotus Connections are also available. More emphasis on social networking than Office tools.
Zoho Notebook Project	Collecting and collaborating on text, line drawings, images, Web pages, video, RSS feeds. Project management (task management, work flow, reports, time tracking, forums, and file sharing). Free or $5/project/month for premium service.
Bluetie	Online collaboration with e-mail, scheduling, to-do lists, contact management, file sharing. Free for less than 20 users, $4.99 user/month after that.
Basecamp	Sharing to-do lists, files, message boards, milestone tracking. Free for a single project, $12/month for three projects with 200 megabytes of storage.
Onehub	Sharing documents, calendars, Web bookmarks; e-mail integration and IM. Manage hub resources; bulletin board.
WorkZone	Collaboration with file sharing; project management; customization; security.

Onehub enables teams to create online workspaces called Hubs to share information, documents, and files from one central location. Tiny widget programs are available for customizing these workspaces by adding capabilities for uploading and moving files, displaying contacts and task lists, and embedding videos.

Evaluating and Selecting Collaboration Software Tools

With so many collaboration tools and services available, how do you choose the right collaboration technology for your firm? To answer this question, you need a framework for understanding just what problems these tools are designed to solve. One framework that has been helpful for us to talk about collaboration tools is the time/space collaboration matrix developed in the early 1990s by a number of collaborative work scholars (Figure 2-12).

The time/space matrix focuses on two dimensions of the collaboration problem: time and space. For instance, you need to collaborate with people in different time zones and you cannot all meet at the same time. Midnight in New York is noon in Bombay, so this makes it difficult to have a video conference (the people in New York are too tired). Time is clearly an obstacle to collaboration on a global scale.

Place (location) also inhibits collaboration in large global or even national and regional firms. Assembling people for a physical meeting is made difficult by the physical dispersion of distributed firms (firms with more than one location), the cost of travel, and the time limitations of managers.

The collaboration technologies we have just described are ways of overcoming the limitations of time and space. Using this time/space framework will help you to choose the most appropriate collaboration and teamwork tools for your firm. Note that some tools are applicable in more than one time/place scenario. For example, Internet collaboration suites such as Lotus Notes have capabilities for both synchronous (instant messaging, electronic meeting tools) and asynchronous (e-mail, wikis, document editing) interactions.

Here's a "to-do" list to get started. If you follow these six steps, you should be led to investing in the correct collaboration software for your firm at a price you can afford, and within your risk tolerance.

1. What are the collaboration challenges facing the firm in terms of time and space? Locate your firm in the time/space matrix. Your firm can occupy more than one cell in the matrix. Different collaboration tools will be needed for each situation.
2. Within each cell of the matrix where your firm faces challenges, exactly what kinds of solutions are available? Make a list of vendor products.
3. Analyze each of the products in terms of their cost and benefits to your firm. Be sure to include the costs of training in your cost estimates, and the costs of involving the information systems department if needed.

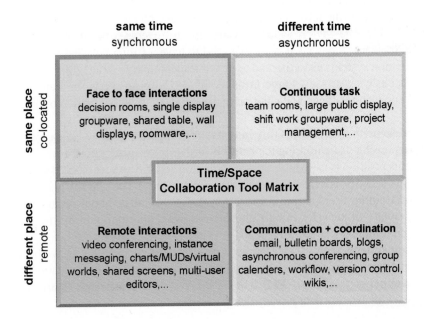

same time synchronous   **different time** asynchronous

same place co-located

Face to face interactions
decision rooms, single display groupware, shared table, wall displays, roomware,...

Continuous task
team rooms, large public display, shift work groupware, project management,...

Time/Space Collaboration Tool Matrix

different place remote

Remote interactions
video conferencing, instance messaging, charts/MUDs/virtual worlds, shared screens, multi-user editors,...

Communication + coordination
email, bulletin boards, blogs, asynchronous conferencing, group calenders, workflow, version control, wikis,...

**Figure 2-12
The Time/Space Collaboration Tool Matrix**
Collaboration technologies can be classified in terms of whether they support interactions at the same or different time or place, and whether these interactions are remote or co-located.

4. Identify the risks to security and vulnerability involved with each of the products. Is your firm willing to put proprietary information into the hands of external service providers over the Internet? Is your firm willing to risk its important operations to systems controlled by other firms? What are the financial risks facing your vendors? Will they be here in three to five years? What would be the cost of making a switch to another vendor in the event the vendor firm fails?

5. Seek the help of potential users to identify implementation and training issues. Some of these tools are easier to use than others.

6. Make your selection of candidate tools, and invite the vendors to make presentations.

2.4 The Information Systems Function in Business

We've seen that businesses need information systems to operate today and that they use many different kinds of systems. But who is responsible for running these systems? Who is responsible for making sure the hardware, software, and other technologies used by these systems are running properly and are up to date? End users manage their systems from a business standpoint, but managing the technology requires a special information systems function.

In all but the smallest of firms, the **information systems department** is the formal organizational unit responsible for information technology services. The information systems department is responsible for maintaining the hardware, software, data storage, and networks that comprise the firm's IT infrastructure. We describe IT infrastructure in detail in Chapter 4.

THE INFORMATION SYSTEMS DEPARTMENT

The information systems department consists of specialists, such as programmers, systems analysts, project leaders, and information systems managers. **Programmers** are highly trained technical specialists who write the software instructions for computers. **Systems analysts** constitute the principal liaisons between the information systems groups and the rest of the organization. It is the systems analyst's job to translate business problems and requirements into information requirements and systems. **Information systems managers** are leaders of teams of programmers and analysts, project managers, physical facility managers, telecommunications managers, or database specialists. They are also managers of computer operations and data entry staff. Also, external specialists, such as hardware vendors and manufacturers, software firms, and consultants, frequently participate in the day-to-day operations and long-term planning of information systems.

In many companies, the information systems department is headed by a **chief information officer (CIO)**. The CIO is a senior manager who oversees the use of information technology in the firm. Today's CIOs are expected to have a strong business background as well as information systems expertise and to play a leadership role in integrating technology into the firm's business strategy. Large firms today also have positions for a chief security officer, chief knowledge officer, and chief privacy officer, all of whom work closely with the CIO.

The **chief security officer (CSO)** is in charge of information systems security for the firm and is responsible for enforcing the firm's information security policy (see Chapter 7). (Sometimes this position is called the chief information security officer [CISO] where information systems security is separated from physical security.) The CSO is responsible for educating and training users and information systems specialists about security, keeping management aware of security threats and breakdowns, and maintaining the tools and policies chosen to implement security.

Information systems security and the need to safeguard personal data have become so important that corporations collecting vast quantities of personal data have established positions for a **chief privacy officer (CPO)**. The CPO is responsible for ensuring that the company complies with existing data privacy laws.

The **chief knowledge officer (CKO)** is responsible for the firm's knowledge management program. The CKO helps design programs and systems to find new sources of knowledge or to make better use of existing knowledge in organizational and management processes. **End users** are representatives of departments outside of the information systems group for whom applications are developed. These users are playing an increasingly large role in the design and development of information systems.

In the early years of computing, the information systems group was composed mostly of programmers who performed highly specialized but limited technical functions. Today, a growing proportion of staff members are systems analysts and network specialists, with the information systems department acting as a powerful change agent in the organization. The information systems department suggests new business strategies and new information-based products and services, and coordinates both the development of the technology and the planned changes in the organization.

INFORMATION SYSTEMS SERVICES

Services provided by the information systems department include the following:
- Computing platforms provide computing services that connect employees, customers, and suppliers into a coherent digital environment, including large mainframes, desktop and laptop computers, and mobile handheld devices.
- Telecommunications services provide data, voice, and video connectivity to employees, customers, and suppliers.
- Data management services store and manage corporate data, and provide capabilities for analyzing the data.
- Application software services provide development and support services for the firm's business systems, including enterprise-wide capabilities, such as enterprise resource planning, customer relationship management, supply chain management, and knowledge management systems, that are shared by all business units.
- Physical facilities management services develop and manage the physical installations required for computing, telecommunications, and data management services.
- IT management services plan and develop the infrastructure, coordinate with the business units for IT services, manage accounting for the IT expenditure, and provide project management services.
- IT standards services provide the firm and its business units with policies that determine which information technology will be used, when, and how.
- IT educational services provide training in system use to employees and offer managers training in how to plan for and manage IT investments.
- IT research and development services provide the firm with research on potential future information systems projects and investments that could help the firm differentiate itself in the marketplace.

In the past, firms generally built their own software and managed their own computing facilities. As our discussion of collaboration systems has shown, many firms are turning to external vendors to provide these services (see also Chapters 4 and 11) and are using their information systems departments to manage these service providers.

2.5 Hands-On MIS Projects

The projects in this section give you hands-on experience analyzing opportunities to improve business processes with new information system applications, using a spreadsheet to improve decision making about suppliers, and using Internet software to plan efficient transportation routes.

MANAGEMENT DECISION PROBLEMS

1. Don's Lumber Company on the Hudson River is one of the oldest retail lumber yards in New York State. It features a large selection of materials for flooring, decks, moldings, windows, siding, and roofing. The prices of lumber and other building materials are constantly changing. When a customer inquires about the price on pre-finished wood flooring, sales representatives consult a manual price sheet and then call the supplier for the most recent price. The supplier in turn uses a manual price sheet, which has been updated each day. Often the supplier must call back Don's sales reps because the company does not have the newest pricing information immediately on hand. Assess the business impact of this situation, describe how this process could be improved with information technology, and identify the decisions that would have to be made to implement a solution. Who would make those decisions?

2. Henry's Hardware is a small family business in Sacramento, California. The owners must use every square foot of store space as profitably as possible. They have never kept detailed inventory or sales records. As soon as a shipment of goods arrives, the items are immediately placed on store shelves. Invoices from suppliers are only kept for tax purposes. When an item is sold, the item number and price are rung up at the cash register. The owners use their own judgment in identifying items that need to be reordered. What is the business impact of this situation? How could information systems help Henry and Kathleen run their business? What data should these systems capture? What decisions could the systems improve?

IMPROVING DECISION MAKING: USE A SPREADSHEET TO SELECT SUPPLIERS

Software skills: Spreadsheet date functions, data filtering, DAVERAGE function
Business skills: Analyzing supplier performance and pricing

In this exercise, you will learn how to use spreadsheet software to improve management decisions about selecting suppliers. You will start with raw transactional data about suppliers organized as a large spreadsheet list. You will use the spreadsheet software to filter the data based on several different criteria to select the best suppliers for your company.

You run a company that manufactures aircraft components. You have many competitors who are trying to offer lower prices and better service to customers, and you are trying to determine whether you can benefit from better supply chain management. In MyMISLab, you will find a spreadsheet file that contains a list of all of the items that your firm has ordered from its suppliers during the past three months. A sample is shown below, but MyMISLab

	B	C	D	E	F	G	H	I	J	K
2				Orders and Suppliers						
3										
4	Vendor No.	Order No.	Item No.	Item Description	Item Cost	Quantity	Cost per order	A/P Terms	Order Date	Arrival Date
5	2	A0111	6489	O-Ring	$ 3.00	900	$ 2,700.00	25	10/10/09	10/18/09
6	6	A0115	5319	Shielded Cable/ft.	$ 1.10	17,500	$ 19,250.00	30	08/20/09	08/31/09
7	6	A0123	4312	Bolt-nut package	$ 3.75	4,250	$ 15,937.50	30	08/25/09	09/01/09
8	6	A0204	5319	Shielded Cable/ft.	$ 1.10	16,500	$ 18,150.00	30	09/15/09	10/05/09
9	6	A0205	5677	Side Panel	$ 195.00	120	$ 23,400.00	30	11/02/09	11/13/09
10	6	A0207	4312	Bolt-nut package	$ 3.75	4,200	$ 15,750.00	30	09/01/09	09/10/09
11	5	A0223	4224	Bolt-nut package	$ 3.95	4,500	$ 17,775.00	30	10/15/09	10/20/09
12	5	A0433	5417	Control Panel	$ 255.00	500	$ 127,500.00	30	10/20/09	10/27/09
13	5	A0443	1243	Airframe fasteners	$ 4.25	10,000	$ 42,500.00	30	08/08/09	08/14/09
14	5	A0446	5417	Control Panel	$ 255.00	406	$ 103,530.00	30	09/01/09	09/10/09
15	2	A0533	9752	Gasket	$ 4.05	1,500	$ 6,075.00	25	09/20/09	09/25/09
16	2	A0555	6489	O-Ring	$ 3.00	1,100	$ 3,300.00	25	10/05/09	10/10/09
17	2	A0622	9752	Gasket	$ 4.05	1,550	$ 6,277.50	25	09/25/09	10/05/09
18	2	A0666	5125	Shielded Cable/ft.	$ 1.15	15,000	$ 17,250.00	25	10/01/09	10/15/09
19	2	A0777	6489	O-Ring	$ 3.00	1,050	$ 3,150.00	25	10/29/09	11/10/09
20	2	A1222	4111	Bolt-nut package	$ 3.55	4,200	$ 14,910.00	25	09/15/09	10/15/09
21	3	A1234	9399	Gasket	$ 3.65	1,250	$ 4,562.50	45	10/01/09	10/06/09
22	3	A1235	9399	Gasket	$ 3.65	1,450	$ 5,292.50	45	10/03/09	10/08/09
23	3	A1344	5454	Control Panel	$ 220.00	550	$ 121,000.00	45	10/01/09	10/14/09
24	3	A1345	9399	Gasket	$ 3.65	1,470	$ 5,365.50	45	10/07/09	10/12/09
25	3	A1346	9399	Gasket	$ 3.65	1,985	$ 7,245.25	45	10/05/09	10/11/09
26	2	A1444	4111	Bolt-nut package	$ 3.55	4,250	$ 15,087.50	25	09/20/09	10/10/09
27	2	A1445	4111	Bolt-nut package	$ 3.55	4,200	$ 14,910.00	25	09/25/09	10/25/09

Sheet3

may have a more recent version of this spreadsheet for this exercise. The fields in the spreadsheet file include vendor name, vendor identification number, purchaser's order number, item identification number and item description (for each item ordered from the vendor), cost per item, number of units of the item ordered (quantity), total cost of each order, vendor's accounts payable terms, order date, and actual arrival date for each order.

Prepare a recommendation of how you can use the data in this spreadsheet database to improve your decisions about selecting suppliers. Some criteria to consider for identifying preferred suppliers include the supplier's track record for on-time deliveries, suppliers offering the best accounts payable terms, and suppliers offering lower pricing when the same item can be provided by multiple suppliers. Use your spreadsheet software to prepare reports to support your recommendations.

ACHIEVING OPERATIONAL EXCELLENCE: USING INTERNET SOFTWARE TO PLAN EFFICIENT TRANSPORTATION ROUTES

In this exercise, you will use the same online software tool that businesses use to map out their transportation routes and select the most efficient route. The MapQuest (www.mapquest.com) Web site includes interactive capabilities for planning a trip. The software on this Web site can calculate the distance between two points and provide itemized driving directions to any location.

You have just started working as a dispatcher for Cross-Country Transport, a new trucking and delivery service based in Cleveland, Ohio. Your first assignment is to plan a delivery of office equipment and furniture from Elkhart, Indiana (at the corner of E. Indiana Ave. and Prairie Street) to Hagerstown, Maryland (corner of Eastern Blvd. N. and Potomac Ave.). To guide your trucker, you need to know the most efficient route between the two cities. Use MapQuest to find the route that is the shortest distance between the two cities. Use MapQuest again to find the route that takes the least time. Compare the results. Which route should Cross-Country use?

LEARNING TRACKS

The following Learning Tracks provide content relevant to topics covered in this chapter:

1. Systems from a Functional Perspective

2. IT Enables Collaboration and Teamwork

3. Challenges of Using Business Information Systems

4. Organizing the Information Systems Function

Review Summary

1 **What are the major features of a business that are important for understanding the role of information systems?** A business is a formal complex organization producing products or services for a profit. Businesses have specialized functions, such as finance and accounting, human resources, manufacturing and production, and sales and marketing. Business organizations are arranged hierarchically into levels of management. A business process is a logically related set of activities that define how specific business tasks are performed. Business firms must monitor and respond to their surrounding environments.

2 **How do systems serve the various levels of management in a business?** Systems serving operational management are transaction processing systems (TPS), such as payroll or order processing, that track the flow of the daily routine transactions necessary to conduct business. Management information systems (MIS) and decision-support systems (DSS) support middle management. Most MIS reports condense information from TPS and are not highly analytical. DSS support management decisions that are unique and rapidly changing using advanced analytical models and data analysis capabilities. Executive support systems (ESS) support senior management by providing data that are often in the form of graphs and charts delivered via portals using many sources of internal and external information.

3 **How do enterprise applications and intranets improve organizational performance?** Enterprise applications are designed to coordinate multiple functions and business processes. Enterprise systems integrate the key internal business processes of a firm into a single software system to improve coordination and decision making. Supply chain management systems help the firm manage its relationship with suppliers to optimize the planning, sourcing, manufacturing, and delivery of products and services. Customer relationship management (CRM) systems coordinate the business processes surrounding the firm's customers. Knowledge management systems enable firms to optimize the creation, sharing, and distribution of knowledge. Intranets and extranets use Internet technology and standards to assemble information from disparate systems and present it to the user in a Web page format. Extranets make portions of private corporate intranets available to outsiders.

4 **Why are systems for collaboration and teamwork so important and what technologies do they use?** Collaboration is working with others to achieve shared and explicit goals. Collaboration and teamwork have become increasingly important in business because of globalization, the decentralization of decision making, and growth in jobs where interaction is the primary value-adding activity. Collaboration is believed to enhance innovation, productivity, quality, and customer service. Effective collaboration today requires a supportive organizational culture as well as information systems and tools for collaborative work. Collaboration tools include e-mail and instant messaging, wikis, videoconferencing systems, virtual worlds, social networking systems, cell phones, and Internet collaboration platforms such as Google Sites/Apps, Microsoft SharePoint, and Lotus Notes.

5 **What is the role of the information systems function in a business?** The information systems department is the formal organizational unit responsible for information technology services. It is responsible for maintaining the hardware, software, data storage, and networks that comprise the firm's IT infrastructure. The department consists of specialists, such as programmers, systems analysts, project leaders, and information systems managers, and is often headed by a CIO.

Key Terms

Business, 41
Business processes, 42
Chief information officer (CIO), 68
Chief knowledge officer (CKO), 69
Chief privacy officer (CPO), 68
Chief security officer (CSO), 68
Collaboration, 56

Customer relationship management (CRM) systems, 55
Data workers, 46
Decision-support systems (DSS), 49
Digital dashboard, 51
Electronic business (e-business), 56
Electronic commerce (e-commerce), 56

E-government, 56
End users, 69
Enterprise applications, 53
Enterprise systems, 54
Executive support systems (ESS), 51
Information systems department, 68
Information systems managers, 68

Review Questions

1. What are the major features of a business that are important for understanding the role of information systems?
- Define a business and describe the major business functions.
- Define business processes and describe the role they play in organizations.
- Identify and describe the different levels in a business firm and their information needs.
- Explain why environments are important for understanding a business.

2. How do systems serve the various levels of management in a business?
- Describe the characteristics of transaction processing systems (TPS) and role they play in a business.
- Describe the characteristics of management information systems (MIS) and explain how MIS differ from TPS and from DSS.
- Describe the characteristics of decision support systems (DSS) and how they benefit businesses.
- Describe the characteristics of executive support systems (ESS) and explain how these systems differ from DSS.

3. How do enterprise applications and intranets improve organizational performance?
- Explain how enterprise applications improve organizational performance.
- Define enterprise systems, supply chain management systems, customer relationship management systems, and knowledge management systems and describe their business benefits.
- Explain how intranets and extranets help firms integrate information and business processes.

4. Why are systems for collaboration and teamwork so important and what technologies do they use?
- Define collaboration and teamwork and explain why they have become so important in business today.
- List and describe the business benefits of collaboration.
- Describe a supportive organizational culture for collaboration.
- List and describe the various types of collaboration and communication systems.

5. What is the role of the information systems function in a business?
- Describe how the information systems function supports a business.
- Compare the roles played by programmers, systems analysts, information systems managers, the chief information officer (CIO), chief security officer (CSO), and chief knowledge officer (CKO).

Discussion Questions

1. How could information systems be used to support the order fulfillment process illustrated in Figure 2-2? What are the most important pieces of information these systems should capture? Explain your answer.

2. Identify the steps that are performed in the process of selecting and checking out a book from your college library and the information that flows among these activities. Diagram the process. Are there any ways this process could be improved to improve the performance of your library or your school? Diagram the improved process.

Video Cases

Video Cases and Instructional Videos illustrating some of the concepts in this chapter are available. Contact your instructor to access these videos.

Collaboration and Teamwork

Describing Management Decisions and Systems

With a team of three or four other students, find a description of a manager in a corporation in *BusinessWeek, Fortune, The Wall Street Journal,* or another business publication or do your research on the Web. Gather information about what the manager's company does and the role he or she plays in the company. Identify the organizational level and business function where this manager works. Make a list of the kinds of decisions this manager has to make and the kind of information the manager would need for those decisions. Suggest how information systems could supply this information. If possible, use Google Sites to post links to Web pages, team communication announcements, and work assignments. Try to use Google Docs to develop a presentation of your findings for the class.

BUSINESS PROBLEM-SOLVING CASE

Innovation and Collaboration at Coca-Cola: It's the Real Thing

The Coca-Cola Company is the largest manufacturer, distributor, and marketer of nonalcoholic beverages, concentrates, and syrups in the world. Coca-Cola owns and maintains more than 450 brands, including Coke, Fanta, Sprite, Minute Maid, and Dasani water, some of which were obtained through acquisitions. The company's corporate headquarters are in Atlanta, Georgia, but Coke has operations in over 200 countries worldwide.

Much of the company's success is a result of its highly recognizable and trusted brand. The Coca-Cola brand is often considered to be the most valuable brand in the world. The brand also holds a unique and important place in American culture. The Coca-Cola brand gives the

company a large competitive advantage in the nonalcoholic beverage market.

Coca-Cola sells its own beverages as well as concentrates and syrups to its bottling companies. Healthy partnerships with bottlers are critical to the financial well-being of the company. The company earned $31.9 billion in revenue in 2008, with more than 70 percent coming from outside the United States.

However, Coca-Cola's continued success isn't a foregone conclusion. The global beverage market is fast-changing, fad-driven, and difficult to control for very long. Fickle customers are constantly switching drinks, while emerging companies create niche products and chip away at Coke's market share. To preserve its market leadership, Coca-Cola needs to constantly innovate and introduce new products more rapidly than its competitors. And it must continue to maintain its brands, its financial strength, its strong distribution system, and its global reach.

For Coke, some of the changes that most effectively fostered innovation and collaboration have come in the form of new information systems. One prominent example involved an overhaul to the company's "digital asset management." As Coke continued to expand its global presence, a growing amount of digital content was scattered in an unorganized fashion. Employees had to spend considerable time searching through a growing mountain of content regarding market demographics, sales figures, images, videos, and cultural information, as well as grapple with disorganized recordkeeping.

Coke's strength is built on images, messages, and marketing savvy, but sales and marketing teams around the globe lacked simple access to this information. So Coke used IBM's Content Manager software to create an online image library and digital archive containing images, documents, and videos, accessible by all employees via a standardized platform through the Web.

The company and its bottlers have made a concerted effort to upgrade their infrastructures to reach their goal of more effective collaboration. In March 2008, Coca-Cola Enterprises (CCE), the company's largest bottling company, announced it would begin using Microsoft collaboration tools, including SharePoint Online for ad hoc team collaboration and content management, Live Meeting for Web conferencing, and Office Communications Server Online for unified communications. Until then, the company had used nonintegrated collaboration tools.

The integrated Microsoft products enhance communication and collaboration across the company. Executives are able to broadcast live video to all of the company's knowledge workers. Employees can schedule LiveMeeting Web conferences using Microsoft Outlook or engage in a chat session using Office Communicator's instant messaging tool and turn it into a phone call. SharePoint provides a platform for a new intranet featuring industry news, video and audio content, executive blogs, and employee polls. CCE eventually wants to extend collaboration capabilities to mobile devices used by its 30,000 employees who stock trucks and replenish vending machines.

Coke continued efforts to foster innovation via information technology by developing the Common Innovation Framework—a system that allows Coca-Cola employees worldwide to search for and reapply concepts used in developing and marketing all of the company's 2,800 beverages. The system combines project management and business intelligence capabilities and is used to develop new beverages, design new equipment, and to create packaging concepts for new and established products. One business unit can mine product ideas by searching for beverage or brand concepts that worked well in other countries. The system helps the company recognize duplicate product ideas and allocate resources efficiently.

Coke Zero is an example of how the Common Innovation Framework is fueling innovation and collaboration at the company. Coke Zero is a recent smash hit for the company. It is marketed as a diet cola without the bitter aftertaste. The Common Innovation Framework allowed managers and personnel in disparate areas of the company and various regions (finance, legal, marketing, R&D) to view the practices that made it successful in other countries, and apply those concepts to future products. Japan is regarded as the most cutting-edge country when it comes to what will be popular; the Common Innovation Framework lets development teams in the United States and Europe see what's popular in Japan and allows them to carry those trends over in their own markets.

Coke relies mostly on independent, local bottlers, but has significant investments in many bottling companies and even owns some bottlers outright. But because Coke owns a controlling stake in only a fraction of the total number of bottlers it uses for its products, it can be a challenge to get all of the approximately 300 bottling companies Coke deals with onto the same platform for the purpose of sharing information.

Coke's Project Scale was implemented to standardize the way the company communicated with its bottlers and vice versa. Coke surveyed its largest bottlers and discovered that 90 percent of their business practices were shared, as well as that most bottlers had planned software upgrades in the upcoming several years. So Coke developed the Coke One bottler model, based on version 6.0 of SAP's ERP platform. Coke One supports 650 business processes common to all bottlers, who were eager to implement the model because they were hoping to upgrade their software anyway.

Coke hoped that the end result of the program would be better communication between the parent company and its bottlers, and by the same token, a more streamlined supply chain and a more cordial relationship between the companies. Some larger bottlers struck their own partnership with other technology companies, as CCE did when they opted out of Coke One. But for smaller bottlers, the program represents readily available intellectual property and opportunities to get better deals, faster implementation of new processes, and higher capability. Project Scale has generally been regarded as a success since its implementation.

To cultivate ties with consumers, Coca-Cola created Mycokerewards.com: a social network that acquires members by appealing to their tastes in sports, music, entertainment, and beverages. The site is an interactive showcase for Coke products and a place where drinkers of any Coke-trademarked beverage can redeem points for items that interest them, in addition to networking with other Coke drinkers with similar interests.

Coke is also innovating within existing social networks like Facebook to market their products. Burn Energy Drinks, a Coke brand developed by Coca-Cola Europe, launched a groundbreaking application, Burn Alter Ego, which combines existing Facebook friendships, avatar mash-up photo technology, and party storytelling. The application allows users to develop a virtual persona which has a "nightlife" that is entirely separate from their own. The more you use your character, the more options you have in customizing your avatar. The application is supposed to add excitement and randomness to existing friendships, and in the process, the developers hope, create more buzz surrounding Burn Energy Drinks.

All of these initiatives to foster innovation and richer collaboration between Coca-Cola employees and consumers figure to help the company remain competitive going forward. But competing industry giant Pepsico has gained market share while Coke has lost ground in the past few years. Like Coca-Cola, it has expanded into faster-growing markets for non-carbonated beverages

and health drinks, and it is a formidable challenger. Other smaller companies threaten to chip away at Coke's dominance in the market. Hopefully, Coke's investment in innovation and collaboration should stand the company in good stead in the years to come.

Sources: Michael Makowski, "Is Your Organization Learning Faster Than Your Competitors? " *Simple Complexity*, May 22, 2009; Bob Evans, "The Global CIO 50: IT Leaders Changing the Business World," *Information Week*, May 23, 2009; Mary Hayes Weier, "Coke Exploits Collaboration Technology To Keep Brand Relevant, *Information Week*, July 19, 2008; and Theresa Lagos, "Coca-Cola Enterprises Leads in Global Collaboration and Next-Generation Business Processes With Cisco Technologies," Reuters.com, April 10, 2008.

Case Study Questions

1. What is Coca-Cola's business strategy? What is the relationship of collaboration and innovation to Coca-Cola's business strategy?

2. How is Coca-Cola using collaboration systems to execute its business model and business strategy? List and describe the collaboration systems and technologies it is using.

3. Why is Coca-Cola's relationship with its bottlers so important? What is Coke doing to improve its ability to collaborate with its bottlers?

4. What are Coca-Cola's prospects for success in the future? Will information systems make a difference? Why or why not?

Achieving Competitive Advantage with Information Systems

CHAPTER 3

STUDENT LEARNING OBJECTIVES

After completing this chapter, you will be able to answer the following questions:

1. How does Porter's competitive forces model help companies develop competitive strategies using information systems?

2. How do the value chain and value web models help businesses identify opportunities for strategic information system applications?

3. How do information systems help businesses use synergies, core competencies, and network-based strategies to achieve competitive advantage?

4. How do competing on a global scale and promoting quality enhance competitive advantage?

5. What is the role of business process management (BPM) in enhancing competitiveness?

CHAPTER OUTLINE

VERIZON OR AT&T: WHICH COMPANY HAS THE BEST DIGITAL STRATEGY?

Verizon and AT&T are the two largest telecommunications companies in the United States. Today their customers do much more than make phone calls. They use their networks to watch high-definition (HD) TV; surf the Internet; send e-mail, text, and video messages; share photos; watch videos online; and conduct videoconferences around the globe. All of these products and services are digital.

Competition in this industry is unusually intense. Both companies are trying to outflank one another by refining their wireless, landline, and high-speed Internet networks and expanding the range of products, applications and services offered to customers. But there are differences. AT&T is staking its growth on the wireless market by aggressively marketing leading-edge high-end devices such as the iPhone. Verizon is betting on its premium television service to homeowners.

For a number of years, Verizon has tried to blunt competition by boasting that its wireless network is the largest and most reliable in the United States. Now, however, it is also focusing on expanding its FiOS TV and high-speed Internet services. FiOS is a bundled communications (Internet, telephone, and TV) service, operating over a

fiber-optic network that extends all the way to individual homes. It delivers Internet service at speeds five times faster than cable competitors, along with over 100 high-definition television channels, over 500 digital channels, and over 2,500 videos on demand.

Verizon's management believes the company "can't roll out FiOS fast enough." Despite prices that average well above $130 for a bundle of Internet, TV and voice services, 20 percent of the homes where FiOS is available sign up for the service.

Verizon's FiOS move is more risky financially than AT&T's, because up-front costs are high and it will take time to generate healthy profit margins on this line of business. Building the fiber system (including extending fiber-optic cabling to individual homes) costs about $4,000 per customer.

AT&T's strategy is more conservative. Why spend so much money on new wires when cell phones are becoming ubiquitous and profitable? Why not partner with other companies to capitalize on their technology innovations? That was the rationale for AT&T contracting with Apple Computer to be the exclusive network for its iPhone. Even though AT&T subsidizes some of the iPhone's cost to consumers, the iPhone's streamlined design, touch screen, exclusive access to the iTunes music service, and 65,000 or so downloadable applications have made it an instant hit. AT&T has been almost neck-and-neck with Verizon in the wireless business. Moreover, AT&T profit margins from the iPhone grow over time because iPhone subscribers are required to sign a two-year contract for a higher-price wireless service plan.

In the long term, however, Verizon's ability to offer TV as part of a bundle of phone, Internet, and television services may give it the competitive edge. Even without an iconic device such as the iPhone, Verizon's wireless business has prospered by relying on network quality and customer service. And Verizon is hedging its bets. In April 2009, Verizon Wireless started talking with Apple, about selling a version of the iPhone that would work on Verizon's network. AT&T's exclusive U.S. rights to the iPhone expire in 2010. If Verizon contracts with Apple to sell the iPhone, the competitive balance will shift again.

Sources: Amol Sharma, "AT&T, Verizon Make Different Calls," *The Wall Street Journal*, January 28, 2009; Amol Sharma and Roger Cheng, "Verizon Widens Lead over AT&T," *The Wall Street Journal*, April 28, 2009; Roger Cheng, "AT&T Gets Another iPhone Boost," *The Wall Street Journal*, July 24, 2009; and Matt Richtel, "Verizon Said to Be in Talks for the iPhone," *The New York Times*, April 28, 2009.

The story of Verizon and AT&T illustrates some of the ways that information systems help businesses compete—and also the challenges of sustaining a competitive advantage. The telecommunications industry in which both companies operate is extremely crowded and competitive, with telecommunications companies vying with cable companies, new upstarts, and each other to provide a wide array of digital services as well as voice transmission. To meet the challenges of surviving and prospering in this environment, each of these companies focused on a different competitive strategy using information technology.

The chapter-opening diagram calls attention to important points raised by this case and this chapter. Both companies saw there were opportunities to use information technology to offer new products and services. AT&T offered enhanced wireless services using the iPhone, while Verizon countered with its FiOS high-capacity Internet, telephone, and digital TV services using fiber-optic landlines. AT&T's strategy emphasized keeping costs low while capitalizing on innovations from other technology vendors. Verizon's strategy involved high up-front costs to build its high-capacity FiOS network infrastructure, and it also invested in providing a high-level of network reliability and customer service.

This case study also shows that it is difficult to sustain a competitive advantage. Exclusive rights to use the highly popular iPhone on its network brought AT&T millions of new customers and enhanced its competitive position. But if Apple allows Verizon to sell a version of the iPhone for its network, AT&T's competitive advantage may disappear.

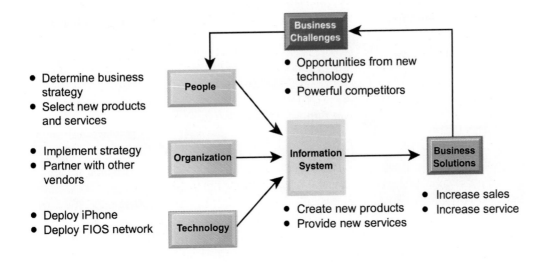

3.1 Using Information Systems to Achieve Competitive Advantage

In almost every industry you examine, you will find that some firms do better than most others. There's almost always a standout firm. In the automotive industry, Toyota is considered a superior performer. In pure online retail, Amazon is the leader; in offline retail Wal-Mart, the largest retailer on earth, is the leader. In online music, Apple's iTunes is considered the leader with more than 75 percent of the downloaded music market, and in the related industry of digital music players, the iPod is the leader. In Web search, Google is considered the leader.

Firms that "do better" than others are said to have a competitive advantage over others: They either have access to special resources that others do not, or they are able to use commonly available resources more efficiently—usually because of superior knowledge and information assets. In any event, they do better in terms of revenue growth, profitability, or productivity growth (efficiency), all of which ultimately in the long run translate into higher stock market valuations than their competitors.

But why do some firms do better than others and how do they achieve competitive advantage? How can you analyze a business and identify its strategic advantages? How can you develop a strategic advantage for your own business? And how do information systems contribute to strategic advantages? One answer to these questions is Michael Porter's competitive forces model.

PORTER'S COMPETITIVE FORCES MODEL

Arguably, the most widely used model for understanding competitive advantage is Michael Porter's **competitive forces model** (see Figure 3-1). This model provides a general view of the firm, its competitors, and the firm's environment. Recall in Chapter 2 we described the importance of a firm's environment and the dependence of firms on environments. Porter's model is all about the firm's general business environment. In this model, five competitive forces shape the fate of the firm.

Figure 3-1
Porter's
Competitive Forces
Model
In Porter's competitive forces model, the strategic position of the firm and its strategies are determined not only by competition with its traditional direct competitors but also by four forces in the industry's environment: new market entrants, substitute products, customers, and suppliers.

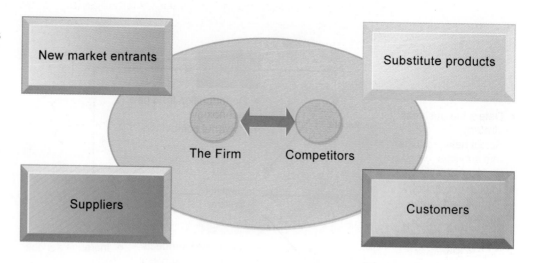

Traditional Competitors

All firms share market space with other competitors who are continuously devising new, more efficient ways to produce by introducing new products and services, and attempting to attract customers by developing their brands and imposing switching costs on their customers.

New Market Entrants

In a free economy with mobile labor and financial resources, new companies are always entering the marketplace. In some industries, there are very low barriers to entry, whereas in other industries, entry is very difficult. For instance, it is fairly easy to start a pizza business or just about any small retail business, but it is much more expensive and difficult to enter the computer chip business, which has very high capital costs and requires significant expertise and knowledge that is hard to obtain. New companies have several possible advantages: They are not locked into old plants and equipment, they often hire younger workers who are less expensive and perhaps more innovative, they are not encumbered by old worn-out brand names, and they are "more hungry" (more highly motivated) than traditional occupants of an industry. These advantages are also their weakness: They depend on outside financing for new plants and equipment, which can be expensive; they have a less-experienced workforce; and they have little brand recognition.

Substitute Products and Services

In just about every industry, there are substitutes that your customers might use if your prices become too high. New technologies create new substitutes all the time. Even oil has substitutes: Ethanol can substitute for gasoline in cars; vegetable oil for diesel fuel in trucks; and wind, solar, coal, and hydro power for industrial electricity generation. Likewise, Internet telephone service can substitute for traditional telephone service, and fiber-optic telephone lines to the home can substitute for cable TV lines. And, of course, an Internet music service that allows you to download music tracks to an iPod is a substitute for CD-based music stores. The more substitute products and services in your industry, the less you can control pricing and the lower your profit margins.

Customers

A profitable company depends in large measure on its ability to attract and retain customers (while denying them to competitors), and charge high prices. The power of customers grows if they can easily switch to a competitor's products and services, or if they can force a business and its competitors to compete on price alone in a transparent marketplace where there is little product differentiation, and all prices are known instantly (such as on the Internet). For instance, in the used college textbook market on the Internet, students (customers) can find multiple suppliers of just about any current college textbook. In this case, online customers have extraordinary power over used-book firms.

Suppliers

The market power of suppliers can have a significant impact on firm profits, especially when the firm cannot raise prices as fast as suppliers can. The more suppliers a firm has, the greater control it can exercise over those suppliers in terms of price, quality, and delivery schedules. For instance, manufacturers of laptop PCs almost always have multiple competing suppliers of key components, such as keyboards, hard drives, and display screens.

INFORMATION SYSTEM STRATEGIES FOR DEALING WITH COMPETITIVE FORCES

So what is a firm to do when it is faced with all these competitive forces? And how can the firm use information systems to counteract some of these forces? How do you prevent substitutes and inhibit new market entrants? How do you become the most successful firm in an industry in terms of profit and share price (two measures of success)?

Basic Strategy 101: Align the IT with the Business Objectives

The basic principle of IT strategy for a business is to ensure the technology serves the business, and not the other way around. The research on IT and business performance has found that (a) the more successfully a firm can align its IT with its business goals, the more profitable it will be, and (b) only about one-quarter of firms achieve alignment of IT with business. About half of a business firm's profits can be explained by alignment of IT with business (Luftman, 2003; Henderson, et al., 1996).

Most businesses get it wrong: IT takes on a life of its own and does not serve management and shareholder interests very well. Instead of business people taking an active role in shaping IT to the enterprise, they ignore it, claim to not understand IT, and tolerate failure in the IT area as just a nuisance to work around. Such firms pay a hefty price in poor performance. Successful firms and managers understand what IT can do and how it works, take an active role in shaping its use, and measure its impact on revenues and profits.

So how do you as a manager achieve this alignment of IT with business? In the following sections, we discuss some basic ways to do this, but here's a summary:

- Identify your business strategy and goals.
- Break these strategic goals down into concrete activities and processes.
- Identify how you will measure progress towards the business goals (e.g. metrics).
- Ask yourself "How can information technology help me achieve progress towards our business goals and how it will improve our business processes and activities?"
- Measure actual performance. Let the numbers speak.

Let's see how this works out in practice. There are four generic strategies, each of which often is enabled by using information technology and systems: low-cost leadership, product differentiation, focus on market niche, and strengthening customer and supplier intimacy.

Low-Cost Leadership

Use information systems to achieve the lowest operational costs and the lowest prices. The classic example is Wal-Mart. By keeping prices low and shelves well stocked using a legendary inventory replenishment system, Wal-Mart became the leading retail business in the United States. Wal-Mart's continuous replenishment system sends orders for new merchandise directly to suppliers as soon as consumers pay for their purchases at the cash register. Point-of-sale terminals record the bar code of each item passing the checkout counter and send a purchase transaction directly to a central computer at Wal-Mart

Supermarkets and large retail stores such as Wal-Mart use sales data captured at the checkout counter to determine which items have sold and need to be reordered. Wal-Mart's continuous replenishment system transmits orders to restock directly to its suppliers. The system enables Wal-Mart to keep costs low while fine-tuning its merchandise to meet customer demands.

headquarters. The computer collects the orders from all Wal-Mart stores and transmits them to suppliers. Suppliers can also access Wal-Mart's sales and inventory data using Web technology.

Because the system replenishes inventory with lightning speed, Wal-Mart does not need to spend much money on maintaining large inventories of goods in its own warehouses. The system also enables Wal-Mart to adjust purchases of store items to meet customer demands. Competitors, such as Sears, have been spending 24.9 percent of sales on overhead. But by using systems to keep operating costs low, Wal-Mart pays only 16.6 percent of sales revenue for overhead. (Operating costs average 20.7 percent of sales in the retail industry.)

Wal-Mart's continuous replenishment system is also an example of an **efficient customer response system**. An efficient customer response system directly links consumer behavior to distribution and production and supply chains. Wal-Mart's continuous replenishment system provides such an efficient customer response. Dell Computer Corporation's assemble-to-order system, described in the following discussion, is another example of an efficient customer response system.

Product Differentiation

Use information systems to enable new products and services, or greatly change the customer convenience in using your existing products and services. For instance, Google continuously introduces new and unique search services on its Web site, such as Google Maps. Apple created iPod, a unique portable digital music player, plus a unique online Web music service where songs can be purchased for $.69 to $1.29 each. Continuing to innovate, Apple introduced an iPod video player and the music and video-playing iPhone.

Manufacturers and retailers are starting to use information systems to create products and services that are customized and personalized to fit the precise specifications of individual customers. Dell Computer Corporation sells directly to customers using assemble-to-order manufacturing. Individuals, businesses, and government agencies can buy computers directly from Dell, customized with the exact features and components they need. They can place their orders directly using a toll-free telephone number or by accessing Dell's Web site. Once Dell's production control receives an order, it directs an assembly plant to assemble the computer using components from an on-site warehouse based on the configuration specified by the customer.

Lands' End customers can use its Web site to order jeans, dress pants, chino pants, and shirts custom-tailored to their own specifications. Customers enter their measurements into a form on the Web site, which then transmits each customer's specifications over a network to a computer that develops an electronic made-to-measure pattern for that customer. The individual patterns are used to drive fabric-cutting equipment at a manufacturing plant. Lands' End has almost no extra production costs because the process does not require additional warehousing, production overruns, and inventories, and the cost to the customer is only slightly higher than that of a mass-produced garment. This ability to offer individually tailored products or services using the same production resources as mass production is called **mass customization**.

Table 3.1 lists a number of companies that have developed IS-based products and services that other firms have found difficult to copy.

Focus on Market Niche

Use information systems to enable a specific market focus, and serve this narrow target market better than competitors. Information systems support this strategy by producing and analyzing data for finely tuned sales and marketing techniques. Information systems enable companies to analyze customer buying patterns, tastes, and preferences closely so that they efficiently pitch advertising and marketing campaigns to smaller and smaller target markets.

The data come from a range of sources—credit card transactions, demographic data, purchase data from checkout counter scanners at supermarkets and retail stores, and data collected when people access and interact with Web sites. Sophisticated software tools find patterns in these large pools of data and infer rules from them that can be used to guide decision making. Analysis of such data drives one-to-one marketing where personal messages can be created based on individualized preferences. For example, Hilton Hotels' OnQ system analyzes detailed data collected on active guests in all of its properties to determine the preferences of each guest and each guest's profitability. Hilton uses this information to give its most profitable customers additional privileges, such as late checkouts. Contemporary customer relationship management (CRM) systems feature analytical capabilities for this type of intensive data analysis (see Chapters 2 and 8).

The Interactive Session on People provides more detail on how skillfully credit card companies are able to mine customer data in order to develop very fine-grained profiles to predict their most profitable cardholders. As you read this case, try to identify the problems faced by credit card companies and whether these solutions are in consumers' best interests.

Strengthen Customer and Supplier Intimacy

Use information systems to tighten linkages with suppliers and develop intimacy with customers. Toyota, Ford, and other automobile manufacturers have information systems that give their suppliers direct access to their production schedules, enabling suppliers to

Amazon: One-click shopping	Amazon holds a patent on one-click shopping that it licenses to other online retailers
Online music: Apple iPod and iTunes	An integrated handheld player backed up with an online library of over 10 million songs
Golf club customization: Ping	Customers can select from more than 1 million different golf club options; a build-to-order system ships their customized clubs within 48 hours
Online person-to-person payment: PayPal.com	Enables transfer of money between individual bank accounts and between bank accounts and credit card accounts

TABLE 3.1

IS-Enabled New Products and Services Providing Competitive Advantage

INTERACTIVE SESSION: PEOPLE   How Much Do Credit Card Companies Know About You?

When Kevin Johnson returned from his honeymoon, a letter from American Express was waiting for him. The letter informed Johnson that AmEx was slashing his credit limit by 60 percent. Why? Not because Johnson missed a payment or had bad credit. The letter stated: "other customers who have used their card at establishments where you recently shopped, have a poor repayment history with American Express." Johnson had started shopping at Wal-Mart. Welcome to the new era of credit card profiling.

Every time you make a purchase with a credit card, a record of that sale is logged into a massive data repository maintained by the card issuer. Each purchase is assigned a four-digit category code that describes the type of purchase that was made. There are separate codes for grocery stores, fast food restaurants, doctors, bars, bail and bond payments, and dating and escort services. Taken together, these codes allow credit card companies to learn a great deal about each of its customers at a glance.

Credit card companies use these data for multiple purposes. First, they use them to target future promotions for additional products more accurately. Users that purchase airline tickets might receive promotions for frequent flyer miles, for example. The data help card issuers guard against credit card fraud by identifying purchases that appear unusual compared to a cardholder's normal purchase history. The card companies also flag users who frequently charge more than their credit limit or demonstrate erratic spending habits. Lastly, these records are used by law enforcement agencies to track down criminals.

Credit card holders with debt, the ones who never fully pay off their balances entirely and thus have to pay monthly interest charges and other fees, have been a major source of profit for credit card issuers. However, the recent financial crisis and credit crunch have turned them into a mounting liability because so many people are defaulting on their payments and even filing for bankruptcy. So the credit card companies are now focusing on mining credit card data to predict cardholders posing the highest risk.

Using complex mathematical formulas and insights from behavioral science, these companies are developing more fine-grained profiles to help them get inside the heads of their customers. The data provide new insights about the relationship of certain types of purchases to a customer's ability or inability to pay off credit card balances and other debt. The card-issuing companies now use this information to deny credit card applications or shrink the amount of credit available to high-risk customers.

These companies are generalizing based on certain types of purchases that may unfairly characterize responsible cardholders as risky. Purchases of second-hand clothing, bail bond services, massages, or gambling might cause card issuers to identify you as a risk, even if you maintain your balance responsibly from month to month. Other behaviors that raise suspicion: using your credit card to get your tires re-treaded, to pay for drinks at a bar, or to obtain a cash advance. In light of the sub-prime mortgage crisis, credit card companies have even begun to consider individuals from Florida, Nevada, California, and other states hardest hit by foreclosures to be risks simply by virtue of their state of residence.

The same fine-grained profiling also identifies the most reliable credit-worthy cardholders. For example, the credit card companies found that people who buy high-quality bird seed and snow rakes to sweep snow off of their roofs are very likely to pay their debts and never miss payments.

Credit card companies are even using their detailed knowledge of cardholder behavior to establish personal connections with the clients that owe them money and convince them to pay off their balances. One 49-year old woman from Missouri in the throes of a divorce owed $40,000 to various credit card companies at one point, including $28,000 to Bank of America. A Bank of America customer service representative studied the woman's profile and spoke to her numerous times, even pointing out one instance where she was erroneously charged twice. The representative forged a bond with the cardholder, and as a result she paid back the entire $28,000 she owed, (even though she failed to repay much of the remainder that she owed to other credit card companies.)

This example illustrates something the credit card companies now know: when cardholders feel more comfortable with companies, as a result of a good relationship with a customer service rep or for any other reason, they're more likely to pay their debts.

It's common practice for credit card companies to use this information to get a better idea of consumer trends, but should they be able to use it to preemptively deny credit or adjust terms of agreements? Law enforcement is not permitted to profile individuals, but it appears that credit card companies are doing just that.

In June 2008, the FTC filed a lawsuit against CompuCredit, a sub-prime credit card marketer. CompuCredit had been using a sophisticated behavioral scoring model to identify customers who they considered to have risky purchasing behaviors and lower these customers' credit limits. CompuCredit settled the suit by crediting $114 million to the accounts of these supposedly risky customers and paid a $2.5 million penalty.

Congress is investigating the extent to which credit card companies use profiling to determine interest rates and policies for their cardholders. The new credit card reform law signed by President Barack Obama in May 2009 requires federal regulators to investigate this. Regulators must also determine whether minority cardholders were adversely profiled by these criteria. The new legislation will also bar card companies from raising interest rates at any time and for any reason on their customers.

If Congress prevails, you're likely to receive far fewer credit card solicitations in the mail and fewer offers of interest-free cards with rates that skyrocket after an initial grace period. You'll also see fewer policies intended to trick or deceive customers, like cash-back rewards for unpaid balances, which actually encourage cardholders not to pay what they owe. But the credit card companies say that to compensate for these changes, they'll need to raise rates across the board, even for good customers.

Sources: Charles Duhigg, "What Does Your Credit-Card Company Know about You?" *The New York Times*, June 17, 2009; "Credit Card Use Is Ripe for Data Mining," *Marketplace*, July 1, 2009; CreditCards.com, "Can Your Lifestyle Hurt Your Credit?" MSN Money, June 30, 2009.

CASE STUDY QUESTIONS

1. What competitive strategy are the credit card companies pursuing? How do information systems support that strategy?

2. What are the business benefits of analyzing customer purchase data and constructing behavioral profiles?

3. Are these practices by credit card companies ethical? Are they an invasion of privacy? Why or why not?

MIS IN ACTION

1. If you have a credit card, make a detailed list of all of your purchases for the past six months. Then write a paragraph describing what credit card companies learned about your interests and behavior from these purchases.

2. How would this information benefit the credit card companies? What other companies would be interested?

decide how and when to ship supplies to the plants where cars are assembled. This allows suppliers more lead time in producing goods. On the customer side, Verizon, described in the chapter-opening case, provides such superior customer service and network reliability that customers are reluctant to change wireless providers. It has the highest customer retention rate among wireless carriers. Strong linkages to customers and suppliers increase switching costs and loyalty to your firm.

Table 3.2 summarizes the competitive strategies we have just described. Some companies focus on one of these strategies, but you will often see companies pursuing several of them simultaneously. For example, Dell Computer has tried to emphasize low cost as well as the ability to customize its personal computers.

Implementing any of these strategies is no simple matter. But it is possible, as evidenced by the many firms that obviously dominate their markets and that have used information systems to enable their strategies. As shown by the cases throughout this book, successfully using information systems to achieve a competitive advantage requires a precise coordination of technology, organizations, and people. Indeed, as many have noted with regard to Wal-Mart, Dell, and Amazon, the ability to successfully implement information systems is not equally distributed, and some firms are much better at it than others. It is not simply a matter of purchasing computers and plugging them into the wall socket. We discuss these topics throughout the book.

TABLE 3.2

Four Basic
Competitive
Strategies

Strategy	Description	Example
Low-cost leadership	Use information systems to produce products and services at a lower price than competitors while enhancing quality and level of service	Wal-Mart
Product differentiation	Use information systems to differentiate products, and enable new services and products	Google, eBay, Apple, Lands' End
Focus on market niche	Use information systems to enable a focused strategy on a single market niche; specialize	AutoNation Harrah's
Customer and supplier intimacy	Use information systems to develop strong ties and loyalty with customers and suppliers	Toyota Corporation Amazon

THE INTERNET'S IMPACT ON COMPETITIVE ADVANTAGE

The Internet has nearly destroyed some industries and has severely threatened more. The Internet has also created entirely new markets and formed the basis for thousands of new businesses. The first wave of e-commerce transformed the business world of books, music, and air travel. In the second wave, eight new industries are facing a similar transformation scenario: telephone services, movies, television, jewelry, real estate, hotels, bill payments, and software. The breadth of e-commerce offerings grows, especially in travel, information clearinghouses, entertainment, retail apparel, appliances, and home furnishings.

For instance, the printed encyclopedia industry and the travel agency industry have been nearly decimated by the availability of substitutes over the Internet. Likewise, the Internet has had a significant impact on the retail, music, book, brokerage, and newspaper industries. At the same time, the Internet has enabled new products and services, new business models, and new industries to spring up every day from eBay and Amazon, to iTunes and Google. In this sense, the Internet is "transforming" entire industries, forcing firms to change how they do business.

Because of the Internet, the traditional competitive forces are still at work, but competitive rivalry has become much more intense (Porter, 2001). Internet technology is based on universal standards that any company can use, making it easy for rivals to compete on price alone and for new competitors to enter the market. Because information is available to everyone, the Internet raises the bargaining power of customers, who can quickly find the lowest-cost provider on the Web. Profits have been dampened. Some industries, such as the travel industry and the financial services industry, have been more impacted than others. Table 3.3 summarizes some of the potentially negative impacts of the Internet on business firms identified by Porter.

However, contrary to Porter's somewhat negative assessment, the Internet also creates new opportunities for building brands and building very large and loyal customer bases that are willing to pay a premium for the brand, for example, Yahoo, eBay, Blue Nile, RedEnvelope, Amazon, and many others. In addition, as with all IT-enabled business initiatives, some firms are far better at using the Internet than other firms are, which creates new strategic opportunities for the successful firms.

THE BUSINESS VALUE CHAIN MODEL

Although the Porter model is very helpful for identifying competitive forces and suggesting generic strategies, it is not very specific about what exactly to do, and it does not provide a

Competitive Force	Impact of the Internet
Substitute products or services	Enables new substitutes to emerge with new approaches to meeting needs and performing functions
Customers' bargaining power	Shifts bargaining power to customers due to the availability of global price and product information
Suppliers' bargaining power	Tends to raise bargaining power over suppliers in procuring products and services; however, suppliers can benefit from reduced barriers to entry and from the elimination of distributors and other intermediaries standing between them and their users
Threat of new entrants	Reduces barriers to entry, such as the need for a sales force, access to channels, and physical assets; it provides a technology for driving business processes that makes other things easier to do
Positioning and rivalry among existing competitors	Widens the geographic market, increasing the number of competitors and reducing differences among competitors; makes it more difficult to sustain operational advantages; puts pressure to compete on price

TABLE 3.3

Impact of the Internet on Competitive Forces and Industry Structure

methodology to follow for achieving competitive advantages. If your goal is to achieve operational excellence, where do you start? Here's where the business value chain model is helpful.

The **value chain model** highlights specific activities in the business where competitive strategies can best be applied (Porter, 1985) and where information systems are most likely to have a strategic impact. This model identifies specific, critical leverage points where a firm can use information technology most effectively to enhance its competitive position. The value chain model views the firm as a series or chain of basic activities that add a margin of value to a firm's products or services. These activities can be categorized as either primary activities or support activities (see Figure 3-2).

Primary activities are most directly related to the production and distribution of the firm's products and services, which create value for the customer. Primary activities include inbound logistics, operations, outbound logistics, sales and marketing, and service. Inbound logistics includes receiving and storing materials for distribution to production. Operations transforms inputs into finished products. Outbound logistics entails storing and distributing finished products. Sales and marketing includes promoting and selling the firm's products. The service activity includes maintenance and repair of the firm's goods and services.

Support activities make the delivery of the primary activities possible and consist of organization infrastructure (administration and management), human resources (employee recruiting, hiring, and training), technology (improving products and the production process), and procurement (purchasing input).

Now you can ask at each stage of the value chain, "How can we use information systems to improve operational efficiency and improve customer and supplier intimacy?" This will force you to critically examine how you perform value-adding activities at each stage and how the business processes might be improved. For example, value chain analysis would indicate that Verizon, described in the chapter-opening case, should improve its processes for product development and quality control. You can also begin to ask how information systems can be used to improve the relationship with customers and with suppliers who lie outside the firm value chain but belong to the firm's extended value chain where they are absolutely critical to your success. Here, supply

Figure 3-2
The Value Chain
Model
This figure provides
examples of systems for
both primary and support
activities of a firm and of
its value partners that
would add a margin of
value to a firm's products
or services.

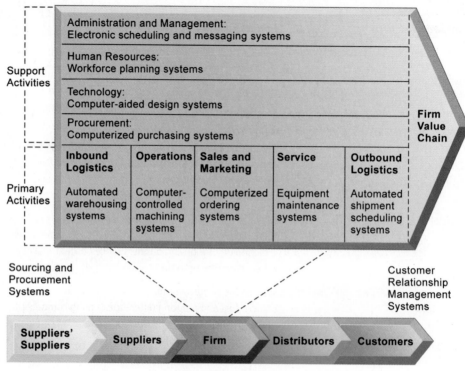

chain management systems that coordinate the flow of resources into your firm, and customer relationship management systems that coordinate your sales and support employees with customers, are two of the most common system applications that result from a business value chain analysis. We discuss these enterprise applications in detail later in Chapter 8.

Using the business value chain model will also cause you to consider benchmarking your business processes against your competitors or others in related industries, and identifying industry best practices. **Benchmarking** involves comparing the efficiency and effectiveness of your business processes against strict standards and then measuring performance against those standards. Industry **best practices** are usually identified by consulting companies, research organizations, government agencies, and industry associations as the most successful solutions or problem-solving methods for consistently and effectively achieving a business objective.

Once you have analyzed the various stages in the value chain at your business, you can come up with candidate applications of information systems. Then, once you have a list of candidate applications, you can decide which to develop first. By making improvements in your own business value chain that your competitors might miss, you can achieve competitive advantage by attaining operational excellence, lowering costs, improving profit margins, and forging a closer relationship with customers and suppliers. If your competitors are making similar improvements, then at least you will not be at a competitive disadvantage—the worst of all cases!

Extending the Value Chain: The Value Web

Figure 3-2 shows that a firm's value chain is linked to the value chains of its suppliers, distributors, and customers. After all, the performance of most firms depends not only on what goes on inside a firm but also on how well the firm coordinates with direct and indirect suppliers, delivery firms (logistics partners, such as FedEx or UPS), and, of course, customers.

How can information systems be used to achieve strategic advantage at the industry level? By working with other firms, industry participants can use information technology to develop industry-wide standards for exchanging information or business transactions electronically, which force all market participants to subscribe to similar standards. Such efforts increase efficiency, making product substitution less likely and perhaps raising entry costs—thus discouraging new entrants. Also, industry members can build industry-wide, IT-supported consortia, symposia, and communications networks to coordinate activities concerning government agencies, foreign competition, and competing industries.

Looking at the industry value chain encourages you to think about how to use information systems to link up more efficiently with your suppliers, strategic partners, and customers. Strategic advantage derives from your ability to relate your value chain to the value chains of other partners in the process. For instance, if you are Amazon.com, you would want to build systems that

- Make it easy for suppliers to display goods and open stores on the Amazon site
- Make it easy for customers to pay for goods
- Develop systems that coordinate the shipment of goods to customers
- Develop shipment tracking systems for customers

In fact, this is exactly what Amazon has done to make it one of the Web's most satisfying online retail shopping sites.

Internet technology has made it possible to create highly synchronized industry value chains called value webs. A **value web** is a collection of independent firms that use information technology to coordinate their value chains to produce a product or service for a market collectively. It is more customer driven and operates in a less linear fashion than the traditional value chain.

Figure 3-3 shows that this value web synchronizes the business processes of customers, suppliers, and trading partners among different companies in an industry or in related industries. These value webs are flexible and adaptive to changes in supply and demand. Relationships can be bundled or unbundled in response to changing market conditions. Firms will accelerate time to market and to customers by optimizing their value web relationships to make quick decisions on who can deliver the required products or services at the right price and location.

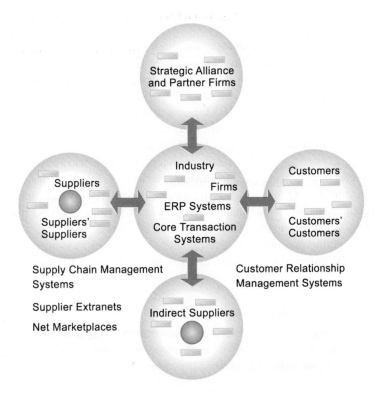

Figure 3-3
The Value Web
The value web is a networked system that can synchronize the value chains of business partners within an industry to respond rapidly to changes in supply and demand.

SYNERGIES, CORE COMPETENCIES, AND NETWORK-BASED STRATEGIES

A large corporation is typically a collection of businesses. Often, the firm is organized financially as a collection of strategic business units, and the returns to the firm are directly tied to the performance of all the strategic business units. For instance, General Electric—one of the largest industrial firms in the world—is a collection of aerospace, heavy manufacturing, electrical appliance, medical imaging, electronics, and financial services firms called business units. Information systems can improve the overall performance of these business units by promoting communication, synergies, and core competencies among the units.

Synergies

The idea of synergies is that when the output of some units can be used as inputs to other units, or two organizations can pool markets and expertise, these relationships lower costs and generate profits. Recent bank and financial firm mergers, such as the merger of Bank of America and Countrywide Financial and JPMorgan Chase and Washington Mutual occurred precisely for this purpose.

One use of information technology in these synergy situations is to tie together the operations of disparate business units so that they can act as a whole. For example, acquiring Countrywide Financial enabled Bank of America to expand its mortgage lending business and acquire a large pool of new customers that might be interested in its credit cards, consumer banking, and other financial products. Information systems would help the merged companies consolidate operations, lower retailing costs, and increase cross-marketing of financial products.

Enhancing Core Competencies

Yet another way to use information systems for competitive advantage is to think about ways that systems can enhance core competencies. The argument is that the performance of all business units can increase insofar as these business units develop, or create, a central core of competencies. A **core competency** is an activity for which a firm is a world-class leader. Core competencies may involve being the world's best miniature parts designer, the best package delivery service, or the best thin-film manufacturer. In general, a core competency relies on knowledge that is gained over many years of experience and a first-class research organization, or simply key people who follow the literature and stay abreast of new external knowledge.

Any information system that encourages the sharing of knowledge across business units enhances competency. Such systems might encourage or enhance existing competencies and help employees become aware of new external knowledge; such systems might also help a business leverage existing competencies to related markets.

For example, Procter & Gamble (P&G), a world leader in brand management and consumer product innovation, uses a series of systems to enhance its core competencies. P&G uses an intranet called InnovationNet to help people working on similar problems share ideas and expertise. The system connects those working in research and development (R&D), engineering, purchasing, marketing, legal affairs, and business information systems around the world, using a portal to provide browser-based access to documents, reports, charts, videos, and other data from various sources. InnovationNet added a directory of subject matter experts who can be tapped to give advice or collaborate on problem solving and product development, and created links to outside research scientists and 150 entrepreneurs who are searching for new, innovative products worldwide.

Network-Based Strategies

Internet and networking technology have spawned strategies that take advantage of firms' abilities to create networks or network with each other. Network-based strategies include the use of network economics and a virtual company model.

Business models based on a network may help firms strategically by taking advantage of **network economics**. In traditional economics—the economics of factories and agriculture—production experiences diminishing returns. The more any given resource is applied to production, the lower the marginal gain in output, until a point is reached where the additional inputs produce no additional outputs. This is the law of diminishing returns, and it is the foundation for most of modern economics.

In some situations, the law of diminishing returns does not work. For instance, in a network, the marginal costs of adding another participant are about zero, whereas the marginal gain is much larger. The larger the number of subscribers in a telephone system or the Internet, the greater the value to all participants because each user can interact with more people. It is no more expensive to operate a television station with 1,000 subscribers than with 10 million subscribers. The value of a community of people grows with size, whereas the cost of adding new members is inconsequential.

From this network economics perspective, information technology can be strategically useful. Internet sites can be used by firms to build *communities of users*—like-minded customers who want to share their experiences. This can build customer loyalty and enjoyment, and build unique ties to customers. EBay, the giant online auction site, and iVillage, an online community for women, are examples. Both businesses are based on networks of millions of users, and both companies have used the Web and Internet communication tools to build communities. The more people offering products on eBay, the more valuable the eBay site is to everyone because more products are listed, and more competition among suppliers lowers prices. Network economics also provide strategic benefits to commercial software vendors. The value of their software and complementary software products increases as more people use them, and there is a larger installed base to justify continued use of the product and vendor support.

Another network-based strategy uses the model of a virtual company to create a competitive business. A **virtual company**, also known as a *virtual organization*, uses networks to link people, assets, and ideas, enabling it to ally with other companies to create and distribute products and services without being limited by traditional organizational boundaries or physical locations. One company can use the capabilities of another company without being physically tied to that company. The virtual company model is useful when a company finds it cheaper to acquire products, services, or capabilities from an external vendor or when it needs to move quickly to exploit new market opportunities and lacks the time and resources to respond on its own.

Fashion companies, such as GUESS, Ann Taylor, Levi Strauss, and Reebok, enlist Hong Kong-based Li & Fung to manage production and shipment of their garments. Li & Fung handles product development, raw material sourcing, production planning, quality assurance, and shipping. Li & Fung does not own any fabric, factories, or machines, outsourcing all of its work to a network of more than 7,500 suppliers in 37 countries all over the world. Customers place orders to Li & Fung over its private extranet. Li & Fung then sends instructions to appropriate raw material suppliers and factories where the clothing is produced. The Li & Fung extranet tracks the entire production process for each order. Working as a virtual company keeps Li & Fung flexible and adaptable so that it can design and produce the products ordered by its clients in short order to keep pace with rapidly changing fashion trends.

DISRUPTIVE TECHNOLOGIES: RIDING THE WAVE

Sometimes a new technology comes along like a tsunami and destroys everything in its path. Some firms are able to create these tsunamis and ride the wave to profits; others learn quickly and are able to swim with the current; still others are obliterated because their products, services, and business models are obsolete. They may be very efficient at doing what no longer needs to be done! There are also cases where no firms benefit, and all the gains go to consumers (firms fail to capture any profits). Business history is filled with examples of **disruptive technologies**. Table 3.4 describes just a few disruptive technologies from the past and some from the likely near-term future.

TABLE 3.4

Disruptive
Technologies: Winners
and Losers

Technology	Description	Winners and Losers
Transistor (1947)	Low-power, compact, semiconductor switch that destroyed the vacuum tube industry	Transistor manufacturing firms win (Texas Instruments), while vacuum tube manufacturers decline (RCA, Sylvania)
Microprocessor chips (1971)	Thousands and eventually millions of transistors on a silicon chip	Microprocessor firms win (Intel, Texas Instruments), while transistor firms (GE) decline
Personal computers (1975)	Small, inexpensive, but fully functional desktop computers	PC manufacturers (HP, Apple, IBM) and chip manufacturers (Intel) prosper, while mainframe (IBM) and minicomputer (DEC) firms lose
PC word processing software (1979)	Inexpensive, limited but functional text editing and formatting for personal computers	PC and software manufacturers (Microsoft, HP, Apple) prosper, while the typewriter industry disappears
World Wide Web (1989)	A global database of digital files and "pages" instantly available	Owners of online content and news benefit, while traditional publishers (newspapers, magazines, broadcast television) lose
Internet music (1998) services	Repositories of downloadable music on the Web with acceptable fidelity	Owners of online music collections (MP3.com; iTunes), telecommunications providers who own Internet backbone (ATT, Verizon), and local Internet service providers win, while record label firms and music retailers lose (Tower Records)
PageRank algorithm	A method for ranking Web pages in terms of their popularity to supplement Web search by key terms	Google wins (it owns the patent), while traditional key word search engines (Alta Vista) lose
Online video search algorithms	Using a family of techniques from speech recognition to text classification in order to make large video collections easily searchable	Online video search companies (Blinkx) win, while traditional search engines at Yahoo!, Amazon, and even Google are challenged
Software as Web service	Using the Internet to provide remote access to online software	Online software services companies (Salesforce.com) win, while traditional "boxed" software companies (Microsoft, SAP, Oracle) lose
Online print services	Using the Internet to provide remote access to digital printers and online designers	Online print process firms gain (digitalpressonline.com), while traditional printers lose (RR Donnelly)

Disruptive technologies are tricky. Firms that invent disruptive technologies as "first movers" do not always benefit if they lack the resources to really exploit the technology or fail to see the opportunity. The MITS Altair 8800 is widely considered the first PC, but its inventors did not take advantage of their first-mover status. Second movers, so-called "fast followers" such as IBM and Microsoft, reaped the rewards. ATMs revolutionized retail banking, but the inventor, Citibank, was copied by other banks, and ultimately all banks used ATMs with the benefits going mostly to the consumers. Google was not a first mover in search but an innovative follower that was able to patent a powerful new search algorithm called PageRank. So far it has been able to hold onto its lead while most other search engines have faded down to small market shares.

The Interactive Session on Organizations explores some of these issues as it examines the Internet's disruptive impact on the television industry. As you read this case, try to identify the problem the television industry is facing, the alternative solutions available to the cable networks and services, and the people, organization, and technology issues that have to be addressed when developing the solution.

3.2 Competing on a Global Scale

Look closely at your jeans or sneakers. Even if they have a U.S. label, they were probably designed in California and stitched together in Hong Kong or Guatemala using materials from China or India. Call up Microsoft Help, or Verizon Help, and chances are good you will be speaking to a customer service representative located in India.

Consider the path to market for a Hewlett-Packard (HP) laptop computer, which is illustrated in Figure 3-4. The idea for the product and initial design came from HP's Laptop Design Team in the United States. HP headquarters in Houston approved the concept. Graphics processors were designed in Canada and manufactured in Taiwan. Taiwan and South Korea provided the liquid-crystal display screens and many of the memory chips. The laptop's hard disk drive came from Japan. Sources in China, Japan, Singapore, South Korea, and the United States supplied other components. Laptop assembly took place in China. Contractors in Taiwan did the machine's engineering design and collaborated with the Chinese manufacturers.

Firms pursuing a global strategy benefit from economies of scale and resource cost reduction (usually wage cost reduction). HP spread design, sourcing, and production for its laptops over multiple countries overseas to reduce logistics, tariffs, and labor costs. Digital content firms that produce Hollywood movies are able to sell millions more copies of DVDs of popular films by using foreign markets.

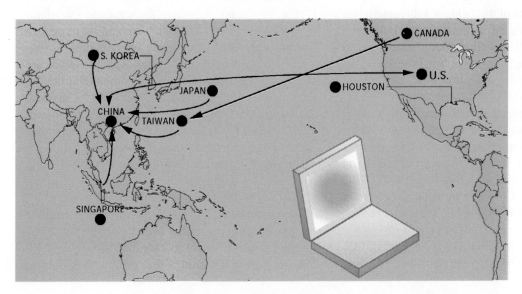

**Figure 3-4
An HP Laptop's
Path to Market**
Hewlett-Packard and other electronics companies assign distribution and production of their products to a number of different countries.

INTERACTIVE SESSION: ORGANIZATIONS   Will TV Succumb to the Internet?

The Internet has transformed the music industry. Sales of CDs in retail music stores have been steadily declining while sales of songs downloaded through the Internet to iPods and other portable music players are skyrocketing. Moreover, the music industry is still contending with millions of people illegally downloading songs for free. Will the television industry have a similar fate?

Widespread use of high-speed Internet access, powerful PCs with high-resolution display screens, iPhones and other mobile handhelds, and leading-edge file-sharing services have made downloading of video content from movies and television shows faster and easier than ever. Free and often illegal downloads of some TV shows are abundant. But the Internet is also providing new ways for television studios to distribute and sell their content, and they are trying to take advantage of that opportunity.

YouTube, which started up in February 2005, quickly became the most popular video-sharing Web site in the world. Even though YouTube's original mission was to provide an outlet for amateur filmmakers, clips of copyrighted Hollywood movies and television shows soon proliferated on the YouTube Web site. It is difficult to gauge how much proprietary content from TV shows winds up on YouTube without the studios' permission. Viacom claimed in a 2008 lawsuit that over 150,000 unauthorized clips of its copyrighted television programs had appeared on YouTube.

YouTube tries to discourage its users from posting illegal clips by limiting the length of videos to 10 minutes each and by removing videos when requested by their copyright owner. YouTube has also implemented Video ID filtering and digital fingerprinting technology that allows copyright owners to compare the digital fingerprints of their videos with material on YouTube and then flag infringing material. Using this technology, it is able to filter many unauthorized videos before they appear on the YouTube Web site. If infringing videos do make it online, they can be tracked using Video ID.

The television industry is also striking back by embracing the Internet as another delivery system for its content. Television broadcast networks such as NBC Universal, Fox, and CNN have put television shows on their own Web sites. In March 2007, NBC Universal, News Corp (the owner of Fox Broadcasting), and ABC Inc. set up Hulu.com, a Web site offering streaming video of television shows and movies from NBC, Fox, ABC, Comedy Central, PBS, USA Network, Bravo, FX, Speed, Sundance, Oxygen,

Onion News Network, and other networks. Hulu also syndicates its hosting to other sites, including AOL, MSN, Facebook, MySpace, Yahoo, and Fancast.com, and allows users to embed Hulu clips in their Web site. The site is free to viewers and supported by advertising commercials. CBS's TV.com and Joost are other popular Web television sites. Content from all of these sites is viewable over iPhones.

What if there are so many TV shows available for free on the Web that "Hulu households" cancel their cable subscriptions to watch free TV online? Cable service operators have begun worrying, especially when the cable networks posted some of their programming on the Web. In July 2009, cable TV operator Comcast Corporation began a trial program to bring some Time Warner network shows, including TBS's *My Boys* and TNT's *The Closer* to the Web. Other cable networks, including A&E and the History Channel, participated in the Comcast test.

By making more television shows available online, but only for cable subscribers, the cable networks hope to preserve and possibly expand the cable TV subscription model in an increasingly digital world. "The vision is you can watch your favorite network's programming on any screen," noted Time Warner Chief Executive Jeff Bewkes. The system used in the Comcast–Time Warner trial is interoperable with cable service providers' systems to authenticate subscribers.

The same technology might also allow cable firms to provide demographic data for more targeted ads and perhaps more sophisticated advertising down the road. Cable programmers also stand to earn more advertising revenue because viewers can't skip ads on TV programs streamed from the Web as they do with traditional TV. Web versions of some television shows in the Comcast–Time Warner trial program, including TNT's *The Closer*, will carry the same number of ads as seen on traditional TV, which amounts to more than four times the ad load on many Internet sites, including Hulu. Many hour-long shows available online are able to accommodate five or six commercial breaks, each with a single 30-second ad. NBC Universal Digital Entertainment has even streamed episodes of series, including *The Office*, with two ads per break. According to research firm eMarketer, these Web-video ads will generate $1.5 billion in ad revenue in 2010 and $2.1 billion in 2011.

Will all of this work out for the cable industry? It's still too early to tell. Although the cable programming companies want an online presence to extend their brands, they don't want to cannibalize TV subscriptions or viewership ratings that generate advertising revenue. Customers accustomed to YouTube and Hulu may rebel if too many ads are shown online. According to Oppenheimer analyst Tim Horan, cable companies will start feeling the impact of customers canceling subscriptions to view online video and TV by 2012. Edward Woo, an Internet and digital media analyst for Wedbush Morgan Securities in Los Angeles predicts that in a few years, "it should get extremely interesting." Hulu and other Web TV and video sites will have much deeper content, and the technology to deliver that content to home viewers will be more advanced.

Sources: Reinhardt Krause, "Cable TV Leaders Plot Strategy Vs. Free Programs on the Web," *Investors Business Daily*, August 18, 2009; Sam Schechner and Vishesh Kumar, "TV Shows Bring Ads Online," *The Wall Street Journal*, July 16, 2009; Sam Schechner and Nat Worden, "Cable Grabs the Web Remote," *The Wall Street Journal*, June 25, 2009; and Kevin Hunt, "The Coming TV-Delivery War: Cable vs. Internet," *The Montana Standard*, July 18, 2009.

CASE STUDY QUESTIONS

1. What competitive forces have challenged the television industry? What problems have these forces created?

2. Describe the impact of disruptive technology on the companies discussed in this case.

3. How have the cable programming and delivery companies responded to the Internet?

4. What people, organization, and technology issues must be addressed to solve the cable industry's problems?

5. Have the cable companies found a successful new business model to compete with the Internet? Why or why not?

MIS IN ACTION

Go to Hulu.com and explore the site. Note all of the TV shows available on the site and pick out three or four of interest to you. View an episode of each of these shows online, then answer the following questions:

1. Did you see any advertisements attached to the programming? What kinds of ads did you see? How were they presented? Do you feel this method of advertising is effective? Why or why not?

2. If more television programs were available online, would you cancel your cable subscription? Why or why not?

THE INTERNET AND GLOBALIZATION

Up until the mid-1990s, competing on a global scale was dominated by huge multinational firms, such as General Electric, General Motors, Toyota, and IBM. These large firms could afford huge investments in factories, warehouses, and distribution centers in foreign countries and proprietary networks and systems that could operate on a global scale. The emergence of the Internet into a full-blown international communications system has drastically reduced the costs of operating on a global scale, deepening the possibilities for large companies but simultaneously creating many opportunities for small and medium-sized firms.

The global Internet, along with internal information systems, puts manufacturing firms in nearly instant contact with their suppliers; Internet telephony permits millions of service calls to U.S. companies to be answered in India and Jamaica, just as easily and cheaply as if the help desk were in New Jersey or California. Likewise, the Internet makes it possible to move very large computer files with hundreds of graphics, or complex industrial designs, across the globe in seconds.

Small and medium-sized firms have created an entirely new class of "micromultinational firms." For instance, CEO Brad Oberwager runs Sundia, a company which sells watermelon juice and fruit in the United States and Europe, out of his San Francisco home. Oberwager has employees in other parts of the United States as well as in India and the Philippines, and they use Web-based information systems to manage and coordinate. A Sundia employee in the Philippines is able to take orders from a Boston grocery store for watermelon juice made from Mexican fruit. The juice is squeezed in Washington State and payment goes to Oberwager in California.

GLOBAL BUSINESS AND SYSTEM STRATEGIES

There are four main ways of organizing businesses internationally: domestic exporter, multinational, franchiser, and transnational, each with different patterns of organizational structure or governance. In each type of global business organization, business functions may be centralized (in the home country), decentralized (to local foreign units), and coordinated (all units participate as equals).

The **domestic exporter** strategy is characterized by heavy centralization of corporate activities in the home country of origin. Production, finance/accounting, sales/marketing, human resources, and strategic management are set up to optimize resources in the home country. International sales are sometimes dispersed using agency agreements or subsidiaries, but foreign marketing is still totally reliant on the domestic home base for marketing themes and strategies. Caterpillar Corporation and other heavy capital equipment manufacturers fall into this category of firm.

A **multinational** strategy concentrates financial management and control out of a central home base while decentralizing production, sales, and marketing operations to units in other countries. The products and services on sale in different countries are adapted to suit local market conditions. The organization becomes a far-flung confederation of production and marketing facilities in different countries. Many financial service firms, along with a host of manufacturers, such as Ford Motor Co. and Intel Corporation fit this pattern.

Franchisers have the product created, designed, financed, and initially produced in the home country but rely heavily on foreign personnel for further production, marketing, and human resources. Food franchisers, such as McDonald's and Starbucks, fit this pattern. McDonald's created a new form of fast-food chain in the United States and continues to rely largely on the United States for inspiration of new products, strategic management, and financing. Nevertheless, local production of some items, local marketing, and local recruitment of personnel are required.

Transnational firms have no single national headquarters but instead have many regional headquarters and perhaps a world headquarters. In a **transnational** strategy, nearly all the value-adding activities are managed from a global perspective without reference to national borders, optimizing sources of supply and demand wherever they appear and taking advantage of any local competitive advantages. There is a strong central management core of decision making but considerable dispersal of power and financial muscle throughout the global divisions. Few companies have actually attained transnational status, but Citigroup, Sony, and Nestlé are attempting this transition.

Nestlé, the largest food and beverage company in the world, is one of the world's most globalized companies, with nearly 250,000 employees at 500 facilities in 200 countries. Nestlé launched a $2.4 billion initiative to adopt a single set of business processes and systems for procurement, distribution, and sales management using mySAP enterprise software. All of Nestlé's worldwide business units use the same processes and systems for making sales commitments, establishing factory production schedules, billing customers, compiling management reports, and reporting financial results. Nestlé has learned how to operate as a single unit on a global scale.

GLOBAL SYSTEM CONFIGURATION

Figure 3-5 depicts four types of systems configurations for global business organizations. *Centralized systems* are those in which systems development and operation occur totally at the domestic home base. *Duplicated systems* are those in which development occurs at the

SYSTEM CONFIGURATION	Strategy			
	Domestic Exporter	Multinational	Franchiser	Transnational
Centralized	X			
Duplicated			X	
Decentralized	x	X	x	
Networked		x		X

Figure 3-5
Global Business Organization and Systems Configurations
The large Xs show the dominant patterns, and the small Xs show the emerging patterns. For instance, domestic exporters rely predominantly on centralized systems, but there is continual pressure and some development of decentralized systems in local marketing regions.

home base but operations are handed over to autonomous units in foreign locations. *Decentralized systems* are those in which each foreign unit designs its own unique solutions and systems. *Networked systems* are those in which systems development and operations occur in an integrated and coordinated fashion across all units.

As can be seen in Figure 3-5, domestic exporters tend to have highly centralized systems in which a single domestic systems development staff develops worldwide applications. Multinationals allow foreign units to devise their own systems solutions based on local needs with few, if any, applications in common with headquarters (the exceptions being financial reporting and some telecommunications applications). Franchisers typically develop a single system, usually at the home base, and then replicate it around the world. Each unit, no matter where it is located, has identical applications. Firms such as Nestle organized along transnational lines use networked systems that span multiple countries using powerful telecommunications networks and a shared management culture that crosses cultural barriers.

3.3 Competing on Quality and Design

Quality has developed from a business buzzword into a very serious goal for many companies. Quality is a form of differentiation. Companies with reputations for high quality, such as Lexus or Nordstrom, are able to charge premium prices for their products and services. Information systems have a major contribution to make in this drive for quality. In the services industries in particular, quality strategies are generally enabled by superior information systems and services.

WHAT IS QUALITY?

Quality can be defined from both producer and customer perspectives. From the perspective of the producer, quality signifies conformance to specifications or the absence of variation from those specifications. The specifications for a telephone might include one that states the strength of the phone should be such that it will not be dented or otherwise damaged by a drop from a four-foot height onto a wooden floor. A simple test will allow this specification to be measured.

A customer definition of quality is much broader. First, customers are concerned with the quality of the physical product—its durability, safety, ease of use, and installation. Second, customers are concerned with the quality of service, by which they mean the accuracy and truthfulness of advertising, responsiveness to warranties, and ongoing product support. Finally, customer concepts of quality include psychological aspects: the company's knowledge of its products, the courtesy and sensitivity of sales and support staff, and the reputation of the product.

Today, as the quality movement in business progresses, the definition of quality is increasingly from the perspective of the customer. Customers are concerned with getting value for their dollar and product fitness, performance, durability, and support.

Many companies have embraced the concept of **total quality management (TQM)**. Total quality management makes quality the responsibility of all people and functions within an organization. TQM holds that the achievement of quality control is an end in itself. Everyone is expected to contribute to the overall improvement of quality—the engineer who avoids design errors, the production worker who spots defects, the sales representative who presents the product properly to potential customers, and even the secretary who avoids typing mistakes. TQM derives from quality management concepts developed by American quality experts, such as W. Edwards Deming and Joseph Juran, but the Japanese popularized it.

Another quality concept that is widely implemented today is six sigma, which Amazon.com used to reduce errors in order fulfillment. **Six sigma** is a specific measure of quality, representing 3.4 defects per million opportunities. Most companies cannot achieve this level of quality but use six sigma as a goal to implement a set of methodologies and techniques for improving quality and reducing costs. Studies have repeatedly shown that the earlier in the business cycle a problem is eliminated, the less it costs the company. Thus, quality improvements not only raise the level of product and service quality but they can also lower costs.

HOW INFORMATION SYSTEMS IMPROVE QUALITY

Let's examine some of the ways companies face the challenge of improving quality to see how information systems can be part of the process.

Reduce Cycle Time and Simplify the Production Process

Studies have shown that probably the best single way to reduce quality problems is to reduce **cycle time**, which refers to the total elapsed time from the beginning of a process to its end. Shorter cycle times mean that problems are caught earlier in the process, often before the production of a defective product is completed, saving some of the hidden costs of producing it. Finally, finding ways to reduce cycle time often means finding ways to simplify production steps. The fewer steps in a process, the less time and opportunity for an error to occur. Information systems help eliminate steps in a process and critical time delays.

800-Flowers, a multimillion-dollar company selling flowers by telephone or over the Web, used to be a much smaller company that had difficulty retaining its customers. It had poor service, inconsistent quality, and a cumbersome manual order-taking process. Telephone representatives had to write each order, obtain credit card approval, determine which participating florist was closest to the delivery location, select a floral arrangement, and forward the order to the florist. Each step in the manual process increased the chance of human error, and the whole process took at least a half hour. Owners Jim and Chris McCann installed a new information system that downloads orders taken in telecenters or over the Web to a central computer and electronically transmits them to local florists. Orders are more accurate and arrive at the florist within two minutes.

Benchmark

Companies achieve quality by using benchmarking to set strict standards for products, services, and other activities, and then measuring performance against those standards. Companies may use external industry standards, standards set by other companies, internally developed high standards, or some combination of the three. L.L.Bean, the Freeport, Maine, outdoor clothing company, used benchmarking to achieve an order-shipping accuracy of 99.9 percent. Its old batch order fulfillment system could not handle the surging volume and variety of items to be shipped. After studying German and Scandinavian companies with leading-edge order fulfillment operations, L.L.Bean carefully redesigned its order fulfillment process and information systems so that orders could be processed as soon as they were received and shipped within 24 hours.

Use Customer Demands to Improve Products and Services

Improving customer service, making customer service the number one priority, will improve the quality of the product itself. Delta Airlines decided to focus on its customers, installing a customer care system at its airport gates. For each flight, the airplane seating chart, reservations, check-in information, and boarding data are linked in a central database. Airline personnel can track which passengers are on board regardless of where they checked in and use this information to help passengers reach their destination quickly, even if delays cause them to miss connecting flights.

Improve Design Quality and Precision

Computer-aided design (CAD) software has made a major contribution to quality improvements in many companies, from producers of automobiles to producers of razor blades. A **computer-aided design (CAD) system** automates the creation and revision of designs, using computers and sophisticated graphics software. The software enables users to create a digital model of a part, a product, or a structure, and make changes to the design on the computer without having to build physical prototypes.

Nikon, which develops and produces cameras, binoculars, and microscopes, uses a 3-D CAD system to reduce the amount of time to design its products while improving their quality. Nikon adopted Catia V5 CAD software from Dassault Systemes and IBM. To refine product design while designing a new camera, Nikon's designers must repeat the process of design creation, evaluation, and modification a large number of times. For example, to move the location of the camera shutter by only .1 millimeter, Nikon's designers will redesign the whole camera to adjust every other detail of design.

CATIA enables Nikon's designers to generate curved surfaces easily and make modifications without creating a new physical mold for each design iteration. Before using these CAD tools, Nikon created product designs by carving out the shape from a block or adding a chunk to that shape. Now, with CATIA, Nikon designers are able to model 3-D shapes on the computer and check modifications immediately. Nikon still has to make design mock-ups, but the CAD software has enabled the company to improve their quality while reducing design lead time down to one-third (IBM, 2009).

Improve Production Precision and Tighten Production Tolerances

For many products, quality can be enhanced by making the production process more precise, thereby decreasing the amount of variation from one part to another. CAD software often produces design specifications for tooling and manufacturing processes, saving additional time and money while producing a manufacturing process with far fewer problems. The user of this software is able to design a more precise production system, a system with tighter tolerances, than could ever be done manually.

3.4 Competing on Business Processes

Technology alone is often not enough to make organizations more competitive, efficient, or quality-oriented. The organization itself needs to be changed to take advantage of the power of information technology. These changes may require minor adjustments in work activities, but, often, entire business processes will need to be redesigned. Business process management (BPM) addresses these needs.

WHAT IS BUSINESS PROCESS MANAGEMENT?

Business process management (BPM) is an approach to business which aims to continuously improve business processes. BPM uses a variety of tools and methodologies to

Computer-aided design (CAD) systems improve the quality and precision of product design by performing much of the design and testing work on the computer.

understand existing processes, design new processes, and optimize those processes. BPM is never concluded because continuous improvement requires continual change. Companies practicing business process management would need to go through the following steps:

1. **Identify processes for change:** One of the most important strategic decisions that a firm can make is not deciding how to use computers to improve business processes, but rather understanding what business processes need improvement. When systems are used to strengthen the wrong business model or business processes, the business can become more efficient at doing what it should not do. As a result, the firm becomes vulnerable to competitors who may have discovered the right business model. Considerable time and cost may also be spent improving business processes that have little impact on overall firm performance and revenue. Managers need to determine what business processes are the most important and how improving these processes will help business performance.

2. **Analyze existing processes:** Existing business processes should be modeled and documented, noting inputs, outputs, resources, and the sequence of activities. The process design team identifies redundant steps, paper-intensive tasks, bottlenecks, and other inefficiencies.

Figure 3-6 illustrates the "as-is" process for purchasing a book from a physical bookstore. Consider what happens when a customer visits a physical bookstore and searches its shelves for a book . If he or she finds the book, that person takes it to the checkout counter and pays for it via credit card, cash, or check. If the customer is unable to locate the book, he or she must ask a bookstore clerk to search the shelves or check the bookstore's inventory records to see if it is in stock. If the clerk finds the book, the customer purchases it and leaves. If the book is not available locally, the clerk inquires about ordering it for the customer, from the bookstore's warehouse or from the book's distributor or publisher. Once the ordered book arrives at the bookstore, a bookstore employee telephones the customer with this information. The customer would have to go to the bookstore again to pick up the book and pay for it. If the bookstore is unable to order the book for the customer, the customer would have to try another bookstore. You can see that this process has many steps and might require the customer to make multiple trips to the bookstore.

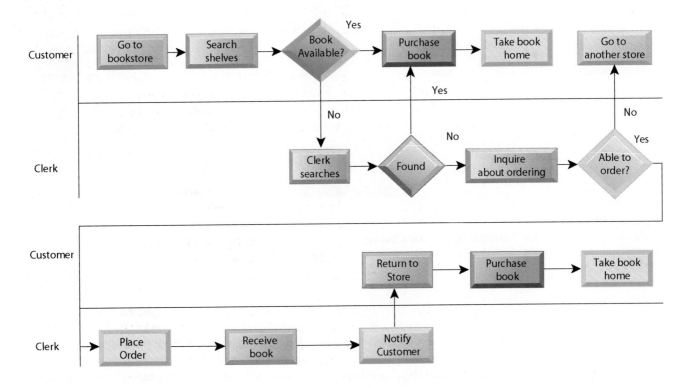

Figure 3-6
As-Is Business Process for Purchasing a Book from a Physical Bookstore
Purchasing a book from a physical bookstore requires many steps to be performed by both the seller and the customer.

3. Design the new process: Once the existing process is mapped and measured in terms of time and cost, the process design team will try to improve the process by designing a new one. A new streamlined "to-be" process will be documented and modeled for comparison with the old process.

Figure 3-7 illustrates how the book purchasing process can be redesigned by taking advantage of the Internet. The customer accesses an online bookstore over the Internet from his or her computer. He or she searches the bookstore's online catalog for the book he or she wants. If the book is available, the customer orders the book online, supplying credit card and shipping address information, and the book is delivered to the customer's home. If the online bookstore does not carry the book, the customer selects another online bookstore and searches for the book again. This process has far fewer steps than that for purchasing the book in a physical bookstore, requires much less effort on the part of the customer, and less sales staff for customer service. The new process is therefore much more efficient and time-saving.

The new process design needs to be justified by showing how much it reduces time and cost or enhances customer service and value. Management first measures the time and cost of the existing process as a baseline. In our example, the time required for purchasing a book from a physical bookstore might range from 15 minutes (if the customer immediately finds what he or she wants) to 30 minutes if the book is in stock but has to be located by sales staff. If the book has to be ordered from another source, the process might take one or two weeks and another trip to the bookstore for the customer. If the customer lives far away from the bookstore, the time to travel to the bookstore would have to be factored in. The bookstore will have to pay the costs for maintaining a physical store and keeping the book in stock, for sales staff on site, and for shipment costs if the book has to be obtained from another location.

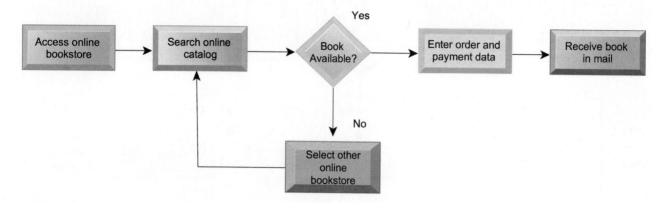

Figure 3-7
Redesigned Process for Purchasing a Book Online
Using Internet technology makes it possible to redesign the process for purchasing a book so that it only has a few steps and consumes much fewer resources.

The new process for purchasing a book online might only take several minutes, although the customer might have to wait several days or weeks to receive the book in the mail and will have to pay a small shipping charge. But the customer saves time and money by not having to travel to the bookstore or make additional visits to pick up the book. Book sellers' costs are lower because they do not have to pay for a physical store location or for local inventory.

4. **Implement the new process:** Once the new process has been thoroughly modeled and analyzed, it must be translated into a new set of procedures and work rules. New information systems or enhancements to existing systems may have to be implemented to support the redesigned process. The new process and supporting systems are rolled out into the business organization. As the business starts using this process, problems are uncovered and addressed. Employees working with the process may recommend improvements.

5. **Continuous measurement:** Once a process has been implemented and optimized, it needs to be continually measured. Why? Processes may deteriorate over time as employees fall back on old methods, or they may lose their effectiveness if the business experiences other changes.

Business Process Reengineering

Many business process improvements are incremental and ongoing, but occasionally, more radical change is required. Our example of a physical bookstore redesigning the book purchasing process so that it can be carried out online is an example of this type of radical, far-reaching change. This radical rethinking and redesign of business processes is called **business process reengineering (BPR)**.

When properly implemented, BPR can lead to dramatic gains in productivity and efficiency, even changing the way the business is run. In some instances, it drives a "paradigm shift" that transforms the nature of the business itself. This actually happened in book retailing when Amazon challenged traditional physical bookstores with its online retail model. By radically rethinking the way a book can be purchased and sold, Amazon and other online bookstores have achieved remarkable efficiencies, cost reductions, and a whole new way of doing business.

BPM poses challenges. Executives report that the largest single barrier to successful business process change is organizational culture. Employees do not like unfamiliar routines, and often try to resist change. This is especially true of business process reengineering projects because the organizational changes are so far-reaching. Managing change is neither simple nor intuitive, and companies committed to extensive process improvement need a good change management strategy (see Chapter 11).

TOOLS FOR BUSINESS PROCESS MANAGEMENT

Over 100 software firms provide tools for various aspects of BPM, including IBM, Oracle, and Tibco. These tools help businesses identify and document processes requiring improvement, create models of improved processes, capture and enforce business rules for performing processes, and integrate existing systems to support new or redesigned processes. BPM software tools also provide analytics for verifying that process performance has been improved and for measuring the impact of process changes on key business performance indicators.

Some BPM tools document and monitor business processes to help firms identify inefficiencies, using software to connect with each of the systems a company uses for a particular process to identify trouble spots. Canadian mutual fund company AIC used Sajus BPM monitoring software to check inconsistencies in its process for updating client accounts whenever they had a transaction. Sajus specializes in "goal-based" process management, which focuses on finding the causes of organizational problems through process monitoring before applying tools to address those problems.

Another category of tools automate some parts of a business process and enforce business rules so that employees perform that process more consistently and efficiently. For example, American National Insurance Company (ANCO), which offers life insurance, medical insurance, property casualty insurance, and investment services, used Pegasystems BPM workflow software to streamline customer service processes across four business groups. The software built rules to guide customer service representatives through a single view of a customer's information that was maintained in multiple systems. By eliminating the need to juggle multiple applications simultaneously to handle customer and agent requests, the improved process increased customer service representative workload capacity by 192 percent.

A third category of tools helps businesses integrate their existing systems to support process improvements. They automatically manage processes across the business, extract data from various sources and databases, and generate transactions in multiple related systems. For example, the Star Alliance of 15 airlines, including United and Lufthansa, used BPM to create common processes shared by all of its members by integrating their existing systems. One project created a new service for frequent fliers on member airlines by consolidating 90 separate business processes across nine airlines and 27 legacy systems. The BPM software documented how each airline processed frequent flier information to help airline managers model a new business process that showed how to share data among the various systems.

3.5 Hands-On MIS Projects

The projects in this section give you hands-on experience identifying information systems to support a business strategy and to solve a customer retention problem, using a database to improve decision making about business strategy, and using Web tools to configure and price an automobile.

MANAGEMENT DECISION PROBLEMS

1. Macy's, Inc., through its subsidiaries, operates approximately 800 department stores in the United States. Its retail stores sell a range of merchandise, including men's, women's, and children's apparel, accessories, cosmetics, home furnishings, and house-

wares. Senior management has decided that Macy's needs to tailor merchandise more to local tastes, that the colors, sizes, brands, and styles of clothing and other merchandise should be based on the sales patterns in each individual Macy's store. For example, stores in Texas might stock clothing in larger sizes and brighter colors than those in New York, or the Macy's on Chicago's State Street might include a greater variety of makeup shades to attract trendier shoppers. How could information systems help Macy's management implement this new strategy? What pieces of data should these systems collect to help management make merchandising decisions that support this strategy?

2. Sprint Nextel has the highest rate of customer churn (the number of customers who discontinue a service) in the cell phone industry, amounting to 2.45 percent. Management wants to know why so many customers are leaving Sprint and what can be done to woo them back. Are customers deserting because of poor customer service, uneven network coverage, or the cost of Sprint cell phone plans? How can the company use information systems to help find the answer? What management decisions could be made using information from these systems?

IMPROVING DECISION MAKING: USING A DATABASE TO CLARIFY BUSINESS STRATEGY

Software skills: Database querying and reporting; database design
Business skills: Reservation systems; customer analysis

In this exercise, you'll use database software to analyze the reservation transactions for a hotel and use that information to fine-tune the hotel's business strategy and marketing activities.

The Presidents' Inn is a small three-story hotel on the Atlantic Ocean in Cape May, New Jersey, a popular northeastern U.S. resort. Ten rooms overlook side streets, 10 rooms have bay windows that offer limited views of the ocean, and the remaining 10 rooms in the front of the hotel face the ocean. Room rates are based on room choice, length of stay, and number of guests per room. Room rates are the same for one to four guests. Fifth and sixth guests must pay an additional $20 charge each per person per day. Guests staying for seven days or more receive a 10 percent discount on their daily room rates.

Business has grown steadily during the past 10 years. Now totally renovated, the inn uses a romantic weekend package to attract couples, a vacation package to attract young families, and a weekday discount package to attract business travelers. The owners currently use a manual reservation and bookkeeping system, which has caused many problems. Sometimes two families have been booked in the same room at the same time. Management does not have immediate data about the hotel's daily operations and income.

In MyMISLab, you will find a database for hotel reservation transactions developed in Microsoft Access. Illustrated below on the next page are some sample records from that database.

Develop some reports that provide information to help management make the business more competitive and profitable. Your reports should answer the following questions:
- What is the average length of stay per room type?
- What is the average number of visitors per room type?
- What is the base income per room (i.e., length of visit multiplied by the daily rate) during a specified period of time?
- What is the strongest customer base?

After answering these questions, write a brief report describing what the database information reveals about the current business situation. Which specific business strategies might be pursued to increase room occupancy and revenue? How could the database be improved to provide better information for strategic decisions?

	Guest First Name	Guest Last Name	Room	Room Type	Arrival Date	Departure Date	No of Guests	Daily Rate	Add New Field
1 Barry	Lloyd	Hayes	Bay-window		12/1/2009	12/4/2009	2	$150.00	
2 Michael	Lunsford	Cleveland	Ocean		12/1/2009	12/9/2009	3	$112.50	
3 Kim	Kyuong	Coolidge	Bay-window		12/4/2009	12/7/2009	1	$150.00	
4 Edward	Holt	Washington	Ocean		12/1/2009	12/3/2009	4	$325.00	
5 Thomas	Collins	Lincoln	Ocean		12/9/2009	12/13/2009	2	$300.00	
6 Paul	Bodkin	Coolidge	Bay-window		12/1/2009	12/3/2009	2	$150.00	
7 Randall	Battenburg	Washington	Ocean		12/4/2009	12/12/2009	2	$292.50	
8 Calvin	Nowotney	Lincoln	Ocean		12/2/2009	12/4/2009	1	$300.00	
9 Homer	Gonzalez	Lincoln	Ocean		12/5/2009	12/7/2009	5	$320.00	
10 David	Sanchez	Jefferson	Bay-window		12/5/2009	12/7/2009	2	$175.00	
11 Buster	Whisler	Jackson	Ocean		12/5/2009	12/8/2009	2	$250.00	
12 Julia	Martines	Reagan	Bay-window		12/10/2009	12/15/2009	1	$150.00	
13 Samuel	Kim	Truman	Side		12/20/2009	12/30/2009	3	$112.50	
14 Arthur	Gottfried	Garfield	Side		12/13/2009	12/15/2009	2	$125.00	
15 Darlene	Shore	Arthur	Ocean		12/24/2009	12/31/2009	5	$198.00	
16 Carlyle	Charleston	Quincy Adams	Bay-window		12/3/2009	12/6/2009	2	$150.00	
17 Albert	Goldstone	Johnson	Ocean		12/5/2009	12/7/2009	3	$250.00	
18 Charlene	Tilson	Van Buren	Bay-window		12/5/2009	12/7/2009	1	$150.00	
19 Everett	Chad	Madison	Ocean		12/10/2009	12/14/2009	2	$275.00	
20 Gerald	Pittsfield	Roosevelt	Ocean		12/5/2009	12/7/2009	2	$275.00	
21 Jamal	Smith	Tyler	Bay-window		12/20/2009	12/23/2009	2	$150.00	
22 Louis	Paris	Jackson	Ocean		12/10/2009	12/14/2009	1	$250.00	
23 Nigel	Stratford	Eisenhower	Ocean		12/14/2009	12/16/2009	2	$200.00	
24 Peter	Willington	Grant	Ocean		12/19/2009	12/21/2009	1	$200.00	
25 Ronald	Cartier	Jefferson	Bay-window		12/24/2009	12/28/2009	4	$175.00	
26 Trista	Leven	Eisenhower	Ocean		12/17/2009	12/20/2009	1	$200.00	

Record: 1 of 30 | No Filter | Search

IMPROVING DECISION MAKING: USING WEB TOOLS TO CONFIGURE AND PRICE AN AUTOMOBILE

Software skills: Internet-based software
Business skills: Researching product information and pricing

In this exercise, you will use software at Web sites for selling cars to find product information about a car of your choice and use that information to make an important purchase decision. You will also evaluate two of these sites as selling tools.

You are interested in purchasing a new Ford Escape (if you are personally interested in another car, domestic or foreign, investigate that one instead). Go to the Web site of CarsDirect (www.carsdirect.com) and begin your investigation. Locate the Ford Escape. Research the various specific automobiles available in that model and determine which you prefer. Explore the full details about the specific car, including pricing, standard features, and options. Locate and read at least two reviews, if possible. Investigate the safety of that model based on the U.S. government crash tests performed by the National Highway Traffic Safety Administration if those test results are available. Explore the features for locating a vehicle in inventory and purchasing directly. Finally, explore the other capabilities of the CarsDirect site for financing.

Having recorded or printed the information you need from CarsDirect for your purchase decision, surf the Web site of the manufacturer, in this case Ford (www.ford.com). Compare the information available on Ford's Web site with that of CarsDirect for the Ford Escape. Be sure to check the price and any incentives being offered (which may not agree with what you found at CarsDirect). Next, find a dealer on the Ford site so that you can view the car before making your purchase decision. Explore the other features of Ford's Web site.

Try to locate the lowest price for the car you want in a local dealer's inventory. Which site would you use to purchase your car? Why? Suggest improvements for the sites of CarsDirect and Ford.

LEARNING TRACKS

The following Learning Tracks provide content relevant to topics covered in this chapter:

1. Challenges of Information Systems for Competitive Advantage
2. Primer on Business Process Management
3. Primer on Business Process Design

Review Summary

1 **How does Porter's competitive forces model help companies develop competitive strategies using information systems?** In Porter's competitive forces model, the strategic position of the firm, and its strategies, are determined by competition with its traditional direct competitors. They are also greatly affected by new market entrants, substitute products and services, suppliers, and customers. Information systems help companies compete by maintaining low costs, differentiating products or services, focusing on market niche, strengthening ties with customer and suppliers, and increasing barriers to market entry with high levels of operational excellence. Information systems are most successful when the technology is aligned with business objectives.

2 **How do the value chain and value web models help businesses identify opportunities for strategic information system applications?** The value chain model highlights specific activities in the business where competitive strategies and information systems will have the greatest impact. The model views the firm as a series of primary and support activities that add value to a firm's products or services. Primary activities are directly related to production and distribution, whereas support activities make the delivery of primary activities possible. A firm's value chain can be linked to the value chains of its suppliers, distributors, and customers. A value web consists of information systems that enhance competitiveness at the industry level by promoting the use of standards and industry-wide consortia, and by enabling businesses to work more efficiently with their value partners.

3 **How do information systems help businesses use synergies, core competences, and network-based strategies to achieve competitive advantage?** Because firms consist of multiple business units, information systems achieve additional efficiencies or enhanced services by tying together the operations of disparate business units. Information systems help businesses leverage their core competencies by promoting the sharing of knowledge across business units. Information systems facilitate business models based on large networks of users or subscribers that take advantage of network economics. A virtual company strategy uses networks to link to other firms so that a company can use the capabilities of other companies to build, market, and distribute products and services. Disruptive technologies provide strategic opportunities, although "first movers" do not necessarily obtain long-term benefit.

4 **How do competing on a global scale and promoting quality enhance competitive advantage?** Information systems and the Internet can help companies operate internationally by facilitating coordination of geographically dispersed units of the company and communication with faraway customers and suppliers. Information systems can enhance quality by simplifying a product or service, facilitating benchmarking, reducing product development cycle time, and improving quality and precision in design and production.

5 **What is the role of business process management (BPM) in enhancing competitiveness?** Organizations often have to change their business processes in order to execute their business strategies successfully. If these business processes use technology, they can be redesigned to make the technology more effective. BPM combines and streamlines the steps in a business process to eliminate repetitive and redundant work and to achieve dramatic improvements in quality, service, and speed. BPM is most effective when it is used to strengthen a good business model and when it strengthens processes that have a major impact on firm performance.

Key Terms

Benchmarking, 90

Business process
  management (BPM), 101

Best practices, 90

Business process
  reengineering (BPR), 104

Competitive forces model, 81

Computer-aided design
  (CAD) system, 101

Core competency, 92

Cycle time, 100

Disruptive technologies, 94

Domestic exporter, 98

Efficient customer response
  system, 84

Franchiser, 99

Mass customization, 85

Multinational, 98

Network economics, 93

Primary activities, 89

Quality, 99

Six sigma, 100

Support activities, 89

Total quality management
  (TQM), 100

Transnational, 98

Value chain model, 89

Value web, 91

Virtual company, 93

Review Questions

1. How does Porter's competitive forces model help companies develop competitive strategies using information systems?
- Define Porter's competitive forces model and explain how it works.
- List and describe four competitive strategies enabled by information systems that firms can pursue.
- Describe how information systems can support each of these competitive strategies and give examples.
- Explain why aligning IT with business objectives is essential for strategic use of systems.

2. How do the value chain and value web models help businesses identify opportunities for strategic information system applications?
- Define and describe the value chain model.
- Explain how the value chain model can be used to identify opportunities for information systems.
- Define the value web and show how it is related to the value chain.
- Explain how the value web helps businesses identify opportunities for strategic information systems.
- Describe how the Internet has changed competitive forces and competitive advantage.

3. How do information systems help businesses use synergies, core competencies, and network-based strategies to achieve competitive advantage?
- Explain how information systems promote synergies and core competencies.
- Describe how promoting synergies and core competencies enhances competitive advantage.
- Explain how businesses benefit by using network economics.
- Define and describe a virtual company and the benefits of pursuing a virtual company strategy.
- Explain how disruptive technologies create strategic opportunities.

4. How do competing on a global scale and promoting quality enhance competitive advantage?
- Describe how globalization has increased opportunities for businesses.
- List and describe the four main ways of organizing a business internationally and the types of systems configuration for global business organizations.
- Define quality and compare the producer and consumer definitions of quality.
- Describe the various ways in which information systems can improve quality.

5. What is the role of business process management (BPM) in enhancing competitiveness?
- Define BPM and explain how it helps firms become more competitive.
- Distinguish between BPM and business process reengineering (BPR).
- List and describe the steps companies should take to make sure BPM is successful.

Discussion Questions

1. It has been said that there is no such thing as a sustainable competitive advantage. Do you agree? Why or why not?

2. What are some of the issues to consider in determining whether the Internet would provide your business with a competitive advantage?

Video Cases

Video Cases and Instructional Videos illustrating some of the concepts in this chapter are available. Contact your instructor to access these videos.

Collaboration and Teamwork

Identifying Opportunities for Strategic Information Systems

With your team of three or four students, select a company described in the *Wall Street Journal*, *Fortune*, *Forbes*, or another business publication. Visit the company's Web site to find additional information about that company and to see how the firm is using the Web. On the basis of this information, analyze the business. Include a description of the organization's features, such as important business processes, culture, structure, and environment, as well as its business strategy. Suggest strategic information systems appropriate for that particular business, including those based on Internet technology, if appropriate. If possible, use Google Sites to post links to Web pages, team communication announcements, and work assignments; to brainstorm; and to work collaboratively on project documents. Try to use Google Docs to develop a presentation of your findings for the class.

BUSINESS PROBLEM-SOLVING CASE

EBay Fine-Tunes Its Strategy

Since its inception, eBay has been synonymous with Internet auctions. The company has been the first and by far the most successful Internet auction business, mushrooming into a gigantic electronic marketplace hosting 25 million sellers all over the world. Founded in 1995 by Pierre Omidyar and originally known as AuctionWeb, eBay has come a long way from its first sale, a broken laser pointer. The company now sells a staggeringly diverse array of goods and is one of the world's most easily recognizable and well-known Web sites.

In 1998, eBay had revenues of $4.8 million in the United States. A decade later in 2008, eBay's marketplaces generated over $8.5 billion in revenue worldwide from selling $60 billion in merchandise. Hundreds of thousands of people support themselves by selling on eBay and many millions more use eBay to supplement their income. During the 2008 holiday season, eBay was the most visited site on the Web, with 85.4 million active visitors.

But while impressive at first glance, eBay's numbers have been slowing down for years. In the very same quarter in which eBay logged 85.4 million visitors, the company's revenue shrank for the first time in the company's history. The biggest cause for eBay's weakening outlook is the same area of the company that propelled it to stardom: its online auction business.

Consumers have indicated a strong preference for fixed-price bulk retailers, like Amazon, which has sustained steady growth despite the economic downturn. For many buyers, the novelty of online auctions has worn off, and these buyers have returned to the easier and simpler method of buying fixed-price goods. Search engines and comparison-shopping sites have also taken away some of eBay's auction business by making items easier to find on other Web sites.

Although the company was slow to diagnose this trend, eBay's leadership has begun taking the necessary steps to meet the shift in demand by consumers from auctions to fixed-price goods. The company unveiled a three-year revival plan in which the overall goal was to create a comprehensive array of marketplaces concentrated in one central online location. Bidding on auctions, clicking on ads, scanning classifieds, and making outright purchases will all be possible from the flagship eBay site and its affiliates.

CEO John Donahoe wants to focus eBay's business on the "secondary market," which includes overstock and out-of-season items as well as the used and antique items that eBay has been known for. He wants the eBay buying experience to emulate that of a low-price bulk retailer such as Costco, where "the inventory is somewhat fluid, but everything they've got is a great deal."

To that end, Donahoe is trying to move eBay away from auctions and toward fixed-price listings. Although this move has appealed to investors, it angered many of the smaller sellers of unique goods that have come to symbolize the company's success. Some longtime sellers chose to move their business elsewhere.

EBay has traditionally derived the bulk of its revenue from fees and commissions associated with its sales transactions. A portion of eBay's revenue comes from direct advertising on the site, and some comes from end-to-end service providers such as PayPal, which increase the ease and speed of eBay transactions. The site imposes several types of fees on sellers, including posting fees for listing items as well as a collection fee on sold items. Traditionally, eBay was seen as a favorable proposition for smaller sellers to find markets for rare goods, or goods that are otherwise difficult to value.

In order to provide more incentive for bulk sellers of fixed-price goods to post their items on the site, eBay significantly adjusted its fee structure as part of its revival plan. The company reduced posting fees for adding an item online and increased the collection fee for sold items. For example, the fee to list a $25 auction item dropped to $1.00 from $1.20, but eBay's sales commission on the same item rose from 5.75 percent to 8.75 percent. In August 2008, eBay lowered its listing fees for all sellers offering fixed-priced items under its "Buy It Now" format.

For bulk sellers, this was a boon. Prior to the change, posting large quantities of items was an expensive undertaking, since only a fraction of those posted items actually sold. Paying these posting fees represented the majority of bulk sellers' se expenditures. But for smaller sellers of unique, expensive items, increasing collection fee percentages meant that they would make significantly less per sale.

EBay also adjusted its search ordering system so that highly rated merchants appear first and receive more exposure. Previously, the first items to be displayed were those for which an auction was about to end. EBay's new search system uses a complicated formula that takes into account an item's price and how well that item's seller ranks in customer satisfaction.

At first glance, this adjustment doesn't benefit any particular group of sellers more than the rest. But eBay also rolled out a rating system that made acquiring a high rating a much more time-consuming undertaking, favoring larger sellers with the time and energy to build a favorable rating. The company also removed the ability of sellers to assign negative ratings to buyers, a feature which many sellers felt protected them against late or non-payment on the part of buyers. The company's reasoning for this change was to stop sellers from rating buyers poorly as revenge for poor customer satisfaction ratings. Smaller sellers were incensed, claiming that the company was unnecessarily mistreating the group that spurred them to market dominance.

Not long ago, eBay's growth strategy focused on expansion in geography and scope and on continuing innovation to enhance the variety and appeal of products on its sites. EBay has always been active in developing and acquiring new products and services that encompass all the activities people perform on the Internet. Earlier this decade, the company fashioned a diversified portfolio of companies with a hand in each of the Internet's big cash pots: shopping, communicating, search, and entertainment. They are now realizing that some of these acquisitions were not good fits with their core business.

PayPal, whose service enables the exchange of money between individuals over the Internet, brings additional transaction-based fee revenue, and has been a significant bright spot for eBay's future prospects. EBay is banking on PayPal becoming the standard payment method for online transactions. The service already receives 40 percent of its business from payment transactions that are not associated with eBay. Management is using PayPal, a high-growth area, to help refocus the business and jump-start stagnant growth.

In 2005, eBay acquired Shopping.com, an online shopping comparison site, and Skype Technologies, which provides a service for free or low-cost voice calls over the Internet. Markets that eBay traditionally had trouble penetrating, such as real estate, travel, new-car sales, and expensive collectibles, require more communication among buyers and sellers than eBay currently offers, and Skype provides voice communication services to help.

But in 2009, eBay announced its plans to unload Skype, admitting its mistake in acquiring the company. EBay assumed that buyers and sellers would use Skype to communicate about transactions, but the feature never caught on as expected. Skype cost eBay $2.6 billion, and eBay stands to recoup only a portion of that initial sum. Investors had urged the company to rid itself of Skype and channel the funds they receive into new growth initiatives.

Despite its mistake in acquiring Skype, eBay is still trying to expand the business via acquisitions. The company also acquired the ticket-reselling Web site StubHub, bought a 25 percent stake in classified ad site Craigslist, and purchased Kurant (now ProStores), whose technology helps users set up online stores. Some analysts report that while many of eBay's individual acquisitions appear to have been successful, they haven't created the synergy that was intended, and diversification has detracted from eBay's core business, auctions.

But that might be what eBay has intended all along. Mom and pop dealers have objected vociferously to most of eBay's recent changes. Donahoe regularly appears on lists of "disliked CEOs," and sellers have voiced their discontent via online forums and shareholder meetings. But Donahoe and the rest of eBay's management maintains that hosting fixed-price sales by reliable retailers makes shopping more customer-friendly and predictable. Will cultivating large sellers dilute eBay's brand and reputation as a dynamic flea market? Or will it steer eBay toward the fastest part of e-commerce growth?

Reports from 2009 appear promising. Despite the unfavorable economic climate, eBay's stock has rallied from lows early in the year, gaining 71%. However, eBay's site traffic is continuing to slowly erode as consumers gravitate towards Amazon and other similar sites. EBay still has a way to go to recoup its dot-com boom glory days. Can the Web's most prominent online auction site change course so dramatically from the formula that made it successful?

Sources: "Is John Donahoe Finally Turning eBay Around?" Kevin Kelleher, www.gigaom.com, June 14, 2009; " Peter Burrows, "EBay Outlines Three-Year Revival Plan," *Business Week*, March 12, 2009; Geoffrey A. Fowler, "Auctions Fade in eBay's Bid for Growth," *The Wall Street Journal*, May 26, 2009, "EBay Retreats in Web Retailing," *The Wall Street Journal*, March 12, 2009, and "EBay to Unload Skype in IPO, Citing Poor Fit," *The Wall Street Journal*, April 15, 2009; Geoffrey A. Fowler and Evan Ramstad, "EBay Looks Abroad for Growth," *The Wall Street Journal*, April 15, 2009; and Brad Stone, "EBay's New Leader Moves Swiftly on a Revamping," *The New York Times*, January 24, 2008.

Case Study Questions

1. Apply the value chain and competitive forces model to eBay.
2. What is eBay's business model and business strategy? How successful has it been?
3. What are the problems that eBay is currently facing? How is eBay trying to solve these problems?
4. Are these good solutions? Why or why not? Are there any other solutions that eBay should consider?
5. What people, organization, and technology factors play a role in eBay's response to its problems?
6. Will eBay be successful in the long run? Why or why not?

Information Technology Infrastructure

PART II

Part II provides the technical foundation for understanding information systems by examining hardware, software, databases, networking technologies, and tools and techniques for security and control. This part answers questions such as these: What technologies and tools do businesses today need to accomplish their work? What do I need to know about these technologies to make sure they enhance the performance of my firm? How are these technologies likely to change in the future?

IT Infrastructure: Hardware and Software

CHAPTER 4

STUDENT LEARNING OBJECTIVES

After completing this chapter, you will be able to answer the following questions:

1. What are the components of IT infrastructure?

2. What are the major computer hardware, data storage, input, and output technologies used in business?

3. What are the major types of computer software used in business?

4. What are the most important contemporary hardware and software trends?

5. What are the principal issues in managing hardware and software technology?

Chapter Outline

CARS.COM'S IT INFRASTRUCTURE DRIVES RAPID BUSINESS GROWTH

If you've ever tried to research or buy a car online, you may have used Cars.com. It's the number one destination for online car shoppers. With comprehensive pricing information, photo galleries, side-by-side comparison tools, videos, and a huge selection of new- and used-car inventory, Cars.com gives millions of car buyers the information they need to make confident buying decisions.

No wonder, then, that the company has experienced explosive growth. In 2008, Cars.com experienced record traffic and dealer leads. Unfortunately, its information systems were unable to keep pace with its aggressive business strategy and expansion. Cars.com's was saddled with a haphazard collection of technologies that had evolved over 10 years that made it difficult to get much work done. It used multiple versions of the Linux operating system, including AGT Linux, which is no longer supported, as well as aging Hewlett-Packard and Sun Microsystems servers running BEA Java. According to the company's Chief Technology Officer Manny Montejano, "Not only did we have multiple pieces of technology from multiple vendors and multiple sources,

but we had multiple versions within those." As a result, Cars.com's information systems staff was spending more time trying to integrate legacy software and systems rather than developing applications to meet new business demands.

Working with Perficient information technology consultants, Cars.com management decided that it would have to replace the firm's entire IT infrastructure in order to achieve its business goals. The project began in January 2007. Cars.com standardized on an IBM platform and a service-oriented architecture (SOA). IBM's WebSphere application server runs on four IBM Power series servers with the P5 chip set using AIX, IBM's version of the Unix operating system. The IBM servers have significantly reduced Cars.com's data center costs because they have lower power, cooling, and space requirements.

The Cars.com application on the application server is written in Java. The IBM Information Server combines data from end users and dealers so it can be integrated with the company's applications. With millions of vehicles in Cars.com's inventory, customers are able to precisely locate what they are looking for. IBM Rational software helps Cars.com programmers rapidly design, develop, and test Java applications. The SOA environment allows the company to build new applications and services more rapidly using plug-and-play technologies.

So far Cars.com's investment in a new IT infrastructure has delivered strong returns. The company can develop new systems much more rapidly, and the information systems department now has the time and resources to take on projects that will help grow the business. For example, the new infrastructure allowed the company to participate in Super Bowl commercials because its systems were now capable of handling large spikes in traffic when its two 30-second ads appeared on TV. The infrastructure also allowed Cars.com become the exclusive provider of used-car listings and exclusive listing service for private-party sellers on Yahoo Autos. Dealer leads have increased 40 percent over 2007. Handling inventory of 2.7 million vehicles, thousands of dealers, and millions of unique Web site visitors each month, Cars.com's new IT infrastructure is clearly up to the task.

Sources: Kevin Helliker, "Americans Renew Their Love for Cars-Online," *The Wall Street Journal*, August 27, 2009; Karen D. Schwartz, "Cars.com Firing on All Cylinders," *eWeek*, June 9 2008; IBM, "Cars.com Turns to IBM Software and SOA Expertise to Drive Rapid Business Growth," April 18, 2008.

Cars.com has an enviable track record as a successful online retail business. Unfortunately, its aggressive growth plans and daily operations were hampered by unmanageable and outdated technology. Cars.com's management felt the best solution was to replace its antiquated IT infrastructure with new computer hardware and software technologies and to standardize on the technology of a single vendor—IBM. This case highlights the critical role that hardware and software investments can play in improving business performance.

The chapter-opening diagram calls attention to important points raised by this case and this chapter. Management decided that the best way to make technology promote business objectives was to overhaul and standardize its IT infrastructure. It now uses more powerful and efficient servers, and a series of IBM software tools along with a service oriented architecture (SOA) that makes it much easier to develop new applications and services. The entire infrastructure is easier to manage and capable of scaling to accomodate spikes in Web site traffic, growing transaction loads, and new business opportunities.

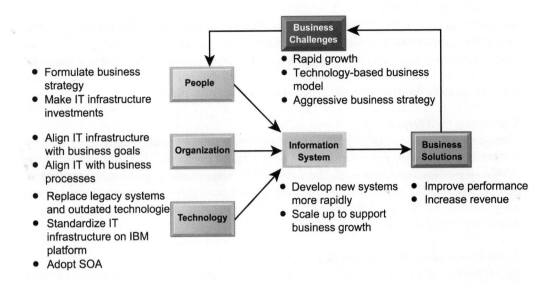

- Formulate business strategy
- Make IT infrastructure investments

- Align IT infrastructure with business goals
- Align IT with business processes
- Replace legacy systems and outdated technologie
- Standardize IT infrastructure on IBM platform
- Adopt SOA

People

Organization

Technology

Business Challenges
- Rapid growth
- Technology-based business model
- Aggressive business strategy

Information System
- Develop new systems more rapidly
- Scale up to support business growth

Business Solutions
- Improve performance
- Increase revenue

4.1 IT Infrastructure: Computer Hardware

If you want to know why American businesses spend about $2 trillion every year on computing and information systems, just consider what it would take for you personally to set up a business or manage a business today. Businesses require a wide variety of computing equipment, software, and communications capabilities simply to operate and solve basic business problems. Obviously, you need computers, and, as it turns out, a wide variety of computers are available, including desktops, laptops, and handhelds.

Do your employees travel or do some work from home? You will want to equip them with laptop computers (over half the computers sold in the U.S. are laptops). If you are employed by a medium to large business, you will also need larger server computers, perhaps an entire data center or server farm with hundreds or even thousands of servers. Google, for instance, is able to answer 300 million queries a day in the United States, most within one second, by using a massive network of over 1 million PC servers linked together to spread the workload.

You will also need plenty of software. Each computer will require an operating system and a wide range of application software capable of dealing with spreadsheets, documents, and data files. Unless you are a single-person business, you will most likely want to have a network to link all the people in your business together and perhaps your customers and suppliers. As a matter of fact, you will probably want several networks: a local-area network connecting employees in your office, and remote access capabilities so employees can share e-mail and computer files while they are out of the office. You will also want all your employees to have access to landline phone systems, cell phone networks, and the Internet. Finally, to make all this equipment and software work harmoniously, you will also need the services of trained people to help you run and manage this technology.

All of the elements we have just described combine to make up the firm's *information technology (IT) infrastructure*, which we first defined in Chapter 1. A firm's IT infrastructure provides the foundation, or platform, for supporting all the information systems in the business.

INFRASTRUCTURE COMPONENTS

Today's IT infrastructure is composed of five major components: computer hardware, computer software, data management technology, networking and telecommunications technology, and technology services (see Figure 4-1). These components must be coordinated with each other.

Computer Hardware

Computer hardware consists of technology for computer processing, data storage, input, and output. This component includes large mainframes, servers, desktop and laptop computers, and mobile devices for accessing corporate data and the Internet. It also includes equipment for gathering and inputting data, physical media for storing the data, and devices for delivering the processed information as output.

Computer Software

Computer software includes both system software and application software. **System software** manages the resources and activities of the computer. **Application software** applies the computer to a specific task for an end user, such as processing an order or generating a mailing list. Today, most system and application software is no longer custom programmed but rather is purchased from outside vendors. We describe these types of software in detail in Section 4.2.

Data Management Technology

In addition to physical media for storing the firm's data, businesses need specialized software to organize the data and make them available to business users. **Data management software** organizes, manages, and processes business data concerned with inventory, customers, and vendors. Chapter 5 describes data management software in detail.

Networking and Telecommunications Technology

Networking and telecommunications technology provides data, voice, and video connectivity to employees, customers, and suppliers. It includes technology for running a company's internal networks, services from telecommunications/telephone services companies, and technology for running Web sites and linking to other computer systems through the Internet. Chapter 6 provides an in-depth description of these technologies.

Technology Services

Businesses need people to run and manage the other infrastructure components we have just described and to train employees in how to use these technologies for their work. Chapter 2 described the role of the information systems department, which is the firm's internal business unit set up for this purpose. Today, many businesses supplement their in-house

Figure 4-1
IT Infrastructure Components
A firm's IT infrastructure is composed of hardware, software, data management technology, networking technology, and technology services.

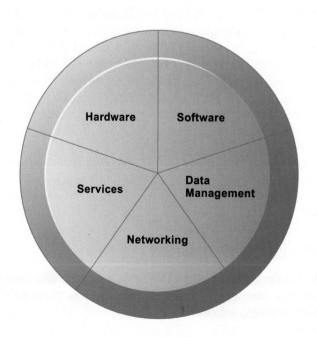

information systems staff with external technology consultants. Even large firms do not have the staff, the skills, the budget, or the necessary experience to implement and run the wide array of technologies that would be required. When businesses need to make major system changes or implement an entirely new IT infrastructure, they typically turn to external consultants to help them with systems integration.

Systems integration means ensuring that the new infrastructure works with the firm's older, so-called legacy systems and that the new elements of the infrastructure work with one another. **Legacy systems** are generally older transaction processing systems created for older computers that continue to be used to avoid the high cost of replacing or redesigning them.

There are many thousands of technology vendors supplying IT infrastructure components and services and an equally large number of ways of putting them together. This chapter is about the hardware and software components of infrastructure you will need to run a business. Chapter 5 describes the data management component, and Chapter 6 is devoted to the networking and telecommunications technology component. Chapter 7 deals with hardware and software for ensuring that information systems are reliable and secure, and Chapter 8 discusses software for enterprise applications.

TYPES OF COMPUTERS

Business firms face many different challenges and problems that can be solved by computers and information systems. In order to be efficient, firms need to match the right computer hardware to the nature of the business challenge, neither overspending nor underspending for the technology.

Computers come in an array of sizes with differing capabilities for processing information, from the smallest handheld devices to the largest mainframes and supercomputers. If you're working alone or with a few other people in a small business, you'll probably be using a desktop or laptop **personal computer (PC)**. You might carry around a mobile device with some computing capability, such as a BlackBerry, iPhone or Palm handheld, or other high-end cell phone. If you're doing advanced design or engineering work requiring powerful graphics or computational capabilities, you might use a **workstation**, which fits on a desktop but has more powerful mathematical and graphics-processing capabilities than a PC.

If your business has a number of computers networked together or maintains a Web site, it will need a **server**. Server computers are specifically optimized to support a computer network, enabling users to share files, software, peripheral devices (such as printers), or other network resources.

Servers have become important components of firms' IT infrastructures because they provide the hardware platform for electronic commerce. By adding special software, they can be customized to deliver Web pages, process purchase and sale transactions, or exchange data with systems inside the company. You will sometimes find many servers linked together to provide all the processing needs for large companies. If your company has to process millions of financial transactions or customer records, you will need multiple servers or a single large mainframe to solve these challenges.

Mainframe computers first appeared in the mid-1960s, and are still used by large banks, insurance companies, stock brokerages, airline reservation systems, and government agencies to keep track of hundreds of thousands, or even millions, of records and transactions. A **mainframe** is a large-capacity, high-performance computer that can process large amounts of data very rapidly. Airlines, for instance, use mainframes to process upwards of 3,000 reservation transactions per second.

IBM, the leading mainframe vendor, has repurposed its mainframe systems so they can be used as giant servers for large-scale enterprise networks and corporate Web sites. A single IBM mainframe can run enough instances of Linux or Windows server software to replace thousands of smaller Windows-based servers.

A **supercomputer** is a specially designed and more sophisticated computer that is used for tasks requiring extremely rapid and complex calculations with thousands of variables, millions of measurements, and thousands of equations. Supercomputers traditionally have been used in engineering analysis of structures, scientific exploration and simulations, and military work, such as classified weapons research and weather forecasting. A few private business firms use supercomputers. For instance, Volvo and most other automobile manufacturers use supercomputers to simulate vehicle crash tests.

If you are a long-term weather forecaster, such as the National Oceanic and Atmospheric Administration (NOAA), or the National Hurricane Center, and your challenge is to predict the movement of weather systems based on hundreds of thousands of measurements, and thousands of equations, you would want access to a supercomputer or a distributed network of computers called a grid.

Grid computing involves connecting geographically remote computers into a single network to create a "virtual supercomputer" by combining the computational power of all computers on the grid. Grid computing takes advantage of the fact that most computers in the United States use their central processing units on average only 25 percent of the time, leaving 75 percent of their capacity available for other tasks. By using the combined power of thousands of PCs and other computers networked together, the grid is able to solve complicated problems at supercomputer speeds at far lower cost.

Private firms are beginning to use computing grids because of their greater reliability than supercomputers, higher capacity, and lower cost. For example, Royal Dutch/Shell Group is using a scalable grid computing platform that improves the accuracy and speed of its scientific modeling applications to find the best oil reservoirs. This platform, which links 1,024 IBM servers running Linux, in effect creates one of the largest commercial Linux supercomputers in the world. The grid adjusts to accommodate the fluctuating data volumes that are typical in this seasonal business. Royal Dutch/Shell Group claims the grid has enabled the company to cut processing time for seismic data, while improving output quality and helping its scientists pinpoint problems in finding new oil supplies.

Computer Networks and Client/Server Computing

Unless you are in a small business with a stand-alone computer, you'll be using networked computers for most processing tasks. The use of multiple computers linked by a communications network for processing is called **distributed processing**. **Centralized processing**, in which all processing is accomplished by one large central computer, is much less common.

One widely used form of distributed processing is **client/server computing**. Client/server computing splits processing between "clients" and "servers." Both are on the network, but each machine is assigned functions it is best suited to perform. The **client** is the user point of entry for the required function and is normally a desktop or laptop computer. The user generally interacts directly only with the client portion of the application. The server provides the client with services. Servers store and process shared data and also perform functions such as managing printers, backup storage, and network activities such as security, remote access, and user authentication. Figure 4-2 illustrates the client/server computing concept. Computing on the Internet uses the client/server model (see Chapter 6).

Figure 4-2
Client/Server Computing
In client/server computing, computer processing is split between client machines and server machines linked by a network. Users interface with the client machines.

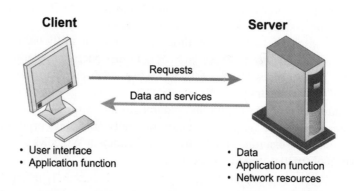

Figure 4-2 illustrates the simplest client/server network, consisting of a client computer networked to a server computer, with processing split between the two types of machines. This is called a *two-tiered client/server architecture*. Whereas simple client/server networks can be found in small businesses, most corporations have more complex, multitiered (often called **N-tier**) **client/server architectures**, in which the work of the entire network is balanced over several different levels of servers, depending on the kind of service being requested (see Figure 4-3).

For instance, at the first level a **Web server** will serve a Web page to a client in response to a request for service. Web server software is responsible for locating and managing stored Web pages. If the client requests access to a corporate system (a product list or price information, for instance), the request is passed along to an **application server**. Application server software handles all application operations between a user and an organization's back-end business systems. The application server may reside on the same computer as the Web server or on its own dedicated computer. Chapters 5 and 6 provide more detail on other pieces of software that are used in multitiered client/server architectures for e-commerce and e-business.

STORAGE, INPUT, AND OUTPUT TECHNOLOGY

In addition to hardware for processing data, you will need technologies for data storage, and input and output. Storage and input and output devices are called *peripheral devices* because they are outside the main computer system unit.

Secondary Storage Technology

Electronic commerce and electronic business, and regulations such as Sarbanes-Oxley, have made storage a strategic technology. The amount of data that companies now need to store is doubling every 12 to 18 months. The principal storage technologies are magnetic disks, optical disc, magnetic tape, and storage networks.

Magnetic Disks The most widely used secondary storage medium today is the **magnetic disk**. PCs have *hard drives*, and large mainframe or midrange computer systems have multiple hard disk drives because they require immense disk storage capacity in the gigabyte and terabyte range. Some older PCs use floppy disks, but they have been largely supplanted by *USB flash drives*, also known as USB drives. A USB flash drive provides portable flash memory storage by plugging into a computer's USB port. It can provide up to 256 gigabytes of portable storage capacity and is small enough to fit into a pocket.

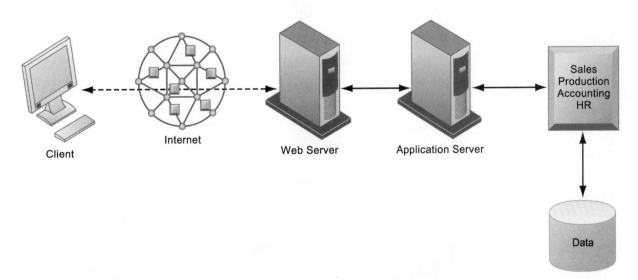

Figure 4-3
A Multitiered Client/Server Network (N-Tier)
In a multitiered client/server network, client requests for service are handled by different levels of servers.

Servers and computers with large storage requirements use a disk technology called *RAID (Redundant Array of Inexpensive Disks).* RAID devices package more than 100 disk drives, a controller chip, and specialized software into a single, large unit delivering data over multiple paths simultaneously.

Optical Discs These discs use laser technology to store large quantities of data, including sound and images, in a highly compact form. They are available for both PCs and large computers. **CD-ROM (compact disk read-only memory)** for PCs is a 4.75-inch compact disc that can store up to 660 megabytes. CD-ROM is read-only storage, but *CD-RW (CD-ReWritable)* discs are rewritable. **Digital video discs (DVDs)** are optical discs the same size as CD-ROMs but of even higher capacity, storing a minimum of 4.7 gigabytes of data. DVDs are now the favored technology for storing video and large quantities of text, graphics, and audio data, and rewritable *(DVD-RW)* discs are widely used in personal computer systems.

Magnetic Tape Some companies still use **magnetic tape,** an older storage technology that is used for secondary storage of large quantities of data that are needed rapidly but not instantly. It stores data sequentially and is relatively slow compared to the speed of other secondary storage media.

Storage Networking Large firms are turning to network-based storage technologies to deal with the complexity and cost of mushrooming storage requirements. **Storage area networks (SANs)** connect multiple storage devices on a separate high-speed network dedicated to storage. The SAN creates a large central pool of storage that can be rapidly accessed and shared by multiple servers (see Figure 4-4).

Input and Output Devices

Human beings interact with computer systems largely through input and output devices. **Input devices** gather data and convert them into electronic form for use by the computer, whereas **output devices** display data after they have been processed. Table 4.1 describes the principal input and output devices.

Figure 4-4
A Storage Area Network (SAN)
A typical SAN consists of a server, storage devices, and networking devices, and is used strictly for storage. The SAN stores data on many different types of storage devices, providing data to the enterprise. The SAN supports communication between any server and the storage unit as well as between different storage devices in the network.

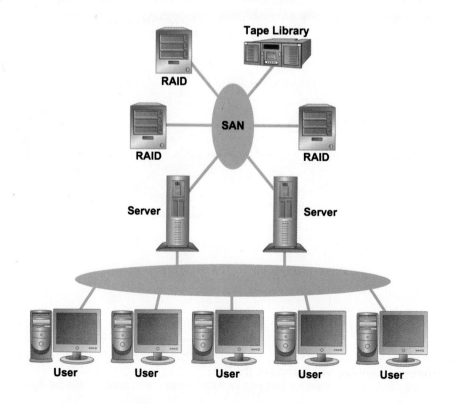

TABLE 4.1

Input and Output Devices

Input Device	Description
Keyboard	Principal method of data entry for text and numerical data.
Computer mouse	Handheld device with point-and-click capabilities that is usually connected to the computer by a cable. The computer user can move the mouse around on a desktop to control the cursor's position on a computer display screen, pushing a button to select a command. Trackballs and touch pads often are used in place of the mouse as pointing devices on laptop PCs.
Touch screen	Device that allows users to interact with a computer by touching the surface of a sensitized display screen. Used in kiosks in airports, retail stores, and restaurants and in multitouch smartphones such as the iPhone.
Optical character recognition	Device that can translate specially designed marks, characters, and codes into digital form. The most widely used optical code is the bar code, which is used in point-of-sale systems in supermarkets and retail stores. The codes can include time, date, and location data in addition to identification data.
Magnetic ink character recognition (MICR)	Technology used primarily in check processing for the banking industry. Characters on the bottom of a check identify the bank, checking account, and check number and are preprinted using special magnetic ink. A MICR reader translates these characters into digital form for the computer.
Pen-based input	Handwriting-recognition devices, such as pen-based tablets, notebooks, and notepads, that convert the motion made by an electronic stylus pressing on a touch-sensitive tablet screen into digital form.
Digital scanner	Device that translates images, such as pictures or documents, into digital form; essential component of image-processing systems.
Audio input	Voice input devices that convert spoken words into digital form for processing by the computer. Microphones and tape cassette players can serve as input devices for music and other sounds.
Sensors	Devices that collect data directly from the environment for input into a computer system. For instance, today's farmers can use sensors to monitor the moisture of the soil in their fields to help them with irrigation.

Output Device	Description
Monitor	Display screen consisting of a flat-panel display or (in older systems) a cathode ray tube (CRT).
Printers	Devices that produce a printed hard copy of information output. They include impact printers (such as dot matrix printers) and nonimpact printers (such as laser, inkjet, and thermal transfer printers).
Audio output	Voice output devices that convert digital output data back into intelligible speech. Other audio output, such as music, can be delivered by speakers connected to the computer.

CONTEMPORARY HARDWARE TRENDS

The exploding power of computer hardware and networking technology has dramatically changed how businesses organize their computing power, putting more of this power on networks. We look at six trends: the emerging mobile digital platform, nanotechnology, cloud computing, autonomic computing, virtualization, and multicore processors.

The Emerging Mobile Digital Platform

Chapter 1 pointed out that new mobile digital computing platforms have emerged as alternatives to PCs and larger computers. Communication devices such as cell phones, and smartphones such as the iPhone and BlackBerry, have taken on many functions of handheld computers, including transmission of data, surfing the Web, transmitting e-mail and instant messages, displaying digital content, and exchanging data with internal corporate systems. The new mobile platform also includes small low-cost lightweight subnotebooks called **netbooks** optimized for wireless communication and Internet access, with core computing functions such as word processing, and digital e-book readers such as Amazon's Kindle with some Web access capabilities.

More and more business computing is moving from PCs and desktop machines to these mobile devices. For example, senior executives at General Motors are using smartphone applications that drill down into vehicle sales information, financial performance, manufacturing metrics, and project management status. At medical device maker AstraTech, sales reps use their smartphones to access Salesforce.com customer relationship management (CRM) applications and sales data, checking data on sold and returned products and overall revenue trends before meeting with customers. Kraft Foods employees use iPhones for e-mail and contacts and for accessing project-related documents, wikis, and blogs on the company's Microsoft SharePoint server.

Nanotechnology

Over the years, microprocessor manufacturers have been able to exponentially increase processing power while shrinking chip size by finding ways to pack more transistors into less space. They are now turning to nanotechnology to shrink the size of transistors down to the width of several atoms. **Nanotechnology** uses individual atoms and molecules to create computer chips and other devices that are thousands of times smaller than current technologies permit. IBM and other research labs have created transistors from nanotubes and other electrical devices and have developed a manufacturing process for producing nanotube processors economically (Figure 4-5).

Portability, ease of use, and low cost have made netbooks increasingly popular computing platforms.

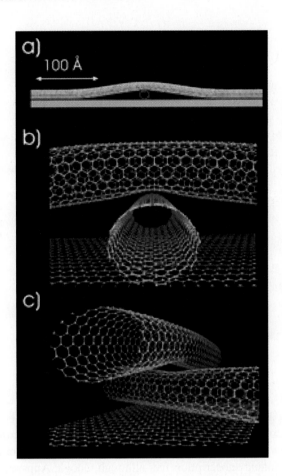

Figure 4-5
Examples of Nanotubes
Nanotubes are tiny tubes about 10,000 times thinner than a human hair. They consist of rolled up sheets of carbon hexagons, have potential uses as minuscule wires or in ultra-small electronic devices, and are very powerful conductors of electrical current.

Cloud Computing

Cloud computing refers to a model of computing in which firms and individuals obtain computing resources and software applications over the Internet (also referred to as "the cloud"). Thousands or even hundreds of thousands computers are located in cloud data centers, where they can be accessed by desktop computers, notebooks, netbooks, entertainment centers, mobile devices, and other client machines linked to the Internet. IBM, HP, Sun Microsystems, Dell, and Amazon operate huge, scalable cloud computing centers that provide both computing power, data storage, and high-speed Internet connections to firms that want to maintain their IT infrastructures remotely. Software firms such as Google, Microsoft, SAP, Oracle, and Salesforce.com sell software applications as services delivered over the Internet. Figure 4-6 illustrates the cloud computing concept.

Cloud computing consists of three different types of services:

- **Cloud infrastructure as a service:** Customers use processing, storage, networking, and other computing resources from cloud service providers to run their information systems. For example, Amazon uses the spare capacity of its IT infrastructure to provide a broadly based cloud environment selling IT infrastructure services. These include its Simple Storage Service (S3) for storing customers' data and its Elastic Compute Cloud (EC2) service for running their applications. Users pay only for the amount of computing and storage capacity they actually use.

- **Cloud platform as a service:** Customers use infrastructure and programming tools hosted by the service provider to develop their own applications. For example, Sun Microsystems offers a Sun Storage Cloud and a Sun Compute Cloud to help software developers, students, and start-ups test and develop new applications over the Internet using Sun's hardware. IBM has a similar Smart Business Application Development & Test service for software development and testing in the cloud.

Figure 4-6
Cloud Computing Platform
In cloud computing, hardware and software capabilities are provided as services over the Internet. Businesses and employees have access to applications and IT infrastructure anywhere at any time using an Internet-connected device.

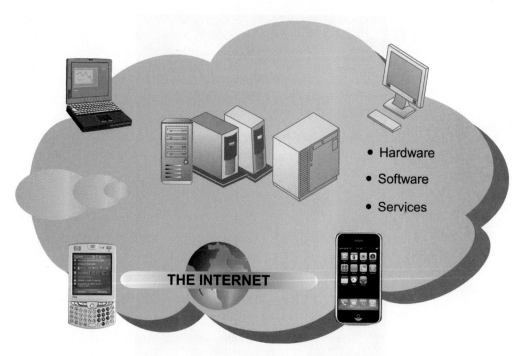

- **Cloud software as a service:** Customers use software hosted by the vendor. Leading examples are Google Apps, which provides common business applications online and Salesforce.com, which leases CRM and related software services over the Internet. Both charge users an annual subscription fee, although Google Apps also has a pared-down free version. Users access these applications from a Web browser, and the data and software are maintained on the providers' remote servers. You can find out more about Salesforce.com and its services in the chapter-ending case study. We will discuss cloud-based software services in greater detail later in this chapter and cloud platform services in Chapter 11.

Since organizations using cloud computing generally do not own the infrastructure, they do not have to make large investments in their own hardware and software. Instead, they purchase their computing services from remote providers and pay only for the amount of computing power they actually use (utility computing) or are billed on a monthly or annual subscription basis. The term **on-demand computing** has also been used to describe such services.

Cloud computing has some drawbacks. Unless users make provisions for storing their data locally, the responsibility of data storage and control is in the hands of the provider. Some companies worry about the security risks related to entrusting their critical data and systems to an outside vendor that also works with other companies. There are also questions of system reliability. Companies expect their systems to be available 24/7 and do not want to suffer any loss of business capability if their IT infrastructures malfunction. When Amazon's cloud went down in July 2008, subscribers were unable to use their systems for eight hours. Another limitation of cloud computing is the possibility of making users dependent on the cloud computing provider.

There are some who believe that cloud computing represents a sea change in the way computing will be performed by corporations as business computing shifts out of private data centers into "the cloud" (Carr, 2008). This remains a matter of debate. Cloud computing is more immediately appealing to small and medium-sized businesses that lack resources to purchase and own their own hardware and software. However, large corporations have huge investments in complex proprietary systems supporting unique business processes, some of which give them strategic advantages. For them, the most likely scenario is a hybrid computing model where firms use their own infrastructure for their most essential core activities and adopt cloud computing for less-critical systems or for additional processing capacity during peak business periods. Cloud computing will gradually shift firms from having a fixed infrastructure capacity toward a more flexible infrastructure, some of it owned by the firm, and some of it rented from giant computer centers owned by computer hardware vendors.

Autonomic Computing

With large systems encompassing many thousands of networked devices, computer systems have become so complex today that some experts believe they may not be manageable in the future. One approach to dealing with this problem from a computer hardware perspective is to employ autonomic computing. **Autonomic computing** is an industry-wide effort to develop systems that can configure themselves, optimize and tune themselves, heal themselves when broken, and protect themselves from outside intruders and self-destruction. Imagine, for instance, a desktop PC that could know it was invaded by a computer virus. Instead of blindly allowing the virus to invade, the PC would identify and eradicate the virus or, alternatively, turn its workload over to another processor and shut itself down before the virus destroyed any files.

You can glimpse some of these capabilities in your desktop system. For instance, virus and firewall protection software can detect viruses on PCs, automatically defeat the viruses, and alert operators. These programs can be updated automatically as the need arises by connecting to an online virus protection service such as McAfee. You can see autonomic computing occur nearly every day on your computer as Microsoft, Apple, and Sun automatically update their users' computers when they are connected to the Internet.

Virtualization and Multicore Processors

As companies deploy hundreds or thousands of servers, many are spending almost as much on electricity to power and cool their systems as they did on purchasing the hardware. The U.S. Environmental Protection Agency estimated that data centers will use more than 2 percent of all U.S. electrical power by 2011. Information technology is believed to contribute about 2 percent of the world's greenhouse gases. Cutting power consumption in data centers has become both a serious business and environmental challenge. The Interactive Session on Organizations examines this problem. As you read this case, try to identify the alternative solutions for this problem and the advantages and disadvantages of each.

This Interactive Session describes organizations curbing hardware proliferation and power consumption by using virtualization to reduce the number of computers required for processing. **Virtualization** presents a set of computing resources (such as computing power or data storage) so that they can all be accessed in ways that are not restricted by physical configuration or geographic location. Server virtualization enables companies to run more than one operating system at the same time on a single machine. Most servers run at just 10 to 15 percent of capacity, and virtualization can boost server utilization rates to 70 percent or higher. Higher utilization rates translate into fewer computers required to process the same amount of work.

For example, the Christus Health network of hospitals and healthcare facilities in the southern and western United States and in Mexico was formerly managing more than 2,000 servers in eight data centers, with 70 percent in the San Antonio data center. In that location, 97 percent of the systems were using 20 percent or less of their processing power, and only 29 percent of available memory. The health care organization used virtualization to consolidate the work of 824 servers onto 83 blade servers, saving $1.8 million, including reductions in electrical power.

Server virtualization software runs between the operating system and the hardware, masking server resources, including the number and identity of physical servers, processors, and operating systems, from server users. VMware is the leading server virtualization software vendor for Windows and Linux systems. Microsoft has built virtualization capabilities into the newest version of Windows Server.

INTERACTIVE SESSION: ORGANIZATIONS   Is Green Computing Good for Business?

Computer rooms are becoming too hot to handle. Data-hungry tasks such as video on demand, music downloads, exchanging photos, and maintaining Web sites require more and more power-hungry machines. Between 2000 and 2007, the total annual cost of electricity for data center servers jumped from $1.3 billion to $2.7 billion in the United States, and from $3.2 billion to $7.2 billion across the world. If this trend persists, the total electricity used by servers in 2010 might be 76 percent higher than 2005, according to a study by Jonathan Kooney, a staff scientist at the Lawrence Berkeley National Laboratory. Gartner Group consultants believe that energy bills, which traditionally accounted for 10 percent of information technology budgets, could soon account for more than 50 percent.

The heat generated from rooms full of servers is causing equipment to fail. Firms are forced to spend even more on cooling their data centers or finding other solutions. Some organizations spend more money to keep their data centers cool than they spend to lease the property itself. It's a vicious cycle, as companies must pay to power their servers, and then pay again to keep them cool and operational. Cooling a server requires roughly the same number of kilowatts of energy as running one. All this additional power consumption has a negative impact on the environment and as well as corporate operating costs.

Some of the world's most prominent firms are tackling their power consumption issues with one eye toward saving the environment and the other toward saving dollars. Google, Microsoft, and HSBC are all building data centers that will take advantage of hydroelectric power. Hewlett-Packard is working on a series of technologies to reduce the carbon footprint of data centers by 75 percent and develop new software and services to measure energy use and carbon emissions. It reduced its power costs by 20 to 25 percent through a consolidation of servers and data centers.

Microsoft's San Antonio data center deploys sensors that measure nearly all power consumption, recycles water used in cooling, and uses internally-developed power management software. Microsoft is also trying to encourage energy-saving software practices by charging business units by the amount of power they consume in the data center rather than the space they take up on the floor.

None of these companies claim that their efforts will save the world, but they do demonstrate recognition of a growing problem and the commencement of the green computing era. And since these companies' technology and processes are more efficient than most

other companies, using their online software services in place of in-house software may also count as a green investment.

PCs typically stay on more than twice the amount of time they are actually being used each day. According to a report by the Alliance to Save Energy, a company with 10,000 desktop PCs will spend more than $165,000 per year in electricity bills if these machines are left on all night. The group estimates that this practice is wasting about $1.7 billion each year in the United States alone.

Although many companies establish default PC power management settings, about 70 percent of employees turn these settings off. PC power management software from BigFix, 1E NightWatchman, and Verdiem locks PC power settings and automatically powers PCs up right before employees arrive for work in the morning.

Miami-Dade County public schools cut the time its PCs were on from 21 hours to 10.3 hours daily by using BigFix to centrally control PC power settings. City University of New York adopted Verdiem's Surveyor software to turn off its 20,000 PCs when they are inactive at night. Surveyor has trimmed 10 percent from CUNY's power bills, creating an annual savings of around $320,000.

Virtualization is a highly effective tool for more cost-effective greener computing because it reduces the number of servers and storage resources in the firm's IT infrastructure. Fulton County, Georgia, which provides services for 988,000 citizens, scrutinizes energy usage when purchasing new information technology. It used VMware virtualization software and a new Fujitsu blade server platform to consolidate underutilized legacy servers so that one machine now performs the work that was formerly performed by eight, saving $44,000 per year in power costs. These efforts also created a more up-to-date IT infrastructure.

Virtualization also encourages the consolidation of people and processes. According to a 2006 International Data Center study, management and administrative expenditures are growing three times faster than expenditures on computing equipment. Virtualization facilitates launching new applications on existing servers, and reduces problems associated with a specific physical server. There are fewer servers to oversee, although they must still be carefully managed and monitored.

Experts note that it's important for companies to measure their energy use and inventory and track their information technology assets both before and after they start their green initiatives. Commonly used metrics used by Microsoft and other companies include power usage effectiveness (PUE), data center infrastructure efficiency (DCIE), and average data center efficiency (ADCE). Health insurer Highmark initially wanted to increase its CPU utilization by 10 percent while reducing power use by 5 percent and eventually by 10 percent. When the company inventoried all of its information technology assets, it found that its information systems staff were hanging onto "dead" servers that served no function but continued to consume power.

Programs to educate employees in energy conservation may also be necessary. In addition to using energy-monitoring tools, Honda Motor Corporation trains its data center administrators how to be more energy efficient. For example, it taught them to decommission unused equipment quickly and to use management tools to ensure servers are being optimized.

Sources: Jim Carlton, "The PC Goes on an Energy Diet," *The Wall Street Journal*, September 8, 2009; Ronan Kavanagh, "IT Virtualization Helps to Go Green," *Information Management Magazine*, March 2009; Ross O. Storey, "Don't Forget the Green IT Imperative," *MIS Asia*, March 23, 2009; J. Nicholas Hoover, "10 Ideas to Power Up Your Green IT Agenda," *Information Week*, September 22, 2008; and Eric Chabrow, "The Wild, Wild Cost of Data Centers," *CIO Insight*, May 2008.

CASE STUDY QUESTIONS

1. What business and social problems does data center power consumption cause?

2. What solutions are available for these problems? Which are environment-friendly?

3. What are the business benefits and costs of these solutions?

4. Should all firms move toward green computing? Why or why not?

MIS IN ACTION

Perform an Internet search on the phrase "green computing" and then answer the following questions:

1. How would you define green computing?

2. Who are some of the leaders of the green computing movement? Which corporations are leading the way? Which environmental organizations are playing an important role?

3. What are the latest trends in green computing? What kind of impact are they having?

4. What can individuals do to contribute to the green computing movement? Is the movement worthwhile?

In addition to reducing hardware and power expenditures, virtualization allows businesses to run their legacy applications on older versions of an operating system on the same server as newer applications. Virtualization also facilitates centralization of hardware administration.

Multicore Processors Another way to reduce power requirements and hardware sprawl is to use multicore processors. A **multicore processor** is an integrated circuit to which two or more processors have been attached for enhanced performance, reduced power consumption, and more efficient simultaneous processing of multiple tasks. This technology enables two processing engines with reduced power requirements and heat dissipation to perform tasks faster than a resource-hungry chip with a single processing core. Today you will find dual-core processors in PCs and quad-core processors in servers. Sun Microsystems's UltraSparc T2 chip for managing Internet workloads has 8 processors, and Intel is working on an 80-processor chip.

4.2 IT Infrastructure: Computer Software

In order to use computer hardware, you will need software, which provides the detailed instructions that direct the computer's work. System software and application software are interrelated and can be thought of as a set of nested boxes, each of which must interact

Figure 4-7
The Major Types of Software
The relationship between the system software, application software, and users can be illustrated by a series of nested boxes. System software—consisting of operating systems, language translators, and utility programs—controls access to the hardware. Application software, including programming languages and "fourth-generation" languages, must work through the system software to operate. The user interacts primarily with the application software.

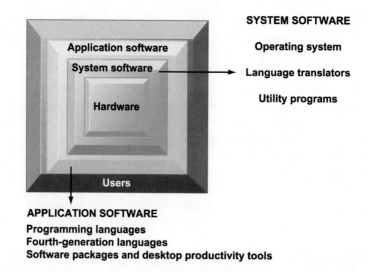

SYSTEM SOFTWARE

Operating system

Language translators

Utility programs

APPLICATION SOFTWARE
Programming languages
Fourth-generation languages
Software packages and desktop productivity tools

closely with the other boxes surrounding it. Figure 4-7 illustrates this relationship. The system software surrounds and controls access to the hardware. Application software must work through the system software in order to operate. End users work primarily with application software. Each type of software must be designed for a specific machine to ensure its compatibility.

OPERATING SYSTEM SOFTWARE

The system software that manages and controls the computer's activities is called the **operating system**. Other system software consists of computer language translation programs that convert programming languages into machine language that can be understood by the computer and utility programs that perform common processing tasks, such as copying, sorting, or computing a square root.

The operating system is the computer system's chief manager, enabling the system to handle many different tasks and users at the same time. The operating system allocates and assigns system resources, schedules the use of computer resources and computer jobs, and monitors computer system activities. The operating system provides locations in primary memory for data and programs, and controls the input and output devices, such as printers, terminals, and telecommunication links. The operating system also coordinates the scheduling of work in various areas of the computer so that different parts of different jobs can be worked on at the same time. Finally, the operating system keeps track of each computer job and may also keep track of who is using the system, of what programs have been run, and of any unauthorized attempts to access the system.

PC, Server, and Mobile Operating Systems

The operating system controls the way users interact with the computer. Contemporary PC operating systems and many types of contemporary application software use a **graphical user interface**, often called a **GUI**, which makes extensive use of icons, buttons, bars, and boxes to perform tasks.

New interface technologies are emerging for both business and home systems. One promising interface technology is **multitouch**, which has been popularized by the iPhone. The Interactive Session on Technology explores multitouch interfaces as alternatives to the GUI. As you read this case, try to identify the problems to be solved by touch interfaces and the people, organization, and technology issues the solution should address.

Table 4.2 compares leading PC and server operating systems. These include the Windows family of operating systems (Windows 7, Windows Vista, Windows Server 2008), UNIX, Linux, and the Macintosh operating system.

TABLE 4.2

Leading PC and Server Operating Systems

Operating System	Features
Windows 7	Most recent Windows operating system for end users, with improved usability, taskbar, performance, and security as well as support for multitouch interfaces.
Windows Vista	Operating system for powerful PCs with versions for home and corporate users. Features desktop searching, multimedia tools, improved security over earlier Windows versions, and synchronization with mobile devices, cameras, and Internet services
Windows Server 2008	Most recent Windows operating system for servers.
UNIX	Used for PCs, workstations, and network servers. Supports multitasking, multiuser processing, and networking. Is portable to different models of computer hardware.
Linux	Open source, reliable alternative to UNIX and Windows operating systems that runs on many different types of computer hardware and can be modified by software developers.
Mac OS X	Operating system for the Macintosh computer that is stable and reliable, with powerful search capabilities, support for video and image processing, and an elegant user interface. Most recent version is Snow Leopard. The iPhone OS operating system is derived from OS X.

The Microsoft Windows family of operating systems has both client and server versions and a streamlined GUI. Windows systems can perform multiple programming tasks simultaneously and have powerful networking capabilities, including the ability to access information from the Internet. **Windows 7** is the latest Windows version. Its improvements over **Windows Vista** and the earlier Windows XP include enhanced usability, faster performance, a new taskbar, support for multitouch interfaces, and additional security enhancements. There are versions for home, small business, and enterprise users. Windows 7 has added a Starter version for small notebook PCs and netbooks that lack the processing capacity and memory for more full-featured versions.

Windows operating systems for network servers provide network management functions, including tools for creating and operating Web sites and other Internet services. Windows Server 2008 has multiple versions for small, medium, and large businesses, including those with massive computer centers and processing requirements.

UNIX is a multiuser, multitasking operating system developed by Bell Laboratories in 1969 to connect various machines together and is highly supportive of communications and networking. UNIX is often used on workstations and servers, and provides the reliability and scalability for running large systems on high-end servers. UNIX can run on many different kinds of computers and can be easily customized. Application programs that run under UNIX can be ported from one computer to run on a different computer with little modification. Graphical user interfaces have been developed for UNIX. Vendors have developed different versions of UNIX that are incompatible, thereby limiting software portability.

INTERACTIVE SESSION: TECHNOLOGY   New to the Touch

When Steve Jobs first demonstrated "the pinch"—the two-finger gesture for zooming in and out of photos and Web pages on the iPhone, he not only shook up the mobile phone industry—the entire digital world took notice. The Apple iPhone's multitouch features dramatized new ways of using touch to interact with software and devices.

Touch interfaces are not new. People use them every day to get money from ATMs or to check into flights at airport kiosks. Academic and commercial researchers have been working on multitouch technology for years. What Apple did was to make multitouch more exciting and relevant, popularizing it just as it did in the 1980s with the mouse and the graphical user interface. (These had also been invented elsewhere.)

Multitouch interfaces are potentially more versatile than single-touch interfaces. They allow you to use one or more fingers to perform special gestures that manipulate lists or objects on a screen without moving a mouse, pressing buttons, turning scroll wheels, or striking keys. They take different actions depending on how many fingers they detect and which gestures a user performs.

The iPhone's multitouch display and software lets you control everything using only your fingers. A panel underneath the display's glass cover senses your touch using electrical fields. It then transmits that information to a LCD screen below it. Special software recognizes multiple simultaneous touch points, (as opposed to the single-touch screen, which recognizes only one touch point.) You can quickly move back and forth through a series of Web pages or photos by "swiping," or placing three fingers on the screen and moving them rapidly sideways. By pinching the image, you can shrink or expand a photo.

Other companies are bringing products with multitouch to the market. Synaptics, a leading supplier of touchpads for laptop makers who compete with Apple, has announced that it is incorporating several multitouch features into its touchpads. Microsoft recently unveiled its Surface computer that runs Windows 7 and lets its business customers use multitouch in a table-top display. Customers of hotels, casinos, and retail stores, will be able to use multitouch finger gestures to move around digital objects such as photos, to play games, and to browse through product options. Surface technology is likely to be integrated into consumer PCs. The Dell Latitude XT tablet PC uses multitouch, which is helpful to people who can't grasp a mouse and want the functionality of a traditional PC. They can use a finger or a stylus instead.

The BlackBerry Storm multitouch screen uses something called "haptic touch," so when you press a button on the screen or on the virtual keyboard it feels as if you're actually pressing on that specific spot. It's tactile, which provides more peace of mind if you're hearing-impaired. If you're visually impaired, this makes typing and clicking a lot easier.

Hewlett-Packard (HP) now has laptops and desktops that use touch technology. Its TouchSmart computer lets you use two fingers at once to manipulate images on the screen or to make on-screen gestures designating specific commands without using cursors or scroll bars. When you can put your finger directly on the screen, you don't need a cursor to show where you are pointing. To move an object, you touch it with a finger and drag it to its new location. Sliding your finger up and down or sideways smoothly scrolls the display.

The TouchSmart makes it possible for home users to engage in a new type of casual computing—leaving written, video, or audio memos for family members, quickly searching for directions before leaving the house, putting on music while preparing dinner. Both consumers and businesses have found other uses as well. According to Alan Reed, HP's vice president and general manager for Business Desktops, "There is untapped potential for touch technology in the business marketplace to engage users in a way that has never been done before."

Chicago's O'Hare Airport integrated a group of TouchSmart PCs into "Explore Chicago" tourist kiosks, allowing visitors to check out a virtual Visitor's Center. TouchSmart computing helped an autistic student to speak to and communicate with others for the first time in the 14 years of his life. Without using the TouchSmart PC's wireless keyboard and mouse, users can hold video chats with remote workers through a built-in Webcam and microphone, access e-mail and the Internet, and manage contacts, calendar items, and photos.

Touch-enabled PCS could also appeal to elementary schools seeking an easy-to-use computer for students in early grades, or a wall-mountable information kiosk-type device for parents and visitors. Touch systems might allow customers to connect, select, and interact with vendors and each other. Customers might use touch to place orders with a retailer, conduct virtual video service calls, or to teach or utilize social networking for business.

Microsoft's new Windows 7 operating system sports multitouch features: When you pair Windows 7 with a touch-screen PC, you can browse online newspapers, flick through photo albums, and shuffle files and folders using nothing but your fingers. To zoom in on something you would place two fingers on the screen of a multitouch-compatible PC and spread them apart. To right-click a file, touch it with one finger and tap the screen with a second.

It's too early to know if the new multitouch interface will ever be as big as the mouse-driven graphical user interface. Although putting your fingers on the screen is the ultimate measure of "cool" in the cell phone market, a "killer application" for touch on the PC has not yet emerged. But

it's already evident that touch has real advantages on devices where a mouse isn't possible or convenient to use, or the decades-old interface of menus and folders is too cumbersome.

Sources: Kathy Sandler, "The Future of Touch," *The Wall Street Journal*, June 2, 2009; Ashlee Vance, "PC Touch Screens Move Ahead," *The New York Times*, June 3, 2009; Suzanne Robitaille, "Multitouch to the Rescue?" Suite101.com, January 22, 2009; Kevin Lau, "HP TouchSmart: More Than Just a PC," GetConnected.com, July 31, 2009; Eric Lai, "HP Aims TouchSmart Desktop PC at Businesses," *Computerworld*, August 1, 2009; Ina Fried, "Touch in Windows 7: Just for Show?" CNET News, July 1, 2009; and Walter Mossberg, "Multitouch Interface Is Starting to Spread Among New Devices," *The Wall Street Journal*, January 31, 2008.

CASE STUDY QUESTIONS

1. What problems does multitouch technology solve?

2. What are the advantages and disadvantages of multitouch interfaces? How useful are they? Explain.

3. Describe three business applications that would benefit from a multitouch interface.

4. What people, organization, and technology issues must be addressed if you or your business was considering systems and computers with multi-touch interfaces?

MIS IN ACTION

1. Describe what you would do differently on your PC if it had multitouch capabilities. How much difference would multitouch make in the way you use your computer?

2. Do a search on "touch computers." and identify additional applications of touch computer screens beyond smartphones. Make a list of these applications and describe the kinds of situations where touch computers are used.

Linux is a UNIX-like operating system that can be downloaded from the Internet free of charge or purchased for a small fee from companies that provide additional tools for the software. It is free, reliable, compactly designed, and capable of running on many different hardware platforms, including servers, handheld computers, and consumer electronics.

Linux has become popular as a robust low-cost alternative to UNIX and the Windows operating systems. For example, E*Trade Financial saves $13 million annually with improved computer performance by running Linux on a series of small inexpensive IBM servers instead of large expensive Sun Microsystems servers running Sun's proprietary version of UNIX.

Linux plays a major role in the back office, running Web servers and local-area networks in about 25 percent of the U.S. server market. Its use in desktop computers is growing steadily. IBM, HP, Intel, Dell, and Sun have made Linux a central part of their offerings to corporations, and major software vendors are starting to provide versions of their products that can run on Linux. Both IBM and Sun offer Linux-based office tools for free or a minimal fee.

Linux is an example of **open source software**, which provides all computer users with free access to its program code, so they can modify the code to fix errors or to make improvements. Open source software is not owned by any company or individual. A global network of programmers and users manages and modifies the software, usually without being paid to do so. Open source software is by definition not restricted to any specific operating system or hardware technology, although most open source software is currently based on a Linux or UNIX.

In addition to these operating systems, new systems for mobile digital devices and cloud-connected computers are emerging. Google's *Chrome OS* serves as a lightweight computer operating system for users who do most of their computing on the Internet and runs on computers ranging from netbooks to desktop computers. It has a minimalist design to take advantage of the Web and cloud computing. *Android* is a mobile operating system initially developed by Google and later the Open Handset Alliance as a flexible, upgradeable mobile device platform. It may eventually be used in small computers. Microsoft has introduced a cloud operating system called *Windows Azure* for its cloud services and platform.

APPLICATION SOFTWARE AND DESKTOP PRODUCTIVITY TOOLS

Today, businesses have access to an array of tools for developing their application software. These include traditional programming languages, fourth-generation languages, application software packages, and desktop productivity tools; software for developing Internet applications; and software for enterprise integration. It is important to know which software tools and programming languages are appropriate for the work your business wants to accomplish.

Application Programming Languages for Business

For business applications, the most important programming languages have been C, C++, Visual Basic, and COBOL. **C** is a powerful and efficient language developed in the early 1970s that combines machine portability with tight control and efficient use of computer resources. C is used primarily by professional programmers to create operating systems and application software, especially for PCs. **C++** is a newer version of C that has all the capabilities of C plus additional features for working with software objects. Unlike traditional programs, which separate data from the actions to be taken on the data, a software **object** combines data and procedures. Chapter 11 describes object-oriented software development in detail. **Visual Basic** is a widely used visual programming tool and environment for creating applications that run on Microsoft Windows operating systems. A **visual programming language** allows users to manipulate graphic or iconic elements to create programs. COBOL (COmmon Business Oriented Language) was developed in the early 1960s for processing large data files with alphanumeric characters (mixed alphabetic and numeric data) and for business reporting. You'll find it today primarily in large legacy business systems.

Fourth-Generation Languages

Fourth-generation languages consist of a variety of software tools that enable end users to develop software applications with minimal or no technical assistance or that enhance professional programmers' productivity. Fourth-generation languages tend to be nonprocedural, or less procedural, than conventional programming languages. Procedural languages require specification of the sequence of steps, or procedures, that tell the computer what to do and how to do it. Nonprocedural languages need only specify what has to be accomplished rather than provide details about how to carry out the task. Some of these nonprocedural languages are *natural languages* that enable users to communicate with the computer using conversational commands resembling human speech.

Table 4.3 shows that there are six categories of fourth-generation languages: PC software tools, query languages, report generators, graphics languages, application generators, and application software packages. The table lists the tools in order of ease of use by nonprogramming end users. End users are most likely to work with PC software tools and query languages. **Query languages** are software tools that provide immediate online answers to requests for information that are not predefined, such as "Who are the highest-performing sales representatives?" Query languages are often tied to data management software (described later in this section) and to database management systems (see Chapter 5).

Table 4.3

Categories of Fourth-Generation Languages

Fourth-Generation Tool	Description	Example	
PC software tools	General-purpose application software packages for PCs.	WordPerfect Microsoft Access	**Oriented toward end users**
Query language	Languages for retrieving data stored in databases or files. Capable of supporting requests for information that are not predefined.	SQL	
Report generator	Extract data from files or databases to create customized reports in a wide range of formats not routinely produced by an information system. Generally provide more control over the way data are formatted, organized, and displayed than query languages.	Crystal Reports	
Graphics language	Retrieve data from files or databases and display them in graphic format. Some graphics software can perform arithmetic or logical operations on data as well.	SAS/Graph Systat	
Application generator	Contain preprogrammed modules that can generate entire applications, including Web sites, greatly speeding development. A user can specify what needs to be done, and the application generator will create the appropriate program code for input, validation, update, processing, and reporting.	WebFOCUS QuickBase	
Application software package	Software programs sold or leased by commercial vendors that eliminate the need for custom-written, in-house software.	Oracle PeopleSoft HCM mySAP ERP	**Oriented toward IS professionals**

Software Packages and Desktop Productivity Tools

Much of the software used in businesses today is not custom programmed but consists of application software packages and desktop productivity tools. A **software package** is a prewritten, precoded, commercially available set of programs that eliminates the need for individuals or organizations to write their own software programs for certain functions. There are software packages for system software, but most package software is application software.

Software packages that run on mainframes and larger computers usually require professional programmers for their installation and support. Desktop productivity software packages for word processing, spreadsheets, data management, presentation graphics, and Web browsers are the most widely used software tools among business and consumer users.

Word Processing Software If you work in an office or attend school, you probably use word processing software every day. **Word processing software** stores text data electronically as a computer file rather than on paper. The word processing software allows the user to make changes in the document electronically, with formatting options to make changes in line spacing, margins, character size, and column width. Microsoft Word and WordPerfect are popular word processing packages.

Most word processing software has advanced features that automate other writing tasks: spelling checkers, style checkers (to analyze grammar and punctuation), thesaurus programs, mail merge programs (which link letters or other text documents with names and addresses in a mailing list), and capabilities for creating and accessing Web pages.

Businesses that need to create highly professional looking brochures, manuals, or books will likely use desktop publishing software for this purpose. Desktop publishing software provides more control over the placement of text, graphics, and photos in the layout of a page than does word processing software. Adobe InDesign and QuarkXpress are two professional publishing packages.

Spreadsheet Software Spreadsheets are valuable for applications in which numerous calculations with pieces of data must be related to each other. **Spreadsheet software** organizes data into a grid of columns and rows. When you change a value or values, all other related values on the spreadsheet will be automatically recomputed.

You will often see spreadsheets in applications that require modeling and "what-if" analysis. After the user has constructed a set of mathematical relationships, the spreadsheet can be recalculated instantaneously using a different set of assumptions. Spreadsheet packages include graphics functions to present data in the form of line graphs, bar graphs, or pie charts, and the ability to read and create Web files. The most popular spreadsheet package is Microsoft Excel. Figure 4-8 illustrates the output from a spreadsheet for a break-even analysis and its accompanying graph.

Data Management Software Although spreadsheet programs are powerful tools for manipulating quantitative data, data management software, which we defined earlier in this chapter, is more suitable for creating and manipulating lists and for combining information from different files. PC database management packages have programming features and easy-to-learn menus that enable nonspecialists to build small information systems.

Data management software typically has facilities for creating files and databases and for storing, modifying, and manipulating data for reports and queries. Popular database manage-

**Figure 4-8
Spreadsheet Software**

Spreadsheet software organizes data into columns and rows for analysis and manipulation. Contemporary spreadsheet software provides graphing abilities for a clear, visual representation of the data in the spreadsheets. This sample break-even analysis is represented as numbers in a spreadsheet as well as a line graph for easy interpretation.

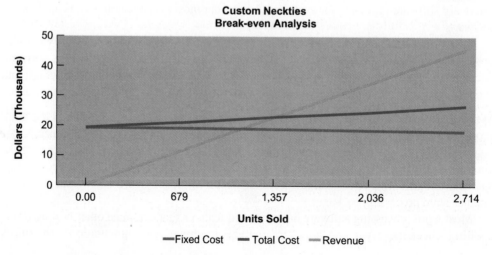

ment software for the personal computer includes Microsoft Access, which has been enhanced to publish data on the Web. We discuss data management software in greater detail in Chapter 5.

Presentation Graphics Users can create professional-quality graphics presentations with **presentation graphics software**. This software can convert numeric data into charts and other types of graphics and can include multimedia displays of sound, animation, photos, and video clips. The leading presentation graphics packages include capabilities for computer-generated slide shows and translating content for the Web. Microsoft PowerPoint and Lotus Freelance Graphics are popular presentation graphics packages.

Software Suites Typically, the major office productivity tools are bundled together as a software suite. Microsoft Office is an example. There are a number of different versions of Office for home and business users, but the core office tools include Word word processing software, Excel spreadsheet software, Access database software, PowerPoint presentation graphics software, and Outlook, a set of tools for e-mail, scheduling, and contact management. Microsoft **Office 2010** is the latest version of this suite. Microsoft has added a Web-based option called Office Web Apps available to businesses and consumers on both a free and subscription basis. Office Web Apps delivers lightweight online versions of Office tools such as Word, Excel, PowerPoint, and One Note via standard Web browsers to PCs, mobile phones, and other Web-enabled devices. Microsoft stores users' data for these online applications and allows some sharing of documents and files.

Competing with Microsoft Office are low-cost office productivity suites such as Sun Microsystems' OpenOffice (which can be downloaded for free over the Internet) and its StarOffice (downloadable for $34.95). However, the real challenge to Microsoft is coming from the cloud. Web-based versions of desktop productivity software are becoming popular because of their convenience, flexibility, and low cost. There are over two million businesses of all sizes using Google Apps, which we introduced in our discussion of collaboration tools in Chapter 2. This online suite includes tools for word processing, spreadsheets, presentations, contact management, messaging, and e-mail) and is available for free or as a more full-featured Premier edition charging businesses $50.

Web Browsers Web browsers Easy-to-use software tools called **web browsers** are used for displaying Web pages and for accessing the Web and other Internet resources. Browsers can display or present graphics, audio, and video information, as well as traditional text, and they allow you to click (or touch) on-screen buttons or highlighted words to link to related Web sites. Web browsers have become the primary interface for accessing the Internet or for using networked systems based on Internet technology. The leading Web browsers today are Microsoft Internet Explorer, Mozilla Firefox, Apple Safari, and Google Chrome. Mobile handhelds have their own specialized Web browsers.

SOFTWARE FOR THE WEB: JAVA, AJAX, AND HTML

There are a number of software tools that that businesses use to build Web sites and applications that run on the Web. Java and Ajax are used for building applications that run on the Web, and HTML is used for creating Web pages.

Java

Java is an operating system-independent, processor-independent, object-oriented programming language that has become a leading interactive programming environment for the Web. Java enables users to work with data on networked systems using Web browsers, reducing the need to write specialized software. At the enterprise level, Java is used for more complex e-commerce and e-business applications that require communication with an organization's back-end transaction processing systems.

Nearly all Web browser software has a Java platform built in. The Java platform has migrated into cell phones, automobiles, music players, game machines, and, finally, into set-top cable television systems serving interactive content.

Java software is designed to run on any computer or computing device, regardless of the specific microprocessor or operating system the device uses. Java achieves this neat trick by using a Java virtual machine built for each type of computer and operating system. The virtual machine enables it to run Java applications. A Macintosh PC, an IBM PC running Windows, a Sun server running UNIX, and even a smart cell phone or PDA can share the same Java application, reducing the costs of software development and creating the same user experience regardless of what kind of computer the user is working with.

In network environments, such as the Internet, Java is used to create miniature programs called *applets* that are designed to reside on centralized network servers. The network delivers to client computers only the applets required for a specific function. With Java applets residing on a network, a user can download only the software functions and data that he or she needs to perform a particular task, such as analyzing the revenue from one sales territory. The user does not need to maintain large software programs or data files on his or her desktop machine.

Ajax

Have you ever filled out a Web order form, made a mistake, and then had to start all over again after a long wait for a new order form page to appear on your computer screen? Or visited a map site, clicked the North arrow once, and waited some time for an entire new page to load? **Ajax** (Asynchronous JavaScript and XML) is another Web development technique for creating interactive Web applications that prevents all of this inconvenience.

Ajax allows a client and server to exchange small pieces of data behind the scene so that an entire Web page does not have to be reloaded each time the user requests a change. So if you click North on a map site, such as Google Maps, the server downloads just that part of the application that changes with no wait for an entirely new map. You can also grab maps in map applications and move the map in any direction without forcing a reload of the entire page. Ajax uses JavaScript programs downloaded to your client to maintain a near-continuous conversation with the server you are using, making the user experience more seamless.

Hypertext Markup Language (HTML)

Hypertext Markup Language (HTML) is a page description language for specifying how text, graphics, video, and sound are placed on a Web page and for creating dynamic links to other Web pages and objects. Using these links, a user need only point at a highlighted keyword or graphic, click on it, and immediately be transported to another document. Table 4.4 illustrates some sample HTML statements.

HTML programs can be custom written, but they also can be created using the HTML authoring capabilities of Web browsers or of popular word processing, spreadsheet, data management, and presentation graphics software packages. HTML editors, such as Adobe Dreamweaver, are more powerful HTML authoring tool programs for creating Web pages.

WEB SERVICES

Web services refer to a set of loosely coupled software components that exchange information with each other using universal Web communication standards and languages. They can exchange information between two different systems regardless of the operating systems or

TABLE 4.4	**Plain English**	**HTML**
Examples of HTML	Subcompact	<TITLE>Automobile</TITLE>
	4 passenger	<LI>4 passenger</LI>
	$16,800	<LI>$16,800</LI>

programming languages on which the systems are based. They can be used to build open-standard, Web-based applications linking systems of two different organizations, and they can be used to create applications that link disparate systems within a single company. Web services are not tied to any one operating system or programming language, and different applications can use them to communicate with each other in a standard way without time-consuming custom coding.

The foundation technology for Web services is **XML**, which stands for **Extensible Markup Language**. This language was developed in 1996 by the World Wide Web Consortium (W3C, the international body that oversees the development of the Web) as a more powerful and flexible markup language than HTML for Web pages. Whereas HTML is limited to describing how data should be presented in the form of Web pages, XML can perform presentation, communication, and storage of data. In XML, a number is not simply a number; the XML tag specifies whether the number represents a price, a date, or a zip code. Table 4.5 illustrates some sample XML statements.

By tagging selected elements of the content of documents for their meanings, XML makes it possible for computers to manipulate and interpret their data automatically and perform operations on the data without human intervention. Web browsers and computer programs, such as order processing or enterprise resource planning (ERP) software, can follow programmed rules for applying and displaying the data. XML provides a standard format for data exchange, enabling Web services to pass data from one process to another.

Web services communicate through XML messages over standard Web protocols. *SOAP*, which stands for *Simple Object Access Protocol*, is a set of rules for structuring messages that enables applications to pass data and instructions to one another. *WSDL* stands for *Web Services Description Language*; it is a common framework for describing the tasks performed by a Web service and the commands and data it will accept so that it can be used by other applications. *UDDI*, which stands for *Universal Description, Discovery, and Integration*, enables a Web service to be listed in a directory of Web services so that it can be easily located. Companies discover and locate Web services through this directory much as they would locate services in the Yellow Pages of a telephone book. Using these protocols, a software application can connect freely to other applications without custom programming for each different application with which it wants to communicate. Everyone shares the same standards.

The collection of Web services that are used to build a firm's software systems constitutes what is known as a service-oriented architecture. A **service-oriented architecture (SOA)** is set of self-contained services that communicate with each other to create a working software application. Business tasks are accomplished by executing a series of these services. Software developers reuse these services in other combinations to assemble other applications as needed.

Virtually all major software vendors, such as IBM, Microsoft, Sun, and HP, provide tools and entire platforms for building and integrating software applications using Web services. IBM includes Web service tools in its WebSphere e-business software platform, and Microsoft has incorporated Web services tools in its Microsoft .NET platform.

Dollar Rent-A-Car's systems use Web services to link its online booking system with the Southwest Airlines Web site. Although both companies' systems are based on different technology platforms, a person booking a flight on Southwest.com can reserve a car from

Plain English	XML
Subcompact	<AUTOMOBILETYPE="Subcompact">
4 passenger	<PASSENGERUNIT="PASS">4</PASSENGER>
$16,800	<PRICE CURRENCY="USD">$16,800</PRICE>

TABLE 4.5

Examples of XML

Dollar without leaving the airline's Web site. Instead of struggling to get Dollar's reservation system to share data with Southwest's information systems, Dollar used Microsoft .NET Web services technology as an intermediary. Reservations from Southwest are translated into Web services protocols, which are then translated into formats that can be understood by Dollar's computers.

Other car rental companies have linked their information systems to airline companies' Web sites before. But without Web services, these connections had to be built one at a time. Web services provide a standard way for Dollar's computers to "talk" to other companies' information systems without having to build special links to each one. Dollar is now expanding its use of Web services to link directly to the systems of a small tour operator and a large travel reservation system as well as a wireless Web site for mobile phones and PDAs. It does not have to write new software code for each new partner's information systems or each new wireless device (see Figure 4-9).

SOFTWARE TRENDS

Today there are many more sources for obtaining software and many more capabilities for users to create their own customized software applications. Expanding use of open source software and cloud-based software tools and services exemplify this trend.

Open Source Software

Arguably the most influential software trend is the movement towards open source software. As noted earlier, open source software is developed by a community of programmers around the world, who make their programs available to users under one of several different licensing schemes. Essentially, users of the software can use the software as is, modify it at will, and even include it in for-profit software applications.

The open source movement started out small in 1983 (when it was called "hippie software"), but it has since grown to be a major part of corporate computing infrastructure, as the foundation for programs such as Linux, and Apache, the most widely used Web server

Figure 4-9
How Dollar Rent-A-Car Uses Web Services

Dollar Rent-A-Car uses Web services to provide a standard intermediate layer of software to "talk" to other companies' information systems. Dollar Rent-A-Car can use this set of Web services to link to other companies' information systems without having to build a separate link to each firm's systems.

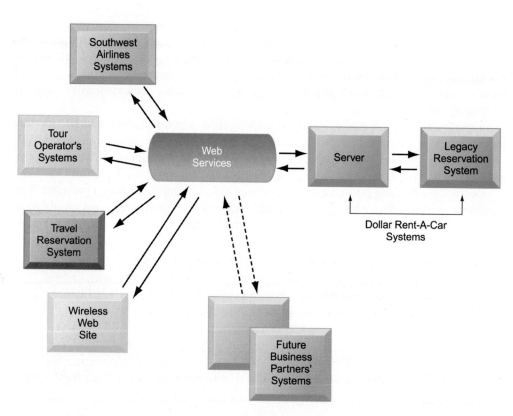

software. Today you can find thousands of open source computer programs to accomplish everything from e-commerce shopping carts and funds clearance to sales force management. Some of the cloud computing applications described in this chapter, such as as Google's Chrome Web browser, are based on open source code.

Cloud-Based Software Tools and Services

In the past, software such as Microsoft Word or Adobe Illustrator came in a box and was designed to operate on a single machine. Today, you're more likely to download the software from the vendor's Web site to your computer or, increasingly, to use the software as a cloud service delivered over the Internet.

Cloud-based software and the data they use are hosted on powerful servers in massive data centers, and can be accessed by anyone with an Internet connection and standard Web browser. Google's numerous Web-based applications, which we described earlier in this chapter and in Chapter 2, are a leading example. Besides Office Web Apps, Microsoft offers other cloud software services, such as its Business Productivity Online Standard Suite for messaging and collaboration.

Mashups and Widgets The software you use for both personal and business tasks may consist of large, self-contained programs, or it may be composed of interchangeable components that integrate freely with other applications on the Internet. Individual users and entire companies mix and match these software components to create their own customized applications and to share information with others. The resulting software applications are called **mashups**. You have performed a mashup if you've ever personalized your Facebook profile or your blog with a capability to display videos or slide shows.

The idea is to take different sources and produce a new work that is "greater than" the sum of its parts. Part of the movement called Web 2.0 (see Chapter 6), and in the spirit of musical mashups, Web mashups combine the capabilities of two or more online applications to create a hybrid that provides more customer value than the original sources alone. For instance, Faceforce integrates Facebook profile information with Salesforce data in real time, providing an instant 360-degree view of customers, prospects, and business associates and a single place to view and manage all contacts.

One area of great innovation is the mashup of mapping software with local content. Google, Yahoo!, and Microsoft now offer tools to allow other applications to pull in information from their map and satellite images with relatively little programming. For example, ZipRealty uses Google Maps and data provided by online real estate community Zillow.com to display a complete list of multiple listing service (MLS) real estate listings for any zip code specified by the user. BidNearBy uses Google Maps and data from eBay's Craigslist to search local auctions and classified listings and display their location on a map view.

The small pieces of software code that enable users to embed content from one site into a Web page or another Web site are called widgets. **Widgets** are small software programs that can be added to Web pages or placed on the desktop (or mobile digital device) to provide additional functionality. For example, the Flixster widget on Facebook profiles transports users to a place where they can list the films they've seen along with their ratings and reviews, view their friends' ratings and reviews, and what's playing in theaters. The iPhone Atom widget delivers news feeds from Google to the iPhone, and there are widgets for displaying Twitter updates on your blog.

Web widgets run inside a Web page or blog. Desktop widgets integrate content from an external source into the user's desktop to provide services such as a calculator, dictionary, or display of current weather conditions. The Yahoo! Weather widget, Apple's Dashboard TV, and Google Desktop Gadgets are examples of desktop widgets.

Widgets can also provide storefront windows for advertising and selling products and services. Amazon and Wal-Mart have toolbar widgets that enable users to search their Web stores while staying on a different Web page. Widgets have become so powerful and useful that Facebook and Google launched programs to attract developers of widgets for their Web sites.

Software As a Service (SaaS) In addition to free or low-cost tools for individuals and businesses provided by Google, Microsoft, or Yahoo!, enterprise software and other complex business functions are available as services from the major commercial software vendors. Instead of buying and installing software programs, subscribing companies rent the same functions from these services, with users paying either on a subscription or per-transaction basis. Services for delivering and providing access to software remotely as a Web-based service are now referred to as **software as a service (SaaS)**.

A leading example is Salesforce.com, which provides on-demand software services for customer relationship management, including sales force automation, partner relationship management, marketing, and customer service. It includes tools for customization, integrating its software with other corporate applications, and creating new applications. You will find out more about Salesforce.com in our chapter-ending case study.

4.3 Managing Hardware and Software Technology

Selection and use of computer hardware and software technology has a profound impact on business performance. We now describe the most important issues you will face when managing hardware and software technology: capacity planning and scalability; determining the total cost of technology assets; determining whether to own and maintain your own hardware, software, and other infrastructure components or lease them from an external technology service provider; and managing mobile platforms and software localization.

CAPACITY PLANNING AND SCALABILITY

E-commerce and e-business are placing heavy new demands on hardware technology. Much larger processing and storage resources are required to process and store the surging digital transactions flowing between different parts of the firm, and between the firm and its customers and suppliers. Many people using a Web site simultaneously place great strains on a computer system, as does hosting large numbers of interactive Web pages with data-intensive graphics or video.

Managers and information systems specialists now need to pay more attention to hardware capacity planning and scalability than before. From an IT perspective, **capacity planning** is the process of predicting when a computer hardware system becomes saturated. It considers factors such as the maximum number of users that the system can accommodate at one time, the impact of existing and future software applications, and performance measures, such as minimum response time for processing business transactions. Capacity planning ensures that the firm has enough computing power for its current and future needs. For example, the Nasdaq Stock Market performs ongoing capacity planning to identify peaks in the volume of stock trading transactions and to ensure it has enough computing capacity to handle large surges in volume when trading is very heavy.

Although information systems specialists perform capacity planning, input from business managers is essential. Business managers need to determine acceptable levels of computer response time and availability for the firm's mission-critical systems to maintain the level of business performance they expect. New applications, mergers and acquisitions, and changes in business volume all impact computer workload and must be considered when planning hardware capacity.

Scalability refers the ability of a computer, product, or system to expand to serve a large number of users without breaking down. Electronic commerce and electronic business both call for scalable IT infrastructures that have the capacity to grow with the business as the size of a Web site and number of visitors increase. Organizations must make sure they have sufficient computer processing, storage, and network resources to handle surging volumes of digital transactions and to make such data immediately available online.

TOTAL COST OF OWNERSHIP (TCO) OF TECHNOLOGY ASSETS

When you calculate how much your hardware and software cost, their purchase price is only the beginning. You must also consider ongoing administration costs for hardware and software upgrades, maintenance, technical support, training, and even utility and real estate costs for running and housing the technology. The **total cost of ownership (TCO)** model can be used to analyze these direct and indirect costs to help determine the actual cost of owning a specific technology. Table 4.6 describes the most important TCO components to consider in a TCO analysis.

When all these cost components are considered, the TCO for a PC might run up to three times the original purchase price of the equipment. "Hidden costs" for support staff, downtime, and additional network management can make distributed client/server architectures—especially those incorporating handheld computers and wireless devices—more expensive than centralized mainframe architectures.

Many large firms are saddled with redundant, incompatible hardware and software because of poor planning. These firms could reduce their TCO through greater centralization and standardization of their hardware and software resources. Companies could reduce the size of the information systems staff required to support their infrastructure if the firm minimized the number of different computer models and pieces of software that employees are allowed to use.

USING TECHNOLOGY SERVICE PROVIDERS

Some of the most important questions facing managers are "How should we acquire and maintain our technology assets? Should we build software applications ourselves or outsource them to an external contractor? Should we purchase and run them ourselves or rent them from external service providers?" In the past, most companies ran their own computer facilities and developed their own software. Today, more and more companies are obtaining their hardware and software technology from external service vendors.

Outsourcing

A number of firms are **outsourcing** the maintenance of their IT infrastructures and the development of new systems to external vendors. They may contract with an external service provider to run their computer center and networks, to develop new software, or to manage all of the components of their IT infrastructures, as did Procter & Gamble (P&G). P&G agreed to pay HP $3 billion to manage its IT infrastructure, computer center opera-

		TABLE 4.6
Hardware acquisition	Purchase price of computer hardware equipment, including computers, terminals, storage, and printers	**Total Cost of Ownership (TCO) Cost Components**
Software acquisition	Purchase or license of software for each user	
Installation	Cost to install computers and software	
Training	Cost to provide training to information systems specialists and end users	
Support	Cost to provide ongoing technical support, help desks, and so forth	
Maintenance	Cost to upgrade the hardware and software	
Infrastructure	Cost to acquire, maintain, and support related infrastructure, such as networks and specialized equipment (including storage backup units)	
Downtime	Lost productivity if hardware or software failures cause the system to be unavailable for processing and user tasks	
Space and energy	Real estate and utility costs for housing and providing power for the technology	

tions, desktop and end-user support, network management, and applications development and maintenance for global operations in 160 countries.

Specialized Web hosting services are available for companies that lack the financial or technical resources to operate their own Web sites. A **Web hosting service** maintains a large Web server, or a series of servers, and provides fee-paying subscribers with space to maintain their Web sites. The subscribing companies may create their own Web pages or have the hosting service, or a Web design firm, create them. Some services offer *co-location*, in which the firm actually purchases and owns the server computer housing its Web site but locates the server in the physical facility of the hosting service.

Firms often retain control over their hardware resources but outsource custom software development or maintenance to outside firms, frequently firms that operate offshore in low-wage areas of the world. When firms outsource software work outside their national borders, the practice is called **offshore software outsourcing**. Until recently, this type of software development involved lower-level maintenance, data entry, and call center operations, but with the growing sophistication and experience of offshore firms, particularly in India, more and more new program development is taking place offshore. Chapter 11 discusses offshore software outsourcing in greater detail.

In order to manage their relationship with an outsourcer or technology service provider, firms will need a contract that includes a **service level agreement (SLA)**. The SLA is a formal contract between customers and their service providers that defines the specific responsibilities of the service provider and the level of service expected by the customer. SLAs typically specify the nature and level of services provided, criteria for performance measurement, support options, provisions for security and disaster recovery, hardware and software ownership and upgrades, customer support, billing, and conditions for terminating the agreement.

Using Cloud Services

Firms now have the option of maintaining their own IT infrastructures or using cloud-based hardware and software services. There are many factors that go into the decision of whether to keep IT infrastructure in-house or turn it over to an external provider. Companies considering the cloud computing model need to carefully assess the costs and benefits of external services, weighing all people, organizational, and technology issues, including the level of service and performance that is acceptable for the business.

Small businesses that typically lack the resources for maintaining their own hardware and software may find it much easier to "rent" infrastructure from another firm and avoid the expense and difficulty of installing, operating, and maintaining hardware and software on their own. For larger businesses, the cost and business advantages are less clear-cut. These firms will have to consider not only the up-front and long-term costs of moving to the cloud but whether cloud computing capabilities are sufficiently secure or reliable for their most critical systems. At the moment, most large companies are likely to maintain most of their infrastructure internally but gradually move non-essential work to cloud services.

One emerging pattern is to off-load peak demand for computing power to remote, large-scale data centers. In this manner, firms reduce their technology expenditures by investing just enough to handle average processing loads and paying for only as much additional computing power as the market demands. This arrangement enables firms to have a more flexible infrastructure, some of it owned by the firm, and some of it rented from giant computer centers run by technology specialists.

The software offered by cloud providers may be suitable for basic desktop functions but not for running large corporate systems with many unique and complex business processes. In some instances, the cost of renting software adds up to more than purchasing and maintaining an application in-house. Yet there may be benefits to using software as a service (SaaS) if it allows the company to focus on core business issues instead of technology challenges.

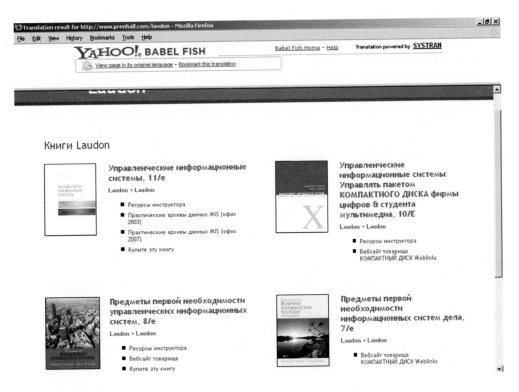

Managing Mobile Platforms

A large firm may have many thousands of wireless devices to configure and monitor, similar to a desktop environment. It will be a challenge to integrate this new platform with the firm's existing IT infrastructure and applications. Central coordination and oversight are essential. Firms will need to inventory all of their mobile devices and develop policies and tools for tracking, updating, and securing them and for controlling the data and applications that run on them.

Gains in productivity and efficiency from equipping employees with mobile computing devices must be balanced against increased costs from integrating these devices into the firm's IT infrastructure and from providing technical support. Other cost components include fees for wireless airtime, end-user training, help desk support, and software for special applications.

Although the cost of a wireless handheld for a corporate employee may run several hundred dollars, the TCO for each device is much higher, ranging from $1,000 to $3,000, according to various consultant estimates. Costs are higher if the mobile devices run many different applications or need to be integrated into back-end systems such as enterprise applications.

MANAGING SOFTWARE LOCALIZATION FOR GLOBAL BUSINESS

If you are operating a global company, all of the management issues we have just described will be affected by the need to create systems that can be realistically used by multiple business units in different countries. Although English has become a kind of standard business language, this is truer at higher levels of companies and not throughout the middle and lower ranks. Software may have to be built with local language interfaces before a new information system can be successfully implemented worldwide.

These interfaces can be costly and messy to build. Menu bars, commands, error messages, reports, queries, online data entry forms, and system documentation may need to be translated into all the languages of the countries where the system will be used. To be truly useful for enhancing productivity of a global workforce, the software interfaces must be easily understood and mastered quickly. The entire process of converting software to operate in a second language is called *software localization.*

Global systems must also consider differences in local cultures and business processes. Cross-functional systems such as enterprise and supply chain management systems are not always compatible with differences in languages, cultural heritages, and business processes in other countries.

In a global systems environment, all of these factors add to the TCO and will influence decisions about whether to outsource or use technology service providers.

4.4 Hands-On MIS Projects

The projects in this section give you hands-on experience in developing solutions for managing IT infrastructures and IT outsourcing, using spreadsheet software to evaluate alternative desktop systems, and using Web research to budget for a sales conference.

MANAGEMENT DECISION PROBLEMS

1. The University of Pittsburgh Medical Center (UPMC) relies on information systems to operate 19 hospitals, a network of other care sites, and international and commercial ventures. Demand for additional servers and storage technology was growing by 20 percent each year. UPMC was setting up a separate server for every application, and its servers and other computers were running a number of different operating systems, including several versions of Unix and Windows. UPMC had to manage technologies from many different vendors, including Hewlett-Packard (HP), Sun Microsystems, Microsoft, and IBM. Assess the impact of this situation on business performance. What factors and management decisions must be considered when developing a solution to this problem?

2. Quantas Airways, Australia's leading airline, faces cost pressures from high fuel prices and lower levels of global airline traffic. To remain competitive, the airline must find ways to keep costs low while providing a high level of customer service. Quantas had a 30-year-old data center. Management had to decide whether to replace its IT infrastructure with newer technology or outsource it. What factors should be considered by Quantas management when deciding whether to outsource? If Quantas decides to outsource, list and describe points that should be addressed in a service level agreement.

IMPROVING DECISION MAKING: USING A SPREADSHEET TO EVALUATE HARDWARE AND SOFTWARE OPTIONS

Software skills: Spreadsheet formulas
Business skills: Technology pricing

In this exercise, you will use spreadsheet software to calculate the cost of alternative desktop systems.

You have been asked to obtain pricing information on hardware and software for an office of 30 people. Using the Internet, get pricing for 30 PC desktop systems (monitors, computers, and keyboards) manufactured by Lenovo, Dell, and HP/Compaq as listed at their respective corporate Web sites. (For the purposes of this exercise, ignore the fact that desktop systems usually come with preloaded software packages.) Also obtain pricing on 15 black and white laser printers manufactured by HP and by Xerox. Each desktop system must satisfy the minimum specifications shown in the following table:

Minimum Desktop Specifications	
Processor speed	3 GHz
Hard drive	250 GB
RAM	3 GB
DVD-ROM speed	16 speed
Monitor (diagonal measurement)	17 inches

Each desktop printer must satisfy the minimum specifications shown in the following table:

Minimum Laser Printer Specifications	
Print speed	20 pages per minute
Print resolution	600 × 600
Network ready?	Yes
Maximum price/unit	$700

After pricing the desktop systems and printers, obtain pricing on 30 copies of the most recent versions of Microsoft Office and Sun StarOffice desktop productivity packages, and on 30 copies of Microsoft Windows 7 Professional. The application software suite packages come in various versions, so be sure that each package contains programs for word processing, spreadsheet analysis, database analysis, graphics preparation, and e-mail.

Prepare a spreadsheet showing your research results for the desktop systems, for the printers, and for the software. Use your spreadsheet software to determine the desktop system, printer, and software combination that will offer both the best performance and pricing per worker. Because every two workers will share one printer (15 printers/30 systems), assume only half a printer cost per worker in the spreadsheet. Assume that your company will take the standard warranty and service contract offered by each product's manufacturer.

IMPROVING DECISION MAKING: USING WEB RESEARCH TO BUDGET FOR A SALES CONFERENCE

Software skills: Internet-based software
Business skills: Researching transportation and lodging costs

In this exercise, you will use software at various online travel sites to arrange transportation and lodging for a large sales force to attend a sales conference at two alternative locations. You will use that information to calculate total travel and lodging costs and decide where to hold the conference.

The Foremost Composite Materials Company is planning a two-day sales conference for October 19–20, starting with a reception on the evening of October 18. The conference consists of all-day meetings that the entire sales force, numbering 125 sales representatives and their 16 managers, must attend. Each sales representative requires his or her own room, and the company needs two common meeting rooms, one large enough to hold the entire sales force plus a few visitors (200) and the other able to hold half the force. Management has set a budget of $110,000 for the representatives' room rentals. The hotel must also have such services as overhead and computer projectors, as well as business center and banquet facilities. It also should have facilities for the company reps to be able to work in their rooms and to enjoy themselves in a swimming pool or gym facility. The company would like to hold the conference in either Miami or Marco Island, Florida.

Foremost usually likes to hold such meetings in Hilton- or Marriott-owned hotels. Use the Hilton and Marriott Web sites to select a hotel in whichever of these cities that would enable the company to hold its sales conference within its budget.

Link to the two sites' home pages, and search them to find a hotel that meets Foremost's sales conference requirements. Once you have selected the hotel, locate flights arriving the afternoon prior to the conference because the attendees will need to check in the day before and attend your reception the evening prior to the conference. Your attendees will be coming from Los Angeles (54), San Francisco (32), Seattle (22), Chicago (19), and Pittsburgh (14). Determine costs of each airline ticket from these cities. When you are finished, create a budget for the conference. The budget will include the cost of each airline ticket, the room cost, and $60 per attendee per day for food.

- What was your final budget?
- Which did you select as the best hotel for the sales conference and why?

LEARNING TRACKS

The following Learning Tracks provide content relevant to topics covered in this chapter:

1. How Computer Hardware Works

2. How Computer Software Works

3. Service Level Agreements

4. Cloud Computing

5. The Open Source Software Initiative

6. Evolution of IT Infrastructure

7. Technology Drivers of IT Infrastructure Evolution

8. IT Infrastructure; Management Opportunities, Challenges, and Solutions

Review Summary

1 **What are the components of IT infrastructure?** IT infrastructure consists of the shared technology resources that provide the platform for the firm's specific information system applications. Major IT infrastructure components include computer hardware, software, data management technology, networking and telecommunications technology, and technology services.

2   **What are the major computer hardware, data storage, input, and output technologies used in business?** Computers are categorized as mainframes, midrange computers, PCs, workstations, or supercomputers. Mainframes are the largest computers, midrange computers are servers, PCs are desktop or laptop machines, workstations are desktop machines with powerful mathematical and graphic capabilities, and supercomputers are sophisticated, powerful computers that can perform massive and complex computations rapidly. Computing power can be further increased by creating a computational grid that combines the computing power of all the computers on a network. In the client/server model of computing, computer processing is split between "clients" and "servers" connected via a network. The exact division of tasks between client and server depends on the application.

The principal secondary storage technologies are magnetic disk, optical disc, and magnetic tape. Optical CD-ROM and DVD discs can store vast amounts of data compactly and some types are rewritable. Storage area networks (SANs) connect multiple storage devices on a separate high-speed network dedicated to storage. The principal input devices are keyboards, computer mice, touch screens, magnetic ink and optical character recognition devices, pen-based instruments, digital scanners, sensors, audio input devices, and radio-frequency identification devices. The principal output devices are display monitors, printers, and audio output devices.

3   **What are the major types of computer software used in business?** The two major types of software are system software and application software. System software coordinates the various parts of the computer system and mediates between application software and computer hardware. Application software is used to develop specific business applications.

The system software that manages and controls the activities of the computer is called the operating system. Leading PC and server operating systems include Windows Vista, Windows 7, Windows Server 2008, UNIX, Linux, and the Macintosh operating system. Linux is a powerful, resilient open source operating system that can run on multiple hardware platforms and is used widely to run Web servers.

The principal programming languages used in business application software include COBOL, C, C++, and Visual Basic. Fourth-generation languages are less procedural than conventional programming languages and enable end users to perform many software tasks that previously required technical specialists. They include popular PC and cloud-based desktop productivity tools, such as word processing, spreadsheet, data management, presentation graphics, and Web browser software. Java is an operating-system- and hardware-independent programming language that is the leading interactive programming environment for the Web. HTML is a page description language for creating Web pages.

Web services are loosely coupled software components based on XML and open Web standards that can work with any application software and operating system. They can be used as components of Web-based applications to link the systems of two different organizations or to link disparate systems of a single company.

4   **What are the most important contemporary hardware and software trends?** Increasingly, computing is taking place on a mobile digital platform. Cloud computing provides hardware and software resources as services delivered over the Internet. In autonomic computing, computer systems have capabilities for automatically configuring and repairing themselves. Open source software is proliferating because it allows users to modify the software at will and use it as a platform for new derivative applications. Mashups and widgets are the building blocks of new software applications and services using the cloud computing model. Software as a service (SaaS) delivers software remotely as an on-demand Web-based service.

5 **What are the principal issues in managing hardware and software technology?**
Managers and information systems specialists need to pay special attention to hardware capacity planning and scalability to ensure that the firm has enough computing power for its current and future needs. Businesses also need to balance the costs and benefits of building and maintaining their own hardware and software versus outsourcing or using an on-demand computing model. The total cost of ownership (TCO) of the organization's technology assets includes not only the original cost of computer hardware and software but also costs for hardware and software upgrades, maintenance, technical support, and training, including the costs for managing and maintaining mobile devices. Companies with global operations need to manage software localization.

Key Terms

Ajax, 138
Application server, 121
Application software, 118
Autonomic computing, 127
C, 134
C++, 134
Capacity planning, 142
CD-ROM (compact disc read-only memory), 122
Centralized processing, 120
Client, 120
Client/server computing, 121
Cloud computing, 125
Data management software, 118
Digital video disc (DVD), 122
Distributed processing, 120
Extensible Markup Language (XML), 139
Fourth-generation languages, 134
Graphical user interface (GUI), 130
Grid computing, 120
Hypertext Markup Language (HTML), 138
Input devices, 122
Java, 137

Legacy systems, 119
Linux, 133
Magnetic disk, 121
Magnetic tape, 122
Mainframe, 119
Mashups, 141
Multicore processor, 129
Multitouch, 130
Nanotechnology, 124
Netbooks, 124
N-tier client/server architectures, 121
Object, 134
Office 2010, 137
Offshore software outsourcing, 144
On-demand computing, 126
Open-source software, 133
Operating system, 130
Output devices, 122
Outsourcing, 143
Personal computer (PC), 119
Presentation graphics software, 137
Query languages, 132
SaaS (software as a service), 142
Scalability, 142
Server, 119

Service level agreement (SLA), 144
Service-oriented architecture (SOA), 139
Software package, 135
Spreadsheet software, 136
Storage area networks (SANs), 122
Supercomputer, 120
System software, 118
Total cost of ownership (TCO), 143
UNIX, 131
Virtualization, 127
Visual Basic, 134
Visual programming language, 134
Web browsers, 137
Web hosting service, 144
Web server, 121
Web services, 138
Widget, 141
Windows 7, 131
Windows Vista, 131
Word processing software, 135
Workstation, 119

Review Questions

1. What are the components of IT infrastructure?
• Define information technology (IT) infrastructure and describe each of its components.

2. What are the major computer hardware, data storage, input, and output technologies used in business?

• List and describes the various type of computers available to businesses today.

• Define the client/server model of computing, and describe the difference between a two-tiered and n-tier client/server architecture.

• List the most important secondary storage media and the strengths and limitations of each.

• List and describe the major computer input and output devices.

3. What are the major types of computer software used in business?

- Distinguish between application software and system software, and explain the role played by the operating system of a computer.
- List and describe the major PC and server operating systems.
- Name and describe each category of fourth-generation software tools, and explain how fourth-generation languages differ from conventional programming languages.
- Name and describe the major desktop productivity software tools.
- Explain how Java and HTML are used in building applications for the Web.
- Define Web services, describe the technologies they use, and explain how Web services benefit businesses.

4. What are the most important contemporary hardware and software trends?

- Define and describe the mobile digital platform, nanotechnology, grid computing, cloud computing, autonomic computing, virtualization, and multicore processing.
- Explain why open source software is so important today and its benefits for business.
- List and describe cloud computing software services, mashups, and widgets, and explain how they benefit individuals and businesses.

5. What are the principal issues in managing hardware and software technology?

- Explain why managers need to pay attention to capacity planning and scalability of technology resources.
- Describe the cost components used to calculate the TCO of technology assets.
- Identify the benefits and challenges of using outsourcing, cloud computing services, and mobile platforms.
- Explain why software localization has become an important management issue for global companies.

Discussion Questions

1. Why is selecting computer hardware and software for the organization an important business decision? What people, organization, and technology issues should be considered when selecting computer hardware and software?

2. Should organizations use software service providers (including cloud services) for all their software needs? Why or why not? What people, organization, and technology factors should be considered when making this decision?

Video Cases

Video Cases and Instructional Videos illustrating some of the concepts in this chapter are available. Contact your instructor to access these videos.

Collaboration and Teamwork

Evaluating Server and Mobile Operating Systems

Form a group with three or four of your classmates. Choose server or mobile operating systems to evaluate. You might research and compare the capabilities and costs of Linux versus the most recent version of the Windows operating system for servers or versus UNIX. Alternatively, you could compare the capabilities of the Android mobile operating system with the Symbian operating system or either of these with the most recent version of the iPhone operating system (iPhone OS). If possible, use Google Sites to post links to Web pages, team communication announcements, and work assignments; to brainstorm; and to work collaboratively on project documents. Try to use Google Docs to develop a presentation of your findings for the class.

BUSINESS PROBLEM-SOLVING CASE

Salesforce.Com: Cloud Software Services Go Mainstream

Salesforce.com Inc., one of the most disruptive technology companies of the past few years, has shaken up the software industry with its innovative business model and resounding success. Salesforce provides customer relationship management (CRM) and other application software solutions in the form of 'software as a service' (SaaS) leased over the Internet, as opposed to software bought and installed on machines locally.

The company was founded in 1999 by former Oracle executive Marc Benioff, and has since grown to 2,600 employees and generated $1.077 billion in revenue in 2009, making it one of the top 50 software companies in the world. Salesforce.com has over 55,000 corporate customers and over 1.5 million subscribers. Salesforce.com attributes its success to the many benefits of its on-demand model of software distribution.

The on-demand model eliminates the need for large up-front capital investments in systems and lengthy implementations on corporate computers. Subscriptions start as low as $9 per user per month for the pared-down Group version for small sales and marketing teams, with monthly subscriptions for more advanced versions for large enterprises starting around $65 per user.

For example, the Minneapolis-based Haagen-Dazs Shoppe owned by Nestle USA calculated it would have had to spend $65,000 for a custom-designed database to help management stay in contact with the company's retail franchises. The company only had to pay $20,000 to establish service with Salesforce, plus a monthly charge of $125 per month for 20 users to use wireless handhelds or the Web to remotely monitor all the Haagen-Dazs franchises across the United States.

Salesforce.com implementations take three months at the longest, and usually less than a month. There is no hardware for subscribers to purchase, scale, and maintain. There are no operating systems, database servers, or application servers to install, no consultants and staff, and no expensive licensing and maintenance fees. The system is accessible via a standard Web browser, and Salesforce.com continually updates its software behind the scenes. There are tools for customizing some features of the software to support a company's unique business processes. Subscribers do not have to make huge up-front hardware and software investments. They can leave if business turns sour or a better system comes along. If they lay people off, they can cut down on the number of Salesforce subscriptions they buy.

Salesforce faces significant challenges as it continues to grow and refine its business. The first challenge comes from increased competition, both from traditional industry leaders and new challengers hoping to replicate Salesforce's success. Microsoft, SAP, and Oracle have rolled out subscription-based versions of their CRM products in response to Salesforce. Smaller competitors like NetSuite, Salesboom.com, and RightNow also have made some inroads against Salesforce's market share.

Salesforce still has plenty of catching up to do to reach the size and market share of its larger competitors. As recently as 2007, SAP's market share was nearly four times as large as Salesforce.com's, and IBM's customer base includes 9,000 software companies that run their applications on IBM software and that are likelier to choose a solution offered by IBM over Salesforce.com.

Salesforce needs to continually prove to customers that it is reliable and secure enough to remotely handle their corporate data and applications. The company has experienced a number of service outages, the most recent of which occurred in early 2009. On January 6, a core network device failed and prevented data in Europe, Japan, and North America from being processed for 38 minutes. Over 177 million transactions were affected. While most of Salesforce's customers accept that IT services provided through the cloud are going to be available slightly less than full time, some customers and critics used the outage as an opportunity to question the soundness of the entire concept of cloud computing. In February, a similar outage occurred, affecting Europe and as well as North America a few hours later.

Thus far, Salesforce.com has experienced only one security breach. In November 2007, a Salesforce employee was the victim of a phishing attack and divulged his corporate password to scammers, exposing Salesforce's customer list. Salesforce clients were subjected to a barrage of highly targeted scams and hacking attempts that appeared authentic. Although this incident raised a red flag, many customers reported that Salesforce's handling of the situation was satisfactory. All of Salesforce's major customers regularly send auditors to Salesforce to check security.

Another challenge for Salesforce.com is to expand its business model into other areas. Salesforce is currently used mostly by sales staff needing to keep track of leads and customer lists. One way the company is trying to provide additional functionality is through a partnership with Google and more specifically Google Apps. Salesforce.com is combining its services with Gmail, Google Docs, Google Talk, and Google Calendar to allow its customers to accomplish more tasks via the

Web. Salesforce also introduced a development tool for integrating with Facebook's social network. Customers are able to build applications that call functions at the Facebook site.

Salesforce has partnered with Apple to distribute its applications for use on its iPhone. The company hopes that it can tap into the large market of iPhone users, pitching the ability to use Salesforce applications anytime, anywhere.

The partnership between Salesforce.com and Google represents a united front against Microsoft, intended to cut into the popularity of Microsoft Office. Currently, Salesforce.com describes the partnership as "primarily a distribution deal," but it could grow stronger based on the idea that businesses prefer to manage customer relationship management and related activities in one place. Salesforce.com and Google both hope that their Salesforce.com for Google Apps initiative will galvanize further growth in on-demand software.

In February 2009, rumors swirled that Oracle was poised to acquire Salesforce. Pundits speculated that the deal was a good one for Oracle because it would take too long to grow its SaaS offerings to the scale that Salesforce had already achieved. Thus far, no such deal has materialized, but some industry observers expect that at some point, Oracle will in fact end up buying Salesforce.

In order to grow its revenues to the levels that industry observers and Wall Street eventually expects, Salesforce will need to change its focus from selling a suite of software applications to providing a broader cloud computing "platform" on which many software companies can deliver applications. As CEO Marc Benioff put it, over the past decade, "we focused on software as a service." In the next decade, Salesforce.com "will really be focused on the platform as a service."

The company has intensified its efforts to provide cloud computing offerings to its customers. The new Salesforce.com Web site places much more emphasis on cloud computing, grouping products into three types of clouds: the Sales Cloud, the Service Cloud, and the Custom Cloud. The Sales and Service clouds consist of applications meant to improve sales and customer service, respectively, but the Custom Cloud is another name for the Force.com application development platform, where customers can develop their own applications for use within the broader Salesforce network.

Force.com provides a set of development tools and IT services that enable users to customize their Salesforce.com customer relationship management applications or to build entirely new applications and run them "in the cloud" on Salesforce.com's data center infrastructure. Salesforce opened up Force.com to other independent software developers and listed their programs on its AppExchange.

Using AppExchange, small businesses can go online and easily download over 800 software applications, some add-ons to Salesforce.com and others that are unrelated, even in non-customer-facing functions such as human resources. Force.com Sites, based on the Force.com development environment, enables users to develop Web pages and register domain names. Pricing is based on site traffic.

Salesforce.com's cloud infrastructure includes two data centers in the United States and a third in Singapore, with others in Europe and Japan planned for the future. Salesforce.com has additionally partnered with Amazon to enable Force.com customers to tap into Amazon's cloud computing services (Elastic Compute Cloud and Simple Storage Service.) Amazon's services handle "cloudburst computing" tasks of Force.com applications that require extra processing power or storage capacity.

Author Solutions, based in Bloomington, Minnesota, uses the Force.com platform to host the applications behind its operations and expand its library of ideas. Authors.com is the largest self-publishing company in the world and published 24,000 titles in 2008, with $100 million in annual revenue and 400 employees. This business is growing at a blistering rate, and had acquired several other companies. It was struggling to manage two databases, two e-commerce systems, and three workflow systems to support its three brands. Senior management decided to consolidate on a single platform.

Salesforce.com was selected for that platform. Author Solutions appreciated the cost savings of up to 75 percent from not having to maintain and manage its own data center and the ability to scale as the company mushroomed. Workflow modifications that once took 30 to 120 hours are accomplished in one-fourth the time. The time and cost for adding a new product, which used to take 120 to 240 hours (and cost $6,000 to $12,000) has been reduced by 75 percent. Within five months after signing with Salesforce, Author Solutions was running its new "publishing enterprise resource planning system," which coordinates all of the processes involved in sourcing and publishing a book—lead tracking, handling of editorial submissions, and corrections. The new platform is able to handle 30 percent more work volume than the old systems with the same number of employees.

The question is whether the audience for Salesforce's AppExchange and Force.com platforms will prove large enough to deliver the level of growth Salesforce wants. It still isn't clear whether the company will generate the revenue it needs to provide cloud computing services on the same scale as Google or Amazon, and also make its cloud computing investments pay off.

Some analysts believe the platform may not be attractive to larger companies for their application needs. Yet another challenge is providing constant availability. Salesforce.com subscribers depend on the service being available 24/7. But thanks to the previously described outages, many companies have rethought their dependency on SaaS. Salesforce.com provides tools to assure customers about its system reliability and also offers PC applications that tie into their services so users can work offline.

Still, a number of companies are reluctant to jump on the SaaS and cloud computing bandwagon. Moreover, it is still not clear whether software delivered over the Web will cost less in the long run. According to Gartner analyst Rob DiSisto, it may be less expensive to subscribe to Salesforce.com's software services for the first few years, but what happens after that? Will the costs of upgrading and managing on-demand software exceed the savings from using Salesforce.com's services?

Sources: Clint Boulton, "Salesforce.com Network Device Failure Shuts Thousands Out of SaaS Apps," *eWeek*, January 7, 2009; Jessi Hempel, "Salesforce Hits Stride," CNN Money.com, March 2, 2009; Charles Babcock, "Salesforce Keeps Tight Control on Cloud Development," *Information Week*, March 27, 2009; "More Books Fewer Worries," *Customer Relationship Management*, August 2009; J. Nicholas Hoover, "Service Outages Force Cloud Adopters to Rethink Tactics," *Information Week*, August 18/25, 2008; Saul Hansell, "How Apple and Facebook Influence Salesforce.com," *The New York Times*, December 17, 2008; Charles Babcock, "Salesforce Ascends Beyond Software As Service," *Information Week*, November 10 2008; Mary Hayes Weier, "Salesforce, Google Show Fruits of Their Collaboration," *Information Week*, April 21, 2008; John Pallatto and Clint Boulton, "An On-Demand Partnership," *eWeek*, April 21, 2008; and Gary Rivlin, "Software for Rent," *The New York Times*, November 13, 2007.

Case Study Questions

1. What are the advantages and disadvantages of the cloud computing model?
2. What are some of the challenges facing Salesforce as it continues its growth? How well will it be able to meet those challenges?
3. What kinds of businesses could benefit from switching to Salesforce and why?
4. What factors would you take into account in deciding whether to use Saleforce.com for your business?
5. Could a company run its entire business using Salesforce.com, Force.com, and App Exchange? Explain your answer.

Foundations of Business Intelligence: Databases and Information Management

CHAPTER 5

STUDENT LEARNING OBJECTIVES

After completing this chapter, you will be able to answer the following questions:

1. How does a relational database organize data, and how does it differ from an object-oriented database?

2. What are the principles of a database management system?

3. What are the principal tools and technologies for accessing information from databases to improve business performance and decision making?

4. What is the role of information policy and data administration in the management of organizational data resources?

5. Why is data quality assurance so important for a business?

CHAPTER OUTLINE

R.R. DONNELLEY TRIES TO MASTER ITS DATA

Right now you are most likely using an R.R. Donnelley product. Chicago-based R.R. Donnelley is a giant commercial printing and service company providing printing services, forms and labels, direct mail, and other services. This textbook probably came off its presses. The company's recent expansion has been fueled by a series of acquisitions, including commercial printer Moore Wallace in 2005 and printing and supply chain management company Banta in January 2007. R.R. Donnelley's revenue has jumped from $2.4 billion in 2003 to $8.4 billion today.

However, all that growth created information management challenges. Each acquired company had its own systems and its own set of customer, vendor, and product data. Coming from so many different sources, the data were often inconsistent, duplicated, or incomplete. For example, different units of the business might each have a different meaning for the entity "customer." One might define "customer" as a specific billing location, while another might define "customer" as the legal parent entity of a company. Donnelley had to use time-consuming manual processes to reconcile the data

stored in multiple systems in order to get a clear enterprise-wide picture of each of its customers, since they might be doing business with several different units of the company. These conditions heightened inefficiencies and costs.

R.R. Donnelley had become so big that it was impractical to store the information from all of its units in a single system. But Donnelley still needed a clear single set of data that was accurate and consistent for the entire enterprise. To solve this problem, R.R. Donnelley turned to master data management (MDM). MDM seeks to ensure that an organization does not use multiple versions of the same piece of data in different parts of its operations by merging disparate records into a single authenticated master file. Once the master file is in place, employees and applications access a single consolidated view of the company's data. It is especially useful for companies such as Donnelley that have data integration problems as a result of mergers and acquisitions.

Implementing MDM is a multi-step process that includes business process analysis, data cleansing, data consolidation and reconciliation, and data migration into a master file of all the company's data. Companies must identify what group in the company "owns" each piece of data and is responsible for resolving inconsistent definitions of data and other discrepancies.

Donnelley launched its MDM program in late 2005 and began creating a single set of identifiers for its customer and vendor data. The company opted for a registry model using Purisma's Data Hub in which customer data continue to reside in the system where they originate but are registered in a master "hub" and cross-referenced so applications can find the data. The data in their source system are not touched.

Nearly a year later, Donnelley brought up its Customer Master Data Store, which integrates the data from numerous systems from Donnelley acquisitions. Data that are outdated, incomplete, or incorrectly formatted are corrected or eliminated. A registry points to where the source data are stored. By having a single consistent enterprise-wide set of data with common definitions and standards, management is able to easily find out what kind of business and how much business it has with a particular customer to identify top customers and sales opportunities. And when Donelley acquires a company, it can quickly see a list of overlapping customers.

Sources: John McCormick, "Mastering Data at R.R. Donnelley," *Information Management Magazine*, March 2009; Loraine Lawson, "Are You Really Ready to Buy a Master Data Management Tool?" *IT BusinessEdge*, June 25, 2009; and www.purisma.com, accessed June 26, 2009.

R.R. Donnelley's experience illustrates the importance of data management for businesses. Donnelley has experienced phenomenal growth, primarily through acquisitions. But its business performance depends on what it can or cannot do with its data. How businesses store, organize, and manage their data has a tremendous impact on organizational effectiveness.

The chapter-opening diagram calls attention to important points raised by this case and this chapter. Management decided that the company needed to centralize the management of the company's data. Data about customers, vendors, products, and other important entities had been stored in a number of different systems and files where they could not be easily retrieved and analyzed. They were often redundant and inconsistent, limiting their usefulness. Management was unable to obtain an enterprise-wide view of all of its customers at all of its acquisitions to market its products and services and provide better service and support.

In the past, R.R. Donnelley had used heavily manual paper processes to reconcile its inconsistent and redundant data and manage its information from an enterprise-wide per-

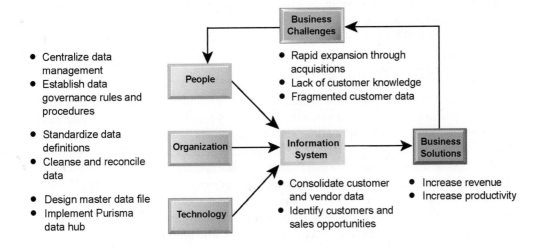

- Centralize data management
- Establish data governance rules and procedures

- Standardize data definitions
- Cleanse and reconcile data

- Design master data file
- Implement Purisma data hub

People

Organization

Technology

Business Challenges

- Rapid expansion through acquisitions
- Lack of customer knowledge
- Fragmented customer data

Information System

- Consolidate customer and vendor data
- Identify customers and sales opportunities

Business Solutions

- Increase revenue
- Increase productivity

spective. This solution was no longer viable as the organization grew larger. A more appropriate solution was to identify, consolidate, cleanse, and standardize customer and other data in a single master data management registry. In addition to using appropriate technology, Donnelley had to correct and reorganize the data into a standard format and establish rules, responsibilities, and procedures for updating and using the data.

A master data management system helps R.R. Donnelley boost profitability by making it easier to identify customers and sales opportunities. It also improves operational efficiency and decision making by having more accurate and complete customer data available and reducing the time required to reconcile redundant and inconsistent data.

5.1 The Database Approach to Data Management

A **database** is a collection of related files containing records on people, places, or things. One of the most successful databases in modern history is the telephone book. The telephone book is a collection of records on people and businesses who use telephones. The telephone book lists four pieces of information for each phone user: last name, first name, address, and phone number. It also contains information on businesses and business categories, such as auto dealers or plumbing suppliers. The telephone book draws its information from a database with files for customers, business classifications, and area codes and geographic regions.

Prior to the development of digital databases, a business would use large filing cabinets filled with paper files to store information on transactions, customers, suppliers, inventory, and employees. They would also use lists, laboriously collated and typed by hand, to quickly summarize the information in paper files. You can still find paper-based manual databases in most doctors' offices where patient records are stored in thousands of paper files.

Needless to say, paper-based databases are extremely inefficient and costly to maintain, often contain inaccurate data, are slow, and make it difficult to access the data in a timely fashion. Paper-based databases are also extremely inflexible. For instance, it would be nearly impossible for a paper-based doctor's office to combine its files on prescriptions with its files on patients in order to produce a list of all people for whom they had prescribed a specific drug. For a modern computer database, this would be very easy. In fact, a powerful feature of computer databases is the ability to quickly relate one set of files to another.

ENTITIES AND ATTRIBUTES

How do you start thinking about the data for your business and how to manage them? The first step is to identify the data you will need to run your business. Typically, you will be using data on categories of information, such as customers, suppliers, employees, orders, products, shippers, and perhaps parts. Each of these generalized categories representing a person, place, or thing on which we store and maintain information is called an **entity**. Each entity has specific characteristics, called **attributes**. For example, the entity SUPPLIER has specific attributes, such as the supplier's name and address, which would most likely include street, city, state, and ZIP code. The entity PART typically has attributes such as part description, price of each part (unit price), and supplier who produced the part.

ORGANIZING DATA IN A RELATIONAL DATABASE

If you stored this information in paper files, you would probably have a file on each entity and its attributes. In an information system, a database organizes the data much the same way, grouping related pieces of data together. The **relational database** is the most common type of database today. Relational databases organize data into two-dimensional tables (called *relations*) with columns and rows. Each table contains data on an entity and its attributes. For the most part, there is one table for each business entity. So, at the most basic level, you will have one table for customers, and a table each for suppliers, parts in inventory, employees, and sales transactions.

Let's look at how a relational database would organize data about suppliers and parts. Take the SUPPLIER table, which is illustrated in Figure 5-1. It consists of a grid of columns and rows of data. Each individual element of data about a supplier, such as the supplier name, street, city, state, and zip code, is stored as a separate **field** within the SUPPLIER table. Each field represents an attribute for the entity SUPPLIER. Fields in a relational database are also called *columns*.

The actual information about a single supplier that resides in a table is called a *row*. Rows are commonly referred to as **records**, or, in very technical terms, as **tuples**.

Note that there is a field for Supplier_Number in this table. This field uniquely identifies each record so that the record can be retrieved, updated, or sorted, and it is called a **key field**. Each table in a relational database has one field that is designated as its **primary key**. This

Figure 5-1
A Relational Database Table
A relational database organizes data in the form of two-dimensional tables. Illustrated here is a table for the entity SUPPLIER showing how it represents the entity and its attributes. Supplier_Number is the key field.

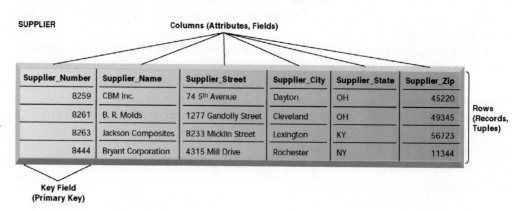

SUPPLIER   Columns (Attributes, Fields)

Supplier_Number	Supplier_Name	Supplier_Street	Supplier_City	Supplier_State	Supplier_Zip
8259	CBM Inc.	74 5th Avenue	Dayton	OH	45220
8261	B. R. Molds	1277 Gandolly Street	Cleveland	OH	49345
8263	Jackson Composites	8233 Micklin Street	Lexington	KY	56723
8444	Bryant Corporation	4315 Mill Drive	Rochester	NY	11344

Rows (Records, Tuples)

Key Field (Primary Key)

key field is the unique identifier for all the information in any row of the table, and this primary key cannot be duplicated.

We could use the supplier's name as a key field. However, if two different suppliers had the same name (which does happen from time to time), supplier name would not uniquely identify each, so it is necessary to assign a special identifier field for this purpose. For example, if you had two suppliers, both named "CBM," but one was based in Dayton and another in St. Louis, it would be easy to confuse them. However, if each has a unique supplier number, such confusion is prevented.

We also see that the address information has been separated into four separate fields: Supplier_Street, Supplier_City, Supplier_State, and Supplier_Zip. Data are separated into the smallest elements that one would want to access separately to make it easy to select only the rows in the table that match the contents of one field, such as all the suppliers in Ohio (OH). The rows of data can also be sorted by the contents of the Supplier_State field to get a list of suppliers by state regardless of their cities.

So far, the SUPPLIER table does not have any information about the parts that a particular supplier provides for your company. PART is a separate entity from SUPPLIER, and fields with information about parts should be stored in a separate PART table (see Figure 5-2).

Why not keep information on parts in the same table as suppliers? If we did that, each row of the table would contain the attributes of both PART and SUPPLIER. Because one supplier could supply more than one part, the table would need many extra rows for a single supplier to show all the parts that supplier provided. We would be maintaining a great deal of redundant data about suppliers, and it would be difficult to search for the information on any individual part because you would not know whether this part is the first or fiftieth part in this supplier's record. A separate table, PART, should be created to store these three fields and solve this problem.

The PART table would also have to contain another field, Supplier_Number, so that you would know the supplier for each part. It would not be necessary to keep repeating all the information about a supplier in each PART record because having a Supplier_ Number field in the PART table allows you to "look up" the data in the fields of the SUPPLIER table.

Notice that Supplier_Number appears in both the SUPPLIER and PART tables. In the SUPPLIER table, Supplier_Number is the primary key. When the field Supplier_Number

PART

Part_Number	Part_Name	Unit_Price	Supplier_Number
137	Door latch	22.00	8259
145	Side mirror	12.00	8444
150	Door molding	6.00	8263
152	Door lock	31.00	8259
155	Compressor	54.00	8261
178	Door handle	10.00	8259

Primary Key   **Foreign Key**

Figure 5-2
The PART Table
Data for the entity PART have their own separate table. Part_Number is the primary key and Supplier_Number is the foreign key, enabling users to find related information from the SUPPLIER table about the supplier for each part.

appears in the PART table it is called a **foreign key** and is essentially a look-up field to look up data about the supplier of a specific part. Note that the PART table would itself have its own primary key field, Part_Number, to uniquely identify each part. This key is not used to link PART with SUPPLIER but might be used to link PART with a different entity.

As we organize data into tables, it is important to make sure that all the attributes for a particular entity apply only to that entity. If you were to keep the supplier's address with the PART record, that information would not really relate only to PART; it would relate to both PART and SUPPLIER. If the supplier's address were to change, it would be necessary to alter the data in every PART record rather than only once in the SUPPLIER record.

ESTABLISHING RELATIONSHIPS

Now that we've broken down our data into a SUPPLIER table and a PART table, we must make sure we understand the relationship between them. A schematic called an **entity-relationship diagram** is used to clarify table relationships in a relational database. The most important piece of information provided by an entity-relationship diagram is the manner in which two tables are related to each other. Tables in a relational database may have one-to-one, one-to-many, and many-to-many relationships.

An example of a one-to-one relationship might be a situation where a human resources system must store confidential data about employees. It might store data, such as the employee name, date of birth, address, and job position in one table, and confidential data about that employee, such as salary or pension benefits, in another table. These two tables pertaining to a single employee would have a one-to-one relationship because each record in the EMPLOYEE table with basic employee data has only one related record in the table storing confidential data.

The relationship between the SUPPLIER and PART entities in our database is a one-to-many relationship: Each supplier can supply more that one part, but each part has only one supplier. For every record in the SUPPLIER table, there may be many related records in the PART table.

Figure 5-3 illustrates how an entity-relationship diagram would depict this one-to-many relationship. The boxes represent entities. The lines connecting the boxes represent relationships. A line connecting two entities that ends in two short marks designates a one-to-one relationship. A line connecting two entities that ends with a crow's foot preceded by a short mark indicates a one-to-many relationship. Figure 5-3 shows that each PART has only one SUPPLIER, but many PARTs can be provided by the same SUPPLIER.

We would also see a one-to-many relationship if we wanted to add a table about orders to our database because one supplier services many orders. The ORDER table would only contain only the Order_Number and Order_Date fields. Figure 5-4 illustrates a report showing an order of parts from a supplier. If you look at the report, you can see that the information on the top-right portion of the report comes from the ORDER table. The actual line items ordered are listed in the lower portion of the report.

Because one order can be for many parts from a supplier, and a single part can be ordered many times on different orders, this creates a many-to-many relationship between the PART and ORDER tables. Whenever a many-to-many relationship exists between two

Figure 5-3
A Simple Entity-Relationship Diagram
This diagram shows the relationship between the entities SUPPLIER and PART.

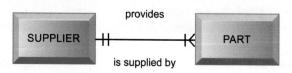

Order Number: 3502
Order Date: 1/15/2010

Supplier Number: 8259
Supplier Name: CBM Inc.
Supplier Address: 74 5th Avenue, Dayton, OH 45220

Order_Number	Part_Number	Part_Quantity	Part_Name	Unit_Price	Extended Price
3502	137	10	Door latch	22.00	$220.00
3502	152	20	Door lock	31.00	620.00
3502	178	5	Door handle	10.00	50.00
			Order Total:		$890.00

Figure 5-4
Sample Order Report
The shaded areas show which data came from the ORDER, SUPPLIER, and LINE_ITEM tables. The database does not maintain data on extended price or order total because they can be derived from other data in the tables.

tables, it is necessary to link these two tables in a table that joins this information. Creating a separate table for a line item in the order would serve this purpose. This table is often called a *join table* or an *intersection relation.* This join table contains only three fields: Order_Number and Part_Number, which are used only to link the ORDER and PART tables, and Part_Quantity. If you look at the bottom-left part of the report, this is the information coming from the LINE_ITEM table.

We would thus wind up with a total of four tables in our database. Figure 5-5 illustrates the final set of tables, and Figure 5-6 shows what the entity-relationship diagram for this set of tables would look like. Note that the ORDER table does not contain data on the extended price because that value can be calculated by multiplying Unit_Price by Part_Quantity. This data element can be derived when needed using information that already exists in the PART and LINE_ITEM tables. Order_Total is another derived field calculated by totaling the extended prices for items ordered.

The process of streamlining complex groups of data to minimize redundant data elements and awkward many-to-many relationships, and increase stability and flexibility is called **normalization.** A database that has been properly designed and normalized will be easy to maintain, and will minimize duplicate data. The Learning Tracks at the end of this chapter direct you to more detailed discussions of database design, normalization, and entity-relationship diagramming in MyMISLab.

Relational database systems try to enforce **referential integrity** rules to ensure that relationships between coupled tables remain consistent. When one table has a foreign key that points to another table, you may not add a record to the table with the foreign key unless there is a corresponding record in the linked table. In the database we have just created, the foreign key Supplier_Number links the PART table to the SUPPLIER table. We may not add a new record to the PART table for a part with supplier number 8266 unless there is a corresponding record in the SUPPLIER table for supplier number 8266. We must also delete the corresponding record in the PART table if we delete the record in the SUPPLIER table for supplier number 8266. In other words, we shouldn't have parts from nonexistent suppliers!

The example provided here for parts, orders, and suppliers is a simple one. Even in a very small business, you will have tables for other important entities, such as customers, shippers, and employees. A very large corporation might have databases with thousands of entities (tables) to maintain. What is important for any business, large or small, is to have a good data model that includes all of its entities and the relationships among them, one that is organized to minimize redundancy, maximize accuracy, and make data easily accessible for reporting and analysis.

PART

Part_Number	Part_Name	Unit_Price	Supplier_Number
137	Door latch	22.00	8259
145	Side mirror	12.00	8444
150	Door molding	6.00	8263
152	Door lock	31.00	8259
155	Compressor	54.00	8261
178	Door handle	10.00	8259

LINE_ITEM

Order_Number	Part_Number	Part_Quantity
3502	137	10
3502	152	20
3502	178	5

ORDER

Order_Number	Order_Date
3502	1/15/2010
3502	1/15/2010
3502	1/15/2010

SUPPLIER

Supplier_Number	Supplier_Name	Supplier_Street	Supplier_City	Supplier_State	Supplier_Zip
8259	CBM Inc.	74 5th Avenue	Dayton	OH	45220
8261	B. R. Molds	1277 Gandolly Street	Cleveland	OH	49345
8263	Jackson Components	8233 Micklin Street	Lexington	KY	56723
8444	Bryant Corporation	4315 Mill Drive	Rochester	NY	11344

Figure 5-5
The Final Database Design with Sample Records
The final design of the database for suppliers, parts, and orders has four tables. The LINE_ITEM table is a join table that eliminates the many-to-many relationship between ORDER and PART.

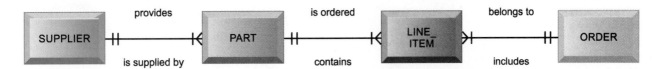

Figure 5-6
Entity-Relationship Diagram for the Database with Four Tables
This diagram shows the relationship between the entities SUPPLIER, PART, LINE_ITEM, and ORDER.

It cannot be emphasized enough: If the business does not get its data model right, the system will not be able to serve the business properly. The company's systems will not be as effective as they could be because they will have to work with data that may be inaccurate, incomplete, or difficult to retrieve. Understanding the organization's data and how they should be represented in a database is perhaps the most important lesson you can learn from this course.

For example, Famous Footwear, a shoe store chain with more than 800 locations in 49 states, could not achieve its goal of having "the right style of shoe in the right store for sale at the right price" because its database was not properly designed for a rapidly adjusting store inventory. The company had an Oracle relational database running on an IBM AS/400 midrange computer, but the database was designed primarily for producing standard reports for management rather than for reacting to marketplace changes. Management could not obtain precise data on specific items in inventory in each of its stores. The company had to work around this problem by building a new database where the sales and inventory data could be better organized for analysis and inventory management.

5.2 Database Management Systems

Now that you have started creating the files and identifying the data required by your business, you will need a database management system to help you manage and use the data. A **database management system (DBMS)** is a specific type of software for creating, storing, organizing, and accessing data from a database. Microsoft Access is a DBMS for desktop systems, whereas DB2, Oracle Database, and Microsoft SQL Server are DBMS for large mainframes and midrange computers. MySQL is a popular open-source DBMS, and Oracle Database Lite is a DBMS for small handheld computing devices. All of these products are relational DBMS that support a relational database.

The DBMS relieves the end user or programmer from the task of understanding where and how the data are actually stored by separating the logical and physical views of the data. The *logical view* presents data as end users or business specialists would perceive them, whereas the *physical view* shows how data are actually organized and structured on physical storage media, such as a hard disk.

The database management software makes the physical database available for different logical views required by users. For example, for the human resources database illustrated in Figure 5-7, a benefits specialist might require a view consisting of the employee's name, social security number, and health insurance coverage. A payroll department member might need data such as the employee's name, social security number, gross pay, and net pay. The data for all of these views is stored in a single database, where it can be more easily managed by the organization.

OPERATIONS OF A RELATIONAL DBMS

In a relational database, tables can be easily combined to deliver data required by users, provided that any two tables share a common data element. Let's return to the database we set up earlier with PART and SUPPLIER tables illustrated in Figures 5-1 and 5-2.

Figure 5-7
Human Resources
Database with
Multiple Views
*A single human
resources database
provides many different
views of data, depending
on the information
requirements of the user.
Illustrated here are two
possible views, one of
interest to a benefits
specialist and one of
interest to a member of
the company's payroll
department.*

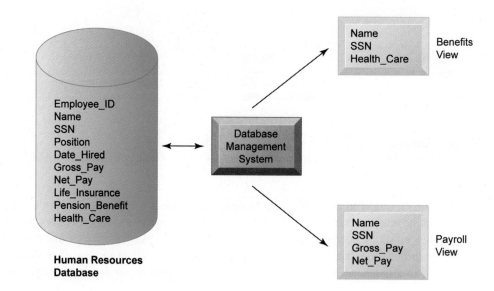

Suppose we wanted to find in this database the names of suppliers who could provide us with part number 137 or part number 150. We would need information from two tables: the SUPPLIER table and the PART table. Note that these two tables have a shared data element: Supplier_Number.

In a relational database, three basic operations, as shown in Figure 5-8, are used to develop useful sets of data: select, project, and join. The *select* operation creates a subset consisting of all records in the file that meet stated criteria. Select creates, in other words, a subset of rows that meet certain criteria. In our example, we want to select records (rows) from the PART table where the Part_Number equals 137 or 150. The *join* operation combines relational tables to provide the user with more information than is available in individual tables. In our example, we want to join the now-shortened PART table (only parts 137 or 150 will be presented) and the SUPPLIER table into a single new table.

The *project* operation creates a subset consisting of columns in a table, permitting the user to create new tables that contain only the information required. In our example, we want to extract from the new table only the following columns: Part_Number, Part_Name, Supplier_Number, and Supplier_Name (see Figure 5-8).

CAPABILITIES OF DATABASE MANAGEMENT SYSTEMS

A DBMS includes capabilities and tools for organizing, managing, and accessing the data in the database. The most important are its data definition capability, data dictionary, and data manipulation language.

DBMS have a **data definition** capability to specify the structure of the content of the database. It would be used to create database tables and to define the characteristics of the fields in each table. This information about the database would be documented in a **data dictionary**. A data dictionary is an automated or manual file that stores definitions of data elements and their characteristics. Microsoft Access has a rudimentary data dictionary capability that displays information about the name, description, size, type, format, and other properties of each field in a table (see Figure 5-9). Data dictionaries for large corporate databases may capture additional information, such as usage, ownership (who in the organization is responsible for maintaining the data), authorization, security, and the individuals, business functions, programs, and reports that use each data element.

Querying and Reporting

DBMS include tools for accessing and manipulating information in databases. Most DBMS have a specialized language called a **data manipulation language** that is used to add, change, delete, and retrieve the data in the database. This language contains commands that

PART

Part_Number	Part_Name	Unit_Price	Supplier_Number
137	Door latch	22.00	8259
145	Side mirror	12.00	8444
150	Door molding	6.00	8263
152	Door lock	31.00	8259
155	Compressor	54.00	8261
178	Door handle	10.00	8259

Select Part_Number = 137 or 150

SUPPLIER

Supplier_Number	Supplier_Name	Supplier_Street	Supplier_City	Supplier_State	Supplier_Zip
8259	CBM Inc.	74 5th Avenue	Dayton	OH	45220
8261	B. R. Molds	1277 Gandolly Street	Cleveland	OH	49345
8263	Jackson Components	8233 Micklin Street	Lexington	KY	56723
8444	Bryant Corporation	4315 Mill Drive	Rochester	NY	11344

Join by Supplier_Number

Part_Number	Part_Name	Supplier_Number	Supplier_Name
137	Door latch	8259	CBM Inc.
150	Door molding	8263	Jackson Components

Project selected columns

Figure 5-8
The Three Basic Operations of a Relational DBMS
The select, join, and project operations enable data from two different tables to be combined and only selected attributes to be displayed.

Figure 5-9
Access Data
Dictionary Features
Microsoft Access has a rudimentary data dictionary capability that displays information about the size, format, and other characteristics of each field in a database. Displayed here is the information maintained in the SUPPLIER table. The small key icon to the left of Supplier_Number indicates that it is a key field.

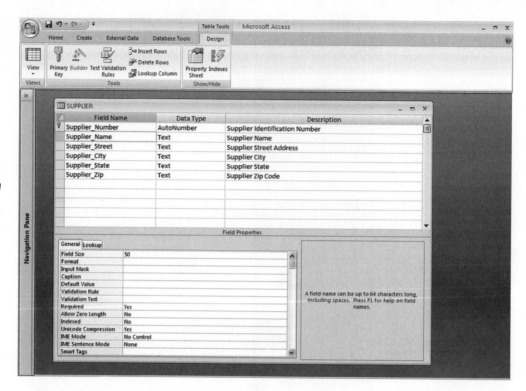

permit end users and programming specialists to extract data from the database to satisfy information requests and develop applications. The most prominent data manipulation language today is **Structured Query Language**, or **SQL**. Figure 5-10 illustrates the SQL query that would produce the new resultant table in Figure 5-8. You can find out more about how to perform SQL queries in our Learning Tracks for this chapter, which can be found in MyMISLab.

Users of DBMS for large and midrange computers, such as DB2, Oracle, or SQL Server, would employ SQL to retrieve information they needed from the database. Microsoft Access also uses SQL, but it provides its own set of user-friendly tools for querying databases and for organizing data from databases into more polished reports.

Microsoft Access has capabilities to help users create queries by identifying the tables and fields they want and the results, and then selecting the rows from the database that meet particular criteria. These actions in turn are translated into SQL commands. Figure 5-11 illustrates how the same query as the SQL query to select parts and suppliers in Figure 5-10 would be constructed using Microsoft Access.

DBMS typically include capabilities for report generation so that the data of interest can be displayed in a more structured and polished format than would be possible just by querying. Crystal Reports is a popular report generator for large corporate DBMS, although it can also be used with Microsoft Access.

Microsoft Access also has capabilities for developing desktop system applications. These include tools for creating data entry screens, reports, and developing the logic for processing transactions. These capabilities are primarily used by information systems specialists.

Figure 5-10
Example of a SQL Query
Illustrated here are the SQL statements for a query to select suppliers for parts 137 or 150. They produce a list with the same results as Figure 5-8.

```
SELECT PART.Part_Number, PART.Part_Name, SUPPLIER.Supplier_Number,
SUPPLIER.Supplier_Name
FROM PART, SUPPLIER
WHERE PART.Supplier_Number = SUPPLIER.Supplier_Number AND
Part_Number = 137 OR Part_Number = 150;
```

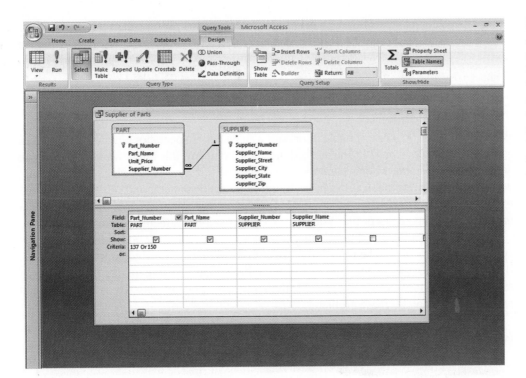

Figure 5-11
An Access Query
Illustrated here is how the query in Figure 5-10 would be constructed using Microsoft Access query-building tools. It shows the tables, fields, and selection criteria used for the query.

OBJECT-ORIENTED DATABASES

Many applications today require databases that can store and retrieve not only structured numbers and characters but also drawings, images, photographs, voice, and full-motion video. DBMS designed for organizing structured data into rows and columns are not well suited to handling graphics-based or multimedia applications. Object-oriented databases are better suited for this purpose.

An **object-oriented DBMS** stores the data and procedures that act on those data as objects that can be automatically retrieved and shared. Object-oriented database management systems (OODBMS) are becoming popular because they can be used to manage the various multimedia components or Java applets used in Web applications, which typically integrate pieces of information from a variety of sources.

Although object-oriented databases can store more complex types of information than relational DBMS, they are relatively slow compared with relational DBMS for processing large numbers of transactions. Hybrid **object-relational DBMS** systems are now available to provide capabilities of both object-oriented and relational DBMS.

5.3 Using Databases to Improve Business Performance and Decision Making

Businesses use their databases to keep track of basic transactions, such as paying suppliers, processing orders, serving customers, and paying employees. But they also need databases to provide information that will help the company run the business more efficiently, and help managers and employees make better decisions. If a company wants to know which product is the most popular or who is its most profitable customer, the answer lies in the data.

For example, by analyzing data from customer credit card purchases, Louise's Trattoria, a Los Angeles restaurant chain, learned that quality was more important than price for most of its customers, who were college-educated and liked fine wine. Acting on this information, the chain introduced vegetarian dishes, more seafood selections, and more expensive wines, raising sales by more than 10 percent.

In a large company, with large databases or large systems for separate functions, such as manufacturing, sales, and accounting, special capabilities and tools are required for analyzing vast quantities of data and for accessing data from multiple systems. These capabilities include data warehousing, data mining, and tools for accessing internal databases through the Web.

DATA WAREHOUSES

What if you wanted concise, reliable information about current operations, trends, and changes across the entire company? If you worked in a large company, this might be difficult because data are often maintained in separate systems, such as sales, manufacturing, or accounting. Some of the data you needed might be found in the sales system, and other pieces in the manufacturing system. Many of these systems are older legacy systems that use outdated data management technologies or file systems where information is difficult for users to access.

You might have to spend an inordinate amount of time locating and gathering the data you needed, or you would be forced to make your decision based on incomplete knowledge. If you wanted information about trends, you might also have trouble finding data about past events because most firms only make their current data immediately available. Data warehousing addresses these problems.

What Is a Data Warehouse?

A **data warehouse** is a database that stores current and historical data of potential interest to decision makers throughout the company. The data originate in many core operational transaction systems, such as systems for sales, customer accounts, and manufacturing, and may include data from Web site transactions. The data warehouse consolidates and standardizes information from different operational databases so that the information can be used across the enterprise for management analysis and decision making.

Figure 5-12 illustrates how a data warehouse works. The data warehouse makes the data available for anyone to access as needed, but it cannot be altered. A data warehouse system also provides a range of ad hoc and standardized query tools, analytical tools, and graphical reporting facilities. Many firms use intranet portals to make the data warehouse information widely available throughout the firm.

The Interactive Session on the Internal Revenue Service (IRS) Compliance Data Warehouse illustrates how data warehouses can serve as powerful tools to enhance decision

Figure 5-12
Components of a Data Warehouse
The data warehouse extracts current and historical data from multiple operational systems inside the organization. These data are combined with data from external sources and reorganized into a central database designed for management reporting and analysis. The information directory provides users with information about the data available in the warehouse.

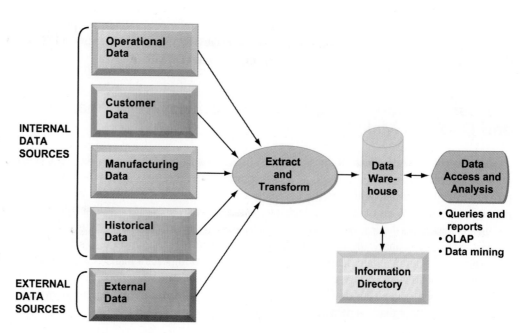

INTERACTIVE SESSION: ORGANIZATIONS   The IRS Uncovers Tax Fraud with a Data Warehouse

The Internal Revenue Service (IRS) is the U.S. government agency that collects taxes and enforces tax law. Since its creation in the 1860s, the IRS has grown by orders of magnitude along with the American population. In 2008, the IRS processed nearly 140 million individual tax returns that pulled in revenue approaching $2 trillion. It's no surprise that any inefficiency in its information systems could result in a great deal of lost revenue for the federal government. Fortunately for the IRS and perhaps unfortunately for some unscrupulous Americans, the IRS and Sybase have teamed up to implement a data warehouse, known as the Compliance Data Warehouse (CDW), that has drastically improved efficiency and increased the amount of money that the IRS collects from delinquent taxpayers.

The IRS needed a data warehouse to organize its accumulated information, which includes personal information of taxpayers and archived tax returns. The data were stored in legacy systems designed to process tax return forms efficiently and organized in many different formats, including hierarchical mainframe databases, Oracle relational databases, and non-database "flat" files. The data in the older style hierarchical databases and "flat" files were nearly impossible to query and analyze and could not easily be combined with the relational data.

The CDW enables highly flexible queries against one of the largest databases in the world, with seven years of individual and business tax return data. Each year 4 terabytes of individual and business tax data are loaded into the system. The database for the data warehouse is relational, with billions of rows and over 200 columns, all with complex links to associated schedules and other attachments. Once the data arrive they are reorganized into the relational structure using standard definitions and formats. IRS researchers can now search and analyze hundreds of millions or even billions of records at one time using a centralized source of accurate and consistent data instead of having to reconcile information from multiple inconsistent sources.

Implementation of the CDW has vastly improved the IRS's ability to manage and make use of the data it had collected. As a result, it allowed the agency to recoup many billions of dollars in tax revenue that was lost under the old system. For example, in 2006, the IRS collected $59.2 billion in additional revenue via 1.4 million audits of taxpayers questioned for underreporting taxes.

The CDW has grown in capacity from 3 terabytes at its creation in the late 1990s to approximately 150 terabytes of data today. It allows users to search through the data with a variety of tools. The CDW initially consisted of Sybase Adaptive Server IQ (relational database software for data warehouses, now called Sybase IQ), Sybase PowerBuilder (application development tools for user reporting and accessing database content), Sybase Open Client (interface between client systems and Sybase servers), Open Database Connectivity (application programming interfaces), Dual Sun Enterprise 6000 servers running Solaris 2.6 (Sun's version of UNIX), and EMC disk arrays. The most important feature of the data warehouse was that it be sufficiently large to accommodate multiple terabytes of data, but also accessible enough to allow queries of its data using many different tools. The components that the IRS selected allowed CDW to do just that.

The implementation of the CDW didn't come without challenges. One of the biggest was that the conversion of the legacy data to the new system was not a uniform process. Because the tax laws have changed many times over the years, the structure of IRS data was not consistent from year to year. This made integration of the data a complicated process. Also, the sheer amount of data that the CDW was slated to manage was far more than anything the IRS had previously handled. Convincing the organization to undergo a sweeping upgrade like a data warehouse implementation was also not easy, since government agencies are normally risk-averse and resist such changes. Data warehouses also tend to require extensive effort and money to keep up to date.

Despite those obstacles, the implementation was a resounding success. The IRS reports that it achieved a 200 to 1 return on investment ratio very shortly after the implementation of the CDW, which cost only $2 million to complete. Much of the savings from the CDW came from the speed and ease with which the system detected mistakes in tax returns. Using the data warehouse, analysts are able to determine patterns in groups of people most likely to cheat on their taxes, such as divorced couples each claiming their children on their tax forms during the same year, people abusing the earned income tax credit or small business tax shelters, or recent college graduates burdened with student loans who might be more likely to fall behind on tax payments. The data warehouse reduced the time it takes to trace mistakes in claims and analyze data from six to eight months to a only few hours.

More recently, the IRS upgraded the way it transports data to its central warehouse. In the early stages of the warehouse's development, the agency transported its data using magnetic tapes that each held just 2 gigabytes. In 2006, it replaced the tapes with 2-terabyte network-attached storage appliances, which are of comparable size to tapes, but hold data equivalent to the amount stored by 1,500 tapes. Also, the storage devices are encrypted, ensuring that the data are safe when being transported, whereas the tapes were not secure and left taxpayer information unprotected while in transit. This change is estimated to save the agency millions of dollars over a five-year period.

The number of audits performed by the IRS suggests that the CDW is working well, resulting in more audits of tax cheats and fewer audits of honest taxpay-

ers. The chances of being audited rose to 1 in 140 in 2006, up from 1 in 377 in 2000. Taxpayers who earned a million dollars or more annually had a 1-in-11 chance of being audited in 2006. In 2003, the chances were 1 in 20 for that same income bracket. But the IRS has been able to reduce the number of audits performed on innocent taxpayers, so the increased number of audits has primarily affected those who are actually at fault.

Sources: Eric Lai, "Been Audited Lately? Blame the IRS's Massive, Superfast Data Warehouse," *Computerworld*, March 22, 2008; www.irs.gov, accessed July 31, 2009; Sybase, "Internal Revenue Service," www.sybase,com, accessed March 25, 2008; and Agency Award: The IRS' Update of the Compliance Data Warehouse Makes Analysis Less Taxing," *Government Computer News*, October 8, 2007.

CASE STUDY QUESTIONS

1. Why was it so difficult for the IRS to analyze the taxpayer data it had collected?

2. What kind of challenges did the IRS encounter when implementing its Compliance Data Warehouse? What management, organization, and technology issues had to be addressed?

3. How did the CDW improve decision making and operations at the IRS? Are there benefits to taxpayers?

4. Do you think data warehouses could be useful in other areas of the federal sector? Which ones? Why or why not?

MIS IN ACTION

Go to the IRS Web site (www.irs.gov), download a 1040 tax return form, and answer the following questions:

1. What are some of the fields from that form that would most likely be included in the Compliance Data Warehouse?

2. How could IRS researchers use these data to determine whether someone was underreporting (cheating on) taxes?

making and operational efficiency. Because taxpayer data were fragmented among many different systems that had been created over the years, the IRS was unable to piece together a complete and comprehensive picture of taxpayers, nor could it easily analyze taxpayer data to identify people likely to cheat on their income tax payments. A data warehouse enabled the IRS to integrate and centralize taxpayer data to perform this task and respond more rapidly to taxpayer queries. As you read this case, try to identify the problem the IRS was facing, what alternative solutions were available to management, and the people, organization, and technology issues that had to be addressed when developing the solution.

Data Marts

Companies often build enterprise-wide data warehouses, where a central data warehouse serves the entire organization, or they create smaller, decentralized warehouses called data marts. A **data mart** is a subset of a data warehouse in which a summarized or highly focused portion of the organization's data is placed in a separate database for a specific population of users. For example, a company might develop marketing and sales data marts to deal with customer information. A data mart typically focuses on a single subject area or line of business, so it usually can be constructed more rapidly and at lower cost than an enterprise-wide data warehouse.

BUSINESS INTELLIGENCE, MULTIDIMENSIONAL DATA ANALYSIS, AND DATA MINING

Once data have been captured and organized in data warehouses and data marts, they are available for further analysis. A series of tools enables users to analyze these data to see new patterns, relationships, and insights that are useful for guiding decision making. These tools for consolidating, analyzing, and providing access to vast amounts of data to help users make better business decisions are often referred to as **business intelligence (BI)**. Principal tools for business intelligence include software for database querying and reporting, tools for multidimensional data analysis (online analytical processing), and data mining tools.

When we think of *intelligence* as applied to humans, we typically think of people's ability to combine learned knowledge with new information and change behaviors in such a way that they succeed at their task or adapt to a new situation. Likewise, business intelligence provides firms with the capability to amass information; develop knowledge about customers, competitors, and internal operations; and change decision-making behavior to achieve higher profitability and other business goals.

For instance, Harrah's Entertainment, the second-largest gambling company in its industry, continually analyzes data about its customers gathered when people play its slot machines or use Harrah's casinos and hotels. Harrah's marketing department uses this information to build a detailed gambling profile, based on a particular customer's ongoing value to the company. For instance, business intelligence lets Harrah's know the favorite gaming experience of a regular customer at one of its Midwest riverboat casinos, along with that person's preferences for room accomodations, restaurants, and entertainment. This information guides management decisions about how to cultivate the most profitable customers, encourage those customers to spend more, and attract more customers with high revenue-generating potential. Business intelligence has improved Harrah's profits so much that it has become the centerpiece of the firm's business strategy.

Figure 5-13 illustrates how business intelligence works. The firm's operational databases keep track of the transactions generated by running the business. These databases feed data to the data warehouse. Managers use business intelligence tools to find patterns and meanings in the data. Managers then act on what they have learned from analyzing the data by making more informed and intelligent business decisions.

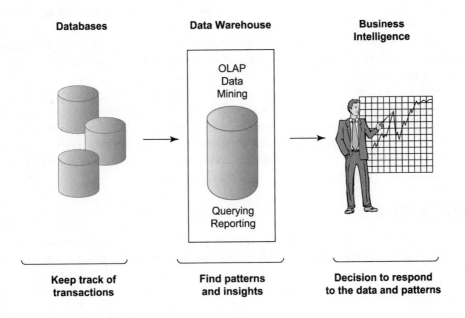

Databases   **Data Warehouse**   **Business Intelligence**

OLAP
Data
Mining

Querying
Reporting

Keep track of
transactions

Find patterns
and insights

Decision to respond
to the data and patterns

Figure 5-13
Business Intelligence
A series of analytical tools works with data stored in databases to find patterns and insights for helping managers and employees make better decisions to improve organizational performance.

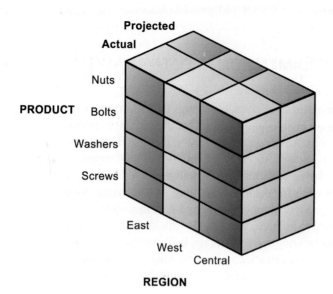

Figure 5-14
Multidimensional Data Model
The view that is showing is product versus region. If you rotate the cube 90 degrees, the face that will show is product versus actual and projected sales. If you rotate the cube 90 degrees again, you will see region versus actual and projected sales. Other views are possible.

This section will introduce you to the most important business intelligence technologies and tools. We will provide more detail about business intelligence applications in the Chapter 10 discussion of decision making.

Online Analytical Processing (OLAP)

Suppose your company sells four different products—nuts, bolts, washers, and screws—in the East, West, and Central regions. If you wanted to ask a fairly straightforward question, such as how many washers sold during the past quarter, you could easily find the answer by querying your sales database. But what if you wanted to know how many washers sold in each of your sales regions and compare actual results with projected sales?

To obtain the answer, you would need to use **online analytical processing (OLAP)**. OLAP supports multidimensional data analysis, enabling users to view the same data in different ways using multiple dimensions. Each aspect of information—product, pricing, cost, region, or time period—represents a different dimension. So, a product manager could use a multidimensional data analysis tool to learn how many washers were sold in the East in June, how that compares with the previous month and the previous June, and how it compares with the sales forecast. OLAP enables users to obtain online answers to ad hoc questions such as these in a fairly rapid amount of time, even when the data are stored in very large databases, such as sales figures for multiple years.

Figure 5-14 shows a multidimensional model that could be created to represent products, regions, actual sales, and projected sales. A matrix of actual sales can be stacked on top of a matrix of projected sales to form a cube with six faces.

If you rotate the cube 90 degrees one way, the face showing will be product versus actual and projected sales. If you rotate the cube 90 degrees again, you will see region versus actual and projected sales. If you rotate 180 degrees from the original view, you will see projected sales and product versus region. Cubes can be nested within cubes to build complex views of data. A company would use either a specialized multidimensional database or a tool that creates multidimensional views of data in relational databases.

DATA MINING

Traditional database queries answer such questions as, "How many units of product number 403 were shipped in February 2010?" OLAP, or multidimensional analysis, supports much more complex requests for information, such as, "Compare sales of product 403 relative to plan by quarter and sales region for the past two years." With OLAP and query-oriented data analysis, users need to have a good idea about the information for which they are looking.

Data mining is more discovery driven. Data mining provides insights into corporate data that cannot be obtained with OLAP by finding hidden patterns and relationships in large databases and inferring rules from them to predict future behavior. The patterns and rules are used to guide decision making and forecast the effect of those decisions. The types of information obtainable from data mining include associations, sequences, classifications, clusters, and forecasts.

- *Associations* are occurrences linked to a single event. For instance, a study of supermarket purchasing patterns might reveal that, when corn chips are purchased, a cola drink is purchased 65 percent of the time, but when there is a promotion, cola is purchased 85 percent of the time. This information helps managers make better decisions because they have learned the profitability of a promotion.

- In *sequences*, events are linked over time. We might find, for example, that if a house is purchased, a new refrigerator will be purchased within two weeks 65 percent of the time, and an oven will be bought within one month of the home purchase 45 percent of the time.

- *Classification* recognizes patterns that describe the group to which an item belongs by examining existing items that have been classified and by inferring a set of rules. For example, businesses such as credit card or telephone companies worry about the loss of steady customers. Classification helps discover the characteristics of customers who are likely to leave and can provide a model to help managers predict who those customers are so that the managers can devise special campaigns to retain such customers.

- *Clustering* works in a manner similar to classification when no groups have yet been defined. A data mining tool can discover different groupings within data, such as finding affinity groups for bank cards or partitioning a database into groups of customers based on demographics and types of personal investments.

- Although these applications involve predictions, *forecasting* uses predictions in a different way. It uses a series of existing values to forecast what other values will be. For example, forecasting might find patterns in data to help managers estimate the future value of continuous variables, such as sales figures.

These systems perform high-level analyses of patterns or trends, but they can also drill down to provide more detail when needed. There are data mining applications for all the functional areas of business, and for government and scientific work. One popular use for data mining is to provide detailed analyses of patterns in customer data for one-to-one marketing campaigns or for identifying profitable customers.

For example, Virgin Mobile Australia uses a data warehouse and data mining to increase customer loyalty and roll out new services. The company created a data warehouse that consolidated data from its enterprise system, customer relationship management system, and customer billing systems in a massive database. Data mining has enabled management to determine the demographic profile of new customers and relate it to the handsets they purchased as well as to the performance of each store and point-of-sale campaign, consumer reactions to new products and services, customer attrition rates, and the revenue generated by each customer.

Predictive analysis uses data mining techniques, historical data, and assumptions about future conditions to predict outcomes of events, such as the probability a customer will respond to an offer or purchase a specific product. For example, the U.S. division of The Body Shop International plc used predictive analysis with its database of catalog, Web, and retail store customers to identify customers who were more likely to make catalog purchases. That information helped the company build a more precise and targeted mailing list for its catalogs, improving the response rate for catalog mailings and catalog revenues.

Data mining is both a powerful and profitable tool, but it poses challenges to the protection of individual privacy. Data mining technology can combine information from many diverse sources to create a detailed "data image" about each of us—our income, our driving habits, our hobbies, our families, and our political interests. The question of whether companies should be allowed to collect such detailed information about individuals is discussed in Chapter 12.

Text Mining and Web Mining

Business intelligence tools deal primarily with data that have been structured in databases and files. However, unstructured data, most in the form of text files, are believed to account for over 80 percent of an organization's useful information. E-mail, memos, call center transcripts, survey responses, legal cases, patent descriptions, and service reports are all valuable for finding patterns and trends that will help employees make better business decisions. **Text mining** tools are now available to help businesses analyze these data. These tools are able to extract key elements from large unstructured data sets, discover patterns and relationships, and summarize the information. Businesses might turn to text mining to analyze transcripts of calls to customer service centers to identify major service and repair issues.

Air Products and Chemicals in Allentown, Pennsylvania, is using text mining to help identify documents that require special record retention procedures to comply with the Sarbanes-Oxley Act. The company has over 9 terabytes of unstructured data (not including e-mail.). SmartDiscovery software from Inxight Software classifies and organizes these data so that the company can apply business rules to a category of documents rather than to individual documents. If a document is found to deal with operations covered by Sarbanes-Oxley, the company will make sure the document meets the law's data retention requirements.

The Web is another rich source of valuable information, some of which can now be mined for patterns, trends, and insights into customer behavior. The discovery and analysis of useful patterns and information from the World Wide Web is called **Web mining**. Businesses might turn to Web mining to help them understand customer behavior, evaluate the effectiveness of a particular Web site, or quantify the success of a marketing campaign. For instance, marketers use Google Trends and Google Insights for Search services, which track the popularity of various words and phrases used in Google search queries, to learn what people are interested in and what they are interested in buying.

Web mining looks for patterns in data through content mining, structure mining, and usage mining. Web content mining is the process of extracting knowledge from the content of Web pages, which may include text, image, audio, and video data. Web structure mining examines data related to the structure of a particular Web site. For example, links pointing to a document indicate the popularity of the document, while links coming out of a document indicate the richness or perhaps the variety of topics covered in the document. Web usage mining examines user interaction data recorded by a Web server whenever requests for a Web site's resources are received. The usage data records the user's behavior when the user browses or performs transactions on the Web site and collects the data in a server log. Analyzing such data helps companies determine the value of particular customers, cross marketing strategies across products, and the effectiveness of promotional campaigns.

DATABASES AND THE WEB

Many companies are using the Web to make some of the information in their internal databases available to customers and business partners. Prospective customers might use a company's Web site to view the company's product catalog or to place an order. The company in turn might use the Web to check inventory availability for that product from its supplier. That supplier in turn may have to check with its own suppliers as well as delivery firms needed to ship the products on time.

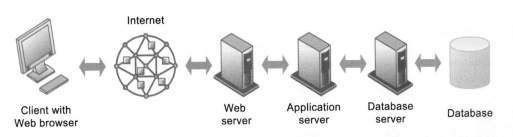

Figure 5-15
Linking Internal Databases to the Web
Users access an organization's internal database through the Web using their desktop PCs and Web browser software.

These actions involve accessing and (in the case of ordering) updating corporate databases through the Web. Suppose, for example, a customer with a Web browser wants to search an online retailer's database for pricing information. Figure 5-15 illustrates how that customer might access the retailer's internal database over the Web. The user would access the retailer's Web site over the Internet using Web browser software on his or her client PC. The user's Web browser software would request data from the organization's database, using HTML commands to communicate with the Web server.

Because many "back-end" databases cannot interpret commands written in HTML, the Web server would pass these requests for data to software that translates HTML commands into SQL so that they can be processed by the DBMS working with the database. In a client/server environment, the DBMS resides on a dedicated computer called a **database server**. The DBMS receives the SQL requests and provides the required data. The information is transferred from the organization's internal database back to the Web server for delivery in the form of a Web page to the user.

Figure 5-15 shows that the software working between the Web server and the DBMS could be on an application server running on its own dedicated computer (see Chapter 4). The application server software handles all application operations, including transaction processing and data access, between browser-based computers and a company's back-end business applications or databases. The application server takes requests from the Web server, runs the business logic to process transactions based on those requests, and provides connectivity to the organization's back-end systems or databases. Alternatively, the software for handling these operations could be a custom program or a CGI script. A CGI script is a compact program using the *Common Gateway Interface (CGI)* specification for processing data on a Web server.

There are a number of advantages to using the Web to access an organization's internal databases. First, everyone knows how to use Web browser software, and employees require much less training than if they used proprietary query tools. Second, the Web interface requires few or no changes to the internal database. Companies leverage their investments in older systems because it costs much less to add a Web interface in front of a legacy system than to redesign and rebuild the system to improve user access. For this reason, most large Fortune 500 firms all have back-end legacy databases running on mainframe computers that are linked to "front-end" software that makes the information available in the form of a Web page to users on request.

Accessing corporate databases through the Web is creating new efficiencies and opportunities, and, in some cases, it is even changing the way business is being done. ThomasNet.com provides an up-to-date directory of information from more than 700,000 suppliers of industrial products, such as chemicals, metals, plastics, rubber, and automotive equipment. Formerly called Thomas Register, the company used to send out huge paper catalogs with this information. Now, it provides this information to users online via its Web site and has become a smaller, leaner company.

Other companies have created entirely new businesses based on access to large databases through the Web. One is the social networking site MySpace, which helps users stay connected with each other or meet new people. MySpace features music, comedy, videos, and "profiles" with information supplied by 175 million users about their age, hometown, dating preferences, marital status, and interests. It maintains a massive database to house and manage all of this content.

5.4 Managing Data Resources

Setting up a database is only a start. In order to make sure that the data for your business remain accurate, reliable, and readily available to those who need it, your business will need special policies and procedures for data management.

ESTABLISHING AN INFORMATION POLICY

Every business, large and small, needs an information policy. Your firm's data are an important resource, and you don't want people doing whatever they want with them. You need to have rules on how the data are to be organized and maintained, and who is allowed to view the data or change them.

An **information policy** specifies the organization's rules for sharing, disseminating, acquiring, standardizing, classifying, and inventorying information. Information policies lay out specific procedures and accountabilities, identifying which users and organizational units can share information, where information can be distributed, and who is responsible for updating and maintaining the information. For example, a typical information policy would specify that only selected members of the payroll and human resources department would have the right to change and view sensitive employee data, such as an employee's salary or social security number, and that these departments are responsible for making sure that such employee data are accurate.

If you are in a small business, the information policy would be established and implemented by the owners or managers. In a large organization, managing and planning for information as a corporate resource often requires a formal data administration function. **Data administration** is responsible for the specific policies and procedures through which data can be managed as an organizational resource. These responsibilities include developing information policy, planning for data, overseeing logical database design and data dictionary development, and monitoring how information systems specialists and end-user groups use data.

A large organization will also have a database design and management group within the corporate information systems division that is responsible for defining and organizing the structure and content of the database, and maintaining the database. In close cooperation with users, the design group establishes the physical database, the logical relations among elements, and the access rules and security procedures. The functions it performs are called **database administration**.

ENSURING DATA QUALITY

A well-designed database and information policy will go a long way toward ensuring that the business has the information it needs. However, additional steps must be taken to ensure that the data in organizational databases are accurate and remain reliable.

What would happen if a customer's telephone number or account balance were incorrect? What would be the impact if the database had the wrong price for the product you sold? Data that are inaccurate, untimely, or inconsistent with other sources of information create serious operational and financial problems for businesses. When faulty data go unnoticed, they often lead to incorrect decisions, product recalls, and even financial losses.

Gartner Group consultants reported that more than 25 percent of the critical data in large Fortune 1000 companies' databases is inaccurate or incomplete, including bad product codes and product descriptions, faulty inventory descriptions, erroneous financial data, incorrect supplier information, and incorrect employee data. A Sirius Decisions study on "The Impact of Bad Data on Demand Creation" found that 10 to 25 percent of customer and prospect records contain critical data errors. Correcting these errors at their source and following best practices for promoting data quality increased the productivity of the sales process and generated a 66 percent increase in revenue (Lager, 2009; Gage and McCormick, 2005).

Some of these data quality problems are caused by redundant and inconsistent data produced by multiple systems feeding a data warehouse. For example, the sales ordering system and the inventory management system might both maintain data on the organization's products. However, the sales ordering system might use the term *Item Number* and the inventory system might call the same attribute *Product Number*. The sales, inventory, or manufacturing systems of a clothing retailer might use different codes to represent values for an attribute. One system might represent clothing size as "extra large," whereas the other system might use the code "XL" for the same purpose. During the design process for the warehouse database, data describing entities, such as a customer, product, or order, should be named and defined consistently for all business areas using the database.

If a database is properly designed and enterprise-wide data standards established, duplicate or inconsistent data elements should be minimal. Most data quality problems, however, such as misspelled names, transposed numbers, or incorrect or missing codes, stem from errors during data input. The incidence of such errors is rising as companies move their businesses to the Web and allow customers and suppliers to enter data into their Web sites that directly update internal systems.

Think of all the times you have received several pieces of the same direct mail advertising on the same day. This is very likely the result of having your name maintained multiple times in a database. Your name may have been misspelled or you used your middle initial on one occasion and not on another or the information was initially entered onto a paper form and not scanned properly into the system. Because of these inconsistencies, the database would treat you as different people! We often receive redundant mail addressed to Laudon, Lavdon, Lauden, or Landon.

Before a new database is in place, organizations need to identify and correct their faulty data and establish better routines for editing data once their database is in operation. Analysis of data quality often begins with a **data quality audit**, which is a structured survey of the accuracy and level of completeness of the data in an information system. Data quality audits can be performed by surveying entire data files, surveying samples from data files, or surveying end users for their perceptions of data quality.

Data cleansing, also known as *data scrubbing*, consists of activities for detecting and correcting data in a database that are incorrect, incomplete, improperly formatted, or redundant. Data cleansing not only corrects data but also enforces consistency among different sets of data that originated in separate information systems. Specialized data-cleansing software is available to automatically survey data files, correct errors in the data, and integrate the data in a consistent company-wide format.

Data quality problems are not just business problems. They also pose serious problems for individuals, affecting their financial condition and even their jobs. The Interactive Session on People describes some of these impacts, as it details the data quality problems in companies that collect and report consumer credit data. As you read this case, look for the people, organization, and technology factors behind this problem, and whether existing solutions are adequate.

INTERACTIVE SESSION: PEOPLE — Credit Bureau Errors—Big People Problems

You've found the car of your dreams, you have a good job and enough money for a down payment. All you need is an auto loan for $14,000. You have a few credit card bills, which you diligently pay off each month. But when you apply for the loan you're turned down. When you ask why, you're told you have an overdue loan from a bank you've never heard of. You've just become one of the millions of people who have been victimized by inaccurate or outdated data in credit bureaus' information systems.

Most data on U.S. consumers' credit histories are collected and maintained by three national credit reporting agencies: Experian, Equifax, and TransUnion. These organizations collect data from various sources to create a detailed dossier of an individual's borrowing and bill paying habits. This information helps lenders assess a person's credit worthiness, the ability to pay back a loan, and can affect the interest rate and other terms of a loan, including whether a loan will be granted in the first place. It can even affect the chances of finding a job, since employers increasingly check credit reports before hiring new employees.

U.S. credit bureaus collect personal information and financial data from a variety of sources, including creditors, lenders, utilities, debt collection agencies, and the courts. These data are aggregated and stored in large databases maintained by the credit bureaus. The credit bureaus then sell this information to other companies to use for credit assessment.

The credit bureaus claim they know which credit cards are in each consumer's wallet, how much is due on the mortgage, and whether the electric bill is paid on time. But if the wrong information gets into their systems, whether through identity theft or errors transmitted by creditors, watch out! Untangling the mess can be almost impossible.

The bureaus understand the importance of providing accurate information to both lenders and consumers. But they also recognize that their own systems are responsible for many credit-report errors. Some mistakes occur because of the procedures for matching loans to individual credit reports.

The sheer volume of information being transmitted from creditors to credit bureaus increases the likelihood of mistakes. Experian, for example, updates 30 million credit reports each day and roughly 2 billion credit reports each month. It matches the identifying personal information in a credit application or credit account with the identifying personal information in a consumer credit file.

Identifying personal information includes items such as first name, last name and middle initial, full current address and zip code, full previous address and zip code, and social security number. The new credit information goes into the consumer credit file that it best matches.

The credit bureaus rarely obtain all the information matching in all the fields, so they have to determine how much variation to allow and still call it a match. Imperfect data lead to imperfect matches. A consumer might provide incomplete or inaccurate information on a credit application. A creditor might submit incomplete or inaccurate information to the credit bureaus. If the wrong person matches better than anyone else, the data could unfortunately go into the wrong account.

Perhaps the consumer didn't write clearly on the account application. Name variations on different credit accounts can also result in less- than-perfect matches. Take the name Edward Jeffrey Johnson. One account may say Edward Johnson. Another may say Ed Johnson. Another might say Edward J. Johnson. Suppose the last two digits of Edward's social security number get transposed—more chance for mismatches.

If the name or social security number on another person's account partially matches the data in your file, the computer might attach that person's data to your record. Your record might likewise be corrupted if workers in companies supplying tax and bankruptcy data from court and government records accidentally transpose a digit or misread a document.

The credit bureaus claim it is impossible for them to monitor the accuracy of the 3.5 billion pieces of credit account information they receive each month. They must continually contend with bogus claims from consumers who falsify lender information or use shady credit-repair companies that challenge all the negative information on a credit report regardless of its validity. To separate the good from the bad, the credit bureaus use an automated e-OSCAR (Electronic Online Solution for Complete and Accurate Reporting) system to forward consumer disputes to lenders for verification.

If your credit report showed an error, the bureaus usually do not contact the lender directly to correct the information. To save money, the bureaus send the consumer's protest and evidence to a data processing center run by a third-party contractor. These contractors rapidly summarize every complaint with a short comment and 2-digit code from a menu of 26 options. For example, the code A3 designates "belongs to another individual with a similar name." These summaries are often too brief to include the background banks need to understand a complaint.

Although this system fixes large numbers of errors (data are updated or corrected for 72 percent of disputes), consumers have few options if the system fails. Consumers who file a second dispute without providing new information might have their dispute dismissed as "frivolous." If the consumer tries to contact the lender that made the error on their own, banks have no obligation to investigate the dispute—unless it's sent by a credit bureau.

Sources: Anne Kadet, "Why Credit Bureaus Can't Get It Right," *Smart Money*, March 2009; "Credit Report Fix a Headache," *Atlanta Journal-Constitution*, June 14, 2009; and Lucy Lazarony, "Your Name Can Mess Up Your Credit Report, Bankrate.com, accessed July 1, 2009.

CASE STUDY QUESTIONS

1. Assess the business impact of credit bureaus' data quality problems (for the credit bureaus, for lenders, for individuals).

2. Are any ethical issues raised by credit bureaus' data quality problems? Explain your answer.

3. Analyze the people, organization, and technology factors responsible for credit bureaus' data quality problems.

4. What can be done to solve these problems?

MIS IN ACTION

Go to the Experian Web site (www.experian.com) and explore the site, with special attention to its services for businesses and small businesses. Then answer the following questions:

1. List and describe five services for businesses and explain how each uses consumer data. Describe the kinds of businesses that would use these services.

2. Explain how each of these services is affected by inaccurate consumer data.

5.5 Hands-On MIS Projects

The projects in this section give you hands-on experience in analyzing data quality problems, establishing company-wide data standards, creating a database for inventory management, and using the Web to search online databases for overseas business resources.

MANAGEMENT DECISION PROBLEMS

1. Emerson Process Management, a global supplier of measurement, analytical, and monitoring instruments and services based in Austin, Texas, had a new data warehouse designed for analyzing customer activity to improve service and marketing. However, the data warehouse was full of inaccurate and redundant data. The data in the warehouse came from numerous transaction processing systems in Europe, Asia, and other locations around the world. The team that designed the warehouse had assumed that sales groups in all these areas would enter customer names and addresses the same way, regardless of their location. In fact, cultural differences combined with complications from absorbing companies that Emerson had acquired led to multiple ways of entering quote, billing, shipping, and other data. Assess the potential business impact of these data quality problems. What decisions have to be made and steps taken to reach a solution?

2. Your industrial supply company wants to create a data warehouse where management can obtain a single corporate-wide view of critical sales information to identify best-selling products in specific geographic areas, key customers, and sales trends. Your sales and product information are stored in several different systems: a divisional sales system

running on a UNIX server and a corporate sales system running on an IBM mainframe. You would like to create a single standard format that consolidates these data from both systems. The following format has been proposed.

PRODUCT_ID	PRODUCT_DESCRIPTION	COST_PER_UNIT	UNITS_SOLD	SALES_REGION	DIVISION	CUSTOMER_ID

The following are sample files from the two systems that would supply the data for the data warehouse:

CORPORATE SALES SYSTEM

PRODUCT_ID	PRODUCT_DESCRIPTION	UNIT_COST	UNITS_SOLD	SALES_TERRITORY	DIVISION
60231	Bearing, 4"	5.28	900,245	Northeast	Parts
85773	SS assembly unit	12.45	992,111	Midwest	Parts

MECHANICAL PARTS DIVISION SALES SYSTEM

PROD_NO	PRODUCT_DESCRIPTION	COST_PER_UNIT	UNITS_SOLD	SALES_REGION	CUSTOMER_ID
60231	4" Steel bearing	5.28	900,245	N.E.	Anderson
85773	SS assembly unit	12.45	992,111	M.W.	Kelly Industries

- What business problems are created by not having these data in a single standard format?
- How easy would it be to create a database with a single standard format that could store the data from both systems? Identify the problems that would have to be addressed.
- Should the problems be solved by database specialists or general business managers? Explain.
- Who should have the authority to finalize a single company-wide format for this information in the data warehouse?

ACHIEVING OPERATIONAL EXCELLENCE: BUILDING A RELATIONAL DATABASE FOR INVENTORY MANAGEMENT

Software skills: Database design, querying, and reporting
Business skills: Inventory management

In this exercise, you will use database software to design a database for managing inventory for a small business. Sylvester's Bike Shop, located in San Francisco, California, sells road, mountain, hybrid, leisure, and children's bicycles. Currently, Sylvester's purchases bikes from three suppliers, but plans to add new suppliers in the near future. This rapidly growing business needs a database system to manage this information.

Initially, the database should house information about suppliers and products. The database will contain two tables: a supplier table and a product table. The reorder level refers to the number of items in inventory that triggers a decision to order more items to prevent a stockout. (In other words, if the number of units of a particular item in inventory falls below the reorder level, the item should be reordered.) The user should be able to perform several queries and produce several managerial reports based on the data contained in the two tables.

Using the information found in the tables in MyMISLab, build a simple relational database for Sylvester's. Once you have built the database, perform the following activities.

- Prepare a report that identifies the five most expensive bicycles. The report should list the bicycles in descending order from most expensive to least expensive, the quantity on hand for each, and the markup percentage for each.

- Prepare a report that lists each supplier, its products, the quantities on hand, and associated reorder levels. The report should be sorted alphabetically by supplier. Within each supplier category, the products should be sorted alphabetically.
- Prepare a report listing only the bicycles that are low in stock and need to be reordered. The report should provide supplier information for the items identified.
- Write a brief description of how the database could be enhanced to further improve management of the business. What tables or fields should be added? What additional reports would be useful?

IMPROVING DECISION MAKING: SEARCHING ONLINE DATABASES FOR OVERSEAS BUSINESS RESOURCES

Software skills: Online databases
Business skills: Researching services for overseas operations

Internet users have access to many thousands of Web-enabled databases with information on services and products in faraway locations. This project develops skills in searching these online databases.

Your company is located in Greensboro, North Carolina, and manufactures office furniture of various types. You have recently acquired several new customers in Australia, and a study you commissioned indicates that, with a presence there, you could greatly increase your sales. Moreover, your study indicates that you could do even better if you actually manufactured many of your products locally (in Australia). First, you need to set up an office in Melbourne to establish a presence, and then you need to begin importing from the United States. You then can plan to start producing locally.

You will soon be traveling to the area to make plans to actually set up an office, and you want to meet with organizations that can help you with your operation. You will need to engage people or organizations that offer many services necessary for you to open your office, including lawyers, accountants, import-export experts, telecommunications equipment and support, and even trainers who can help you to prepare your future employees to work for you.

Start by searching for U.S. Department of Commerce advice on doing business in Australia. Then try the following online databases to locate companies that you would like to meet with during your upcoming trip: Australian Business Register (abr.gov.au), Australia Trade Now (australiatradenow.com), and the Nationwide Business Directory of Australia (www.nationwide.com.au). If necessary, you could also try search engines such as Yahoo! and Google.

- List the companies you would contact on your trip to determine whether they can help you with these and any other functions you think are vital to establishing your office.
- Rate the databases you used for accuracy of name, completeness, ease of use, and general helpfulness.
- What does this exercise tell you about the design of databases?

LEARNING TRACKS

The following Learning Tracks provide content relevant to topics covered in this chapter:

1. Database Design, Normalization, and Entity-Relationship Diagramming
2. Introduction to SQL
3. Hierarchical and Network Data Models

Review Summary

1 **How does a relational database organize data, and how does it differ from an object-oriented database?** The relational database is the primary method for organizing and maintaining data today in information system. It organizes data in two-dimensional tables with rows and columns called relations. Each table contains data about an entity and its attributes. Each row represents a record and each column represents an attribute or field. Each table also contains a key field to uniquely identify each record for retrieval or manipulation. An entity-relationship diagram graphically depicts the relationship between entities (tables) in a relational database. The process of breaking down complex groupings of data and streamlining them to minimize redundancy and awkward many-to-many relationships is called normalization. An object-oriented database management system (DBMS) stores data and procedures that act on the data as objects, and it can handle multimedia as well as characters and numbers.

2 **What are the principles of a database management system?** A DBMS consists of software that permits centralization of data and data management so that businesses have a single consistent source for all their data needs. A single database services multiple applications. The DBMS separates the logical and physical views of data so that the user does not have to be concerned with the data's physical location. The principal capabilities of a DBMS includes a data definition capability, a data dictionary capability, and a data manipulation language.

3 **What are the principal tools and technologies for accessing information from databases to improve business performance and decision making?** A data warehouse consolidates current and historical data from many different operational systems in a central database designed for reporting and analysis. Data warehouses support multidimensional data analysis, also known as online analytical processing (OLAP). OLAP represents relationships among data as a multidimensional structure, which can be visualized as cubes of data and cubes within cubes of data. Data mining analyzes large pools of data, including the contents of data warehouses, to find patterns and rules that can be used to predict future behavior and guide decision making. Text mining tools help businesses analyze large unstructured data sets consisting of text. Web mining tools focus on analyzing useful patterns and information fromo the World Wide Web, examining the structure of Web sites, activities of Web site users, and the contents of Web pages. Conventional databases can be linked to the Web or a Web interface to facilitate user access to an organization's internal data.

4 **What is the role of information policy and data administration in the management of organizational data resources?** Developing a database environment requires policies and procedures for managing organizational data as well as a good data model and database technology. A formal information policy governs the maintenance, distribution, and use of information in the organization. In large corporations, a formal data administration function is responsible for information policy, as well as for data planning, data dictionary development, and monitoring data usage in the firm.

5 **Why is data quality assurance so important for a business?** Data that are inaccurate, incomplete, or inconsistent create serious operational and financial problems for businesses if they lead to inaccurate decisions about the actions that should be taken by the firm. Assuring data quality involves using enterprise-wide data standards, databases designed to minimize inconsistent and redundant data, data quality audits, and data cleansing software.

Key Terms

Attributes, 160	Database administration, 178	Object-relational DBMS, 169
Business intelligence (BI), 173	Database management system (DBMS), 165	Online analytical processing (OLAP), 174
Data administration, 178	Database server, 177	Predictive analysis, 175
Data cleansing, 179	Entity, 160	Primary key, 160
Data dictionary, 166	Entity-relationship diagram, 162	Records, 160
Data manipulation language, 166	Field, 160	Referential integrity, 163
Data mart, 172	Foreign key, 162	Relational database, 160
Data mining, 175	Information policy, 178	Structured Query Language (SQL), 168
Data quality audit, 179	Key field, 160	Text mining, 176
Data warehouse, 170	Normalization, 163	Tuples, 160
Database, 159	Object-oriented DBMS, 169	Web mining, 176

Review Questions

1. How does a relational database organize data, and how does it differ from an object-oriented database?
- Define and explain the significance of entities, attributes, and key fields.
- Define a relational database and explain how it organizes and stores information.
- Explain the role of entity-relationship diagrams and normalization in database design.
- Define an object-oriented database and explain how it differs from a relational database.

2. What are the principles of a database management system?
- Define a database management system (DBMS), describe how it works, and explain how it benefit organizations.
- Define and compare the logical and a physical view of data.
- Define and describe the three operations of a relational database management system.
- Name and describe the three major capabilities of a DBMS.

3. What are the principal tools and technologies for accessing information from databases to improve business performance and decision making?
- Define a data warehouse and describe how it works.
- Define business intelligence and explain how it is related to database technology.
- Describe the capabilities of online analytical processing (OLAP).
- Define data mining, describe what types of information can be obtained from it, and explain how does it differs from OLAP.
- Explain how text mining and Web mining differ from conventional data mining.
- Explain how users can access information from a company's internal databases through the Web.

4. What is the role of information policy and data administration in the management of organizational data resources?
- Define information policy and data administration and explain how they help organizations manage their data.

5. Why is data quality assurance so important for a business?
- List and describe the most common data quality problems.
- List and describe the most important tools and techniques for assuring data quality.

Discussion Questions

1. It has been said that you do not need database management software to create a database environment. Discuss.

2. To what extent should end users be involved in the selection of a database management system and database design?

Video Cases

Video Cases and Instructional Videos illustrating some of the concepts in this chapter are available. Contact your instructor to access these videos.

Collaboration and Teamwork

Identifying Entities and Attributes in an Online Database

With a group of two or three of your fellow students, select an online database to explore, such as AOL Music or the Internet Movie Database. Explore these Web sites to see what information they provide. Then list the entities and attributes that they must keep track of in their databases. Diagram the relationship between the entities you have identified. If possible, use Google Sites to post links to Web pages, team communication announcements, and work assignments; to brainstorm; and to work collaboratively on project documents. Try to use Google Docs to develop a presentation of your findings for the class.

BUSINESS PROBLEM-SOLVING CASE

Trouble with the Terrorist Watch-List Database

In the aftermath of the 9-11 attacks, both critics and defenders of the information systems employed by the U.S. intelligence community united to help analyze what went wrong and how to prevent future terrorist incidents. The FBI's Terrorist Screening Center, or TSC, was established to organize and standardize information about suspected terrorists from multiple government agencies into a single list to enhance communication between agencies. A database of suspected terrorists known as the terrorist watch list was created. Multiple agencies had been maintaining separate lists and these agencies lacked a consistent process to share relevant information.

Records in the TSC database contain sensitive but unclassified information on terrorist identities, such as name and date of birth, that can be shared with other screening agencies. Classified information about the people in the watch list is maintained in other law enforcement and intelligence agency databases. Records for the watch list database are provided by two sources: The National Counterterrorism Center (NCTC) managed by the Office of the Director of National Intelligence provides identifying information on individuals with ties to international terrorism. The FBI provides identifying information on individuals with ties to purely domestic terrorism.

These agencies collect and maintain terrorist information and nominate individuals for inclusion in the TSC's consolidated watch list. They are required to follow strict procedures established by the head of the agency concerned and approved by the U.S. Attorney General. TSC staff must review each record submitted before it is added to the database. An individual will remain on the watch list until the respective department or agency that nominated that person to the list determines that the person should be removed from the list and deleted from the database.

The TSC watch list database is updated daily with new nominations, modifications to existing records, and deletions. Since its creation, the list has grown to 400,000 people, recorded as 1.1 million names and aliases, and is continuing to grow at a rate of 200,000 records each year. Information on the list is distributed to a wide range of government agency systems for use in efforts to deter or detect the movements of known or suspected terrorists.

Recipient agencies include the FBI, CIA, National Security Agency (NSA), Transportation Security Administration (TSA), Department of Homeland Security, State Department, Customs and Border Protection, Secret Service, U.S. Marshal Service, and the White House. Airlines use data supplied by the TSA system in their NoFly and Selectee lists for prescreening passengers, while the U.S. Customs and Border Protection system uses the watch list data to help screen travelers entering the United States. The State Department system screens applicants for visas to enter the United States and U.S. residents applying for passports, while state and local law enforcement agencies use the FBI system to help with arrests, detentions, and other criminal justice activities. Each of these agencies receives the subset of data in the watch list that pertains to its specific mission.

When an individual makes an airline reservation, arrives at a U.S. port of entry, applies for a U.S. visa, or is stopped by state or local police within the United States, the frontline screening agency or airline conducts a name-based search of the individual against the records from the terrorist watch list database. When the computerized name-matching system generates a "hit" (a potential name match) against a watch list record, the airline or agency will review each potential match. Matches that are clearly positive or exact matches that are inconclusive (uncertain or difficult to verify) are referred to the applicable screening agency's intelligence or operations center and to the TSC for closer examination. In turn, TSC checks its databases and other sources, including classified databases maintained by the NCTC and FBI to confirm whether the individual is a positive, negative, or inconclusive match to the watch list record. TSC creates a daily report summarizing all positive matches to the watch list and distributes them to numerous federal agencies.

While unification of various terrorism watch lists has been a positive step combating terrorists, the project has been a slow and painstaking one, requiring the integration of at least 12 different databases. Two years after the process of integration took place, 10 of the 12 databases had been processed. The remaining 2 databases (the U.S. Immigration and Customs Enforcement's Automatic Biometric Identification System and the FBI's Integrated Fingerprint Identification System) are both fingerprint databases. There is still more work to be done to optimize the usefulness of the terrorist watch list.

Reports from both the Government Accountability Office and the Office of the Inspector General assert that the list contains inaccuracies and that government departmental policies for nomination and removal from the lists are not uniform. There has also been public out-cry resulting from the size of the list and well-publicized incidents of obvious non-terrorists finding that they are included on the list.

Information about the process for inclusion on the list must necessarily be carefully protected if the list is to be effective against terrorists. On the other hand, for inno-cent people who are unnecessarily inconvenienced, the inability to ascertain how they came to be on the list is upsetting. The specific criteria for inclusion on the list are not public knowledge. We do know, however, that government agencies populate their watch lists by per-forming wide sweeps of information gathered on travel-ers, using many misspellings and alternate variations of the names of suspected terrorists. This often leads to the inclusion of people that do not belong on watch lists, known as "false positives." It also results in some people being listed multiple times under different spellings of their names.

While these selection criteria may be effective for tracking as many potential terrorists as possible, they also lead to many more erroneous entries on the list than if the process required more finely tuned information to add new entries. Notable examples of "false positives" include U.S. Marine Daniel Brown, who was stopped at the airport for additional screening after an 8-month tour in Iraq; senator Ted Kennedy, who had been repeatedly delayed in the past because his name resembled an alias once used by a suspected terrorist; and John Anderson, a 6-year-old boy who was stopped at an airport for addi-tional investigation despite his young age. Like Kennedy, Anderson may have been added because his name is the same or similar to a different suspected ter-rorist.

These incidents call attention to the quality and accu-racy of the data in the TSC consolidated terrorist watch list. In June 2005, a report by the Department of Justice's Office of the Inspector General found inconsis-tent record counts, duplicate records, and records that lacked data fields or had unclear sources for their data. Although TSC subsequently enhanced its efforts to iden-tify and correct incomplete or inaccurate watch list records, the Inspector General noted in September 2007 that TSC management of the watch list still showed some weaknesses.

Given the option between a list that tracks every potential terrorist at the cost of unnecessarily tracking some innocents, and a list that fails to track many terror-ists in an effort to avoid tracking innocents, many would choose the list that tracked every terrorist despite the drawbacks. But to make matters worse for those already inconvenienced by wrongful inclusion on the list, there is currently no simple and quick redress process for innocents that hope to remove themselves from it.

The number of requests for removal from the watch list continues to mount, with over 24,000 requests recorded (about 2,000 each month) and only 54 percent of them resolved. The average time to process a request in 2008 was 40 days, which is not fast enough to keep pace with the number of requests for removal coming in. As a result, law-abiding travelers that inexplicably find themselves on the watch list are left with no easy way to remove themselves from it.

In February 2007, the Department of Homeland Security instituted its Traveler Redress Inquiry Program (TRIP) to help people that have been erroneously added to terrorist watch lists remove themselves and avoid extra screening and questioning. John Anderson's mother claimed that, despite her best efforts, she was unable to remove her son from the watch lists. Senator Kennedy reportedly was only able to remove himself from the list by personally bringing up the matter to Tom Ridge, then the Director of the Department of Homeland Security.

Security officials say that mistakes such as the one that led to Anderson and Kennedy's inclusion on no-fly and consolidated watch lists occur due to the matching of imperfect data in airline reservation systems with imper-fect data on the watch lists. Many airlines don't include gender, middle name, or date of birth in their reserva-tions records, which increases the likelihood of false matches.

One way to improve screening and help reduce the number of people erroneously marked for additional investigation would be to use a more sophisticated sys-tem involving more personal data about individuals on the list. The TSA is developing just such a system, called "Secure Flight," but it has been continually delayed due to privacy concerns regarding the sensitivity and safety of the data it would collect. Other similar surveillance programs and watch lists, such as the NSA's attempts to gather information about suspected terrorists, have drawn criticism for potential privacy violations.

Additionally, the watch list has drawn criticism because of its potential to promote racial profiling and discrimination. Some allege that they were included by virtue of their race and ethnic descent, such as David Fathi, an attorney for the ACLU of Iranian descent, and Asif Iqbal, a U.S. citizen of Pakistani descent with the same name as a Guantanamo detainee. Outspoken critics of U.S. foreign policy, such as some elected officials and university professors, have also found themselves on the list.

A report released in early May 2009 by Department of Justice Inspector General Glenn A. Fine found that the FBI had incorrectly kept nearly 24,000 people on its own watch list that supplies data to the terrorist watch list on the basis of outdated or irrelevant information. Examining nearly 69,000 referrals to the FBI list, the report found that 35 percent of those people remained on the list despite inadequate justification. Even more worrisome, the list did not contain the names of people who should have been listed because of their terrorist ties. FBI officials claim that the bureau has made improvements, including better training, faster processing of referrals, and requiring field office supervisors to review watch-list nominations for accuracy and completeness.

The sooner these improvements are made, the better. In early 2008, it was revealed that 20 known terrorists were not correctly listed on the consolidated watch list. (Whether these individuals were able to enter the U.S. as a result is unclear.) And in June 2009, the TSA announced that at least six men suspected or convicted of crimes threatening national security had retained their federal aviation licenses, including a Libyan sentenced to 27 years in prison by a Scottish court for the 1988 bombing of Pam Am Flight 103 over Scotland.

Sources: Eric Lichtblau, "Justice Dept. Finds Flaws in F.B.I. Terror List," *The New York Times*, May 7, 2009; Spencer S. Hsu, "GAO Cites Gun Sales to Those on Watch List," *The Washington Post*, June 23, 2009; Matthew L. Wald, "6 Considered Threats Kept Licenses for Aviation," *The New York Times*, June 26, 2009; Bob Egelko, "Watch-list Name Confusion Causes Hardship," *San Francisco Chronicle*, March 20, 2008; Siobhan Gorman, "NSA's Domestic Spying Grows as Agency Sweeps Up Data," *The Wall Street Journal*, March 10, 2008; Ellen Nakashima, "Reports Cite Lack of Uniform Policy for Terrorist Watch List," *The Washington Post*, March 18, 2008; Scott McCartney, "When Your Name is Mud at the Airport," *The Wall Street Journal*, January 29, 2008; Audrey Hudson, "Airport Watch List Now Reviewed Often," *The Washington Times*, April 11, 2008; Mimi Hall, "Terror Watch List Swells to More Than 755,000," *USA Today*, October 23, 2007; and "Justice Department Report Tells of Flaws in Terrorist Watch List," CNN.com, September 7, 2007.

Case Study Questions

1. What concepts in this chapter are illustrated in this case?

2. Why was the consolidated terror watch list created? What are the benefits of the list?

3. Describe some of the weaknesses of the watch list. What people, organization, and technology factors are responsible for these weaknesses?

4. If you were responsible for the management of the TSC watch list database, what steps would you take to correct some of these weaknesses?

5. Do you believe that the terrorist watch list represents a significant threat to individuals' privacy or Constitutional rights? Why or why not?

Telecommunications, the Internet, and Wireless Technology

CHAPTER 6

STUDENT LEARNING OBJECTIVES

After completing this chapter, you will be able to answer the following questions:

1. What are the principal components of telecommunications networks and key networking technologies?

2. What are the main telecommunications transmission media and types of networks?

3. How do the Internet and Internet technology work, and how do they support communication and e-business?

4. What are the principal technologies and standards for wireless networking, communication, and Internet access?

5. Why are radio frequency identification (RFID) and wireless sensor networks valuable for business?

Chapter Outline

LOS ANGELES INTERNATIONAL AIRPORT SOARS WITH NEW NETWORKING TECHNOLOGY

What does it take today to be a state-of-the art international airport? Los Angeles World Airports (LAWA) is trying to answer this question. LAWA is the department of the City of Los Angeles, California, that owns and operates Los Angeles International Airport (LAX), the Van Nuys Airport, the LA/Ontario International Airport, and the LA/Palmdale Regional Airport. These airports' physical facilities and IT infrastructure were out of date. The new generation of giant aircraft with very large wingspans didn't fit most of LAWA's existing airport gates. What's more, LAWA needed more powerful computing and networking capabilities to make its operations more efficient and convenient for travelers.

To recapture its place among first-rate international airports, LAWA began upgrading both physical facilities and IT infrastructure at Los Angeles International Airport's Tom Bradley Terminal in late 2006. All projects will be completed by 2013. The terminal will

almost double in size, and the entire airport will have a new Ethernet local-area network (LAN). LAX's network is linked to LAWA's other airports.

LAWA management wants to make its network available to the 70 airlines that use its airports to generate additional revenue and defray costs. The airlines will be billed for these technologies on a usage basis. Larger airlines will probably continue to use their own telecommunications lines and networks, but many smaller airlines will opt for using the LAWA network to avoid the expense of purchasing and maintaining their own technology.

LAWA is relying increasingly on technology for virtually everything, and a wireless network is critical. The airport's wireless Wi-Fi network will expand throughout the entire airport. For a fee, passengers are able to access the Internet from any public areas, from curbside to the nose of the aircraft. When planes arrive at the gate, they can use wireless connections to order parts and relay instructions to maintenance staff. Wireless handheld devices are used for monitoring and checking bags. Wireless devices called COWs (common use on wheels) can be wheeled directly to passengers standing in long lines to help them obtain tickets and check in. The COWs tie into the airport's common-use systems and have a flight information display screen on top. The flexibility provided by wireless technology made it possible reorganize work activities to increase efficiency and customer service.

In May 2009, LAWA launched a new intranet site for its approximately 4,000 employees. The intranet provides staff members with the latest news about the airports and airport/-airline business, along with chat rooms, blogs, and wikis to share knowledge and expertise. The majority of LAWA employees have access to the intranet from their desktop computers. Employees who don't have a desktop computer were recently supplied with a handheld version of the intranet. LAWA is considering opening some portions of the intranet to city officials, councilmen, and perhaps local community groups who could benefit from the information.

Sources: Eileen Feretic, "The Future of Flight," *Baseline*, June 2009; "CIO Profiles: Dom Nessi: Deputy Executive Director and CIO, Los Angeles World Airports, *Information Week*, May 4. 2009; and www.airport-la.com, accessed July 12, 2009.

Los Angeles World Airports illustrates some of the powerful new capabilities and opportunities provided by contemporary networking technology. LAWA added a powerful local-area network to connect devices and aircraft within its airports and wireless Wi-Fi technology to support wireless devices and Internet access. These technologies improved customer service and increased efficiency for both airports and airlines.

The chapter-opening diagram calls attention to important points raised by this case and this chapter. LAWA has to compete with other airports as an international destination or stopping point for many airlines. If it didn't upgrade to a state-of-the-art physical or technology infrastructure, it would lose business from the growing number of international flights using giant airplanes. Its image as an airport for international flights would suffer.

Management decided to expand the airports and implement new networking technology, including a powerful local-area network for the airport, Wi-Fi wireless networking, wireless devices for check-in and Internet access, and a new intranet. These improvements made the airport easier to use for both passengers and airlines, saving time and operating costs. LAWA had to redesign its ticketing, check-in, and other processes to take advantage of the new technology.

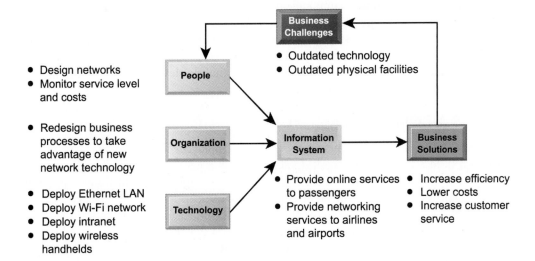

- Design networks
- Monitor service level and costs

- Redesign business processes to take advantage of new network technology

- Deploy Ethernet LAN
- Deploy Wi-Fi network
- Deploy intranet
- Deploy wireless handhelds

People

Organization

Technology

Business Challenges
- Outdated technology
- Outdated physical facilities

Information System

Business Solutions

- Provide online services to passengers
- Provide networking services to airlines and airports

- Increase efficiency
- Lower costs
- Increase customer service

6.1 Telecommunications and Networking in Today's Business World

If you run or work in a business, you can't do without networks. You need to communicate rapidly with your customers, suppliers, and employees. Until about 1990, you used the postal system or telephone system with voice or fax for business communication. Today, however, you and your employees use computers and e-mail, the Internet, cell phones, and mobile computers connected to wireless networks for this purpose. Networking and the Internet are now nearly synonymous with doing business.

NETWORKING AND COMMUNICATION TRENDS

Firms in the past used two fundamentally different types of networks: telephone networks and computer networks. Telephone networks historically handled voice communication, and computer networks handled data traffic. Telephone networks were built by telephone companies throughout the twentieth century using voice transmission technologies (hardware and software), and these companies almost always operated as regulated monopolies throughout the world. Computer networks were originally built by computer companies seeking to transmit data between computers in different locations.

Thanks to continuing telecommunications deregulation and information technology innovation, telephone and computer networks are slowly converging into a single digital network using shared Internet-based standards and equipment. Telecommunications providers, such as AT&T and Verizon, today offer data transmission, Internet access, cellular telephone service, and television programming as well as voice service. Cable companies, such as Cablevision and Comcast, now offer voice service and Internet access. Computer networks have expanded to include Internet telephone and limited video services. Increasingly, all of these voice, video, and data communications are based on Internet technology.

Both voice and data communication networks have also become more powerful (faster), more portable (smaller and mobile), and less expensive. For instance, the typical Internet connection speed in 2000 was 56 kilobits per second, but today more than 60 percent of U.S. Internet users have high-speed **broadband** connections provided by telephone and cable TV companies running at 1 to 15 million bits per second. The cost for this service has fallen exponentially, from 25 cents per kilobit in 2000 to a fraction of a cent today.

Increasingly, voice and data communication, as well as Internet access, are taking place over broadband wireless platforms, such as cell phones, handheld digital devices like Kindles, and PCs in wireless networks. In a few years, more than half the Internet users in the United States will use smartphones and mobile netbooks to access the Internet. In 2009, 73 million Americans access the Internet through mobile devices, and this number is expected to double by 2013 (eMarketer, 2009).

WHAT IS A COMPUTER NETWORK?

If you had to connect the computers for two or more employees together in the same office, you would need a computer network. Exactly what is a network? In its simplest form, a network consists of two or more connected computers. Figure 6-1 illustrates the major hardware, software, and transmission components used in a simple network: a client computer and a dedicated server computer, network interfaces, a connection medium, network operating system software, and either a hub or a switch.

Each computer on the network contains a network interface device called a **network interface card (NIC)**. Most personal computers today have this card built into the motherboard. The connection medium for linking network components can be a telephone wire, coaxial cable, or radio signal in the case of cell phone and wireless local-area networks (Wi-Fi networks).

The **network operating system (NOS)** routes and manages communications on the network and coordinates network resources. It can reside on every computer in the network, or it can reside primarily on a dedicated server computer for all the applications on the network. A server computer is a computer on a network that performs important network functions for client computers, such as serving up Web pages, storing data, and storing the network operating system (and hence controlling the network). Server software, such as Microsoft Windows Server, Linux, and Novell Open Enterprise Server, are the most widely used network operating systems.

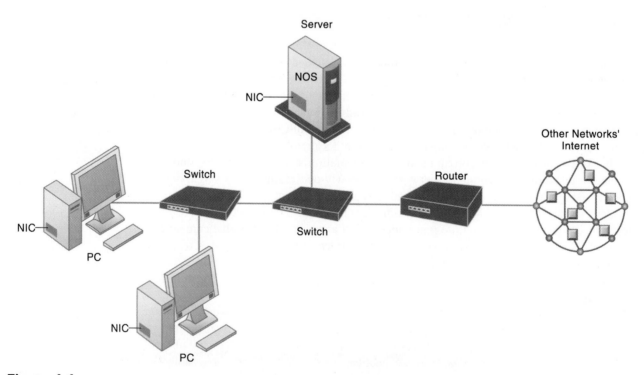

Figure 6-1
Components of a Simple Computer Network
Illustrated here is a very simple computer network, consisting of computers, a network operating system residing on a dedicated server computer, cable (wiring) connecting the devices, network interface cards (NIC), switches, and a router.

Most networks also contain a switch or a hub acting as a connection point between the computers. **Hubs** are very simple devices that connect network components, sending a packet of data to all other connected devices. A **switch** has more intelligence than a hub and can filter and forward data to a specified destination on the network.

What if you want to communicate with another network, such as the Internet? You would need a router. A **router** is a communications processor used to route packets of data through different networks, ensuring that the data sent gets to the correct address.

Networks in Large Companies

The network we've just described might be suitable for a small business. But what about large companies with many different locations and thousands of employees? As a firm grows, and collects hundreds of small local-area networks, these networks can be tied together into a corporate-wide networking infrastructure. The network infrastructure for a large corporation consists of a large number of these small local-area networks linked to other local-area networks and to firmwide corporate networks. A number of powerful servers support a corporate Web site, a corporate intranet, and perhaps an extranet. Some of these servers link to other large computers supporting back-end systems.

Figure 6-2 provides an illustration of these more complex, larger scale corporate-wide networks. Here you can see that the corporate network infrastructure supports a mobile sales force using cell phones, mobile employees linking to the company Web site, internal company networks using mobile wireless local-area networks (Wi-Fi networks), and a videoconferencing system to support managers across the world. In addition to these computer networks, the firm's infrastructure usually includes a separate telephone network that handles most voice data. Many firms are dispensing with their traditional telephone networks and using Internet telephones that run on their existing data networks (described later).

As you can see from this figure, a large corporate network infrastructure uses a wide variety of technologies—everything from ordinary telephone service and corporate data networks to Internet service, wireless Internet, and wireless cell phones. One of the major

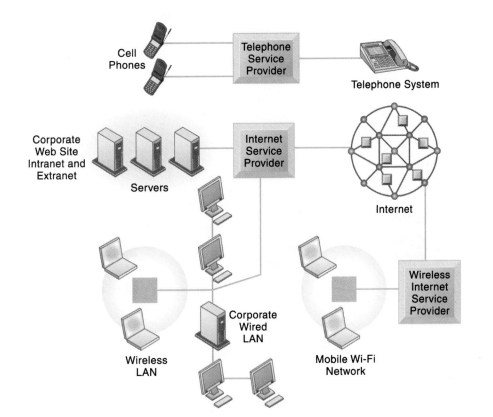

Figure 6-2
Corporate Network Infrastructure
Today's corporate network infrastructure is a collection of many different networks from the public switched telephone network, to the Internet, to corporate local-area networks linking workgroups, departments, or office floors.

problems facing corporations today is how to integrate all the different communication networks and channels into a coherent system that enables information to flow from one part of the corporation to another, from one system to another. As more and more communication networks become digital, and based on Internet technologies, it will become easier to integrate them.

KEY DIGITAL NETWORKING TECHNOLOGIES

Contemporary digital networks and the Internet are based on three key technologies: client/server computing, the use of packet switching, and the development of widely used communications standards (the most important of which is Transmission Control Protocol/Internet Protocol, or TCP/IP) for linking disparate networks and computers.

Client/Server Computing

We introduced client/server computing in Chapter 5. Client/server computing is a distributed computing model in which some of the processing power is located within small, inexpensive client computers, and resides literally on desktops, laptops, or in handheld devices. These powerful clients are linked to one another through a network that is controlled by a network server computer. The server sets the rules of communication for the network and provides every client with an address so others can find it on the network.

Client/server computing has largely replaced centralized mainframe computing in which nearly all of the processing takes place on a central large mainframe computer. Client/server computing has extended computing to departments, workgroups, factory floors, and other parts of the business that could not be served by a centralized architecture. The Internet is the largest implementation of client/server computing.

Packet Switching

Packet switching is a method of slicing digital messages into parcels called packets, sending the packets along different communication paths as they become available, and then reassembling the packets once they arrive at their destinations (see Figure 6-3). Prior to the development of packet switching, computer networks used leased, dedicated telephone circuits to communicate with other computers in remote locations. In circuit-switched networks, such as the telephone system, a complete point-to-point circuit is assembled, and then communication can proceed. These dedicated circuit-switching techniques were expensive and wasted available communications capacity—the circuit was maintained regardless of whether any data were being sent.

Figure 6-3
Packed-Switched Networks and Packet Communications
Data are grouped into small packets, which are transmitted independently over various communications channels and reassembled at their final destination.

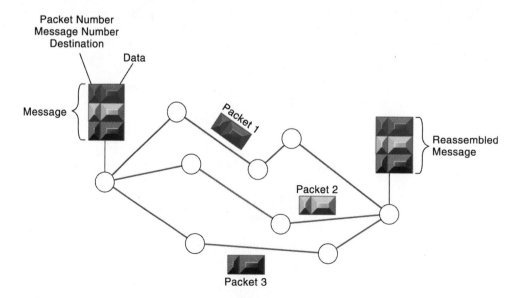

Packet switching makes much more efficient use of the communications capacity of a network. In packet-switched networks, messages are first broken down into small fixed bundles of data called packets. The packets include information for directing the packet to the right address and for checking transmission errors along with the data. The packets are transmitted over various communications channels using routers, each packet traveling independently. Packets of data originating at one source will be routed through many different paths and networks before being reassembled into the original message when they reach their destinations.

TCP/IP and Connectivity

In a typical telecommunications network, diverse hardware and software components need to work together to transmit information. Different components in a network communicate with each other only by adhering to a common set of rules called protocols. A **protocol** is a set of rules and procedures governing transmission of information between two points in a network.

In the past, many diverse proprietary and incompatible protocols often forced business firms to purchase computing and communications equipment from a single vendor. But today corporate networks are increasingly using a single, common, worldwide standard called **Transmission Control Protocol/ Internet Protocol (TCP/IP)**. TCP/IP was developed during the early 1970s to support U.S. Department of Defense Advanced Research Projects Agency (DARPA) efforts to help scientists transmit data among different types of computers over long distances.

TCP/IP uses a suite of protocols, the main ones being TCP and IP. TCP refers to the Transmission Control Protocol (TCP), which handles the movement of data between computers. TCP establishes a connection between the computers, sequences the transfer of packets, and acknowledges the packets sent. IP refers to the Internet Protocol (IP), which is responsible for the delivery of packets and includes the disassembling and reassembling of packets during transmission. Figure 6-4 illustrates the four-layered Department of Defense reference model for TCP/IP.

1. Application layer. The Application layer enables client application programs to access the other layers and defines the protocols that applications use to exchange data. One of these application protocols is the Hypertext Transfer Protocol (HTTP), which is used to transfer Web page files.
2. Transport layer. The Transport layer is responsible for providing the Application layer with communication and packet services. This layer includes TCP and other protocols.
3. Internet layer. The Internet layer is responsible for addressing, routing, and packaging data packets called IP datagrams. The Internet Protocol is one of the protocols used in this layer.

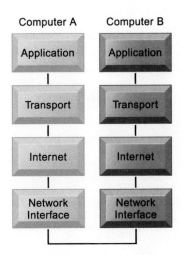

Figure 6-4
The Transmission Control Protocol/Internet Protocol (TCP/IP) Reference Model
This figure illustrates the four layers of the TCP/IP reference model for communications.

4. Network Interface layer. At the bottom of the reference model, the Network Interface layer is responsible for placing packets on and receiving them from the network medium, which could be any networking technology.

Two computers using TCP/IP are able to communicate even if they are based on different hardware and software platforms. Data sent from one computer to the other passes downward through all four layers, starting with the sending computer's Application layer and passing through the Network Interface layer. After the data reach the recipient host computer, they travel up the layers and are reassembled into a format the receiving computer can use. If the receiving computer finds a damaged packet, it asks the sending computer to retransmit it. This process is reversed when the receiving computer responds.

6.2 Communications Networks

Let's look more closely at alternative networking technologies available to businesses.

SIGNALS: DIGITAL VS. ANALOG

There are two ways to communicate a message in a network: either using an analog signal or a digital signal. An *analog signal* is represented by a continuous waveform that passes through a communications medium and has been used for voice communication. The most common analog devices are the telephone handset, the speaker on your computer, or your iPod earphone, all of which create analog wave forms that your ear can hear.

A *digital signal* is a discrete, binary waveform, rather than a continuous waveform. Digital signals communicate information as strings of two discrete states: one bit and zero bits, which are represented as on–off electrical pulses. Computers use digital signals and require a **modem** to convert these digital signals into analog signals that can be sent over (or received from) telephone lines, cable lines, or wireless media that use analog signals (see Figure 6-5). *Modem* stands for modulator-demodulator. Cable modems connect your computer to the Internet using a cable network. DSL modems connect your computer to the Internet using a telephone company's land line network. Wireless modems perform the same function as traditional modems, connecting your computer to a wireless network that could be a cell phone network, or a Wi-Fi network. Without modems, computers could not communicate with one another using analog networks (which include the telephone system and cable networks).

TYPES OF NETWORKS

There are many different kinds of networks and ways of classifying them. One way of looking at networks is in terms of their geographic scope (see Table 6.1).

Local-Area Networks
If you work in a business that uses networking, you are probably connecting to other employees and groups via a local-area network. A **local-area network (LAN)** is designed to

TABLE 6.1

Types of Networks

Type	Area
Local-area network (LAN)	Up to 500 meters (half a mile); an office or floor of a building
Campus-area network (CAN)	Up to 1,000 meters (a mile); a college campus or corporate facility
Metropolitan-area network (MAN)	A city or metropolitan area
Wide-area network (WAN)	A transcontinental or global area

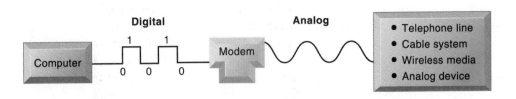

Figure 6-5
Functions of the Modem
A modem is a device that translates digital signals into analog form (and vice versa) so that computers can transmit data over analog networks such as telephone and cable networks.

connect personal computers and other digital devices within a half-mile or 500-meter radius. LANs typically connect a few computers in a small office, all the computers in one building, or all the computers in several buildings in close proximity. LANs also are used to link to long-distance wide-area networks (WANs, described later in this section) and other networks around the world using the Internet.

Review Figure 6-1, which could serve as a model for a small LAN that might be used in an office. One computer is a dedicated network file server, providing users with access to shared computing resources in the network, including software programs and data files. The server determines who gets access to what and in which sequence. The router connects the LAN to other networks, which could be the Internet or another corporate network, so that the LAN can exchange information with networks external to it. The most common LAN operating systems are Windows, Linux, and Novell. Each of these network operating systems supports TCP/IP as their default networking protocol.

Ethernet is the dominant LAN standard at the physical network level, specifying the physical medium to carry signals between computers, access control rules, and a standardized set of bits used to carry data over the system. Originally, Ethernet supported a data transfer rate of 10 megabits per second (Mbps). Newer versions, such as Fast Ethernet and Gigabit Ethernet, support data transfer rates of 100 Mbps and 1 gigabits per second (Gbps), respectively, and are used in network backbones.

The LAN illustrated in Figure 6-1 uses a client/server architecture where the network operating system resides primarily on a single file server, and the server provides much of the control and resources for the network. Alternatively, LANs may use a peer-to-peer architecture. A **peer-to-peer** network treats all processors equally and is used primarily in small networks with 10 or fewer users. The various computers on the network can exchange data by direct access and can share peripheral devices without going through a separate server.

In LANs using the Windows Server family of operating systems, the peer-to-peer architecture is called the *workgroup network model* in which a small group of computers can share resources, such as files, folders, and printers, over the network without a dedicated server. The Windows *domain network model*, in contrast, uses a dedicated server to manage the computers in the network.

Larger LANs have many clients and multiple servers, with separate servers for specific services, such as storing and managing files and databases (file servers or database servers), managing printers (print servers), storing and managing e-mail (mail servers), or storing and managing Web pages (Web servers).

Sometimes LANs are described in terms of the way their components are connected together, or their **topology**. There are three major LAN topologies: star, bus, and ring (see Figure 6-6).

In a **star topology**, all devices on the network connect to a single hub. Figure 6-6 illustrates a simple star topology in which all network traffic flows through the hub. In an *extended star network*, multiple layers of hubs are organized into a hierarchy.

In a **bus topology**, one station transmits signals, which travel in both directions along a single transmission segment. All of the signals are broadcast in both directions to the entire network. All machines on the network receive the same signals, and software installed on the client computers enables each client to listen for messages addressed specifically to it. The bus topology is the most common Ethernet topology.

Figure 6-6
Network Topologies
The three basic network topologies are the star, bus, and ring.

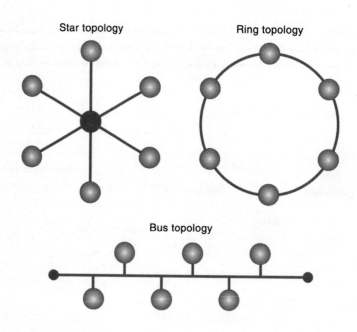

A **ring topology** connects network components in a closed loop. Messages pass from computer to computer in only one direction around the loop, and only one station at a time may transmit. The ring topology is primarily found in older LANs using Token Ring networking software.

Metropolitan- and Wide-Area Networks

Wide-area networks (WANs) span broad geographical distances—entire regions, states, continents, or the entire globe. The most universal and powerful WAN is the Internet. Computers connect to a WAN through public networks, such as the telephone system or private cable systems, or through leased lines or satellites. A **metropolitan-area network (MAN)** is a network that spans a metropolitan area, usually a city and its major suburbs. Its geographic scope falls between a WAN and a LAN.

PHYSICAL TRANSMISSION MEDIA

Networks use different kinds of physical transmission media, including twisted wire, coaxial cable, fiber optics, and media for wireless transmission. Each has advantages and limitations. A wide range of speeds is possible for any given medium depending on the software and hardware configuration.

Twisted Wire

Twisted wire consists of strands of copper wire twisted in pairs and is an older type of transmission medium. Many of the telephone systems in buildings had twisted wires installed for analog communication, but they can be used for digital communication as well. Although an older physical transmission medium, the twisted wires used in today's LANs, such as CAT5, can obtain speeds up to 1 Gbps. Twisted-pair cabling is limited to a maximum recommended run of 100 meters (328 feet).

Coaxial Cable

Coaxial cable, similar to that used for cable television, consists of thickly insulated copper wire, which can transmit a larger volume of data than twisted wire. Cable was used in early LANs and is still used today for longer (more than 100 meters) runs in large buildings. Coaxial has speeds up to 1 Gbps.

Fiber Optics and Optical Networks

Fiber-optic cable consists of bound strands of clear glass fiber, each the thickness of a human hair. Data are transformed into pulses of light, which are sent through the fiber-optic cable by a laser device at rates varying from 500 kilobits to several trillion bits per second in experimental settings. Fiber-optic cable is considerably faster, lighter, and more durable than wire media, and is well suited to systems requiring transfers of large volumes of data. However, fiber-optic cable is more expensive than other physical transmission media and harder to install.

Until recently, fiber-optic cable had been used primarily for the high-speed network backbone, which handles the major traffic. Now cellular phone companies such as Verizon are starting to bring fiber lines into the home for new types of services, such as Verizon's Fiber Optic Services (FiOS) Internet service that provides up 50 Mbps download speeds.

Wireless Transmission Media

Wireless transmission is based on radio signals of various frequencies. There are three kinds of wireless networks used by computers: microwave, cellular, and Wi-Fi networks. **Microwave** systems, both terrestrial and celestial, transmit high-frequency radio signals through the atmosphere and are widely used for high-volume, long-distance, point-to-point communication. Microwave signals follow a straight line and do not bend with the curvature of the earth. Therefore, long-distance terrestrial transmission systems require that transmission stations be positioned about 37 miles apart. Long-distance transmission is also possible by using communication satellites as relay stations for microwave signals transmitted from terrestrial stations.

Communication satellites use microwave transmission and are typically used for transmission in large, geographically dispersed organizations that would be difficult to network using cabling media or terrestrial microwave, as well as for home Internet service, especially in rural areas. For instance, the global energy company BP p.l.c. uses satellites for real-time data transfer of oil field exploration data gathered from searches of the ocean floor. Using geosynchronous satellites, exploration ships transfer these data to central computing centers in the United States for use by researchers in Houston, Tulsa, and suburban Chicago. Figure 6-7 illustrates how this system works. Satellites are also used for home television and Internet service. The two major satellite Internet providers (Dish Network and DirectTV) have about 30 million subscribers, and about 17 percent of all U.S. households access the Internet using satellite services (eMarketer, 2009).

Cellular systems also use radio waves and a variety of different protocols to communicate with radio antennas (towers) placed within adjacent geographic areas called cells. Communications transmitted from a **cell phone** to a local cell pass from antenna to antenna—cell to cell—until they reach their final destination.

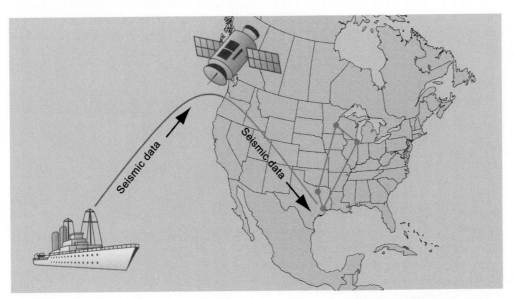

Figure 6-7
BP's Satellite Transmission System
Communication satellites help BP transfer seismic data between oil exploration ships and research centers in the United States.

Wireless networks are supplanting traditional wired networks for many applications and creating new applications, services, and business models. In Section 6.4, we provide a detailed description of the applications and technology standards driving the "wireless revolution."

Transmission Speed

The total amount of digital information that can be transmitted through any telecommunications medium is measured in bits per second (bps). One signal change, or cycle, is required to transmit one or several bits; therefore, the transmission capacity of each type of telecommunications medium is a function of its frequency. The number of cycles per second that can be sent through that medium is measured in **hertz**—one hertz is equal to one cycle of the medium.

The range of frequencies that can be accommodated on a particular telecommunications channel is called its **bandwidth**. The bandwidth is the difference between the highest and lowest frequencies that can be accommodated on a single channel. The greater the range of frequencies, the greater the bandwidth and the greater the channel's transmission capacity. Table 6.2 compares the transmission speeds of the major types of media.

6.3 The Global Internet

We all use the Internet, and many of us can't do without it. It's become an indispensable personal and business tool. But what exactly is the Internet? How does it work, and what does Internet technology have to offer for business? Let's look at the most important Internet features.

WHAT IS THE INTERNET?

The Internet has become the world's most extensive, public communication system that now rivals the global telephone system in reach and range. It's also the world's largest implementation of client/server computing and internetworking, linking millions of individual networks all over the world. This global network of networks began in the early 1970s as a U.S. Department of Defense network to link scientists and university professors around the world.

Most homes and small businesses connect to the Internet by subscribing to an Internet service provider. An **Internet service provider (ISP)** is a commercial organization with a permanent connection to the Internet that sells temporary connections to retail subscribers. EarthLink, NetZero, AT&T, and Time Warner are ISPs. Individuals also connect to the Internet through their business firms, universities, or research centers that have designated Internet domains.

There are a variety of services for ISP Internet connections. Connecting via a traditional telephone line and modem, at a speed of 56.6 kilobits per second (Kbps) used to be the most common form of connection worldwide, but it is quickly being replaced by broadband

TABLE 6.2		
Typical Speeds of Telecommunications Transmission Media	**Medium**	**Speed**
	Twisted wire	Up to 1 Gbps
	Microwave	Up to 10 Mbps
	Satellite	Up to 10 Mbps
	Coaxial cable	Up to 1 Gbps
	Fiber-optic cable	Up to 6+ Tbps

Mbps = megabits per second
Gbps = gigabits per second
Tbps = terabits per second

connections. Digital subscriber line (DSL), cable, and satellite Internet connections, and T lines provide these broadband services.

Digital subscriber line (DSL) technologies operate over existing telephone lines to carry voice, data, and video at transmission rates ranging from 385 Kbps all the way up to 9 Mbps. **Cable Internet connections** provided by cable television vendors use digital cable coaxial lines to deliver high-speed Internet access to homes and businesses. They can provide high-speed access to the Internet of up to 10 Mbps. In areas where DSL and cable services are unavailable, it is possible to access the Internet via satellite, although some satellite Internet connections have slower upload speeds than other broadband services.

T1 and T3 are international telephone standards for digital communication. They are leased, dedicated lines suitable for businesses or government agencies requiring high-speed guaranteed service levels. **T1 lines** offer guaranteed delivery at 1.54 Mbps, and T3 lines offer delivery at 45 Mbps.

INTERNET ADDRESSING AND ARCHITECTURE

The Internet is based on the TCP/IP networking protocol suite described earlier in this chapter. Every computer on the Internet is assigned a unique **Internet Protocol (IP) address**, which currently is a 32-bit number represented by four strings of numbers ranging from 0 to 255 separated by periods. For instance, the IP address of www.microsoft.com is 207.46.250.119.

When a user sends a message to another user on the Internet, the message is first decomposed into packets using the TCP protocol. Each packet contains its destination address. The packets are then sent from the client to the network server and from there on to as many other servers as necessary to arrive at a specific computer with a known address. At the destination address, the packets are reassembled into the original message.

The Domain Name System

Because it would be incredibly difficult for Internet users to remember strings of 12 numbers, the **Domain Name System (DNS)** converts IP addresses to domain names. The **domain name** is the English-like name that corresponds to the unique 32-bit numeric IP address for each computer connected to the Internet. DNS servers maintain a database containing IP addresses mapped to their corresponding domain names. To access a computer on the Internet, users need only specify its domain name.

DNS has a hierarchical structure (see Figure 6-8). At the top of the DNS hierarchy is the root domain. The child domain of the root is called a top-level domain, and the child domain

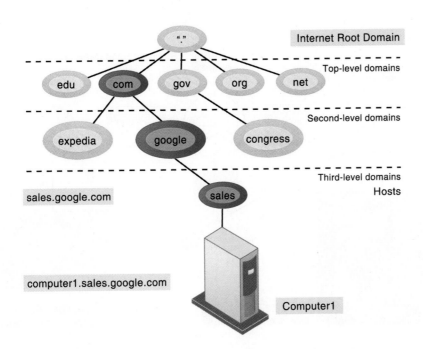

Figure 6-8
The Domain Name System
Domain Name System is a hierarchical system with a root domain, top-level domains, second-level domains, and host computers at the third level.

of a top-level domain is called is a second-level domain. Top-level domains are two- and three-character names you are familiar with from surfing the Web, for example, .com, .edu, .gov, and the various country codes such as .ca for Canada or .it for Italy. Second-level domains have two parts, designating a top-level name and a second-level name—such as buy.com, nyu.edu, or amazon.ca. A host name at the bottom of the hierarchy designates a specific computer on either the Internet or a private network.

The most common domain extensions currently available and officially approved are shown in the following list. Countries also have domain names such as .uk, .au, and .fr (United Kingdom, Australia, and France, respectively). In the future, this list will expand to include many more types of organizations and industries.

.com   Commercial organizations/businesses

.edu   Educational institutions

.gov   U.S. government agencies

.mil   U.S. military

.net   Network computers

.org   Nonprofit organizations and foundations

.biz   Business firms

.info   Information providers

Internet Architecture and Governance

Internet data traffic is carried over transcontinental high-speed backbone networks that generally operate today in the range of 45 Mbps to 2.5 Gbps (see Figure 6-9). These trunk lines are typically owned by long distance telephone companies (called *network service providers*) or by national governments. Local connection lines are owned by regional telephone and cable television companies in the United States that connect retail users in homes and businesses to the Internet. The regional networks lease access to ISPs, private companies, and government institutions.

Figure 6-9
Internet Network Architecture
The Internet backbone connects to regional networks, which in turn provide access to Internet service providers, large firms, and government institutions. Network access points (NAPs) and metropolitan-area exchanges (MAEs) are hubs where the backbone intersects regional and local networks and where backbone owners connect with one another.

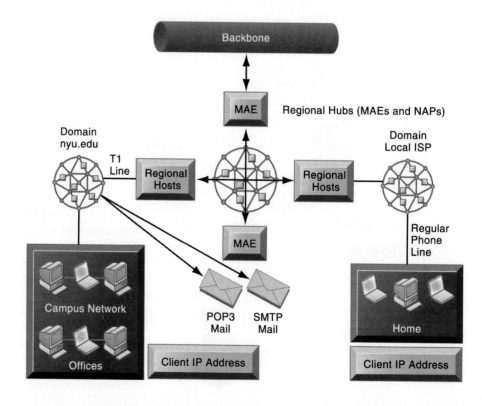

Each organization pays for its own networks and its own local Internet connection services, a part of which is paid to the long-distance trunk line owners. Individual Internet users pay ISPs for using their service, and they generally pay a flat subscription fee, no matter how much or how little they use the Internet. A debate is now raging on whether this arrangement should continue or whether heavy Internet users who download large video and music files should pay more for the bandwidth they consume. The Interactive Session on Organizations explores this topic, as it examines the pros and cons of network neutrality.

No one "owns" the Internet, and it has no formal management. However, worldwide Internet policies are established by a number of professional organizations and government bodies, including the Internet Architecture Board (IAB), which helps define the overall structure of the Internet; the Internet Corporation for Assigned Names and Numbers (ICANN), which assigns IP addresses; and the World Wide Web Consortium (W3C), which sets Hypertext Markup Language and other programming standards for the Web.

These organizations influence government agencies, network owners, ISPs, and software developers with the goal of keeping the Internet operating as efficiently as possible. The Internet must also conform to the laws of the sovereign nation-states in which it operates, as well as the technical infrastructures that exist within the nation-states. Although in the early years of the Internet and the Web there was very little legislative or executive interference, this situation is changing as the Internet plays a growing role in the distribution of information and knowledge, including content that some find objectionable.

The Future Internet: IPv6 and Internet2

The Internet was not originally designed to handle the transmission of massive quantities of data and billions of users. Because many corporations and governments have been given large blocks of millions of IP addresses to accommodate current and future workforces, and because of sheer Internet population growth, the world will run out of available IP addresses using the existing addressing convention by 2012 or 2013. Under development is a new version of the IP addressing schema called *Internet Protocol version 6 (IPv6)*, which contains 128-bit addresses (2 to the power of 128), or more than a quadrillion possible unique addresses.

Internet2 and Next-Generation Internet (NGI) are consortia representing 200 universities, private businesses, and government agencies in the United States that are working on a new, robust, high-bandwidth version of the Internet. They have established several new high-performance backbone networks with bandwidths ranging from 2.5 Gbps to 9.6 Gbps. Internet2 research groups are developing and implementing new technologies for more effective routing practices; different levels of service, depending on the type and importance of the data being transmitted; and advanced applications for distributed computation, virtual laboratories, digital libraries, distributed learning, and tele-immersion. These networks do not replace the public Internet, but they do provide test beds for leading-edge technology that may eventually migrate to the public Internet.

INTERNET SERVICES AND COMMUNICATION TOOLS

The Internet is based on client/server technology. Individuals using the Internet control what they do through client applications on their computers, such as Web browser software. The data, including e-mail messages and Web pages, are stored on servers. A client uses the Internet to request information from a particular Web server on a distant computer, and the server sends the requested information back to the client over the Internet. Chapters 4 and 5 describe how Web servers work with application servers and database servers to access information from an organization's internal information systems applications and their associated databases. Client platforms today include not only PCs and other computers but also cell phones, small handheld digital devices, and other information appliances.

What kind of Internet user are you? Do you primarily use the Net to do a little e-mail and look up phone numbers? Or are you online all day, watching YouTube videos, downloading music files, or playing massively multiplayer online games? If you're the latter, you are consuming a great deal of bandwidth, and hundreds of millions of people like you might start to slow the Internet down. YouTube consumed as much bandwidth in 2007 as the entire Internet did in 2000. That's one of the arguments being made today for charging Internet users based on the amount of transmission capacity they use.

According to one November 2007 report, a research firm projected that user demand for the Internet could outpace network capacity by 2011.

If this happens, the Internet might not come to a screeching halt, but users would be faced with sluggish download speeds and slow performance of YouTube, Facebook, and other data-heavy services. (Heavy use of iPhones in urban areas such as New York and San Francisco has already degraded service on the AT&T wireless network.)

Other researchers believe that as digital traffic on the Internet grows, even at a rate of 50 percent per year, the technology for handling all this traffic is advancing at an equally rapid pace.

In addition to these technical issues, the debate about metering Internet use centers around the concept of network neutrality. Network neutrality is the idea that Internet service providers must allow customers equal access to content and applications, regardless of the source or nature of the content. Presently, the Internet is indeed neutral: all Internet traffic is treated equally on a first-come, first-served basis by Internet backbone owners. The Internet is neutral because it was built on phone lines, which are subject to "common carriage" laws. These laws require phone companies to treat all calls and customers equally. They cannot offer extra benefits to customers willing to pay higher premiums for faster or clearer calls, a model known as tiered service.

Now telecommunications and cable companies want to be able to charge differentiated prices based on the amount of bandwidth consumed by content being delivered over the Internet. In June 2008, Time Warner Cable started testing metered pricing for its Internet access service in the city of Beaumont, Texas. Under the pilot program, Time Warner charged customers an additional $1 per month for each gigabyte of content they downloaded or sent over the bandwidth limit of their monthly plan. The company reported that 5 percent of its customers had been using half the capacity

on its local lines without paying any more than low-usage customers, and that metered pricing was "the fairest way" to finance necessary investments in its network infrastructure.

This is not how Internet service has worked traditionally and contradicts the goals of network neutrality. Advocates of net neutrality are pushing Congress to regulate the industry, requiring network providers to refrain from these types of practices. The strange alliance of net neutrality advocates includes MoveOn.org, the Christian Coalition, the American Library Association, every major consumer group, many bloggers and small businesses, and some large Internet companies like Google and Amazon.

Internet service providers point to the upsurge in piracy of copyrighted materials over the Internet. Comcast, the second largest Internet service provider in the United States, reported that illegal file sharing of copyrighted material was consuming 50 percent of its network capacity. At one point Comcast slowed down transmission of BitTorrent files, used extensively for piracy and illegal sharing of copyrighted materials, including video. Comcast drew fierce criticism for its handling of BitTorrent packets, and the FCC ruled that Comcast had to stop slowing peer-to-peer traffic in the name of network management. Comcast then filed a lawsuit challenging the FCC's authority to enforce network neutrality.

Net neutrality advocates argue that the risk of censorship increases when network operators can selectively block or slow access to certain content. There are already many examples of Internet providers restricting access to sensitive materials (such as anti-Bush comments from an online Pearl Jam concert, a text-messaging program from pro-choice group NARAL, or access to competitors like Vonage). Pakistan's government blocked access to anti-Muslim sites and YouTube as a whole in response to content they deemed defamatory to Islam.

Proponents of net neutrality also argue that a neutral Internet encourages everyone to innovate without permission from the phone and cable companies or other authorities, and this level playing field has spawned countless new businesses. Allowing unrestricted information flow becomes essential to free markets and democracy as commerce and society increasingly move online.

Network owners believe regulation like the bills proposed by net neutrality advocates will impede U.S. competitiveness by stifling innovation and hurt customers who will benefit from "discriminatory" network practices. U.S. Internet service lags behind other many other nations in overall speed, cost, and quality of service, adding credibility to the providers' arguments.

Network neutrality advocates counter that U.S. carriers already have too much power due to lack of options for service. Without sufficient competition, the carriers have more freedom to set prices and policies, and customers cannot seek recourse via other options. Carriers can discriminate in favor of their own content. Even broadband users in large metropolitan areas lack many options for service. With enough options for Internet access, net neutrality would not be such a pressing issue. Dissatisfied consumers could simply switch to providers who enforce net neutrality and allow unlimited Internet use.

On September 21, 2009, the U.S. Federal Communications Commission (FCC) announced its intention to formalize a set of rules supporting net neu-

trality based on principles that the FCC has embraced since August 2005. These rules entitle consumers to lawful Internet content, applications, and services of their choice, and to use devices of their choice to connect to the Internet. The rules also support competition among Internet network, application, service, and content providers. Two new rules would prevent ISPs from discriminating against particular content and ensure disclosure of their network management practices. For the first time, all of these rules would be applied to wireless companies.

Sources: Fawn Johnson and Amy Schatz, "FCC Chairman Proposes 'Net Neutrality' Rules," *The Wall Street Journal*, September 21, 2009; Grant Gross, "FCC Chairman Calls for Formal Net Neutrality Rules," *IDG News Service*, September 21, 2009; Joanie Wexler: "Net Neutrality: Can We Find Common Ground?" *Network World*, April 1, 2009; Andy Dornan, "Is Your Network Neutral?" *Information Week*, May 18, 2008; Steve Lohr, "Video Road Hogs Stir Fear of Internet Traffic Jam," *The New York Times*, March 13, 2008; and Peter Burrows, "The FCC, Comcast, and Net Neutrality," *Business Week*, February 26, 2008.

CASE STUDY QUESTIONS

1. What is network neutrality? Why has the Internet operated under net neutrality up to this point in time?

2. Who's in favor of network neutrality? Who's opposed? Why?

3. What would be the impact on individual users, businesses, and government if Internet providers switched to a tiered service model?

4. Are you in favor of legislation enforcing network neutrality? Why or why not?

MIS IN ACTION

1. Visit the Web site of the Open Internet Coalition and select five member organizations. Then visit the Web site of each of these organizations or surf the Web to find out more information about each. Write a short essay explaining why each organization is in favor of network neutrality.

2. Calculate how much bandwidth you consume when using the Internet every day. How many e-mails do you send daily and what is the size of each? (Your e-mail program may have e-mail file size information.) How many music and video clips do you download daily and what is the size of each? If you view YouTube often, surf the Web to find out the size of a typical YouTube file. Add up the number of e-mail, audio, and video files you transmit or receive on a typical day.

Internet Services

A client computer connecting to the Internet has access to a variety of services. These services include e-mail, electronic discussion groups, chatting and instant messaging, **Telnet**, **File Transfer Protocol (FTP)**, and the Web. Table 6.3 provides a brief description of these services.

Each Internet service is implemented by one or more software programs. All of the services may run on a single server computer, or different services may be allocated to different machines. Figure 6-10 illustrates one way that these services can be arranged in a multitiered client/server architecture.

TABLE 6.3

Major Internet Services

Capability	Functions Supported
E-mail	Person-to-person messaging; document sharing
Chatting and instant messaging	Interactive conversations
Newsgroups	Discussion groups on electronic bulletin boards
Telnet	Logging on to one computer system and doing work on another
File Transfer Protocol (FTP)	Transferring files from computer to computer
The Web	Retrieving, formatting, and displaying information (including text, audio, graphics, and video) using hypertext links

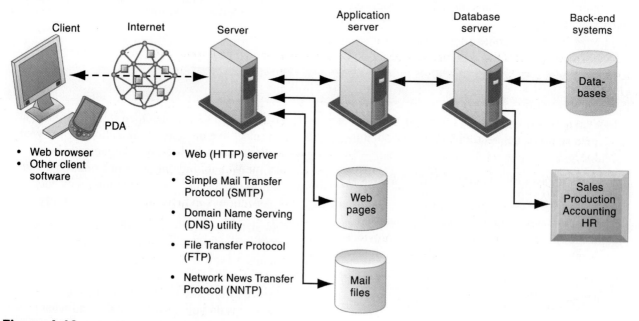

Figure 6-10
Client/Server Computing on the Internet
Client computers running Web browser and other software can access an array of services on servers over the Internet. These services may all run on a single physical server or on multiple specialized physical servers.

E-mail enables messages to be exchanged from computer to computer, with capabilities for routing messages to multiple recipients, forwarding messages, and attaching text documents or multimedia files to messages. Although some organizations operate their own internal electronic mail systems, most e-mail today is sent through the Internet. The costs of e-mail is far lower than equivalent voice, postal, or overnight delivery costs, making the Internet a very inexpensive and rapid communications medium. Most e-mail messages arrive anywhere in the world in a matter of seconds.

Nearly 90 percent of U.S. workplaces have employees communicating interactively using **chat** or instant messaging tools. Chatting enables two or more people who are simultaneously connected to the Internet to hold live, interactive conversations. Chat systems now support voice and video chat as well as written conversations. Many online retail businesses offer chat services on their Web sites to attract visitors, to encourage repeat purchases, and to improve customer service.

Instant messaging is a type of chat service that enables participants to create their own private chat channels. The instant messaging system alerts the user whenever someone on his or her private list is online so that the user can initiate a chat session with other individuals. Instant messaging systems for consumers include Yahoo! Messenger, Google Talk, and Windows Live Messenger. Companies concerned with security use proprietary instant messaging systems such as Lotus Sametime.

Newsgroups are worldwide discussion groups posted on Internet electronic bulletin boards on which people share information and ideas on a defined topic, such as radiology or rock bands. Anyone can post messages on these bulletin boards for others to read. Many thousands of groups exist that discuss almost all conceivable topics.

Employee use of e-mail, instant messaging, and the Internet is supposed to increase worker productivity, but the accompanying Interactive Session on People shows that this may not always be the case. Many company managers now believe they need to monitor and even regulate their employees' online activity. But is this ethical? Although there are some strong business reasons why companies may need to monitor their employees' e-mail and Web activities, what does this mean for employee privacy?

Voice over IP

The Internet has also become a popular platform for voice transmission and corporate networking. **Voice over IP (VoIP)** technology delivers voice information in digital form using packet switching, avoiding the tolls charged by local and long distance telephone networks (see Figure 6-11). Calls that would ordinarily be transmitted over public telephone networks would travel over the corporate network based on the Internet Protocol, or the public Internet. Voice calls can be made and received with a desktop computer equipped with a microphone and speakers or with a VoIP-enabled telephone.

Telecommunications service providers (such as Verizon) and cable firms (such as Time Warner and Cablevision) provide VoIP services. Skype offers free VoIP worldwide using a peer-to-peer network, and Google has its own free VoIP service.

Although there are up-front investments required for an IP phone system, VoIP can reduce communication and network management costs by 20 to 30 percent. For example, VoIP saves Virgin Entertainment Group $700,000 per year in long distance bills. In addition to lowering long distance costs and eliminating monthly fees for private lines, an IP network provides a single voice-data infrastructure for both telecommunications and computing services. Companies no longer have to maintain separate networks or provide support services and personnel for each different type of network.

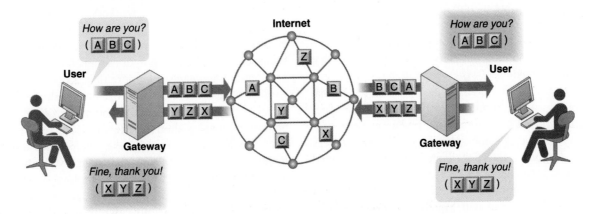

Figure 6-11
How Voice over IP Works
An VoIP phone call digitizes and breaks up a voice message into data packets that may travel along different routes before being reassembled at the final destination. A processor nearest the call's destination, called a gateway, arranges the packets in the proper order and directs them to the telephone number of the receiver or the IP address of the receiving computer.

INTERACTIVE SESSION: PEOPLE   Monitoring Employees on Networks: Unethical or Good Business?

As Internet use has exploded worldwide, so have the use of e-mail and the Web for personal business at the workplace. Several management problems have emerged: First, checking e-mail, responding to instant messages, or sneaking in a brief YouTube or MySpace video create a series of nonstop interruptions that divert employee attention from the job tasks they are supposed to be performing. According to Basex, a New York City business research company, these distractions take up as much as 28 percent of the average U.S. worker's day and result in $650 billion in lost productivity each year!

Second, these interruptions are not necessarily work-related. A number of studies have concluded that at least 25 percent of employee online time is spent on non-work-related Web surfing, and perhaps as many as 90 percent of employees receive or send personal e-mail at work.

Many companies have begun monitoring their employee use of e-mail, blogs, and the Internet, sometimes without their knowledge. A recent American Management Association (AMA) survey of 304 U.S. companies of all sizes found that 66 percent of these companies monitor employee e-mail messages and Web connections. Although U.S. companies have the legal right to monitor employee Internet and e-mail activity while they are at work, is such monitoring unethical, or is it simply good business?

Managers worry about the loss of time and employee productivity when employees are focusing on personal rather than company business. Too much time on personal business, on the Internet or not, can mean lost revenue or overbilled clients. Some employees may be charging time they spend trading their personal stocks online or pursuing other personal business to clients, thus overcharging the clients.

If personal traffic on company networks is too high, it can also clog the company's network so that legitimate business work cannot be performed. Schemmer Associates, an architecture firm in Omaha, Nebraska, and Potomac Hospital in Woodridge, Virginia, found their computing resources were limited by a lack of bandwidth caused by employees using corporate Internet connections to watch and download video files.

When employees use e-mail or the Web at employer facilities or with employer equipment, anything they do, including anything illegal, carries the company's name. Therefore, the employer can be traced and held liable. Management in many firms fear that racist, sexually explicit, or other potentially offensive material accessed or traded by their employees could result in adverse publicity and even lawsuits for the firm. Even if the company is found not to be liable, responding to lawsuits could cost the company tens of thousands of dollars.

Companies also fear leakage of confidential information and trade secrets through e-mail or blogs. A recent survey conducted by the American Management Association and the ePolicy Institute found that 14 percent of the employees polled admitted they had sent confidential or potentially embarrassing company e-mails to outsiders.

U.S. companies have the legal right to monitor what employees are doing with company equipment during business hours. The question is whether electronic surveillance is an appropriate tool for maintaining an efficient and positive workplace. Some companies try to ban all personal activities on corporate networks—zero tolerance. Others block employee access to specific Web sites or social sites or limit personal time on the Web.

For example, Enterprise Rent-A-Car blocks employee access to certain social sites and monitors the Web for employees' online postings about the company. Ajax Boiler in Santa Ana, California, uses software from SpectorSoft Corporation that records all the Web sites employees visit, time spent at each site, and all e-mails sent. Flushing Financial Corporation installed software that prevents employees from sending e-mail to specified addresses and scans e-mail attachments for sensitive information. Schemmer Associates uses OpenDNS to categorize and filter Web content and block unwanted video.

Some firms have fired employees who have stepped out of bounds. One-third of the companies surveyed in the AMA study had fired workers for misusing the Internet on the job. Among managers who fired employees for Internet misuse, 64 percent did so because the employees' e-mail contained inappropriate or offensive language, and more than 25 percent fired workers for excessive personal use of e-mail.

No solution is problem free, but many consultants believe companies should write corporate policies on employee e-mail and Internet use. The policies should include explicit ground rules that state, by position or level, under what circumstances employees can use company facilities for e-mail, blogging, or Web surfing. The policies should also inform employees whether these activities are monitored and explain why.

IBM now has "social computing guidelines" that cover employee activity on sites such as Facebook and

Twitter. The guidelines urge employees not to conceal their identities, to remember that they are personally responsible for what they publish, and to refrain from discussing controversial topics that are not related to their IBM role.

The rules should be tailored to specific business needs and organizational cultures. For example, although some companies may exclude all employees from visiting sites that have explicit sexual material, law firms or hospital employees may require access to these sites. Investment firms will need to allow many of their employees access to other investment sites. A company dependent on widespread information sharing, innovation, and independence could very well find that monitoring creates more problems than it solves.

Sources: Michelle Conline and Douglas MacMillan, "Web 2.0: Managing Corporate Reputations," *Business Week*, May 20, 2009; Dana Mattioli, "Leaks Grow in a World of Blogs," *The Wall Street Journal*, July 20, 2009; James Wong, "Drafting Trouble-Free Social Media Policies," Law.com, June 15, 2009; Nancy Gohring, "Over 50 Percent of Companies Fire Workers for E-Mail, Net Abuse," *InfoWorld*, February 28, 2008; Bobby White, "The New Workplace Rules: No Video-Watching," *The Wall Street Journal*, March 4, 2008; and Maggie Jackson, "May We Have Your Attention, Please?" *Business Week*, June 23, 2008.

CASE STUDY QUESTIONS

1. Should managers monitor employee e-mail and Internet usage? Why or why not?

2. Describe an effective e-mail and Web use policy for a company.

3. Should managers inform employees that their Web behavior is being monitored? Or should managers monitor secretly? Why or why not?

MIS IN ACTION

Explore the Web site of online employee monitoring software such as Websense, Barracuda Networks, MessageLabs, or SpectorSoft, and answer the following questions.

1. What employee activities does this software track? What can an employer learn about an employee by using this software?

2. How can businesses benefit from using this software?

3. How would you feel if your employer used this software where you work to monitor what you are doing on the job? Explain your response.

Another advantage of VoIP is its flexibility. Unlike the traditional telephone network, phones can be added or moved to different offices without rewiring or reconfiguring the network. With VoIP, a conference call is arranged by a simple click-and-drag operation on the computer screen to select the names of the conferees. Voice mail and e-mail can be combined into a single directory.

Unified Communications

In the past, each of the firm's networks for wired and wireless data, voice communications, and videoconferencing operated independently of each other and had to be managed separately by the information systems department. Now, however, firms are able to merge disparate communications modes into a single universally accessible service using unified communications technology. **Unified communications** integrates disparate channels for voice communications, data communications, instant messaging, e-mail, and electronic conferencing into a single experience where users can seamlessly switch back and forth between different communication modes. Presence technology shows whether a person is available to receive a call. Companies will need to examine how work flows and business processes will be altered by this technology in order to gauge its value.

CenterPoint Properties, a major Chicago area industrial real estate company, used unified communications technology to create collaborative Web sites for each of its real estate deals. Each Web site provides a single point for accessing structured and unstructured data. Integrated presence technology lets team members e-mail, instant message, call, or videoconference with one click.

Virtual Private Networks

What if you had a marketing group charged with developing new products and services for your firm with members spread across the United States? You would want to be able to e-mail each other and communicate with the home office without any chance that outsiders could intercept the communications. In the past, one answer to this problem was to work with large private networking firms who offered secure, private, dedicated networks to customers. But this was an expensive solution. A much less-expensive solution is to create a virtual private network within the public Internet.

A **virtual private network (VPN)** is a secure, encrypted, private network that has been configured within a public network to take advantage of the economies of scale and management facilities of large networks, such as the Internet (see Figure 6-12). A VPN provides your firm with secure, encrypted communications at a much lower cost than the same capabilities offered by traditional non-Internet providers who use their private networks to secure communications. VPNs also provide a network infrastructure for combining voice and data networks.

Several competing protocols are used to protect data transmitted over the public Internet, including *Point-to-Point Tunneling Protocol (PPTP)*. In a process called tunneling, packets of data are encrypted and wrapped inside IP packets. By adding this wrapper around a network message to hide its content, business firms create a private connection that travels through the public Internet.

THE WEB

You've probably used the Web to download music, to find information for a term paper, or to obtain news and weather reports. The Web is the most popular Internet service. It's a system with universally accepted standards for storing, retrieving, formatting, and displaying information using a client/server architecture. Web pages are formatted using hypertext with embedded links that connect documents to one another and that also link pages to other objects, such as sound, video, or animation files. When you click a graphic and a video clip plays, you have clicked a hyperlink. A typical **Web site** is a collection of Web pages linked to a home page.

Hypertext

Web pages are based on a standard Hypertext Markup Language (HTML), which formats documents and incorporates dynamic links to other documents and pictures stored in the

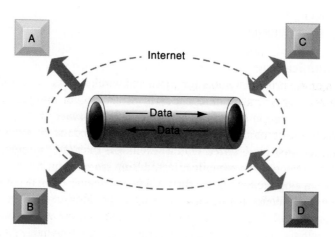

Figure 6-12
A Virtual Private Network Using the Internet
This VPN is a private network of computers linked using a secure "tunnel" connection over the Internet. It protects data transmitted over the public Internet by encoding the data and "wrapping" them within the Internet Protocol (IP). By adding a wrapper around a network message to hide its content, organizations can create a private connection that travels through the public Internet.

same or remote computers (see Chapter 4). Web pages are accessible through the Internet because Web browser software operating your computer can request Web pages stored on an Internet host server using the **Hypertext Transfer Protocol (HTTP)**. HTTP is the communications standard used to transfer pages on the Web. For example, when you type a Web address in your browser, such as www.sec.gov, your browser sends an HTTP request to the sec.gov server requesting the home page of sec.gov.

HTTP is the first set of letters at the start of every Web address, followed by the domain name, which specifies the organization's server computer that is storing the document. Most companies have a domain name that is the same as or closely related to their official corporate name. The directory path and document name are two more pieces of information within the Web address that help the browser track down the requested page. Together, the address is called a **uniform resource locator (URL)**. When typed into a browser, a URL tells the browser software exactly where to look for the information. For example, in the URL http://www.megacorp.com/content/features/082602.html, *http* names the protocol used to display Web pages, *www.megacorp.com* is the domain name, *content/features* is the directory path that identifies where on the domain Web server the page is stored, and *082602.html* is the document name and the name of the format it is in (it is an HTML page).

Web Servers

A Web server is software for locating and managing stored Web pages. It locates the Web pages requested by a user on the computer where they are stored and delivers the Web pages to the user's computer. Server applications usually run on dedicated computers, although they can all reside on a single computer in small organizations.

The most common Web server in use today is Apache HTTP Server, which controls 46 percent of the market. Apache is an open source product that is free of charge and can be downloaded from the Web. Microsoft Internet Information Services is the second most commonly used Web server, with a 22 percent market share.

Searching for Information on the Web

No one knows for sure how many Web pages there really are. The surface Web is the part of the Web that search engines visit and about which information is recorded. For instance, Google visited about 50 billion in 2008 although publicly it acknowledges indexing more than 25 billion. But there is a "deep Web" that contains an estimated 800 billion additional pages, many of them proprietary (such as the pages of *The Wall Street Journal* Online, which cannot be visited without an access code) or that are stored in protected corporate databases.

Search Engines Obviously, with so many Web pages, finding specific Web pages that can help you or your business, nearly instantly, is an important problem. The question is, how can you find the one or two pages you really want and need out of billions of indexed Web pages? **Search engines** attempt to solve the problem of finding useful information on the Web nearly instantly, and, arguably, they are the "killer app" of the Internet era. Today's search engines can sift through HTML files, files of Microsoft Office applications, PDF files, as well as audio, video, and image files. There are hundreds of different search engines in the world, but the vast majority of search results are supplied by three top providers: Google, Yahoo!, and Microsoft's recently released Bing search engine.

Web search engines started out in the early 1990s as relatively simple software programs that roamed the nascent Web, visiting pages and gathering information about the content of each page. The first search engines were simple keyword indexes of all the pages they visited, leaving the user with lists of pages that may not have been truly relevant to their search.

In 1994, Stanford University computer science students David Filo and Jerry Yang created a hand-selected list of their favorite Web pages and called it "Yet Another Hierarchical Officious Oracle," or Yahoo!. Yahoo! was not initially a search engine but rather an edited selection of Web sites organized by categories the editors found useful, but it has since developed its own search engine capabilities.

In 1998, Larry Page and Sergey Brin, two other Stanford computer science students, released their first version of Google. This search engine was different: Not only did it index each Web page's words but it also ranked search results based on the relevance of each page. Page patented the idea of a page ranking system (PageRank System), which essentially measures the popularity of a Web page by calculating the number of sites that link to that page as well as the number of pages which it links to. Brin contributed a unique Web crawler program that indexed not only keywords on a page but also combinations of words (such as authors and the titles of their articles). These two ideas became the foundation for the Google search engine. Figure 6-13 illustrates how Google works.

Search engine Web sites are so popular that many people use them as their home page, the page where they start (see Chapter 9). As useful as they are, no one expected search engines to be big money makers. Today, however, search engines are the foundation for the fastest growing form of marketing and advertising, search engine marketing.

Search engines have become major shopping tools by offering what is now called **search engine marketing**. When users enter a search term at Google, Bing, Yahoo!, or any of the other sites serviced by these search engines, they receive two types of listings: sponsored links, for which advertisers have paid to be listed (usually at the top of the search results page), and unsponsored "organic" search results. In addition, advertisers can purchase small text boxes on the side of search results pages. The paid, sponsored advertisements are the fastest growing form of Internet advertising and are powerful new marketing tools that precisely match consumer interests with advertising messages at the right moment. Search engine marketing monetizes the value of the search process. In 2009, search engine marketing generated $12.2 billion in revenue, half of all online advertising. Ninety eight percent of Google's annual revenue of $22 billion comes from search engine marketing (eMarketer, 2009).

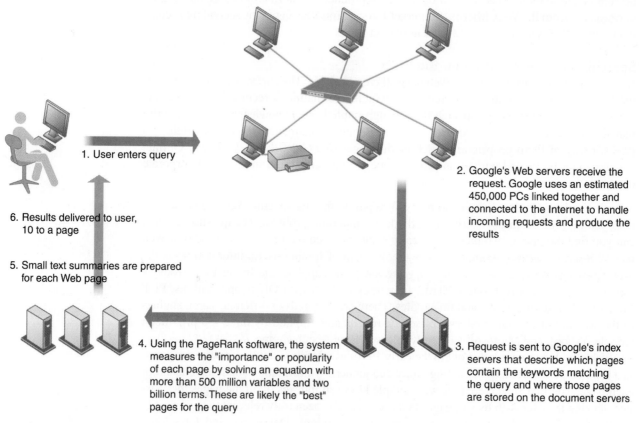

1. User enters query

2. Google's Web servers receive the request. Google uses an estimated 450,000 PCs linked together and connected to the Internet to handle incoming requests and produce the results

6. Results delivered to user, 10 to a page

5. Small text summaries are prepared for each Web page

4. Using the PageRank software, the system measures the "importance" or popularity of each page by solving an equation with more than 500 million variables and two billion terms. These are likely the "best" pages for the query

3. Request is sent to Google's index servers that describe which pages contain the keywords matching the query and where those pages are stored on the document servers

Figure 6-13
How Google Works
The Google search engine is continuously crawling the Web, indexing the content of each page, calculating its popularity, and storing the pages so that it can respond quickly to user requests to see a page. The entire process takes about one-half second.

Because search engine marketing is so effective, companies are starting to optimize their Web sites for search engine recognition. The better optimized the page is, the higher a ranking it will achieve in search engine result listings. **Search engine optimization (SEO)** is the process of improving the quality and volume of Web traffic to a Web site by employing a series of techniques that help a Web site achieve a higher ranking with the major search engines when certain keywords and phrases are put in the search field. One technique is to make sure that the keywords used in the Web site description match the keywords likely to be used as search terms by prospective customers. For example, your Web site is more likely to be among the first ranked by search engines if it uses the keyword "lighting" rather than "lamps" if most prospective customers are searching for "lighting." It is also advantageous to link your Web site to as many other Wet sites as possible because search engines evaluate such links to determine the popularity of a Web page and how it is linked to other content on the Web. The assumption is the more links there are to a Web site, the more useful the Web site must be.

In 2008, about 100 million people each day in the United States alone used a search engine, producing over 17 billion searches a month. There are hundreds of search engines but the top three (Google, Yahoo!, and Bing) account for 90 percent of all searches (see Figure 6-14).

Although search engines were originally built to search text documents, the explosion in online video and images has created a demand for search engines that can quickly find specific videos. The words "dance," "love," "music," and "girl" are all exceedingly popular in titles of YouTube videos, and searching on these keywords produces a flood of responses even though the actual contents of the video may have nothing to do with the search term. Searching videos is challenging because computers are not very good or quick at recognizing digital images. Some search engines have started indexing movies scripts so it will be possible to search on dialogue to find a movie. One of the most popular video search engines is Blinkx.com, which stores 18 million hours of video and employs a large group of human classifiers who check the contents of uploaded videos against their titles.

Intelligent Agent Shopping Bots Chapter 11 describes the capabilities of software agents with built-in intelligence that can gather or filter information and perform other tasks to assist users. **Shopping bots** use intelligent agent software for searching the Internet for shopping information. Shopping bots such as MySimon or Google Product Search can help people interested in making a purchase filter and retrieve information about products of interest, evaluate competing products according to criteria the users have established, and negotiate with vendors for price and delivery terms. Many of these shopping agents search

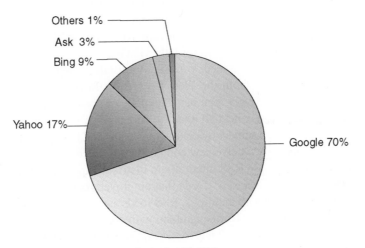

Figure 6-14
Top U.S. Web Search Engines
Google is the most popular search engine on the Web, handling 70 percent of all Web searches.

Sources: Based on data from SeoConsultants.com, September 25, 2009.

the Web for pricing and availability of products specified by the user and return a list of sites that sell the item along with pricing information and a purchase link.

Web 2.0

Today's Web sites don't just contain static content—they enable people to collaborate, share information, and create new services and content online. **Web 2.0** refers to these second-generation interactive Internet-based services. If you have shared photos over the Internet at Flickr or another photo site, posted a video to YouTube, created a blog, used Wikipedia, or added a widget to your Facebook page, you've used some of these Web 2.0 services.

Web 2.0 has four defining features: interactivity, real-time user control, social participation (sharing), and user-generated content. The technologies and services behind these features include cloud computing, software mashups and widgets, blogs, RSS, wikis, and social networks.

Mashups and widgets, which we introduced in Chapter 4, are software services that enable users and system developers to mix and match content or software components to create something entirely new. For example, Yahoo's photo storage and sharing site Flickr combines photos with other information about the images provided by users and tools to make it usable within other programming environments.

These software applications run on the Web itself instead of the desktop. With Web 2.0, the Web is not just a collection of destination sites, but a source of data and services that can be combined to create applications users need. Web 2.0 tools and services have fueled the creation of social networks and other online communities where people can interact with one another in the manner of their choosing.

A **blog**, the popular term for a Weblog, is a personal Web site that typically contains a series of chronological entries (newest to oldest) by its author, and links to related Web pages. The blog may include a *blogroll* (a collection of links to other blogs) and *trackbacks* (a list of entries in other blogs that refer to a post on the first blog). Most blogs allow readers to post comments on the blog entries as well. The act of creating a blog is often referred to as "blogging." Blogs are either hosted by a third-party site such as Blogger.com, LiveJournal.com, TypePad.com, and Xanga.com, or prospective bloggers can download software such as Movable Type to create a blog that is housed by the user's ISP.

Blog pages are usually variations on templates provided by the blogging service or software. Therefore, millions of people without HTML skills of any kind can post their own Web pages and share content with others. The totality of blog-related Web sites is often referred to as the **blogosphere**. Although blogs have become popular personal publishing tools, they also have business uses (see Chapters 9 and 10).

If you're an avid blog reader, you might use RSS to keep up with your favorite blogs without constantly checking them for updates. **RSS**, which stands for Rich Site Summary or Really Simple Syndication, syndicates Web site content so that it can be used in another setting. RSS technology pulls specified content from Web sites and feeds it automatically to users' computers, where it can be stored for later viewing.

To receive an RSS information feed, you need to install aggregator or news reader software that can be downloaded from the Web. (Microsoft Internet Explorer includes RSS reading capabilities.) Alternatively, you can establish an account with an aggregator Web site. You tell the aggregator to collect all updates from a given Web page, or list of pages, or gather information on a given subject by conducting Web searches at regular intervals. Once subscribed, you automatically receive new content as it is posted to the specified Web site.

A number of businesses use RSS internally to distribute updated corporate information. Wells Fargo uses RSS to deliver news feeds that employees can customize to see the business news of greatest relevance to their jobs. RSS feeds are so popular that online publishers are developing ways to present advertising along with content.

Blogs allow visitors to add comments to the original content, but they do not allow visitors to change the original posted material. **Wikis**, in contrast, are collaborative Web sites where visitors can add, delete, or modify content on the site, including the work of previous authors. Wiki comes from the Hawaiian word for "quick."

Wiki software typically provides a template that defines layout and elements common to all pages, displays user-editable software program code, and then renders the content into an HTML-based page for display in a Web browser. Some wiki software allows only basic text formatting, whereas other tools allow the use of tables, images or even interactive elements, such as polls or games. Most wikis provide capabilities for monitoring the work of other users and correcting mistakes.

Because wikis make information sharing so easy, they have many business uses. For example, Motorola sales representatives use wikis for sharing sales information. Instead of developing a different pitch for every client, reps reuse the information posted on the wiki. The U.S. Department of Homeland Security's National Cyber Security Center deployed a wiki to facilitate collaboration among federal agencies on cybersecurity. NCSC and other agencies use the wiki for real-time information sharing on threats, attacks, and responses and as a repository for technical and standards information.

Social networking sites enable users to build communities of friends and professional colleagues. Members each typically create a "profile," a Web page for posting photos, videos, MP3 files, and text, and then share these profiles with others on the service identified as their "friends" or contacts. Social networking sites are highly interactive, offer real-time user control, rely on user-generated content, and are broadly based on social participation and sharing of content and opinions. Leading social networking sites include Facebook, MySpace (each with over 100 million members), and LinkedIn (for professional contacts).

For many, social networking sites are the defining Web 2.0 application, and one that will radically change how people spend their time online; how people communicate and with whom; how business people stay in touch with customers, suppliers, and employees; how providers of goods and services learn about their customers; and how advertisers reach potential customers. The large social networking sites are also morphing into application development platforms where members can create and sell software applications to other members of the community. Facebook alone had over 1 million developers who created over 350,000 applications for gaming, video sharing, and communicating with friends and family. We will talk more about business applications of social networking in Chapters 9 and 10, and you can find social networking discussions in many other chapters of the text. You can also find a more detailed discussion of Web 2.0 in our Learning Tracks.

Web 3.0: The Future Web

Every day about 100 million Americans enter 500 million queries to search engines. How many of these 500 million queries produce a meaningful result (a useful answer in the first three listings)? Arguably, fewer than half. Google, Yahoo!, Microsoft, and Amazon are all trying to increase the odds of people finding meaningful answers to search engine queries. But with over 50 billion Web pages indexed, the means available for finding the information you really want are quite primitive, based on the words used on the pages, and the relative popularity of the page among people who use those same search terms. In other words, it's hit and miss.

To a large extent, the future of the Web involves developing techniques to make searching the 50 billion Web pages more productive and meaningful for ordinary people. Web 1.0 solved the problem of obtaining access to information. Web 2.0 solved the problem of sharing that information with others, and building new Web experiences. **Web 3.0** is the promise of a future Web where all this digital information, all these contacts, can be woven together into a single meaningful experience.

Sometimes this is referred to as the **Semantic Web**. "Semantic" refers to meaning. Most of the Web's content today is designed for humans to read and for computers to display, not for computer programs to analyze and manipulate. Search engines can discover when a particular term or keyword appears in a Web document, but they do not really understand its meaning or how it relates to other information on the Web. You can check this out on Google by entering two searches. First, enter "Paris Hilton". Next, enter "Hilton in Paris". Because Google does not understand ordinary English, it has no idea that you are interested in the Hilton Hotel in Paris in the second search. Because it cannot understand the meaning of pages it has indexed, Google's search engine returns the most popular pages for those queries where "Hilton" and "Paris" appear on the pages.

First described in a 2001 *Scientific American* article, the Semantic Web is a collaborative effort led by the World Wide Web Consortium to add a layer of meaning atop the existing Web to reduce the amount of human involvement in searching for and processing Web information (Berners-Lee et al., 2001).

Views on the future of the Web vary, but they generally focus on ways to make the Web more "intelligent," with machine-facilitated understanding of information promoting a more intuitive and effective user experience. For instance, let's say you want to set up a party with your tennis buddies at a local restaurant Friday night after work. One problem is that you had earlier scheduled to go to a movie with another friend. In a Semantic Web 3.0 environment, you would be able to coordinate this change in plans with the schedules of your tennis buddies, the schedule of your movie friend, and make a reservation at the restaurant all with a single set of commands issued as text or voice to your handheld smartphone. Right now, this capability is beyond our grasp.

Work proceeds slowly on making the Web a more intelligent experience, in large part because it is difficult to make machines, including software programs, that are truly intelligent like humans. But there are other views of the future Web. Some see a 3-D Web where you can walk through pages in a 3-D environment. Others point to the idea of a pervasive Web that controls everything from the lights in your living room, to your car's rear view mirror, not to mention managing your calendar and appointments.

Other complementary trends leading toward a future Web 3.0 include more widespread use of cloud computing and SaaS business models, ubiquitous connectivity among mobile platforms and Internet access devices, and the transformation of the Web from a network of separate siloed applications and content into a more seamless and interoperable whole. These more modest visions of the future Web 3.0 are more likely to be realized in the near term.

6.4 The Wireless Revolution

If you have a cell phone, do you use it for taking and sending photos, sending text messages, or downloading music clips? Do you take your laptop to class or to the library to link up to the Internet? If so, you're part of the wireless revolution! Cell phones, laptops, and small handheld devices have morphed into portable computing platforms that let you perform some of the computing tasks you used to do at your desk.

Wireless communication helps businesses more easily stay in touch with customers, suppliers, and employees and provides more flexible arrangements for organizing work. Wireless technology has also created new products, services, and sales channels, which we discuss in Chapter 9.

If you require mobile communication and computing power or remote access to corporate systems, you can work with an array of wireless devices, including cell phones, **smartphones**, and wireless-enabled personal computers. We introduced smartphones in our discussions of the mobile digital platform in Chapters 1 and 4. In addition to voice transmission, they feature capabilities for e-mail, messaging, wireless Internet access, digital photography, and personal information management. The features of the iPhone and BlackBerry illustrate the extent to which cellphones have evolved into small mobile computers.

CELLULAR SYSTEMS

Digital cellular service uses several competing standards. In Europe and much of the rest of the world outside the United Sates, the standard is Global System for Mobile Communication (GSM). GSM's strength is its international roaming capability. There are GSM cell phone systems in the United States, including T-Mobile and AT&T Wireless.

The major standard in the United States is Code Division Multiple Access (CDMA), which is the system used by Verizon and Sprint. CDMA was developed by the military during World War II. It transmits over several frequencies, occupies the entire spectrum, and randomly assigns users to a range of frequencies over time. In general, CDMA is cheaper to implement, is more efficient in its use of spectrum, and provides higher quality throughput of voice and data than GSM.

Earlier generations of cellular systems were designed primarily for voice and limited data transmission in the form of short text messages. Wireless carriers now offer more powerful cellular networks called third-generation **(3G) networks**, with transmission speeds ranging from 144 Kbps for mobile users in, say, a car, to more than 2 Mbps for stationary users. This is sufficient transmission capacity for video, graphics, and other rich media, in addition to voice, making 3G networks suitable for wireless broadband Internet access. Many of the cellular handsets available today are 3G-enabled, including the newest version of Apple's iPhone.

3G networks are widely used in Japan, South Korea, Taiwan, Hong Kong, Singapore, and parts of northern Europe. In U.S. locations without 3G coverage, U.S. cellular carriers have upgraded their networks to support higher-speed transmission. These interim *2.5G networks* provide data transmission rates ranging from 60 to 354 Kbps, enabling cell phones to be used for Web access, music downloads, and other broadband services. AT&T's EDGE network used by the first-generation iPhone is an example. PCs equipped with a special card can use these broadband cellular services for anytime, anywhere wireless Internet access.

The next evolution in wireless communication, called **4G networks**, is entirely packet-switched and capable of providing between 1 Mbps and 1 Gbps speeds, with premium quality and high security. Voice, data, and high-quality streaming video will be available to users anywhere, anytime. Commercial deployment of 4G networks will take place within the next few years. Telecommunications companies such as Sprint, Verizon, and NTT DoCoMo have started rolling out 4G systems. You can find out more about cellular generations in the Learning Tracks for this chapter.

WIRELESS COMPUTER NETWORKS AND INTERNET ACCESS

If you have a laptop computer, you might be able to use it to access the Internet as you move from room to room in your dorm, or table to table in your university library. An array of technologies provide high-speed wireless access to the Internet for PCs and other wireless handheld devices as well as for cell phones. These new high-speed services have extended Internet access to numerous locations that could not be covered by traditional wired Internet services.

Bluetooth

Bluetooth is the popular name for the 802.15 wireless networking standard, which is useful for creating small **personal-area networks (PANs)**. It links up to eight devices within a 10-meter area using low-power, radio-based communication and can transmit up to 722 Kbps in the 2.4-GHz band.

Wireless phones, pagers, computers, printers, and computing devices using Bluetooth communicate with each other and even operate each other without direct user intervention (see Figure 6-15). For example, a person could direct a notebook computer to send a document file wirelessly to a printer. Bluetooth connects wireless keyboards and mice to PCs or cell phones to earpieces without wires. Bluetooth has low-power requirements, making it appropriate for battery-powered handheld computers, cell phones, or PDAs.

Although Bluetooth lends itself to personal networking, it has uses in large corporations. For example, FedEx drivers use Bluetooth to transmit the delivery data captured by their handheld PowerPad computers to cellular transmitters, which forward the data to corporate computers. Drivers no longer need to spend time docking their handheld units physically in the transmitters, and Bluetooth has saved FedEx $20 million per year.

Figure 6-15
A Bluetooth Network (PAN)
Bluetooth enables a variety of devices, including cell phones, PDAs, wireless keyboards and mice, PCs, and printers, to interact wirelessly with each other within a small 30-foot (10-meter) area. In addition to the links shown, Bluetooth can be used to network similar devices to send data from one PC to another, for example.

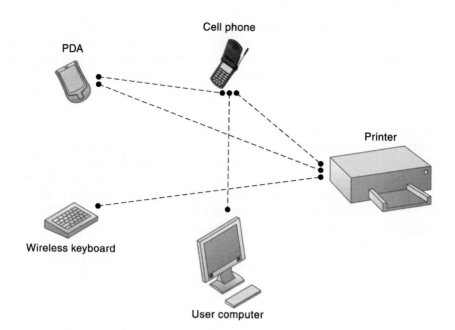

Wi-Fi

The 802.11 set of standards for wireless LANs is also known as **Wi-Fi**. There are three standards in this family: 802.11a, 802.11b, and 802.11g. 802.11n is a new standard for increasing the speed and capacity of wireless networking.

The 802.11a standard can transmit up to 54 Mbps in the unlicensed 5-GHz frequency range and has an effective distance of 10 to 30 meters. The 802.11b standard can transmit up to 11 Mbps in the unlicensed 2.4-GHz band and has an effective distance of 30 to 50 meters, although this range can be extended outdoors by using tower-mounted antennas. The 802.11g standard can transmit up to 54 Mbps in the 2.4-GHz range. 802.11n can transmit at more than 600 Mbps.

802.11b was the first wireless standard to be widely adopted for wireless LANs and wireless Internet access. 802.11g is increasingly used for this purpose, and systems capable of handling 802.11n are becoming available.

In most Wi-Fi communications, wireless devices communicate with a wired LAN using access points. An access point is a box consisting of a radio receiver/transmitter and antennas that links to a wired network, router, or hub.

Figure 6-16 illustrates an 802.11 wireless LAN operating in infrastructure mode that connects a small number of mobile devices to a larger wired LAN. Most wireless devices are client machines. The servers that the mobile client stations need to use are on the wired LAN. The access point controls the wireless stations and acts as a bridge between the main wired LAN and the wireless LAN. (A bridge connects two LANs based on different technologies.) The access point also controls the wireless stations.

Laptop PCs now come equipped with chips to receive Wi-Fi signals. Older models may need an add-in wireless network interface card.

Wi-Fi and Wireless Internet Access

The 802.11 standard also provides wireless access to the Internet using a broadband connection. In this instance, an access point plugs into an Internet connection, which could come from a cable TV line or DSL telephone service. Computers within range of the access point use it to link wirelessly to the Internet.

Businesses of all sizes are using Wi-Fi networks to provide low-cost wireless LANs and Internet access. Wi-Fi hotspots are springing up in hotels, airport lounges, libraries, cafes, and college campuses to provide mobile access to the Internet. Dartmouth College is one of many campuses where students now use Wi-Fi for research, course work, and entertainment.

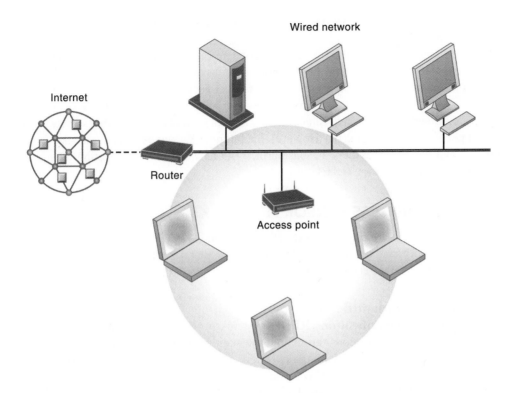

Figure 6-16
An 802.11 Wireless LAN
Mobile laptop computers equipped with network interface cards link to the wired LAN by communicating with the access point. The access point uses radio waves to transmit network signals from the wired network to the client adapters, which convert them into data that the mobile device can understand. The client adapter then transmits the data from the mobile device back to the access point, which forwards the data to the wired network.

Hotspots typically consist of one or more access points positioned on a ceiling, wall, or other strategic spot in a public place to provide maximum wireless coverage for a specific area. Users in range of a hotspot are able to access the Internet from laptops, handhelds, or cell phones that are Wi-Fi enabled, such as Apple's iPhone. Some hotspots are free or do not require any additional software to use; others may require activation and the establishment of a user account by providing a credit card number over the Web.

Wi-Fi technology poses several challenges, however. Right now, users cannot freely roam from hotspot to hotspot if these hotspots use different Wi-Fi network services. Unless the service is free, users would need to log on to separate accounts for each service, each with its own fees.

One major drawback of Wi-Fi is its weak security features, which make these wireless networks vulnerable to intruders. We provide more detail about Wi-Fi security issues in Chapter 8.

Another drawback of Wi-Fi networks is susceptibility to interference from nearby systems operating in the same spectrum, such as wireless phones, microwave ovens, or other wireless LANs. Wireless networks based on the 802.11n specification solve this problem by using multiple wireless antennas in tandem to transmit and receive data and technology to coordinate multiple simultaneous radio signals. This technology is called *MIMO* (*multiple input multiple output*).

WiMax

A surprisingly large number of areas in the United States and throughout the world do not have access to Wi-Fi or fixed broadband connectivity. The range of Wi-Fi systems is no more than 300 feet from the base station, making it difficult for rural groups that don't have cable or DSL service to find wireless access to the Internet.

The IEEE developed a new family of standards known as WiMax to deal with these problems. **WiMax**, which stands for Worldwide Interoperability for Microwave Access, is the popular term for IEEE Standard 802.16, known as the "Air Interface for Fixed Broadband Wireless Access Systems." WiMax has a wireless access range of up to 31 miles, compared to 300 feet for Wi-Fi and 30 feet for Bluetooth, and a data transfer rate of up to 75

Mbps. The 802.16 specification has robust security and quality-of-service features to support voice and video.

WiMax antennas are powerful enough to beam high-speed Internet connections to rooftop antennas of homes and businesses that are miles away. Cellular handsets and laptops with WiMax capabilities are appearing in the marketplace. Clearwire, which is owned by Sprint Nextel, is using WiMax technology as the foundation for the 4G networks it is deploying throughout the United States. Clearwire plans expects to offer this service to 120 million people by the end of 2010. However, the future of WiMax is cloudy because Verizon Wireless and wireless providers are basing their 4G networks on a competing technology called Long-Term Evolution (LTE).

RFID AND WIRELESS SENSOR NETWORKS

Mobile technologies are creating new efficiencies and ways of working throughout the enterprise. In addition to the wireless systems we have just described, radio frequency identification systems and wireless sensor networks are having a major impact.

Radio Frequency Identification

Radio frequency identification (RFID) systems provide a powerful technology for tracking the movement of goods throughout the supply chain. RFID systems use tiny tags with embedded microchips containing data about an item and its location to transmit radio signals over a short distance to RFID readers. The RFID readers then pass the data over a network to a computer for processing. Unlike bar codes, RFID tags do not need line-of-sight contact to be read.

The RFID tag is electronically programmed with information that can uniquely identify an item plus other information about the item, such as its location, where and when it was made, or its status during production. Embedded in the tag is a microchip for storing the data. The rest of the tag is an antenna that transmits data to the reader.

The reader unit consists of an antenna and radio transmitter with a decoding capability attached to a stationary or handheld device. The reader emits radio waves in ranges anywhere from 1 inch to 100 feet, depending on its power output, the radio frequency employed, and surrounding environmental conditions. When an RFID tag comes within the range of the reader, the tag is activated and starts sending data. The reader captures these data, decodes them, and sends them back over a wired or wireless network to a host computer for further processing (see Figure 6-17). Both RFID tags and antennas come in a variety of shapes and sizes.

Active RFID tags are powered by an internal battery and typically enable data to be rewritten and modified. Active tags can transmit for hundreds of feet but may cost several dollars and upward per tag. Automated toll-collection systems such as New York's E-ZPass use active RFID tags.

Passive RFID tags do not have their own power source and obtain their operating power from the radio frequency energy transmitted by the RFID reader. They are smaller, lighter, and less expensive than active tags, but only have a range of several feet.

In inventory control and supply chain management, RFID systems capture and manage more detailed information about items in warehouses or in production than bar coding systems. If a large number of items are shipped together, RFID systems track each pallet, lot, or even unit item in the shipment. This technology may help companies such as Wal-Mart improve receiving and storage operations by improving their ability to "see" exactly what stock is stored in warehouses or on retail store shelves.

Wal-Mart has installed RFID readers at store receiving docks to record the arrival of pallets and cases of goods shipped with RFID tags. The RFID reader reads the tags a second time just as the cases are brought onto the sales floor from backroom storage areas. Software combines sales data from Wal-Mart's point-of-sale systems and the RFID data regarding the number of cases brought out to the sales floor. The program determines which items will soon be depleted and automatically generates a list of items to pick in the warehouse to

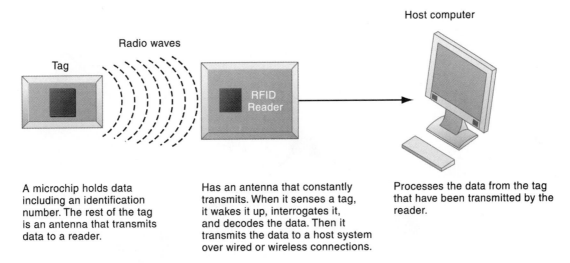

A microchip holds data including an identification number. The rest of the tag is an antenna that transmits data to a reader.

Has an antenna that constantly transmits. When it senses a tag, it wakes it up, interrogates it, and decodes the data. Then it transmits the data to a host system over wired or wireless connections.

Processes the data from the tag that have been transmitted by the reader.

Figure 6-17
How RFID Works
RFID uses low-powered radio transmitters to read data stored in a tag at distances ranging from 1 inch to 100 feet. The reader captures the data from the tag and sends them over a network to a host computer for processing.

replenish store shelves before they run out. This information helps Wal-Mart reduce out-of-stock items, increase sales, and further shrink its costs.

The cost of RFID tags used to be too high for widespread use, but now it is less than 10 cents per passive tag in the United States. As the price decreases, RFID is starting to become cost-effective for some applications.

In addition to installing RFID readers and tagging systems, companies may need to upgrade their hardware and software to process the massive amounts of data produced by RFID systems—transactions that could add up to tens or hundreds of terabytes.

Software is used to filter, aggregate, and prevent RFID data from overloading business networks and system applications. Applications often need to be redesigned to accept large volumes of frequently generated RFID data and to share those data with other applications. Major enterprise software vendors, including SAP and Oracle-PeopleSoft, now offer RFID-ready versions of their supply chain management applications.

Wireless Sensor Networks

If your company wanted state-of-the art technology to monitor building security or detect hazardous substances in the air, it might deploy a wireless sensor network. **Wireless sensor networks (WSNs)** are networks of interconnected wireless devices that are embedded into the physical environment to provide measurements of many points over large spaces. These devices have built-in processing, storage, and radio frequency sensors and antennas. They are linked into an interconnected network that routes the data they capture to a computer for analysis.

These networks range from hundreds to thousands of nodes. Because wireless sensor devices are placed in the field for years at a time without any maintenance or human intervention, they must have very low power requirements and batteries capable of lasting for years.

Figure 6-18 illustrates one type of wireless sensor network, with data from individual nodes flowing across the network to a server with greater processing power. The server acts as a gateway to a network based on Internet technology.

Wireless sensor networks are valuable in areas such as monitoring environmental changes, monitoring traffic or military activity, protecting property, efficiently operating and managing machinery and vehicles, establishing security perimeters, monitoring supply chain management, or detecting chemical, biological, or radiological material.

Figure 6-18
A Wireless Sensor Network

The small circles represent lower-level nodes and the larger circles represent high-end nodes. Lower-level nodes forward data to each other or to higher-level nodes, which transmit data more rapidly and speed up network performance.

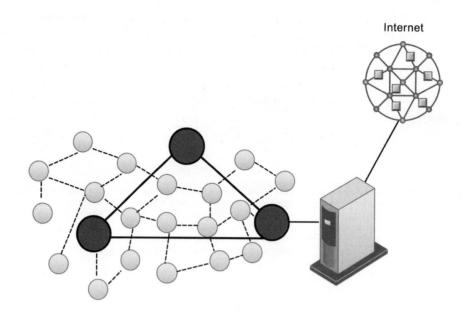

Internet

6.5 Hands-On MIS Projects

The projects in this section give you hands-on experience evaluating and selecting communications technology, using spreadsheet software to improve selection of telecommunications services, and using Web search engines for business research.

MANAGEMENT DECISION PROBLEMS

1. Your company supplies ceramic floor tiles to Home Depot, Lowe's, and other home improvement stores. You have been asked to start using radio frequency identification tags on each case of tiles you ship to help your customers improve the management of your products and those of other suppliers in their warehouses. Use the Web to identify the cost of hardware, software, and networking components for an RFID system for your company. What factors should be considered? What are the key decisions that have to be made in determining whether your firm should adopt this technology?

2. BestMed Medical Supplies Corporation sells medical and surgical products and equipment from over 700 different manufacturers to hospitals, health clinics, and medical offices. The company employs 500 people at seven different locations in western and midwestern states, including account managers, customer service and support representatives, and warehouse staff. Employees communicate via traditional telephone voice services, e-mail, instant messaging, and cell phones. Management is inquiring about whether the company should adopt a system for unified communications. What factors should be considered? What are the key decisions that have to be made in determining whether to adopt this technology? Use the Web, if necessary, to find out more about unified communications and its costs.

IMPROVING DECISION MAKING: USING SPREADSHEET SOFTWARE TO EVALUATE WIRELESS SERVICES

Software skills: Spreadsheet formulas, formatting
Business skills: Analyzing telecommunications services and costs

In this project, you'll use the Web to research alternative wireless services and use spreadsheet software to calculate wireless service costs for a sales force.

You would like to equip your sales force of 35 based in Cincinnati, Ohio, with mobile phones that have capabilities for voice transmission, text messaging, and taking and sending photos. Use the Web to select a wireless service provider that provides nationwide service as well as good service in your home area. Examine the features of the mobile handsets offered by each of these vendors. Assume that each of the 35 salespeople will need to spend three hours per day during business hours (8 a.m. to 6 p.m.) on mobile voice communication, send 30 text messages per day, and five photos per week. Use your spreadsheet software to determine the wireless service and handset that will offer the best pricing per user over a two-year period. For the purposes of this exercise, you do not need to consider corporate discounts.

ACHIEVING OPERATIONAL EXCELLENCE: USING WEB SEARCH ENGINES FOR BUSINESS RESEARCH

Software skills: Web search tools
Business skills: Researching new technologies

This project will help develop your Internet skills in using Web search engines for business research.

You want to learn more about ethanol as an alternative fuel for motor vehicles. Use the following search engines to obtain that information: Yahoo!, Google, and Bing. If you wish, try some other search engines as well. Compare the volume and quality of information you find with each search tool. Which tool is the easiest to use? Which produced the best results for your research? Why?

LEARNING TRACKS

The following Learning Tracks provide content relevant to topics covered in this chapter:

1. Computing and Communications Services Provided by Commercial Communications Vendors

2. Broadband Network Services and Technologies

3. Cellular System Generations

4. Wireless Applications for Customer Relationship Management, Supply Chain Management, and Healthcare

5. Web 2.0

Review Summary

1 **What are the principal components of telecommunications networks and key networking technologies?** A simple network consists of two or more connected computers. Basic network components include computers, network interfaces, a connection medium, network operating system software, and either a hub or a switch. The networking infrastructure for a large company includes the traditional telephone system, mobile cellular communication, wireless local-area networks, videoconferencing systems, a corporate Web site, intranets, extranets, and an array of local and wide-area networks, including the Internet.

Contemporary networks have been shaped by the rise of client/server computing, the use of packet switching, and the adoption of Transmission Control Protocol/Internet Protocol (TCP/IP) as a universal communications standard for linking disparate networks and computers, including the Internet. Protocols provide a common set of rules that enable communication among diverse components in a telecommunications network.

2 **What are the main telecommunications transmission media and types of networks?** The principal physical transmission media are twisted copper telephone wire, coaxial copper cable, fiber-optic cable, and wireless transmission. Twisted wire enables companies to use existing wiring for telephone systems for digital communication, although it is relatively slow. Fiber-optic and coaxial cable are used for high-volume transmission but are expensive to install. Microwave and communications satellites are used for wireless communication over long distances.

Local-area networks (LANs) connect PCs and other digital devices together within a 500-meter radius and are used today for many corporate computing tasks. Network components may be connected together using a star, bus, or ring topology. Wide-area networks (WANs) span broad geographical distances, ranging from several miles to continents, and are private networks that are independently managed. Metropolitan-area networks (MANs) span a single urban area.

Digital subscriber line (DSL) technologies, cable Internet connections, and T1 lines are often used for high-capacity Internet connections.

Cable Internet connections provide high-speed access to the Web or corporate intranets at speeds of up to 10 Mbps. A T1 line supports a data transmission rate of 1.544 Mbps.

3 **How do the Internet and Internet technology work, and how do they support communication and e-business?** The Internet is a worldwide network of networks that uses the client/server model of computing and the TCP/IP network reference model. Every computer on the Internet is assigned a unique numeric IP address. The Domain Name System (DNS) converts IP addresses to more user-friendly domain names. Worldwide Internet policies are established by organizations and government bodies, such as the Internet Architecture Board (IAB) and the World Wide Web Consortium (W3C).

Major Internet services include e-mail, newgroups, chatting, instant messaging, Telnet, FTP, and the Web. Web pages are based on Hypertext Markup Language (HTML) and can display text, graphics, video, and audio. Web site directories, search engines, and RSS technology help users locate the information they need on the Web. RSS, blogs, social networking, and wikis are features of Web 2.0.

Firms are also starting to realize economies by using VoIP technology for voice transmission and by using virtual private networks (VPNs) as low-cost alternatives to private WANs.

4 **What are the principal technologies and standards for wireless networking, communication, and Internet access?** Cellular networks are evolving toward high-speed, high-bandwidth, digital packet-switched transmission. Broadband 3G networks are capable of transmitting data at speeds ranging from 144 Kbps to more than 2 Mbps. 4G networks capable of transmission speeds that could reach 1 Gbps are starting to be rolled out.

Major cellular standards include Code Division Multiple Access (CDMA), which is used primarily in the United States, and Global System for Mobile Communications (GSM), which is the standard in Europe and much of the rest of the world.

Standards for wireless computer networks include Bluetooth (802.15) for small personal-area networks (PANs), Wi-Fi (802.11) for local-area networks (LANs), and WiMax (802.16) for metropolitan-area networks (MANs).

5   Why are radio frequency identification (RFID) and wireless sensor networks valuable for business? Radio frequency identification (RFID) systems provide a powerful technology for tracking the movement of goods by using tiny tags with embedded data about an item and its location. RFID readers read the radio signals transmitted by these tags and pass the data over a network to a computer for processing. Wireless sensor networks (WSNs) are networks of interconnected wireless sensing and transmitting devices that are embedded into the physical environment to provide measurements of many points over large spaces.

Key Terms

3G networks, 219
4G networks, 219
Bandwidth, 202
Blog, 216
Blogosphere, 216
Bluetooth, 219
Broadband, 193
Bus topology, 199
Cable Internet
    connections, 203
Cell phone, 201
Chat, 208
Coaxial cable, 200
Digital subscriber line (DSL),
    203
Domain name, 203
Domain Name System
    (DNS), 203
E-mail, 208
Fiber-optic cable, 201
File Transfer Protocol
    (FTP), 207
Hertz, 202
Hotspots, 221
Hubs, 195
Hypertext Transfer Protocol
    (HTTP), 213
Instant messaging, 2

Internet Protocol (IP)
    address, 203
Internet service provider
    (ISP), 202
Internet2, 205
Local-area network (LAN),
    198
Metropolitan-area network
    (MAN), 200
Microwave, 201
Modem, 198
Network interface card
    (NIC), 194
Network operating system
    (NOS), 194
Packet switching, 196
Peer-to-peer, 199
Personal-area networks
    (PANs), 219
Protocol, 197
Radio frequency identification (RFID), 222
Ring topology, 200
Router, 195
RSS, 216
Search engines, 213
Search engine marketing, 214
Search engine optimization
    (SEO), 215

Semantic Web, 217
Shopping bots, 215
Smartphones, 218
Social networking, 217
Star topology, 199
Switch, 195
T1 lines, 203
Telnet, 207
Topology, 199
Transmission Control
    Protocol/Internet Protocol
    (TCP/IP), 197
Twisted wire, 200
Unified communications, 211
Uniform resource locator
    (URL), 213
Virtual private network
    (VPN), 212
Voice over IP (VoIP), 209
Web 2.0, 216
Web 3.0, 217
Web site, 212
Wide-area networks (WANs),
    200
Wi-Fi, 220
Wiki, 216
WiMax, 221
Wireless sensor networks
    (WSNs), 223

Review Questions

1. What are the principal components of telecommunications networks and key networking technologies?
   - Describe the features of a simple network and the network infrastructure for a large company.
   - Name and describe the principal technologies and trends that have shaped contemporary telecommunications systems.

2. What are the main telecommunications transmission media and types of networks?
   - Name the different types of physical transmission media and compare them in terms of speed and cost.
   - Define a LAN, and describe its components and the functions of each component.
   - Name and describe the principal network topologies.

3. How do the Internet and Internet technology work, and how do they support communication and e-business?
- Define the Internet, describe how it works, and explain how it provides business value.
- Explain how the Domain Name System (DNS) and IP addressing system work.
- List and describe the principal Internet services.
- Define and describe VoIP and virtual private networks, and explain how they provide value to businesses.
- List and describe alternative ways of locating information on the Web.
- Compare Web 2.0 and Web 3.0.

4. What are the principal technologies and standards for wireless networking, communications, and Internet access?
- Define Bluetooth, Wi-Fi, WiMax, and 3G networks.
- Describe the capabilities of each and for which types of applications each is best suited.

5. Why are RFID and wireless sensor networks (WSNs) valuable for business?
- Define RFID, explain how it works, and describe how it provides value to businesses.
- Define WSNs, explain how they work, and describe the kinds of applications that use them.

Discussion Questions

1. It has been said that within the next few years, smartphones will become the single most important digital device we own. Discuss the implications of this statement.

2. Should all major retailing and manufacturing companies switch to RFID? Why or why not?

Video Cases

Video Cases and Instructional Videos illustrating some of the concepts in this chapter are available. Contact your instructor to access these videos.

Collaboration and Teamwork

Evaluating Smartphones

Form a group with three or four of your classmates. Compare the capabilities of Apple's iPhone with a smartphone handset from another vendor with similar features. Your analysis should consider the purchase cost of each device, the wireless networks where each device can operate, service plan and handset costs, and the services available for each device. You should also consider other capabilities of each device, including the ability to integrate with existing corporate or PC applications. Which device would you select? What criteria would you use to guide your selection? If possible, use Google Sites to post links to Web pages, team communication announcements, and work assignments; to brainstorm; and to work collaboratively on project documents. Try to use Google Docs to develop a presentation of your findings for the class.

BUSINESS PROBLEM-SOLVING CASE

Google Versus Microsoft: Clash of the Technology Titans

Google and Microsoft, two of the most prominent technology companies to arise in the past several decades, are poised to square off for dominance of the workplace and the Internet. The battle is already well underway. Google has dominated the Internet, while Microsoft has dominated the desktop. But both are increasingly seeking to grow into the other's core businesses. The competition between the companies is becoming fierce.

Differences in the strategies and business models of the two companies illustrate why this conflict will shape our technological future. Google began as one search company among many. But the effectiveness of its PageRank search algorithm and online advertising services, along with its ability to attract the best and brightest minds in the industry, have catapulted Google to global prominence. The company's extensive infrastructure allows them to offer the fastest search speeds and a variety of Web-based products. Google believes that online applications will be one of its next big businesses, as its core search and search-advertising businesses mature.

Microsoft achieved its giant stature on the strength of its Windows operating system and Office desktop productivity applications, which are used by over 500 million people worldwide. Sometimes vilified for its anti-competitive practices, the company and its products are nevertheless staples for businesses and consumers looking to improve their productivity with computer-based tasks.

Today, the two companies have very different visions for the future, influenced by the continued development of the Internet and increased availability of broadband Internet connections. Google believes that the maturation of the Internet will allow more and more computing tasks to be performed via the Web, on computers sitting in remote data centers rather than on your desktop or computers owned by individual business firms. This idea is known as cloud computing, and it is central to Google's business model going forward. Microsoft, on the other hand, has built its success around the model of desktop computing. Microsoft's goal is to embrace the Internet while persuading consumers to retain the desktop as the focal point for computing tasks.

With a vast array of Internet-based products and tools for online search, online advertising, digital mapping, online collaboration, digital photo management, digital radio broadcasting, blogging, social networking, and online video viewing, Google has pioneered cloud computing. It is banking on the idea that Internet-based computing will supplant desktop computing as the way most people work with their computers. Users would use various connectivity devices to access applications from remote servers stored in data centers, as opposed to working locally from their machine.

One advantage to the cloud computing model is that users would not be tied to a particular machine to access information or do work. Another is that Google would be responsible for most of the maintenance of the data centers that house these applications. But the disadvantages of the model are the requirement of an Internet connection to use the applications, as well as the security concerns surrounding Google's handling of your information. Google is banking on the increasing ubiquity of the Internet and availability of broadband and Wi-Fi connections to offset these drawbacks.

Microsoft already has several significant advantages to help remain relevant even if cloud computing is as good as Google advertises. The company has a well-established and popular set of applications that many consumers and businesses feel comfortable using. When Microsoft launches a new product, users of Office products and Windows can be sure that they will know how to use the product and that it will work with their system.

Cloud computing nevertheless represents a threat to Microsoft's core business model, which revolves around the desktop as the center for nearly all computing tasks. If, rather than buying software from Microsoft, consumers can instead buy access to applications stored on remote servers for a much cheaper cost, the desktop suddenly no longer occupies that central position. In the past, Microsoft used the popularity of its Windows operating system (found on 95 percent of the world's personal computers) and Office to destroy competing products such as Netscape Navigator, Lotus 1-2-3, and WordPerfect. But Google's offerings are Web-based, and thus not reliant on Windows or Office. Google believes that the vast majority of computing tasks, around 90 percent, can be done in the cloud. Microsoft disputes this claim, calling it grossly overstated.

Microsoft clearly wants to bolster its Internet presence in the event that Google is correct. It tried to acquire Yahoo in early 2008 for $45 billion, and failed. Microsoft wanted not only to bolster its Internet presence but also to end the threat of an advertising deal between Google and Yahoo. In June 2008, those chances diminished further due to a partnership between Google and Yahoo under which Yahoo outsourced a portion of its advertising to Google. Google planned to deliver some of its ads alongside some of the less profitable areas of Yahoo's search, since Google's technology is far more sophisticated and generates more revenue per search than any competitor. Microsoft struck back in July 2009 by reaching a deal with Yahoo in which Yahoo will use the Bing search engine.

Microsoft's new goals are to "innovate and disrupt in search, win in display ads, reinvent portal and social media experiences." Although Microsoft faces considerable hurdles in achieving these goals, it has made some progress. In May 2009, Microsoft launched a new Internet search engine called Bing, which has received very favorable reviews for the quality of its results as well as its features and design. Bing still ranks behind Yahoo and Google in popularity, but it is attracting many users. Microsoft hopes it will help it muscle in on Google's core market in Internet search advertising.

In the meantime, Google is developing a new operating system based on its Chrome Web browser. The Google Chrome Operating System is initially intended for use in low-cost netbook computers (see Chapter 4), but will be able to power full-size PCs. The operating system is fast, lightweight, and capable of getting a user onto the Web in a few seconds, and will further Google's vision of Internet-based computing.

The centerpiece of Google's efforts to encroach on Microsoft's turf is its Google Apps suite. These are a series of Web-based applications that include Gmail, instant messaging, calendar, word processing, presentation, and spreadsheet applications (Google Docs), and tools for creating collaborative Web sites. These applications are simpler versions of Microsoft's Office applications, and Google is offering basic versions of them for free, and "Premier" editions for a fraction of Microsoft's price. Subscribing to the Premier edition of Google Apps costs $50 per year per person, as opposed to approximately $500 per person to purchase Microsoft Office.

Google believes that most Office users don't need the advanced features of Word, Excel, and other Office applications, and have a great deal to gain by switching to Google Apps. Small businesses, for example, might prefer cheaper, simpler versions of word processing, spreadsheet, and electronic presentation applications because they don't require the complex features of Microsoft Office. Microsoft disputes this, saying that Office is a result of many years and dollars of research indicating what consumers want, and that consumers are very satisfied with their products. Many businesses agree, saying that they are reluctant to move away from Office because it is the "safe choice." These firms are often concerned that their data is not stored on-site and that they may be in violation of laws like Sarbanes-Oxley as a result, which requires that companies

maintain and report their data to the government upon request.

Microsoft is countering by offering more software features and Web-based services to bolster its online presence. These include SharePoint, a Web-based collaboration and document management platform (see Chapter 2) and Microsoft Office Live, providing Web-based services for e-mail, project management, and organizing information, as well as online extensions to Office.

In September 2009, Microsoft unveiled its Web-hosted Office Web Apps version of its new Office 2010 desktop suite. Office Web Apps include Word for word processing, Excel for spreadsheets, PowerPoint for presentations, and One Note for gathering and sharing information. A free ad-supported version of Office Web is available to consumers via Microsoft's Windows Live online service. Other versions will be available for businesses for a fee. Users of Office Web Apps who have the desktop version of Office will be able to switch seamlessly between the two tools.

Microsoft hopes that such lightweight and Web-based versions of its products will blunt competition from Google Docs and other popular options without curtailing the profitability of its products that still run on PC desktops or corporate servers. Microsoft's Windows 7 operating system has a version that runs well on the tiny netbooks.

The battle between Google and Microsoft isn't just being waged in the area of office productivity tools, Web browsers, and operating systems. The two companies are trading blows in a multitude of other fields, including Web maps, online video, cell phone software, and online health record keeping tools. Salesforce.com (see the case study at the end of Chapter 4) represents the site of another conflict between the two giants. Microsoft has attempted to move in on the software as a service (SaaS) model popularized by Salesforce.com, offering a competing CRM product for a fraction of the cost. Google has gone the opposite route, partnering with Salesforce to integrate their CRM applications with Google Apps and creating a new sales channel to market Google Apps to businesses that have already adopted Salesforce CRM software.

Both companies are attempting to open themselves up as platforms to developers. Google has already launched its Google App Engine, which allows outside programmers to develop and launch their own applications for minimal cost. In a move that represented a drastic change from their previous policy, Microsoft announced that it would reveal many key details of its software that had previously been kept secret. Programmers will have an easier time building services that work with Microsoft programs. Microsoft's secrecy once helped them control the marketplace by forcing other companies to use

Windows rather than develop alternatives, but if they can't do the same to Google Apps, it makes sense to try a different approach to attract developers.

Time will tell whether or not Microsoft is able to fend off Google's challenge to its dominance in the tech industry. Many other prominent companies have fallen victim to paradigm shifts, such as mainframes to personal computers, traditional print media to Internet distribution, and, if Google has its way, personal computers to cloud computing.

Sources: Jessica E. Vascellaro, "Google Strives to Help Online Software Catch Up," *The Wall Street Journal*, July 15, 2009; Neil McAllister, "Sneak Peek: Microsoft Office Web Apps," *InfoWorld*, September 18, 2009; Miguel Helft, "Bing Delivers Credibility to Microsoft," *The New York Times*, July 14, 2009 and "Google's Free Phone Manager Could Threaten a Variety of Services," *The New York Times*, March 12, 2009; Jessica Hodgson, "Microsoft to Offer Office over Web as It Responds to Google Threat," *The Wall Street Journal*, July 14, 2009; Miguel Helft and Ashlee Vance, "Google Ploans a PC Operating System," *The New York Times*, July 8, 2009; Clint Boulton,"Microsoft Marks the Spot," *eWeek*, May 5, 2008; Andy Kessler, "The War for the Web," *The Wall Street Journal*, May 6, 2008; John Pallatto and Clint Boulton, "An On-Demand Partnership" and Clint Boulton, "Google Apps Go to School," *eWeek*, April 21, 2008; Miguel Helft, "Google and Salesforce Join to Fight Microsoft." *The New York Times*, April 14, 2008; and Robert A. Guth, Ben Worthen, and Charles Forelle, "Microsoft to Allow Software Secrets on Internet," *The Wall Street Journal*, February 22, 2008.

Case Study Questions

1. Define and compare the business strategies and business models of Google and Microsoft.

2. Has the Internet taken over the PC desktop as the center of the action? Why or why not?

3. Why has Microsoft attempted to acquire Yahoo? How does it affect its business model? Do you believe this is a good move?

4. What is the significance of Google Apps to Google's future success?

5. Would you use Google Apps instead of Microsoft Office applications for computing tasks? Why or why not?

6. Which company and business model do you believe will prevail in this epic struggle? Justify your answer.

Securing Information Systems

STUDENT LEARNING OBJECTIVES

After completing this chapter, you will be able to answer the following questions:

1. Why are information systems vulnerable to destruction, error, and abuse?

2. What is the business value of security and control?

3. What are the components of an organizational framework for security and control?

4. What are the most important tools and technologies for safeguarding information resources?

CHAPTER OUTLINE

BOSTON CELTICS SCORE BIG POINTS AGAINST SPYWARE

While the Boston Celtics were fighting for a spot in the playoffs several years ago, another fierce battle was being waged by its information systems. Jay Wessel, the team's vice president of technology, was trying to score points against computer spyware. Wessel and his IT staff manage about 100 laptops issued to coaches and scouts, and sales, marketing, and finance employees, and these machines were being overwhelmed by malware (malicious software).

Like any sports franchise, the Celtics are on the road a great deal of time during the playing season. Coaches, recruiters, and other staff members are at away games 40 or more times each season, using their mobile laptop computers to review plays and update the status of players. They continually sign onto the Internet and connect to the Celtics' internal network from airports, hotels, and other public places. According to Wessel, "Hotel Internet connections are a hotbed for spyware activity." People would bring laptops that had been infected on the road back to team headquarters in Boston and clog up the network. Moreover, the spyware was affecting the accessibility and performance of the Celtics' proprietary statistical database created with Microsoft SQL Server,

which the coaches use to prepare for each game. Wessel and his staff were overwhelmed spending too much time trying to rid the machines and the network of infections.

During one playoff battle, a torrent of spyware poured into the laptops via a bad Internet connection in an Indiana hotel. At that point, Wessel decided to take a more aggressive stance toward spyware. His options were limited because his staff is small and the company does not have many resources for dealing with security. The security software solutions that the Celtics had been using (Aladdin eSafe Security Gateway and Webroot Spy Sweeper) were too unwieldy. The only way the Celtics could run a video-editing suite used for scouting new players was to temporarily remove these products.

Wessel decided to use Mi5 Networks' Webgate security appliance as a solution. The tool sits between the Celtics' corporate firewall and network, where it stops spyware from entering the Celtics' corporate network and prevents machines that have already been infected from connecting to the network. Webgate also prevents machines infected with spyware from transmitting data back to the source of the spyware.

Infected machines are quarantined and cleaned up by Wessel's staff. Webgate provides an executive summary screen for Wessel to review a list of infected machines, internal botnet activity, remote attacks, and spyware attempts to surreptitiously communicate with its authors. To supplement Webgate, the Celtics use SurfControl (now part of Websense) to filter e-mail and Web surfing activity, Trend Micro antivirus software, SonicWALL firewall and intrusion detection technology, and Aladdin eSafe for additional malware detection.

Since installing Webgate and these other tools, the Celtics' network has been spyware-free. Laptop performance, which used to be slowed down by malicious software, has improved, the corporate network runs much faster, and calls are down to the Celtics' IT help desk. Wessel is quick to point out that this security system would not work without user education. Employees are required to sign an acceptable use policy that states what they are allowed to do on their work machines, and they are explicitly discouraged from visiting Web sites that could transmit more malware to the Celtics' network.

Sources: Mi5 Networks, "Boston Celtics Shut Out Spyware with Mi5 Webgate Appliance," www.mi5networks.com, accessed September 19, 2009; Doug Bartholomew, "The Boston Celtics' New Malware Point Guard," *Baseline Magazine*, January 2008; and Bill Brenner, "Boston Celtics Face Off Against Spyware," SearchSecurity.com, accessed June 23, 2008.

The problems created by spyware for the Boston Celtics illustrate some of the reasons why businesses need to pay special attention to information system security. Malicious spyware that had infected coaches' and employees' laptops when they were on the road impaired performance of the company's internal systems, making it difficult for employees to obtain the information they needed to perform their jobs.

The chapter-opening diagram calls attention to important points raised by this case and this chapter. The Boston Celtics coaches and other staff members need to use their laptops to connect to the company's internal systems while they are traveling with the team. Linking to public Wi-Fi networks at hotels and airports exposed the laptops to malicious spyware, which the laptops then transmitted to corporate systems. The company was spending too much time and money ridding its systems of malware. Management decided to invest in new security technology to provide additional layers of protection. It also revised security procedures requiring infected laptops to be quarantined so they could not infect corporate systems. The chosen solution has kept the Celtics' systems free of spyware and speeded up system performance.

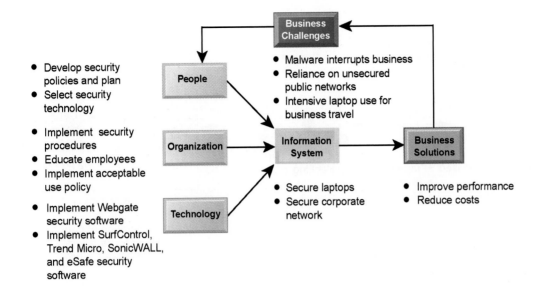

- Develop security policies and plan
- Select security technology

- Implement security procedures
- Educate employees
- Implement acceptable use policy

- Implement Webgate security software
- Implement SurfControl, Trend Micro, SonicWALL, and eSafe security software

People

Organization

Technology

Business Challenges
- Malware interrupts business
- Reliance on unsecured public networks
- Intensive laptop use for business travel

Information System
- Secure laptops
- Secure corporate network

Business Solutions
- Improve performance
- Reduce costs

7.1 System Vulnerability and Abuse

Can you imagine what would happen if you tried to link to the Internet without a firewall or antivirus software? Your computer would be disabled in a few seconds, and it might take you many days to recover. If you used the computer to run your business, you might not be able to sell to your customers or place orders with your suppliers while it was down. And you might find that your computer system had been penetrated by outsiders, who perhaps stole or destroyed valuable data, including confidential payment data from your customers. If too much data were destroyed or divulged, your business might never be able to operate!

In short, if you operate a business today, you need to make security and control a top priority. **Security** refers to the policies, procedures, and technical measures used to prevent unauthorized access, alteration, theft, or physical damage to information systems. **Controls** are methods, policies, and organizational procedures that ensure the safety of the organization's assets; the accuracy and reliability of its records; and operational adherence to management standards.

WHY SYSTEMS ARE VULNERABLE

When large amounts of data are stored in electronic form, they are vulnerable to many more kinds of threats than when they existed in manual form. Through communications networks, information systems in different locations are interconnected. The potential for unauthorized access, abuse, or fraud is not limited to a single location but can occur at any access point in the network. Figure 7-1 illustrates the most common threats against contemporary information systems. They can stem from technical, organizational, and environmental factors compounded by poor management decisions. In the multi-tier client/server computing environment illustrated here, vulnerabilities exist at each layer and in the communications between the layers. Users at the client layer can cause harm by introducing errors or by accessing systems without authorization. It is possible to access data flowing over networks, steal valuable data during transmission, or alter messages without authorization. Radiation may disrupt a network at various points as well. Intruders can launch denial-of-service attacks or malicious software to disrupt the operation of Web sites. Those capable of penetrating corporate systems can destroy or alter corporate data stored in databases or files.

Systems malfunction if computer hardware breaks down, is not configured properly, or is damaged by improper use or criminal acts. Errors in programming, improper installation, or unauthorized changes cause computer software to fail. Power failures, floods, fires, or other natural disasters can also disrupt computer systems.

Figure 7-1
Contemporary Security Challenges and Vulnerabilities
The architecture of a Web-based application typically includes a Web client, a server, and corporate information systems linked to databases. Each of these components presents security challenges and vulnerabilities. Floods, fires, power failures, and other electrical problems can cause disruptions at any point in the network.

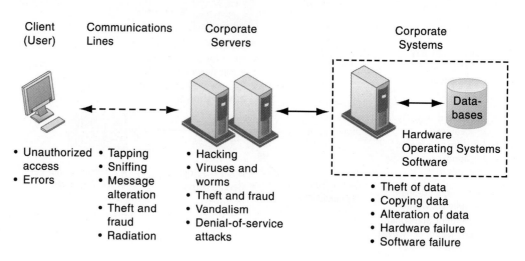

Client (User)	Communications Lines	Corporate Servers	Corporate Systems
• Unauthorized access	• Tapping	• Hacking	Hardware Operating Systems Software
• Errors	• Sniffing	• Viruses and worms	• Theft of data
	• Message alteration	• Theft and fraud	• Copying data
	• Theft and fraud	• Vandalism	• Alteration of data
	• Radiation	• Denial-of-service attacks	• Hardware failure
			• Software failure

Domestic or offshore partnering with another company adds to system vulnerability if valuable information resides on networks and computers outside the organization's control. Without strong safeguards, valuable data could be lost, destroyed, or could fall into the wrong hands, revealing important trade secrets or information that violates personal privacy.

The growing use of mobile devices for business computing adds to these woes. Portability makes cell phones and smartphones easy to lose or steal, and their networks are vulnerable to access by outsiders. Smartphones used by corporate executives may contain sensitive data such as sales figures, customer names, phone numbers, and e-mail addresses. Intruders may be able to access internal corporate networks through these devices. Unauthorized downloads may introduce disabling software.

Internet Vulnerabilities

Large public networks, such as the Internet, are more vulnerable than internal networks because they are virtually open to anyone. The Internet is so huge that when abuses do occur, they can have an enormously widespread impact. When the Internet becomes part of the corporate network, the organization's information systems are even more vulnerable to actions from outsiders.

Computers that are constantly connected to the Internet by cable modems or digital subscriber line (DSL) are more open to penetration by outsiders because they use fixed Internet addresses where they can be easily identified. (With dial-up service, a temporary Internet address is assigned for each session.) A fixed Internet address creates a fixed target for hackers.

Telephone service based on Internet technology (see Chapter 6) is more vulnerable than the switched voice network if it does not run over a secure private network. Voice over IP (VoIP) traffic over the public Internet is not encrypted, so anyone with a network can listen in on conversations. Hackers can intercept conversations or shut down voice service by flooding servers supporting VoIP with bogus traffic.

Vulnerability has also increased from widespread use of e-mail, instant messaging (IM), and peer-to-peer (P2P) file-sharing programs. E-mail may contain attachments that serve as springboards for malicious software or unauthorized access to internal corporate systems. Employees may use e-mail messages to transmit valuable trade secrets, financial data, or confidential customer information to unauthorized recipients. Popular instant messaging applications for consumers do not use a secure layer for text messages, so they can be intercepted and read by outsiders during transmission over the public Internet. IM activity over the Internet can in some cases be used as a back door to an otherwise secure network. Sharing files over P2P networks, such as those for illegal music sharing, may also transmit alicious software or expose information on either individual or corporate computers to outsiders.

Wireless Security Challenges

Is it safe to log onto a wireless network at an airport, library, or other public location? It depends on how vigilant you are. Even the wireless network in your home is vulnerable because Wi-Fi radio transmissions are easy to scan. Both Bluetooth and Wi-Fi networks are susceptible to hacking by eavesdroppers. Although the range of Wi-Fi networks is only several hundred feet, it can be extended up to one-fourth of a mile using external antennae. Local-area networks (LANs) using the 802.11 standard can be easily penetrated by outsiders armed with laptops, wireless cards, external antennae, and hacking software. Hackers use these tools to detect unprotected networks, monitor network traffic, and, in some cases, gain access to the Internet or to corporate networks.

Wi-Fi transmission technology was designed to make it easy for stations to find and hear one another. The *service set identifiers (SSIDs)* identifying the access points in a Wi-Fi network are broadcast multiple times and can be picked up fairly easily by intruders' sniffer programs (see Figure 7-2). Wireless networks in many locations do not have basic protections against **war driving**, in which eavesdroppers drive by buildings or park outside and try to intercept wireless network traffic.

A hacker can employ an 802.11 analysis tool to identify the SSID. (Windows XP, Vista , and Windows 7 have capabilities for detecting the SSID used in a network and automatically configuring the radio NIC within the user's device.) An intruder that has associated with an access point by using the correct SSID is capable of accessing other resources on the network, using the Windows operating system to determine which other users are connected to the network, access their computer hard drives, and open or copy their files.

Intruders also use the information they have gleaned to set up rogue access points on a different radio channel in physical locations close to users to force a user's radio NIC to associate with the rogue access point. Once this association occurs, hackers using the rogue access point can capture the names and passwords of unsuspecting users.

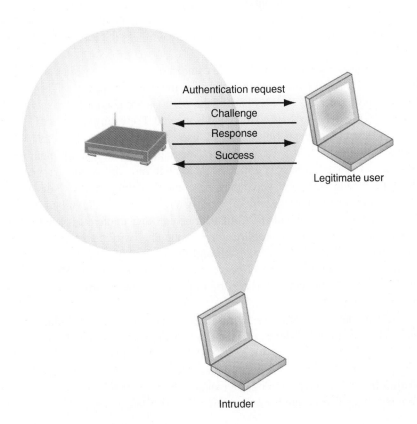

Figure 7-2
Wi-Fi Security Challenges
Many Wi-Fi networks can be penetrated easily by intruders using sniffer programs to obtain an address to access the resources of a network without authorization.

Authentication request

Challenge

Response

Success

Legitimate user

Intruder

The initial security standard developed for Wi-Fi, called *Wired Equivalent Privacy (WEP)*, is not very effective. WEP is built into all standard 802.11 products, but its use is optional. Many users neglect to use WEP security features, leaving them unprotected. The basic WEP specification calls for an access point and all of its users to share the same 40-bit encrypted password, which can be easily decrypted by hackers from a small amount of traffic. Stronger encryption and authentication systems are now available, but users must be willing to install them.

MALICIOUS SOFTWARE: VIRUSES, WORMS, TROJAN HORSES, AND SPYWARE

Malicious software programs are referred to as **malware** and include a variety of threats, such as computer viruses, worms, and Trojan horses. A **computer virus** is a rogue software program that attaches itself to other software programs or data files in order to be executed, usually without user knowledge or permission. Most computer viruses deliver a "payload." The payload may be relatively benign, such as the instructions to display a message or image, or it may be highly destructive—destroying programs or data, clogging computer memory, reformatting a computer's hard drive, or causing programs to run improperly. Viruses typically spread from computer to computer when humans take an action, such as sending an e-mail attachment or copying an infected file.

Most recent attacks have come from **worms**, which are independent computer programs that copy themselves from one computer to other computers over a network. (Unlike viruses, they can operate on their own without attaching to other computer program files and rely less on human behavior in order to spread from computer to computer. This explains why computer worms spread much more rapidly than computer viruses.) Worms destroy data and programs as well as disrupt or even halt the operation of computer networks.

Worms and viruses are often spread over the Internet from files of downloaded software, from files attached to e-mail transmissions, or from compromised e-mail messages or instant messaging. Viruses have also invaded computerized information systems from "infected" disks or infected machines. E-mail worms are currently the most problematic.

There are now more than 200 viruses and worms targeting mobile phones, such as Cabir, Commwarrior, and Frontal.A. Frontal.A, for example, installs a corrupted file that causes phone failure and prevents the user from rebooting. Mobile device viruses could pose serious threats to enterprise computing because so many wireless devices are now linked to corporate information systems.

Web 2.0 applications, such as blogs, wikis, and social networking sites such as Facebook and MySpace, have emerged as new conduits for malware or spyware. These applications allow users to post software code as part of the permissible content, and such code can be launched automatically as soon as a Web page is viewed. For example, in August 2008, malicious hackers targeted unsuspecting Facebook users via postings on the site's Wall feature, which is used by members to leave each other messages. Impersonating members' friends, malicious hackers posted messages urging users to click on a link to view a video that transported them to a rogue Web page where they were told to download a new version of Adobe's Flash player in order to view the video. If users authorized the download, the site would install a Trojan horse, Troj/Dloadr-BPL, that funneled other malicious code to their PCs. In July 2009, hackers exploited vulnerabilities in the popular TwitPic add-on service to Twitter. They stole Britney Spears' Twitter log-on and then sent "tweets" (short text messages) claiming to the singer's followers that Spears had died (Acohido, 2009; Perez, 2008).

Table 7.1 describes the characteristics of some of the most harmful worms and viruses that have appeared to date.

Over the past decade, worms and viruses have cause billions of dollars of damage to corporate networks, e-mail systems, and data. According to Consumer Reports' State of the Net 2009 survey, U.S. consumers lost $7.5 billion because of malware and online scams, and the majority of these losses came from malware (Consumer Reports, 2009).

A **Trojan horse** is a software program that appears to be benign but then does something other than expected. The Trojan horse is not itself a virus because it does not replicate but is

TABLE 7.1

Examples of Malicious Code

Name	Type	Description
Conficker (aka Downadup, Downup)	Worm	First detected in November 2008. Uses flaws in Windows software to take over machines and link them into a virtual computer that can be commanded remotely. Has more than 5 million computers worldwide under its control. Difficult to eradicate.
Storm	Worm/ Trojan horse	First identified in January 2007. Spreads via e-mail spam with a fake attachment. Infected up to 10 million computers, causing them to join its zombie network of computers engaged in criminal activity.
Sasser.ftp	Worm	First appeared in May 2004. Spread over the Internet by attacking random IP addresses. Causes computers to continually crash and reboot, and infected computers to search for more victims. Affected millions of computers worldwide, disrupting British Airways flight check-ins, operations of British coast guard stations, Hong Kong hospitals, Taiwan post office branches, and Australia's Westpac Bank. Sasser and its variants caused an estimated $14.8 billion to $18.6 billion in damages worldwide.
Mydoom.A	Worm	First appeared on January 26, 2004. Spreads as an e-mail attachment. Sends e-mail to addresses harvested from infected machines, forging the sender's address. At its peak, this worm lowered global Internet performance by 10 percent and Web page loading times by as much as 50 percent. Was programmed to stop spreading after February 12, 2004.
Sobig.F	Worm	First detected on August 19, 2003. Spreads via e-mail attachments and sends massive amounts of mail with forged sender information. Deactivated itself on September 10, 2003, after infecting more than 1 million PCs and doing $5 to $10 billion in damage.
ILOVEYOU	Virus	First detected on May 3, 2000. Script virus written in Visual Basic script and transmitted as an attachment to e-mail with the subject line ILOVEYOU. Overwrites music, image, and other files with a copy of itself and did an estimated $10 billion to $15 billion in damage.
Melissa	Macro virus/ worm	First appeared in March 1999. Word macro script mailed infected Word files to first 50 entries in user's Microsoft Outlook address book. Infected 15 to 29 percent of all business PCs, causing $300 million to $600 million in damage.

often a way for viruses or other malicious code to be introduced into a computer system. The term *Trojan horse* is based on the huge wooden horse used by the Greeks to trick the Trojans into opening the gates to their fortified city during the *Trojan War*. Once inside the city walls, Greek soldiers hidden in the horse revealed themselves and captured the city.

Another example of a modern-day Trojan horse is Pushdo Trojan, which uses electronic greeting-card lures in e-mail to trick Windows users into launching an executable program. Once the Trojan is executed, it pretends to be an Apache Web server and tries to deliver executable malware programs to the infected Windows machines.

At the moment, **SQL injection attacks** are the largest malware threat. SQL injection attacks take advantage of vulnerabilities in poorly coded Web application software to introduce malicious program code into a company's systems and networks. These vulnerabilities occur when a Web application fails to properly validate or filter data entered by a user on a Web page, which might occur when ordering something online. An attacker uses this input validation error to send a rogue SQL query to the underlying database to access the database, plant malicious code, or access other systems on the network. Large Web applications have hundreds of places for inputting user data, each of which creates an opportunity for an SQL injection attack.

A large number of Web-facing applications are believed to have SQL injection vulnerabilities, and tools are available for hackers to check Web applications for these vulnerabilities. Such tools are able to locate a data entry field on a Web page form, enter data into it, and check the response to see if shows vulnerability to a SQL injection.

Some types of **spyware** also act as malicious software. These small programs install themselves surreptitiously on computers to monitor user Web surfing activity and serve up advertising. Thousands of forms of spyware have been documented.

Many users find such spyware annoying and some critics worry about its infringement on computer users' privacy. Some forms of spyware are especially nefarious. **Keyloggers** record every keystroke made on a computer to steal serial numbers for software, to launch Internet attacks, to gain access to e-mail accounts, to obtain passwords to protected computer systems, or to pick up personal information such as credit card numbers. Other spyware programs reset Web browser home pages, redirect search requests, or slow performance by taking up too much memory.

HACKERS AND COMPUTER CRIME

A **hacker** is an individual who intends to gain unauthorized access to a computer system. Within the hacking community, the term *cracker* is typically used to denote a hacker with criminal intent, although in the public press, the terms hacker and cracker are used interchangeably. Hackers and crackers gain unauthorized access by finding weaknesses in the security protections employed by Web sites and computer systems, often taking advantage of various features of the Internet that make it an open system that is easy to use.

Hacker activities have broadened beyond mere system intrusion to include theft of goods and information, as well as system damage and **cybervandalism**, the intentional disruption, defacement, or even destruction of a Web site or corporate information system. For example, cybervandals have turned many of the MySpace "group" sites, which are dedicated to interests such as home beer brewing or animal welfare, into cyber-graffiti walls, filled with offensive comments and photographs.

Spoofing and Sniffing

Hackers attempting to hide their true identities often spoof, or misrepresent, themselves by using fake e-mail addresses or masquerading as someone else. **Spoofing** also may involve redirecting a Web link to an address different from the intended one, with the site masquerading as the intended destination. For example, if hackers redirect customers to a fake Web site that looks almost exactly like the true site, they can then collect and process orders, effectively stealing business as well as sensitive customer information from the true site. We provide more detail on other forms of spoofing in our discussion of computer crime.

A **sniffer** is a type of eavesdropping program that monitors information traveling over a network. When used legitimately, sniffers help identify potential network trouble spots or criminal activity on networks, but when used for criminal purposes, they can be damaging and very difficult to detect. Sniffers enable hackers to steal proprietary information from anywhere on a network, including e-mail messages, company files, and confidential reports.

Denial-of-Service Attacks

In a **denial-of-service (DoS) attack**, hackers flood a network server or Web server with many thousands of false communications or requests for services to crash the network. The network receives so many queries that it cannot keep up with them and is thus unavailable to service legitimate requests. A **distributed denial-of-service (DDoS)** attack uses numerous computers to inundate and overwhelm the network from numerous launch points. For example, during the 2009 Iranian election protests, foreign activists trying to help the opposition engaged in DDoS attacks against Iran's government. The official Web site of the Iranian government (ahmedinejad.ir) was rendered inaccessible on several occasions.

Although DoS attacks do not destroy information or access restricted areas of a company's information systems, they often cause a Web site to shut down, making it impossible for legitimate users to access the site. For busy e-commerce sites, these attacks are costly; while the site is shut down, customers cannot make purchases. Especially vulnerable are small and midsize businesses whose networks tend to be less protected than those of large corporations.

Perpetrators of DoS attacks often use thousands of "zombie" PCs infected with malicious software without their owners' knowledge and organized into a **botnet**. Hackers create these botnets by infecting other people's computers with bot malware that opens a back door through which an attacker can give instructions. The infected computer then becomes a slave, or zombie, serving a master computer belonging to someone else. Once a hacker infects enough computers, her or she can use the amassed resources of the botnet to launch DDos attacks, phishing campaigns, or unsolicited "spam" e-mail.

The chapter-ending case study describes multiple waves of DDoS attacks targeting a number of Web sites of government agencies and other organizations in South Korea and the United States in July 2009. The attacker used a botnet that took control of 65,000 computers and was able to cripple some of these sites for several days. Most of the bots originated from China and North Korea. Botnet attacks thought to have originated in Russia were responsible for crippling the Web sites of the Estonian government in April 2007 and the Georgian government in July 2008.

Computer Crime

Most hacker activities are criminal offenses, and the vulnerabilities of systems we have just described make them targets for other types of computer crime as well. For example, in early July 2009, U.S. federal agents arrested Sergey Aleynikov, a computer programmer at investment banking firm Goldman Sachs, for stealing proprietary computer programs used in making lucrative rapid-fire trades in the financial markets. The software brought Goldman many millions of dollars of profits per year and, in the wrong hands, could have been used to manipulate financial markets in unfair ways. **Computer crime** is defined by the U.S. Department of Justice as "any violations of criminal law that involve a knowledge of computer technology for their perpetration, investigation, or prosecution." Table 7.2 provides examples of the computer as a target of crime and as an instrument of crime.

No one knows the magnitude of the computer crime problem—how many systems are invaded, how many people engage in the practice, or the total economic damage. According to the 2008 CSI Computer Crime and Security Survey of 522 companies, participants' average annual loss from computer crime and security attacks was close to $500,000 (Richardson, 2008). Many companies are reluctant to report computer crimes because the crimes may involve employees, or the company fears that publicizing its vulnerability will hurt its reputation. The most economically damaging kinds of computer crime are DoS attacks, introducing viruses, theft of services, and disruption of computer systems.

IDENTITY THEFT

With the growth of the Internet and electronic commerce, identity theft has become especially troubling. **Identity theft** is a crime in which an imposter obtains key pieces of personal information, such as social security identification numbers, driver's license numbers, or credit card numbers, to impersonate someone else. The information may be used to obtain credit, merchandise, or services in the name of the victim or to provide the thief with false credentials. According to Javelin Strategy and Research, 4.7 percent of Americans were victims of identity theft in 2008 and they suffered losses totaling $48 billion (Javelin, 2009).

TABLE 7.2

Examples of
Computer Crime

Computers as Targets of Crime

Breaching the confidentiality of protected computerized data

Accessing a computer system without authority

Knowingly accessing a protected computer to commit fraud

Intentionally accessing a protected computer and causing damage, negligently or deliberately

Knowingly transmitting a program, program code, or command that intentionally causes damage to a protected computer

Threatening to cause damage to a protected computer

Computers as Instruments of Crime

Theft of trade secrets

Unauthorized copying of software or copyrighted intellectual property, such as articles, books, music, and video

Schemes to defraud

Using e-mail for threats or harassment

Intentionally attempting to intercept electronic communication

Illegally accessing stored electronic communications, including e-mail and voice mail

Transmitting or possessing child pornography using a computer

Identify theft has flourished on the Internet, with credit card files a major target of Web site hackers. Moreover, e-commerce sites are wonderful sources of customer personal information—name, address, and phone number. Armed with this information, criminals are able to assume new identities and establish new credit for their own purposes.

One increasingly popular tactic is a form of spoofing called **phishing**. Phishing involves setting up fake Web sites or sending e-mail or text messages that look like those of legitimate businesses to ask users for confidential personal data. The message instructs recipients to update or confirm records by providing social security numbers, bank and credit card information, and other confidential data either by responding to the e-mail message, by entering the information at a bogus Web site, or by calling a telephone number. EBay, PayPal, Amazon, Wal-Mart, and a variety of banks, are among the top spoofed companies.

New phishing techniques called evil twins and pharming are harder to detect. **Evil twins** are wireless networks that pretend to offer trustworthy Wi-Fi connections to the Internet, such as those in airport lounges, hotels, or coffee shops. The bogus network looks identical to a legitimate public network. Fraudsters try to capture passwords or credit card numbers of unwitting users who log on to the network.

Pharming redirects users to a bogus Web page, even when the individual types the correct Web page address into his or her browser. This is possible if pharming perpetrators gain access to the Internet address information stored by Internet service providers to speed up Web browsing and the ISP companies have flawed software on their servers that allows the fraudsters to hack in and change those addresses.

The Interactive Session on Organizations describes the largest instance of identity theft to date in which hackers penetrated the corporate systems of TJX Corporation, Hannaford Brothers, 7-Eleven, and other major retailers and stole over 130 million credit and debit card numbers. As you read this case, pay attention to the people, organizational, and technology issues raised by this problem and whether these companies implemented effective solutions.

The U.S. Congress addressed the threat of computer crime in 1986 with the Computer Fraud and Abuse Act. This act makes it illegal to access a computer system without

INTERACTIVE SESSION: ORGANIZATIONS   The Worst Data Theft Ever

On August 17, 2009, 28-year-old Alberto Gonzalez of Miami was charged along with two Russian accomplices with carrying out the largest hacking and identity-theft crime in U.S. history. Federal prosecutors alleged that the three had masterminded a global scheme to steal more than 130 million credit and debit card numbers between 2006 and 2008 by hacking into the computer systems of companies that included the Hannaford Bros. supermarket chain, 7-Eleven, and Heartland Payment Systems, a credit card processing company.

The group used a network of computers in New Jersey, California, Illinois, Latvia, the Netherlands, and the Ukraine to infiltrate the computer systems of targeted companies, using sophisticated techniques to evade detection by antivirus software. They planted software programs in these companies' computer networks that enabled them to steal more data in the future as well as "sniffer" programs to capture card data while they were being transmitted between computer systems. An unspecified number of the stolen credit and debit card numbers were sold online and used to make unauthorized purchases and withdrawals from banks.

Gonzalez and his group have been responsible for other major data thefts as well. On September 18, 2009, Gonzalez pleaded guilty to 19 counts of criminal activity and credit card fraud in attacks against Barnes and Noble, OfficeMax, Boston Market, and Sports Authority. Gonzalez was also responsible for stealing 40 million credit and debit card numbers from TJX Cos., the parent company of T.J. Maxx.

The data thefts at Hannaford, Heartland, and 7-Eleven Stores were carried out using SQL injection attacks, which we defined earlier in this chapter. SQL injection attacks are well understood, and security experts have warned retailers about them for years. Nevertheless, many companies still use older versions of Microsoft SQL Server database management software that allow attackers to take control of the database with a SQL injection.

Gonzalez and his ring started using SQL injection attacks around August 2007. Before that time, they penetrated corporate systems by exploiting weak wireless security. The thieves drove around and scanned retailers' wireless networks to identify network vulnerabilities and then installed sniffer programs that tapped into the networks for processing credit cards, intercepting customers' debit and credit card numbers and PINs (personal identification numbers).

These techniques enabled the group to siphon off more than 40 million credit and debit-card numbers

from TJX in July 2005. Gonzalez's team identified a vulnerable network at a Marshall's department store in Miami and used it to install a sniffer program on the computers of the chain's parent company, TJX. The group was then able to access the central TJX database, which stored customer transactions for T.J. Maxx, Marshalls, HomeGoods, and A.J. Wright stores in the United States and Puerto Rico, and for Winners and HomeSense stores in Canada.

TJX was still using the old Wired Equivalent Privacy (WEP) encryption system, which is relatively easy for hackers to crack. Other companies had switched to the more secure Wi-Fi Protected Access (WPA) standard with more complex encryption, but TJX at that time had not made the change. An auditor later found that TJX had also neglected to install firewalls and data encryption on many of the computers using the wireless network, and didn't properly install another layer of security software it had purchased. TJX acknowledged in a Securities and Exchange Commission filing that it transmitted credit card data to banks without encryption, violating credit card company guidelines. TJX also retained cardholder data in its systems much longer than stipulated by industry rules for storing such data.

In March 2008, TJX management agreed to strengthen the company's information system security. It also agreed to have third-party auditors review security measures every 2 years for the next 20 years. TJX has already spent over $202 million to deal with its data theft, including legal settlements. Forrester Research estimates that the cost to TJX for the data breach could surpass $1 billion over five years, including costs for consultants, security upgrades, attorney fees, and additional marketing to reassure customers.

Hannaford Bros. also started implementing additional security safeguards. It updated firewalls, installed a round-the-clock security monitoring and detection service from IBM, and also began encrypting traffic flowing over a private network from its store registers to its credit card processor. (The existing Payment Card Industry Data Security Standard [PCI DSS] guidelines, which apply to all companies processing credit cards, only require encryption of data transmitted over public networks.)

Sources: Jaikumar Vijayan, "SQL Injection Attacks Led to Hartland, Hannaford Breaches," *Chief Security Officer*, August 19, 2009; Dan Kaplan, "After Breach, Hannaford Details IT Security Remodel," *SC Magazine*, April 23, 2009; Brad Stone, "3 Indicted in Theft of 130 Million Card Numbers," *The New York Times*, August 18, 2009 and "11 Charged in Theft of 41 Million Card Numbers," *The New York Times*, August 6, 2008; Siobhan Gorman, "Arrest in Epic Cyber Swindle," *The Wall Street Journal*, August 19, 2009; Andrew Conry-Murray, Dan Berthiaume, "Data Breaches Cause Concern," *eWeek*, April 7, 2008; and "T.J. Maxx Probe Reveals Data Brach Worse Than Originally Thought," *Information Week*, February 21, 2007.

CASE STUDY QUESTIONS

1. List and describe the security control weaknesses at Hannaford Bros. and TJX Companies.

2. What people, organization, and technology factors contributed to these problems?

3. What was the business impact of the TJX and Hannaford data losses on these companies and consumers?

4. Were the solutions adopted by TJX and Hannaford effective? Why or why not?

5. Who should be held liable for the losses caused by the use of fraudulent credit cards in this case? TJX and Hannaford? The banks issuing the credit cards? The consumers? Justify your answer.

6. What solutions would you suggest to prevent the problems?

MIS IN ACTION

Explore the Web site of the PCI Security Standards Council (www.pcisecuritystandards.org) and review the PCI Data Security Standard (PCI DSS).

1. Based on the details in this case study, how well was TJX complying with the PCI DSS. What requirements did it fail to meet?

2. Would complying with this standard have prevented the theft of credit card data from TJX? Why or why not?

authorization. Most states have similar laws, and nations in Europe have comparable legislation. Congress also passed the National Information Infrastructure Protection Act in 1996 to make virus distribution and hacker attacks that disable Web sites federal crimes. U.S. legislation, such as the Wiretap Act, Wire Fraud Act, Economic Espionage Act, Electronic Communications Privacy Act, E-Mail Threats and Harassment Act, and Child Pornography Act, covers computer crimes involving intercepting electronic communication, using electronic communication to defraud, stealing trade secrets, illegally accessing stored electronic communications, using e-mail for threats or harassment, and transmitting or possessing child pornography.

Click Fraud

When you click on an ad displayed by a search engine, the advertiser typically pays a fee for each click, which is supposed to direct potential buyers to its products. **Click fraud** occurs when an individual or computer program fraudulently clicks on an online ad without any intention of learning more about the advertiser or making a purchase. Click fraud has become a serious problem at Google and other Web sites that feature pay-per-click online advertising.

Some companies hire third parties (typically from low-wage countries) to fraudulently click on a competitor's ads to weaken them by driving up their marketing costs. Click fraud can also be perpetrated with software programs doing the clicking, and botnets are often used for this purpose. Search engines such as Google attempt to monitor click fraud but have been reluctant to publicize their efforts to deal with the problem.

Global Threats: Cyberterrorism and Cyberwarfare

The cybercriminal activities we have described—launching malware, denial-of- service attacks, and phishing probes—are borderless. Computer security firm Sophos reported that 37 percent of the malware it identified in 2008 originated in the United States, while 28 percent came from China, and 9 percent from Russia (Sophos, 2009). The global nature of the Internet makes it possible for cybercriminals to operate—and to do harm—anywhere in the world.

Concern is mounting that the vulnerabilities of the Internet or other networks make digital networks easy targets for digital attacks by terrorists, foreign intelligence services, or other groups seeking to create widespread disruption and harm. Such cyberattacks might target the software that runs electrical power grids, air traffic control systems, or networks of major banks and financial institutions. At least 20 countries, including China, Russia, and the United States, are believed to be developing offensive and defensive cyberwarfare capabilities. The chapter-ending case study discusses this problem in greater detail.

INTERNAL THREATS: EMPLOYEES

We tend to think the security threats to a business originate outside the organization. In fact, company insiders pose serious security problems. Employees have access to privileged information, and in the presence of sloppy internal security procedures, they are often able to roam throughout an organization's systems without leaving a trace.

Studies have found that user lack of knowledge is the single greatest cause of network security breaches. Many employees forget their passwords to access computer systems or allow co-workers to use them, which compromises the system. Malicious intruders seeking system access sometimes trick employees into revealing their passwords by pretending to be legitimate members of the company in need of information. This practice is called **social engineering.**

Both end users and information systems specialists are also a major source of errors introduced into information systems. End users introduce errors by entering faulty data or by not following the proper instructions for processing data and using computer equipment. Information systems specialists may create software errors as they design and develop new software or maintain existing programs.

SOFTWARE VULNERABILITY

Software errors pose a constant threat to information systems, causing untold losses in productivity. Growing complexity and size of software programs, coupled with demands for timely delivery to markets, have contributed to an increase in software flaws or vulnerabilities. For example, a computer programming error at the New York City Housing Authority was responsible for miscalculating rents for hundreds of welfare families between September 2008 and May 2009. The affected families were billed an average of $183 more for rent than what was supposed to be charged and threatened with eviction for failing to pay the higher amount (Fernandez, 2009).

A major problem with software is the presence of hidden **bugs** or program code defects. Studies have shown that it is virtually impossible to eliminate all bugs from large programs. The main source of bugs is the complexity of decision-making code. A relatively small program of several hundred lines will contain tens of decisions leading to hundreds or even thousands of different paths. Important programs within most corporations are usually much larger, containing tens of thousands or even millions of lines of code, each with many times the choices and paths of the smaller programs.

Zero defects cannot be achieved in larger programs. Complete testing simply is not possible. Fully testing programs that contain thousands of choices and millions of paths would require thousands of years. Even with rigorous testing, you would not know for sure that a piece of software was dependable until the product proved itself after much operational use.

Flaws in commercial software not only impede performance but also create security vulnerabilities that open networks to intruders. Each year security firms identify about 5,000 software vulnerabilities in Internet and PC software. For instance, in 2008, Symantec identified 47 vulnerabilities in Microsoft Internet Explorer, 99 in Mozilla browsers, and 40 in Apple Safari. Some of these vulnerabilities are critical (Symantec, 2009).

To correct software flaws once they are identified, the software vendor creates small pieces of software called **patches** to repair the flaws without disturbing the proper operation of the software. An example is Microsoft's Windows Vista Service Pack 2, released in

April 2009, which includes some security enhancements to counter malware and hackers. It is up to users of the software to track these vulnerabilities, test, and apply all patches. This process is called *patch management.*

Because a company's IT infrastructure is typically laden with multiple business applications, operating system installations, and other system services, maintaining patches on all devices and services used by a company is often time-consuming and costly. Malware is being created so rapidly that companies have very little time to respond between the time a vulnerability and a patch are announced and the time malicious software appears to exploit the vulnerability.

7.2 Business Value of Security and Control

Many firms are reluctant to spend heavily on security because it is not directly related to sales revenue. However, protecting information systems is so critical to the operation of the business that it deserves a second look.

Companies have very valuable information assets to protect. Systems often house confidential information about individuals' taxes, financial assets, medical records, and job performance reviews. They also can contain information on corporate operations, including trade secrets, new product development plans, and marketing strategies. Government systems may store information on weapons systems, intelligence operations, and military targets. These information assets have tremendous value, and the repercussions can be devastating if they are lost, destroyed, or placed in the wrong hands. One study estimated that when the security of a large firm is compromised, the company loses approximately 2.1 percent of its market value within two days of the security breach, which translates into an average loss of $1.65 billion in stock market value per incident (Cavusoglu, Mishra, and Raghunathan, 2004).

Inadequate security and control may result in serious legal liability. Businesses must protect not only their own information assets but also those of customers, employees, and business partners. Failure to do so may open the firm to costly litigation for data exposure or theft. An organization can be held liable for needless risk and harm created if the organization fails to take appropriate protective action to prevent loss of confidential information, data corruption, or breach of privacy. For example, BJ's Wholesale Club was sued by the U.S. Federal Trade Commission for allowing hackers to access its systems and steal credit and debit card data for fraudulent purchases. Banks that issued the cards with the stolen data sought $13 million from BJ's to compensate them for reimbursing card holders for the fraudulent purchases. A sound security and control framework that protects business information assets can thus produce a high return on investment. Strong security and control also increase employee productivity and lower operational costs.

LEGAL AND REGULATORY REQUIREMENTS FOR ELECTRONIC RECORDS MANAGEMENT

Recent U.S. government regulations are forcing companies to take security and control more seriously by mandating the protection of data from abuse, exposure, and unauthorized access. Firms face new legal obligations for the retention and storage of electronic records as well as for privacy protection.

If you work in the healthcare industry, your firm will need to comply with the Health Insurance Portability and Accountability Act (HIPAA) of 1996. **HIPAA** outlines medical security and privacy rules and procedures for simplifying the administration of healthcare billing and automating the transfer of healthcare data between healthcare providers, payers, and plans. It requires members of the healthcare industry to retain patient information for six years and ensure the confidentiality of those records. It specifies privacy, security, and electronic transaction standards for healthcare providers handling patient information, providing penalties for breaches of medical privacy, disclosure of patient records by e-mail, or unauthorized network access.

If you work in a firm providing financial services, your firm will need to comply with the Financial Services Modernization Act of 1999, better known as the **Gramm-Leach-Bliley Act** after its congressional sponsors. This act requires financial institutions to ensure the security and confidentiality of customer data. Data must be stored on a secure medium, and special security measures must be enforced to protect such data on storage media and during transmittal.

If you work in a publicly traded company, your company will need to comply with the Public Company Accounting Reform and Investor Protection Act of 2002, better known as the **Sarbanes-Oxley Act** after its sponsors Senator Paul Sarbanes of Maryland and Representative Michael Oxley of Ohio. This Act was designed to protect investors after the financial scandals at Enron, WorldCom, and other public companies. It imposes responsibility on companies and their management to safeguard the accuracy and integrity of financial information that is used internally and released externally. One of the Learning Tracks for this chapter discusses Sarbanes-Oxley in detail.

Sarbanes-Oxley is fundamentally about ensuring that internal controls are in place to govern the creation and documentation of information in financial statements. Because information systems are used to generate, store, and transport such data, the legislation requires firms to consider information systems security and other controls required to ensure the integrity, confidentiality, and accuracy of their data. Each system application that deals with critical financial reporting data requires controls to make sure the data are accurate. Controls to secure the corporate network, prevent unauthorized access to systems and data, and ensure data integrity and availability in the event of disaster or other disruption of service are essential as well.

ELECTRONIC EVIDENCE AND COMPUTER FORENSICS

Security, control, and electronic records management have become essential for responding to legal actions. Much of the evidence today for stock fraud, embezzlement, theft of company trade secrets, computer crime, and many civil cases is in digital form. In addition to information from printed or typewritten pages, legal cases today increasingly rely on evidence represented as digital data stored on flash drives, CDs, and computer hard disk drives, as well as in e-mail, instant messages, and e-commerce transactions over the Internet. E-mail is currently the most common type of electronic evidence.

In a legal action, a firm is obligated to respond to a discovery request for access to information that may be used as evidence, and the company is required by law to produce those data. The cost of responding to a discovery request can be enormous if the company has trouble assembling the required data or the data have been corrupted or destroyed. Courts now impose severe financial and even criminal penalties for improper destruction of electronic documents.

An effective electronic document retention policy ensures that electronic documents, e-mail, and other records are well organized, accessible, and neither retained too long nor discarded too soon. It also reflects an awareness of how to preserve potential evidence for computer forensics. **Computer forensics** is the scientific collection, examination, authentication, preservation, and analysis of data held on or retrieved from computer storage media in such a way that the information can be used as evidence in a court of law. It deals with the following problems:

- Recovering data from computers while preserving evidential integrity
- Securely storing and handling recovered electronic data
- Finding significant information in a large volume of electronic data
- Presenting the information to a court of law

Electronic evidence may reside on computer storage media in the form of computer files and as *ambient data*, which are not visible to the average user. An example might be a file that has been deleted on a PC hard drive. Data that a computer user may have deleted on computer storage media can be recovered through various techniques. Computer forensics experts try to recover such hidden data for presentation as evidence.

An awareness of computer forensics should be incorporated into a firm's contingency planning process. The CIO, security specialists, information systems staff, and corporate legal counsel should all work together to have a plan in place that can be executed if a legal need arises. You can find out more about computer forensics in the Learning Tracks for this chapter.

7.3 Establishing a Framework for Security and Control

Even with the best security tools, your information systems won't be reliable and secure unless you know how and where to deploy them. You'll need to know where your company is at risk and what controls you must have in place to protect your information systems. You'll also need to develop a security policy and plans for keeping your business running if your information systems aren't operational.

INFORMATION SYSTEMS CONTROLS

Information systems controls are both manual and automated and consist of both general controls and application controls. **General controls** govern the design, security, and use of computer programs and the security of data files in general throughout the organization's information technology infrastructure. On the whole, general controls apply to all computerized applications and consist of a combination of hardware, software, and manual procedures that create an overall control environment.

General controls include software controls, physical hardware controls, computer operations controls, data security controls, controls over implementation of system processes, and administrative controls. Table 7.3 describes the functions of each of these controls.

Application controls are specific controls unique to each computerized application, such as payroll or order processing. They include both automated and manual procedures that ensure that only authorized data are completely and accurately processed by that application. Application controls can be classified as (1) input controls, (2) processing controls, and (3) output controls.

Input controls check data for accuracy and completeness when they enter the system. There are specific input controls for input authorization, data conversion, data editing, and error handling. *Processing controls* establish that data are complete and accurate during updating. *Output controls* ensure that the results of computer processing are accurate, complete, and properly distributed. You can find more detail about application and general controls in our Learning Tracks.

RISK ASSESSMENT

Before your company commits resources to security and information systems controls, it must know which assets require protection and the extent to which these assets are vulnerable. A risk assessment helps answer these questions and determine the most cost-effective set of controls for protecting assets.

A **risk assessment** determines the level of risk to the firm if a specific activity or process is not properly controlled. Not all risks can be anticipated and measured, but most businesses will be able to acquire some understanding of the risks they face. Business managers working with information systems specialists should try to determine the value of information assets, points of vulnerability, the likely frequency of a problem, and the potential for damage. For example, if an event is likely to occur no more than once a year, with a maximum of a $1,000 loss to the organization, it is not be wise to spend $20,000 on the design and maintenance of a control to protect against that event. However, if that same event could occur at least once a day, with a potential loss of more than $300,000 a year, $100,000 spent on a control might be entirely appropriate.

TABLE 7.3

General Controls

Type of General Control	Description
Software controls	Monitor the use of system software and prevent unauthorized access of software programs, system software, and computer programs.
Hardware controls	Ensure that computer hardware is physically secure, and check for equipment malfunction. Organizations that are critically dependent on their computers also must make provisions for backup or continued operation to maintain constant service.
Computer operations controls	Oversee the work of the computer department to ensure that programmed procedures are consistently and correctly applied to the storage and processing of data. They include controls over the setup of computer processing jobs and backup and recovery procedures for processing that ends abnormally.
Data security controls	Ensure that valuable business data files on either disk or tape are not subject to unauthorized access, change, or destruction while they are in use or in storage.
Implementation controls	Audit the systems development process at various points to ensure that the process is properly controlled and managed.
Administrative controls	Formalize standards, rules, procedures, and control disciplines to ensure that the organization's general and application controls are properly executed and enforced.

Table 7.4 illustrates sample results of a risk assessment for an online order processing system that processes 30,000 orders per day. The likelihood of each exposure occurring over a one-year period is expressed as a percentage. The next column shows the highest and lowest possible loss that could be expected each time the exposure occurred and an average loss calculated by adding the highest and lowest figures together and dividing by two. The expected annual loss for each exposure can be determined by multiplying the average loss by its probability of occurrence.

This risk assessment shows that the probability of a power failure occurring in a one-year period is 30 percent. Loss of order transactions while power is down could range from $5,000 to $200,000 (averaging $102,500) for each occurrence, depending on how long processing is halted. The probability of embezzlement occurring over a yearly period is about 5 percent, with potential losses ranging from $1,000 to $50,000 (and averaging $25,500) for each occurrence. User errors have a 98 percent chance of occurring over a yearly period, with losses ranging from $200 to $40,000 (and averaging $20,100) for each occurrence.

TABLE 7.4

Online Order Processing Risk Assessment

Exposure	Probability of Occurrence (%)	Loss Range/ Average ($)	Expected Annual Loss ($)
Power failure	30%	$5,000–$200,000 ($102,500)	$30,750
Embezzlement	5%	$1,000–$50,000 ($25,500)	$1,275
User error	98%	$200–$40,000 ($20,100)	$19,698

3

250 Part II: Information Technology Infrastructure

Once the risks have been assessed, system builders will concentrate on the control points with the greatest vulnerability and potential for loss. In this case, controls should focus on ways to minimize the risk of power failures and user errors because anticipated annual losses are highest for these areas.

SECURITY POLICY

Once you've identified the main risks to your systems, your company will need to develop a security policy for protecting the company's assets. A **security policy** consists of statements ranking information risks, identifying acceptable security goals, and identifying the mechanisms for achieving these goals. What are the firm's most important information assets? Who generates and controls this information in the firm? What existing security policies are in place to protect the information? What level of risk is management willing to accept for each of these assets? Is it willing, for instance, to lose customer credit data once every 10 years? Or will it build a security system for credit card data that can withstand the once-in-a-hundred-year disaster? Management must estimate how much it will cost to achieve this level of acceptable risk.

The security policy drives policies determining acceptable use of the firm's information resources and which members of the company have access to its information assets. An **acceptable use policy (AUP)** defines acceptable uses of the firm's information resources and computing equipment, including desktop and laptop computers, wireless devices, telephones, and the Internet. The policy should clarify company policy regarding privacy, user responsibility, and personal use of company equipment and networks. A good AUP defines unacceptable and acceptable actions for every user and specifies consequences for noncompliance. For example, security policy at Unilever, the giant multinational consumer goods company, requires every employee equipped with a laptop mobile handheld device to use a company-specified device and employ a password or other method of identification when logging onto the corporate network.

Authorization policies determine differing levels of access to information assets for different levels of users. **Authorization management systems** establish where and when a user is permitted to access certain parts of a Web site or a corporate database. Such systems allow each user access only to those portions of a system that person is permitted to enter, based on information established by a set of access rules.

The authorization management system knows exactly what information each user is permitted to access as shown in Figure 7-3. This figure illustrates the security allowed for two sets of users of an online personnel database containing sensitive information, such as employees' salaries, benefits, and medical histories. One set of users consists of all employees who perform clerical functions, such as inputting employee data into the system. All individuals with this type of profile can update the system but can neither read nor update sensitive fields, such as salary, medical history, or earnings data. Another profile applies to a divisional manager, who cannot update the system but who can read all employee data fields for his or her division, including medical history and salary. These profiles are based on access rules supplied by business groups. The system illustrated in Figure 7-3 provides very fine-grained security restrictions, such as allowing authorized personnel users to inquire about all employee information except that in confidential fields, such as salary or medical history.

DISASTER RECOVERY PLANNING AND BUSINESS CONTINUITY PLANNING

If you run a business, you need to plan for events such as power outages, floods, earthquakes, or terrorist attacks that will prevent your information systems and your business from operating. **Disaster recovery planning** devises plans for the restoration of computing and communications services after they have been disrupted. Disaster recovery plans focus primarily on

```
╔══════════════════════════════════════════════════════════════╗
║                      SECURITY PROFILE 1                        ║
║   User:  Personnel Dept. Clerk                                 ║
║                                                                ║
║   Location:  Division 1                                        ║
║                                                                ║
║   Employee Identification                                      ║
║   Codes with This Profile:            00753, 27834, 37665, 44116║
║  ─────────────────────────────────────────────────────────────║
║   Data Field                                    Type of Access ║
║   Restrictions                                                 ║
║  ─────────────────────────────────────────────────────────────║
║   All employee data for                      Read and Update  ║
║   Division 1 only                                              ║
║                                                                ║
║        • Medical history data                 None            ║
║        • Salary                                None            ║
║        • Pensionable earnings                  None            ║
╚══════════════════════════════════════════════════════════════╝
```

```
╔══════════════════════════════════════════════════════════════╗
║                      SECURITY PROFILE 2                        ║
║   User:  Divisional Personnel Manager                          ║
║                                                                ║
║   Location:  Division 1                                        ║
║                                                                ║
║   Employee Identification                                      ║
║   Codes with This Profile:     27321                           ║
║  ─────────────────────────────────────────────────────────────║
║   Data Field                                    Type of Access ║
║   Restrictions                                                 ║
║  ─────────────────────────────────────────────────────────────║
║   All employee data for                        Read Only      ║
║   Division 1 only                                              ║
╚══════════════════════════════════════════════════════════════╝
```

Figure 7-3
Security Profiles for a Personnel System
These two examples represent two security profiles or data security patterns that might be found in a personnel system. Depending on the security profile, a user would have certain restrictions on access to various systems, locations, or data in an organization.

the technical issues involved in keeping systems up and running, such as which files to back up and the maintenance of backup computer systems or disaster recovery services.

For example, MasterCard maintains a duplicate computer center in Kansas City, Missouri, to serve as an emergency backup to its primary computer center in St. Louis. Rather than build their own backup facilities, many firms contract with disaster recovery firms, such as Comdisco Disaster Recovery Services in Rosemont, Illinois, and SunGard Availability Services, headquartered in Wayne, Pennsylvania. These disaster recovery firms provide hot sites housing spare computers at locations around the country where subscribing firms can run their critical applications in an emergency. For example, Champion Technologies, which supplies chemicals used in oil and gas operations, is able to switch its enterprise systems from Houston to a SunGard hot site in Scottsdale, Arizona, in two hours.

Business continuity planning focuses on how the company can restore business operations after a disaster strikes. The business continuity plan identifies critical business processes and determines action plans for handling mission-critical functions if systems go down. For example, Deutsche Bank, which provides investment banking and asset management services in 74 different countries, has a well-developed business continuity plan that it continually updates and refines. It maintains full-time teams in Singapore, Hong Kong, Japan, India, and Australia to coordinate plans addressing loss of facilities, personnel, or critical systems so that the company can continue to operate when a catastrophic event occurs. Deutsche Bank's plan distinguishes between processes critical for business survival and those critical to crisis support and is coordinated with the company's disaster recovery planning for its computer centers.

Business managers and information technology specialists need to work together on both types of plans to determine which systems and business processes are most critical to the company. They must conduct a business impact analysis to identify the firm's most critical systems and the impact a systems outage would have on the business. Management must determine the maximum amount of time the business can survive with its systems down and which parts of the business must be restored first.

THE ROLE OF AUDITING

How does management know that information systems security and controls are effective? To answer this question, organizations must conduct comprehensive and systematic audits. An **MIS audit** examines the firm's overall security environment as well as controls governing individual information systems. The auditor should trace the flow of sample transactions through the system and perform tests, using, if appropriate, automated audit software. The MIS audit may also examine data quality.

Security audits review technologies, procedures, documentation, training, and personnel. A thorough audit will even simulate an attack or disaster to test the response of the technology, information systems staff, and business employees.

The audit lists and ranks all control weaknesses and estimates the probability of their occurrence. It then assesses the financial and organizational impact of each threat. Figure 7-4 is a sample auditor's listing of control weaknesses for a loan system. It includes a section for notifying management of such weaknesses and for management's response. Management is expected to devise a plan for countering significant weaknesses in controls.

7.4 Technologies and Tools for Protecting Information Resources

Businesses have an array of tools and technologies for protecting their information resources. They include tools and technologies for securing systems and data, ensuring system availability, and ensuring software quality.

ACCESS CONTROL

Access control consists of all the policies and procedures a company uses to prevent improper access to systems by unauthorized insiders and outsiders. To gain access a user must be authorized and authenticated. **Authentication** refers to the ability to know that a person is who he or she claims to be. Access control software is designed to

Figure 7-4
Sample Auditor's List of Control Weaknesses
This chart is a sample page from a list of control weaknesses that an auditor might find in a loan system in a local commercial bank. This form helps auditors record and evaluate control weaknesses and shows the results of discussing those weaknesses with management, as well as any corrective actions taken by management.

Function: Loans Location: Peoria, IL	Prepared by: J. Ericson Date: June 16, 2010		Received by: T. Benson Review date: June 28, 2010	
Nature of Weakness and Impact	Chance for Error/Abuse		Notification to Management	
	Yes/No	Justification	Report date	Management response
User accounts with missing passwords	Yes	Leaves system open to unauthorized outsiders or attackers	5/10/10	Eliminate accounts without passwords
Network configured to allow some sharing of system files	Yes	Exposes critical system files to hostile parties connected to the network	5/10/10	Ensure only required directories are shared and that they are protected with strong passwords
Software patches can update production programs without final approval from Standards and Controls group	No	All production programs require management approval; Standards and Controls group assigns such cases to a temporary production status		

allow only authorized users to use systems or to access data using some method for authentication.

Authentication is often established by using passwords known only to authorized users. An end user uses a password to log on to a computer system and may also use passwords for accessing specific systems and files. However, users often forget passwords, share them, or choose poor passwords that are easy to guess, which compromises security. Password systems that are too rigorous hinder employee productivity. When employees must change complex passwords frequently, they often take shortcuts, such as choosing passwords that are easy to guess or writing down their passwords at their workstations in plain view. Passwords can also be "sniffed" if transmitted over a network or stolen through social engineering.

New authentication technologies, such as tokens, smart cards, and biometric authentication, overcome some of these problems. A **token** is a physical device, similar to an identification card, that is designed to prove the identity of a single user. Tokens are small gadgets that typically fit on key rings and display passcodes that change frequently. A **smart card** is a device about the size of a credit card that contains a chip formatted with access permission and other data. (Smart cards are also used in electronic payment systems.) A reader device interprets the data on the smart card and allows or denies access.

Biometric authentication uses systems that read and interpret individual human traits, such as fingerprints, irises, and voices, in order to grant or deny access. Biometric authentication is based on the measurement of a physical or behavioral trait that makes each individual unique. It compares a person's unique characteristics, such as the fingerprints, face, or retinal image, against a stored profile of these characteristics to determine whether there are any differences between these characteristics and the stored profile. If the two profiles match, access is granted. Fingerprint and facial recognition technologies are just beginning to be used for security applications. PC laptops are starting to be equipped with fingerprint identification devices.

FIREWALLS, INTRUSION DETECTION SYSTEMS, AND ANTIVIRUS SOFTWARE

Without protection against malware and intruders, connecting to the Internet would be very dangerous. Firewalls, intrusion detection systems, and antivirus software have become essential business tools.

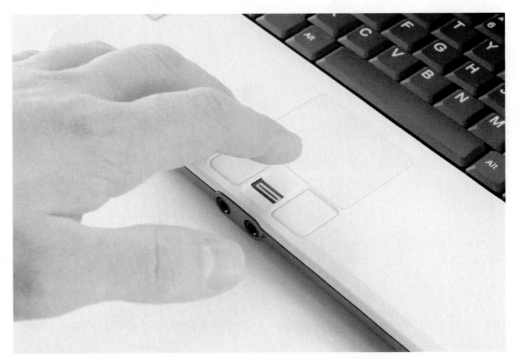

This PC has a biometric fingerprint reader for fast yet secure access to files and networks. New models of PCs are starting to use biometric identification to authenticate users.

Firewalls

Firewalls prevent unauthorized users from accessing private networks. A firewall is a combination of hardware and software that controls the flow of incoming and outgoing network traffic. It is generally placed between the organization's private internal networks and distrusted external networks, such as the Internet, although firewalls can also be used to protect one part of a company's network from the rest of the network (see Figure 7-5).

The firewall acts like a gatekeeper who examines each user's credentials before access is granted to a network. The firewall identifies names, IP addresses, applications, and other characteristics of incoming traffic. It checks this information against the access rules that have been programmed into the system by the network administrator. The firewall prevents unauthorized communication into and out of the network.

In large organizations, the firewall often resides on a specially designated computer separate from the rest of the network, so no incoming request directly accesses private network resources. There are a number of firewall screening technologies, including static packet filtering, stateful inspection, Network Address Translation, and application proxy filtering. They are frequently used in combination to provide firewall protection.

Packet filtering examines selected fields in the headers of data packets flowing back and forth between the trusted network and the Internet, examining individual packets in isolation. This filtering technology can miss many types of attacks. *Stateful inspection* provides additional security by determining whether packets are part of an ongoing dialogue between a sender and a receiver. It sets up state tables to track information over multiple packets. Packets are accepted or rejected based on whether they are part of an approved conversation or whether they are attempting to establish a legitimate connection.

Network Address Translation (NAT) can provide another layer of protection when static packet filtering and stateful inspection are employed. NAT conceals the IP addresses of the

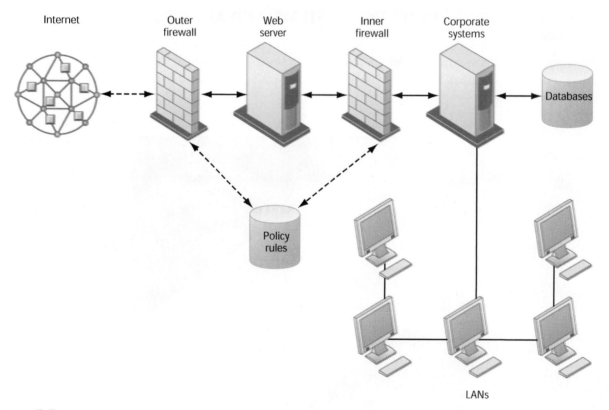

Figure 7-5
A Corporate Firewall
The firewall is placed between the firm's private network and the public Internet or another distrusted network to protect against unauthorized traffic.

organization's internal host computer(s) to prevent sniffer programs outside the firewall from ascertaining them and using that information to penetrate internal systems.

Application proxy filtering examines the application content of packets. A proxy server stops data packets originating outside the organization, inspects them, and passes a proxy to the other side of the firewall. If a user outside the company wants to communicate with a user inside the organization, the outside user first "talks" to the proxy application and the proxy application communicates with the firm's internal computer. Likewise, a computer user inside the organization goes through the proxy to talk with computers on the outside.

To create a good firewall, an administrator must maintain detailed internal rules identifying the people, applications, or addresses that are allowed or rejected. Firewalls can deter, but not completely prevent, network penetration by outsiders and should be viewed as one element in an overall security plan.

Intrusion Detection Systems

In addition to firewalls, commercial security vendors now provide intrusion detection tools and services to protect against suspicious network traffic and attempts to access files and databases. **Intrusion detection systems** feature full-time monitoring tools placed at the most vulnerable points or "hot spots" of corporate networks to detect and deter intruders continually. The system generates an alarm if it finds a suspicious or anomalous event. Scanning software looks for patterns indicative of known methods of computer attacks, such as bad passwords, checks to see if important files have been removed or modified, and sends warnings of vandalism or system administration errors. Monitoring software examines events as they are happening to discover security attacks in progress. The intrusion detection tool can also be customized to shut down a particularly sensitive part of a network if it receives unauthorized traffic.

Antivirus and Antispyware Software

Defensive technology plans for both individuals and businesses must include antivirus protection for every computer. **Antivirus software** is designed to check computer systems and drives for the presence of computer viruses. Often the software eliminates the virus from the infected area. However, most antivirus software is effective only against viruses already known when the software was written. To remain effective, the antivirus software must be continually updated. Antivirus products are available for many different types of mobile and handheld devices in addition to servers, workstations, and desktop PCs.

Leading antivirus software vendors, such as Avira, McAfee, Symantec, and Trend Micro, have enhanced their products to include protection against spyware. Antispyware software tools such as Ad-Aware, Spybot S&D, and Spyware Doctor are also very helpful.

Unified Threat Management Systems

To help businesses reduce costs and improve manageability, security vendors have combined into a single appliance various security tools, including firewalls, virtual private networks, intrusion detection systems, and Web content filtering and antispam software. These comprehensive security management products are called **unified threat management (UTM)** systems. Although initially aimed at small and medium-sized businesses, UTM products are available for all sizes of networks. Leading UTM vendors include Crossbeam, Fortinet, and Check Point, and networking vendors such as Cisco Systems and Juniper Networks provide some UTM capabilities in their equipment.

SECURING WIRELESS NETWORKS

Despite its flaws, WEP provides some margin of security if Wi-Fi users remember to activate it. A simple first step to thwart hackers is to assign a unique name to your network's SSID and instruct your router not to broadcast it. Corporations can further improve Wi-Fi security by using it in conjunction with virtual private network (VPN) technology when accessing internal corporate data.

In June 2004, the Wi-Fi Alliance industry trade group finalized the 802.11i specification (also referred to as Wi-Fi Protected Access 2 or WPA2) that replaces WEP with stronger security standards. Instead of the static encryption keys used in WEP, the new standard uses much longer keys that continually change, making them harder to crack. It also employs an encrypted authentication system with a central authentication server to ensure that only authorized users access the network.

ENCRYPTION AND PUBLIC KEY INFRASTRUCTURE

Many businesses use encryption to protect digital information that they store, physically transfer, or send over the Internet. **Encryption** is the process of transforming plain text or data into cipher text that cannot be read by anyone other than the sender and the intended receiver. Data are encrypted by using a secret numerical code, called an encryption key, that transforms plain data into cipher text. The message must be decrypted by the receiver.

Two methods for encrypting network traffic on the Web are SSL and S-HTTP. **Secure Sockets Layer (SSL)** and its successor Transport Layer Security (TLS) enable client and server computers to manage encryption and decryption activities as they communicate with each other during a secure Web session. **Secure Hypertext Transfer Protocol (S-HTTP)** is another protocol used for encrypting data flowing over the Internet, but it is limited to individual messages, whereas SSL and TLS are designed to establish a secure connection between two computers.

The capability to generate secure sessions is built into Internet client browser software and servers. The client and the server negotiate what key and what level of security to use. Once a secure session is established between the client and the server, all messages in that session are encrypted.

There are two alternative methods of encryption: symmetric key encryption and public key encryption. In symmetric key encryption, the sender and receiver establish a secure Internet session by creating a single encryption key and sending it to the receiver so both the sender and receiver share the same key. The strength of the encryption key is measured by its bit length. Today, a typical key will be 128 bits long (a string of 128 binary digits).

The problem with all symmetric encryption schemes is that the key itself must be shared somehow among the senders and receivers, which exposes the key to outsiders who might just be able to intercept and decrypt the key. A more secure form of encryption called **public key encryption** uses two keys: one shared (or public) and one totally private as shown in Figure 7-6. The keys are mathematically related so that data encrypted with one key can be decrypted using only the other key. To send and receive messages, communicators first create separate pairs of private and public keys. The public key is kept in a directory and the private key must be kept secret. The sender encrypts a message with the recipient's public key. On receiving the message, the recipient uses his or her private key to decrypt it.

Digital certificates are data files used to establish the identity of users and electronic assets for protection of online transactions (see Figure 7-7). A digital certificate system uses a trusted third party, known as a certificate authority (CA), to validate a user's identity. There are many CAs in the United States and around the world, including VeriSign, IdenTrust, and Australia's KeyPost.

The CA verifies a digital certificate user's identity offline. This information is put into a CA server, which generates an encrypted digital certificate containing owner identification information and a copy of the owner's public key. The certificate authenticates that the public key belongs to the designated owner. The CA makes its own public key available publicly either in print or perhaps on the Internet. The recipient of an encrypted message uses the CA's public key to decode the digital certificate attached to the message, verifies it was issued by the CA, and then obtains the sender's public key and identification information contained in the certificate. Using this information, the recipient can send an encrypted reply. The digital certificate system would enable, for example, a credit card user and a merchant to validate that their digital certificates were issued by an

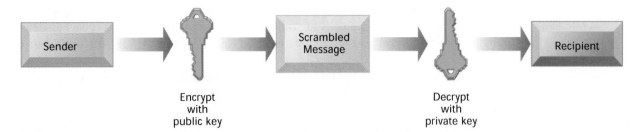

Figure 7-6
Public Key Encryption
A public key encryption system can be viewed as a series of public and private keys that lock data when they are transmitted and unlock the data when they are received. The sender locates the recipient's public key in a directory and uses it to encrypt a message. The message is sent in encrypted form over the Internet or a private network. When the encrypted message arrives, the recipient uses his or her private key to decrypt the data and read the message.

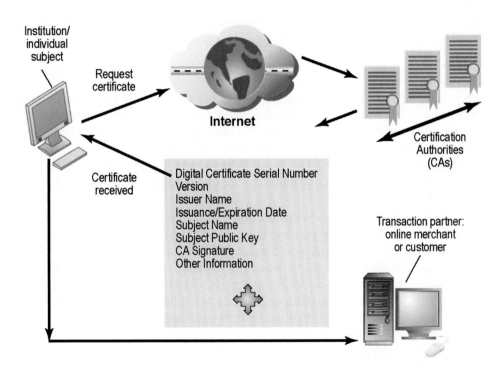

Figure 7-7
Digital Certificates
Digital certificates help establish the identity of people or electronic assets. They protect online transactions by providing secure, encrypted, online communication.

authorized and trusted third party before they exchange data. **Public key infrastructure (PKI)**, the use of public key cryptography working with a certificate authority, is now widely used in e-commerce.

ENSURING SYSTEM AVAILABILITY

As companies increasingly rely on digital networks for revenue and operations, they need to take additional steps to ensure that their systems and applications are always available. Firms such as those in the airline and financial services industries with critical applications requiring online transaction processing have traditionally used fault-tolerant computer systems for many years to ensure 100-percent availability. In **online transaction processing**, transactions entered online are immediately processed by the computer. Multitudinous changes to databases, reporting, and requests for information occur each instant.

Fault-tolerant computer systems contain redundant hardware, software, and power supply components that create an environment that provides continuous, uninterrupted service. Fault-tolerant computers use special software routines or self-checking logic built into their circuitry to detect hardware failures and automatically switch to a backup device. Parts from these computers can be removed and repaired without disruption to the computer system.

Fault tolerance should be distinguished from **high-availability computing**. Both fault tolerance and high-availability computing try to minimize downtime. **Downtime** refers to periods of time in which a system is not operational. However, high-availability computing helps firms recover quickly from a system crash, whereas fault tolerance promises continuous availability and the elimination of recovery time altogether.

High-availability computing environments are a minimum requirement for firms with heavy e-commerce processing or for firms that depend on digital networks for their internal operations. High-availability computing requires backup servers, distribution of processing across multiple servers, high-capacity storage, and good disaster recovery and business continuity plans. The firm's computing platform must be extremely robust with scalable processing power, storage, and bandwidth.

Researchers are exploring ways to make computing systems recover even more rapidly when mishaps occur, an approach called **recovery-oriented computing**. This work includes designing systems that recover quickly, and implementing capabilities and tools to help operators pinpoint the sources of faults in multi-component systems and easily correct their mistakes.

Controlling Network Traffic: Deep Packet Inspection

Have you ever tried to use your campus network and found it was very slow? It may be because your fellow students are using the network to download music or watch YouTube. Bandwith-consuming applications such as file-sharing programs, Internet phone service, and online video are able to clog and slow down corporate networks, degrading performance. For example, Ball Sate University in Muncie, Indiana, found its network had slowed because a small minority of students were using peer-to-peer file sharing programs to download movies and music.

A technology called **deep packet inspection (DPI)** helps solve this problem. DPI examines data files and sorts out low-priority online material while assigning higher priority to business-critical files. Based on the priorities established by a network's operators, it decides whether a specific data packet can continue to its destination or should be blocked or delayed while more important traffic proceeds. Using a DPI system from Allot Communications, Ball State was able to cap the amount of file-sharing traffic and assign it a much lower priority. Ball State's preferred network traffic speeded up.

Security Outsourcing

Many companies, especially small businesses, lack the resources or expertise to provide a secure high-availability computing environment on their own. They can outsource many security functions to **managed security service providers (MSSPs)** that monitor network activity and perform vulnerability testing and intrusion detection. SecureWorks, BT Counterpane, VeriSign, and Symantec are leading providers of MSSP services.

SECURITY ISSUES FOR CLOUD COMPUTING AND THE MOBILE DIGITAL PLATFORM

Although cloud computing and the emerging mobile digital platform have the potential to deliver powerful benefits, they pose new challenges to system security and reliability. We now describe some of these challenges and how they should be addressed.

Security in the Cloud

When processing takes place in the cloud, accountability and responsibility for protection of sensitive data still reside with the company owning that data. Understanding how the cloud computing provider organizes its services and manages the data is critical. The Interactive Session on Technology details some of the cloud security issues that should be addressed.

Cloud users need to confirm that regardless of where their data are stored or transferred, they are protected at a level that meets their corporate requirements. They should stipulate that the cloud provider store and process data in specific jurisdictions according to the privacy rules of those jurisdictions. Cloud clients should find how the cloud provider segregates their corporate data from those of other companies and ask for proof that encryption mechanisms are sound. It's also important to know how the cloud provider will respond if a disaster strikes, whether the provider will be able to completely restore your data, and how long this should take. Cloud users should also ask whether cloud providers will submit to external audits and security certifications. These kinds of controls can be written into the service level agreement (SLA) before signing with a cloud provider.

Securing Mobile Platforms

Malware targeting mobile devices is not as extensive as that targeting computers, but is spreading nonetheless using e-mail, text messages, Bluetooth, and file downloads from the Web via Wi-Fi or cellular networks. If mobile devices are performing many of the functions of PCs, they need to be secured like desktops and laptops against malware, theft, accidental loss, unauthorized access, and hacking attempts. Mobile devices accessing corporate systems and data require special protection.

Companies should make sure that their corporate security policy includes mobile devices, with additional details on how mobile devices should be supported, protected, and used. Guidelines should stipulate required software and procedures for remote access of corporate systems. At this time, the security for smartphones is not as well developed as for larger devices. These devices may not be able to fully protect sensitive information, especially data transmitted via e-mail attachments and data stored locally on the devices.

ENSURING SOFTWARE QUALITY

In addition to implementing effective security and controls, organizations can improve system quality and reliability by employing software metrics and rigorous software testing. Software metrics are objective assessments of the system in the form of quantified measurements. Ongoing use of metrics allows the information systems department and end users to jointly measure the performance of the system and identify problems as they occur. Examples of software metrics include the number of transactions that can be processed in a specified unit of time, online response time, the number of payroll checks printed per hour, and the number of known bugs per hundred lines of program code. For metrics to be successful, they must be carefully designed, formal, objective, and used consistently.

Early, regular, and thorough testing will contribute significantly to system quality. Many view testing as a way to prove the correctness of work they have done. In fact, we know that all sizable software is riddled with errors, and we must test to uncover these errors.

Good testing begins before a software program is even written by using a *walkthrough*— a review of a specification or design document by a small group of people carefully selected based on the skills needed for the particular objectives being tested. Once developers start writing software programs, coding walkthroughs also can be used to review program code. However, code must be tested by computer runs. When errors are discovered, the source is found and eliminated through a process called *debugging*. You can find out more about the various stages of testing required to put an information system into operation in Chapter 11. Our Learning Tracks also contain descriptions of methodologies for developing software programs that also contribute to software quality.

INTERACTIVE SESSION: TECHNOLOGY   How Secure Is the Cloud?

New York-based investment banking and financial services firm Cowen and Co. has moved its global sales systems to the cloud using Salesforce.com. So far, Cowen's CIO Daniel Flax is pleased. Using cloud services has helped the company lower up-front technology costs, decrease downtime, and support additional services. But he's trying to come to grips with cloud security issues. Cloud computing security is indeed cloudy, and this lack of transparency is troubling to many. One of the biggest risks of cloud computing is that it is highly distributed. Cloud applications and application mashups reside in virtual libraries in large remote data centers and server farms that supply business services and data management to multiple corporate clients. To save money and keep costs low, cloud computing providers often distribute work to data centers around the globe where work can be accomplished most efficiently. When you use the cloud, you may not know precisely where your data are being hosted, and you might not even know the country where they are being stored.

The dispersed nature of cloud computing makes it difficult to track unauthorized activity. Virtually all cloud providers use encryption, such as Secure Sockets Layer (SSL) to secure the data they handle while the data are being transmitted. But if the data are stored on devices that also store other companies' data, it's important to ensure these stored data are encrypted as well.

Indian Harvest Specialtifoods, a Bemidji, Minnesota-based company that distributes rice, grains, and legumes to restaurants worldwide, relies on cloud software provider NetSuite to ensure that its data sent to the cloud are fully protected. Mike Mullin, Indian Harvest's IT director, feels that using SSL to encrypt the data gives him some level of confidence that the data are secure. He also points out that his company and other users of cloud services need to pay attention to their own security practices, especially access controls. "Your side of the infrastructure is just as vulnerable, if not more vulnerable, than the provider's side," he observes.

One way to deal with these problems is to use a cloud vendor that is a public company, which is required by law to disclose how it manages information. Salesforce.com meets this requirement, with strict processes and guidelines for managing its data centers. "We know our data are in the U.S. and we have a report on the very data centers that we're talking about," says Flax.

Another alternative is to use a cloud provider that give subscribers the option to choose where their cloud computing work takes place. For example, Terremark Worldwide Inc. is giving its subscriber Agora Games the option to choose where its applications run. Terremark has a Miami facility but is adding other locations. In the past, Agora had no say over where Terremark hosted its applications and data.

Even if your data are totally secure in the cloud, you may not be able to prove it. Some cloud providers don't meet current compliance requirements regarding security, and some of those providers, such as Amazon, have asserted that they don't intend to meet those rules and won't allow compliance auditors on-site.

There are laws restricting where companies can send and store some types of information—personally identifiable information in the European Union (EU), government work in the United States, or applications that employ certain encryption algorithms. Companies required to meet these regulations involving protected data either in the United States or the EU won't be able to use public cloud providers.

Some of these regulations call for proof that systems are securely managed, which may require confirmation from an independent audit. Large cloud providers are unlikely to allow another company's auditors to inspect their data centers. Microsoft found a way to deal with this problem that may be helpful. The company reduced 26 different types of audits to a list of 200 necessary controls for meeting compliance standards that were applied to its data center environments and services. Microsoft does not give every customer or auditor access to its data centers, but its compliance framework allows auditors to order from a menu of tests and receive the results.

Companies expect their systems to be running 24/7, but cloud providers haven't always been able to provide this level of service. Millions of customers of Salesforce.com suffered a 38-minute outage in early January 2009 and others several years earlier. The January 2009 outage locked more than 900,000 subscribers out of crucial applications and data needed to transact business with customers. Users of Amazon's cloud services experienced downtime several times in 2008. (In July 2008 they lost service for 8 hours.)

Agreements for services such as Amazon EC2 and Microsoft Azure state that these companies are not going to be held liable for data losses or fines or other legal penalties when companies use their services. Both vendors offer guidance on how to use their cloud platforms securely, and they may still be able to protect data better than some companies' homegrown facilities.

Salesforce.com had been building up and redesigning its infrastructure to ensure better service. The company invested $50 million in Mirrorforce technology, a mirroring system that creates a duplicate database in a separate location and synchronizes the data instantaneously. If one database is disabled, the other takes over. Salesforce.com added two data centers on the East and West coasts in addition to its Silicon Valley facility. The company distributed processing for its larger customers among these centers to balance its database load.

Sources: John Edwards, "Cutting Through the Fog of Cloud Security," *Computerworld*, February 23, 2009; Wayne Rash, "Is Cloud Computing Secure? Prove It," *eWeek*, September 21, 2009; Robert Lemos, ,"Five Lessons from Microsoft on Cloud Security," *Computerworld*, August 25, 2009; Mike Fratto, "Cloud Control," *Information Week*, January 26, 2009.

CASE STUDY QUESTIONS

1. What security and control problems are described in this case?

2. What people, organization, and technology factors contribute to these problems?

3. How secure is cloud computing? Explain your answer.

4. If you were in charge of your company's information systems department, what issues would you want to clarify with prospective vendors?

5. Would you entrust your corporate systems to a cloud computing provider? Why or why not?

MIS IN ACTION

Go to www.trust.salesforce.com, then answer the following questions:

1. Click on Security and describe Salesforce.com's security provisions. How helpful are these?

2. Click on Best Practices and describe what subscribing companies can do to tighten security. How helpful are these guidelines?

3. If you ran a business, would you feel confident about using Salesforce.com's on-demand service? Why or why not?

7.5 Hands-On MIS Projects

The projects in this section give you hands-on experience analyzing security vulnerabilities, using spreadsheet software for risk analysis, and using Web tools to research security outsourcing services.

MANAGEMENT DECISION PROBLEMS

1. K2 Network operates online game sites used by about 16 million people in over 100 countries. Players are allowed to enter a game for free, but must buy digital "assets" from K2, such as swords to fight dragons, if they want to be deeply involved. The games can accomodate millions of players at once and are played simultaneously by people all over the world. Prepare a security analysis for this Internet-based business. What kinds of threats should it anticipate? What would be their impact on the business? What steps can it take to prevent damage to its Web sites and continuing operations?

2. A survey of your firm's information technology infrastructure has produced the following security analysis statistics:

High-risk vulnerabilities include non-authorized users accessing applications, guessable passwords, user names matching the password, active user accounts with missing passwords, and the existence of unauthorized programs in application systems. Medium-risk vulnerabilities include the ability of users to shut down the system without being logged on, passwords and screen saver settings that were not established for PCs, and outdated versions of software still being stored on hard drives. Low-risk vulnerabilities include the inability of users to change their passwords, user passwords that have not been changed periodically, and passwords that were smaller than the minimum size specified by the company.

SECURITY VULNERABILITIES BY TYPE OF COMPUTING PLATFORM

Platform	Number of Computers	High Risk	Medium Risk	Low Risk	Total Vulnerabilities
Windows Server (corporate applications)	1	11	37	19	
Windows 7 Enterprise (high-level administrators)	3	56	242	87	
Linux (e-mail and printing services)	1	3	154	98	
Sun Solaris (UNIX) (E-commerce and Web servers)	2	12	299	78	
Windows 7 Enterprise user desktops and laptops with office productivity tools that can also be linked to the corporate network running corporate applications and intranet	195	14	16	1,237	

- Calculate the total number of vulnerabilities for each platform. What is the potential impact of the security problems for each computing platform on the organization?
- If you only have one information systems specialist in charge of security, which platforms should you address first in trying to eliminate these vulnerabilities? Second? Third? Last? Why?
- Identify the types of control problems illustrated by these vulnerabilities and explain the measures that should be taken to solve them.
- What does your firm risk by ignoring the security vulnerabilities identified?

IMPROVING DECISION MAKING: USING SPREADSHEET SOFTWARE TO PERFORM A SECURITY RISK ASSESSMENT

Software skills: Spreadsheet formulas and charts
Business skills: Risk assessment

This project uses spreadsheet software to calculate anticipated annual losses from various security threats identified for a small company.

Mercer Paints is a small but highly regarded paint manufacturing company located in Alabama. The company has a network in place linking many of its business operations. Although the firm believes that its security is adequate, the recent addition of a Web site has become an open invitation to hackers. Management requested a risk assessment. The risk assessment identified a number of potential exposures. These exposures, their associated probabilities, and average losses are summarized in the following table.

MERCER PAINTS RISK ASSESSMENT

Exposure	Probability of Occurrence (%)	Average Loss ($)
Malware attack	60%	$75,000
Data loss	12%	$70,000
Embezzlement	3%	$30,000
User errors	95%	$25,000
Threats from hackers	95%	$90,000
Improper use by employees	5%	$5,000
Power failure	15%	$300,000

- In addition to the potential exposures listed, you should identify at least three other potential threats to Mercer Paints, assign probabilities, and estimate a loss range.
- Use spreadsheet software and the risk assessment data to calculate the expected annual loss for each exposure.
- Present your findings in the form of a chart. Which control points have the greatest vulnerability? What recommendations would you make to Mercer Paints? Prepare a written report that summarizes your findings and recommendations.

IMPROVING DECISION MAKING: EVALUATING SECURITY OUTSOURCING SERVICES

Software skills: Web browser and presentation software
Business skills: Evaluating business outsourcing services

Businesses today have a choice of whether to outsource the security function or maintain their own internal staff for this purpose. This project will help develop your Internet skills in using the Web to research and evaluate security outsourcing services.

As an information systems expert in your firm, you have been asked to help management decide whether to outsource security or keep the security function within the firm. Search the Web to find information to help you decide whether to outsource security and to locate security outsourcing services.

- Present a brief summary of the arguments for and against outsourcing computer security for your company.
- Select two firms that offer computer security outsourcing services, and compare them and their services.
- Prepare an electronic presentation for management summarizing your findings. Your presentation should make the case on whether or not your company should outsource computer security. If you believe your company should outsource, the presentation should identify which security outsourcing service should be selected and justify your selection.

LEARNING TRACKS

The following Learning Tracks provide content relevant to topics covered in this chapter:

1. The Booming Job Market in IT Security
2. The Sarbanes-Oxley Act
3. Computer Forensics
4. General and Application Controls for Information Systems
5. Software Vulnerability and Reliability
6. Management Challenges of Security and Control

Review Summary

1 **Why are information systems vulnerable to destruction, error, and abuse?**
Digital data are vulnerable to destruction, misuse, error, fraud, and hardware or software failures. The Internet is designed to be an open system and makes internal corporate systems more vulnerable to actions from outsiders. Hackers can unleash denial-of-service (DoS) attacks or penetrate corporate networks, causing serious system disruptions. Wi-Fi networks

can easily be penetrated by intruders using sniffer programs to obtain an address to access the resources of the network. Computer viruses and worms can disable systems and Web sites. The dispersed nature of cloud computing makes it difficult to track unauthorized activity or to apply controls from afar. Software presents problems because software bugs may be impossible to eliminate and because software vulnerabilities can be exploited by hackers and malicious software. End users often introduce errors.

2 **What is the business value of security and control?** Lack of sound security and control can cause firms relying on computer systems for their core business functions to lose sales and productivity. Information assets, such as confidential employee records, trade secrets, or business plans, lose much of their value if they are revealed to outsiders or if they expose the firm to legal liability. New laws, such as HIPAA, the Sarbanes-Oxley Act, and the Gramm-Leach-Bliley Act, require companies to practice stringent electronic records management and adhere to strict standards for security, privacy, and control. Legal actions requiring electronic evidence and computer forensics also require firms to pay more attention to security and electronic records management.

3 **What are the components of an organizational framework for security and control?** Firms need to establish a good set of both general and application controls for their information systems. A risk assessment evaluates information assets, identifies control points and control weaknesses, and determines the most cost-effective set of controls. Firms must also develop a coherent corporate security policy and plans for continuing business operations in the event of disaster or disruption. The security policy includes policies for acceptable use and authorization. Comprehensive and systematic MIS auditing helps organizations determine the effectiveness of security and controls for their information systems.

4 **What are the most important tools and technologies for safeguarding information resources?** Firewalls prevent unauthorized users from accessing a private network when it is linked to the Internet. Intrusion detection systems monitor private networks from suspicious network traffic and attempts to access corporate systems. Passwords, tokens, smart cards, and biometric authentication are used to authenticate system users. Antivirus software checks computer systems for infections by viruses and worms and often eliminates the malicious software, while antispyware software combats intrusive and harmful spyware programs. Encryption, the coding and scrambling of messages, is a widely used technology for securing electronic transmissions over unprotected networks. Digital certificates combined with public key encryption provide further protection of electronic transactions by authenticating a user's identity. Companies can use fault-tolerant computer systems or create high-availability computing environments to make sure that their information systems are always available. Use of software metrics and rigorous software testing help improve software quality and reliability.

Key Terms

Acceptable use policy (AUP), 250
Access control, 252
Antivirus software, 255
Application controls, 248
Authentication, 252
Authorization management systems, 250
Authorization policies, 250

Biometric authentication, 253
Botnet, 241
Bugs, 245
Business continuity planning, 251
Click fraud, 244
Computer crime, 241
Computer forensics, 247
Computer virus, 238

Controls, 235
Cybervandalism, 240
Deep packet inspection (DPI), 258
Denial-of-service (DoS) attack, 240
Digital certificates, 256
Disaster recovery planning, 250

Review Questions

1. Why are information systems vulnerable to destruction, error, and abuse?
- List and describe the most common threats against contemporary information systems.
- Define malware and distinguish among a virus, a worm, and a Trojan horse.
- Define a hacker and explain how hackers create security problems and damage systems.
- Define computer crime. Provide two examples of crime in which computers are targets and two examples in which computers are used as instruments of crime.
- Define identity theft and phishing and explain why identity theft is such a big problem today.
- Describe the security and system reliability problems created by employees.
- Explain how software defects affect system reliability and security.

2. What is the business value of security and control?
- Explain how security and control provide value for businesses.
- Describe the relationship between security and control and recent U.S. government regulatory requirements and computer forensics.

3. What are the components of an organizational framework for security and control?
- Define general controls and describe each type of general control.
- Define application controls and describe each type of application control.
- Describe the function of risk assessment and explain how it is conducted for information systems.
- Define and describe the following: security policy, acceptable use policy, authorization policy.
- Explain how MIS auditing promotes security and control.

4. What are the most important tools and technologies for safeguarding information resources?
- Name and describe three authentication methods.
- Describe the roles of firewalls, intrusion detection systems, and antivirus software in promoting security.
- Explain how encryption protects information.
- Describe the role of encryption and digital certificates in a public key infrastructure.
- Distinguish between fault-tolerant and high-availability computing, and between disaster recovery planning and business continuity planning.
- Identify and describe the security problems posed by cloud computing.
- Describe measures for improving software quality and reliability

Discussion Questions

1. Security isn't simply a technology issue, it's a business issue. Discuss.

2. If you were developing a business continuity plan for your company, where would you start? What aspects of the business would the plan address?

Video Cases

Video Cases and Instructional Videos illustrating some of the concepts in this chapter are available. Contact your instructor to access these videos.

Collaboration and Teamwork

Evaluating Security Software Tools

With a group of three or four students, use the Web to research and evaluate security products from two competing vendors, such as antivirus software, firewalls, or antispyware software. For each product, describe its capabilities, for what types of businesses it is best suited, and its cost to purchase and install. Which is the best product? Why? If possible, use Google Sites to post links to Web pages, team communication announcements, and work assignments; to brainstorm; and to work collaboratively on project documents. Try to use Google Docs to develop a presentation of your findings for the class.

BUSINESS PROBLEM-SOLVING CASE

Are We Ready for Cyberwarfare?

For most of us, the Internet is a tool we use for e-mail, news, entertainment, socializing, and shopping. But for computer security experts affiliated with government agencies and private contractors, as well as their hacker counterparts from across the globe, the Internet has become a battlefield—a war zone where cyberwarfare is becoming more frequent and hacking techniques are becoming more advanced. Cyberwarfare poses a unique and daunting set of challenges for security experts, not only in detecting and preventing intrusions but also in tracking down perpetrators and bringing them to justice.

Cyberwarfare can take many forms. Often, hackers use botnets, massive networks of computers that they control thanks to spyware and other malware, to launch large-scale DDoS attacks on their target's servers. But other methods exist that allow intruders to access secure computers remotely and copy or delete e-mail and files from the machine, or even to remotely monitor users of a machine using more sophisticated software. For cyber-criminals, the benefit of cyberwarfare is that they can

compete with traditional superpowers for a fraction of the cost of, for example, building up a nuclear arsenal. Because more and more modern technological infrastructure will rely on the Internet to function, cyberwarriors will have no shortage of targets at which to take aim.

Cyberwarfare also involves defending against these types of attacks. That's a major focus of U.S. intelligence agencies. While the U.S. is currently at the forefront of cyberwarfare technologies, it's unlikely to maintain technological dominance because of the relatively low cost of the technologies needed to mount these types of attacks.

In fact, hackers worldwide have already begun doing so in earnest. In July 2009, 27 American and South Korean government agencies and other organizations were hit by a DDoS attack. An estimated 65,000 computers belonging to foreign botnets flooded the Web sites with access requests. Affected sites included those of the White House, the Treasury, the Federal Trade

Commission, the Defense Department, the Secret Service, the New York Stock Exchange, and the Washington Post, in addition to the Korean Defense Ministry, National Assembly, the presidential Blue House, and several others. The attacks were not sophisticated, but were widespread and prolonged, succeeding in slowing down most of the U.S. sites and forcing several South Korean sites to stop operating. North Korea or pro-North Korean groups were suspected to be behind the attacks, but the Pyongyang government denied any involvement.

The lone positive from the attacks was that only the Web sites of these agencies were affected. However, other intrusions suggest that hackers already have the potential for much more damaging acts of cyberwarfare. The Federal Aviation Administration (FAA), which oversees the airline activity of the United States, has already been subject to successful attacks on its systems, including one in 2006 that partially shut down air-traffic data systems in Alaska.

In 2007 and 2008, computer spies broke into the Pentagon's $300 billion Joint Strike Fighter project. Intruders were able to copy and siphon off several terabytes of data related to design and electronics systems, potentially making it easier to defend against the fighter when it's eventually produced. The intruders entered through vulnerabilities of two or three contractors working on the fighter jet project. Fortunately, computers containing the most sensitive data were not connected to the Internet, and were therefore inaccessible to the intruders. Former U.S. officials say that this attack originated in China, and that China had been making steady progress in developing online-warfare techniques. China rebutted these claims, stating that the U.S. media was subscribing to outdated, Cold War-era thinking in blaming them, and that Chinese hackers were not skilled enough to perpetrate an attack of that magnitude.

In April 2009, cyberspies infiltrated the U.S. electrical grid, using weak points where computers on the grid are connected to the Internet, and left behind software programs whose purpose is unclear, but which presumably could be used to disrupt the system. Reports indicated that the spies originated in computer networks in China and Russia. Again, both nations denied the charges. In response to these and other intrusions, Congress is considering legislation that would require all critical infrastructure companies to meet newer, tougher cybersecurity standards. As of this writing, most federal agencies get passing marks for meeting the requirements of the Federal Information Security Management Act, the most recent set of standards passed into law. But as cyberwarfare technologies develop and become more advanced, the standards imposed by this legislation will likely be insufficient to defend against attacks.

In each incident of cyberwarfare, the governments of the countries suspected to be responsible have roundly denied the charges with no repercussions. How could this be possible? The major reason is that tracing identities of specific attackers through cyberspace is next to impossible, making deniability simple.

While the task is hard enough for government agencies with the resources and expertise to tackle these problems, two groups, the Information Warfare Monitor (IWM) and Citizen Lab, share the goal of empowering non-government groups with investigative tools that have traditionally been available only to law enforcement agencies. These groups have made some surprising breakthroughs in tracking down cybercriminals and identifying their techniques.

Nart Villeneuve, who works for both groups, found that a Chinese equivalent to Skype was used for surveillance by a major Chinese wireless carrier, and that a spy system he and other investigators dubbed "Ghostnet" was spying on South Asian government-owed computers worldwide. An audit of the Dalai Lama's office network in Dharamsala, India, which had endured consistent attacks from hackers, spurred the discovery. The operation was thought to be sponsored by the Chinese government, which has traditionally been antagonistic to the Dalai Lama and his expelled Tibetan government. The IWM used a free program called Wireshark to capture inbound and outbound Internet traffic from the exiled Tibetan government's computers. The program detected that the Ghostnet system had installed secret surveillance software on computers remotely and was able to access files and e-mail.

The real worry for security experts and government officials is an act of cyberwar against a critical resource, such as the electric grid, financial system, or communications systems. First of all, the United States has no clear policy about how the country would respond to that level of a cyberattack. Although the electric grid was accessed by hackers, it hasn't yet actually been attacked. A three-year study of U.S. cybersecurity recommended that such a policy be created and made public. It also suggested that the United States attempt to find common ground with other nations to join forces in preventing these attacks.

Secondly, the effects of such an attack would likely be devastating. Mike McConnell, the former director of national intelligence, stated that if even a single large American bank were successfully attacked, "it would have an order-of-magnitude greater impact on the global economy" than the World Trade Center attacks, and that "the ability to threaten the U.S. money supply is the equivalent of today's nuclear weapon." Such an attack would have a catastrophic effect on the U.S. financial system, and by extension, the world economy.

Lastly, many industry analysts are concerned that the organization of our cybersecurity is messy, with no clear leader among our intelligence agencies. Several different agencies, including the Pentagon and the National Security Agency (NSA), have their sights on being the leading agency in the ongoing efforts to combat cyberwarfare. In June 2009, Secretary of Defense Robert Gates ordered the creation of the first headquarters designed to coordinate government cybersecurity efforts, tentatively called Cybercom. Cybercom's purpose will be to coordinate the operation and protection of military and Pentagon computer networks in the hopes of resolving this organizational tangle.

President Obama had previously announced his intention to expand on the $17 billion program approved in 2008. Much of that sum will presumably go to Cybercom as it coordinates efforts to restrict access to government computers and protect systems that run the stock exchanges, clear global banking transactions, and manage the air traffic control system. Its ultimate goal will be to prevent catastrophic cyberattacks against the United States. But some insiders suggest that it might not be able to effectively organize the governmental agencies without direct access to the President, which it currently lacks. Nevertheless, the first task of the office would be to organize the various components and capabilities scattered across the four armed services.

In confronting this problem, one critical question has arisen: how much control over enforcing cybersecurity should be given to American spy agencies, since they are prohibited from acting on American soil? Cyberattacks know no borders, so distinguishing between American soil and foreign soil means domestic agencies will be unnecessarily inhibited in their ability to fight cybercrime. For example, if the NSA was investigating the source of a cyberattack on government Web sites, and determined that the attack originated from American servers, under our current laws, it would not be able to investigate further.

Some experts believe that there is no effective way for a domestic agency to conduct computer operations without entering prohibited networks within the United States, or even conducting investigations in countries that are American allies. The NSA has already come under heavy fire for its surveillance actions after 9-11, and this has the potential to raise similar privacy concerns. Preventing terrorist or cyberwar attacks may require examining some e-mail messages from other countries or giving intelligence agencies more access to networks or Internet service providers. There is a need for an open debate about what constitutes a violation of privacy and what is acceptable during "cyber-wartime," which is essentially all the time. The law may need to be changed to accommodate effective cybersecurity techniques, but it's unclear that this can be done without eroding some privacy rights that we consider essential.

One way around this would be to entrust some of the work to private defense contractors. Many contractors are hoping to garner valuable government contracts to both develop defense systems for our networks as well as to create offensive measures to disable enemy networks. Teams of highly skilled computer engineers at major defense contractors are at work on this today, and might be able to circumvent the restrictions holding government agencies back from surveillance within the U.S.

As for these offensive measures, it's unclear how strong the United States' offensive capabilities for cyberwarfare are. The government closely guards this information, almost all of which is classified. But former military and intelligence officials indicate that our cyberwarfare capabilities have dramatically increased in sophistication in the past year or two. And because tracking cybercriminals has proven so difficult, it may be that the best defense is a strong offense.

Sources: Hoover, J. Nicholas. "Cybersecurity Balancing Act." *Information Week*, April 27, 2009; David E. Sanger, John Markoff, and Thom Shanker, "U.S. Steps Up Effort on Digital Defenses," *The New York Times*, April 28, 2009; John Markoff and Thom Shanker. "Panel Advises Clarifying U.S. Plans on Cyberwar." *The New York Times*, April 30, 2009; Siobhan Gorman and Evan Ramstad, "Cyber Blitz Hits U.S., Korea," *The Wall Street Journal*, July 9, 2009; Lolita C. Baldor, "White House Among Targets of Sweeping Cyber Attack," Associated Press, July 8, 2009; Choe Sang-Hun, "Cyberattacks Hit U.S. and South Korean Web Sites," *The New York Times*, July 9, 2009; Siobhan Gorman, "FAA's Air-Traffic Networks Breached by Hackers," *The Wall Street Journal*, May 7, 2009; Thom Shanker, "New Military Command for Cyberspace," *The New York Times*, June 24, 2009; David E. Sanger and Thom Shanker, "Pentagon Plans New Arm to Wage Wars in Cyberspace," *The New York Times*, May 29, 2009; Lolita C. Baldor, "Obama Setting Up Better Security for Computers," Associated Press, May 29, 2009; Christopher Drew and John Markoff. "Contractors Vie for Plum Work, Hacking for U.S.," *The New York Times*, May 31, 2009; Thom Shanker and David E. Sanger, "Privacy May Be a Victim in Cyberdefense Plan," *The New York Times*, June 13, 2009; Siobhan Gorman, August Cole, and Yochi Dreazen, "Computer Spies Breach Fighter-Jet Project," *The Wall Street Journal*, April 21, 2009; Carlos Tejada and Juliet Ye, "Computer Spying: China Responds," *The Wall Street Journal*, April 22, 2008; Gorman, Siobhan. "Electricity Grid in U.S. Penetrated by Spies." *The Wall Street Journal* (April 8, 2009); "Has Power Grid Been Hacked? U.S. Won't Say." Reuters, April 8, 2009; Markoff, John. "Vast Spy System Loots Computers in 103 Countries." *The New York Times* (March 29, 2009); Markoff, John, "Tracking Cyberspies Through the Web Wilderness," *The New York Times*, May 12, 2009.

Case Study Questions

1. Is cyberwarfare a serious problem? Why or why not?

2. Assess the people, organization, and technology factors that have created this problem.

3. What solutions have been proposed? Do you think they will be effective? Why or why not?

4. Are there other solutions for this problem that should be pursued? What are they?

Key System Applications for the Digital Age

PART III

Part III examines the core information system applications businesses are using today to improve operational excellence and decision making. These applications include enterprise systems; systems for supply chain management, customer relationship management, and knowledge management; e-commerce applications; decision-support systems; and executive support systems. This part answers questions such as these: How can enterprise applications improve business performance? How do firms use e-commerce to extend the reach of their businesses? How can systems improve decision making and help companies make better use of their knowledge assets?

Achieving Operational Excellence and Customer Intimacy: Enterprise Applications

CHAPTER 8

STUDENT LEARNING OBJECTIVES

After completing this chapter, you will be able to answer the following questions:

1. How do enterprise systems help businesses achieve operational excellence?

2. How do supply chain management systems coordinate planning, production, and logistics with suppliers?

3. How do customer relationship management systems help firms achieve customer intimacy?

4. What are the challenges posed by enterprise applications?

5. How are enterprise applications used in platforms for new cross-functional services?

CHAPTER OUTLINE

ENTERPRISE APPLICATIONS HELP SEVERSTAL CREATE A GLOBAL PRODUCTION PLATFORM

Severstal ("Northern Steel") is one of Russia's largest steelmakers. It operates primarily in Russia but maintains facilities in the Ukraine, Kazakhstan, the United Kingdom, France, Italy, the United States, and Africa. With more than 100,000 employees worldwide and more than US $22.4 billion in revenue in 2008, it's on its way to redefining global steel making.

Some U.S. firms have left the steel production market because it's very capital-intensive. Severstal's not worried about that. This company's managers are convinced that they are at the helm of a global profitability leader in the steel and mining industry.

Severstal's corporate strategy calls for providing high-margin value-added products in attractive niche markets worldwide while keeping costs low. The company is developing a global platform for best-practice sharing and competencies development. Severstal wants to leverage best practices and technologies across its global operations and improve efficiencies by locating mills closer to key automotive customers. In 2004, for example, Severstal North America purchased Rouge Industries in Dearborn

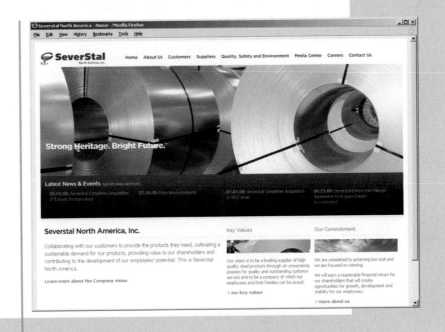

Michigan, originally part of Henry Ford's massive River Rouge manufacturing complex, to gain access to the U.S. market for automotive steel. Severstal North America (SNA) is now the fourth-largest integrated steel maker in the United States.

Most of Severstal's customers have operations throughout the world and the want to be supplied with the same quality steel in North America, Europe, and Russia. Severstal's strategy "is to create a global production platform that can supply high-quality steel to customers, wherever they are located," says Sergei Kuznetsov, Severstal North America's chief financial officer.

All these plans call for a flexible IT infrastructure that is agile enough to meet changing global business requirements and support efficient growth. SNA's IT infrastructure was a hodgepodge of different systems, including Oracle PeopleSoft Enterprise for financials, Indus Enterprise PAC for purchasing and maintenance, and a variety of custom systems. Information was unable to flow freely across different functional areas.

Instead of upgrading its existing applications, SNA standardized on Oracle E-Business Suite 12, an enterprise applications suite that includes integrated modules for financials, purchasing, enterprise asset management, manufacturing, and order management. The applications in Oracle E-Business Suite are integrated, making it easier to access data from different functional areas for decision making while creating more efficient workflows and enhancing productivity. Instead of optimizing individual business processes, the company is able to optimize end-to-end processes. For example, SNA's procure-to-pay processes are integrated with its purchasing system.

The new system also reduced the time required to close the company's books from 10 days to 5 days or less, providing more timely and higher-quality information to the Severstal parent company in Russia. Oracle iSupplier Portal, Oracle iProcurement, and Oracle Sourcing include capabilities for electronic quoting and self-service applications, facilitating communication and collaboration with SNA's suppliers and business partners. As Severstal grows organically or through acquisitions, the Oracle software will help it integrate the new units on the same platform.

Sources: David A. Kelly, "Managing in a Global Economy: SeverStal," *Profit Magazine*, February 2008; Anna V. Schevchenko, "Severstal Global Master Data Project," October 15-16, 2008; and www.severstalna.com, accessed July 5, 2009.

Severstal's efforts to create a global IT infrastructure identifies some of the issues that organizations need to consider if they want to use global and enterprise-wide systems. In order to operate as a global business, the company had to have the right set of business processes and information systems in place. It needed to access company-wide information from all of its different global operating locations and business functions so that management could manage the company as a single global entity.

The chapter-opening diagram calls attention to important points raised by this case and this chapter. Severstal is trying to generate profits in a competitive and capital-intensive industry by providing products that can command higher prices in niche markets, but it still needs to keep its operating costs low. It adopted a global production model to meet this challenge. Severstal could have upgraded its existing systems with newer technology, but these legacy information systems did not support global business processes and information flows. Instead, the company replaced them with a set of enterprise applications from Oracle. The new systems integrate disparate business functions and business processes and enable the company to create new cross-functional company-wide processes. The company is now able to respond flexibly to opportunities all over the world.

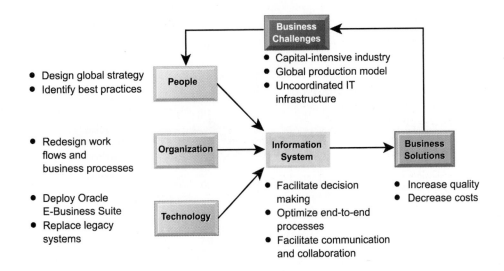

- Design global strategy
- Identify best practices

People

Business Challenges
- Capital-intensive industry
- Global production model
- Uncoordinated IT infrastructure

- Redesign work flows and business processes

Organization

- Deploy Oracle E-Business Suite
- Replace legacy systems

Technology

Information System
- Facilitate decision making
- Optimize end-to-end processes
- Facilitate communication and collaboration

Business Solutions
- Increase quality
- Decrease costs

8.1 Enterprise Systems

Around the globe, companies are increasingly becoming more connected, both internally and with other companies. If you run a business, you'll want to be able to react instantaneously when a customer places a large order or when a shipment from a supplier is delayed. You may also want to know the impact of these events on every part of the business and how the business is performing at any point in time, especially if you're running a large company. Enterprise systems provide the integration to make this possible. Let's look at how they work and what they can do for the firm.

WHAT ARE ENTERPRISE SYSTEMS?

Imagine that you had to run a business based on information from tens or even hundreds of different databases and systems, none of which could speak to one another? Imagine your company had 10 different major product lines, each produced in separate factories, and each with separate and incompatible sets of systems controlling production, warehousing, and distribution.

For example, Alcoa, the world's leading producer of aluminum and aluminum products with operations spanning 41 countries and 500 locations, had initially been organized around lines of business, each of which had its own set of information systems. Many of these systems were redundant and inefficient. Alcoa's costs for executing requisition-to-pay and financial processes were much higher and its cycle times were longer than those of other companies in its industry. (Cycle time refers to the total elapsed time from the beginning to the end of a process.) The company could not operate as a single worldwide entity.

In this situation, without integrated systems, your decision making would often be based on manual hard copy reports, often out of date, and it would be difficult to really understand what is happening in the business as whole. Sales personnel might not be able to tell at the time they place an order whether the ordered items are in inventory, and manufacturing could not easily use sales data to plan for new production. You now have a good idea of why firms need a special enterprise system to integrate information.

Chapter 2 introduced enterprise systems, also known as enterprise resource planning (ERP) systems, which are based on a suite of integrated software modules and a common central database. The database collects data from many different divisions and departments in a firm, and from a large number of key business processes in manufacturing and production, finance and accounting, sales and marketing, and human resources, making the data available for applications that support nearly all of an organization's internal business

Figure 8-1
How Enterprise Systems Work
Enterprise systems feature a set of integrated software modules and a central database that enables data to be shared by many different business processes and functional areas throughout the enterprise.

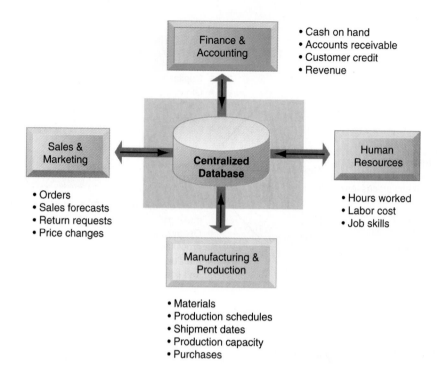

activities. When new information is entered by one process, the information is made immediately available to other business processes (see Figure 8-1).

If a sales representative places an order for tire rims, for example, the system verifies the customer's credit limit, schedules the shipment, identifies the best shipping route, and reserves the necessary items from inventory. If inventory stock were insufficient to fill the order, the system schedules the manufacture of more rims, ordering the needed materials and components from suppliers. Sales and production forecasts are immediately updated. General ledger and corporate cash levels are automatically updated with the revenue and cost information from the order. Users could tap into the system and find out where that particular order was at any minute. Management could obtain information at any point in time about how the business was operating. The system could also generate enterprise-wide data for management analyses of product cost and profitability.

ENTERPRISE SOFTWARE

Enterprise software is built around thousands of predefined business processes that reflect best practices. Table 8.1 describes some of the major business processes supported by enterprise software.

Companies implementing this software would have to first select the functions of the system they wished to use and then map their business processes to the predefined business processes in the software. (One of our Learning Tracks shows how SAP enterprise software handles the procurement process for a new piece of equipment.) To implement a new enterprise system, Tasty Baking Company identified its existing business processes and then translated them into the business processes built into the SAP ERP software it had selected. A firm would use configuration tables provided by the software to tailor a particular aspect of the system to the way it does business. For example, the firm could use these tables to select whether it wants to track revenue by product line, geographical unit, or distribution channel.

If the enterprise software does not support the way the organization does business, companies can rewrite some of the software to support the way their business processes work. However, enterprise software is unusually complex, and extensive customization may degrade system performance, compromising the information and process integration that are the main benefits of the system. If companies want to reap the maximum benefits from

TABLE 8.1

Business Processes Supported by Enterprise Systems

Financial and accounting processes, including general ledger, accounts payable, accounts receivable, fixed assets, cash management and forecasting, product-cost accounting, cost-center accounting, asset accounting, tax accounting, credit management, and financial reporting

Human resources processes, including personnel administration, time accounting, payroll, personnel planning and development, benefits accounting, applicant tracking, time management, compensation, workforce planning, performance management, and travel expense reporting

Manufacturing and production processes, including procurement, inventory management, purchasing, shipping, production planning, production scheduling, material requirements planning, quality control, distribution, transportation execution, and plant and equipment maintenance

Sales and marketing processes, including order processing, quotations, contracts, product configuration, pricing, billing, credit checking, incentive and commission management, and sales planning

enterprise software, they must change the way they work to conform to the business processes in the software. To ensure it obtained these benefits, Tasty Baking Company deliberately planned for customizing less than 5 percent of the system and made very few changes to the SAP software itself. It used as many tools and features that were already built into the SAP software as it could. SAP has more than 3,000 configuration tables for its enterprise software. Identifying the organization's business processes to be included in the system and then mapping them to the processes in the enterprise software is often a major effort.

Major enterprise software vendors include SAP, Oracle (with its acquisition of PeopleSoft), and Infor Global Solutions. There are versions of enterprise software packages designed for small businesses and versions obtained through software service providers over the Web. Although initially designed to automate the firm's internal "back-office" business processes, enterprise systems have become more externally oriented and capable of communicating with customers, suppliers, and other organizations.

BUSINESS VALUE OF ENTERPRISE SYSTEMS

Enterprise systems provide value both by increasing operational efficiency and by providing firmwide information to help managers make better decisions. Large companies with many operating units in different locations have used enterprise systems to enforce standard practices and data so that everyone does business the same way worldwide.

Coca-Cola, for instance, implemented a SAP enterprise system to standardize and coordinate important business processes in 200 countries. Lack of standard, company-wide business processes prevented the company from leveraging its worldwide buying power to obtain lower prices for raw materials and from reacting rapidly to market changes. Severstal, described in the chapter-opening case, implemented its enterprise system to standardize global business processes for similar reasons.

Enterprise systems help firms respond rapidly to customer requests for information or products. Because the system integrates order, manufacturing, and delivery data, manufacturing is better informed about producing only what customers have ordered, procuring exactly the right amount of components or raw materials to fill actual orders, staging production, and minimizing the time that components or finished products are in inventory.

After implementing enterprise software from Oracle, Alcoa eliminated many redundant processes and systems. The enterprise system helped Alcoa reduce requisition-to-pay cycle time (the total elapsed time from the time a purchase requisition is generated to the time the payment for the purchase is made) by verifying receipt of goods and automatically generating receipts for payment. Alcoa's accounts payable transaction processing dropped 89 percent. Alcoa was able to centralize financial and procurement activities, which helped the company reduce nearly 20 percent of its worldwide costs.

Enterprise systems provide valuable information for improving management decision making. Corporate headquarters has access to up-to-the-minute data on sales, inventory, and production, and uses this information to create more accurate sales and production forecasts. Enterprise software includes analytical tools for using data captured by the system to evaluate overall organizational performance. Enterprise system data have common standardized definitions and formats that are accepted by the entire organization. Performance figures mean the same thing across the company. Enterprise systems allow senior management to easily find out at any moment how a particular organizational unit is performing, determine which products are most or least profitable, and calculate costs for the company as a whole.

For example, Alcoa's enterprise system includes functionality for global human resources management that shows correlations between investment in employee training and quality, measures the company-wide costs of delivering services to employees, and measures the effectiveness of employee recruitment, compensation, and training.

8.2 Supply Chain Management Systems

If you manage a small firm that makes a few products or sells a few services, chances are you will have a small number of suppliers. You could coordinate your supplier orders and deliveries using a telephone and fax machine. But if you manage a firm that produces more complex products and services, then you will have hundreds of suppliers, and your suppliers will each have their own set of suppliers. Suddenly, you are in a situation where you will need to coordinate the activities of hundreds or even thousands of other firms in order to produce your products and services. Supply chain management systems, which we introduced in Chapter 2, are an answer to these problems of supply chain complexity and scale.

THE SUPPLY CHAIN

A firm's **supply chain** is a network of organizations and business processes for procuring raw materials, transforming these materials into intermediate and finished products, and distributing the finished products to customers. It links suppliers, manufacturing plants, distribution centers, retail outlets, and customers to supply goods and services from source through consumption. Materials, information, and payments flow through the supply chain in both directions.

Goods start out as raw materials and, as they move through the supply chain, are transformed into intermediate products (also referred to as components or parts), and finally, into finished products. The finished products are shipped to distribution centers and from there to retailers and customers. Returned items flow in the reverse direction from the buyer back to the seller.

Let's look at the supply chain for Nike sneakers as an example. Nike designs, markets, and sells sneakers, socks, athletic clothing, and accessories throughout the world. Its primary suppliers are contract manufacturers with factories in China, Thailand, Indonesia, Brazil, and other countries. These companies fashion Nike's finished products.

Nike's contract suppliers do not manufacture sneakers from scratch. They obtain components for the sneakers—the laces, eyelets, uppers, and soles—from other suppliers and then assemble them into finished sneakers. These suppliers in turn have their own suppliers. For example, the suppliers of soles have suppliers for synthetic rubber, suppliers for chemicals used to melt the rubber for molding, and suppliers for the molds into which to pour the rubber. Suppliers of laces have suppliers for their thread, for dyes, and for the plastic lace tips.

Figure 8-2 provides a simplified illustration of Nike's supply chain for sneakers; it shows the flow of information and materials among suppliers, Nike, Nike's distributors, retailers, and customers. Nike's contract manufacturers are its primary suppliers. The suppliers of soles, eyelets, uppers, and laces are the secondary (Tier 2) suppliers. Suppliers to these suppliers are the tertiary (Tier 3) suppliers.

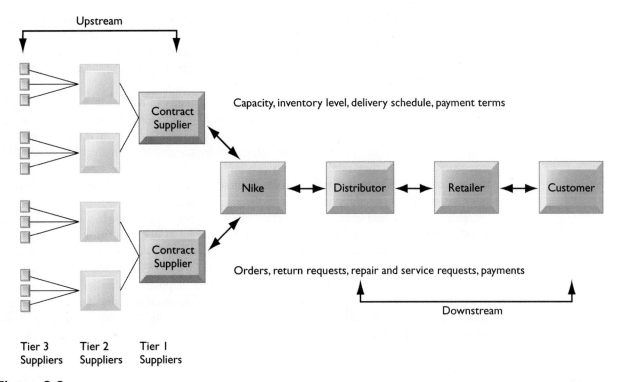

Figure 8-2
Nike's Supply Chain
This figure illustrates the major entities in Nike's supply chain and the flow of information upstream and downstream to coordinate the activities involved in buying, making, and moving a product. Shown here is a simplified supply chain, with the upstream portion focusing only on the suppliers for sneakers and sneaker soles.

The *upstream* portion of the supply chain includes the company's suppliers, the suppliers' suppliers, and the processes for managing relationships with them. The *downstream* portion consists of the organizations and processes for distributing and delivering products to the final customers. Companies doing manufacturing, such as Nike's contract suppliers of sneakers, also manage their own *internal supply chain* processes for transforming materials, components, and services furnished by their suppliers into finished products or intermediate products (components or parts) for their customers and for managing materials and inventory.

The supply chain illustrated in Figure 8-2 has been simplified. It only shows two contract manufacturers for sneakers and only the upstream supply chain for sneaker soles. Nike has hundreds of contract manufacturers turning out finished sneakers, socks, and athletic clothing, each with its own set of suppliers. The upstream portion of Nike's supply chain would actually comprise thousands of entities. Nike also has numerous distributors and many thousands of retail stores where its shoes are sold, so the downstream portion of its supply chain is also large and complex.

INFORMATION SYSTEMS AND SUPPLY CHAIN MANAGEMENT

Inefficiencies in the supply chain, such as parts shortages, underutilized plant capacity, excessive finished goods inventory, or high transportation costs, are caused by inaccurate or untimely information. For example, manufacturers may keep too many parts in inventory because they do not know exactly when they will receive their next shipments from their suppliers. Suppliers may order too few raw materials because they do not have precise information on demand. These supply chain inefficiencies waste as much as 25 percent of a company's operating costs.

If a manufacturer had perfect information about exactly how many units of product customers wanted, when they wanted them, and when they could be produced, it would be possible to implement a highly efficient **just-in-time strategy**. Components would arrive exactly at the moment they were needed and finished goods would be shipped as they left the assembly line.

In a supply chain, however, uncertainties arise because many events cannot be foreseen—uncertain product demand, late shipments from suppliers, defective parts or raw materials, or production process breakdowns. To satisfy customers, manufacturers often deal with such uncertainties and unforeseen events by keeping more material or products in inventory than what they think they may actually need. The *safety stock* acts as a buffer for the lack of flexibility in the supply chain. Although excess inventory is expensive, low fill rates are also costly because business may be lost from canceled orders.

One recurring problem in supply chain management is the **bullwhip effect**, in which information about the demand for a product gets distorted as it passes from one entity to the next across the supply chain. A slight rise in demand for an item might cause different members in the supply chain—distributors, manufacturers, suppliers, secondary suppliers (suppliers' suppliers), and tertiary suppliers (suppliers' suppliers' suppliers)—to stockpile inventory so each has enough "just in case." These changes ripple throughout the supply chain, magnifying what started out as a small change from planned orders, creating excess inventory, production, warehousing, and shipping costs (see Figure 8-3).

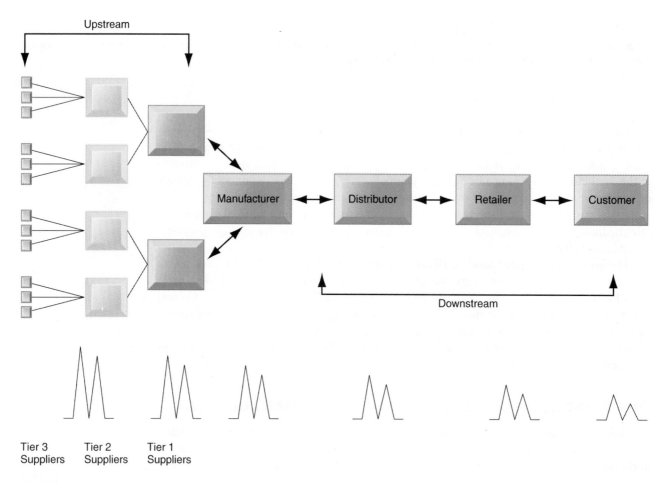

Figure 8-3
The Bullwhip Effect
Inaccurate information can cause minor fluctuations in demand for a product to be amplified as one moves further back in the supply chain. Minor fluctuations in retail sales for a product can create excess inventory for distributors, manufacturers, and suppliers.

For example, Procter & Gamble (P&G) found it had excessively high inventories of its Pampers disposable diapers at various points along its supply chain because of such distorted information. Although customer purchases in stores were fairly stable, orders from distributors would spike when P&G offered aggressive price promotions. Pampers and Pampers' components accumulated in warehouses along the supply chain to meet demand that did not actually exist. To eliminate this problem, P&G revised its marketing, sales, and supply chain processes and used more accurate demand forecasting.

The bullwhip is tamed by reducing uncertainties about demand and supply when all members of the supply chain have accurate and up-to-date information. If all supply chain members share dynamic information about inventory levels, schedules, forecasts, and shipments, they have more precise knowledge about how to adjust their sourcing, manufacturing, and distribution plans. Supply chain management systems provide the kind of information that helps members of the supply chain make better purchasing and scheduling decisions. Table 8.2 describes how firms benefit from these systems.

SUPPLY CHAIN MANAGEMENT SOFTWARE

Supply chain software is classified as either software to help businesses plan their supply chains (supply chain planning) or software to help them execute the supply chain steps (supply chain execution). **Supply chain planning systems** enable the firm to model its existing supply chain, generate demand forecasts for products, and develop optimal sourcing and manufacturing plans. Such systems help companies make better decisions such as determining how much of a specific product to manufacture in a given time period; establishing inventory levels for raw materials, intermediate products, and finished goods; determining where to store finished goods; and identifying the transportation mode to use for product delivery.

For example, if a large customer places a larger order than usual or changes that order on short notice, it can have a widespread impact throughout the supply chain. Additional raw materials or a different mix of raw materials may need to be ordered from suppliers. Manufacturing may have to change job scheduling. A transportation carrier may have to reschedule deliveries. Supply chain planning software makes the necessary adjustments to production and distribution plans. Information about changes is shared among the relevant supply chain members so that their work can be coordinated. One of the most important—and complex—supply chain planning functions is **demand planning**, which determines how much product a business needs to make to satisfy all of its customers' demands.

Whirlpool Corporation, which produces washing; machines, dryers, refrigerators, ovens, and other home appliances, uses supply chain planning systems to make sure what it produces matches customer demand. The company uses supply chain planning software

---

Information from supply chain management systems helps firms

Decide when and what to produce, store, and move

Rapidly communicate orders

Track the status of orders

Check inventory availability and monitor inventory levels

Reduce inventory, transportation, and warehousing costs

Track shipments

Plan production based on actual customer demand

Rapidly communicate changes in product design

TABLE 8.2

How Information Systems Facilitate Supply Chain Management

from i2 Technologies, that includes modules for Master Scheduling, Deployment Planning, and Inventory Planning. Whirlpool also installed i2's Web-based tool for Collaborative Planning, Forecasting, and Replenishment (CPFR) for sharing and combining its sales forecasts with those of its major sales partners. Improvements in supply chain planning combined with new state-of-the-art distribution centers helped Whirlpool increase availability of products in stock when customers needed them to 97 percent, while reducing the number of excess finished goods in inventory by 20 percent and forecasting errors by 50 percent (Barrett, 2009).

Supply chain execution systems manage the flow of products through distribution centers and warehouses to ensure that products are delivered to the right locations in the most efficient manner. They track the physical status of goods, the management of materials, warehouse and transportation operations, and financial information involving all parties. Haworth Incorporated's Warehouse Management System (WMS) is an example. Haworth is a world-leading manufacturer and designer of office furniture, with distribution centers in four different states. The WMS tracks and controls the flow of finished goods from Haworth's distribution centers to its customers. Acting on shipping plans for customer orders, the WMS directs the movement of goods based on immediate conditions for space, equipment, inventory, and personnel. Manugistics and i2 Technologies (both acquired by JDA Software) are major supply chain management software vendors, and enterprise software vendors SAP and Oracle PeopleSoft offer supply chain management modules.

The Interactive Session on Technology describes how supply chain management software improves operational performance and decision making at Procter & Gamble. This multinational giant manages global supply chains for more than 300 brands, each of which has many different configurations. Its supply chains are numerous and complex. P&G has many supply chain management applications. The one described here is for inventory optimization.

GLOBAL SUPPLY CHAINS AND THE INTERNET

Before the Internet, supply chain coordination was hampered by the difficulties of making information flow smoothly among disparate internal supply chain systems for purchasing, materials management, manufacturing, and distribution. It was also difficult to share information with external supply chain partners because the systems of suppliers, distributors, or logistics providers were based on incompatible technology platforms and standards. Enterprise systems supply some integration of internal supply chain processes but they are not designed to deal with external supply chain processes.

Some supply chain integration is supplied inexpensively using Internet technology. Firms use intranets to improve coordination among their internal supply chain processes, and they use extranets to coordinate supply chain processes shared with their business partners (see Figure 8-4).

Using intranets and extranets, all members of the supply chain are instantly able to communicate with each other, using up-to-date information to adjust purchasing, logistics, manufacturing, packaging, and schedules. A manager will use a Web interface to tap into suppliers' systems to determine whether inventory and production capabilities match demand for the firm's products. Business partners will use Web-based supply chain management tools to collaborate online on forecasts. Sales representatives will access suppliers' production schedules and logistics information to monitor customers' order status.

Global Supply Chain Issues

More and more companies are entering international markets, outsourcing manufacturing operations, and obtaining supplies from other countries as well as selling abroad. Their supply chains extend across multiple countries and regions. There are additional complexities and challenges to managing a global supply chain.

INTERACTIVE SESSION: TECHNOLOGY   Procter & Gamble Tries to Optimize Inventory

The shampoo and lipstick aisles at Target and Wal-Mart hardly seem like battlegrounds, but they are actually sites for an unending struggle among consumer products companies for retail shelf space. No company knows this better than Procter & Gamble (P&G), one of the world's largest consumer goods companies, with annual revenue surpassing $76 billion and 138,000 employees in 80 countries. The company sells more than 300 brands worldwide, including Cover Girl cosmetics, Olay skin care, Crest, Charmin, Tide, Pringles, and Pampers.

Demand variability for P&G's products from its Beauty division is very high. A popular eye shadow or lipstick color may quickly fall out of favor, while fashion trends call for new products continually to come on-stream. Major retail outlets such as Wal-Mart and Target compete by offering brand-name products at the lowest price possible.

In response to these pressures, P&G is constantly searching for ways to reduce supply chain costs and improve efficiency throughout its entire manufacturing and distribution network. It recently implemented a multi-echelon inventory optimization system to manage its supply chain more efficiently.

The supply chains of a company as large as P&G are extremely complicated, featuring thousands of suppliers, manufacturing facilities, and markets. Even the slightest of changes at any part of the supply chain has significant effects on all of the other participants. What's more, because P&G's supply chains are so extensive, the chance for any errors or inefficiencies to occur are greater than with smaller, more compact supply chains. Inventory optimization for a company as large as P&G is therefore critical to cutting costs and increasing revenues. P&G was already renowned for its supply chain management, successfully reducing its surplus inventory with sales and operations planning, better forecasting, just-in-time delivery strategies, and vendor-managed inventory activity. But multi-echelon inventory optimization has provided the company with a new means to achieve even higher levels of efficiency.

Multi-echelon networks are networks in which products are located in a variety of locations along their path to distribution, some of which are in different "echelons", or tiers, of the enterprise's distribution network. For example, large retailers' distribution networks often consist of a regional distribution center and a larger number of forward distribution centers. The presence of multiple echelons in a distribution network makes inventory management more difficult because each echelon is isolated from other echelons, so changes in inventory made by one echelon may have unpredictable consequences on the others.

Multi-echelon inventory optimization seeks to minimize the total inventory in all of the echelons of a company's supply chain. This is more complicated than traditional inventory optimization because of the additional lead times between each echelon, the bullwhip effect, and the need to synchronize orders and control costs between echelons. Companies with this level of complexity in their supply chains must replenish and divide their inventories at each distribution point along the supply chain, as opposed to just one distribution point or even just the inventory of the initial supplier. Each point in the supply chain is also unaware of the inventory levels of points beyond those that they have immediate contact with, which creates a lack of visibility up and down the supply chain.

The multi-echelon approach to inventory management consists of the following factors: multiple independent forecast updates in each echelon; accounting for all lead times and variations in lead times; management of the bullwhip effect; creation of visibility up and down the demand chain; synchronized order strategies; and appropriate modeling of the effects of different echelons' replenishment strategies on one another.

P&G prefers to develop its own analytical tools, but in this case turned to Optiant for its PowerChain Suite multi-echelon inventory optimization solution. Gillette, which P&G was preparing to acquire at the time, had already begun using Optiant software with strong results.

PowerChain Suite determines appropriate inventory configurations that can adapt smoothly to quickly changing demand. The solution uses mathematical models, based on award-winning research from MIT, which balance costs, resources, and customer service to arrive at these configurations. PowerChain tools pool inventory to minimize risk across products, components, and customers and also coordinate inventory policy across different items. (When inventory is available at the same time, this helps reduce early stock). PowerChain enables companies to design new supply chains and to model their end-to-end supply chain. They then can quickly evaluate the cost and performance of alternate supply chain structures and sourcing options to make better decisions. Optiant has provided supply chain management for other leading manufacturers such as Black & Decker, HP, IKEA, Imation, Intel, Kraft, Microsoft, and Sonoco.

P&G's beauty division served as the pilot project for the adoption of the Optiant software. Beauty is one of the company's largest, most complicated, and most profitable divisions. P&G believed that if multi-echelon inventory strategies could increase profitability at this division, it would work at any unit of the company.

The Optiant software first configured P&G's existing cosmetics supply chain, pulling in the previous 18 months of demand data and using the previous three months' demand variability. It then optimized the inventory strategy within that supply chain, aiming for target service levels above 99 percent. A third step identified alternate supply chain designs, and the final step created an optimal redesign of the supply network.

Results have been impressive. P&G's beauty division trimmed its total inventory by 3 to 7 percent and maintained service levels above 99 percent. In the first fiscal year after implementation of the new software, the division's earnings rose 13 percent and sales rose 7 percent. Inventory days on hand were down by eight days compared to the previous fiscal year. The results were so successful that P&G began rolling out multi-echelon inventory strategies across all of its various manufacturing branches.

Sources: "Optiant Adds New Inventory Optimization Capabilities and Centralized Administration Portal," *Supply& Demand Chain Executive*, February 27, 2009; John Kerr, "Procter & Gamble Takes Inventory Up a Notch," *Supply Chain Management Review*, February 13, 2008; Optiant, "Optiant Announces Multi-Echelon Inventory Optimization Enterprise Agreement with P&G," October 17, 2007; and www. optiant.com accessed July 17, 2009.

CASE STUDY QUESTIONS

1. Why are larger supply chains more difficult to manage? List several reasons.

2. Why is supply chain management so important at a company such as P&G?

3. How did inventory optimization impact operations and decision making at P&G?

4. Why wouldn't a small company derive much benefit from multi-echelon inventory optimization as a large company? Explain your answer.

MIS IN ACTION

1. Surf the Web for the ingredients of a Procter & Gamble product such as Crest toothpaste or Cover Girl lipstick or look for the list of ingredients on the packaging for these products in a retail store. Make a list of the ingredients for the product you selected.

2. Use the Web to find the major suppliers for each of these ingredients and their locations.

3. What did you learn from your investigation about P&G's supply chains for these products? What factors would determine price and availability of these products?

Figure 8-4
Intranets and Extranets for Supply Chain Management
Intranets integrate information from isolated business processes within the firm to help manage its internal supply chain. Access to these private intranets can also be extended to authorized suppliers, distributors, logistics services, and, sometimes, to retail customers to improve coordination of external supply chain processes.

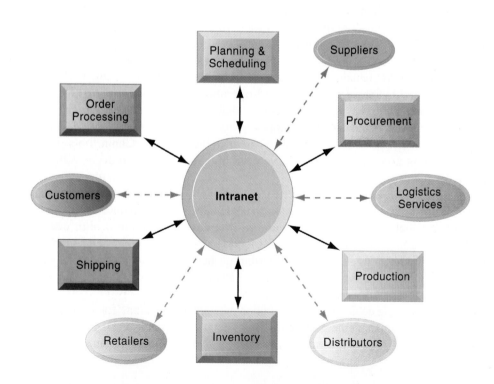

Global supply chains typically span greater geographic distances and time differences than domestic supply chains and have participants from a number of different countries. Although the purchase price of many goods might be lower abroad, there are often additional costs for transportation, inventory (the need for a larger buffer of safety stock), and local taxes or fees. Performance standards may vary from region to region or from nation to nation. Supply chain management may need to reflect foreign government regulations and cultural differences. All of these factors impact how a company takes orders, plans distribution, sizes warehousing, and manages inbound and outbound logistics throughout the global markets it services.

The Internet helps companies manage many aspects of their global supply chains, including sourcing, transportation, communications, and international finance. Today's apparel industry, for example, relies heavily on outsourcing to contract manufacturers in China and other low-wage countries. Apparel companies are starting to use the Web to manage their global supply chain and production issues.

For example, Koret of California, a subsidiary of apparel maker Kellwood Co., uses e-SPS Web-based software to gain end-to-end visibility into its entire global supply chain. E-SPS features Web-based software for sourcing, work-in-progress tracking, production routing, product development tracking, problem identification and collaboration, delivery-date projections, and production-related inquiries and reports.

As goods are being sourced, produced, and shipped, communication is required among retailers, manufacturers, contractors, agents, and logistics providers. Many, especially smaller companies, still share product information over the phone, via e-mail, or through faxes. These methods slow down the supply chain and also increase errors and uncertainty. With e-SPS, all supply chain members communicate through a Web-based system. If one of Koret's vendors makes a change in the status of a product, everyone in the supply chain sees the change.

In addition to contract manufacturing, globalization has encouraged outsourcing warehouse management, transportation management, and related operations to third-party logistics providers, such as UPS Supply Chain Solutions and Schneider Logistics Services. These logistics services offer Web-based software to give their customers a better view of their global supply chains. Customers are able to check a secure Web site to monitor inventory and shipments, helping them run their global supply chains more efficiently.

Demand-Driven Supply Chains: From Push to Pull Manufacturing and Efficient Customer Response

In addition to reducing costs, supply chain management systems facilitate efficient customer response, enabling the workings of the business to be driven more by customer demand. (We introduced efficient customer response systems in Chapter 3.)

Earlier supply chain management systems were driven by a push-based model (also known as build-to-stock). In a **push-based model**, production master schedules are based on forecasts or best guesses of demand for products, and products are "pushed" to customers. With new flows of information made possible by Web-based tools, supply chain management more easily follows a **pull-based model**. In a pull-based model, also known as a demand-driven model or build-to-order, actual customer orders or purchases trigger events in the supply chain. Transactions to produce and deliver only what customers have ordered move up the supply chain from retailers to distributors to manufacturers and eventually to suppliers. Only products to fulfill these orders move back down the supply chain to the retailer. Manufacturers use only actual order demand information to drive their production schedules and the procurement of components or raw materials, as illustrated in Figure 8-5. Wal-Mart's continuous replenishment system and Dell Computer's assemble-to-order system, both described in Chapter 3, are examples of the pull-based model.

The Internet and Internet technology make it possible to move from sequential supply chains, where information and materials flow sequentially from company to company, to concurrent supply chains, where information flows in many directions simultaneously among members of a supply chain network. Members of the network immediately adjust to

Figure 8-5
Push- Versus Pull-Based Supply Chain Models
The difference between push- and pull-based models is summarized by the slogan "Make what we sell, not sell what we make."

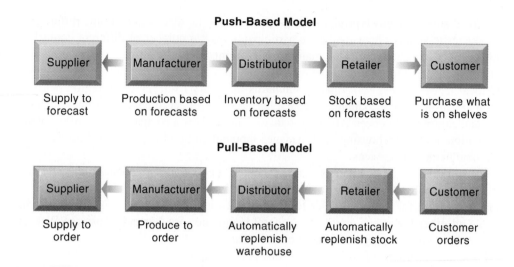

changes in schedules or orders. Ultimately, the Internet could create a "digital logistics nervous system" throughout the supply chain (see Figure 8-6).

BUSINESS VALUE OF SUPPLY CHAIN MANAGEMENT SYSTEMS

You have just read how supply chain management systems enable firms to streamline both their internal and external supply chain processes and provide management with more accurate information about what to produce, store, and move. By implementing a networked and integrated supply chain management system, companies match supply to demand, reduce inventory levels, improve delivery service, speed product time to market, and use assets more effectively.

Total supply chain costs represent the majority of operating expenses for many businesses and in some industries approach 75 percent of the total operating budget. Reducing supply chain costs has a major impact on firm profitability.

In addition to reducing costs, supply chain management systems help increase sales. If a product is not available when a customer wants it, customers often try to purchase it from

Figure 8-6
The Future Internet-Driven Supply Chain
The future Internet-driven supply chain operates like a digital logistics nervous system. It provides multidirectional communication among firms, networks of firms, and e-marketplaces so that entire networks of supply chain partners can immediately adjust inventories, orders, and capacities.

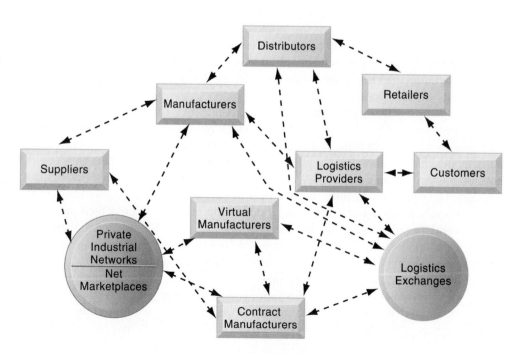

someone else. More precise control of the supply chain enhances the firm's ability to have the right product available for customer purchases at the right time.

8.3 Customer Relationship Management Systems

You've all heard phrases such as "the customer is always right" or "the customer comes first." Today these words ring more true than ever. Because competitive advantage based on an innovative new product or service is often very short lived, companies are realizing that their only enduring competitive strength may be their relationships with their customers. Some say that the basis of competition has switched from who sells the most products and services to who "owns" the customer, and that customer relationships represent a firm's most valuable asset.

WHAT IS CUSTOMER RELATIONSHIP MANAGEMENT?

What kinds of information would you need to build and nurture strong, long-lasting relationships with customers? You'd want to know exactly who your customers are, how to contact them, whether they are costly to service and sell to, what kinds of products and services they are interested in, and how much money they spend on your company. If you could, you'd want to make sure you knew each of your customers well, as if you were running a small-town store. And you'd want to make your good customers feel special.

In a small business operating in a neighborhood, it is possible for business owners and managers to really know their customers on a personal, face-to-face basis. But in a large business operating on a metropolitan, regional, national, or even global basis, it is impossible to "know your customer" in this intimate way. In these kinds of businesses there are too many customers and too many different ways that customers interact with the firm (over the Web, the phone, fax, and face-to-face). It becomes especially difficult to integrate information from all theses sources and to deal with the large numbers of customers.

A large business's processes for sales, service, and marketing tend to be highly compartmentalized, and these departments do not share much essential customer information. Some information on a specific customer might be stored and organized in terms of that person's account with the company. Other pieces of information about the same customer might be organized by products that were purchased. There is no way to consolidate all of this information to provide a unified view of a customer across the company.

This is where customer relationship management systems help. Customer relationship management (CRM) systems, which we introduced in Chapter 2, capture and integrate customer data from all over the organization, consolidate the data, analyze the data, and then distribute the results to various systems and customer touch points across the enterprise. A **touch point** (also known as a contact point) is a method of interaction with the customer, such as telephone, e-mail, customer service desk, conventional mail, Web site, wireless device, or retail store.

Well-designed CRM systems provide a single enterprise view of customers that is useful for improving both sales and customer service. Such systems likewise provide customers with a single view of the company regardless of what touch point the customer uses (see Figure 8-7).

Good CRM systems provide data and analytical tools for answering questions such as these: "What is the value of a particular customer to the firm over his or her lifetime?" "Who are our most loyal customers?" (It can cost six times more to sell to a new customer than to an existing customer.) "Who are our most profitable customers?" and "What do these profitable customers want to buy?" Firms use the answers to these questions to acquire new customers, provide better service and support to existing customers, customize their offerings more precisely to customer preferences, and provide ongoing value to retain profitable customers.

Figure 8-7
Customer
Relationship
Management (CRM)
CRM systems examine
customers from a
multifaceted perspective.
These systems use a set
of integrated applications
to address all aspects of
the customer relation-
ship, including customer
service, sales, and
marketing.

CRM SOFTWARE

Commercial CRM software packages range from niche tools that perform limited functions, such as personalizing Web sites for specific customers, to large-scale enterprise applications that capture myriad interactions with customers, analyze them with sophisticated reporting tools, and link to other major enterprise applications, such as supply chain management and enterprise systems. The more comprehensive CRM packages contain modules for **partner relationship management (PRM)** and **employee relationship management (ERM)**.

PRM uses many of the same data, tools, and systems as customer relationship management to enhance collaboration between a company and its selling partners. If a company does not sell directly to customers but rather works through distributors or retailers, PRM helps these channels sell to customers directly. It provides a company and its selling partners with the ability to trade information and distribute leads and data about customers, integrating lead generation, pricing, promotions, order configurations, and availability. It also provides a firm with tools to assess its partners' performances so it can make sure its best partners receive the support they need to close more business.

ERM software deals with employee issues that are closely related to CRM, such as setting objectives, employee performance management, performance-based compensation, and employee training. Major CRM application software vendors include Oracle-owned Siebel and PeopleSoft CRM, SAP, Salesforce.com, and Microsoft Dynamics CRM.

Customer relationship management systems typically provide software and online tools for sales, customer service, and marketing. We briefly describe some of these capabilities.

Sales Force Automation (SFA)

Sales force automation modules in CRM systems help sales staff increase their productivity by focusing sales efforts on the most profitable customers, those who are good candidates for sales and services. CRM systems provide sales prospect and contact information, product information, product configuration capabilities, and sales quote generation capabilities. Such software can assemble information about a particular customer's past purchases to help the salesperson make personalized recommendations. CRM software enables sales, marketing, and delivery departments to easily share customer and prospect information. It increases each salesperson's efficiency in reducing the cost per sale as well as the cost of acquiring new customers and retaining old ones. CRM software also has capabilities for sales forecasting, territory management, and team selling.

Customer Service

Customer service modules in CRM systems provide information and tools to increase the efficiency of call centers, help desks, and customer support staff. They have capabilities for assigning and managing customer service requests.

One such capability is an appointment or advice telephone line: When a customer calls a standard phone number, the system routes the call to the correct service person, who inputs information about that customer into the system only once. Once the customer's data are in the system, any service representative can handle the customer relationship. Improved access to consistent and accurate customer information help call centers handle more calls per day and decrease the duration of each call. Thus, call centers and customer service groups achieve greater productivity, reduced transaction time, and higher quality of service at lower cost. The customer is happier because he or she spends less time on the phone restating his or her problem to customer service representatives.

The Interactive Session on Organizations describes another CRM capability for improving customer service and operational efficiency. Implementation of Enkata software helped JP Morgan Chase increase its rate of first-call resolution, which takes place when a call center agent is able resolve a customer service issue during the first call.

CRM systems may also include Web-based self-service capabilities: The company Web site can be set up to provide inquiring customers' personalized support information as well as the option to contact customer service staff by phone for additional assistance.

Marketing

CRM systems support direct-marketing campaigns by providing capabilities for capturing prospect and customer data, for providing product and service information, for qualifying leads for targeted marketing, and for scheduling and tracking direct-marketing mailings or e-mail (see Figure 8-8). Marketing modules also include tools for analyzing marketing and customer data, identifying profitable and unprofitable customers, designing products and services to satisfy specific customer needs and interests, and identifying opportunities for cross-selling.

Cross-selling is the marketing of complementary products to customers. (For example, in financial services, a customer with a checking account might be sold a money market account or a home improvement loan.) CRM tools also help firms manage and execute marketing campaigns at all stages, from planning to determining the rate of success for each campaign.

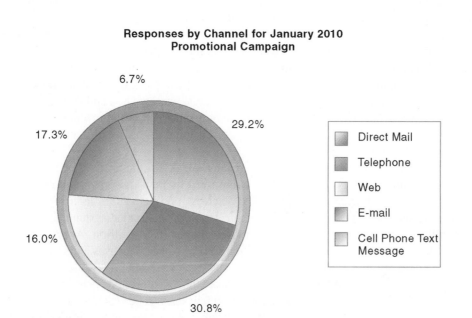

Responses by Channel for January 2010 Promotional Campaign

6.7%
29.2%
17.3%
16.0%
30.8%

- Direct Mail
- Telephone
- Web
- E-mail
- Cell Phone Text Message

Figure 8-8
How CRM Systems Support Marketing
Customer relationship management software provides a single point for users to manage and evaluate marketing campaigns across multiple channels, including e-mail, direct mail, telephone, the Web, and wireless messages.

If you have a credit card, there's a good chance that it is from Chase. Chase Card Services is the division of JP Morgan Chase that specializes in credit cards, offering an array of credit card products such as the Chase Rewards Platinum Visa card. As one of the largest credit card issuers in the United States, the company fields a correspondingly large amount of calls from people seeking customer service for their credit card accounts. Each of Chase's 6,000 call center agents worldwide at the company's 11 call centers fields field up to 120 calls per day. The company handles slightly less than 200 million calls each year from a customer base of 100 million.

Even a small reduction of 1 percent to the amount of calls received results in savings of millions of dollars and improved customer service for Chase. Achieving such a reduction is easier said than done, however. In 2006, Chase Card Services attempted to accomplish this by improving first-call resolution. First-call resolution is when a call center agent is able to resolve a customer's issues during the initial call to customer service without requiring additional calls.

The problem was that the company's record keeping did not give an accurate account of current rates of first-call resolution. Chase had previously tried tracking first-call resolution rates by having agents log the content and results of each call they received. But this task was time-consuming and was not standardized, since agents tended to record results subjectively and not in a uniform way. Company policies for some customer requests were also far from ideal for increasing first-call resolution. For example, agents were only able to process balance transfers for customers calling from their homes, and the fee structure underwent multiple changes over a short span, prompting repeat calls.

To improve call center efficiency, Chase contracted with Enkata Technologies to implement a performance and talent management system.

The system monitors and tags each call with the topic and length of the call as well as the length of time the agent that handled the call has been working. It doesn't require agents to perform any action to acquire this information; it tracks calls automatically by keeping track of the keyboard strokes of each agent.

As soon as an agent clicks on the feature of the account that the customer is calling about, the Enkata system automatically identifies the reason for the call. Proprietary algorithms match the reason and caller identification to the amount of time predetermined for each type of call.

The system then monitors discrepancies in call time, depending on the reason for the call. For example, a call from a customer requiring card activation should be a quick call, so the system will pinpoint card activation calls that take longer than normal, or fee dispute calls that are shorter than normal. But sometimes customers have multiple reasons for calling, which would have been very difficult to track prior to the implementation of Enkata's system. Now Enkata separates each individual reason for calling and organizes them into a sequence, so that a call with multiple issues to resolve is analyzed using the appropriate time frame.

By separating and organizing reasons for calling into distinct categories, Chase is able to determine criteria for declaring particular calls "resolved."

For example, a card activation call will be considered resolved after only a few days without a follow-up call, but a disputed fee call won't be considered resolved until the customer received another statement without any complaints. This method gives Chase much more accurate data on first-call resolution, a feat which is regarded as very difficult and impressive in the industry.

Enkata compiles this data and distributes it to Chase Card Services in the form of weekly reports on call type and length, call handling times, repeat call rates, and other performance measures that allow both agents and supervisors to monitor their performance. The system also connects reports with call recordings to assist managers in coaching and evaluating their agents. When the system was still being implemented, Enkata used historical call data gathered prior to the implementation to create initial reports. Chase Card Services executives considered this initial upload of data to be the most time- consuming part of the implementation. Once the implementation was complete, the company hoped that improvements in the interpretation and management of this information would lead to improvements in agent performance, customer satisfaction, and customer retention.

The results speak for themselves. Chase Card Services improved its first-call resolution rate to 91 percent, an increase of 3 percent, in its first year after the implementation of the Enkata system. That represented a total savings of $8 million. Approximately $2.5 million of that total savings was a direct result of the average call time decreasing by two seconds.

The company hopes to reach its goal of 95 percent within the next few years. A perfect rate of 100 percent first-call resolution is not feasible because some addi-

tional calls after the first are acceptable under certain circumstances, such as a customer remembering a charge that he or she had initially disputed.

Within three months time, 30 percent of agents that had scored below the acceptable rate for first-call resolution improved to an acceptable rate. And although the number of active customer accounts grew by 5.2 percent in the six months after implementation of the system, call volume decreased 8.3 percent over that same span.

Encouraged by these successes, Chase Card Services is now looking to expand the capabilities of the system to classify calls into even more categories, and to link their collected data to marketing programs to foster cross-selling and upselling.

Sources: Marshall Lager, "Credit Where Due," *Customer Relationship Management*, April 2008; and Michele Heller, "How Chase Got Control of Call-Center Expenses," *American Banker*, February 26, 2008.

CASE STUDY QUESTIONS

1. What functions of customer relationship management systems are illustrated in this case?

2. Why is the call center so important for Chase Card Services? How could Chase's call centers help it improve relationships with customers?

3. Describe the problem at Chase call centers. What management, organization, or technology factors contributed to the problem?

4. How did using Enkata improve operational performance and decision making? Give examples.

5. What management, organization, or technology factors would have to be considered in implementing the Enkata solution?

MIS IN ACTION

Visit the Enkata Web site and explore the features of its products, then answer the following questions:

1. How could Enkata's system be used for analyzing customer service at another type of business (such as a cell phone provider or clothing retailer with catalog and Web ordering, for example)?

2. What kinds of questions might customers call in to ask? What kinds of problems might call center agents encounter in answering these questions? How could Enkata software help?

Figure 8-9 illustrates the most important capabilities for sales, service, and marketing processes that would be found in major CRM software products. Like enterprise software, this software is business-process driven, incorporating hundreds of business processes thought to represent best practices in each of these areas. To achieve maximum benefit, companies need to revise and model their business processes to conform to the best-practice business processes in the CRM software.

Figure 8-10 illustrates how a best practice for increasing customer loyalty through customer service might be modeled by CRM software. Directly servicing customers provides firms with opportunities to increase customer retention by singling out profitable long-term customers for preferential treatment. CRM software can assign each customer a score based on that person's value and loyalty to the company and provide that information to help call centers route each customer's service request to agents who can best handle that customer's needs. The system would automatically provide the service agent with a detailed profile of that customer that included his or her score for value and loyalty. The service agent would use this information to present special offers or additional service to the customer to encourage the customer to keep transacting business with the company. You will find more information on other best-practice business processes in CRM systems in our Learning Tracks.

Figure 8-9
CRM Software
Capabilities
The major CRM software products support business processes in sales, service, and marketing, integrating customer information from many different sources. Included are support for both the operational and analytical aspects of CRM.

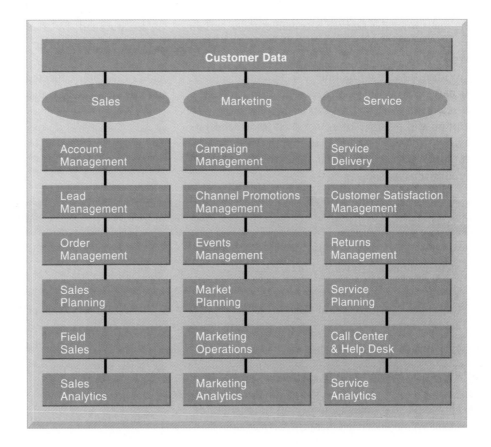

Figure 8-10
Customer Loyalty Management Process Map
This process map shows how a best practice for promoting customer loyalty through customer service would be modeled by customer relationship management software. The CRM software helps firms identify high-value customers for preferential treatment.

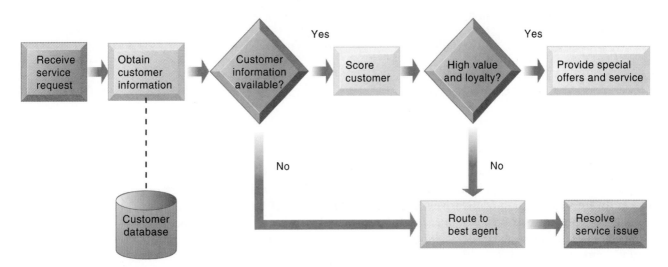

OPERATIONAL AND ANALYTICAL CRM

All of the applications we have just described support either the operational or analytical aspects of customer relationship management. **Operational CRM** includes customer-facing applications, such as tools for sales force automation, call center and customer service

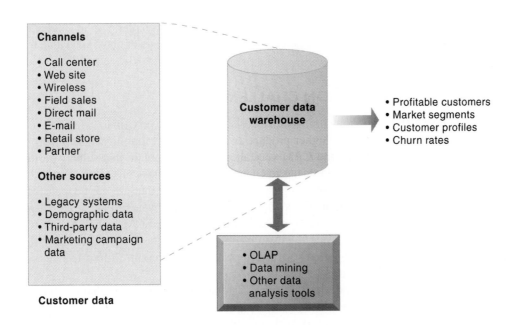

**Figure 8-11
Analytical CRM Data
Warehouse**
*Analytical CRM uses a
customer data ware-
house and tools to
analyze customer data
collected from the firm's
customer touch points
and from other sources.*

support, and marketing automation. **Analytical CRM** includes applications that analyze customer data generated by operational CRM applications to provide information for improving business performance.

Analytical CRM applications are based on data warehouses that consolidate the data from operational CRM systems and customer touch points for use with online analytical processing (OLAP), data mining, and other data analysis techniques (see Chapter 5). Customer data collected by the organization might be combined with data from other sources, such as customer lists for direct-marketing campaigns purchased from other companies or demographic data. Such data are analyzed to identify buying patterns, to segments for targeted marketing, and to pinpoint profitable and unprofitable customers (see Figure 8-11).

Another important output of analytical CRM is the customer's lifetime value to the firm. **Customer lifetime value (CLTV)** is based on the relationship between the revenue produced by a specific customer, the expenses incurred in acquiring and servicing that customer, and the expected life of the relationship between the customer and the company.

BUSINESS VALUE OF CUSTOMER RELATIONSHIP MANAGEMENT SYSTEMS

Companies with effective customer relationship management systems realize many benefits, including increased customer satisfaction, reduced direct-marketing costs, more effective marketing, and lower costs for customer acquisition and retention. Information from CRM systems increases sales revenue by identifying the most profitable customers and segments for focused marketing and cross-selling.

Customer churn is reduced as sales, service, and marketing better respond to customer needs. The **churn rate** measures the number of customers who stop using or purchasing products or services from a company. It is an important indicator of the growth or decline of a firm's customer base.

8.4 Enterprise Applications: New Opportunities and Challenges

Many firms have implemented enterprise systems and systems for supply chain management and customer relationship because they are such powerful instruments for achieving operational excellence and enhancing decision making. But precisely because they are so powerful in changing the way the organization works, they are challenging to implement. Let's briefly examine some of these challenges, as well as new ways of obtaining value from these systems.

ENTERPRISE APPLICATION CHALLENGES

Promises of dramatic reductions in inventory costs, order-to-delivery time, as well as more efficient customer response and higher product and customer profitability make enterprise systems and systems for SCM and CRM very alluring. But to obtain this value, you must clearly understand how your business has to change to use these systems effectively.

Enterprise applications involve complex pieces of software that are very expensive to purchase and implement. It might take a large company several years to complete a large-scale implementation of an enterprise system or a system for SCM or CRM. The total implementation cost of a large system, including software, database tools, consulting fees, personnel costs, training, and perhaps hardware costs, might amount to four to five times the initial purchase price for the software.

Enterprise applications require not only deep-seated technological changes but also fundamental changes in the way the business operates. Companies must make sweeping changes to their business processes to work with the software. Employees must accept new job functions and responsibilities. They must learn how to perform a new set of work activities and understand how the information they enter into the system can affect other parts of the company. This requires new organizational learning.

Supply chain management systems require multiple organizations to share information and business processes. Each participant in the system may have to change some of its processes and the way it uses information to create a system that best serves the supply chain as a whole.

Some firms experienced enormous operating problems and losses when they first implemented enterprise applications because they did not understand how much organizational change was required.

- Kmart had trouble getting products to store shelves when it implemented supply chain management software from i2 Technologies in July 2000. The i2 software did not work well with Kmart's promotion-driven business model, which creates sharp spikes and drops in demand for products, and it was not designed to handle the massive number of products stocked in Kmart stores.
- A mistake-laden Oracle implementation rolled out in October 2005 caused Overstock.com's order tracking system to go down for a full week and contributed to a third-quarter loss of $14.5 million. Overstock.com had tried to replace a homegrown system with an Oracle enterprise system. A rush to implement caused early design problems. The new system recorded customer refunds transaction-by-transaction rather than in batches (as did the old homegrown system). Overstock's ERP development team did not synchronize this change properly with the company's accounts receivable system, so that the accounts receivable balance did not accurately reflect all of these refunds. In October 2008, Overstock had to re-state more than 5 years of earnings, with a revenue reduction of $12.9 million and increased losses of $10.3 million.

Enterprise applications also introduce "switching costs." Once you adopt an enterprise application from a single vendor, such as SAP, Oracle, or others, it is very costly to switch vendors, and your firm becomes dependent on the vendor to upgrade its product and maintain your installation.

Enterprise applications are based on organization-wide definitions of data. You'll need to understand exactly how your business uses its data and how the data would be organized in a customer relationship management, supply chain management, or enterprise system. CRM systems typically require some data cleansing work.

In a nutshell, it takes a lot of work to get enterprise applications to work properly. Everyone in the organization must be involved. For the most part, companies that have successfully implemented CRM, SCM, and enterprise systems, the results have justified the effort.

NEXT-GENERATION ENTERPRISE APPLICATIONS

Today, enterprise application vendors are delivering more value by becoming more flexible, Web-enabled, and capable of integration with other systems. Stand-alone enterprise systems, customer relationship systems, and supply chain management systems are becoming a thing of the past.

The major enterprise software vendors have created what they call *enterprise solutions*, *enterprise suites*, or *e-business suites* to make their customer relationship management, supply chain management, and enterprise systems work closely with each other, and link to systems of customers and suppliers. SAP Business Suite, Oracle e-Business Suite, and Microsoft's Dynamics suite (aimed at mid-sized companies) are examples, and they now utilize Web services and service-oriented architecture (SOA, see Chapter 4).

SAP's next-generation enterprise applications are based on its enterprise service-oriented architecture. It incorporates SOA standards and uses its NetWeaver tool as an integration platform linking SAP's own applications and also Web services developed by independent software vendors. The goal is to make enterprise applications easier to implement and manage.

For example, the current version of SAP enterprise software combines key applications in finance, logistics and procurement, and human resources administration into a core ERP component. Businesses then extend these applications by linking to function-specific Web services such as employee recruiting or collections management provided by SAP and other vendors. SAP provides over 500 Web services through its Web site.

Oracle also has included SOA and business process management capabilities into its Fusion middleware products. Businesses can use Oracle tools to customize Oracle's applications without breaking the entire application.

Next-generation enterprise applications also include open source and on-demand solutions. Compared to commercial enterprise application software, open source products such as Compiere, Open for Business (OFBiz), and Openbravo are not as mature, nor do they include as much support. However, companies such as small manufacturers are choosing this option because there are no software licensing fees. (Support and customization for open source products cost extra.)

The most explosive growth in software as a service (SaaS) offerings has been for customer relationship management. Salesforce.com has been the leader in hosted CRM solutions, but Oracle and SAP have also developed SaaS capabilities. SaaS versions of enterprise systems are available from smaller vendors such as NetSuite and Plex Online.

SAP now offers an on-demand enterprise software solution called Business ByDesign for small and medium businesses in select countries. For large businesses, SAP's on-site software is the only version available. However, SAP is hosting function-specific applications (such as e-sourcing and expense management) available by subscription that integrate with customers' on-site SAP Business Suite systems. The major enterprise application vendors also offer portions of their products that work on mobile handhelds. You can find out more about this topic in our Learning Track on Wireless Applications for Customer Relationship Management, Supply Chain Management, and Healthcare.

Salesforce.com and Oracle now include some Web 2.0 capabilities that enable organizations to identify new ideas more rapidly, improve team productivity, and deepen interactions with customers. For example, Salesforce Ideas allows employees, customers, and business partners to suggest and then vote on new ideas. Dell Computer deployed this technology as Dell IdeaStorm (dellideastorm.com) to enable customers to suggest and vote on new concepts and feature changes in Dell products. Ideas contributed on the service encouraged Dell to add higher-resolution screens to the Dell 1530 laptop (Greenfield, 2008).

Service Platforms

Another way of extending enterprise applications is to use them to create service platforms for new or improved business processes that integrate information from multiple functional areas. These enterprise-wide service platforms provide a greater degree of cross-functional integration than traditional enterprise applications. A **service platform** integrates multiple applications from multiple business functions, business units, or business partners to deliver a seamless experience for the customer, employee, manager, or business partner.

For instance, the order-to-cash process involves receiving an order and seeing it all the way through obtaining payment for the order. This process begins with lead generation, marketing campaigns, and order entry, which are typically supported by CRM systems. Once the order is received, manufacturing is scheduled and parts availability is verified—processes that are usually supported by enterprise software. The order is then handled by processes for distribution planning, warehousing, order fulfillment, and shipping, which are usually supported by supply chain management systems. Finally, the order is billed to the customer, which is handled by either enterprise financial applications or accounts receivable. If the purchase at some point required customer service, customer relationship management systems would again be invoked.

A service such as order-to-cash requires data from enterprise applications and financial systems to be further integrated into an enterprise-wide composite process. To accomplish this, firms need software tools that use existing applications as building blocks for new cross-enterprise processes (see Figure 8-12). Enterprise application vendors provide middleware and tools that use XML and Web services for integrating enterprise applications with older legacy applications and systems from other vendors.

Increasingly, these new services are delivered through portals. Portal software integrates information from enterprise applications and disparate in-house legacy systems, presenting it to users through a Web interface so that the information appears to be coming from a single source. For example, Valero Energy, North America's largest refiner, used SAP NetWeaver Portal to create a service for wholesale clients to view their account information all at once. SAP NetWeaver Portal provides an interface to clients' invoice, price, electronic funds, and credit card transaction data stored in SAP's customer relationship management system data warehouse as well as in non-SAP systems.

Figure 8-12
Order-to-Cash Service
Order-to-cash is a composite process that integrates data from individual enterprise systems and legacy financial applications. The process must be modeled and translated into a software system using application integration tools.

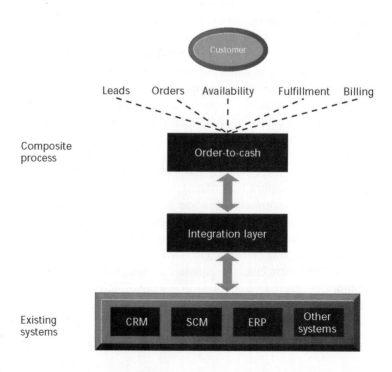

8.5 Hands-On MIS Projects

The projects in this section give you hands-on experience analyzing business process integration, suggesting supply chain management and customer relationship management applications, using database software to manage customer service requests, and evaluating supply chain management business services.

MANAGEMENT DECISION PROBLEMS

1. Toronto-based Mercedes-Benz Canada, with a network of 55 dealers, did not know enough about its customers. Dealers provided customer data to the company on an ad hoc basis. Mercedes did not force dealers to report this information, and its process for tracking dealers that failed to report was cumbersome. There was no real incentive for dealers to share information with the company. How could customer relationship management (CRM) and partner relationship management (PRM) systems help solve this problem?

2. Office Depot sells a wide range of office products and services in the United States and internationally, including general office supplies, computer supplies, business machines (and related supplies), and office furniture. The company tries to offer a wider range of office supplies at lower cost than other retailers by using just-in-time replenishment and tight inventory control systems. It uses information from a demand forecasting system and point-of-sale data to replenish its inventory in its 1,600 retail stores. Explain how these systems help Office Depot minimize costs and any other benefits they provide. Identify and describe other supply chain management applications that would be especially helpful to Office Depot.

IMPROVING DECISION MAKING: USING DATABASE SOFTWARE TO MANAGE CUSTOMER SERVICE REQUESTS

Software skills: Database design; querying and reporting
Business skills: Customer service analysis

In this exercise, you'll use database software to develop an application that tracks customer service requests and analyzes customer data to identify customers meriting priority treatment.

Prime Service is a large service company that provides maintenance and repair services for close to 1,200 commercial businesses in New York, New Jersey, and Connecticut. Its customers include businesses of all sizes. Customers with service needs call into its customer service department with requests for repairing heating ducts, broken windows, leaky roofs, broken water pipes, and other problems. The company assigns each request a number and writes down the service request number, identification number of the customer account, the date of the request, the type of equipment requiring repair, and a brief description of the problem. The service requests are handled on a first-come-first-served basis. After the service work has been completed, Prime calculates the cost of the work, enters the price on the service request form, and bills the client.

Management is not happy with this arrangement because the most important and profitable clients—those with accounts of more than $70,000—are treated no differently from its clients with small accounts. It would like to find a way to provide its best customers with better service. Management would also like to know which types of service problems occur the most frequently so that it can make sure it has adequate resources to address them.

Prime Service has a small database with client account information, which can be found in MyMISLab. A sample is shown on the next page, but the Web site may have a more recent version of this database for this exercise. The database table includes fields for the account ID, company (account) name, street address, city, state, zip code, account size (in dollars), contact last name, contact first name, and contact telephone number. The contact is the name

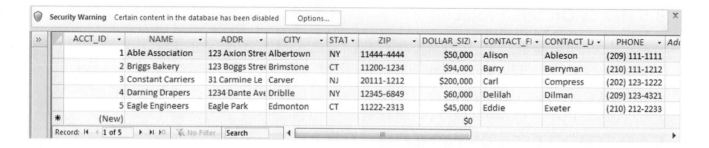

of the person in each company who is responsible for contacting Prime about maintenance and repair work. Use your database software to design a solution that would enable Prime's customer service representatives to identify the most important customers so that they could receive priority service. Your solution will require more than one table. Populate your database with at least 15 service requests. Create several reports that would be of interest to management, such as a list of the highest- and lowest-priority accounts or a report showing the most frequently occurring service problems. Create a report showing customer service representatives which service calls they should respond to first on a specific date.

ACHIEVING OPERATIONAL EXCELLENCE: EVALUATING SUPPLY CHAIN MANAGEMENT SERVICES

Software skills: Web browser and presentation software
Business skills: Evaluating supply chain management services

Trucking companies no longer merely carry goods from one place to another. Some also provide supply chain management services to their customers and help them manage their information. In this project, you'll use the Web to research and evaluate two of these business services.

Investigate the Web sites of two companies, UPS Logistics and Schneider Logistics, to see how these companies' services can be used for supply chain management. Then respond to the following questions:

- What supply chain processes can each of these companies support for their clients?
- How can customers use the Web sites of each company to help them with supply chain management?
- Compare the supply chain management services provided by these companies. Which company would you select to help your firm manage its supply chain? Why?

LEARNING TRACKS

The following Learning Tracks provide content relevant to topics covered in this chapter:

1. SAP Business Process Map

2. Business Processes in Supply Chain Management and Supply Chain Metrics

3. Best-Practice Business Processes in CRM Software

4 Wireless Applications for Customer Relationship Mangement, Supply Chain Management, and Healthcare

Review Summary

1 **How do enterprise systems help businesses achieve operational excellence?** Enterprise software is based on a suite of integrated software modules and a common central database. The database collects data from and feeds the data into numerous applications that can support nearly all of an organization's internal business activities. When new information is entered by one process, the information is made available immediately to other business processes.

Enterprise systems support organizational centralization by enforcing uniform data standards and business processes throughout the company and a single unified technology platform. The firmwide data generated by enterprise systems helps managers evaluate organizational performance.

2 **How do supply chain management systems coordinate planning, production, and logistics with suppliers?** Supply chain management systems automate the flow of information among members of the supply chain so they can use it to make better decisions about when and how much to purchase, produce, or ship. More accurate information from supply chain management systems reduces uncertainty and the impact of the bullwhip effect.

Supply chain management software includes software for supply chain planning and for supply chain execution. Internet technology facilitates the management of global supply chains by providing the connectivity for organizations in different countries to share supply chain information. Improved communication among supply chain members also facilitates efficient customer response and movement toward a demand-driven model.

3 **How do customer relationship management systems help firms achieve customer intimacy?** Customer relationship management (CRM) systems integrate and automate customer-facing processes in sales, marketing, and customer service, providing an enterprise-wide view of customers. Companies can use this customer knowledge when they interact with customers to provide them with better service or to sell new products and services. These systems also identify profitable or nonprofitable customers or opportunities to reduce the churn rate.

The major customer relationship management software packages provide capabilities for both operational CRM and analytical CRM. They often include modules for managing relationships with selling partners (partner relationship management) and for employee relationship management.

4 **What are the challenges posed by enterprise applications?** Enterprise applications are difficult to implement. They require extensive organizational change, large new software investments, and careful assessment of how these systems will enhance organizational performance. Enterprise applications cannot provide value if they are implemented atop flawed processes or if firms do not know how to use these systems to measure performance improvements. Employees require training to prepare for new procedures and roles. Attention to data management is essential.

5 **How are enterprise applications used in platforms for new cross-functional services?** Service platforms integrate data and processes from the various enterprise applications (customer relationship management, supply chain management, and enterprise systems), as well as from disparate legacy applications to create new composite business processes. Web services tie various systems together. The new services are delivered through enterprise portals, which can integrate disparate applications so that information appears to be coming from a single source. Open source, mobile, and cloud versioins of some of these products are becoming available.

Key Terms

Analytical CRM, 291
Bullwhip effect, 278
Churn rate, 291
Cross-selling, 287
Customer lifetime value (CLTV), 391
Demand planning, 279

Employee relationship management (ERM), 286
Enterprise software, 274
Just-in-time strategy, 278
Operational CRM, 290
Partner relationship management (PRM), 286
Pull-based model, 283

Push-based model, 283
Service platform, 294
Supply chain, 276
Supply chain execution systems, 280
Supply chain planning systems, 279
Touch point, 285

Review Questions

1. How do enterprise systems help businesses achieve operational excellence?
- Define an enterprise system and explain how enterprise software works.
- Describe how enterprise systems provide value for a business.

2. How do supply chain management systems coordinate planning, production, and logistics with suppliers?
- Define a supply chain and identify each of its components.
- Explain how supply chain management systems help reduce the bullwhip effect and how they provide value for a business.
- Define and compare supply chain planning systems and supply chain execution systems.
- Describe the challenges of global supply chains and how Internet technology can help companies manage them better.
- Distinguish between a push-based and pull-based model of supply chain management and explain how contemporary supply chain management systems facilitate a pull-based model.

3. How do customer relationship management systems help firms achieve customer intimacy?
- Define customer relationship management and explain why customer relationships are so important today.
- Describe how partner relationship management (PRM) and employee relationship management (ERM) are related to customer relationship management (CRM).
- Describe the tools and capabilities of customer relationship management software for sales, marketing, and customer service.
- Distinguish between operational and analytical CRM.

4. What are the challenges posed by enterprise applications?
- List and describe the challenges posed by enterprise applications
- Explain how these challenges can be addressed.

5. How are enterprise applications used in platforms for new cross-functional services?
- Define a service platform and describe the tools for integrating data from enterprise applications.
- How are enterprise applications taking advantage of cloud computing, wireless technology, Web 2.0, and open source technology?

Discussion Questions

1. Supply chain management is less about managing the physical movement of goods and more about managing information. Discuss the implications of this statement.

2. If a company wants to implement an enterprise application, it had better do its homework. Discuss the implications of this statement.

Video Cases

Video Cases and Instructional Videos illustrating some of the concepts in this chapter are available. Contact your instructor to access these videos.

Collaboration and Teamwork

Analyzing Enterprise Application Vendors

With a group of three or four students, use the Web to research and evaluate the products of two vendors of enterprise application software. You could compare, for example, the SAP and Oracle enterprise systems, the supply chain management systems from i2 and SAP, or the customer relationship management systems of Oracle's Siebel CRM and Salesforce.com. Use what you have learned from these companies' Web sites to compare the software packages you have selected in terms of business functions supported, technology platforms, cost, and ease of use. Which vendor would you select? Why? Would you select the same vendor for a small business as well as a large one? If possible, use Google Sites to post links to Web pages, team communication announcements, and work assignments; to brainstorm; and to work collaboratively on project documents. Try to use Google Docs to develop a presentation of your findings for the class.

BUSINESS PROBLEM-SOLVING CASE

Border States Industries Fuels Rapid Growth with ERP

Border States Industries Inc. (BSE) is a wholesale distributor for the construction, industrial, utility, and data communications markets. The company is headquartered in Fargo, North Dakota, and has 57 sales offices in states along the U.S. borders with Canada and Mexico as well as in South Dakota, Wisconsin, Iowa, and Missouri. BSE has 1,400 employees and is wholly employee-owned through its employee stock ownership plan. For the fiscal year ending March 31, 2008, BSE earned revenues of over US $880 million.

BSE's goal is to provide customers with what they need whenever they need it, including providing custom services beyond delivery of products. Thus, the company is not only a wholesale distributor but also a provider of supply chain solutions, with extensive service operations such as logistics, job-site trailers, and kitting (packaging individually separate but related items together as one

unit). BSE has distribution agreements with more than 9,000 product vendors.

BSE had relied on its own legacy ERP system called Rigel since 1988 to support its core business processes. However, Rigel had been designed exclusively for electrical wholesalers, and by the mid-1990s, the system could not support BSE's new lines of business and extensive growth.

At that point, BSE's management decided to implement a new ERP system and selected the enterprise software from SAP AG. The ERP solution included SAP's modules for sales and distribution, materials management, financials and controlling, and human resources.

BSE initially budgeted $6 million for the new system, with a start date of November 1, 1998. Senior management worked with IBM and SAP consulting to implement the system. Although close involvement of management was one key ingredient in the systems' success, day-to-day operations suffered while managers were working on the project.

BSE also decided to customize the system extensively. It wrote its own software to enable the ERP system to interface automatically with systems from other vendors, including Taxware Systems, Inc., Innovis Inc., and TOP-CALL International GmbH. The Taxware system enables BSE to comply with the sales tax requirements of all the states and municipalities where it conducts business. The Innovis system supports electronic data interchange (EDI) so that BSE could electronically exchange purchase and payment transactions with its suppliers. The TOPCALL system enables BSE to fax customers and vendors directly from the SAP system.

At the time of this implementation, BSE had no experience with SAP software, and few consultants familiar with the version of the SAP software that BSE was using. Instead of adopting the best-practice business processes embedded in the SAP software, BSE hired consultants to further customize the SAP software to make its new SAP system look like its old Rigel system in certain areas. For example, it tried to make customer invoices resemble the invoices produced by the old Rigel system.

Implementing these changes required so much customization of the SAP software that BSE had to delay the launch date for the new ERP system until February 1, 1999. By that time, continued customization and tuning raised total implementation costs to $9 million (an increase of 50 percent).

Converting and cleansing data from BSE's legacy system took far longer than management had anticipated. The first group of "expert users" were trained too early in the project and had to be retrained when the new system finally went live. BSE never fully tested the system as it would be used in a working production environment before the system actually went live.

For the next five years, BSE continued to use its SAP ERP system successfully as it acquired several small companies and expanded its branch office infrastructure to 24 states. As the business grew further, profits and inventory turns increased. However, the Internet brought about the need for additional changes, as customers sought to transact business with BSE through an e-commerce storefront. BSE automated online credit card processing and special pricing agreements (SPAs) with designated customers. Unfortunately, the existing SAP software did not support these changes, so the company had to process thousands of SPAs manually.

To process a credit card transaction in a branch office, BSE employees had to leave their desks, walk over to a dedicated credit card processing system in the back office, manually enter the credit card numbers, wait for transaction approval, and then return to their workstations to continue processing sales transactions.

In 2004, BSE began upgrading its ERP system to a more recent version of the SAP software. The software included new support for bills of material and kitting, which were not available in the old system. This functionality enabled BSE to provide better support to utility customers because it could prepare kits that could be delivered directly to a site.

This time the company kept customization to a minimum and used the SAP best practices for wholesale distribution embedded in the software. It also replaced TOPCALL with software from Esker for faxing and e-mailing outbound invoices, order acknowledgments, and purchase orders and added capabilities from Vistex Inc. to automate SPA rebate claims processing. BSE processes over 360,000 SPA claims each year, and the Vistex software enabled BSE to reduce rebate fulfillment time to 72 hours and transaction processing time by 63 percent. In the past, it took 15 to 30 days for BSE to receive rebates from vendors.

BSE budgeted $1.6 million and 4.5 months for implementation, which management believed was sufficient for a project of this magnitude. This time there were no problems. The new system went live on its target date and cost only $1.4 million to implement—14 percent below budget.

In late 2006, BSE acquired a large company that was anticipated to increase sales volume by 20 percent each year. This acquisition added 19 new branches to BSE. These new branches were able to run BSE's SAP software within a day after the acquisition had been completed. BSE now tracks 1.5 million unique items with the software.

Since BSE first deployed SAP software in 1998, sales have increased 300 percent, profits have climbed more than 500 percent, 60 percent of accounts payable transactions take place electronically using EDI, and SPA processing has been reduced by 63 percent. The company turns over its inventory more than four times per year. Instead of waiting 15 to 20 days for monthly financial statements, monthly and year-to-date financial results are available within a day after closing the books. Manual work for handling incoming mail, preparing bank deposits, and taking checks physically to the bank has been significantly reduced. Over 60 percent of vendor invoices arrive electronically, which has reduced staff size in accounts payable and the number of transaction errors. Transaction costs are lower.

The number of full-time BSE employees did increase in the information systems area to support the SAP software. BSE had initially expected to have 3 IT staff supporting the system, but needed 8 people when the first ERP implementation went live in 1999 and 11 by 2006 to support additional SAP software and the new acquisition. BSE's information technology (IT) costs rose by approximately $3 million per year after the first SAP implementation. However, sales expanded during the same period, so the increased overhead for the system produced a cost increase of only .5 percent of total sales.

BSE management has pointed out that much of the work that was automated by the ERP systems has been in the accounting department and involved activities that were purely transactional. This has freed up resources for adding more employees who work directly with customers trying to reduce costs and increase sales.

In the past, BSE had maintained much of its data outside its major corporate systems using PC-based Microsoft Access database and Excel spreadsheet software. Management lacked a single company-wide version of corporate data because the data were fragmented into so many different systems. Now the company is standardized on one common platform and the information is always current and available to management. Management can obtain a picture of how the entire business is performing at any moment in time. Since the SAP system makes all of BSE's planning and budgeting data available online, management is able to make better and quicker decisions.

In 2006, Gartner Group Consultants performed an independent evaluation of BSE's ERP implementation. Gartner interviewed top executives and analyzed BSE data on the impact of the ERP system on BSE's business process costs, using costs as a percentage of sales as its final metric for assessing the financial impact of SAP software. Cost categories analyzed included costs of goods sold, overhead and administration, warehousing costs, IT support, and delivery.

Gartner's analysis validated that the SAP software implementation cost from 1998 to 2001 did indeed total $9 million and that this investment was paid back by savings from the new ERP system within 2.5 years. Between 1998 and 2006, the SAP software implemented by BSE produced total savings of $30 million,

approximately one-third of BSE's cumulative earnings during the same period. As a percentage of sales, warehouse costs went down 1 percent, delivery costs decreased by .5 percent, and total overhead costs declined by 1.5 percent. Gartner calculated the total return on investment (ROI) for the project between 1998 and 2006 was $3.3 million per year, or 37% of the original investment.

BSE is now focusing on providing more support for Internet sales, including online ordering, inventory, order status, and invoice review, all within a SAP software environment. The company implemented SAP NetWeaver Master Data Management to provide tools to manage and maintain catalog data and prepare the data for publication online and in traditional print media. The company is using SAP's Web Dynpro development environment to enable wireless warehouse and inventory management activities to interact with the SAP software. And it is using SAP NetWeaver Business Intelligence software to learn more about customers, their buying habits, and opportunities to cross-sell and upsell products.

Sources: Jim Shepherd and Aurelie Cordier, "Wholesale Distributor Uses ERP Solution to Fuel Rapid Growth," AMR Research, 2009; SAP AG, "Border States Industries: SAP Software Empowers Wholesale Distributor," 2008; www.borderstateselectric.com, accessed July 7, 2009; and "Border States (BSE)," 2008 ASUG Impact Award.

Case Study Questions

1. What problems was Border States Industries encountering as it expanded? What people, organization, and technology factors were responsible for these problems?
2. How easy was it to develop a solution using SAP ERP software? Explain your answer.
3. List and describe the benefits from the SAP software.
4. How much did the new system solution transform the business? Explain your answer.
5. How successful was this solution for BSE? Identify and describe the metrics used to measure the success of the solution.
6. If you had been in charge of SAP's ERP implementations, what would you have done differently?

E-commerce: Digital Markets, Digital Goods

CHAPTER

9

STUDENT LEARNING OBJECTIVES

After completing this chapter, you will be able to answer the following questions:

1. What are the unique features of e-commerce, digital markets, and digital goods?

2. What are the principal e-commerce business and revenue models?

3. How has e-commerce has transformed marketing?

4. How has e-commerce affected business-to-business transactions?

5. What is the role of m-commerce in business, and what are the most important m-commerce applications?

6. What issues must be addressed when building an e-commerce Web site?

CHAPTER OUTLINE

NEXON GAMES: E-COMMERCE GOES SOCIAL

If you like to play online games, you may already be familiar with MapleStory. It's an online role-playing game in which players assume the identities of warriors, magicians, and thieves to collectively fight monsters. You can play the game for free, but if you want your avatar to have a new outfit, wacky hairstyle, or funny pet, you'll need to pay for these extras. And if you want your MapleStory characters to marry each other in an elaborate Las Vegas ceremony attended by other in-game buddies, it will cost $20 to $29.

MapleStory is a recent creation of Nexon Holdings Inc., the world leader in massively multiplayer online role-playing games. Nexon is headquartered in South Korea, with branch offices in China, Japan, and the United States. Nexon pioneered the "item" (microtransactions) business model, where users can access the full game for free but later opt to pay for game enhancements (items). Nexon is a real pioneer in the development of the "fremium" business model where some content is free, but premium content or service is charged for. Nexon charges players anywhere from 30 cents to $30 each for virtual "items" to enhance their game experiences. MapleStory has 92 million users globally, with over 6 million registered in North America. In 2007, players world-

wide purchased more than 1.3 million articles of clothing and over 1 million hair makeovers for their MapleStory characters.

One source of Nexon's popularity is the ability to socialize with other users. According to Min Kim, vice president of marketing at Nexon's U.S. division, "we sell social experiences, not packaged products." During much of the last decade, most games were played alone. As the Internet and PCs developed more capabilities for rich-media experiences, solitary gaming has given way to social gaming. Whether it's integrated instant messaging, voice over IP, or text messaging, there are now multiple mechanisms for players to communicate with their friends. Video games now attract a whole new type of consumer—people who want to have a social experience.

In 2009, Nexon America introduced a new, free service initiative called BlockParty that will centralize all of Nexon's games into one online portal and combine it with a social network designed to expand players' gaming experience. According to Nexon America executives, BlockParty is one part game, one part portal with a twist of social networking. Nexon America's goal for BlockParty is to create the biggest online party with great games and awesome gamers.

Other popular Nexon games include Mabinogi, Combat Arms, and Dungeon Fighter Online. Mabinogi allows players to participate in mundane tasks such as farming, writing music, and marrying as well as fighting. The game continuously evolves through the release of patches (termed "Generations" and "Chapters") that introduce new areas to explore and advance the story line. Combat Arms is a first-person shooter with over 3 million registered players featuring highly advanced graphics, and Dungeon Fighter Online is a unique fighting game where players choose one of several different "classes". Nexon games feature forums where players are invited to socialize with friends, share hints, or just hang out.

Nexon looks like it has a winning formula for success online. Despite the recession, 2009 revenues are estimated to be $349 million, up 29 percent from 2008. Prepaid cards used to purchase Nexon game items are now the second best-selling entertainment gift card (after Apple's iTunes Store) at Target Stores.

Sources: Mike Crouch, "Nexon America Unveils BlockParty," Melodika.net, October 6, 2009; Yukari Iwatani Kane, "Online Gaming—the Family Edition," *The Wall Street Journal*, March 26, 2009; Nick Wingfield, "Korea's Nexon Bets on Sales of Virtual Gear for Free Online Games," *The Wall Street Journal*, May 23, 2008; Kara Swisher, "Playing with Others," *The Wall Street Journal*, June 9, 2008; and www.nexon.com, accessed May 25, 2008.

Nexon's online games exemplify the new face of e-commerce. Selling physical goods on the Internet is still important, but much of the excitement and interest now centers around services and social experiences—social networking, photo sharing, sharing music, sharing ideas, and multiplayer online games where users communicate and interact with other users. The ability to link with other users and with other Web sites has spawned a huge wave of new businesses built around linking and sharing.

The chapter-opening diagram calls attention to important points raised by this case and this chapter. The business challenge facing Nexon is that Internet technology is changing rapidly, along with consumer tastes. Nexon customers want to play games online in a Web 2.0 environment with other friends in a social atmosphere. Customers wanted games with a virtual life quality so they could differentiate their warriers and game characters, and enrich their social experiences online. To meet these changing market requirements, Nexon needed to marry its strength in game design and online delivery, with the growing market demand for social interaction. Nexon pioneered in the microtransactions business model and became a leading provider of massively multiplayer online games. The company provides games replete with action and interactivity where players can socialize with friends or other players. By playing up social features of online games, and providing the ability to make online micropayments for small purchases, Nexon's games have huge numbers of users and a continuing stream of revenue.

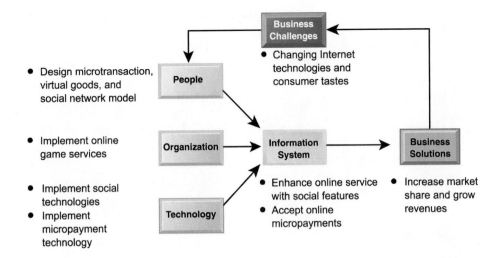

9.1 E-commerce and the Internet

Have you ever purchased music over the Web? Have you ever used the Web to search for information about your sneakers before you bought them in a retail store? If so, you've participated in e-commerce. So have hundreds of millions of people around the globe. And although most purchases still take place through traditional channels, e-commerce continues to grow rapidly and to transform the way many companies do business.

E-COMMERCE TODAY

E-commerce refers to the use of the Internet and the Web to transact business. More formally, e-commerce is about digitally enabled commercial transactions between and among organizations and individuals. For the most part, this means transactions that occur over the Internet and the Web. Commercial transactions involve the exchange of value (e.g., money) across organizational or individual boundaries in return for products and services.

E-commerce began in 1995 when one of the first Internet portals, Netscape.com, accepted the first ads from major corporations and popularized the idea that the Web could be used as a new medium for advertising and sales. No one envisioned at the time what would turn out to be an exponential growth curve for e-commerce retail sales, which doubled and tripled in the early years. E-commerce grew at double-digit rates until the recession of 2008–2009 when growth slowed to a crawl. In 2009, e-commerce revenues were flat (Figure 9-1), not bad considering that traditional retail sales were shrinking by 5% annually. In fact, e-commerce during the recession was the only stable segment in retail. Some online retailers forged ahead at a record pace: Amazon's 2009 revenues were up 25 percent over 2008 sales (eMarketer, 2009; U.S. Census, 2009).

Mirroring the history of many technological innovations, such as the telephone, radio, and television, the very rapid growth in e-commerce in the early years created a market bubble in e-commerce stocks. Like all bubbles, the "dot-com" bubble burst (in March 2001). A large number of e-commerce companies failed during this process. Yet for many others, such as Amazon, eBay, Expedia, and Google, the results have been more positive: soaring revenues, fine-tuned business models that produce profits, and rising stock prices. By 2006, e-commerce revenues returned to solid growth, and have continued to be the fastest growing form of retail trade in the United States, Europe, and Asia.

- Online consumer sales grew to an estimated $228 billion in 2009, an increase of more than 1 percent since 2008 (including travel services and digital downloads), with 123 million people purchasing online and 152 million shopping and gathering information but not necessarily purchasing (eMarketer, 2009).

Figure 9-1
The Growth of
E-commerce

Retail e-commerce
revenues grew 15%–25%
a year until the recession
of 2008–2009, when they
slowed measurably. In
2010, e-commerce
revenues are expected to
begin growing again at
an estimated 10% annual
clip.

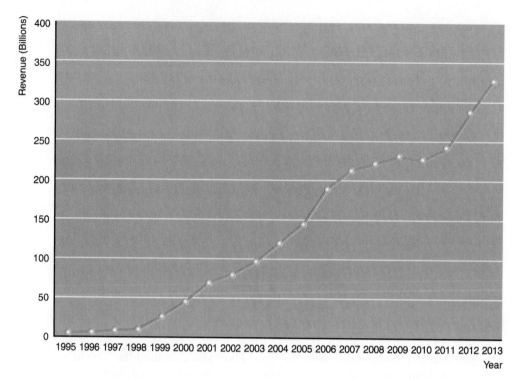

- The number of individuals online in the United States expanded to 199 million in 2009, up from 147 million in 2004. In the world, over 1.4 billion people are now connected to the Internet. Growth in the overall Internet population has spurred growth in e-commerce.
- About 73 million Americans now access the Internet using a smartphone such as an iPhone or a BlackBerry. Mobile e-commerce has begun a rapid growth based on apps, ringtones, downloaded entertainment, and location-based services.
- On the average day, 143 million people go online, 113 million send e-mail, 100 million use a search engine, 20 million read a blog, 6 million write on their blogs, 13 million share music on peer-to-peer networks, 40 million work on their social network profile, 24 million visit Wikipedia, and 32 million watch a video. (Pew Internet, 2009).
- B2B e-commerce-use of the Internet for business-to-business commerce and collaboration among business partners expanded 2 percent to more than $3.7 trillion.

The e-commerce revolution is still unfolding. Individuals and businesses will increasingly use the Internet to conduct commerce as more products and services come online and households switch to broadband telecommunications. More industries will be transformed by e-commerce, including travel reservations, music and entertainment, news, software, education, and finance. Table 9.1 highlights these new e-commerce developments.

WHY E-COMMERCE IS DIFFERENT

Why has e-commerce grown so rapidly? The answer lies in the unique nature of the Internet and the Web. Simply put, the Internet and e-commerce technologies are much more rich and powerful than previous technology revolutions like radio, television, and the telephone. Table 9.2 describes the unique features of the Internet and Web as a commercial medium. Let's explore each of these unique features in more detail.

Ubiquity

In traditional commerce, a marketplace is a physical place, such as a retail store, that you visit to transact business. E-commerce is ubiquitous, meaning that is it available just about everywhere, at all times. It makes it possible to shop from your desktop, at home, at work, or even from your car, using mobile commerce. The result is called a **marketspace**—a market-

TABLE 9.1

The Growth of E-commerce

Business Transformation

- E-commerce remains the fastest growing form of commerce when compared to physical retail stores, services, and entertainment.

- The first wave of e-commerce transformed the business world of books, music, and air travel. In the second wave, nine new industries are facing a similar transformation scenario: marketing and advertising, telecommunications, movies, television, jewelry, real estate, hotels, bill payments, and software.

- The breadth of e-commerce offerings grows, especially in the services economy of social networking, travel, information clearinghouses, entertainment, retail apparel, appliances, and home furnishings.

- The online demographics of shoppers broaden to match that of ordinary shoppers.

- Pure e-commerce business models are refined further to achieve higher levels of profitability, whereas traditional retail brands, such as Sears, JC Penney, L.L. Bean, and Wal-Mart, use e-commerce to retain their dominant retail positions.

- Small businesses and entrepreneurs continue to flood the e-commerce marketplace, often riding on the infrastructures created by industry giants, such as Amazon and eBay.

- Mobile e-commerce begins to take off in the United States with location-based services and entertainment downloads including e-books.

Technology Foundations

- Wireless Internet connections (Wi-Fi, WiMax, and 3G smart phones) grow rapidly.

- Powerful handheld mobile devices support music, Web surfing, and entertainment as well as voice communication. Podcasting takes off as a medium for distribution of video, radio, and user-generated content.

- The Internet broadband foundation becomes stronger in households and businesses as transmission prices fall. More than 80 million households had broadband cable or DSL access to the Internet in 2009—about 72 percent of all households in the United States (eMarketer, 2009).

- Social networking software and sites such as Facebook, MySpace, Twitter, LinkedIn and thousands of others become a major new platform for e-commerce, marketing, and advertising.

- New Internet-based models of computing, such as cloud computing, software as a service (SaaS), and Web 2.0 software greatly reduce the cost of e-commerce Web sites.

New Business Models Emerge

- More than half the Internet user population join an online social networks, contribute to social bookmarking sites, create blogs, and share photos. Together these sites create a massive online audience as large as television that is attractive to marketers.

- The traditional advertising business model is severely disrupted as Google and other technology players such as Microsoft and Yahoo! seek to dominate online advertising, and expand into offline ad brokerage for television and newspapers.

- Newspapers and other traditional media adopt online, interactive models but are losing advertising revenues to the online players despite gaining online readers.

- Online entertainment business models offering television, movies, music, sports, and e-books surge, with cooperation among the major copyright owners in Hollywood and New York with the Internet distributors like Google, YouTube, Facebook, and Microsoft.

TABLE 9.2

Eight Unique Features of E-commerce Technology

E-commerce Technology Dimension	Business Significance
Ubiquity. Internet/Web technology is available everywhere: at work, at home, and elsewhere via mobile devices.	The marketplace is extended beyond traditional boundaries and is removed from a temporal and geographic location. "Marketspace" anytime. is created; shopping can take place anywhere. Customer convenience is enhanced, and shopping costs are reduced.
Global Reach. The technology reaches across national boundaries, around the Earth.	Commerce is enabled across cultural and national boundaries seamlessly and without modification. The marketspace includes, potentially, billions of consumers and millions of businesses worldwide.
Universal Standards. There is one set of technology standards, namely Internet standards.	With one set of technical standards across the globe, disparate computer systems can easily communicate with each other.
Richness. Video, audio, and text messages are possible.	Video, audio, and text marketing messages are integrated into a single marketing message and consumer experience.
Interactivity. The technology works through interaction with the user.	Consumers are engaged in a dialog that dynamically adjusts the experience to the individual, and makes the consumer a co-participant in the process of delivering goods to the market.
Information Density. The technology reduces information costs and raises quality.	Information processing, storage, and communication costs drop dramatically, whereas currency, accuracy, and timeliness improve greatly. Information becomes plentiful, cheap, and more accurate.
Personalization/Customization. The technology allows personalized messages to be delivered to individuals as well as groups.	Personalization of marketing messages and customization of products and services are based on individual characteristics.
Social Technology. User content generation and social networking.	New Internet social and business models enable user content creation and distribution, and support social networks.

place extended beyond traditional boundaries and removed from a temporal and geographic location.

From a consumer point of view, ubiquity reduces **transaction costs**—the costs of participating in a market . To transact business, it is no longer necessary that you spend time or money traveling to a market, and much less mental effort is required to make a purchase.

Global Reach

E-commerce technology permits commercial transactions to cross cultural and national boundaries far more conveniently and cost effectively than is true in traditional commerce. As a result, the potential market size for e-commerce merchants is roughly equal to the size of the world's online population (estimated to be more than 1.5 billion, and growing rapidly).

In contrast, most traditional commerce is local or regional—it involves local merchants or national merchants with local outlets. Television and radio stations and newspapers, for instance, are primarily local and regional institutions with limited, but powerful, national networks that can attract a national audience but not easily cross national boundaries to a global audience.

Universal Standards

One strikingly unusual feature of e-commerce technologies is that the technical standards of the Internet and, therefore, the technical standards for conducting e-commerce are universal standards. They are shared by all nations around the world and enable any computer to link with any other computer regardless of the technology platform each is using. In contrast, most traditional commerce technologies differ from one nation to the next. For instance, television and radio standards differ around the world, as does cell telephone technology.

The universal technical standards of the Internet and e-commerce greatly lower **market entry costs**—the cost merchants must pay simply to bring their goods to market. At the same time, for consumers, universal standards reduce **search costs**—the effort required to find suitable products.

Richness

Information **richness** refers to the complexity and content of a message. Traditional markets, national sales forces, and small retail stores have great richness: They are able to provide personal, face-to-face service using aural and visual cues when making a sale. The richness of traditional markets makes them powerful selling or commercial environments. Prior to the development of the Web, there was a trade-off between richness and reach: The larger the audience reached, the less rich the message. The Web makes it possible to deliver rich messages with text, audio, and video simultaneously to large numbers of people.

Interactivity

Unlike any of the commercial technologies of the twentieth century, with the possible exception of the telephone, e-commerce technologies are interactive, meaning they allow for two-way communication between merchant and consumer. Television, for instance, cannot ask viewers any questions or enter into conversations with them, and it cannot request that customer information be entered into a form. In contrast, all of these activities are possible on an e-commerce Web site. Interactivity allows an online merchant to engage a consumer in ways similar to a face-to-face experience but on a massive, global scale.

Information Density

The Internet and the Web vastly increase **information density**—the total amount and quality of information available to all market participants, consumers, and merchants alike. E-commerce technologies reduce information collection, storage, processing, and communication costs while greatly increasing the currency, accuracy, and timeliness of information.

Information density in e-commerce markets make prices and costs more transparent. **Price transparency** refers to the ease with which consumers can find out the variety of prices in a market; **cost transparency** refers to the ability of consumers to discover the actual costs merchants pay for products.

There are advantages for merchants as well. Online merchants can discover much more about consumers than in the past. This allows merchants to segment the market into groups who are willing to pay different prices and permits the merchants to engage in **price discrimination**—selling the same goods, or nearly the same goods, to different targeted groups at different prices. For instance, an online merchant can discover a consumer's avid interest in expensive, exotic vacations and then pitch high-end vacation plans to that consumer at a premium price, knowing this person is willing to pay extra for such a vacation. At the same time, the online merchant can pitch the same vacation plan at a lower price to a more price-sensitive consumer. Information density also helps merchants differentiate their products in terms of cost, brand, and quality.

Personalization/Customization

E-commerce technologies permit **personalization**: Merchants can target their marketing messages to specific individuals by adjusting the message to a person's name, interests, and past purchases. The technology also permits **customization**—changing the delivered product or service based on a user's preferences or prior behavior. Given the interactive nature of e-commerce technology, much information about the consumer can be gathered in the marketplace at the moment of purchase. With the increase in information density, a great deal of information about the consumer's past purchases and behavior can be stored and used by online merchants.

The result is a level of personalization and customization unthinkable with traditional commerce technologies. For instance, you may be able to shape what you see on television by selecting a channel, but you cannot change the content of the channel you have chosen. In contrast, the *Wall Street Journal* Online allows you to select the type of news stories you want to see first and gives you the opportunity to be alerted when certain events happen.

You can see these features of e-commerce at work in the Interactive Session on Technology. Turner Sports New Media operates a series of Web sites for NASCAR, the NBA, and other sports organizations. It uses interactivity and richness, and is able to combine the reach of cable TV with deep relationships with consumers. For instance, at the Major League Baseball Web site (mlb.com) you can watch the postseason games from any of four different camera angles! Your choice.

Social Technology: User Content Generation and Social Networking

In contrast to previous technologies, the Internet and e-commerce technologies have evolved to be much more social by allowing users to create and share with their personal friends (and a larger worldwide community) content in the form of text, videos, music, or photos. Using these forms of communication, users are able to create new social networks and strengthen existing ones.

All previous mass media in modern history, including the printing press, use a broadcast model (one-to-many) where content is created in a central location by experts (professional writers, editors, directors, and producers) and audiences are concentrated in huge numbers to consume a standardized product. The new Internet and e-commerce empower users to create and distribute content on a large scale, and permit users to program their own content consumption. The Internet provides a unique many-to-many model of mass communications.

KEY CONCEPTS IN E-COMMERCE: DIGITAL MARKETS AND DIGITAL GOODS IN A GLOBAL MARKETPLACE

The location, timing, and revenue models of business are based in some part on the cost and distribution of information. The Internet has created a digital marketplace where millions of people all over the world are able to exchange massive amounts of information directly, instantly, and for free. As a result, the Internet has changed the way companies conduct business and increased their global reach.

The Internet reduces information asymmetry. An **information asymmetry** exists when one party in a transaction has more information that is important for the transaction than the other party. That information helps determine their relative bargaining power. In digital markets, consumers and suppliers can "see" the prices being charged for goods, and in that sense digital markets are said to be more "transparent" than traditional markets.

For example, before auto retailing sites appeared on the Web, there was a significant information asymmetry between auto dealers and customers. Only the auto dealers knew the manufacturers' prices, and it was difficult for consumers to shop around for the best price. Auto dealers' profit margins depended on this asymmetry of information. Today's consumers have access to a legion of Web sites providing competitive pricing information, and three-fourths of U.S. auto buyers use the Internet to shop around for the best deal. Thus, the Web has reduced the information asymmetry surrounding an auto purchase. The Internet has also helped businesses seeking to purchase from other businesses reduce information asymmetries and locate better prices and terms.

Digital markets are very flexible and efficient because they operate with reduced search and transaction costs, lower **menu costs** (merchants' costs of changing prices), price discrimination, and the ability to change prices dynamically based on market conditions. In

INTERACTIVE SESSION: TECHNOLOGY   Turner Sports Marries TV and the Internet, then Goes Social

Sports are hot on the Internet. Sports Web sites in the United States drew over 86 million monthly visitors in 2009; next to social networks, sports sites were the most popular destination sites. The single-site leader in sports sites is ESPN (23 million monthly visitors and owned by Disney), but close behind are a family of sites like NASCAR.com, PGA.com, MLB.com (Major League Baseball), NBA.com, and a host of related sites, that are all operated by Turner Sports Inc. The Turner Sports sites collectively draw even more fans than ESPN. In 2009, Turner Sports is embracing the techniques and technologies of social media to promote its clients' Web programs, making Turner the leading innovator in Internet sports programming. In the past few years, Turner Sports established itself as an innovator through its ability to combine TV and the Web more successfully than rivals. Turner's success allows them to both sell more ads and persuade sports leagues such as the PGA Tour and NASCAR to pay Turner millions per year to run their Web operations. Turner's formula is to provide rich, interactive features that use TV and the Web simultaneously to enhance the viewer's experience. With today's new social media, this formula is hitting on all cylinders.

Turner Sports is the division of Turner Broadcasting System responsible for sports broadcasts on Turner cable channels (TBS, TNT, and Peachtree TV) and for operating a family of online interactive properties for professional sports organizations. While Turner dominated cable television sports since its inception in 1975, it was late coming to the Internet and creating an integrated Web-TV platform. Turner's Internet sports program started out in 2001 with NASCAR.com. By 2006, Turner had added PGA.com and PGATour.com, and in early 2008 reached an agreement with the NBA to jointly manage NBA.com, which has 5.5 million unique monthly visitors. Turner's latest target is Major League Soccer's Web operations, which, oddly enough, are managed by Major League Baseball. Turner earns fees for managing the sites and splits ad revenues with each league. With each site that Turner Sports New Media manages, its goal is to get fans switching between TV and unique features on their desktops or laptops. For example, PGATour.com visitors can watch play on certain holes, watch a certain player, get aerial views of the course, and get tips from pros on the site while events are in progress.

Many sports leagues don't like to relinquish control of their Web sites to outside organizations, preferring to handle their Web operations themselves in order to control their brands and Web site content. In the case of Turner Sports, the same business that controls your cable TV distribution also can control your Web distribution. For instance, the NFL recently reacquired rights to its Web site back from CBS. But Turner's value proposition to sports leagues is a compelling one. Turner offers to provide an integrated platform that connects the league's television broadcasts with its Web site activities. Why rely on two or more separate organizations when its all "media"? The league's official site will benefit from Turner's reach and the Web's relationship with consumers. Turner's experience with running Web sites is extensive, as is it's track record for success in increasing site traffic and developing innovative interactive applications. Marketers can place ads in multiple formats (TV and the Internet).

Turner's oldest client is NASCAR, and the recent contract extension signed between the two suggests that NASCAR is more than happy with Turner's results. NASCAR.com has been one of the top three sports league sites on the Internet in the past few years. Since Turner assumed control of the league's Web rights, the site has seen double-digit growth in page views and an increase in average monthly unique visitors of 25 percent over the last 7 years. Over the past calendar year the site had 1.4 billion page views. Turner will continue to operate NASCAR.com through 2014, collaborating on content creation, e-commerce, and race ticket sales. Turner will continue to have oversight over news content, broadband coverage, wireless platforms, video downloads, and ad sales, and will seek to provide fans with better information and NASCAR merchandise.

Turner has implemented a wide array of cutting-edge applications and offerings to NASCAR.com, including TrackPass, its most interactive feature. TrackPass is a premium service that consists of several interactive applications, including TrackPass Scanner, TrackPass PitCommand, and TrackPass RaceView. RaceView renders each car digitally and offers a multitude of camera angles and viewing options for each and every car and driver. Users can pause, rewind, and replay live races and listen to any driver's in-car audio, in addition to a variety of other features that give the viewer unparalleled customization over how they watch and enjoy each race.

Other features that Turner has implemented on NASCAR.com include a 24-hour news center, live streaming for some races, a social networking "community" section, an extensive video library, live and interactive broadband shows, and a merchandise superstore.

Turner's contract extension with the NBA extends the longest-running partnership between a league and programming network in professional sports to a whopping 32 years. The contract also grants Turner Sports access to the NBA.com network, which includes WNBA.com and NBADleague.com in addition to the flagship site. Under the contract, TNT will continue to televise NBA games, broaden their Internet involvement, and jointly manage NBA's digital businesses along with the league. These businesses include NBA TV (a 24-hour digital TV network), operating the NBA.com network of sites, NBA League Pass, advertising, and availability of TNT's on-air TV talent for NBA.com's interactive features. Turner is likely to develop features like TrackPass RaceView for NBA games to provide a similar level of richness and customizability to the viewer experience.

One feature that Turner hopes to further develop is TNT NBA Overtime—a broadband feature on NBA.com that streams TNT-televised games, highlights, exclusive interviews, expert analysis, and more, which users can get live, delayed, and on demand. Turner's contract with the NBA is slated to run through the 2015–16 NBA season. If Turner's track record continues, NBA.com will continue to be an example of rich, interactive media done right. But Internet technologies change rapidly, and Turner is just starting to exploit the power of social media.

In April 2009, Turner Sports announced its new social media marketing campaign that utilizes Facebook, YouTube, and Twitter to promoted TNT's "40 Games in 40 Nights" coverage of the 2009 NBA Playoffs. The campaign includes player-specific videos on YouTube, messaging on Facebook coordinated with sponsored ads, and a special program to encourage Facebook users to "Become a Fan" of the NBA. Turner Sports is adding to its social media campaign with a coordinated Twitter full-court press featuring updates from popular announcers, with links to the NBA's Twitter page.

Turner is starting to experiment with user-generated content and Web experience control in a 2009 deal with MLB.com to give online fans user-controlled cameras to view every MLB postseason game through a subscription service at MLB.com/Postseason.TV. Users can control their experience of the games. To promote more user involvement at NASCAR.com, NASCAR announced a new program called "NASCAR Citizen Journalist," where the best-known independent NASCAR bloggers and Web site operators are republished at NASCAR.com.

Sources: "MLB.com, Turner Sports, and FOX Sports Give Fans Live User-Controlled Views for Every MLB Postseason Game," Reuters, October 6, 2009; "ComScore Media Metrix Ranks Top 50 US Web Properties," ComScore, September 21, 2009; "NASCAR Openly Embraces Changing Media Landscape," NASCAR Press Release, June 2, 2009; "Turner Sports Engages Fans Online Through Robust Social Media Campaign for 2009 NBA Playoffs," Time Warner Inc. Press Release, April 14, 2009.

CASE STUDY QUESTIONS

1. Describe the unique features of e-commerce technology illustrated in this case.

2. How does the Web enhance the TV businesses for the companies discussed in this case? How does it add value?

3. Why is NASCAR TrackPass a good example of Turner Sports New Media's value to sports league sites?

4. Do you think Turner Sports will be successful migrating its content to social media sites where its viewers are moving? Why or why not?

MIS IN ACTION

Visit PGA.com, PGATour.com, or NASCAR.com, explore the Web site, and then answer the following questions:

1. What unique features of e-commerce technology can you find on the site? What purposes do they serve?

2. How does the Web site promote TV viewing? How does it create value for the company?

3. What e-commerce business and revenue models are being used?

dynamic pricing, the price of a product varies depending on the demand characteristics of the customer or the supply situation of the seller.

These new digital markets may either reduce or increase switching costs, depending on the nature of the product or service being sold, and they may cause some extra delay in gratification. Unlike a physical market, you can't immediately consume a product such as clothing purchased over the Web (although immediate consumption is possible with digital music downloads and other digital products.)

Digital markets provide many opportunities to sell directly to the consumer, bypassing intermediaries, such as distributors or retail outlets. Eliminating intermediaries in the distribution channel can significantly lower purchase transaction costs. To pay for all the steps in a traditional distribution channel, a product may have to be priced as high as 135 percent of its original cost to manufacture.

Figure 9-2 illustrates how much savings result from eliminating each of these layers in the distribution process. By selling directly to consumers or reducing the number of intermediaries, companies are able to raise profits while charging lower prices. The removal of organizations or business process layers responsible for intermediary steps in a value chain is called **disintermediation**.

Disintermediation is affecting the market for services. Airlines and hotels operating their own reservation sites online earn more per ticket because they have eliminated travel agents as intermediaries. Table 9.3 summarizes the differences between digital markets and traditional markets.

Digital Goods

The Internet digital marketplace has greatly expanded sales of digital goods. **Digital goods** are goods that can be delivered over a digital network. Music tracks, video, Hollywood movies, software, newspapers, magazines, and books can all be expressed, stored, delivered, and sold as purely digital products. Currently, most of these products are sold as physical goods, for example, CDs, DVDs, newspapers, and hard-copy books. But the Internet offers the possibility of delivering all these products on demand as digital products.

In general, for digital goods, the marginal cost of producing another unit is about zero (it costs nothing to make a copy of a music file). However, the cost of producing the original first unit is relatively high—in fact, it is nearly the total cost of the product because there are few other costs of inventory and distribution. Costs of delivery over the Internet are very low, marketing costs remain the same, and pricing can be highly variable. (On the Internet, the merchant can change prices as often as desired because of low menu costs.)

The impact of the Internet on the market for these kinds of digital goods is nothing short of revolutionary, and we see the results around us every day. Businesses dependent on physical products for sales—such as bookstores, book publishers, music labels, and film studios—face the possibility of declining sales and even destruction of their businesses. Newspapers and magazines are losing readers to the Internet, and losing advertisers even as online newspaper readership soars. Record label companies are losing sales to Internet piracy, and record stores are going out of business. Video rental firms, such as Blockbuster, based on a physical DVD market and physical stores have lost sales to NetFlix using an Internet catalog and streaming video model. Hollywood studios as well face the prospect that Internet pirates will distribute their product as a digital stream, bypassing Hollywood's monopoly on DVD rentals and sales, which now accounts for more than half of industry film revenues. Table 9.4 describes digital goods and how they differ from traditional physical goods.

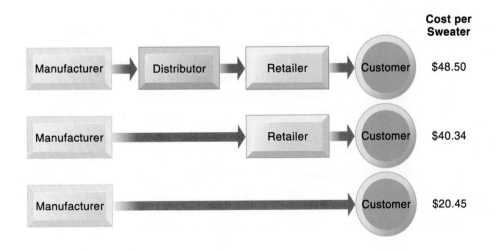

Figure 9-2
The Benefits of Disintermediation to the Consumer
The typical distribution channel has several intermediary layers, each of which adds to the final cost of a product, such as a sweater. Removing layers lowers the final cost to the consumer.

TABLE 9.3

Digital Markets
Compared to
Traditional Markets

	Digital Markets	Traditional Market
Information asymmetry	Asymmetry reduced	Asymmetry high
Search costs	Low	High
Transaction costs	Low (sometimes virtually nothing)	High (time, travel)
Delayed gratification	High (or lower in the case of a digital good)	Lower: purchase now
Menu costs	Low	High
Dynamic pricing	Low cost, instant	High cost, delayed
Price discrimination	Low cost, instant	High cost, delayed
Market segmentation	Low cost, moderate precision	High cost, less precision
Switching costs	Higher/lower (depending on product characteristics)	High
Network effects	Strong	Weaker
Disintermediation	More possible/likely	Less possible/unlikely

TABLE 9.4

How the Internet
Changes the Markets
for Digital Goods

	Digital Goods	Traditional Goods
Marginal cost/unit	Zero	Greater than zero , high
Cost of production	High (most of the cost)	Variable
Copying cost	Approximately zero	Greater than zero, high
Distributed delivery cost	Low	High
Inventory cost	Low	High
Marketing cost	Variable	Variable
Pricing	More variable (bundling, random pricing games)	Fixed, based on unit costs

9.2 E-commerce: Business and Technology

E-commerce has grown from a few advertisements on early Web portals in 1995, to over 5 percent of all retail sales in 2010 (an estimated $245 billion), surpassing the mail order catalog business. E-commerce is a fascinating combination of business models and new information technologies. Let's start with a basic understanding of the types of e-commerce, and then describe e-commerce business and revenue models. We'll also cover new technologies that help companies reach over 200 million online consumers in the United States, and an estimated 600 million more worldwide.

TYPES OF E-COMMERCE

There are many ways to classify electronic commerce transactions. One is by looking at the nature of the participants in the electronic commerce transaction. The three major electronic commerce categories are business-to-consumer (B2C) e-commerce, business-to-business (B2B) e-commerce, and consumer-to-consumer (C2C) e-commerce.

- **Business-to-consumer (B2C)** electronic commerce involves retailing products and services to individual shoppers. BarnesandNoble.com, which sells books, software, and music to individual consumers, is an example of B2C e-commerce.

- **Business-to-business (B2B)** electronic commerce involves sales of goods and services among businesses. ChemConnect's Web site for buying and selling chemicals and plastics is an example of B2B e-commerce.

- **Consumer-to-consumer (C2C)** electronic commerce involves consumers selling directly to consumers. For example, eBay, the giant Web auction site, enables people to sell their goods to other consumers by auctioning their merchandise off to the highest bidder, or for a fixed price. Craigslist is the most widely used platform used by consumers to buy and sell directly from others.

Another way of classifying electronic commerce transactions is in terms of the platforms used by participants in a transaction. Until recently, most e-commerce transactions took place using a personal computer connected to the Internet over wired networks. Two wireless mobile alternatives have emerged: mobile smartphones and dedicated e-readers like the Kindle using cellular networks, and mobile smartphones and small tablet computers using Wi-Fi wireless networks. The use of handheld wireless devices for purchasing goods and services from any location has been termed **mobile commerce** or **m-commerce**. Both business-to-business and business-to-consumer e-commerce transactions can take place using m-commerce technology, which we discuss in detail in Section 9.3.

E-COMMERCE BUSINESS MODELS

Changes in the economics of information described earlier have created the conditions for entirely new business models to appear, while destroying older business models. Table 9.5 describes some of the most important Internet business models that have emerged. All, in one way or another, use the Internet to add extra value to existing products and services or to provide the foundation for new products and services.

Portal

Portals such as Google, Bing, Yahoo, MSN, and AOL offer powerful Web search tools as well as an integrated package of content and services, such as news, e-mail, instant messaging, maps, calendars, shopping, music downloads, video streaming, and more, all in one place. Initially, portals were primarily "gateways" to the Internet. Today, however, the portal business model provides a destination site where users start their Web searching and linger to read news, find entertainment, meet other people, (and be exposed to advertising). Portals generate revenue primarily by attracting very large audiences, charging advertisers for ad placement, collecting referral fees for steering customers to other sites, and charging for premium services. In 2009, portals generated an estimated $36 billion in revenues. Although there are hundreds of portal/search engine sites, the top five sites (Google, Yahoo, MSN/Bing, AOL, and Ask.com) gather more than 95 percent of the Internet traffic because of their superior brand recognition (Nielsen Online, 2009).

E-tailer

Online retail stores, often called **e-tailers**, come in all sizes, from giant Amazon with 2009 revenues of more than $20 billion, to tiny local stores that have Web sites. E-tailers are similar to the typical bricks-and-mortar storefront, except that customers only need to connect to the Internet to check their inventory and place an order. Altogether online retail generated about $131 billion in revenues for 2009. The value proposition of e-tailers is to provide convenient, low-cost shopping 24/7, offering large selections and consumer choice. Some e-tailers, such as Walmart.com or Staples.com, referred to as "bricks-and-clicks," are subsidiaries or divisions of existing physical stores and carry the same products. Others, however, operate only in the virtual world, without any ties to physical locations. Amazon.com, BlueNile.com, and Drugstore.com are examples of this type of e-tailer.

TABLE 9.5

Internet Business
Models

Category	Description	Examples
E-tailer	Sells physical products directly to consumers or to individual businesses.	Amazon.com RedEnvelope.com
Transaction broker	Saves users money and time by processing online sales transactions and generating a fee each time a transaction occurs.	ETrade.com Expedia.com
Market creator	Provides a digital environment where buyers and sellers can meet, search for products, display products, and establish prices for those products. Can serve consumers or B2B e-commerce, generating revenue from transaction fees.	eBay.com Priceline.com ChemConnect.com
Content provider	Creates revenue by providing digital content, such as digital news, music, photos, or video, over the Web. The customer may pay to access the content, or revenue may be generated by selling advertising space.	WSJ.com GettyImages.com iTunes.com Games.com
Community provider	Provides an online meeting place where people with similar interests can communicate and find useful information.	iVillage.com MySpace.com Facebook.com
Portal	Provides initial point of entry to the Web along with specialized content and other services.	Yahoo.com Bing.com Google.com
Service Provider	Provides Web 2.0 applications such as photo sharing, video sharing, and user-generated content as services. Provide other services such as online data storage and backup.	Google Apps Photobucket.com Xdrive.com

Several other variations of e-tailers—such as online versions of direct mail catalogs, online malls, and manufacturer-direct online sales—also exist.

Content Provider

While e-commerce began as a retail product channel, it has increasingly turned into a global content channel. "Content" is defined broadly to include all forms of intellectual property. **Intellectual property** refers to all forms of human expression that can be put into a tangible medium such as text, CDs, DVDs, or stored on any digital (or other) media, including the Web. Content providers distribute information content, such as digital video, music, photos, text, and artwork, over the Web. The value proposition of online content providers is that consumers can find a wide range of content online, conveniently, and purchase this content inexpensively, to be played, or viewed, on multiple computer devices or smartphones.

Providers do not have to be the creators of the content (although sometimes they are like Disney.com), and are more likely to be Internet-based distributors of content produced and created by others. For example, Apple sells music tracks at its iTunes Store, but it does not create or commission new music.

The phenomenal popularity of iTunes and Apple's iPod portable music player have inspired a new form of digital content delivery called podcasting. **Podcasting** is a method of publishing audio or video broadcasts via the Internet, allowing subscribing users to download audio or video files onto their personal computers or portable music players.

Estimates vary, but total download and subscription media revenues are somewhere between $4 billion and $8 billion annually. They are the fastest growing segment within e-commerce, growing at an estimated 20 percent annual rate (eMarketer, 2009).

Transaction Broker

Sites that process transactions for consumers normally handled in person, by phone, or by mail are transaction brokers. The largest industries using this model are financial services and travel services. The online transaction broker's primary value propositions are savings of money and time, as well as providing an extraordinary inventory of financial products and travel packages, in a single location. Online stock brokers and travel booking services charge fees that are considerably less than traditional versions of these services.

Market Creator

Market creators build a digital environment in which buyers and sellers can meet, display products, search for products, and establish prices. The value proposition of online market creators is that they provide a platform where sellers can easily display their wares and where purchasers can buy directly from sellers. Online auction markets like eBay and Priceline are good examples of the market creator business model. Another example is Amazon's Merchants platform (and similar programs at eBay) where merchants are allowed to set up stores on Amazon's Web site and sell goods at fixed prices to consumers. This is reminiscent of open air markets where the market creator operates a facility (a town square) where merchants and consumers meet. Online market creators will generate about $14 billion in revenues for 2009.

Service Provider

While e-tailers sell products online, service providers offer services online. There's been an explosion in online services. Web 2.0 applications, photo sharing, and online sites for data backup and storage all use a service provider business model. Software is no longer a physical product with a CD in a box, but increasingly software as a service (SaaS) that you subscribe to online rather than purchase from a retailer (see Chapter 4). Google has led the way in developing online software service applications such as Google Apps, Gmail, and online data storage services.

Community Provider

Community providers are sites that create a digital online environment where people with similar interests can transact (buy and sell goods); share interests, photos, videos; communicate with like-minded people; receive interest-related information; and even play out fantasies by adopting online personalities called avatars. The social networking sites Facebook, MySpace, LinkedIn, and Twitter, online communities such as iVillage, and hundreds of other smaller, niche sites such as Doostang and Sportsvite, all offer users community building tools and services. Social networking sites have been the fastest growing Web sites in recent years, often doubling their audience size in a year. However, they are struggling to achieve profitability. The Interactive Session on Organizations and chapter-ending case study explore this topic.

E-COMMERCE REVENUE MODELS

A firm's **revenue model** describes how the firm will earn revenue, generate profits, and produce a superior return on investment. Although there are many different e-commerce revenue models that have been developed, most companies rely on one, or some combination, of the following six revenue models: advertising, sales, subscription, free/freemium, transaction fee, and the affiliate model.

Advertising Revenue Model

In the advertising revenue model, a Web site generates revenue by attracting a large audience of visitors who can then be exposed to advertisements. The advertising model is the most widely used revenue model in e-commerce, and arguably, without advertising revenues the Web would be a vastly different experience from what it is now. Content on the Web—everything from news to videos and opinions—is "free" to visitors because advertisers pay

Twitter, the social networking site based on 140-character text messages, is the buzz social networking phenomenon of the year. Like all social networking sites, such as Facebook, MySpace, YouTube, Flickr, and others, Twitter provides a platform for users to express themselves by creating content and sharing it with their "followers," who sign up to receive someone's "tweets." And like most social networking sites, Twitter faces the problem of how to make money. As of October 2009, Twitter has failed to generate revenue as its management ponders how best to exploit the buzz and user base it has created.

Twitter began as a Web-based version of popular text messaging services provided by cell phone carriers. Executives in a podcasting company called Odeo were searching for a new revenue-producing product or service. In March 2006 they created a stand-alone, private company called Twitter.

The basic idea was to marry short text messaging on cell phones with the Web and its ability to create social groups. You start by establishing a Twitter account online, and identifying the friends that you would like to receive your messages. By sending a text message called a "tweet" to a short code on your cell phone (40404), you can tell your friends what you are doing, your location, and whatever else you might want to say. You are limited to 140 characters, but there is no installation and no charge. This social network messaging service to keep buddies informed was a smash success.

Coming up with solid numbers for Twitter is not easy because the firm is not releasing any "official" figures. By September 2009, Twitter, according to some estimates, had around 20 million unique monthly users in the United States, and perhaps 50 million worldwide. Industry observers believe Twitter is the third largest social networking site behind Facebook and MySpace.

The number of individual tweets is also known only by the company. According to the company, by early 2007, Twitter had transmitted 20,000 tweets, which jumped to 60,000 tweets in a few months. During the Iranian rebellion in June 2009, there were reported to be over 200,000 tweets per hour worldwide. On the other hand, experts believe that 80 percent of tweets are generated by only 10 percent of users, and that the median number of tweet readers per tweet is 1 (most Tweeters tweet to one follower). Even more disturbing is that Twittter has a 60 percent churn rate: only 40 percent of users remain more than one month. Obviously, many users lose interest in learning about their friends' break-fast menu, and many feel "too connected" to their "friends," who in fact may only be distant acquaintances, if that. On the other hand, celebrities such as Britney Spears have hundreds of thousands of "friends" who follow their activities, making Twitter a marvelous, free public relations tool. Twitter unfortunately does not make a cent on these activities.

The answer to these questions about unique users, numbers of tweets, and churn rate are critical to understanding the business value of Twitter as a firm. To date, Twitter has generated losses and has unknown revenues, but in February 2009, it raised a $35 million in a deal that valued the company at $255 million. The following September, Twitter announced it had raised $100 million in additional funding, from private equity firms, previous investors, and mutual fund giant T. Rowe Price, based on a company valuation of a staggering $1 billion!

So how can Twitter make money from its users, and their tweets? What's their business model and how might it evolve over time? Twitter's main asset is user attention and audience size (eyeballs per day). An equally important asset is the database of tweets that contains real-time, spontaneous comments, observations, and opinions of the audience, and the search engine that mines those tweets for patterns.

Yet another asset has emerged in the last year: Twitter is a powerful alternative media platform for the distribution of news, videos, and pictures. Once again, no one predicted that Twitter would be the first to report on terrorist attacks in Mumbai, the landing of a passenger jet in the Hudson River, or the Iranian rebellion in June 2009.

How can these assets be monetized? Twitter could ask users to pay a subscription fee, especially for premium services such as videos and music downloads. However, it may be too late for this idea because users have come to expect the service to be free. Twitter could sell display ads or text ads on its screens, something it is testing in Japan. But social media sites are known to be poor advertising venues with very low response rates, although this could change with better targeting. Twitter could charge advertisers to pay a fee for inserting messages into individual tweets. Message your friend to meet you in Times Square, and the message contains an ad for a nearby restaurant. Twitter could charge service providers such as doctors, dentists, lawyers, and hair salons for providing their customers with unexpected appointment availabilities.

Twitter's most likely steady revenue source might be the intelligence embedded in its database of hundreds of millions of real-time tweets. Major firms such as Starbucks, Amazon, Intuit (makers of QuickBooks and the Mint.com site), and Dell have used Twitter to understand how their customers are reacting to products, services and Web sites, and then making corrections or changes in those services and products.

The company is coy about announcing its business model. In a nod to Apple's iTunes and Amazon's merchant services, Twitter has turned over its messaging capabilities and software platform to others, one of which is CoTweet.com, a company that organizes multiple Twitter exchanges for customers so they can be tracked more easily. Google is selling ad units based around a company's last five tweets (ads are displayed to users who have created or viewed tweets about a company). Twitter is not charging for this service. In the meantime, observers wonder if Twitter is twittering away its assets.

Sources: Alexei Oreskovic, "Twitter Snags $100 Million Investment, New Backers," *Reuters*, September 25, 2009; Claire Cain Miller, "Putting Twitter's World to Use," *The New York Times*, April 14, 2009; Jon Fine, "Twitter Makes a Racket. But Revenues?" *BusinessWeek*, April 9, 2009; Jessica Vascallaro, "Firms Seek Profit in Twitter's Chatter," *The Wall Street Journal*, March 26, 2009; Taylor Buley, "Twitter's Analytical Business Plan," *Forbes*, February 15, 2009; Ben Kunz, "The Trouble With Twitter," *BusinessWeek*, August 18, 2008.

CASE STUDY QUESTIONS

1. Based on your reading in this chapter, how would you characterize Twitter's business model?

2. If Twitter is to have a revenue model, which of the revenue models described in this chapter would work?

3. What is the most important asset that Twitter has, and how could it monetize this asset?

4. What impact will a high customer churn rate have on Twitter's potential advertising revenue?

MIS IN ACTION

1. Go to Twitter.com and enter a search on your favorite (or least favorite) car. Can you find the company's official site? What else do you find? Describe the results and characterize the potential risks and rewards for companies that would like to advertise to Twitter's audience.

2. How would you improve Twitter's Web site to make it more friendly for large advertisers?

3. Teenagers are infrequent users of Twitter because they use their cell phones for texting, and most users are adults 18–34 years of age. Find five users of Twitter and ask them how long they have used the service, are they likely to continue using the service, and how would they feel about banner ads appearing on their Twitter Web screen and phone screens. Are loyal users of Twitter less likely (or more likely) to tolerate advertising on Twitter?

the production and distribution costs in return for the right to expose visitors to ads. Companies will spend an estimated $240 billion on advertising in 2009, and an estimated $24 billion of that amount on online advertising (in the form of a paid message on a Web site, paid search listing, video, widget, game, or other online medium, such as instant messaging). In the last five years, advertisers have increased online spending and cut outlays on traditional channels such as radio, television, and newspapers.

Web sites with the largest viewership or that attract a highly specialized, differentiated viewership and are able to retain user attention ("stickiness") are able to charge higher advertising rates. Yahoo, for instance, derives nearly all its revenue from display ads (banner ads) and to a lesser extent search engine text ads. Ninety-eight percent of Google's revenue derives from selling keywords to advertisers in an auction-like market (the AdSense program).

Sales Revenue Model

In the sales revenue model, companies derive revenue by selling goods, information, or services to customers. Companies such as Amazon.com (which sells books, music, and other products), LLBean.com, and Gap.com, all have sales revenue models. Content providers make money by charging for downloads of entire files such as music tracks (iTunes Store) or books or for downloading music and/or video streams (Hulu.com TV shows–see Chapter 3). Apple has pioneered and strengthened the acceptance of micropayments. **Micropayment systems** provide content providers with a cost-effective method for processing high volumes of very small monetary transactions (anywhere from $.25 to $5.00 per transaction). MyMISLab has a Learning Track with more detail on micropayment and other e-commerce payment systems.

Subscription Revenue Model

In the subscription revenue model, a Web site offering content or services charges a subscription fee for access to some or all of its offerings on an ongoing basis. Content providers often use this revenue model. For instance, the online version of *Consumer Reports* provides access to premium content, such as detailed ratings, reviews, and recommendations, only to subscribers, who have a choice of paying a $5.95 monthly subscription fee or a $26.00 annual fee. The *Wall Street Journal* has the largest online subscription newspaper with more than 1 million online subscribers. To be successful, the subscription model requires that the content be perceived as a having high added value, differentiated, and not readily available elsewhere nor easily replicated. Companies successfully offering content or services online on a subscription basis include Match.com and eHarmony (dating services), Ancestry.com and Genealogy.com (genealogy research), Microsoft's Xboxlive.com (video games), and Rhapsody.com (music).

Free/Fremium Revenue Model

In the **free/fremium** revenue model, firms offer basic services or content for free, while charging a premium for advanced or special features. For example, Google offers free applications, but charges for premium services. The Flickr photo-sharing service offers free basic services for sharing photos with friends and family, and also sells a $24.95 "premium" package that provides users unlimited storage, high-definition video storage and play back, and freedom from display advertising. The idea is to attract very large audiences with free services, and then to convert some of this audience to pay a subscription for premium services. One problem with this model is converting people from being "free loaders" into paying customers. "Free" can be a powerful model for losing money.

Transaction Fee Revenue Model

In the **transaction fee revenue model**, a company receives a fee for enabling or executing a transaction. For example, eBay provides an online auction marketplace and receives a small transaction fee from a seller if the seller is successful in selling an item. E*Trade, an online stockbroker, receives transaction fees each time it executes a stock transaction on behalf of a customer. The transaction revenue model enjoys wide acceptance in part because the true cost of using the platform is not immediately apparent to the user.

Affiliate Revenue Model

In the **affiliate revenue model**, Web sites (called "affiliate Web sites) send visitors to other Web sites in return for a referral fee or percentage of the revenue from any resulting sales. For example, MyPoints makes money by connecting companies to potential customers by offering special deals to its members. When members take advantage of an offer and make a purchase, they earn "points" they can redeem for free products and services, and MyPoints receives a referral fee. Community feedback sites such as Epinions receive much of their revenue from steering potential customers to Web sites where they make a purchase. Amazon uses affiliates who steer business to the Amazon Web site by placing the Amazon logo on their blogs. Personal blogs may be involved in affiliate marketing. Some bloggers are paid directly by manufacturers, or receive free products, for speaking highly of products and providing links to sales channels.

WEB 2.0, SOCIAL NETWORKING AND THE WISDOM OF CROWDS

One of the fastest growing areas of e-commerce revenues are Web 2.0 online services, which we described in Chapter 6. The most popular Web 2.0 service is social networking, online meeting places where people can meet their friends and their friends' friends. Every month over 80 million Internet users in the United States visit a social networking site like Facebook, MySpace, LinkedIn, and hundreds of others.

Social networking sites link people through their mutual business or personal connections, enabling them to mine their friends (and their friends' friends) for sales leads, job-hunting tips, or new friends. MySpace, Facebook, and Friendster appeal to people who are primarily interested in extending their friendships, while LinkedIn focuses on job networking for professionals.

Social networking sites and online communities offer new possibilities for e-commerce. Networking sites like Facebook and MySpace sell banner, video, and text ads; sell user preference information to marketers; and sell products such as music, videos, and e-books. Corporations set up their own Facebook and MySpace profiles to interact with potential customers. For example, Procter & Gamble set up a MySpace profile page for Crest toothpaste soliciting "friends" for a fictional character called "Miss Irresistable." Business firms can also "listen" to what social networkers are saying about their products, and obtain valuable feedback from consumers. At user-generated content sites like YouTube, high-quality video content is used to display advertising, and Hollywood studios have set up their own channels to market their products. The chapter-ending case study provides a detailed discussion of social networking on Facebook.

At **social shopping** sites like Kaboodle, ThisNext, and Stylehive you can swap shopping ideas with friends. Facebook offers this same service on a voluntary basis. Online communities are also ideal venues to employ viral marketing techniques. Online viral marketing is like traditional word-of-mouth marketing except that the word can spread across an online community at the speed of light, and go much further geographically than a small network of friends.

The Wisdom of Crowds

Creating sites where thousands, even millions, of people can interact offers business firms new ways to market and advertise, to discover who likes (or hates) their products. In a phenomenon called "**the wisdom of crowds,**" some argue that large numbers of people can make better decisions about a wide range of topics or products than a single person or even a small committee of experts (James Surowiecki, 2004).

Obviously this is not always the case, but it can happen in interesting ways. In marketing, the "wisdom of crowds" concept suggests that firms should consult with thousands of their customers first as a way of establishing a relationship with them, and second, to better understand how their products and services are used and appreciated (or rejected). Actively soliciting the comments of your customers builds trust and sends the message to your customers that you care what they are thinking, and that you need their advice.

Beyond merely soliciting advice, firms can be actively helped in solving some business problems using what is called **crowdsourcing**. For instance, in 2006, Netflix announced a contest in which it offered to pay $1 million to the person or team who comes up with a method for improving by 10 pecent Netflix's prediction of what movies customers would like as measured against their actual choices. By 2009, Netflix received 44,014 entries from 5,169 teams in 186 countries. The winning team improved a key part of Netflix's business: a recommender system that recommends to its customers what new movies to order based on their personal past movie choices and the choices of millions of other customers who are like them (Howe, 2008).

Firms can also use the wisdom of crowds in the form of **prediction markets**. Prediction markets are established as peer-to-peer betting markets where participants make bets on specific outcomes of, say, quarterly sales of a new product, designs for new products, or political elections. The world's largest commercial prediction market is Betfair, founded in 2000, where you bet for or against specific outcomes on football games, horse races, and whether or not the Dow Jones will go up or down in a single day. Iowa Electronic Markets (IEM) is an academic market focused on elections. You can place bets on the outcome of local and national elections.

E-COMMERCE MARKETING

While e-commerce and the Internet have changed entire industries and enable new business models, no industry has been more affected than marketing and marketing communications. The Internet provides marketers with new ways of identifying and communicating with millions of potential customers at costs far lower than traditional media, including search engine marketing, data mining, recommender systems, and targeted e-mail. The Internet enables **long tail marketing**. Before the Internet, reaching a large audience was very expensive, and marketers had to focus on attracting the largest number of consumers with popular hit products, whether music, Hollywood movies, books, or cars. In contrast, the Internet allows marketers to inexpensively find potential customers for which demand is very low, people on the far ends of the bell (normal) curve. For instance, the Internet makes it possible to sell independent music profitably to very small audiences. There's always some demand for almost any product. Put a string of such long tail sales together and you have a profitable business.

The Internet also provides new ways—often instantaneous and spontaneous—to gather information from customers, adjust product offerings, and increase customer value. Table 9.6 describes the leading marketing and advertising formats used in e-commerce.

Many e-commerce marketing firms use behavioral targeting techniques to increase the effectiveness of banner, rich media, and video ads. **Behavioral targeting** refers to tracking the click-streams (history of clicking behavior) of individuals on thousands of Web sites for the purpose of understanding their interests and intentions, and exposing them to advertisements which are uniquely suited to their behavior. Ultimately, this more precise understanding of the customer leads to more efficient marketing (the firm pays for ads only to those shoppers who are most interested in their products) and larger sales and revenues. Unfortunately, behavioral targeting of millions of Web users also leads to the invasion of personal privacy without user consent (see our discussion in Chapter 12).

Behavioral targeting takes place at two levels: at individual Web sites and on various advertising networks that track users across thousands of Web sites. All Web sites collect data on visitor browser activity and store it in a database. They have tools to record the site that users visited prior to coming to the Web site, where these users go when they leave that site, the type of operating system they use, browser information, and even some location data. They also record the specific pages visited on the particular site, the time spent on each page of the site, the types of pages visited, and what the visitors purchased (see Figure 9-3). Firms analyze this information about customer interests and behavior to develop precise profiles of existing and potential customers.

This information enables firms to understand how well their Web site is working, create unique personalized Web pages that display content or ads for products or services of special interest to each user, improve the customer's experience, and create additional value through a better understanding of the shopper (see Figure 9-4). By using personalization technology to modify the Web pages presented to each customer, marketers achieve some of the benefits of using individual salespeople at dramatically lower costs. For instance, General Motors will show a Chevrolet banner ad to women emphasizing safety and utility, while men will receive different ads emphasizing power and ruggedness.

What if you are a large national advertising company with many different clients trying to reach millions of consumers? What if you were a large global manufacturer trying to reach potential consumers for your products? With millions of Web sites, working with each one would be impractical. Advertising networks solve this problem by creating a network of several thousand of the most popular Web sites visited by millions of people, tracking the behavior of these users across the entire network, building profiles of each user, and then selling these profiles to advertisers. Looking for young, single consumers, with college degrees, living in the Northeast, in the 18–34 age range who are interested purchasing a

TABLE 9.6

Online Marketing and Advertising Formats Revenue (Billions)

Marketing Format	2009 Revenue	Description
Search engine	$11.95	Text ads targeted at precisely what the customer is looking for at the moment of shopping and purchasing. Sales oriented.
Display ads	$4.65	Banner ads (pop-ups and leave-behinds) with interactive features; increasingly behaviorally targeted to individual Web activity. Brand development and sales.
Classified	$2.67	Job, real estate, and services ads; interactive, rich media, and personalized to user searches. Sales and branding.
Affiliate and blog marketing	$1.76	Blog and Web site marketing steers customers to parent sites; interactive, personal, and often with video. Sales orientation.
Rich media	$1.69	Animations, games, and puzzles. Interactive, targeted, and entertaining. Branding orientation.
Video	$1.05	Fastest growing format, engaging and entertaining; behaviorally targeted, interactive. Branding and sales.
E-mail	$.39	Effective, targeted marketing tool with interactive and rich media potential. Sales oriented.
Sponsorships	$.32	Online games, puzzle, contests, and coupon sites sponsored by firms to promote products. Sales orientation.

The shopper clicks on the home page. The store can tell that the shopper arrived from the Yahoo! portal at 2:30 PM (which might help determine staffing for customer service centers) and how long she lingered on the home page (which might indicate trouble navigating the site).

The shopper clicks on blouses, clicks to select a woman's white blouse, then clicks to view the same item in pink. The shopper clicks to select this item in a size 10 in pink and clicks to place it in her shopping cart. This information can help the store determine which sizes and colors are most popular.

From the shopping cart page, the shopper clicks to close the browser to leave the Web site without purchasing the blouse. This action could indicate the shopper changed her mind or that she had a problem with the Web site's checkout and payment process. Such behavior might signal that the Web site was not well designed.

Figure 9-3
Web Site Visitor Tracking
E-commerce Web sites have tools to track a shopper's every step through an online store. Close examination of customer behavior at a Web site selling women's clothing shows what the store might learn at each step and what actions it could take to increase sales.

European car? Not a problem. Advertising networks can identify and deliver hundreds of hundreds of thousands of people who fit this profile to expose to ads for European cars as they move from one Web site to another. Estimates vary, but behaviorally targeted ads are ten times more likely to produce a consumer response than a randomly chosen banner or video ad (see Figure 9-5).

Figure 9-4
Web Site
Personalization
Firms can create unique personalized Web pages that display content or ads for products or services of special interest to individual users, improving the customer experience and creating additional value.

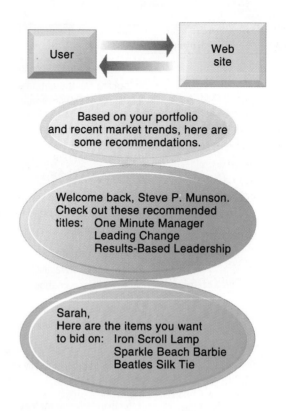

Figure 9-5
How an Advertising Network such as Doubleclick Works
Advertising networks have become controversial among privacy advocates because of their ability to track individual consumers across the Internet. We discuss privacy issues further in Chapter 12.

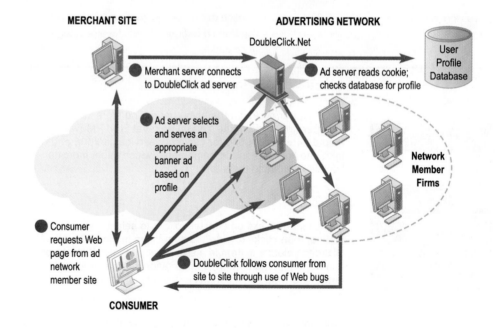

B2B E-COMMERCE: NEW EFFICIENCIES AND RELATIONSHIPS

The trade between business firms (business-to-business commerce or B2B) represents a huge marketplace. The total amount of B2B trade in the United States in 2009 is about $11.5 trillion, with B2B e-commerce (online B2B) contributing about $3.36 trillion of that amount (U.S. Census Bureau, 2009a, b; authors' estimates). By 2013, B2B e-commerce should grow to about $4.75 trillion in the United States, assuming an average growth rate of about 9 percent. The process of conducting trade among business firms is complex and requires significant human intervention, and therefore, it consumes significant resources. Some firms estimate that each corporate purchase order for support products costs them, on average, at least $100 in administrative overhead. Administrative overhead includes processing paper, approving purchase decisions, spending time using the telephone and fax machines to search for products and arrange for purchases, arranging for shipping, and receiving the goods . Across the economy, this adds up to trillions of dollars annually being spent for procurement processes that could potentially be automated. If even just a portion of inter-firm trade were automated, and parts of the entire procurement process assisted by the Internet, then literally trillions of dollars might be released for more productive uses, consumer prices potentially would fall, productivity would increase, and the economic wealth of the nation would expand. This is the promise of B2B e-commerce. The challenge of B2B e-commerce is changing existing patterns and systems of procurement, and designing and implementing new Internet-based B2B solutions.

Business-to-business e-commerce refers to the commercial transactions that occur among business firms. Increasingly these transactions are flowing through a variety of different Internet-enabled mechanisms. About 80 percent of online B2B e-commerce is still based on proprietary systems for **electronic data interchange (EDI)**. Electronic data interchange enables the computer-to-computer exchange between two organizations of standard transactions such as invoices, bills of lading, shipment schedules, or purchase orders. Transactions are automatically transmitted from one information system to another through a network, eliminating the printing and handling of paper at one end and the inputting of data at the other. Each major industry in the United States and much of the rest of the world has EDI standards that define the structure and information fields of electronic documents for that industry.

EDI originally automated the exchange of documents such as purchase orders, invoices, and shipping notices. Although some companies still use EDI for document automation, firms engaged in just-in-time inventory replenishment and continuous production use EDI as a system for continuous replenishment. Suppliers have online access to selected parts of the purchasing firm's production and delivery schedules and automatically ship materials and goods to meet prespecified targets without intervention by firm purchasing agents (see Figure 9-6).

Although many organizations still use private networks for EDI, they are increasingly Web-enabled because Internet technology provides a much more flexible and low-cost platform for linking to other firms. Businesses are able to extend digital technology to a wider range of activities and broaden their circle of trading partners.

Take procurement, for example. **Procurement** involves not only purchasing goods and materials but also sourcing, negotiating with suppliers, paying for goods, and making delivery arrangements. Businesses can now use the Internet to locate the most low-cost supplier, search online catalogs of supplier products, negotiate with suppliers, place orders, make payments, and arrange transportation. They are not limited to partners linked by traditional EDI networks.

The Internet and Web technology enable businesses to create new electronic storefronts for selling to other businesses with multimedia graphic displays and interactive features similar to those for B2C commerce. Alternatively, businesses can use Internet technology to

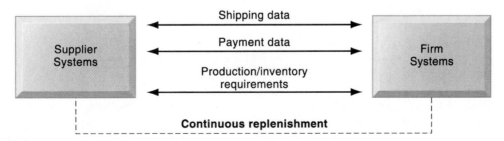

Figure 9-6
Electronic Data Interchange (EDI)
Companies use EDI to automate transactions for B2B e-commerce and continuous inventory replenishment. Suppliers can automatically send data about shipments to purchasing firms. The purchasing firms can use EDI to provide production and inventory requirements and payment data to suppliers.

Figure 9-7
A Private Industrial Network
A private industrial network, also known as a private exchange, links a firm to its suppliers, distributors, and other key business partners for efficient supply-chain management and other collaborative commerce activities.

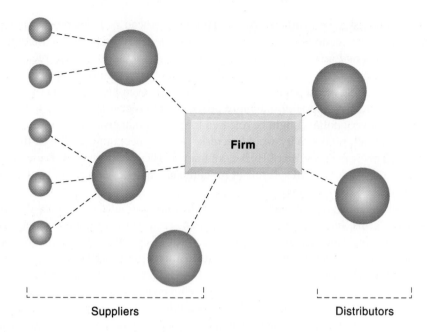

Suppliers   Distributors

create extranets or electronic marketplaces for linking to other businesses for purchase and sale transactions.

Private industrial networks typically consist of a large firm using an extranet to link to its suppliers and other key business partners (see Figure 9-7). The network is owned by the buyer, and it permits the firm and designated suppliers, distributors, and other business partners to share product design and development, marketing, production scheduling, inventory management, and unstructured communication, including graphics and e-mail. Another term for a private industrial network is a **private exchange**.

An example is VW Group Supply, which links the Volkswagen Group and its suppliers. VW Group Supply handles 90 percent of all global purchasing for Volkswagen, including all automotive and parts components.

Net marketplaces, which are sometimes called e-hubs, provide a single, digital marketplace based on Internet technology for many different buyers and sellers (see Figure 9-8). They are industry owned or operate as independent intermediaries between buyers and sellers. Net marketplaces generate revenue from purchase and sale transac-

Figure 9-8
A Net Marketplace
Net marketplaces are online marketplaces where multiple buyers can purchase from multiple sellers.

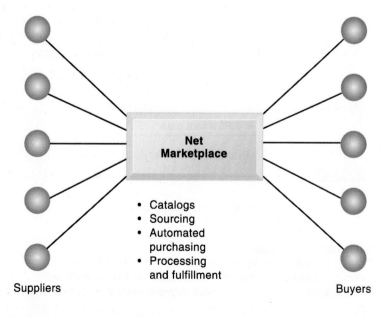

Suppliers   Buyers

tions and other services provided to clients. Participants in Net marketplaces can establish prices through online negotiations, auctions, or requests for quotations, or they can use fixed prices.

There are many different types of Net marketplaces and ways of classifying them. Some Net marketplaces sell direct goods and some sell indirect goods. *Direct goods* are goods used in a production process, such as sheet steel for auto body production. *Indirect goods* are all other goods not directly involved in the production process, such as office supplies or products for maintenance and repair. Some Net marketplaces support contractual purchasing based on long-term relationships with designated suppliers, and others support short-term spot purchasing, where goods are purchased based on immediate needs, often from many different suppliers.

Some Net marketplaces serve vertical markets for specific industries, such as automobiles, telecommunications, or machine tools, whereas others serve horizontal markets for goods and services that can be found in many different industries, such as office equipment or transportation.

Exostar is an example of an industry-owned Net marketplace, focusing on long-term contract purchasing relationships and on providing common networks and computing platforms for reducing supply chain inefficiencies. This aerospace and defense industry-sponsored Net marketplace was founded jointly by BAE Systems, Boeing, Lockheed Martin, Raytheon, and Rolls-Royce plc to connect these companies to their suppliers and facilitate collaboration. More than 16,000 trading partners in the commercial, military, and government sectors use Exostar's sourcing, e-procurement, and collaboration tools for both direct and indirect goods.

Exchanges are independently owned third-party Net marketplaces that connect thousands of suppliers and buyers for spot purchasing. Many exchanges provide vertical markets for a single industry, such as food, electronics, or industrial equipment, and they primarily deal with direct inputs. For example, Gotopaper enables a spot market for paper, board, and kraft among buyers and sellers in the paper industries from over 75 countries.

Exchanges proliferated during the early years of e-commerce, but many have failed. Suppliers were reluctant to participate because the exchanges encouraged competitive bidding that drove prices down and did not offer any long-term relationships with buyers or services to make lowering prices worthwhile. Many essential direct purchases are not conducted on a spot basis because they require contracts and consideration of issues such as delivery timing, customization, and quality of products.

9.3 The Mobile Digital Platform and Mobile E-commerce

Walk down the street in any major metropolitan area and count how many people are pecking away at their iPhones or BlackBerries. Ride the trains, fly the planes, and you'll see your fellow travelers reading an online newspaper, watching a video on their phone, or reading a novel on their Kindle. In five years, the majority of Internet users in the United States will rely on mobile devices as their primary device for accessing the Internet. M-commerce has taken off.

In 2009, m-commerce represented less than 10 percent of all e-commerce, with about $5 billion in annual revenues generated by selling music, videos, ring tones, applications, movies, television, and location-based services like local restaurant locators and traffic updates. However, m-commerce is the fastest growing form of e-commerce, expanding at a rate of 50 percent or more per year, and is estimated to grow to $27 billion in 2013 (see Figure 9-9). In 2009, there were an estimated 3 billion cell phone subscribers worldwide, with over 600 million in China and 281 million in the United States (eMarketer, 2009).

M-COMMERCE SERVICES AND APPLICATIONS

The main areas of growth in mobile e-commerce are location-based services, about $134 million in revenue in 2009; software application sales at stores such as iTunes (about $3

Figure 9-9
Consolidated
Mobile Commerce
Revenues
Mobile e-commerce is the fastest growing type of B2C e-commerce although it represents only a small part of all e-commerce in 2009.

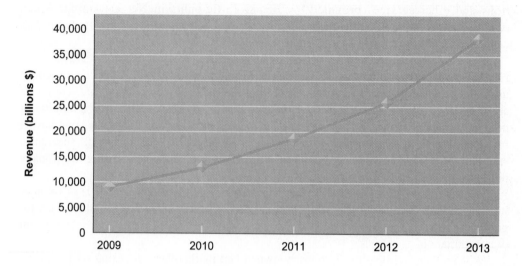

billion); entertainment downloads of ringtones, music, video, and TV shows (about $1 billion); mobile display advertising ($760 million); direct shopping services such as Slifter ($200 million); and e-book sales ($100 million).

M-commerce applications have taken off for services that are time-critical, that appeal to people on the move, or that accomplish a task more efficiently than other methods. They are especially popular in Europe, Japan, South Korea, and other countries with strong wireless broadband infrastructures. The following sections describe some examples.

Location-Based Services

Wikitude.me provides a special kind of browser for smart phones equipped with a built-in global positioning system (GPS) and compass that can identify your precise location and where the phone is pointed. Using information from over 800,000 points of interest available on Wikipedia, plus thousands of other local sites, the browser overlays information about points of interest you are viewing, and displays that information on your smartphone screen, superimposed on a map or photograph that you just snapped. For example, users can point their smart phone cameras towards mountains from a tour bus and see the names and heights of the mountains displayed on the screen. Lost in a European medieval city, or downtown Los Angeles? Open up the Wikitude browser, point your camera at a building, and then find the address and other interesting details. Wikitude.me also allows users to geo-tag the world around them, and then submit the tags to Wikitude in order to share content with other users.

Banking and Financial Services

Banks and credit card companies are rolling out services that let customers manage their accounts from their mobile devices. JPMorgan Chase and Bank of America customers can use their cell phones to check account balances, transfer funds, and pay bills.

Wireless Advertising

Although the mobile advertising market is currently small ($760 million), it is rapidly growing (up 17 percent from last year and expected to grow to over $3.3 billion by 2013), as more and more companies seek ways to exploit new databases of location-specific information. For example, in May 2009, Alcatel-Lucent announced a new service to be managed by 1020 Placecast that will identify cell phone users within a specified distance of an advertiser's nearest outlet and notify them about the outlet's address and phone number, perhaps including a link to a coupon or other promotion. 1020 Placecast's clients include Hyatt, FedEx, and Avis Rent A Car.

Burger King and Suburu have recently run trial campaigns using Useful Networks' Store Finder application that allowed users to click a mobile banner ad to find the nearest store location. The trial showed that the location-enabled campaign significantly increased Store Finder conversion rates compared to users who had to manually enter zip codes to find locations.

Loopt is a free social networking application that allows you to share your status and track the location of friends via smartphones such as the iPhone, BlackBerry, and over 100 other mobile devices. Loopt has more than 1 million users. Loopt doesn't sell information to advertisers, but does post ads based on user location. Loopt's target is to deal with advertisers at the walking level (within 200 to 250 meters).

Yahoo! displays ads on its mobile home page for companies such as Pepsi, Procter & Gamble, Hilton, Nissan, and Intel. Google is displaying ads linked to cell phone searches by users of the mobile version of its search engine, while Microsoft offers banner and text advertising on its MSN Mobile portal in the United States. Ads are starting to be embedded in downloadable applications such as games and videos.

Games and Entertainment

Cell phones are quickly turning into portable entertainment platforms. Mobile phone services offer downloadable digital games, music, and ringtones. More and more handset models combine the features of a cell phone and a portable music player.

Users of broadband services from the major wireless vendors can download on-demand video clips, news clips, and weather reports. MobiTV, offered by Sprint and AT&T Wireless, features live TV programs, including MSNBC and Fox Sports. Film companies are starting to produce short films explicitly designed to play on mobile phones. User-generated content is also appearing in mobile form. Facebook, MySpace, YouTube, and other social networking sites have versions for mobile devices.

9.4 Building an E-commerce Web Site

Building a successful e-commerce site requires a keen understanding of business, technology, and social issues, as well as a systematic approach. A complete treatment of the topic is beyond the scope of this text, and students should consult books devoted to just this topic (Laudon and Traver, 2010). The two most important management challenges in building a successful e-commerce site are (1) developing a clear understanding of your business objectives and (2) knowing how to choose the right technology to achieve those objectives.

PIECES OF THE SITE-BUILDING PUZZLE

Let's assume you are a manager for a medium-sized, industrial parts firm of around 10,000 employees worldwide, operating in eight countries in Europe, Asia, and North America. Senior management has given you a budget of $1 million to build an e-commerce site within one year. The purpose of this site will be to sell and service the firm's 20,000 customers, who are mostly small machine and metal fabricating shops around the world. Where do you start?

First, you must be aware of the main areas where you will need to make decisions On the organizational and human resources fronts, you will have to bring together a team of individuals who possess the skill sets needed to build and manage a successful e-commerce site. This team will make the key decisions about technology, site design, and the social and information policies that will be applied at your site. The entire site development effort must be closely managed if you hope to avoid the disasters that have occurred at some firms.

You will also need to make decisions about your site's hardware, software, and telecommunications infrastructure. The demands of your customers should drive your choices of technology. Your customers will want technology that enables them to find what they want easily, view the product, purchase the product, and then receive the product from your warehouses quickly. You will also have to carefully consider your site's design. Once you have identified the key decision areas, you will need to think about a plan for the project.

BUSINESS OBJECTIVES, SYSTEM FUNCTIONALITY, AND INFORMATION REQUIREMENTS

Planning needs to answer the question, "What do we want the e-commerce site to do for our business?" The key lesson to be learned here is to let the business decisions drive the technology, not the reverse. This will ensure that your technology platform is aligned with your business. We will assume here that you have identified a business strategy and chosen a business model to achieve your strategic objectives. (Review Chapter 3.) But how do you translate your strategies, business models, and ideas into a working e-commerce site?

Your planning should identify the specific business objectives for your site, and then develop a list of system functionalities and information requirements. Business objectives are simply capabilities you want your site to have. System functionalities are types of information systems capabilities you will need to achieve your business objectives. The information requirements for a system are the information elements that the system must produce in order to achieve the business objectives.

Table 9.7 describes some basic business objectives, system functionalities, and information requirements for a typical e-commerce site. The objectives must be translated into a description of system functionalities and ultimately into a set of precise information requirements. The specific information requirements for a system typically are defined in much greater detail than Table 9.7 indicates (see Chapter 11). The business objectives of an e-commerce site are similar to those of a physical retail store, but they must be provided entirely in digital form, twenty-four hours a day, seven days a week.

TABLE 9.7

System Analysis: Business Objectives, System Functionality, and Information Requirements for a Typical E-commerce Site

Business Objective	System Functionality	Information Requirements
Display goods	Digital catalog	Dynamic text and graphics catalog
Provide product information (content)	Product database	Product description, stocking numbers, inventory levels
Personalize/customize product	Customer on-site tracking	Site log for every customer visit; data mining capability to identify common customer paths and appropriate responses
Execute a transaction payment	Shopping cart/payment system	Secure credit card clearing; multiple options
Accumulate customer information	Customer database	Name, address, phone, and e-mail for all customers; online customer registration
Provide after-sale customer support	Sales database	Customer ID, product, date, payment, shipment date
Coordinate marketing/advertising	Ad server, e-mail server, e-mail, campaign manager, ad banner manager	Site behavior log of prospects and customers linked to e-mail and banner ad campaigns
Understand marketing effectiveness	Site tracking and reporting system	Number of unique visitors, pages visited, products purchased, identified by marketing campaign
Provide production and supplier links	Inventory management system	Product and inventory levels, supplier ID and contact, order quantity data by product

BUILDING THE WEB SITE: IN-HOUSE VERSUS OUTSOURCING

There are many choices for building and maintaining Web sites. Much depends on how much money you are willing to spend. Choices range from outsourcing the entire Web site development to an external vendor to building everything yourself (in-house). You also have a second decision to make: will you host (operate) the site on your firm's own servers or will you outsource the hosting to a Web host provider? There are some vendors who will design, build, and host your site, while others will either build or host (but not both). Figure 9-10 illustrates the alternatives.

The Building Decision

If you elect to build your own site, there are a range of options. Unless you are fairly skilled, you should use a pre-built template to create the Web site. For example, Yahoo Merchant Solutions, Amazon Stores, and eBay all provide templates that merely require you to input text, graphics, and other data, as well as the infrastructure to run the Web site once it has been created. This is the least costly and simplest solution but you will be limited to the "look and feel" and functionality provided by the template and infrastructure.

If you have some experience with computers, you might decide to build the site yourself. There is a broad variety of tools, ranging from those that help you build everything truly "from scratch," such as Adobe Dreamweaver, Adobe InDesign, and Microsoft Expression, to top-of-the-line prepackaged site-building tools that can create sophisticated sites customized to your needs.

The decision to build a Web site on your own has a number of risks. Given the complexity of features such as shopping carts, credit card authentication and processing, inventory management, and order processing, development costs are high, as are the risks of doing a poor job. You will be reinventing what other specialized firms have already built, and your staff may face a long, difficult learning curve, delaying your entry to market. Your efforts could fail. On the positive side, you may able to build a site that does exactly what you want, and develop the in-house knowledge to revise the site rapidly if necessitated by a changing business environment.

If you choose more expensive site-building packages, you will be purchasing state-of-the art software that is well tested. You could get to market sooner. However, to make a sound decision, you will have to evaluate many different software packages and this can take a long time. You may have to modify the packages to fit your business needs and perhaps hire additional outside consultants to do the modifications. Costs rise rapidly as modifications mount. (We discuss this problem in greater detail in Chapter 11.) A $4,000 package can easily become a $40,000 to $60,000 development project.

In the past, bricks-and-mortar retailers typically designed their e-commerce sites themselves (because they already had the skilled staff and IT infrastructure in place to do this). Today, however, larger retailers rely heavily on external vendors to provide sophisticated Web site capabilities, while also maintaining a substantial internal staff. Medium-size start-ups will often purchase a sophisticated package and then modify it to suit their needs. Very small mom-and-pop firms seeking simple storefronts will use templates.

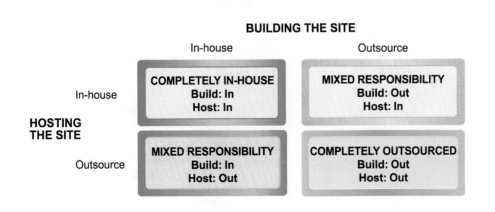

BUILDING THE SITE

	In-house	Outsource
In-house	**COMPLETELY IN-HOUSE** Build: In Host: In	**MIXED RESPONSIBILITY** Build: Out Host: In
HOSTING THE SITE		
Outsource	**MIXED RESPONSIBILITY** Build: In Host: Out	**COMPLETELY OUTSOURCED** Build: Out Host: Out

Figure 9-10
Choices in Building and Hosting Web Sites
You have a number of alternatives to consider when building and hosting an e-commerce site.

The Hosting Decision

Now let's look at the hosting decision. Most businesses choose to outsource hosting and pay a company to host their Web site, which means that the hosting company is responsible for ensuring the site is "live" or accessible, twenty-four hours a day. By agreeing to a monthly fee, the business need not concern itself with technical aspects of setting up and maintaining a Web server, telecommunications links, or specialized staffing.

With a **co-location** agreement, your firm purchases or leases a Web server (and has total control over its operation) but locates the server in a vendor's physical facility. The vendor maintains the facility, communications lines, and the machinery. In this case, you do not purchase the server, but rent its capabilities on a monthly basis. There is an extraordinary range of prices for co-hosting, ranging from $4.95 a month, to several hundred thousands of dollars per month depending on the size of the Web site, bandwidth, storage, and support requirements. Very large providers (such as IBM and Qwest) achieve large economies of scale by establishing huge "server farms" located strategically around the country and the globe. What this means is that the cost of pure hosting has fallen as fast as the fall in server prices, dropping about 50 percent every year.

Web Site Budgets

Simple Web sites can be built and hosted with a first-year cost of $5,000 or less. The Web sites of large firms with high levels of interactivity and linkage to corporate systems can cost several hundred thousand to millions of dollars a year to create and operate. For instance, in September 2006, Bluefly, which sells women's and men's designer clothes online, embarked on the process of developing an improved version of its Web site based on software from Art Technology Group (ATG). It launched the new site in August 2008. To date, it has invested over $5.3 million in connection with the redevelopment of the Web site (Bluefly, Inc., 2009).

Figure 9-11 provides some idea of the relative size of various Web site cost components. In general, the cost of hardware, software, and telecommunications for building and operating a Web site has fallen dramatically (by over 50 percent) since 2000, making it possible for very small entrepreneurs to create fairly sophisticated sites. At the same time, the costs of system maintenance and content creation have risen to make up more than half of typical Web site budgets. Providing content and smooth 24/7 operations are both very labor-intensive.

9.5 Hands-On MIS Projects

The projects in this section give you hands-on experience developing e-commerce strategies for businesses, using spreadsheet software to research the profitability of an e-commerce company, and using Web tools to research and evaluate e-commerce hosting services.

Figure 9-11
Components of a
Web Site Budget

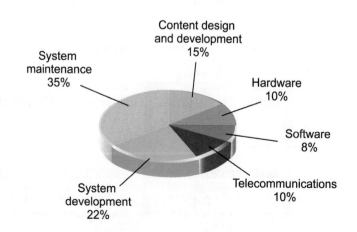

MANAGEMENT DECISION PROBLEMS

1. Columbiana is a small, independent island in the Caribbean. It wants to develop its tourist industry and attract more visitors. The island has many historical buildings, forts, and other sites, along with rain forests and striking mountains. A few first-class hotels and several dozen less-expensive accommodations can be found along its beautiful white sand beaches. The major airlines have regular flights to Columbiana, as do several small airlines. Columbiana's government wants to increase tourism and develop new markets for the country's tropical agricultural products. How can a Web presence help? What Internet business model would be appropriate? What functions should the Web site perform?

2. Explore the Web sites of the following companies: Blue Nile, J.Crew, Circuit City, Black&Decker, Peet's Coffee & Tea, and Priceline. Determine which of these Web sites would benefit most from adding a company-sponsored blog to the Web site. List the business benefits of the blog. Specify the intended audience for the blog. Decide who in the company should author the blog, and select some topics for the blog.

IMPROVING DECISION MAKING: USING SPREADSHEET SOFTWARE TO ANALYZE A DOT-COM BUSINESS

Software skills: Spreadsheet downloading, formatting, and formulas
Business skills: Financial statement analysis

Publicly traded companies, including those specializing in e-commerce, are required to file financial data with the U.S. Securities and Exchange Commission. By analyzing this information, you can determine the profitability of an e-commerce company and the viability of its business model.

Pick one e-commerce company on the Internet, for example, Ashford, Buy.com, Yahoo, or Priceline. Study the Web pages that describe the company and explain its purpose and structure. Use the Web to find articles that comment on the company. Then visit the Securities and Exchange Commission's Web site at www.sec.gov and select Filings & Forms to access the company's 10-K (annual report) form showing income statements and balance sheets. Select only the sections of the 10-K form containing the desired portions of financial statements that you need to examine, and download them into your spreadsheet. (MyMISLab provides more detailed instructions on how to download this 10-K data into a spreadsheet.) Create simplified spreadsheets of the company's balance sheets and income statements for the past three years.

- Is the company a dot-com success, borderline business, or failure? What information dictates the basis of your decision? Why? When answering these questions, pay special attention to the company's three-year trends in revenues, costs of sales, gross margins, operating expenses, and net margins.
- Prepare an overhead presentation (with a minimum of five slides), including appropriate spreadsheets or charts, and present your work to your professor and classmates.

ACHIEVING OPERATIONAL EXCELLENCE: EVALUATING E-COMMERCE HOSTING SERVICES

Software skills: Web browser software
Business skills: Evaluating e-commerce hosting services

This project will help develop your Internet skills in commercial services for hosting an e-commerce site for a small start-up company.

You would like to set up a Web site to sell towels, linens, pottery, and tableware from Portugal and are examining services for hosting small business Internet storefronts. Your Web site should be able to take secure credit card payments and to calculate shipping costs and taxes. Initially, you would like to display photos and descriptions of 40 different products. Visit Yahoo! Small Business, GoDaddy, and Volusion and compare the range of e-commerce hosting services they offer to small businesses, their capabilities, and costs. Also examine the tools they provide for creating an e-commerce site. Compare these services and decide which you would use if you were actually establishing a Web store. Write a brief report indicating your choice and explaining the strengths and weaknesses of each.

LEARNING TRACKS

The following Learning Tracks provide content relevant to topics covered in this chapter:

1. Building a Web page
2. E-commerce Challenges: The Story of Online Groceries
3. Build an E-commerce Business Plan
4. Hot New Careers in E-commerce

Review Summary

1 **What are the unique features of e-commerce, digital markets, and digital goods?** E-commerce involves digitally enabled commercial transactions between and among organizations and individuals. Unique features of e-commerce technology include ubiquity, global reach, universal technology standards, richness, interactivity, information density, capabilities for personalization and customization, and social technology.

Digital markets are said to be more "transparent" than traditional markets, with reduced information asymmetry, search costs, transaction costs, and menu costs, along with the ability to change prices dynamically based on market conditions. Digital goods, such as music, video, software, and books, can be delivered over a digital network. Once a digital product has been produced, the cost of delivering that product digitally is extremely low.

2 **What are the principal e-commerce business and revenue models?** The principal e-commerce business models are e-tailers, transaction brokers, market creators, content providers, community providers, service providers, and portals. The principal e-commerce revenue models are advertising, sales, subscription, free/freemium, transaction fee, and affiliate.

3 **How has e-commerce transformed marketing?** The Internet provides marketers with new ways of identifying and communicating with millions of potential customers at costs far lower than traditional media. Crowdsourcing utilizing the "wisdom of crowds" helps companies learn from customers in order to improve product offerings and increase customer value. Behavioral targeting techniques increase the effectiveness of banner, rich media, and video ads.

4 **How has e-commerce affected business-to-business transactions?** B2B e-commerce generates efficiencies by enabling companies to locate suppliers, solicit bids, place orders, and track shipments in transit electronically. Net marketplaces provide a single, digital marketplace for many buyers and sellers. Private industrial networks link a firm with its suppliers and other strategic business partners to develop highly efficient and responsive supply chains.

5 **What is the role of m-commerce in business, and what are the most important m-commerce applications?** M-commerce is especially well-suited for location-based applications, such as finding local hotels and restaurants, monitoring local traffic and weather, and providing personalized location-based marketing. Mobile phones and handhelds are being used for mobile bill payment, banking, securities trading, transportation schedule updates, and downloads of digital content, such as music, games, and video clips. M-commerce requires wireless portals and special digital payment systems that can handle micropayments.

6 **What issues must be addressed when building an e-commerce Web site?** Building a successful e-commerce site requires a clear understanding of the business objectives to be achieved by the site and selection of the right technology to achieve those objectives. E-commerce sites can be built and hosted in-house or partially or fully outsourced to external service providers.

Key Terms

Affiliate revenue model, 320

Behavioral marketing, 322

Business-to-business (B2B) electronic commerce, 315

Business-to-consumer (B2C) electronic commerce, 315

Co-location, 332

Community providers, 317

Consumer-to-consumer (C2C) electronic commerce, 315

Cost Transparency, 309

Crowdsourcing, 321

Customization, 309

Digital goods, 313

Disintermediation, 313

Dynamic pricing, 312

Electronic data interchange (EDI), 325

E-tailer, 315

Exchanges, 327

Free/freemium revenue model, 320

Information asymmetry, 310

Information density, 309

Intellectual property, 316

Long tail marketing, 322

Market creator, 317

Market entry costs, 309

Marketspace, 306

Menu costs, 310

Micropayment systems, 320

Mobile commerce (m-commerce), 315

Net marketplaces, 326

Personalization, 309

Podcasting, 316

Prediction market, 321

Price discrimination, 309

Price transparency, 309

Private exchange, 326

Private industrial networks, 326

Procurement, 325

Revenue model, 317

Richness, 309

Search costs, 309

Social shopping, 321

Transaction costs, 308

Transaction fee revenue model, 320

Wisdom of crowds, 321

Review Questions

1. What are the unique features of e-commerce, digital markets, and digital goods?

- Name and describe four business trends and three technology trends shaping e-commerce today.
- List and describe the eight unique features of e-commerce.
- Define a digital market and digital goods and describe their distinguishing features.

2. What are the principal e-commerce business and revenue models?

- Name and describe the principal e-commerce business models.
- Name and describe the e-commerce revenue models.

3. How has e-commerce transformed marketing?

- Explain how social networking and the "wisdom of crowds" help companies improve their marketing.
- Define behavioral targeting and explain how it works at individual Web sites and on advertising networks.

4. How has e-commerce affected business-to-business transactions?

  • Explain how Internet technology supports business-to-business electronic commerce.
  • Define and describe Net marketplaces and explain how they differ from private industrial networks (private exchanges).

5. What is the role of m-commerce in business, and what are the most important m-commerce applications?

  • List and describe important types of m-commerce services and applications.
  • Describe some of the barriers to m-commerce.

6. What issues must be addressed when building an e-commerce Web site?

  • List and describe each of the factors that go into the building of an e-commerce Web site.
  • List and describe four business objectives, four system functionalities, and four information requirements of a typical e-commerce Web site.
  • List and describe each of the options for building and hosting e-commerce Web sites.

Discussion Questions

1. How does the Internet change consumer and supplier relationships?

2. The Internet may not make corporations obsolete, but the corporations will have to change their business models. Do you agree? Why or why not?

Video Cases

Video Cases and Instructional Videos illustrating some of the concepts in this chapter are available. Contact your instructor to access these videos.

Collaboration and Teamwork

Performing a Competitive Analysis of E-commerce Sites

Form a group with three or four of your classmates. Select two businesses that are competitors in the same industry and that use their Web sites for electronic commerce. Visit these Web sites. You might compare, for example, the Web sites for iTunes and Napster, Amazon.com and BarnesandNoble.com, or E*Trade and Scottrade. Prepare an evaluation of each business's Web site in terms of its functions, user friendliness, and ability to support the company's business strategy. Which Web site does a better job? Why? Can you make some recommendations to improve these Web sites? If possible, use Google Sites to post links to Web pages, team communication announcements, and work assignments; to brainstorm; and to work collaboratively on project documents. Try to use Google Docs to develop a presentation of your findings for the class.

BUSINESS PROBLEM-SOLVING CASE

Facebook's Dilemma: Profits (Theirs) versus Privacy (Yours)

Facebook is the largest social networking site in the world and a pioneer of the social networking industry. Founded in 2004 by Mark Zuckerberg, the site had over 300 million worldwide users by the fall of 2009. Facebook allows users to create a profile and join various types of self-contained networks, including college-wide, workplace, and regional networks. The site includes a wide array of tools that allow users to connect and interact with other users, including messaging, groups, photo-sharing, and user-created applications.

Facebook was originally open only to a small handful of colleges, but the site has grown explosively since it opened its doors to all college students and eventually the general public. Facebook is now one of the most recognizable sites on the Web. Compared to its biggest rival, MySpace, Facebook's interface is simple and clean, and tends to attract those looking for a crisp, more structured social networking environment. With MySpace fading from view in the rearview mirror, Twitter has emerged as the most viable future challenger to Facebook's social networking dominance. But the company has taken many steps to fend off Twitter and other competitors as it continues its quest for dominance on the Web, not to mention profitability.

Facebook represents a unique opportunity for advertisers to reach highly targeted audiences based on their demographic information, hobbies, personal preferences, and other narrowly specified criteria in a comfortable and engaging environment. Businesses can place advertisements that are fully integrated into primary features of the site, such as the News Feed, a continually updating list of news stories about members' friends' activities on Facebook. Firms and individuals also can create Facebook pages for viewers to learn more about and interact with them. For example, a restaurant can advertise by having Facebook place items in the News Feeds of its customers indicating that those people ate there recently. Blockbuster had recent rentals and reviews of its movies appearing in similar fashion. Many companies, including eBay, Sony Pictures, *The New York Times*, and Verizon maintain Facebook pages where users can learn more about these companies' products and services.

For advertisers, Facebook represents a gold mine of opportunity because of the information the site has gathered and because of the richness of the social networking environment. The site has amassed a huge audience. It's also an extremely "sticky" site. According to comScore, the typical Facebook user spends an average of 169 minutes per month there, compared to 13 minutes per month at Google News.

Despite these advantages, Facebook's path to profitability has not been smooth. It's a very expensive site to maintain. Users upload more than 2 billion photos and 14 million videos each month and share more than 2 billion pieces of content, such as news stories, photos, and blog posts each week. Maintaining and transmitting such vast amounts of data requires huge expenditures for servers and networking. Facebook's traffic continues to rise at a healthy rate, and the company's sales reached about $265 million in 2008, but the company continues to spend more money than it earns.

Attempts to sell online ads on Facebook and other social networking sites have not been successful. Banner ads sell for as little as 15 cents per 1,000 clicks, compared to $8 per 1,000 clicks on a targeted portal such as Yahoo! Auto because Facebook members largely ignore them. More than 70 percent of Facebook users are outside the United States, and much less likely to make online purchases. Social networkers don't like banner ads interfering with their banter.

The company has also encountered more than its fair share of controversy, mostly concerning its handling and usage of the extensive information it collects from its users. Though users contribute most of their information to Facebook willingly, the privacy and user controls over the information granted to Facebook are the biggest concerns most users have with the site.

To truly capitalize on the massive audience and immersive environment of the site, Facebook needs to innovate and find new ways to grow revenue that do not alienate the very users that the company is depending on to spur its growth. The personal information collected on the site represents a mother lode to advertisers, but one that will remain largely untapped if Facebook users do not feel comfortable enough or have sufficient incentive to share it.

Facebook's dilemma is finding a way to turn a profit and increase revenues using the information its users voluntarily provide without violating privacy (and creating a firestorm of user protests). Thus far, its attempts to do so have not been successful. In fact, Facebook is a prime example of a senior management that just didn't get it when it comes to members' sense of their privacy.

In December 2007, Facebook CEO Mark Zuckerberg announced the Beacon Program, sponsored by over 40 large firms, that would track what Facebook members purchased at their corporate sites, send the information to Facebook, who would then share that information with their friends without asking permission. In a few days, hundreds of thousands of members had organized a fierce resistance to the program. Management then declared that members could opt-out of the program and turn it off completely. Coca-Cola withdrew from sponsorship because it thought the program was an opt-in program only. Other corporate sponsors started pulling out from the program, as member resistance mounted. In 2009, Beacon still exists, but keeps a lower profile. Many open source programs exist on the Internet to block Beacon, and the Firefox Web browser has a Beacon Blocker add-on to prevent corporate sites from sending any information to Facebook.

In a similar gaffe, in February 2009, Facebook sought to change its information retention and collection policy (Terms of Service), granting Facebook nearly unlimited data collection and control over user-generated information forever, without redress. If you were a photographer and shared your photos with your friends on Facebook, you would lose your ownership of the content under the new policy. Management acted without warning, provided no opportunity for public comment, and applied the new policy to personal information that had been collected under the old policy. Over 100,000 people joined various blog sites and privacy groups to protest, based on the belief that their information belonged to them, not Facebook. Within days the firm retreated to the old policy, and set up user forums to discuss the Terms of Service and user attitudes about personal information.

In the meantime, however, millions of people on Facebook continue to use third-party quiz applications (such as "Which Cocktail Best Suits Your Personality?") without realizing the extent to which developers of the quizzes and other applications have access to personal information. Facebook's default privacy settings allow nearly unfettered access to a user's profile information. Only "sensitive information" such as contact information is not available.

Facebook has also come under fire for its handling of the personal information of people who attempt to remove their profiles from the site. Facebook offers users the ability to deactivate their accounts, but the company's servers maintain copies of the information contained in those accounts indefinitely. The company's reasoning for this is that reactivating accounts is far easier if Facebook retains copies of profile content and other personal information. Users that attempted to delete their accounts were met with resistance and often required outside assistance from watchdog groups. One user spent two months attempting to delete his profile unsuccessfully while still receiving updates and messages through the site.

In August 2009, Facebook announced a simplification of its privacy policy in response to a Canadian ruling that the site was unlawfully retaining information from deleted accounts. Facebook will now require third-party application developers to conform to a more rigid set of rules regarding the use of users' information, and will reach out to users to better communicate its simplified privacy options. Users will now easily be able to choose between account deletion and account deactivation.

Currently, one of Facebook's most promising prospects to become profitable involves the development of applications for use on Facebook Platform. Facebook Platform, launched in May 2007, opened up the site to serve as a "platform" for applications that are independently developed by third parties. These applications consist of games, plug-in features for user profiles, and other programs, which are fully integrated with the Facebook site.

Facebook Platform makes Facebook's environment even more engaging, and gives developers unparalleled exposure for their applications. There are currently more than 350,000 applications on the Facebook Platform. A small percentage of these applications have turned into viable businesses. Companies attracting large numbers of users to their applications on Facebook are able to sell goods, services, or advertising. All of these applications earn advertising revenue.

It's currently unclear whether Facebook will generate significant revenue from these applications. Some believe that Facebook applications are "the next big thing" and that traditional advertisers will gravitate towards Facebook to reach highly targeted audiences with their applications. On the flip side, others believe Facebook's own popularity will injure its chances to attract advertisers to its site, claiming that the engaging and immersive environment that draws visitors to the site makes users less likely to click on ads. Skeptics also believe that the current application system, where applications tend to support one another via advertising through other applications without the aid of extensive external advertising, is an unsustainable model over the long term. So far, only 250 Facebook applications have attracted more than 1 million users per month, and 60 percent failed to attract even 100 daily users.

Twitter, one of Facebook's largest rivals, experienced explosive growth in 2009. Eager to maintain its dominance in the marketplace, Facebook wasted no time in making several moves in response. Facebook's purchase of FriendFeed and its rollout of the Facebook Lite variant suggest its desire to offer an alternative to Twitter's pared-down design.

FriendFeed allows users to aggregate all of the content from the social media sites they belong to (Facebook and Twitter included) in one central location. Industry analysts have described FriendFeed's user base as most popular among "uber social geeks," but Facebook is more interested in incorporating the technology behind FriendFeed with their own site.

More specifically, Facebook sees opportunities to harness FriendFeed's aggregation technology to develop a richer, more developed internal search engine. By organizing personal information, status updates, and other Facebook activity into a user friendly format, users will more easily be able to search for anything or anyone they want on Facebook. What's unclear is the extent to which that information will be available outside the "walled garden" of Facebook—for example, to advertisers.

Facebook Lite is a stripped-down, simplified version of the richer Facebook interface. Only the basic features of the site are offered: making comments, viewing photos, and accepting friend requests. Facebook Lite was intended for users in countries without widespread access to broadband Internet connections, and the company hopes that this option will help it continue its growth into emerging Internet marketplaces, but it's probably no coincidence that its design looks much like Twitter's.

Given that Facebook's growth outstripped Twitter's in the month prior to these moves, it looks like the reigning social media champion is poised to retain its edge. But Facebook's goals are even loftier: The site hopes to outstrip Microsoft, Google, and other tech giants as a portal for sharing information seamlessly throughout the globe. The company still has a ways to go before it should be grouped with the other titans of their industry.

In 2007, Microsoft purchased a small stake in Facebook, buying 1.6 percent of the company for $246 million. That investment put Facebook's valuation at approximately $15 billion. Since then, other valuations have been as low as $3.7 billion or as large as $10 billion, representing the uncertainty surrounding Facebook's eventual profitability. The precipitous drop in valuation suggests that investors lack confidence that Facebook will be as profitable as was initially expected. In many ways, users' insistence on privacy has been the major stumbling block.

The initial furor and subsequent acceptance of the News Feed feature shows that Facebook users' stances on their privacy may be subject to change or persuasion, and many users may not even be aware or care about the dissemination of their personal information. Even if they did, the benefits of being a part of Facebook, thanks to its large audience and wealth of features and content, may still outweigh the reservations its users have regarding their privacy. But it appears that enough Facebook users are concerned and aware of their privacy to prevent services as invasive as Beacon's initial incarnation from becoming realities.

Sources: Brad Stone, "Tinker Away, Facebook Says," *The New York Times*, May 3, 2009; Jessica E. Vascellaro, "Facebook Opens Site to Developers of Services." *The Wall Street Journal*, April 27, 2009; Jessi Hempl, "Is Facebook Losing Its Glow?" *Fortune*, April 15, 2009; "How Facebook Is Taking Over Our Lives," *Fortune*, March 2, 2009; Julia Angwin, "Facebook: Can It Be Tamed?" *The Wall Street Journal*, April 21, 2009; Carl Bialik, "Facebook Users-and Research-Need Further Study," *The Wall Street Journal*, April 22, 2009; Brian Stelter, "Facebook's Users Ask Who Owns Information," *The New York Times*, February 17, 2009; Jessica E. Vascellaro, "Facebook Seeks Input from Users on Policies," *The Wall Street Journal*, February 27, 2009 and Facebook's About Face on Data, February 19, 2009; Brad Stone, "Is Facebook Growing Up too Fast?" *The New York Times*, March 29, 2009; www.facebook.com, accessed October 14, 2009; "Facebook Aims to Extend Its Reach Across the Web," *The New York Times*, December 2, 2008; and Jessica E. Vascellaro, "Facebook Pushes New Service," *The Wall Street Journal*, December 5, 2008.

Case Study Questions

1. What concepts in this chapter are illustrated in this case?
2. What is the role of e-commerce and Web 2.0 technologies in Facebook's widespread popularity?
3. Describe the weaknesses of Facebook's privacy policies and features. What people, organization, and technology factors have contributed to those weaknesses?
4. Does Facebook have a viable business model? Explain your answer.
5. If you were responsible for coordinating Facebook's advertising, how would you balance the desire to become increasingly profitable with the need to protect the privacy of your users?

Improving Decision Making and Managing Knowledge

CHAPTER 10

STUDENT LEARNING OBJECTIVES

After completing this chapter, you will be able to answer the following questions:

1. What are the different types of decisions, and how does the decision-making process work?

2. How do information systems help people working individually and in groups make decisions more effectively?

3. What are the business benefits of using intelligent techniques in decision making and knowledge management?

4. What types of systems are used for enterprise-wide knowledge management, and how do they provide value for businesses?

5. What are the major types of knowledge work systems, and how do they provide value for firms?

CHAPTER OUTLINE

P&G MOVES FROM PAPER TO PIXELS FOR KNOWLEDGE MANAGEMENT

Procter & Gamble (P&G) is a global leader in the development of market-leading consumer and healthcare products. With 2009 sales topping $79 billion, P&G has over 300 brands, including Crest, Tide, Folgers coffee, and Pampers. But there's another side to P&G that's less widely known: It is one of the world's great research organizations and holders of global patents. The company's research and development organization includes over 7,500 scientists and 22 research centers in 12 countries. P&G got to the top—and stays on top—by continually creating an ongoing stream of innovative new products. At this company, knowledge sharing is key to success and survival.

P&G's organizational culture explicitly promotes knowledge sharing. It supports numerous communities of practice that link people doing similar work in different business units. Researchers publish monthly reports on their projects. And P&G has undertaken a number of knowledge-sharing initiatives to connect its global knowledge

341

community. An InnovationNet (INet) intranet houses over 5 million research-related documents in digital format that can be accessed from a browser-based portal. MyInet is an enhancement that helps researchers locate experts in the company who are doing related work and keep track of relevant innovations in other areas of the firm. MyInet users are able to specify topics of interest and be notified of any new documents pertaining to those topics.

Even with these leading-edge knowledge management efforts, P&G was still awash in paper documents. For companies developing drugs and over-the-counter medications, regulatory issues, research and development, and potential litigation create an avalanche of documents and files. Researchers, clinicians, quality-control staff, marketing specialists, and other internal P&G staff members and external partners must exchange and share these documents. In the past, storing all those documents meant filling up filing cabinets, producing microfiche, managing indexes, and renting warehouses to store the paperwork. Digging through these paper records to locate a document was a long and laborious process that threatened to slow down the pace of research and development work.

P&G recently rolled out an electronic document management system called eLab Notebook to store such information electronically. The new system uses Adobe LiveCycle software to create a searchable archive of Portable Document Format (PDF) files and a common set of tools that can be used around the globe. After a researcher has collected all the data, the LiveCycle PDF generator creates a PDF document and prompts the person who created the file to add a digital signature. Then LiveCycle Reader Extensions embed usage rights within the document, specifying which people in the company are allowed to access it.

The new system changed work flow. P&G had to train employees who had been accustomed to working with paper to use the eLab application and change the way they worked.

The eLab Notebook program is saving time and money. Researchers no longer have to spend several hours per week archiving paper files from their experiments. Other P&G employees are able to rapidly retrieve large volumes of data required by government regulators, outside partners, or buyers. An initial study showed that productivity increased between 5 and 10 percent.

Sources: "Leading Consumer Goods Manufacturer Streamlined and Enhanced Security of Research and Development Processes with Adobe LiveCycle Solutions," Adobe Systems, 2009; Matt Hamblen, "Finding Star Employees with Bright Ideas, *Computerworld*, September 14, 2009; and Samuel Greengard, "A Document Management Case Study: Procter & Gamble," *Baseline Magazine*, September 2008.

P&G's experience shows how organizational performance can benefit by making organizational knowledge more easily available. Collaborating and communicating with practitioners and experts, facilitating access to knowledge, and using that knowledge to improve business processes and innovate are vital to success and survival.

The chapter-opening diagram calls attention to important points raised by this case and this chapter. Procter & Gamble is highly knowledge-intensive and has an innovation-drive business model. Much of the essential information and knowledge for research and development was not easily accessible because it was stored in many different paper documents. Delays in accessing research and development documents and other vital information created inefficiencies that threatened to impair P&G's business performance. In order to benefit from document management technology, P&G had to make changes in its work flow and train employees in the new system. Because R&D documents are immediately available, the new INet system has made P&G much more efficient.

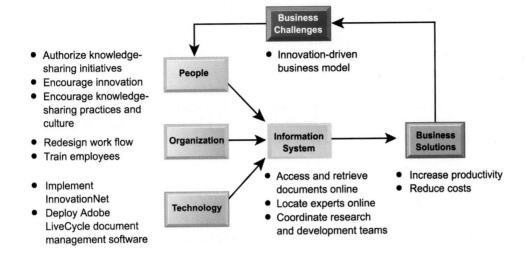

- Authorize knowledge-sharing initiatives
- Encourage innovation
- Encourage knowledge-sharing practices and culture

- Redesign work flow
- Train employees

- Implement InnovationNet
- Deploy Adobe LiveCycle document management software

Business Challenges

- Innovation-driven business model

People

Organization

Technology

Information System

- Access and retrieve documents online
- Locate experts online
- Coordinate research and development teams

Business Solutions

- Increase productivity
- Reduce costs

10.1 Decision Making and Information Systems

One of the main contributions of information systems has been to improve decision making, both for individuals and groups. Decision making in businesses used to be limited to management. Today, lower-level employees are responsible for some of these decisions, as information systems make information available to lower levels of the business. But what do we mean by better decision making? How does decision making take place in businesses and other organizations? Let's take a closer look.

BUSINESS VALUE OF IMPROVED DECISION MAKING

What does it mean to the business to be able to make a better decision? What is the monetary value to the business of better, improved decision making? Table 10.1 attempts to measure the monetary value of improved decision making for a small U.S. manufactur-

TABLE 10.1

Business Value of Enhanced Decision Making

Example Decision Value	Decision Maker	Number of Annual Decisions	Estimated Value to Firm of a Single Improved Decision	Annual
Allocate support to most valuable customers	Accounts manager	12	$100,000	$1,200,000
Predict call center daily demand	Call Center management	4	150,000	600,000
Decide parts inventory levels daily	Inventory manager	365	5,000	1,825,000
Identify competitive bids from major suppliers	Senior management	1	2,000,000	2,000,000
Schedule production to fill orders	Manufacturing manager	150	10,000	1,500,000

ing firm with $280 million in annual revenue and 140 employees. The firm has identified a number of key decisions where new system investments might improve the quality of decision making. The table provides selected estimates of annual value (in the form of cost savings or increased revenue) from improved decision making in selected areas of the business.

We can see from Table 10.1 that decisions are made at all levels of the firm, and that some of these decisions are common, routine, and numerous. Although the value of improving any single decision may be small, improving hundreds of thousands of "small" decisions adds up to a large annual value for the business.

TYPES OF DECISIONS

Chapter 2 showed that there are different levels in an organization. Each of these levels has different information requirements for decision support and responsibility for different types of decisions (see Figure 10-1). Decisions are classified as structured, semistructured, and unstructured.

Unstructured decisions are those in which the decision maker must provide judgment, evaluation, and insight to solve the problem. Each of these decisions is novel, important, and nonroutine, and there is no well-understood or agreed-on procedure for making them.

Structured decisions, by contrast, are repetitive and routine, and they involve a definite procedure for handling them so that they do not have to be treated each time as if they were new. Many decisions have elements of both types of decisions and are **semistructured**, where only part of the problem has a clear-cut answer provided by an accepted procedure. In general, structured decisions are more prevalent at lower organizational levels, whereas unstructured problems are more common at higher levels of the firm.

Senior executives face many unstructured decision situations, such as establishing the firm's five- or ten-year goals or deciding new markets to enter. Answering the question "Should we enter a new market?" would require access to news, government reports, and industry views, as well as high-level summaries of firm performance. However, the answer would also require senior managers to use their own best judgment and poll other managers for their opinions.

Middle management faces more structured decision scenarios, but their decisions may include unstructured components. A typical middle-level management decision might be "Why is the reported order fulfillment showing a decline over the past six months at a distribution center in Minneapolis?" This middle manager could obtain a report from the

**Figure 10-1
Information
Requirements of
Key Decision-
Making Groups
in a Firm**
Senior managers, middle managers, operational managers, and employees have different types of decisions and information requirements.

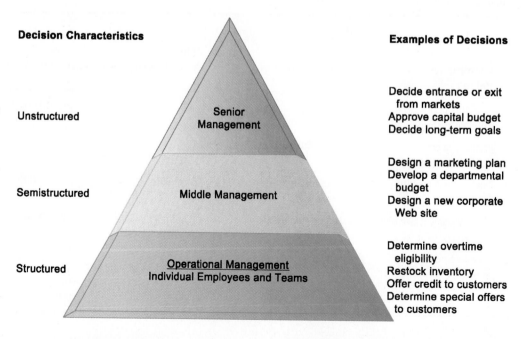

Decision Characteristics

Examples of Decisions

Unstructured — Senior Management

Decide entrance or exit from markets
Approve capital budget
Decide long-term goals

Semistructured — Middle Management

Design a marketing plan
Develop a departmental budget
Design a new corporate Web site

Structured — Operational Management
Individual Employees and Teams

Determine overtime eligibility
Restock inventory
Offer credit to customers
Determine special offers to customers

firm's enterprise system or distribution management system on order activity and operational efficiency at the Minneapolis distribution center. This is the structured part of the decision. But before arriving at an answer, this middle manager will have to interview employees and gather more unstructured information from external sources about local economic conditions or sales trends.

Operational management and rank-and-file employees tend to make more structured decisions. For example, a supervisor on an assembly line has to decide whether an hourly paid worker is entitled to overtime pay. If the employee worked more than eight hours on a particular day, the supervisor would routinely grant overtime pay for any time beyond eight hours that was clocked on that day.

A sales account representative often has to make decisions about extending credit to customers by consulting the firm's customer database that contains credit information. If the customer met the firm's prespecified criteria for granting credit, the account representative would grant that customer credit to make a purchase. In both instances, the decisions are highly structured and are routinely made thousands of times each day in most large firms. The answer has been preprogrammed into the firm's payroll and accounts receivable systems.

THE DECISION-MAKING PROCESS

Making a decision is a multistep process. Simon (1960) described four different stages in decision making: intelligence, design, choice, and implementation (see Figure 10-2). These stages correspond to the four steps in problem-solving used throughout this book.

Intelligence consists of discovering, identifying, and understanding the problems occurring in the organization—why is there a problem, where, and what effects it is having on the firm.

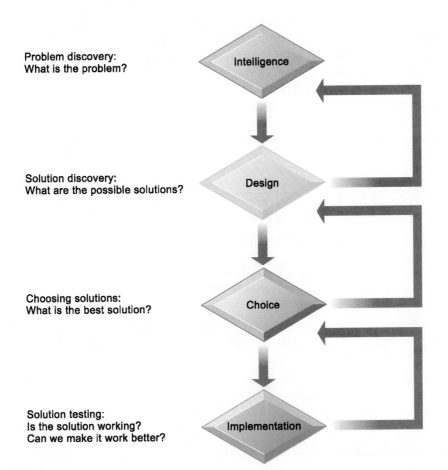

Problem discovery:
What is the problem?

Intelligence

Solution discovery:
What are the possible solutions?

Design

Choosing solutions:
What is the best solution?

Choice

Solution testing:
Is the solution working?
Can we make it work better?

Implementation

Figure 10-2
Stages in Decision Making
The decision-making process can be broken down into four stages.

Design involves identifying and exploring various solutions to the problem.

Choice consists of choosing among solution alternatives.

Implementation involves making the chosen alternative work and continuing to monitor how well the solution is working.

What happens if the solution you have chosen does not work? Figure 10-2 shows that you can return to an earlier stage in the decision-making process and repeat it, if necessary. For instance, in the face of declining sales, a sales management team may decide to pay the sales force a higher commission for making more sales to spur on the sales effort. If this does not produce sales increases, managers would need to investigate whether the problem stems from poor product design, inadequate customer support, or a host of other causes that call for a different solution.

QUALITY OF DECISIONS AND DECISION MAKING

How can you tell if a decision has become "better" or the decision-making process "improved"? Accuracy is one important dimension of quality: In general, we think decisions are "better" if they accurately reflect the real-world data. Speed is another dimension: We tend to think that the decision-making process should be efficient, even speedy. For instance, when you apply for car insurance, you want the decision making by the insurance firm to be fast and accurate. But there are many other dimensions of quality in decisions and the decision-making process to consider. Which is important for you will depend on the business firm where you work, the various parties involved in the decision, and your own personal values. Table 10.2 describes some quality dimensions for decision making. When we describe how systems "improve decisions and the decision-making process" in this chapter, we are referencing the dimensions in this table.

SYSTEMS AND TECHNOLOGIES FOR SUPPORTING DECISIONS

There are four kinds of systems for supporting the different levels and types of decisions we have just described. We introduced these systems in Chapter 2. *Management information systems* (*MIS*) deliver routine reports and summaries of transaction-level data to middle- and operational-level managers to provide answers to structured and semistructured decision problems. *Decision support systems* (*DSS*) provide analytical models or tools for analyzing large quantities of data and supportive interactive queries for middle managers who face semistructured decision situations. *Executive support systems* (*ESS*) are systems that provide senior management, making primarily unstructured decisions, with external information (news, stock analyses, and industry

---

TABLE 10.2

Qualities of Decisions and the Decision-Making Process

Quality Dimension	Description
Accuracy	Decision reflects reality
Comprehensiveness	Decision reflects a full consideration of the facts and circumstances
Fairness	Decision faithfully reflects the concerns and interests of affected parties
Speed (efficiency)	Decision making is efficient with respect to time and other resources, including the time and resources of affected parties, such as customers
Coherence	Decision reflects a rational process that can be explained to others and made understandable
Due process	Decision is the result of a known process and can be appealed to a higher authority

trends) and high-level summaries of firm performance. *Group decision-support systems (GDSS)* are specialized systems that provide a group electronic environment in which managers and teams can collectively make decisions and design solutions for unstructured and semistructured problems.

Decision making is also enhanced by intelligent techniques and knowledge management systems. **Intelligent techniques** consist of expert systems, case-based reasoning, genetic algorithms, neural networks, fuzzy logic, and intelligent agents. These technologies aid decision makers by capturing individual and collective knowledge, discovering patterns and behaviors in very large quantities of data, and generating solutions to problems that are too large and complex for human beings to solve on their own.

Knowledge management systems, which we introduced in Chapter 2, and knowledge work systems provide tools for knowledge discovery, communication, and collaboration that make knowledge more easily available to decision makers and integrate it into the business processes of the firm.

10.2 Systems for Decision Support

Exactly how do these different types of systems for supporting decisions affect a business? What can today's decision-support systems do for a business? Let's look more closely at how each major type of decision-support system works and provides value.

MANAGEMENT INFORMATION SYSTEMS (MIS)

Management information systems, which we introduced in Chapter 2, help managers monitor and control the business by providing information on the firm's performance. They typically produce fixed, regularly scheduled reports based on data extracted and summarized from the firm's underlying transaction processing systems (TPS). The formats for these reports are often specified in advance. A typical MIS report might show a summary of monthly or annual sales for each of the major sales territories of a company. Sometimes, MIS reports are exception reports, highlighting only exceptional conditions, such as when the sales quotas for a specific territory fall below an anticipated level or employees have exceeded their spending limits in a dental care plan.

Traditional MIS produce primarily hard-copy reports. Today, many of these reports are available online through an intranet, and more MIS reports can be generated on demand. Table 10.3 provides some examples of MIS applications.

TABLE 10.3

Examples of MIS Applications

Company	MIS Application
California Pizza Kitchen	Inventory Express application "remembers" each restaurant's ordering patterns and compares the amount of ingredients used per menu item to predefined portion measurements established by management. The system identifies restaurants with out-of-line portions and notifies their managers so that corrective actions can be taken.
PharMark	Extranet MIS identifies patients with drug-use patterns that place them at risk for adverse outcomes.
Black & Veatch	Intranet MIS tracks construction costs for various projects across the United States.
Taco Bell	Total Automation of Company Operations (TACO) system provides information on food, labor, and period-to-date costs for each restaurant.

DECISION-SUPPORT SYSTEMS (DSS)

Whereas MIS primarily address structured problems, DSS support semistructured and unstructured problem analysis. The earliest DSS were heavily model-driven, using some type of model to perform "what-if" and other kinds of analyses. In a what-if analysis, a model is developed, various input factors are changed, and the output changes are measured (see the following section). DSS analysis capabilities were based on a strong theory or model combined with a good user interface that made the system easy to use.

The voyage-estimating DSS described in Chapter 2 and P&G's inventory optimization system described in Chapter 8 are examples of model-driven DSS. Another example is a "media modeling" system developed by Chrysler Corporation to predict how effectively its advertisements translate into sales. The system calculates how much spending on advertisements is required to meet specified sales targets by determining how much Web traffic the company needs to generate to produce that level of sales activity. The model considers the impact on sales of economic factors such as fuel prices and unemployment rates and the types of Web activities that translate into actual auto sales (Steel, 2009).

Some DSS are data-driven, using online analytical processing (OLAP) and data mining to analyze large pools of data in large corporate systems. The business intelligence applications described in Chapter 5 are examples of these data-driven DSS. They support decision making by enabling users to extract valuable information that was previously buried in large quantities of data.

The Interactive Session on People is another example of this type of DSS. It describes school districts' move to quantify and analyze student performance data to make better decisions about how to allocate resources to enhance student and teacher performance. As you read this case, try to identify the problem school districts are facing, what alternative solutions are available, and how well the chosen solution is working.

Components of DSS

Figure 10-3 illustrates the components of a DSS. They include a database of data used for query and analysis; a software system with models, data mining, and other analytical tools; and a user interface.

**Figure 10-3
Overview of a
Decision-Support
System**
*The main components of
the DSS are the DSS
database, the DSS
software system, and the
user interface. The DSS
database may be a small
database residing on a
PC or a large data
warehouse.*

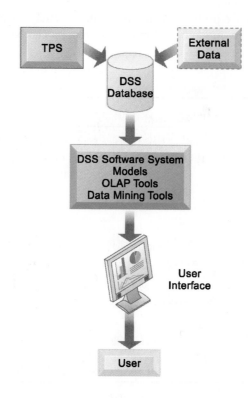

INTERACTIVE SESSION: PEOPLE   Data-Driven Schools

As more and more reports suggest that American schoolchildren are falling behind those from other countries, improving our schools has become an increasingly urgent mission for the nation. Actually achieving that improvement is a difficult task. One approach gaining sway is more intensive use of information systems to measure educational performance at the individual and school district level and identify problem areas requiring additional resources and intervention.

The 139,000-student Montgomery County public school system in Rockville, Maryland, is at the forefront of the push for data-driven DSS in schools. Forty employees at the school district's Office of Shared Accountability generate reports on how many students take algebra in middle school or read below grade level. The district's Edline and M-Stat systems alert principals to individuals with patterns of failing so they can receive extra resources, such as after-school tutoring, study sessions, and special meetings with parents.

Earlier this decade, Montgomery County school superintendent Jerry Weast predicted that the increasing stratification between students in what he called the "green zone" (white and wealthy students) and students in the "red zone" (poor and minority students) would weigh down the school district as a whole. Having exhausted other options, administrators initiated a plan to create a data collection system for test scores, grades, and other data useful for identifying students with problems and speeding up interventions to improve their learning and educational performance.

Principals access and analyze student performance data to help make instructional decisions over the course of the year, as opposed to only when annual standardized test data arrives. This way, teachers can meet the needs of students who require additional instruction or other types of intervention before they fall behind. Test scores, grades, and other data are entered into the system in real time, and can be accessed in real time. In the past, school data were disorganized, and trends in individual student performance as well as overall student body performance were difficult to diagnose.

Kindergarten teachers are now able to monitor their students' success in reading words, noting which words each student struggles with on a Palm handheld device. The device calculates the accuracy with which the student reads each passage and, over time, provides information about what sorts of problems the student consistently encounters. Also, when students begin to deviate from their normal academic patterns, like getting a rash of poor grades, the system sends alerts to parents and school administrators. In many cases, this quicker response is enough to help the student reverse course before failing.

Many parents in Montgomery County have expressed concern that the new systems are an excessive and unnecessary expenditure. In the short term, President Obama's stimulus plan provides increased funding to schools over the next two years. Projects like these are likely to become more popular as it becomes clearer that a data-driven approach yields quantifiable results. But will they become the standard in American schools? The long-term sustainability of these systems is still unclear.

In Montgomery County, one of the primary goals of the implementation of data-driven systems was to close the achievement gap between white and minority students in the lower grades. Teachers and administrators would use different types of information organized by the DSS to identify gifted students earlier and challenge them with a more appropriate course load of more Advanced Placement classes. Data collected on each child would offer teachers insight into what methods worked best for each individual.

The results are very impressive. In Montgomery County, 90 percent of kindergartners were able to read at the level required by standardized testing, with minimal differences among racial and socioeconomic groups. These numbers are up from 52 percent of African-Americans, 42 percent of Latinos, and 44 percent of low-income students just seven years ago. Also, the system has effectively identified students with abilities at an earlier age. The number of African American students who passed at least one AP test at Montgomery has risen from 199 earlier this decade to 1,152 this year; the number of Latino students went from 218 to 1,336.

Some critics claim that the emphasis on closing the achievement gap between different student populations is shortchanging gifted students and those with disabilities. "Green zone" parents question whether their children are receiving enough attention and resources with so much emphasis being placed on the improving the red zone. Green zone districts in Montgomery County receive $13,000 per student, compared with $15,000 in the red zone. Red zone classes have only 15 students in kindergarten and 17 in the first and second grades, compared with 25 and 26 in the green zone. School administrators counter that the system not only provides appropriate help for underperforming students, but also that it provides the additional challenges that are vital to a gifted child's development.

Other evidence suggests that the gains in reducing the achievement gap earlier in childhood erode as children get older. Among eighth graders in Montgomery County, approximately 90 percent of white and Asian eighth graders tested proficient or advanced in math on state tests, compared with only half of African-Americans and Hispanics. African-American and Hispanic SAT scores were over three hundred points below those of whites and Asians. Still, the data-driven implementation has been responsible for some large improvements over past statistics. Some of the red zone schools have seen the most dramatic improvement in test scores and graduation rates.

In many ways, the data-driven systems build from the wealth of standardized testing information created by the No Child Left Behind Act passed during the Bush presidency. Some parents and educators complain about the amount and frequency of standardized testing, suggesting that children should be spending more time on projects and creative tasks. But viable alternative strategies to foster improvement in struggling school districts are difficult to develop.

It's not just students that are subject to this data-driven approach. Montgomery County teachers have been enrolled in a similar program that identifies struggling teachers and supplies data to help them improve. In many cases, contracts and tenure make it difficult to dismiss less effective teachers. To try and solve this problem, teachers unions and administrators have teamed up to develop a peer review program that pairs underperforming teachers with a mentor who provides guidance and support.

After two years, teachers who fail to achieve results appear before a larger panel of teachers and principals that makes a decision regarding their potential termination or extension of another year of peer review. But teachers are rarely terminated in the program—instead, they're given tangible evidence of things they're doing well and things they can improve based on data that's been collected on their day-to-day performance, student achievement rates, and many other metrics.

Not all teachers have embraced the data-driven approach. The Montgomery Education Association, the county's main teachers' union, estimates that keeping a "running record" of student results on reading assessments and other testing adds about three to four hours to teachers' weekly workloads. According to Raymond Myrtle, principal of Highland Elementary in Silver Spring, "this is a lot of hard work. A lot of teachers don't want to do it. For those who don't like it we suggested they do something else." To date, 11 of 33 teachers at Highland have left the district or are teaching at other Montgomery schools.

Sources: John Hechinger, "Data-Driven Schools See Rising Scores," *The Wall Street Journal*, June 12, 2009. Daniel de Vise, "Throwing a Lifeline to Struggling Teachers," *Washington Post*, June 29, 2009; and Daniel de Vise, "The Results, Warts and All, of Data-Driven Problem Solving," *Washington Post*, May 1, 2007.

CASE STUDY QUESTIONS

1. Identify and describe the problem discussed in the case.

2. How do data-driven DSS provide a solution to this problem? What are the inputs and outputs of these systems?

3. What people, organization, and technology issues must be addressed by this solution?

4. How successful is this solution? Explain your answer.

5. Should all school districts use such a data-driven approach to education? Why or why not?

MIS IN ACTION

Explore the Web site of the Montgomery County, Maryland School District and then answer the following questions:

1. Select one of the district's elementary, middle, or high schools and describe the data available on that particular school. What kinds of decisions do these data support? How do these data help school officials improve educational performance?

2. Click the Schools tab, and then click School Survey Results link, select one of the district's schools, and then read the survey results. How do these surveys help decision makers improve educational quality?

The **DSS database** is a collection of current or historical data from a number of applications or groups. It may be a small database residing on a PC that contains a subset of corporate data that has been downloaded and possibly combined with external data. Alternatively, the DSS database may be a massive data warehouse that is continuously updated by major corporate TPS (including enterprise systems and data generated by Web site transactions). The data in DSS databases are generally extracts or copies of production databases so that using the DSS does not interfere with critical operational systems.

The **DSS software system** contains the software tools that are used for data analysis. It may contain various OLAP tools, data mining tools, or a collection of mathematical and analytical models that easily can be made accessible to the DSS user. A **model** is an abstract representation that illustrates the components or relationships of a phenomenon. A model can be a physical model (such as a model airplane), a mathematical model (such as an equation), or a verbal model (such as a description of a procedure for writing an order).

Statistical modeling helps establish relationships, such as relating product sales to differences in age, income, or other factors between communities. Optimization models determine optimal resource allocation to maximize or minimize specified variables, such as cost or time. A classic use of optimization models is to determine the proper mix of products within a given market to maximize profits. P&G uses optimization models to determine how to maximize its return on investment from the organization of its supply chain.

Forecasting models often are used to forecast sales. The user of this type of model might supply a range of historical data to project future conditions and the sales that might result from those conditions. The decision maker could vary those future conditions (entering, for example, a rise in raw materials costs or the entry of a new, low-priced competitor in the market) to determine how new conditions might affect sales.

Sensitivity analysis models ask what-if questions repeatedly to determine the impact on outcomes of changes in one or more factors. *What-if analysis*—working forward from known or assumed conditions—allows the user to vary certain values to test results to better predict outcomes if changes occur in those values. What happens if we raise product price by 5 percent or increase the advertising budget by $100,000? What happens if we keep the price and advertising budgets the same? Spreadsheet software, such as Microsoft Excel, is often used for this purpose (see Figure 10-4). Backward sensitivity analysis software helps decision makers with goal seeking: If I want to sell 1 million product units next year, how much must I reduce the price of the product?

The DSS user interface permits easy interaction between users of the system and the DSS software tools. Many DSS today have Web interfaces to take advantage of graphic displays, interactivity, and ease of use.

Using Spreadsheet Pivot Tables to Support Decision Making

Managers also use spreadsheets to identify and understand patterns in business information. For instance, let's a take a look at one day's worth of transactions at the online firm Online Management Training Inc. (OMT Inc.), which sells online management training videos and

			Variable Cost per Unit			
Total fixed costs	19000					
Variable cost per unit	3					
Average sales price	17					
Contribution margin	14					
Break-even point	1357					
Sales	1357	2	3	4	5	6
Price	14	1583	1727	1900	2111	2375
	15	1462	1583	1727	1900	2111
	16	1357	1462	1583	1727	1900
	17	1267	1357	1462	1583	1727
	18	1188	1267	1357	1462	1583

Figure 10-4
Sensitivity Analysis
This table displays the results of a sensitivity analysis of the effect of changing the sales price of a necktie and the cost per unit on the product's break-even point. It answers the question, "What happens to the break-even point if the sales price and the cost to make each unit increase or decrease?"

books to corporations and individuals who want to improve their management techniques. On a single day, the firm experienced 517 order transactions. Figure 10-5 shows the first 25 records of transactions produced at the firm's Web site on that day. The names of customers and other identifiers have been removed from this list.

You can think of this list as a database composed of transaction records (the rows). The fields (column headings) for each customer record are: customer ID, region of purchase, payment method, source of contact (e-mail versus Web banner ad), amount of purchase, the product purchased (either online training or a book), and time of day (in 24 hour time).

There is a great deal of valuable information in this transaction list that could help managers answer important questions and make important decisions:

- Where do most of our customers come from? The answer might tell managers where to spend more marketing resources or to initiate new marketing efforts.
- Are there regional differences in the sources of our customers? Perhaps in some regions, e-mail is the most effective marketing tool, whereas in other regions, Web banner ads are more effective. The answer to this more complicated question could help managers develop a regional marketing strategy.
- Where are the average purchases higher? The answer might tell managers where to focus marketing and sales resources or to pitch different messages to different regions.
- What form of payment is the most common? The answer could be used to emphasize in advertising the most preferred means of payment.
- Are there any times of day when purchases are most common? Do people buy products while at work (likely during the day) or at home (likely in the evening)?
- Are there regional differences in the average purchase? If one region is much more lucrative, managers could focus their marketing and advertising resources on that region.

Notice that these questions often involve multiple dimensions: region and average purchase, time of day and average purchase, payment type and average purchase, and region, source of customer, and purchase. Also, some of the dimensions are categorical, such as payment type, region, and source. If the list were small, you could simply inspect the list and find patterns in the data. But this is impossible when you have a list of over 500 transactions.

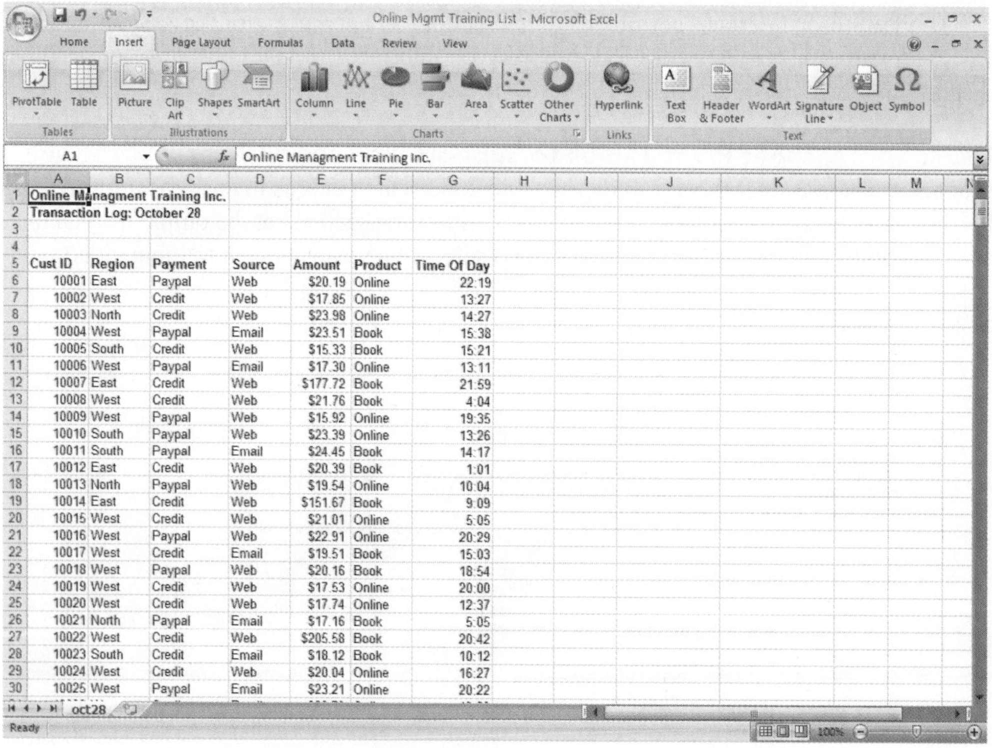

Online Managment Training Inc.

Transaction Log: October 28

Cust ID	Region	Payment	Source	Amount	Product	Time Of Day
10001	East	Paypal	Web	$20.19	Online	22:19
10002	West	Credit	Web	$17.85	Online	13:27
10003	North	Credit	Web	$23.98	Online	14:27
10004	West	Paypal	Email	$23.51	Book	15:38
10005	South	Credit	Web	$15.33	Book	15:21
10006	West	Paypal	Email	$17.30	Online	13:11
10007	East	Credit	Web	$177.72	Book	21:59
10008	West	Credit	Web	$21.76	Book	4:04
10009	West	Paypal	Web	$15.92	Online	19:35
10010	South	Paypal	Web	$23.39	Online	13:26
10011	South	Paypal	Email	$24.45	Book	14:17
10012	East	Credit	Web	$20.39	Book	1:01
10013	North	Paypal	Web	$19.54	Online	10:04
10014	East	Credit	Web	$151.67	Book	9:09
10015	West	Credit	Web	$21.01	Online	5:05
10016	West	Paypal	Web	$22.91	Online	20:29
10017	West	Credit	Email	$19.51	Book	15:03
10018	West	Paypal	Web	$20.16	Book	18:54
10019	West	Credit	Web	$17.53	Online	20:00
10020	West	Credit	Web	$17.74	Online	12:37
10021	North	Paypal	Email	$17.16	Book	5:05
10022	West	Credit	Web	$205.58	Book	20:42
10023	South	Credit	Email	$18.12	Book	10:12
10024	West	Credit	Web	$20.04	Online	16:27
10025	West	Paypal	Email	$23.21	Online	20:22

Figure 10-5 Sample List of Transactions for Online Management Training Inc.
This list shows a portion of the order transactions for Online Management Training Inc. on October 28, 2009.

Fortunately, the spreadsheet pivot table provides a powerful tool for answering such questions using large data sets. A **pivot table** is a table that displays two or more dimensions of data in a convenient format. Microsoft Excel's PivotTable capability makes it easy to analyze lists and databases by automatically extracting, organizing, and summarizing the data.

For instance, let's take the first question, "Where do our customers come from?" We will start with region and ask the question "How many customers come from each region?" To find the answer using Excel 2007, you would create a pivot table by selecting the range of data, fields you want to analyze, and a location for the PivotTable report, as illustrated in Figure 10-6. The pivot table shows most customers come from the Western region.

Does the source of the customer make a difference in addition to region? We have two sources of customers: e-mail campaigns and online banner advertising. In a few seconds, you can find the answer shown in Figure 10-7. The pivot table shows that Web banner advertising produces most of the customers, and this is true of all the regions.

You can use pivot tables to answer all the questions we have posed about the Online Management Training data. The complete Excel file for these examples is available in MyMISLab. The Hands-On MIS section of this chapter asks you to find answers to a number of other questions regarding this data file.

Data Visualization and Geographic Information Systems

Data from information systems can be made easier for users to digest and act on by using graphics, charts, tables, maps, digital images, three-dimensional presentations, animations, and other data visualization technologies. By presenting data in graphical form, **data visualization** tools help users see patterns and relationships in large amounts of data that would be difficult to discern if the data were presented as traditional lists of text.

Geographic information systems (GIS) are a special category of DSS that use data visualization technology to analyze and display data for planning and decision making in the form of digitized maps. The software assembles, stores, manipulates, and displays geographically referenced information, tying data to points, lines, and areas on a map. GIS have modeling capabilities, enabling managers to change data and automatically revise business scenarios.

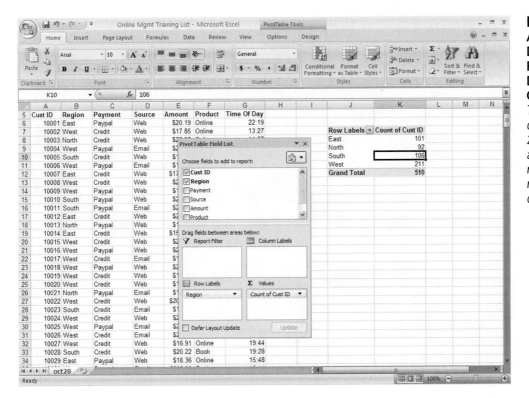

Figure 10-6
A Pivot Table That Determines the Regional Distribution of Customers
This pivot table was created using Excel 2007 to quickly produce a table showing the relationship between region and number of customers.

Figure 10-7
A Pivot Table That Examines Customer Regional Distribution and Advertising Source
In this pivot table, we can examine where customers come from in terms of region and advertising source.
It appears nearly about 70 percent of the customers respond to Web banner ads, and there are some regional variations.

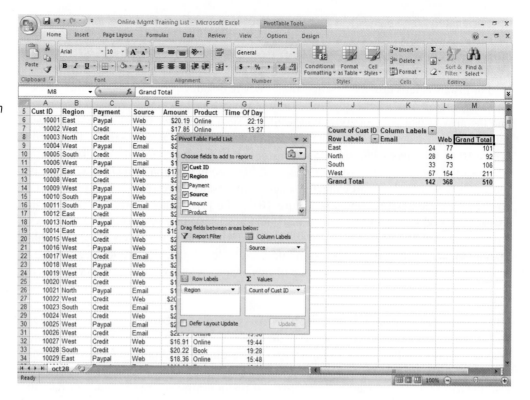

GIS support decisions that require knowledge about the geographic distribution of people or other resources. For example, GIS might be used to help state and local governments calculate emergency response times to natural disasters, to help retail chains identify profitable new store locations, or to help banks identify the best locations for installing new branches or automatic teller machine (ATM) terminals.

Somerset County, New Jersey, developed a GIS based on ESRI software to provide Web access to geospatial data about flood conditions. The system provides information that helps emergency responders and county residents prepare for floods and enables emergency managers to make decisions more quickly.

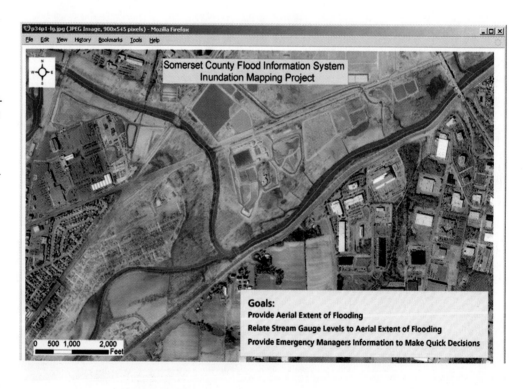

Web-Based Customer Decision-Support Systems

DSS based on the Web and the Internet support decision making by providing online access to various databases and information pools along with software for data analysis. **Customer decision-support systems (CDSS)** support the decision-making process of an existing or potential customer.

People interested in purchasing a product or service can use Internet search engines, intelligent agents, online catalogs, Web directories, newsgroup discussions, e-mail, and other tools to help them locate the information they need to help with their decision. Companies have developed specific customer Web sites where all the information, models, or other analytical tools for evaluating alternatives are concentrated in one location. Web-based DSS have become especially popular in the financial services area because so many people are trying to manage their own assets and retirement savings. For example, the T. Rowe Price Web site offers a series of online tools and planning guides for college planning, retirement planning, investment planning, tax planning, and estate planning.

EXECUTIVE SUPPORT SYSTEMS

If you were a senior executive and you wanted a picture of the overall performance of your firm, where would you find that information? You would turn to an executive support system. Executive support systems (ESS), which we introduced in Chapter 2, help solve unstructured and semistructured problems by focusing on the information needs of senior management. Contemporary ESS bring together data from many different internal and external sources, including data from the Web, often through a portal. These systems provide easy-to-use analytical tools and online displays to help users select, access, and tailor the data as needed.

You can think of ESS as generalized computing, communications, and graphic systems that, similar to a zoom lens, can focus quickly on detailed problems or retract back for a broad view of the company. ESS have a capability to **drill down**, moving from a piece of summary data to lower and lower levels of detail. Some display a high-level view of firm performance in the form of a *digital dashboard*. A digital dashboard displays on a single screen all of the critical measurements for piloting a company, similar to the cockpit of an airplane or an automobile dashboard. The dashboard presents key performance indicators as graphs and charts, providing a one-page overview of all the critical measurements necessary to make key executive decisions.

ESS help senior executives monitor organizational performance, track activities of competitors, identify changing market conditions, spot problems, identify opportunities, and forecast trends. Employees lower down in the corporate hierarchy also use these systems to monitor and measure business performance in their areas of responsibility.

GROUP DECISION-SUPPORT SYSTEMS

The systems we have just described focus primarily on helping you make a decision acting alone. But what if you are part of a team and need to make a decision as a group? You would use a special category of systems called group decision-support systems (GDSS) for this purpose.

A **group decision-support system (GDSS)** is an interactive computer-based system for facilitating the solution of unstructured problems by a set of decision makers working together as a group in the same location or in different locations. Groupware and Web-based tools for videoconferencing and electronic meetings described earlier in this text support some group decision processes, but their focus is primarily on communication. GDSS, however, provide tools and technologies geared explicitly toward group decision making.

GDSS-guided meetings take place in conference rooms with special hardware and software tools to facilitate group decision making. The hardware includes computer and networking equipment, overhead projectors, and display screens. Special electronic meeting software collects, documents, ranks, edits, and stores the ideas offered in a decision-making meeting. The more elaborate GDSS use a professional facilitator and support staff. The facilitator selects the software tools and helps organize and run the meeting.

A sophisticated GDSS provides each attendee with a dedicated desktop computer under that person's individual control. No one will be able to see what individuals do on their computers until those participants are ready to share information. Their input is transmitted over a network to a central server that stores information generated by the meeting and makes it available to all on the meeting network. Data can also be projected on a large screen in the meeting room.

GDSS make it possible to increase meeting size while at the same time increasing productivity because individuals contribute simultaneously rather than one at a time. A GDSS promotes a collaborative atmosphere by guaranteeing contributors' anonymity so that attendees can focus on evaluating the ideas themselves without fear of personally being criticized or of having their ideas rejected based on the contributor. GDSS software tools follow structured methods for organizing and evaluating ideas and for preserving the results of meetings, enabling nonattendees to locate needed information after the meeting. The effectiveness of GDSS depends on the nature of the problem and the group and on how well a meeting is planned and conducted.

10.3 Intelligent Systems for Decision Support

A number of intelligent techniques for enhancing decision making are based on **artificial intelligence (AI)** technology, which consists of computer-based systems (both hardware and software) that attempt to emulate human behavior and thought patterns. These techniques include expert systems, case-based reasoning, fuzzy logic, neural networks, genetic algorithms, and intelligent agents.

EXPERT SYSTEMS

What if employees in your firm had to make decisions that required some special knowledge, such as how to formulate a fast-drying sealing compound or how to diagnose and repair a malfunctioning diesel engine, but all the people with that expertise had left the firm? Expert systems are one type of decision-making aid that could help you out. An **expert system** captures human expertise in a limited domain of knowledge as a set of rules in a software system that can be used by others in the organization. These systems typically perform a limited number of tasks that can be performed by professionals in a few minutes or hours, such as diagnosing a malfunctioning machine or determining whether to grant credit for a loan. They are useful in decision-making situations where expertise is expensive or in short supply.

How Expert Systems Work

Human knowledge must be modeled or represented in a form that a computer can process. Expert systems model human knowledge as a set of rules that collectively are called the **knowledge base**. Expert systems can have from 200 to as many as 10,000 of these rules, depending on the complexity of the decision-making problem. These rules are much more interconnected and nested than in a traditional software program (see Figure 10-8).

The strategy used to search through the collection of rules and formulate conclusions is called the **inference engine**. The inference engine works by searching through the rules and "firing" those rules that are triggered by facts gathered and entered by the user.

Expert systems provide businesses with an array of benefits, including improved decisions, reduced errors, reduced costs, reduced training time, and improved quality and service. For example, Con-Way Transportation built an expert system called Line-haul to automate and optimize planning of overnight shipment routes for its nationwide

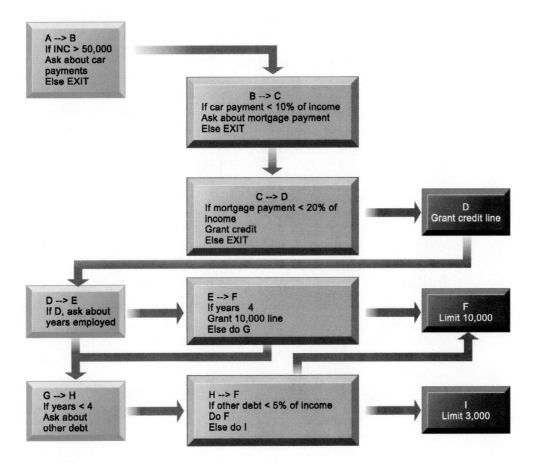

Figure 10-8
Rules in an Expert System
An expert system contains a set of rules to be followed when used. The rules are interconnected, the number of outcomes is known in advance and is limited, there are multiple paths to the same outcome, and the system can consider multiple rules at a single time. The rules illustrated are for a simple credit-granting expert system.

freight-trucking business. The expert system captures the business rules that dispatchers follow when assigning drivers, trucks, and trailers to transport 50,000 shipments of heavy freight each night across 25 U.S. states and Canada and when plotting their routes. Line-haul runs on a Sun platform and uses data on daily customer shipment requests, available drivers, trucks, trailer space, and weight stored in an Oracle database. The expert system uses thousands of rules and 100,000 lines of program code written in C++ to crunch the numbers and create optimum routing plans for 95 percent of daily freight shipments. Con-Way dispatchers tweak the routing plan provided by the expert system and relay final routing specifications to field personnel responsible for packing the trailers for their nighttime runs. Con-Way recouped its $3 million investment in the system within two years by reducing the number of drivers, packing more freight per trailer, and reducing damage from rehandling. The system also reduces dispatchers' arduous nightly tasks.

Although expert systems lack the robust and general intelligence of human beings, they can provide benefits to organizations if their limitations are well understood. Only certain classes of problems can be solved using expert systems. Virtually all successful expert systems deal with problems of classification in which there are relatively few alternative outcomes and in which these possible outcomes are all known in advance. Expert systems are much less useful for dealing with unstructured problems typically encountered by managers.

CASE-BASED REASONING

Expert systems primarily capture the knowledge of individual experts, but organizations also have collective knowledge and expertise that they have built up over the years. This organizational knowledge can be captured and stored using case-based reasoning. In **case-based reasoning (CBR)**, knowledge and past experiences of human specialists are represented as cases and stored in a database for later retrieval when the user encounters a new case with similar parameters. The system searches for stored cases with problem characteristics similar to the new one, finds the closest fit, and applies the solutions of the old case to the new case. Successful solutions are tagged to the new case and both are stored together with the other cases in the knowledge base. Unsuccessful solutions also are appended to the case database along with explanations as to why the solutions did not work (see Figure 10-9).

You'll find case-based reasoning in diagnostic systems in medicine or customer support where users can retrieve past cases whose characteristics are similar to the new case. The system suggests a solution or diagnosis based on the best-matching retrieved case.

FUZZY LOGIC SYSTEMS

Most people do not think in terms of traditional IF-THEN rules or precise numbers. Humans tend to categorize things imprecisely, using rules for making decisions that may have many shades of meaning. For example, a man or a woman may be *strong* or *intelligent*. A company may be *large, medium*, or *small* in size. Temperature may be *hot, cold, cool*, or *warm*. These categories represent a range of values.

Fuzzy logic is a rule-based technology that represents such imprecision by creating rules that use approximate or subjective values. It describes a particular phenomenon or

Figure 10-9
How Case-Based Reasoning Works
Case-based reasoning represents knowledge as a database of past cases and their solutions. The system uses a six-step process to generate solutions to new problems encountered by the user.

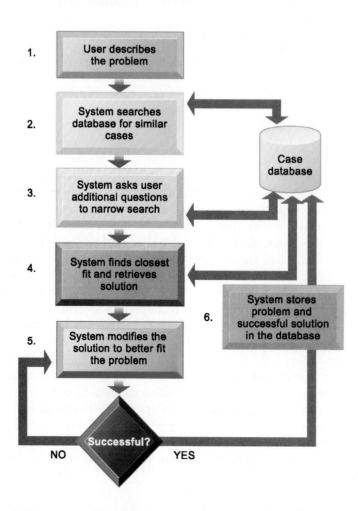

process linguistically and then represents that description in a small number of flexible rules.

Let's look at the way fuzzy logic would represent various temperatures in a computer application to control room temperature automatically. The terms (known as *membership functions*) are imprecisely defined so that, for example, in Figure 10-10, cool is between 45 degrees and 70 degrees, although the temperature is most clearly cool between about 60 degrees and 67 degrees. Note that *cool* is overlapped by *cold* or *norm*. To control the room environment using this logic, the programmer would develop similarly imprecise definitions for humidity and other factors, such as outdoor wind and temperature. The rules might include one that says, "If the temperature is *cool* or *cold* and the humidity is low while the outdoor wind is high and the outdoor temperature is low, raise the heat and humidity in the room." The computer would combine the membership function readings in a weighted manner and, using all the rules, raise and lower the temperature and humidity.

Fuzzy logic provides solutions to problems requiring expertise that is difficult to represent in the form of crisp IF-THEN rules. In Japan, Sendai's subway system uses fuzzy logic controls to accelerate so smoothly that standing passengers need not hold on. Fuzzy logic allows incremental changes in inputs to produce smooth changes in outputs instead of discontinuous ones, making it useful for consumer electronics and engineering applications.

NEURAL NETWORKS

Neural networks are used for solving complex, poorly understood problems for which large amounts of data have been collected. They find patterns and relationships in massive amounts of data that would be too complicated and difficult for a human being to analyze. Neural networks discover this knowledge by using hardware and software that parallel the processing patterns of the biological or human brain. Neural networks "learn" patterns from large quantities of data by sifting through data, searching for relationships, building models, and correcting over and over again the model's own mistakes.

A neural network has a large number of sensing and processing nodes that continuously interact with each other. Figure 10-11 represents one type of neural network comprising an input layer, a hidden processing layer, and an output layer. Humans "train" the network by feeding it a set of training data for which the inputs produce a known set of outputs or

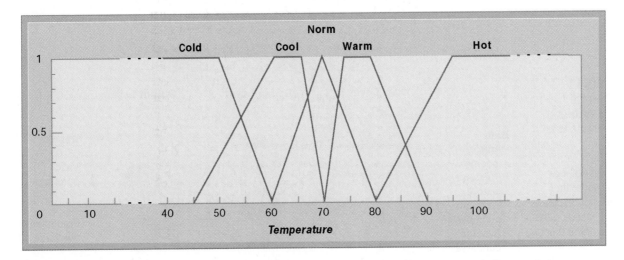

Figure 10-10
Fuzzy Logic for Temperature Control
The membership functions for the input called "temperature" are in the logic of the thermostat to control the room temperature. Membership functions help translate linguistic expressions, such as warm, into numbers that the computer can manipulate.

conclusions. This helps the computer learn the correct solution by example. As the computer is fed more data, each case is compared with the known outcome. If it differs, a correction is calculated and applied to the nodes in the hidden processing layer. These steps are repeated until a condition, such as corrections being less than a certain amount, is reached. The neural network in Figure 10-11 has learned how to identify a fraudulent credit card purchase. Also, self-organizing neural networks can be trained by exposing them to large amounts of data and allowing them to discover the patterns and relationships in the data.

Whereas expert systems seek to emulate or model a human expert's way of solving problems, neural network builders claim that they do not program solutions and do not aim to solve specific problems. Instead, neural network designers seek to put intelligence into the hardware in the form of a generalized capability to learn. In contrast, the expert system is highly specific to a given problem and cannot be retrained easily.

Neural network applications in medicine, science, and business address problems in pattern classification, prediction, financial analysis, and control and optimization. In medicine, neural network applications are used for screening patients for coronary artery disease, for diagnosing patients with epilepsy and Alzheimer's disease, and for performing pattern recognition of pathology images. The financial industry uses neural networks to discern patterns in vast pools of data that might help investment firms predict the performance of equities, corporate bond ratings, or corporate bankruptcies. Visa International uses a neural network to help detect credit card fraud by monitoring all Visa transactions for sudden changes in the buying patterns of cardholders.

There are many puzzling aspects of neural networks. Unlike expert systems, which typically provide explanations for their solutions, neural networks cannot always explain why they arrived at a particular solution. They may not perform well if their training covers too little or too much data. In most current applications, neural networks are best used as aids to human decision makers instead of substitutes for them.

The Interactive Session on Technology describes other applications that have benefited from pattern recognition technology. In this case, the applications are based on **machine learning**, a related AI technology focusing on algorithms and techniques allowing computers to "learn" by extracting information using computation and statistical methods. Inductive machine learning methods extract rules and patterns out of massive data sets. Both neural networks and machine learning techniques are used in data mining.

GENETIC ALGORITHMS

Genetic algorithms are useful for finding the optimal solution for a specific problem by examining a very large number of alternative solutions for that problem. They are based on

Figure 10-11
How a Neural Network Works
A neural network uses rules it "learns" from patterns in data to construct a hidden layer of logic. The hidden layer then processes inputs, classifying them based on the experience of the model. In this example, the neural network has been trained to distinguish between valid and fraudulent credit card purchases.

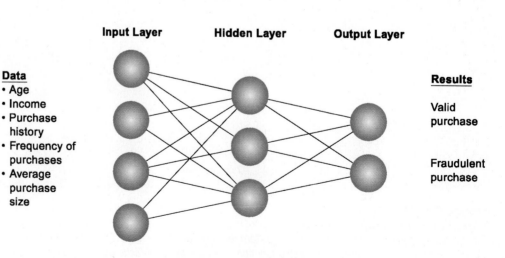

INTERACTIVE SESSION: TECHNOLOGY   Reality Mining

Deciding where to eat when you're going out to dinner with friends can sometimes be a tricky process. You might not know where to go or which restaurant other people like you tend to enjoy most. Imagine selecting your destination based on a "heat map" on your iPhone displaying where people like you and your friends were eating, showing larger crowds as brighter spots on the map. Sense Networks, Inc., based in New York City and founded in 2003 by Gregory Skibiski, Sandy Pentland, and Tony Jebara, is hoping to make that vision a reality. The company specializes in "location-based mobile networking" products, and its founding team consists of computer scientists from Columbia and MIT.

Sense Networks's goal is to harness location-based data from cell phone users tracked by global positioning systems (GPSs), cell phone towers, or local Wi-Fi networks to create a variety of consumer and business products. Because the volume of data captured by these technologies is so enormous, it has been challenging to extract any meaningful information. Sense Networks is attempting to make sense of these data using complex algorithms, and to use the result to reveal economic trends, optimal location for offices and new stores, better ways to advertise, and more.

Tracking GPS information gives insight into people's routines and allows Sense to develop probabilities for where people will go. A requirement for this type of analysis is a very large set of data to analyze over a multi-year span. Jebara claims that his statistical models are accurate, but require a large volume of data over a sufficiently long time period. In order to acquire a sufficient amount of location data to begin with, Sense initially acquired information from taxicab companies, which use GPS in their cars to track their drivers' location, and other publicly available information like weather information.

Sense has two ongoing projects aimed at different audiences: Macrosense and Citysense. Macrosense is an application aimed at the enterprise, offering businesses valuable information about their customers and aiding in important location-based decision making. Citysense is a consumer application intended for the individual, offering similar types of information to help with smaller-scale decisions.

Macrosense applies complex statistical algorithms to make sense of massive sets of location-based data and make predictions or recommendations based on the data. The software could let businesses know where their customers go after leaving their store, as well as where their competitors' customers go. It would track any notable trends in people's habits over time; how far customers will travel to reach your store or your competitors' store; which places in a city are "influence points" where people stop and diverge, as opposed to which places are simply points en-route; or where to locate a store and what places in other cities most resemble that location.

Macrosense employs powerful machine learning algorithms that process time-stamped location data and metadata streams from a variety of sources, including GPS, Wi-Fi positioning, cell tower triangulation, RFID, and other sensors. According to the Sense Web site, these algorithms process 487,500 dimensions to each location in a city, "identifying a unique and complex 'DNA' that describes it completely." These are based on movement to and from the location and where people go after leaving a location. After the initial location data have been processed, Macrosense's MVE (minimum-value embedding) algorithm summarizes high-volume data compactly for analysis.

Citysense, another Sense product in development, is a software package that uses location data to show where people are going and maps their activity. It will not only answer "where is everyone right now" but "where is everyone like me right now." Subscribers who download the software to their mobile phones agree to be tracked and placed into a "tribe" of people with similar interests and behaviors. The software learns its user's patterns over time and suggests destinations or displays where people with similar patterns are going. The service does not ask for personal information. It is currently being alpha tested in San Francisco.

If Sense's products are successful and give individuals and businesses accurate location-based information, Sense has a chance to capitalize on a market that is currently untapped. Macrosense and Citysense are likely to generate prolific demand from businesses and individuals looking to achieve a deeper understanding of their environments. For example, Kinetic, the outdoor advertising unit of the WPP advertising firm, learned from Citysense data that one "tribe" frequented bars in San Francisco's Marina district where a certain beer promotion did well. Kinetic encouraged the beer company to extend the promotion to other bars in the city that attracted like-minded people.

However, privacy questions remain: cellular phone companies are not allowed to share customers' location data without their consent, and these technologies may expose cell phone companies to liability without their actually having done anything wrong. It's not clear whether the benefits of Citysense are significant enough for individuals to relinquish their privacy and allow themselves to be tracked. Citysense has tried to address this issue by providing buttons to "delete any data acquired in the last 24 hours" and to "delete all historical data." After these deletions are made, personalized services will no longer operate, but Citysense wants users to have this choice.

Sense Networks is also trying to have its products contribute toward the public good. Its charitable foundation is working with mobile operator Vodafone, the

Centers for Disease Control (CDC) and other organizations to build an early-warning system for modeling and predicting the spread of tuberculosis in South Africa.

Sources: Stephen Baker, "Mapping a New Mobile Internet," *Business Week*, February 26, 2009; "Sensors and Sensitivity," *The Economist*, June 4, 2009; and Michael Fitzgerald, "Predicting Where You'll Go and What You'll Like," *The New York Times*, June 22, 2008.

CASE STUDY QUESTIONS

1. Why might businesses be interested in location-based mobile networking?

2. What technological developments have set the stage for the growth of Sense Networks and the success of their products?

3. Do you feel that the privacy risks surrounding Citysense are significant? Would you sign up to use Sense Networks services? Why or why not?

MIS IN ACTION

Explore the Sense Networks Web site and then answer the following question:

1. Give examples of three different businesses that might benefit from this technology and explain why they would benefit.

2. Give examples of three decisions that could be made by these businesses using information from Sense Networks applications.

techniques inspired by evolutionary biology, such as inheritance, mutation, selection, and crossover (recombination).

A genetic algorithm works by representing a solution as a string of 0s and 1s. The genetic algorithm searches a population of randomly generated strings of binary digits to identify the right string representing the best possible solution for the problem. As solutions alter and combine, the worst ones are discarded and the better ones survive to go on to produce even better solutions.

In Figure 10-12, each string corresponds to one of the variables in the problem. One applies a test for fitness, ranking the strings in the population according to their level of desirability as possible solutions. After the initial population is evaluated for fitness, the algorithm then produces the next generation of strings, consisting of strings that survived the fitness test plus offspring strings produced from mating pairs of strings, and tests their fitness. The process continues until a solution is reached.

Genetic algorithms are used to solve complex problems that are very dynamic and complex, involving hundreds or thousands of variables or formulas. The problem must be one where the range of possible solutions can be represented genetically and criteria can be established for evaluating fitness. Genetic algorithms expedite the solution because they can evaluate many solution alternatives quickly to find the best one. For example, General Electric engineers used genetic algorithms to help optimize the design for jet turbine aircraft engines, where each design change required changes in up to 100 variables. The supply chain management software from i2 Technologies uses genetic algorithms to optimize production-scheduling models, incorporating hundreds of thousands of details about customer orders, material and resource availability, manufacturing and distribution capability, and delivery dates.

INTELLIGENT AGENTS

Intelligent agent technology helps businesses and decision makers navigate through large amounts of data to locate and act on information that is considered important. **Intelligent agents** are software programs that work in the background without direct

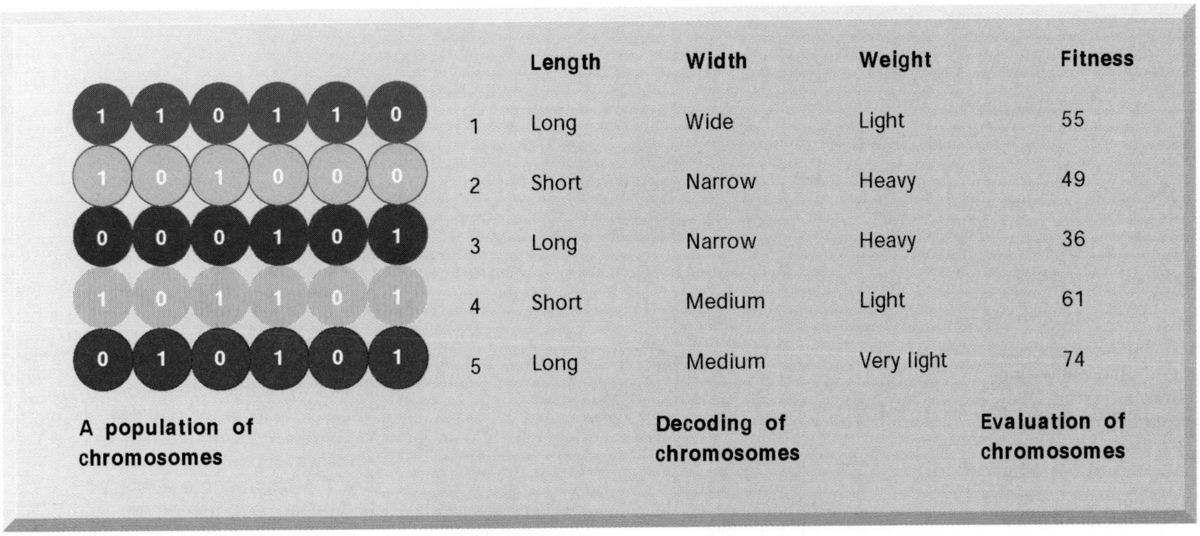

		Length	Width	Weight	Fitness
1 1 0 1 1 0	1	Long	Wide	Light	55
1 0 1 0 0 0	2	Short	Narrow	Heavy	49
0 0 0 1 0 1	3	Long	Narrow	Heavy	36
1 0 1 1 0 1	4	Short	Medium	Light	61
0 1 0 1 0 1	5	Long	Medium	Very light	74

A population of chromosomes	Decoding of chromosomes	Evaluation of chromosomes

Figure 10-12
The Components of a Genetic Algorithm
This example illustrates an initial population of "chromosomes," each representing a different solution. The genetic algorithm uses an iterative process to refine the initial solutions so that the better ones, those with the higher fitness, are more likely to emerge as the best solution.

human intervention to carry out specific, repetitive, and predictable tasks for an individual user, business process, or software application. The agent uses a limited built-in or learned knowledge base to accomplish tasks or make decisions on the user's behalf, such as deleting junk e-mail, scheduling appointments, or finding the cheapest airfare to California.

There are many intelligent agent applications today in operating systems, application software, e-mail systems, mobile computing software, and network tools. Of special interest to business are intelligent agents that search for information on the Internet. Chapter 6 describes how shopping bots help consumers find products they want and assists them in comparing prices and other features.

Procter & Gamble (P&G) used intelligent agent technology to make its supply chain more efficient (see Figure 10-13). It modeled a complex supply chain as a group of semiautonomous "agents" representing individual supply-chain components, such as trucks, production facilities, distributors, and retail stores. The behavior of each agent is programmed to follow rules that mimic actual behavior, such as "order an item when it is out of stock." Simulations using the agents enable the company to perform what-if analyses on inventory levels, in-store stockouts, and transportation costs.

Using intelligent agent models, P&G discovered that trucks should often be dispatched before being fully loaded. Although transportation costs would be higher using partially loaded trucks, the simulation showed that retail store stockouts would occur less often, thus reducing the amount of lost sales, which would more than make up for the higher distribution costs. Agent-based modeling has saved P&G $300 million annually on an investment of less than 1 percent of that amount.

10.4 Systems for Managing Knowledge

Systems for knowledge management improve the quality and utilization of knowledge used in the decision-making process. **Knowledge management** refers to the set of business processes developed in an organization to create, store, transfer, and apply knowl-

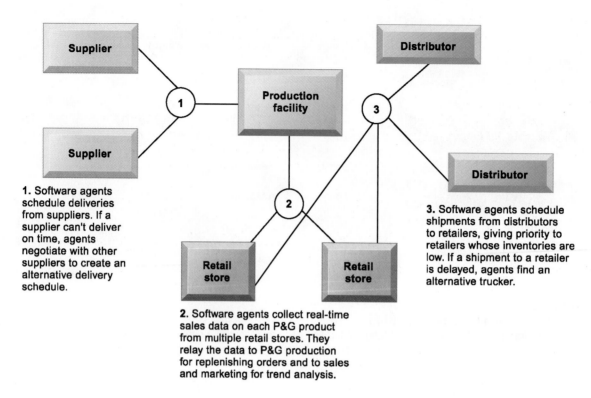

Figure 10-13
Intelligent Agents in P&G's Supply Chain Network
Intelligent agents are helping Procter & Gamble shorten the replenishment cycles for products, such as a box of Tide.

edge. Knowledge management increases the ability of the organization to learn from its environment and to incorporate knowledge into its business processes and decision making.

Knowledge that is not shared and applied to the problems facing firms and managers does not add any value to the business. Knowing how to do things effectively and efficiently in ways that other organizations cannot duplicate is a major source of profit and competitive advantage. Why? Because the knowledge you generate about your own production processes, and about your customers, usually stays within your firm and cannot be sold or purchased on the open market. In this sense, self-generated business knowledge is a strategic resource and can provide strategic advantage. Businesses will operate less effectively and efficiently if this unique knowledge is not available for decision making and ongoing operations. There are two major types of knowledge management systems: enterprise-wide knowledge management systems and knowledge work systems.

ENTERPRISE-WIDE KNOWLEDGE MANAGEMENT SYSTEMS

Firms must deal with at least three kinds of knowledge. Some knowledge exists within the firm in the form of structured text documents (reports and presentations). Decision makers also need knowledge that is semistructured, such as e-mail, voice mail, chat room exchanges, videos, digital pictures, brochures, or bulletin board postings. In still other cases, there is no formal or digital information of any kind, and the knowledge resides in the heads of employees. Much of this knowledge is **tacit knowledge** and is rarely written down.

Enterprise-wide knowledge management systems deal with all three types of knowledge. Enterprise-wide knowledge management systems are general-purpose, firmwide systems that collect, store, distribute, and apply digital content and knowledge. These systems include capabilities for searching for information, storing both structured and unstructured data, and locating employee expertise within the firm. They also include supporting technologies such as portals, search engines, collaboration tools, and learning management systems.

Enterprise Content Management Systems

Businesses today need to organize and manage both structured and semistructured knowledge assets. **Structured knowledge** is explicit knowledge that exists in formal documents, as well as in formal rules that organizations derive by observing experts and their decision-making behaviors. But, according to experts, at least 80 percent of an organization's business content is semistructured or unstructured—information in folders, messages, memos, proposals, e-mails, graphics, electronic slide presentations, and even videos created in different formats and stored in many locations.

Enterprise content management systems help organizations manage both types of information. They have capabilities for knowledge capture, storage, retrieval, distribution, and preservation to help firms improve their business processes and decisions. Such systems include corporate repositories of documents, reports, presentations, and best practices, as well as capabilities for collecting and organizing semistructured knowledge such as e-mail (see Figure 10-14). Major enterprise content management systems also enable users to access external sources of information, such as news feeds and research, and to communicate via e-mail, chat/instant messaging, discussion groups, and videoconferencing.

A key problem in managing knowledge is the creation of an appropriate classification scheme to organize information into meaningful categories. Once the categories for classifying knowledge have been created, each knowledge object needs to be "tagged," or classified, so that it can be easily retrieved. Enterprise content management systems have capabilities for tagging, interfacing with corporate databases where the documents are stored, and creating an enterprise portal environment for employees to use when searching for corporate knowledge. Open Text, EMC Corporation, IBM, and Oracle are leading vendors of enterprise content management software.

The Department of Watershed Management of the City of Atlanta, which provides residents with drinking water and wastewater services, uses Open Text enterprise content management tools to help it manage the 1.35 million documents it uses annually. The system provides a central repository for organizing and storing both structured and unstructured content, including plans, drawings, maps, progress reports, operations and maintenance documents, and legal, financial, and purchasing documents. The enterprise content management system helps the department comply with federal and state regulations for records management and also improves collaboration, workflows, and customer service (Open Text, 2009).

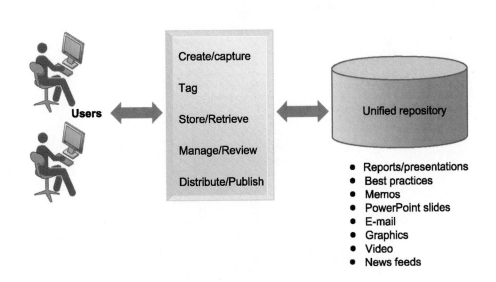

Figure 10-14
An Enterprise Content Management System
An enterprise content management system has capabilities for classifying, organizing, and managing structured and semistructured knowledge and making it available throughout the enterprise.

Firms in publishing, advertising, broadcasting, and entertainment have special needs for storing and managing unstructured digital data such as photographs, graphic images, video, and audio content. **Digital asset management systems** help them classify, store, and distribute these digital objects.

Knowledge Network Systems

Knowledge network systems, also known as *expertise location and management systems*, address the problem that arises when the appropriate knowledge is not in the form of a digital document but instead resides in the memory of expert individuals in the firm. Knowledge network systems provide an online directory of corporate experts in well-defined knowledge domains and use communication technologies to make it easy for employees to find the appropriate expert in a company. Some knowledge network systems go further by systematizing the solutions developed by experts and then storing the solutions in a knowledge database as a best-practices or frequently asked questions (FAQs) repository (see Figure 10-15). AskMe-Realcom and Oracle's Tacit Software are leading knowledge network system vendors.

Collaboration Tools and Learning Management Systems

We have already discussed the role of collaboration tools in information sharing and teamwork in Chapters 2 and 6. Social bookmarking and learning management systems feature additional capabilities for sharing and managing knowledge.

Social bookmarking makes it easier to search for and share information by allowing users to save their bookmarks to Web pages on a public Web site and tag these bookmarks with keywords. These tags can be used to organize and search for the documents. Lists of tags can be shared with other people to help them find information of interest. The

Figure 10-15
An Enterprise Knowledge Network System
A knowledge network maintains a database of firm experts, as well as accepted solutions to known problems, and then facilitates the communication between employees looking for knowledge and experts who have that knowledge. Solutions created in this communication are then added to a database of solutions in the form of frequently asked questions (FAQs), best practices, or other documents.

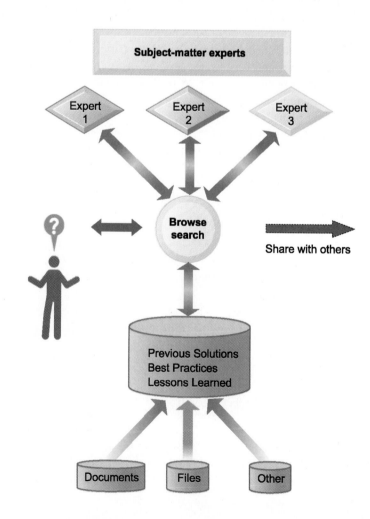

user-created taxonomies created for shared bookmarks and social tagging are called **folk-sonomies**. Delicious and Digg are two popular social bookmarking sites.

Suppose, for example, that you are on a corporate team researching wind power. If you did a Web search and found relevant Web pages on wind power, you would click on a bookmarking button on a social bookmarking site and create a tag identifying each Web document you found to link it to wind power. By clicking on the "tags" button at the social networking site, you would be able to see a list of all the tags you created and select the documents you need.

Companies need ways to keep track of and manage employee learning and to integrate it more fully into their knowledge management and other corporate systems. A **learning management system (LMS)** provides tools for the management, delivery, tracking, and assessment of various types of employee learning and training.

For example, Total Access Communication Public Company Limited, known as dtac, deployed Softscape's learning management system to automate learning and development processes across its entire workforce. Dtac is the second largest mobile phone operator in Thailand. In addition to student registration, Softscape's Learning & Development suite includes capabilities for site administration, curriculum management, course management, class scheduling, instructional administration (waitlists, attendance, grading, scoring, notifications), distance learning, educational asset management, evaluations, and transcripts. (Softscape, 2009).

KNOWLEDGE WORK SYSTEMS

The enterprise-wide knowledge systems we have just described provide a wide range of capabilities used by many, if not all, the workers and groups in an organization. Firms also have specialized systems for knowledge workers to help them create new knowledge for improving the firm's business processes and decision making. **Knowledge work systems (KWS)** are specialized systems for engineers, scientists, and other knowledge workers that are designed to promote the creation of knowledge and to ensure that new knowledge and technical expertise are properly integrated into the business.

Requirements of Knowledge Work Systems

Knowledge work systems give knowledge workers the specialized tools they need, such as powerful graphics, analytical tools, and communications and document management. These systems require great computing power to handle the sophisticated graphics or complex calculations necessary for such knowledge workers as scientific researchers, product designers, and financial analysts. Because knowledge workers are so focused on knowledge in the external world, these systems also must give the worker quick and easy access to external databases. They typically feature user-friendly interfaces that enable users to perform needed tasks without having to spend a lot of time learning how to use the computer. Figure 10-16 summarizes the requirements of knowledge work systems.

Knowledge workstations often are designed and optimized for the specific tasks to be performed. Design engineers need graphics with enough power to handle three-dimensional, computer-aided design (CAD) systems. However, financial analysts are more interested in access to a myriad of external databases and technology for efficiently storing and accessing massive amounts of financial data.

Examples of Knowledge Work Systems

Major knowledge work applications include CAD systems (which we introduced in Chapter 3), virtual reality systems for simulation and modeling, and financial workstations.

Contemporary CAD systems are capable of generating realistic-looking three-dimensional graphic designs that can be rotated and viewed from all sides. Architects from Skidmore, Owings, & Merrill LLP used a three-dimensional CAD program called Revit to work out the creative and technical details of the design for the Freedom Tower at the site of the former World Trade Center. The software enabled the architects to strip

**Figure 10-16
Requirements of
Knowledge Work
Systems**
*Knowledge work
systems require strong
links to external
knowledge bases in
addition to specialized
hardware and software.*

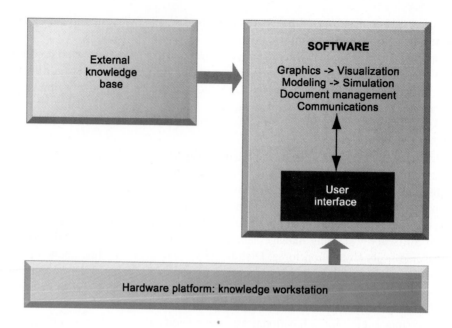

away the outer layer to manipulate the shape of the floors. Changes appeared immediately in the entire model, and the software automatically recalculated the technical details in the blueprints.

Virtual reality systems use interactive graphics software to create computer-generated simulations that are so close to reality that users almost believe they are participating in a real-world situation. In many virtual reality systems, the user dons special clothing, headgear, and equipment, depending on the application. The clothing contains sensors that record the user's movements and immediately transmit that information back to the computer. For instance, to walk through a virtual reality simulation of a house, you would need garb that monitors the movement of your feet, hands, and head. You also would need goggles containing video screens and sometimes audio attachments and feeling gloves so that you are immersed in the computer feedback.

Virtual reality is just starting to provide benefits in educational, scientific, and business work. For example, neuroradiologists at New York's Beth Israel Medical Center use the Siemens Medical Systems 3D Virtuoso System to peek at the interplay of tiny blood vessels or take a fly-through of the aorta. Surgeons at New York University School of Medicine use three-dimensional modeling to target brain tumors more precisely, thereby reducing bleeding and trauma during surgery.

Virtual reality applications developed for the Web use a standard called **Virtual Reality Modeling Language (VRML)**. VRML is a set of specifications for interactive, three-dimensional modeling on the World Wide Web that organize multiple media types, including animation, images, and audio, to put users in a simulated real-world environment. VRML is platform independent, operates over a desktop computer, and requires little bandwidth.

DuPont, the Wilmington, Delaware, chemical company, created a VRML application called HyperPlant, which enables users to access three-dimensional data over the Internet using Web browser software. Engineers can go through three-dimensional models as if they were physically walking through a plant, viewing objects at eye level. This level of detail reduces the number of mistakes they make during construction of oil rigs, oil plants, and other structures.

The financial industry is using specialized **investment workstations** to leverage the knowledge and time of its brokers, traders, and portfolio managers. Firms such as Merrill Lynch and UBS Financial Services have installed investment workstations that integrate a wide range of data from both internal and external sources, including contact management data, real-time and historical market data, and research reports. Previously, financial professionals had to spend considerable time accessing data from separate systems and piecing together the information they needed. By providing one-stop information faster and with fewer errors, the workstations streamline the entire investment process from stock selection to updating client records.

10.5 Hands-On MIS Projects

The projects in this section give you hands-on experience designing a knowledge portal, identifying opportunities for DSS, using a spreadsheet pivot table to analyze sales data, and using intelligent agents to research products for sale on the Web.

MANAGEMENT DECISION PROBLEMS

1. U.S. Pharma Corporation is headquartered in New Jersey but has research sites in Germany, France, the United Kingdom, Switzerland, and Australia. Research and development of new pharmaceuticals is key to ongoing profits, and U.S. Pharma researches and tests thousands of possible drugs. The company's researchers need to share information with others within and outside the company, including the U.S. Food and Drug Administration, the World Health Organization, and the International Federation of Pharmaceutical Manufacturers & Associations. Also critical is access to health information sites, such as the U.S. National Library of Medicine and to industry conferences and professional journals. Design a knowledge portal for U.S. Pharma's researchers. Include in your design specifications relevant internal systems and databases, external sources of information, and internal and external communication and collaboration tools. Design a home page for your portal.

2. Applebee's is the largest casual dining chain in the world, with 1,970 locations throughout the U.S. and nearly 20 other countries worldwide. The menu features beef, chicken, and pork items, as well as burgers, pasta, and seafood. The Applebee's CEO wants to make the restaurant more profitable by developing menus that are tastier and contain more items that customers want and are willing to pay for despite rising costs for gasoline and agricultural products. How might information systems help management implement this strategy? What pieces of data would Applebee's need to collect? What kinds of reports would be useful to help management make decisions on how to improve menus and profitability?

IMPROVING DECISION MAKING: USING PIVOT TABLES TO ANALYZE SALES DATA

Software skills: Pivot tables
Business skills: Analyzing sales data

This project gives you an opportunity to learn how to use Excel's PivotTable functionality to analyze a database or data list.

Use the data file for Online Management Training Inc. described earlier in the chapter. This is a list of the sales transactions at OMT for one day. You can find this spreadsheet file at MyMISLab.

Use Excel's PivotTable to help you answer the following questions:

- Where are the average purchases higher? The answer might tell managers where to focus marketing and sales resources, or pitch different messages to different regions.
- What form of payment is the most common? The answer could be used to emphasize in advertising the most preferred means of payment.

- Are there any times of day when purchases are most common? Do people buy are products while at work (likely during the day) or at home (likely in the evening)?
- What's the relationship between region, type of product purchased, and average sales price?

We provide instructions on how to use Excel PivotTables in our Learning Tracks.

IMPROVING DECISION MAKING: USING INTELLIGENT AGENTS FOR COMPARISON SHOPPING

Software skills: Web browser and shopping bot software
Business skills: Product evaluation and selection

This project will give you experience using shopping bots to search online for products, find product information, and find the best prices and vendors.

You have decided to purchase a new digital camera. Select a digital camera you might want to purchase, such as the Canon PowerShot SX120 or the Olympus Stylus-7010. To purchase the camera as inexpensively as possible, try several of the shopping bot sites, which do the price comparisons for you. Visit MySimon (www.mysimon.com), BizRate.com (www.bizrate.com), and Google Product Search. Compare these shopping sites in terms of their ease of use, number of offerings, speed in obtaining information, thoroughness of information offered about the product and seller, and price selection. Which site or sites would you use and why? Which camera would you select and why? How helpful were these sites for making your decision?

LEARNING TRACKS

The following Learning Tracks provide content relevant to topics covered in this chapter:

1. Building and Using Pivot Tables
2. How an Expert System Inference Engine Works
3. Challenges of Implementing and Using Knowledge Management Systems

Review Summary

1 **What are the different types of decisions, and how does the decision-making process work?** Decisions may be structured, semistructured, or unstructured, with structured decisions clustering at the operational level of the organization and unstructured decisions at the strategic level. Decision making can be performed by individuals or groups and includes employees as well as operational, middle, and senior managers. There are four stages in decision making: intelligence, design, choice, and implementation.

2 **How do information systems help people working individually and in groups make decisions more effectively?** Systems specifically designed to help managers and employees make better decisions include management information systems (MIS), decision-support systems (DSS), group decision-support systems (GDSS), and executive support systems (ESS).

MIS provide information on firm performance to help managers monitor and control the business, often in the form of fixed regularly scheduled reports based on data summarized from the firm's transaction processing systems. MIS support structured decisions and some semistructured decisions.

Decision-support systems combine data, sophisticated analytical models and tools, and user-friendly software into a single powerful system that can support semistructured or unstructured decision making. Geographic information systems (GIS) uses data visualization technology to analyze and display data for planning and decision making with digitized maps.

Group decision-support systems (GDSS) help people meeting together in a group arrive at decisions more efficiently. GDSS feature special conference room facilities where participants contribute their ideas using networked computers and software tools for organizing ideas, gathering information, ranking and setting priorities, and documenting meeting sessions.

Executive support systems (ESS) help senior managers with unstructured problems by combining data from internal and external sources for high-level overviews or drilling down to detailed transaction data.

3 **What are the business benefits of using intelligent techniques in decision making and knowledge management?** Expert systems capture tacit knowledge from a limited domain of human expertise and express that knowledge in the form of rules. The strategy used to search through the knowledge base is called the *inference engine*. Case-based reasoning represents organizational knowledge as a database of cases that can be continually expanded and refined.

Fuzzy logic is a software technology for expressing knowledge in the form of rules that use approximate or subjective values. Neural networks consist of hardware and software that attempt to mimic the thought processes of the human brain. Neural networks are notable for their ability to learn without programming and to recognize patterns in massive amounts of data.

Genetic algorithms develop solutions to particular problems using genetically based processes, such as fitness, crossover, and mutation. Intelligent agents are software programs with built-in or learned knowledge bases that carry out specific, repetitive, and predictable tasks for an individual user, business process, or software application.

4 **What types of systems are used for enterprise-wide knowledge management, and how do they provide value for businesses?** Enterprise content management systems feature databases and tools for organizing and storing structured documents and semistructured knowledge, such as e-mail or rich media. Knowledge network systems provide directories and tools for locating firm employees with special expertise who are important sources of tacit knowledge. Often these systems include group collaboration tools, portals to simplify information access, search tools, and tools for classifying information based on a taxonomy that is appropriate for the organization. Learning management systems provide tools for the management, delivery, tracking, and assessment of various types of employee learning and training.

5 **What are the major types of knowledge work systems, and how do they provide value for firms?** Knowledge work systems (KWS) support the creation of new knowledge and its integration into the organization. KWS require easy access to an external knowledge base; powerful computer hardware that can support software with intensive graphics, analysis, document management, and communications capabilities; and a user-friendly interface.

Key Terms

Artificial intelligence
   (AI), 356
Case-based reasoning
   (CBR), 358
Choice, 346
Customer decision-support
   systems (CDSS), 355
Data visualization, 353
Design, 346
Digital asset management
   systems, 366
Drill down, 355
DSS database, 351
DSS software system, 351
Enterprise content manage-
   ment systems, 365
Enterprise-wide knowledge
   management systems, 364
Expert system, 356

Folksonomies, 367
Fuzzy logic, 358
Genetic algorithms, 360
Geographic information
   systems (GIS), 353
Group decision-support
   systems (GDSS), 355
Implementation, 346
Intelligence, 345
Inference engine, 356
Intelligent agents, 362
Intelligent techniques, 347
Investment workstations, 368
Knowledge base, 356
Knowledge management, 363
Knowledge network
   systems, 366
Knowledge work systems
   (KWS), 367

Learning management system
   (LMS), 367
Machine learning, 360
Model, 351
Neural networks, 359
Pivot table, 353
Semistructured
   decisions, 344
Sensitivity analysis, 351
Social bookmarking, 366
Structured decisions, 344
Structured knowledge, 365
Tacit knowledge, 364
Unstructured decisions, 344
Virtual reality systems, 368
Virtual Reality Modeling
   Language (VRML), 368

Review Questions

1. What are the different types of decisions, and how does the decision-making process work?
- List and describe the different decision-making levels and decision-making groups in organizations and their decision-making requirements.
- Distinguish between an unstructured, semistructured, and structured decision.
- List and describe the stages in decision making.

2. How do information systems help people working individually and in groups make decisions more effectively?
- Distinguish between a decision-support system (DSS) and a management information system (MIS).
- List and describe the three basic components of a DSS.
- Define a geographic information system (GIS), and explain how it supports decision making.
- Define a customer decision-support system (CDSS), and explain how the Internet is used for this purpose.
- Define an executive support system (ESS), and explain how its capabilities enhance managerial decision making and provide value for a business.
- Define a group decision-support system (GDSS), explaining how it works and the problems it solves.

3. What are the business benefits of using intelligent techniques in decision making and knowledge management?
- Define an expert system, describe how it works, and explain its value to business.
- Define case-based reasoning, and explain how it differs from an expert system.
- Define a neural network, and describe how it works and how it benefits businesses.
- Define and describe fuzzy logic, genetic algorithms, and intelligent agents. Explain how each works and the kinds of problems for which each is suited.

4. What types of systems are used for enterprise-wide knowledge management, and how do they provide value for businesses?
- Define knowledge management, and explain its value to businesses.
- Define and describe the various types of enterprise-wide knowledge systems, and explain how they provide value for businesses.
- Describe how the various types of collaboration tools and learning management systems facilitate knowledge management.

5. What are the major types of knowledge work systems, and how do they provide value for firms?
- Define knowledge work systems, and describe the generic requirements of knowledge work systems.
- Describe how the following systems support knowledge work: computer-aided design (CAD), virtual reality, and investment workstations.

Discussion Questions

1. If businesses used DSS, GDSS, and ESS more widely, would they make better decisions? Why or why not?

2. Describe various ways that knowledge management systems could help firms with sales and marketing or with manufacturing and production.

Video Cases

Video Cases and Instructional Videos illustrating some of the concepts in this chapter are available. Contact your instructor to access these videos.

Teamwork

Designing a University GDSS

With three or four of your classmates, identify several groups in your university that might benefit from a GDSS. Design a GDSS for one of those groups, describing its hardware, software, and people elements. If possible, use Google Sites to post links to Web pages, team communication announcements, and work assignments; to brainstorm; and to work collaboratively on project documents. Try to use Google Docs to develop a presentation of your findings for the class.

BUSINESS PROBLEM-SOLVING CASE

HSBC's Mortgage Lending Decisions and the Big Melt

It isn't often that the American financial system, and its world counterpart, has a near-death experience. The last time was the 1930s. Beginning in 2007 and extending through 2009, American and global financial systems failed, melted down, and were rescued only by concerted central bank interventions in all the major industrial countries. The United States directly invested about 1 trillion dollars in U.S. financial institutions, and guaranteed an estimated $14 trillion dollars in private debt.

The complete history of this period has not been written. Many causes, involving many different actors, have been identified. Some have likened the big melt to a "perfect storm" where a number of storm systems just happened to combine to form a much larger, lethal storm. But one cause was the failure of decision-making models, both the model builders and the financial managers who relied on those models.

One of the major players in this crisis was HSBC Holdings PLC, the third largest bank in the world based on market value, and the largest bank in Europe. In the financial meltdown of 2008—2009, HSBC joined the other major money center banks in a collective failure. HSBC weathered the turmoil in the financial markets better than most of its rivals, mainly because it had profited from continuing growth in Asia, where it generates about 65 percent of its pretax profit. But the company's stock prices have fallen by half from their pre-crisis high, and HSBC had to shed over 6,000 employees, close over a thousand branches worldwide, and write off its mortgage generating unit in the United States called Household International.

Senior managers at HSBC had observed the incredible rise in U.S. home prices in the period 1990—2000, and closely followed the subprime mortgage market which drove home sales ever higher in the United States. In order to participate in this frothy market, HSBC bought Household International in 2002 for $15 billion. Household was one of the largest originators of consumer credit and subprime mortgages in the United States.

Subprime mortgages are targeted toward low-income borrowers who represent a higher risk of default when compared to prime borrowers. Some subprime mortgages were "stated-income" mortgages where applicants did not have to prove their incomes but simply stated them on an application. Sixty percent of these applicants were found to have inflated their incomes by 50 percent or more. Many also exaggerated their employment positions to coincide with the inflated income. As a result, they received approval for loans that were much

larger than they could actually afford. Adding risk, most subprime loans were variable rate loans where interest rates rose steeply after a few years.

Why on earth would banks and credit lenders like Household lend money to people who were unlikely to pay it back? The answer lies in modern tools of "risk management" and financial innovation. The risk management part involved selling the risk to other institutions and individuals who did not understand the risks they were taking. The financial innovation part was a relatively new instrument invented in the 1990s called a "collateralized debt obligation" or CDO. Lenders would originate mortgages, bundle thousands of them together, create a new financial instrument that offered high interest based on the cash flow of the subprime mortgages in the bundle, and then sell this instrument around the world as a "safe investment" in the rising U.S. home market. There seemed to be an insatiable market for CDOs, which offered slightly higher rates than safer government bonds. Similar lending practices were adopted in the United Kingdom, including Ireland, less so on the European continent, and in Asia. Reckless practices were extended to other forms of credit including credit cards (even prisoners were offered credit cards), and personal loans.

Welcome to the new world of risk management and the distribution of risk over millions of investors! The risk finally was passed onto whoever wound up with the debt instrument in their hands, a kind of financial musical chairs. When the music stopped, those left holding the bag included pension funds, municipal governments, and millions of individuals throughout the world all looking for slightly higher returns. Ultimately, governments around the world ended up guaranteeing much of this debt estimated to be well over $15 trillion in mortgages alone.

Unfortunately, the banks' practices were based on models using rosy assumptions that home price values would rise over long periods of time, and that collapse in one credit market would not spread across the globe to all financial markets because the developed markets of the West were now "de-coupled" from the emerging markets. The really fundamental assumptions in these models were that home prices in the United States had not experienced a long-term secular decline in prices since the 1930s, that the prices of homes historically were normally distributed, and that therefore, the risks could be estimated, understood, and priced into the instruments. As it turned out, all of these assumptions were wrong. The assumption on the stability of home prices over many decades was like saying the average wind in New Orleans over the last 50 years was 8 miles per hour from the southeast, without explaining that sometimes the wind goes over 100 miles per hour (which occurred during Hurricane Katrina).

With the purchase of Household International, HSBC began aggressively growing its mortgage and credit business in the United States. Household's CEO William Aldinger had touted his company's ability to assess credit risk using modeling techniques designed by 150 PhDs. The system, called the Worldwide Household International Revolving Lending System, or Whirl, helped Household underwrite credit card debt and support collection services in the United States, Mexico, the United Kingdom, and the Middle East.

Lenders such as HSBC who are analyzing applicants for credit cards, car loans, and fixed-rate mortgages use a credit rating from Fair Isaac Corp. of Minneapolis called a FICO score. However, FICO scores had not yet been proven reliable tools for predicting the performance, during a weakening housing market, of second-lien loans or of adjustable rate mortgages (ARMs) taken out by subprime borrowers. Data on subprime borrowers who made small or no down payments were scarce, and the FICO scores did not adequately distinguish between loans where borrowers had put their own money down and loans with no down payment. Nor did the models take into account what would happen if housing prices fell to the point where the amount owed on some mortgages exceeded the value of the homes they covered. By 2007, 12 percent of the total $8.4 trillion U.S. mortgage market consisted of subprime mortgages, up from just 7.5 percent near the end of 2001.

As the U.S. real estate market slowed in 2006, and then collapsed in 2008, home values fell drastically, by 30 percent in some hot markets. Subprime mortgages were all adjustable rate mortgages that started out with below-market rates, usually 4 percent, but then rose to 8 percent and even 10 percent within a few years. When interest rates rose, many borrowers were unable to make their mortgage payments and defaulted on their loans. HSBC anticipated seeing the number of delinquent and defaulted accounts grow, but not to the level that actually occurred.

In its quest for higher revenue, HSBC began buying up subprime loans from other sources. In 2005 and 2006, with the housing boom in its final stages, HSBC bought billions of dollars of subprime loans (including nearly $4 billion in second-lien loans) from as many as 250 wholesale mortgage companies, that had acquired the loans from independent brokers and banks. Second-lien loans are piggyback loans which allow home owners unable to make a down payment for a house to qualify for a mortgage by borrowing the down payment amount. The surge increased the bank's second-lien to a total of $10.24 billion.

HSBC even accepted pools that included stated-income loans. These are loans for which the borrower simply states his or her income with providing any documentation to verify it. According to Martin Eakes, CEO of the Center for Responsible Lending, 90 percent of stated-income loan applicants declare their incomes to be higher than they are in IRS records. Sixty percent of these people inflate their incomes by 50 percent or more. Many also exaggerate their employment positions to coincide with the inflated income. As a result, they receive approval for loans that are much larger than they can actually afford.

In 2005, Bobby Mehta, the top HSBC executive in the United States, described the development of the bank's mortgage portfolio as disciplined. He reported to investors, "We've done them conservatively based on analytics and based on our ability to earn a good return for the risks that we undertake." HSBC stated it had a process for forecasting how many of the loans it purchased from wholesalers were likely to default. First, the bank would tell the wholesaler what types of loans it was interested in, based on the income and credit scores of the borrowers. Once the wholesaler offered a pool of mortgages, HSBC analysts evaluated the lot to determine whether it met HSBC standards.

In early 2007, HSBC shook up Wall Street when it announced a much higher percentage of its subprime loans defaulted than it had anticipated. It would have to make provisions for $10.6 billion in bad debt stemming from loan delinquencies in 2006. The percentage of all HSBC Mortgage Services loans that were overdue by 60 days or more jumped from 2.95 to over 4 percent in 2009. In short, the subprime mortgage market was in distress, and profits from the high-risk loans were disappearing. By 2009, HSBC had taken a cumulative bad loan charge of $53 billion. It wrote off the entire $15 billion purchase price of Household, and still retained on its books over $62 billion in home mortgages, some of which surely will default.

HSBC was one of the fortunate banks that did not have to take a government bailout. But with so many mortgages originated in 2005 and 2006 and interest rate hikes in 2008 and 2009, HSBC is facing another onslaught of delinquencies and defaults over the next two years. The Center for Responsible Lending predicted that 20 percent of subprime mortgages sold during those two years will result in foreclosure.

HSBC adopted business analytics software from Experian-Scorex to help support the decision making of its credit application processing staff. The software provides users with the ability to consistently deploy scoring models and portfolio segmentation. It also includes tools for managing customer relationships and improving risk management decisions. By using these tools, HSBC hopes to be able to create strategies for individual applicants, assess the value of each applicant, and then customize a loan offer that suits the customer's needs as well as the bank's business.

HSBC also made changes in both personnel and policy. The company ceased originating and purchasing stated-income loans and boosted the required FICO score for some loans. Tom Detelich, who had led the transition from Household to HSBC's consumer lending business, was appointed head of HSBC Mortgage Services. HSBC doubled the number of customer representatives who call on borrowers who have missed payments and discuss payment plans that are more manageable. Those operations now run seven days a week. HSBC is also utilizing information technology to pinpoint ahead of time which customers are most in danger of failing to meet their monthly payments once their ARMs jump from their initial teaser interest rates to higher rates. In some cases, the adjustment can increase a monthly payment by $500.

Major investment banks like Bear Stearns and Lehman Brothers failed in the fall of 2008 because they were holding massive amounts of unsold CDOs and other derivative products, as did AIG, the single largest insurer of these instruments. Critical attention turned to the models used to support what turned out to be a very risky activity. While most blamed the models, and modeling in general, others pointed a finger not at modeling as an activity, but at the faulty application of the modeling, poor assumptions encouraged by senior executives who did not want to understand the "real" risks they were taking as long as they made money, and the failure to take into account human behavioral issues. These human behavioral factors included bankers around the world acting like herds rather independent decision makers, all relying on the same convenient models and assumptions, which predicted incredible profits and a rosy future. The models also failed to understand that when one multitrillion dollar credit market collapsed in a global banking system, other credit markets would shut down, and major financial institutions and millions of ordinary citizens would panic, run for the exits, and just stop borrowing, lending, and spending. In fact, there is no model for inter-market risk or for the behavioral factors that drive correlation across markets.

Sources: Saul Hansell, "How Wall Street Lied to Its Computers," *The New York Times*, September 18, 2009; Steve Lohr, "Wall Street's Math Wizards Forgot a Few Variables," *The New York Times*, September 13, 2009; Julia Werdigier, "HSBC Seeks $18 Billion in Capital and Cuts 6,100 Jobs," *The New York Times*, March 13, 2009; Jeffrey Goldfarb, "HSBC is Hardier Than Most Banks," *The New York Times*, March 2, 2009; Joe Nocera, "Risk Mismanagement," *The New York Times*, January 4, 2009; Steve Lohr, "In Modeling Risk, the Human Factor Was Left Out," November 5, 2008; Carrick Mollenkamp, Serena Ng, Liam Pleven, and Randall Smith. "Behind AIG's Fall, Risk Models Failed to Pass Real-World Test," *The Wall Street Journal*, October 31, 2008; Carrick Mollenkamp, "In Home-Lending Push, Banks Misjudged Risk," *The Wall Street Journal*, February 8, 2007; and "HSBC Implements Experian-Scorex Decision Support Software," www.finextra.com, February 23, 2007.

Case Study Questions

1. What problem did HSBC face in this case? What people, technology, and organization factors were responsible for the problem? Did HSBC management correctly identify the problem?
2. HSBC had sophisticated information systems and analytical tools for predicting the risk presented by subprime mortgage applicants. Why did HSBC still run into trouble?
3. What solutions is HSBC relying on to deal with its problem going forward? Will these solutions be sufficient to turn the subprime mortgage business around? Are there additional factors for which HSBC has not accounted? What are they?
4. HSBC made a decision to pursue subprime mortgages as a segment of its business. Explain how this was a structured, unstructured, or semistructured decision. Then, present your opinion about where in the decision-making process HSBC went wrong. Finally, apply the decision quality concepts of accuracy and comprehensiveness to this case.
5. Do you think one solution to HSBC's poor risk management practices is more and better information supplied to decision makers, or is something else required to improve its risk management?

Building and Managing Systems

PART IV

Part IV shows how to use the knowledge acquired in earlier chapters to analyze and design information system solutions to business problems. This part answers questions such as these: How can I develop a solution to an information system problem that provides genuine business benefits? How can the firm adjust to the changes introduced by the new system solution? What alternative approaches are available for building system solutions? What broader ethical and social issues should be addressed when building and using information systems?

Building Information Systems and Managing Projects

11

STUDENT LEARNING OBJECTIVES

After completing this chapter, you will be able to answer the following questions:

1. What are the core problem-solving steps for developing new information systems?

2. What are the alternative methods for building information systems?

3. What are the principal methodologies for modeling and designing systems?

4. How should information systems projects be selected and evaluated?

5. How should information systems projects be managed?

CHAPTER OUTLINE

A NEW ORDERING SYSTEM FOR GIRL SCOUT COOKIES

Peanut Butter Petites, Caramel DeLites, Thin Mints—Girl Scout Cookies have been American favorites since the organization's first cookie drive in 1917. The Girl Scouts have been so successful selling cookies that cookie sales are a major source of funding for this organization. The Girl Scouts sell so many cookies that collecting, counting, and organizing the annual avalanche of orders has become a tremendous challenge.

The Girl Scouts' traditional cookie-ordering process depended on mountains of paperwork. During the peak sales period in January, each Girl Scout marked her sales on an individual order card and turned the card in to the troop leader when she was finished. The troop leader would transfer the information onto a five-part form and give this form to a community volunteer who tabulated the orders. From there, the orders data passed to a regional council headquarters, where they would be batched into final orders for the manufacturer, ABC Cookies. In addition to ordering, Girl Scout volunteers and troop members had to coordinate cookie deliveries, from the manufacturer to regional warehouses, to local drop-off sites, to each scout, and to the customers themselves.

The Patriots' Trail Girl Scout Council, representing 65 communities and 18,000 Girl Scouts in the greater Boston area, sold more than 1.6 million boxes of eight different cookie varieties in 2004 alone. According to its associate executive director Deborah Deacetis, the paperwork had become "overwhelming." "It changed hands too many times. There was a lot of opportunity for error, because of all the added columns, multiple prices per box, and calculations that had to be made by different people, all on deadline."

The Patriots' Trail Council first looked into building a computerized system using Microsoft Access database management and application development tools. But this alternative would have cost $25,000 to develop and would have taken at least three to four months to get the system up and running. It was too time-consuming, complex, and expensive for the Girl Scouts. In addition to Microsoft Access software, the Girl Scouts would have to purchase a server to run the system, plus pay for networking and Web site maintenance services so the system could be made available on the Web.

After consulting with management consultants Dovetail Associates, the council selected Intuit's QuickBase for Corporate Workgroups. QuickBase is a hosted Web-based software service for small businesses and corporate workgroups. It is especially well suited for building simple database applications very quickly and does not require a great deal of training to use. QuickBase is customizable and designed to collect, organize, and share data among teams in many different locations.

A Dovetail consultant created a working QuickBase prototype with some basic functions for the Girl Scouts within a few hours. It only took two months to build, test, and implement the entire system using this software. The cost for developing the entire system was a fraction of the Microsoft Access solution. The Girl Scouts do not have to pay for any hardware, software, or networking services because QuickBase runs everything for them on its servers. QuickBase costs $500 per month for organizations with 100 users and $1,500 per month for organizations with up to 500 users. It is very easy to use.

The QuickBase solution eliminates paperwork and calculation errors by providing a clear central source of data for the entire council and easy online entry of cookie orders over the Web. Troop leaders collect the Girl Scouts' order cards and enter them directly into the QuickBase system using their home computers linked to the Web. With a few mouse clicks, the council office consolidates the unit totals and transmits the orders electronically to ABC Cookies.

In the past, the council relied on volunteers to handle their paperwork, dropping it off at the council office or mailing it in. "Now we have a way to actually watch the orders coming in," Deacetis notes. As local orders come in, local section leaders can track the data in real time.

The Patriots' Trail Girl Scout Council also uses the QuickBase system to manage the Cookie Cupboard warehouse, where volunteers pick up their cookie orders. Volunteers use the system to make reservations so that the warehouse can prepare the orders in advance, saving time and inventory management costs. The trucking companies that deliver cookie shipments now receive their instructions electronically through QuickBase so that they can create efficient delivery schedules.

Since its implementation, the QuickBase system has cut paperwork by more than 90 percent, reduced errors to 1 percent, and reduced the time spent by volunteers by 50 percent. The old system used to take two months to tally the orders and determine which Scouts should be rewarded for selling the most cookies. Now that time has been cut to 48 hours.

Sources: www.girlscoutseasternmass.org/cookies, accessed October 29, 2009 and "Girl Scouts Unite Behind Order Tracking," *Customer Relationship Management*, May 2005.

The experience of the Patriots' Trail Girl Scout Council illustrates some of the steps required to design and build new information systems. It also illustrates some of the benefits of a new system solution. The Girl Scouts had an outdated manual paper-based system for processing cookie orders that was excessively time-consuming and error ridden. The Girl Scouts tried several alternative solutions before opting for a new ordering system based on the QuickBase software service. In this chapter, we will examine the Girl Scouts' search for a system solution as we describe each step of building a new information system using the problem-solving process.

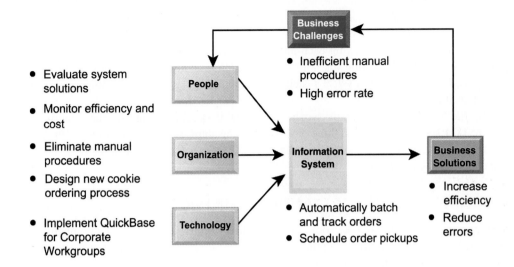

11.1 Problem Solving and Systems Development

We have already described the problem-solving process and how it helps us analyze and understand the role of information systems in business. This problem-solving process is especially valuable when we need to build new systems. A new information system is built as a solution to a problem or set of problems the organization perceives it is facing. The problem may be one in which managers and employees believe that the business is not performing as well as expected, or it may come from the realization that the organization should take advantage of new opportunities to perform more effectively.

Let's apply this problem-solving process to system building. Figure 11-1 illustrates the four steps we would need to take: (1) define and understand the problem, (2) develop alternative solutions, (3) choose the best solution, and (4) implement the solution.

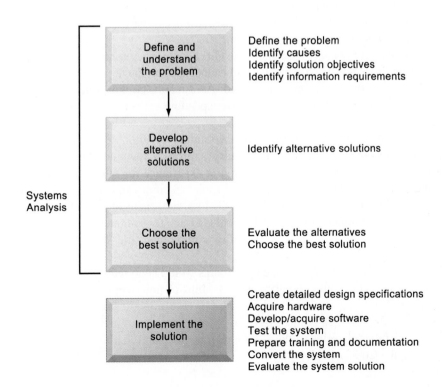

Figure 11-1
Developing an Information System Solution
Developing an information system solution is based on the problem-solving process.

Before a problem can be solved, it first must be properly defined. Members of the organization must agree that a problem actually exists and that it is serious. The problem must be investigated so that it can be better understood. Next comes a period of devising alternative solutions, then one of evaluating each alternative and selecting the best solution. The final stage is one of implementing the solution, in which a detailed design for the solution is specified, translated into a physical system, tested, introduced to the organization, and further refined as it is used over time.

In the information systems world, we have a special name for these activities. Figure 11-1 shows that the first three problem-solving steps, where we identify the problem, gather information, devise alternative solutions, and make a decision about the best solution, are called **systems analysis**.

DEFINING AND UNDERSTANDING THE PROBLEM

Defining the problem may take some work because various members of the company may have different ideas about the nature of the problem and its severity. What caused the problem? Why is it still around? Why wasn't it solved long ago? Systems analysts typically gather facts about existing systems and problems by examining documents, work papers, procedures, and system operations and by interviewing key users of the system.

Information systems problems in the business world typically result from a combination of people, organization, and technology factors. When identifying a key issue or problem, ask what kind of problem it is: Is it a people problem, an organizational problem, a technology problem, or a combination of these? What people, organizational, and technological factors contributed to the problem?

Once the problem has been defined and analyzed, it is possible to make some decisions about what should and can be done. What are the objectives of a solution to the problem? Is the firm's objective to reduce costs, increase sales, or improve relationships with customers, suppliers, or employees? Do managers have sufficient information for decision making? What information is required to achieve these objectives?

At the most basic level, the **information requirements** of a new system identify who needs what information, where, when, and how. Requirements analysis carefully defines the objectives of the new or modified system and develops a detailed description of the functions that the new system must perform. A system designed around the wrong set of requirements will either have to be discarded because of poor performance or will need to undergo major modifications. Section 11.2 describes alternative approaches to eliciting requirements that help minimize this problem.

Let's return to our opening case about the Girl Scouts. The problem here is that the Girl Scout ordering process is heavily manual and cannot support the large number of volunteers and cookie orders that must be coordinated. As a result, cookie ordering is extremely inefficient with high error rates and volunteers spending excessive time organizing orders and deliveries.

Organizationally, the Girl Scouts are a voluntary organization distributed across a large area, with cookie sales as the primary source of revenue. The Scouts rely on volunteers with little or no business or computer experience for sales and management of orders and deliveries. They have almost no financial resources and volunteers are strapped for time. The Girl Scout cookie-ordering process requires many steps and coordination of multiple groups and organizations—individual Girl Scouts, volunteers, the council office, the cookie manufacturing factory, trucking companies, and the Cookie Cupboard warehouse.

The objectives of a solution for the Girl Scouts would be to reduce the amount of time, effort, and errors in the cookie-ordering process. Information requirements for the solution include the ability to rapidly total and organize order transactions for transmittal to ABC Cookies; the ability to track orders by type of cookie, troop, and individual Girl Scout; the ability to schedule deliveries to the Cookie Cupboard; and the ability to schedule order pickups from the Cookie Cupboard.

DEVELOPING ALTERNATIVE SOLUTIONS

What alternative solutions are possible for achieving these objectives and meeting these information requirements? The systems analysis lays out the most likely paths to follow given the nature of the problem. Some possible solutions do not require an information system solution but instead call for an adjustment in management, additional training, or refinement of existing organizational procedures. Some, however, do require modifications to the firm's existing information systems or an entirely new information system.

EVALUATING AND CHOOSING SOLUTIONS

The systems analysis includes a **feasibility study** to determine whether each proposed solution is feasible, or achievable, from a financial, technical, and organizational standpoint. The feasibility study establishes whether each alternative solution is a good investment, whether the technology needed for the system is available and can be handled by the firm's information systems staff, and whether the organization is capable of accommodating the changes introduced by the system.

A written systems proposal report describes the costs and benefits, and advantages and disadvantages of each alternative solution. Which solution is best in a financial sense? Which works best for the organization? The systems analysis will detail the costs and benefits of each alternative and the changes that the organization will have to make to use the solution effectively. We provide a detailed discussion of how to determine the business value of systems and manage change in the following section. On the basis of this report, management will select what it believes is the best solution for the company.

The Patriots' Trail Girl Scouts had three alternative solutions. One was to streamline existing processes, continuing to rely on manual procedures. However, given the large number of Girl Scouts and cookie orders, as well as relationships with manufacturers and shippers, redesigning and streamlining a manual ordering and delivery process would not have provided many benefits. The Girl Scouts needed an automated solution that accurately tracked thousands of order and delivery transactions, reduced paperwork, and created a central real-time source of sales data that could be accessed by council headquarters and individual volunteers.

A second alternative was to custom-build a cookie-ordering system using Microsoft Access. This alternative was considered too time-consuming, expensive, and technically challenging for the Girl Scouts. It required $25,000 in initial programming costs, plus the purchase of hardware and networking equipment to run the system and link it to the Internet, as well as trained staff to run and maintain the system.

The third alternative was to rapidly create a system using an application service provider. QuickBase provides templates and tools for creating simple database systems in very short periods, provides the hardware for running the application and Web site, and can be accessed by many different users over the Web. This solution does not require the Girl Scouts to purchase any hardware, software, or networking technology or to maintain any information system staff to support the system. This last alternative was the most feasible for the Girl Scouts.

IMPLEMENTING THE SOLUTION

The first step in implementing a system solution is to create detailed design specifications. **Systems design** shows how the chosen solution should be realized. The system design is the model or blueprint for an information system solution and consists of all the specifications that will deliver the functions identified during systems analysis. These specifications should address all of the technical, organization, and people components of the system solution. Table 11.1 lists the types of specifications that would be produced during system design.

TABLE 11.1

**System Design
Specifications**

Output	Medium and content
	Timing
Input	Flow
	Data entry
User interface	Feedback and error handling
Database	Logical data model
	Volume and speed requirements
	File and record specifications
Processing	Program logic and computations
Manual procedures	What activities, who, when, how, and where
Security and controls	Access controls
	Input, processing, and output controls
Conversion	Testing method
	Conversion strategy
Training and documentation	Training modules and platforms
	Systems, user, and operations documentation
Organizational changes	Process design
	Organizational structure changes

A Dovetail Associates consultant elicited information requirements and created a design for the new Girl Scout cookie system. Table 11.2 shows some of the design specifications for the new system.

Completing Implementation

In the final steps of implementing a system solution, the following activities would be performed:

- *Hardware selection and acquisition.* System builders select appropriate hardware for the application. They would either purchase the necessary computers and networking hardware or lease them from a technology provider.

- *Software development and programming.* Software is custom programmed in-house or purchased from an external source, such as an outsourcing vendor, an application software package vendor, or an application service provider.

The Girl Scouts did not have to purchase additional hardware or software. QuickBase offers templates for generating simple database applications. Dovetail consultants used the QuickBase tools to rapidly create the software for the system. The system runs on QuickBase servers.

- *Testing.* The system is thoroughly tested to ensure it produces the right results. The **testing** process requires detailed testing of individual computer programs, called **unit testing**, as well as **system testing**, which tests the performance of the information system as a whole. **Acceptance testing** provides the final certification that the system is ready to be used in a production setting. Information systems tests are evaluated by users and reviewed by management. When all parties are satisfied that the new system meets their standards, the system is formally accepted for installation.

The systems development team works with users to devise a systematic test plan. The **test plan** includes all of the preparations for the series of tests we have just described.

TABLE 11.2

Design Specifications for the Girl Scout Cookie System

Output	Online reports
	Hard copy reports
	Online queries
	Order transactions for ABC Cookies
	Delivery tickets for the trucking firm
Input	Order data entry form
	Troop data entry form
	Girl Scout data entry form
	Shipping/delivery data entry form
User interface	Graphical Web interface
Database	Database with cookie order file, delivery file, troop contact file
Processing	Calculate order totals by type of cookie and number of boxes
	Track orders by troop and individual Girl Scout
	Schedule pickups at the Cookie Cupboard
	Update Girl Scout and troop data for address and member changes
Manual procedures	Girl Scouts take orders with paper forms
	Troop leaders collect order cards from Scouts and enter the order data online
Security and controls	Online passwords
	Control totals
Conversion	Input Girl Scout and troop data
	Transfer factory and delivery data
	Test system
Training and documentation	System guide for users
	Online practice demonstration
	Online training sessions
	Training for ABC Cookies and trucking companies to accept data and instructions automatically from the Girl Scout system
Organizational changes	Job design: Volunteers no longer have to tabulate orders
	Process design: Take orders on manual cards but enter them online into the system
	Schedule order pickups from the Cookie Cupboard online

Figure 11-2 shows a sample from a test plan that might have been used for the Girl Scout cookie system. The condition being tested is online access of an existing record for a specific Girl Scout troop.

- *Training and documentation.* End users and information system specialists require training so that they will be able to use the new system. Detailed **documentation** showing how the system works from both a technical and end-user standpoint must be prepared.

Figure 11-2
A Sample Test Plan for the Girl Scout Cookie System

When developing a test plan, it is imperative to include the various conditions to be tested, the requirements for each condition tested, and the expected results. Test plans require input from both end users and information systems specialists.

Test Case Number: GS02-010

Prepared by: A. Nelson   Date: February 15, 2010

Objective: This subtest checks for accessing an existing troop record

Specific Environment: QuickBase for WorkGroups

Procedure Description:
Click on My Troop Summary link.
Enter Troop Number

Expected Result:
When user clicks on My Troop Summary, the Troop Summary screen appears.
When user enters the correct Troop Number, the Troop record appears.
When user enters the wrong Troop Number, the error message "Wrong Troop Number" appears.

Test Results:
All OK.

The Girl Scout cookie system provides an online practice area for users to practice entering data into the system by following step-by-step instructions. Also available on the Web is a step-by-step instruction guide for the system that can be downloaded and printed as a hard-copy manual.

- *Conversion* is the process of changing from the old system to the new system. There are three main conversion strategies: the parallel strategy, the direct cutover strategy, and the phased approach strategy.

  In a **parallel strategy**, both the old system and its potential replacement are run together for a time until everyone is assured that the new one functions correctly. The old system remains available as a backup in case of problems. The **direct cutover strategy** replaces the old system entirely with the new system on an appointed day, carrying the risk that there is no system to fall back on if problems arise. A **phased approach** introduces the system in stages (such as first introducing the modules for ordering Girl Scout cookies and then introducing the modules for transmitting orders and instructions to the cookie factory and shipper).

- *Production and maintenance.* After the new system is installed and conversion is complete, the system is said to be in **production**. During this stage, users and technical specialists review the solution to determine how well it has met its original objectives and to decide whether any revisions or modifications are in order. Changes in hardware, software, documentation, or procedures to a production system to correct errors, meet new requirements, or improve processing efficiency are termed **maintenance.**

The Girl Scouts continued to improve and refine their QuickBase cookie system. The system was made more efficient for users with slow Internet connections. Other recent enhancements include capabilities for paying for orders more rapidly, entering troop information and initial orders without waiting for a specified starting date, and receiving online confirmation for reservations to pick up orders from the Cookie Cupboard.

Managing the Change

Developing a new information systems solution is not merely a matter of installing hardware and software. The business must also deal with the organizational changes that the new solution will bring about—new information, new business processes, and perhaps new reporting relationships and decision-making power. A very well-designed solution may not work unless it is introduced to the organization very carefully. The process of planning change in an organization so that it is implemented in an orderly and effective manner is so critical to the success or failure of information system solutions that we devote the next section to a detailed discussion of this topic.

To manage the transition from the old manual cookie-ordering processes to the new system, the Girl Scouts would have to inform troop leaders and volunteers about changes in cookie-ordering procedures, provide training, and provide resources for answering any questions that arose as parents and volunteers started using the system. They would need to work with ABC Cookies and their shippers on new procedures for transmitting and delivering orders.

11.2 Alternative Systems-Building Approaches

There are alternative methods for building systems using the basic problem-solving model we have just described. These alternative methods include the traditional systems lifecycle, prototyping, end-user development, application software packages, and outsourcing.

TRADITIONAL SYSTEMS DEVELOPMENT LIFECYCLE

The **systems development lifecycle (SDLC)** is the oldest method for building information systems. The lifecycle methodology is a phased approach to building a system, dividing systems development into a series of formal stages, as illustrated in Figure 11-3. Although systems builders can go back and forth among stages in the lifecycle, the systems lifecycle is predominantly a "waterfall" approach in which tasks in one stage are completed before work for the next stage begins.

This approach maintains a very formal division of labor between end users and information systems specialists. Technical specialists, such as system analysts and programmers, are responsible for much of the systems analysis, design, and implementation work; end users are limited to providing information requirements and reviewing the technical staff's work. The lifecycle also emphasizes formal specifications and paperwork, so many documents are generated during the course of a systems project.

The systems lifecycle is still used for building large complex systems that require rigorous and formal requirements analysis, predefined specifications, and tight controls over the systems-building process. However, this approach is also time-consuming and expensive to use. Tasks in one stage are supposed to be completed before work for the next stage

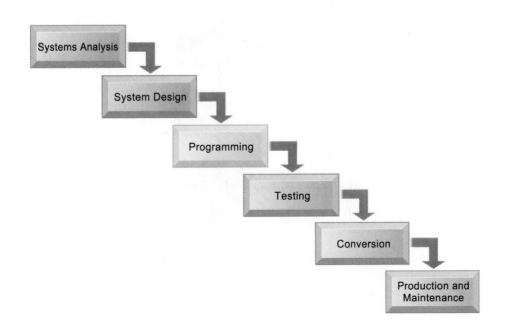

**Figure 11-3
The Traditional Systems Development Lifecycle**
The systems development lifecycle partitions systems development into formal stages, with each stage requiring completion before the next stage can begin.

begins. Activities can be repeated, but volumes of new documents must be generated and steps retraced if requirements and specifications need to be revised. This encourages freezing of specifications relatively early in the development process. The lifecycle approach is also not suitable for many small desktop systems, which tend to be less structured and more individualized.

PROTOTYPING

Prototyping consists of building an experimental system rapidly and inexpensively for end users to evaluate. The prototype is a working version of an information system or part of the system, but it is intended as only a preliminary model. Users interact with the prototype to get a better idea of their information requirements, refining the prototype multiple times. (The chapter-opening case describes how Dovetail Associates used QuickBase to create a prototype that helped the Patriots' Trail Girl Scout Council refine their specifications for their cookie-ordering system.) When the design is finalized, the prototype will be converted to a polished production system. Figure 11-4 shows a four-step model of the prototyping process.

Step 1: *Identify the user's basic requirements.* The system designer (usually an information systems specialist) works with the user only long enough to capture the user's basic information needs.

Step 2: *Develop an initial prototype.* The system designer creates a working prototype quickly, using tools for rapidly generating software.

Step 3: *Use the prototype.* The user is encouraged to work with the system to determine how well the prototype meets his or her needs and to make suggestions for improving the prototype.

Step 4: *Revise and enhance the prototype.* The system builder notes all changes the user requests and refines the prototype accordingly. After the prototype has been revised, the cycle returns to Step 3. Steps 3 and 4 are repeated until the user is satisfied.

Figure 11-4
The Prototyping Process
The process of developing a prototype consists of four steps. Because a prototype can be developed quickly and inexpensively, systems builders can go through several iterations, repeating steps 3 and 4, to refine and enhance the prototype before arriving at the final operational one.

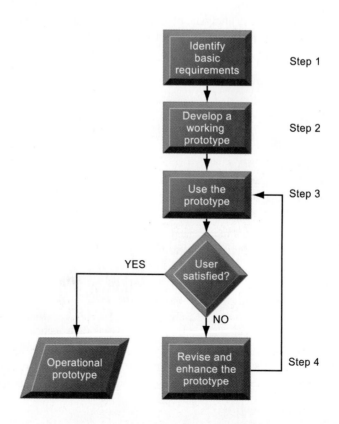

Prototyping is especially useful in designing an information system's user interface. Because prototyping encourages intense end-user involvement throughout the systems-development process, it is more likely to produce systems that fulfill user requirements.

However, rapid prototyping may gloss over essential steps in systems development, such as thorough testing and documentation. If the completed prototype works reasonably well, management may not see the need to build a polished production system. Some hastily constructed systems do not easily accommodate large quantities of data or a large number of users in a production environment.

END-USER DEVELOPMENT

End-user development allows end users, with little or no formal assistance from technical specialists, to create simple information systems, reducing the time and steps required to produce a finished application. Using fourth-generation languages, graphics languages, and PC software tools, end users can access data, create reports, and develop entire information systems on their own, with little or no help from professional systems analysts or programmers.

For example, Elie Tahari Ltd., a leading designer of women's fashions, uses Information Builders Inc.'s WebFOCUS software to enable authorized users to obtain self-service reports on orders, inventory, sales, and finance. Sales executives use the system to view their accounts, to determine what merchandise is selling, and to see what customers have ordered. Users can also create ad hoc reports by themselves to obtain specific pieces of information or more detailed data (Information Builders, 2009).

On the whole, end-user-developed systems are completed more rapidly than those developed with conventional programming tools. Allowing users to specify their own business needs improves requirements gathering and often leads to a higher level of user involvement and satisfaction with the system. However, fourth-generation tools still cannot replace conventional tools for some business applications because they cannot easily handle the processing of large numbers of transactions or applications with extensive procedural logic and updating requirements.

End-user development also poses organizational risks because systems are created rapidly, without a formal development methodology, testing, and documentation. To help organizations maximize the benefits of end-user applications development, management should require cost justification of end-user information system projects and establish hardware, software, and quality standards for user-developed applications.

PURCHASING SOLUTIONS: APPLICATION SOFTWARE PACKAGES AND OUTSOURCING

Chapter 4 points out that the software for most systems today is not developed in-house but is purchased from external sources. Firms may choose to purchase a software package from a commercial vendor, rent the software from a service provider, or outsource the development work to another firm. Selection of the software or software service is often based on a **Request for Proposal (RFP)**, which is a detailed list of questions submitted to external vendors to see how well they meet the requirements for the proposed system.

Application Software Packages

Most new information systems today are built using an application software package or preprogrammed software components. Many applications are common to all business organizations—for example, payroll, accounts receivable, general ledger, or inventory control. For such universal functions with standard processes that do not change a great deal over time, a generalized system will fulfill the requirements of many organizations.

If a software package can fulfill most of an organization's requirements, the company does not have to write its own software. The company saves time and money by using the prewritten, predesigned, pretested software programs from the package.

Many packages include capabilities for customization to meet unique requirements not addressed by the package software. **Customization** features allow a software package to be modified to meet an organization's unique requirements without destroying the integrity of the packaged software. However, if extensive customization is required, additional programming and customization work may become so expensive and time-consuming that it negates many of the advantages of software packages. If the package cannot be customized, the organization will have to adapt to the package and change its procedures.

The Interactive Session on Technology describes the experience of Zimbra, a software company that selected a software package solution for its new marketing automation system. As you read this case, try to identify the problem this company was facing, what alternative solutions were available to management, why a software package was an appropriate solution, and how well the chosen solution worked.

Outsourcing

If a firm does not want to use its internal resources to build or operate information systems, it can outsource the work to an external organization that specializes in providing these services. Software service providers, which we describe in Chapter 4, are one form of outsourcing. An example would be the Girl Scouts leasing the software and hardware from QuickBase to run their cookie-ordering system. Subscribing companies use the software and computer hardware of the service provider as the technical platform for their systems. In another form of outsourcing, a company would hire an external vendor to design and create the software for its system, but that company would operate the system on its own computers.

The outsourcing vendor might be domestic or in another country. Domestic outsourcing is driven primarily by the fact that outsourcing firms possess skills, resources, and assets that their clients do not have. Installing a new supply chain management system in a very large company might require hiring an additional 30–50 people with specific expertise in supply chain management software licensed, say, from JDA/Manugistics or another vendor. Rather than hire permanent new employees, most of whom would need extensive training in the software package, and then release them after the new system is built, it makes more sense, and is often less expensive, to outsource this work for a 12-month period.

In the case of offshore outsourcing, the decision tends to be much more cost-driven. A skilled programmer in India or Russia earns about U.S. $10,000 per year, compared to $70,000 per year for a comparable programmer in the United States. The Internet and low-cost communications technology have drastically reduced the expense and difficulty of coordinating the work of global teams in faraway locations. In addition to cost savings, many offshore outsourcing firms offer world-class technology assets and skills.

For example, Pinnacle West Capital Corporation, which sells and delivers electricity and energy-related services to 1 million customers in the western United States, turned to outsourcing to reduce operational costs. It contracted with the Indian software and service provider Wipro Ltd. to handle its application development. Wipro develops Pinnacle West's applications, services system enhancements, and provides 24-hour system support. Outsourcing to Wipro helped Pinnacle West accomplish 12 months of development work in 7 months while reducing computer processing and application development costs .

There is a very strong chance that at some point in your career, you'll be working with offshore outsourcers or global teams. Your firm is most likely to benefit from outsourcing if it takes the time to evaluate all the risks and to make sure outsourcing is appropriate for its particular needs. Any company that outsources its applications must thoroughly understand

INTERACTIVE SESSION: TECHNOLOGY   Zimbra Zooms Ahead with OneView

Zimbra is a software company whose flagship product is its Zimbra Collaboration Suite (ZCS), an open source e-mail collaboration suite that relies heavily on Ajax to provide a variety of business functions. Purchased by Yahoo in 2007, the company now has accumulated 50 million paid mailboxes. In addition to e-mail, ZCS combines contact lists, a shared calendar, instant messaging, hosted documents, search, and VoIP into one package, and can be used on any mobile Web browser.

As an open source software company, Zimbra uses viral marketing models, word-of-mouth marketing, and open standards to grow its business. Customers are as free to criticize Zimbra and ZCS as they are to praise the company and its flagship offering. For the most part, this strategy has proven very successful for the company thus far.

Zimbra makes sales via its Web site and offers both free and commercial versions. Zimbra's business model hinges on driving large numbers of visitors to its Web site, allowing them to try the most basic version of the software for free, and then persuading them to purchase one of its more full-featured commercial versions. Zimbra has over 200,000 visitors to its Web site each week.

Zimbra's sales process begins when one of these 200,000 weekly visitors downloads a 60-day trial version. Salespeople try to identify which people using the trial version are most likely to upgrade to one of its commercial versions and then contact these people via e-mail and telephone to try to close the sale.

To make this work, Zimbra's sales team needs capabililities for weeding out the interested buyers from its huge volume of Web visitors. As Greg Armanini, Zimbra's director of marketing pointed out, the sales team will be overwhelmed with a ton of unqualified leads unless sales and marketing automation tools are able to focus sales reps only on the leads that will generate revenue. Zimbra uses its Web site to track visitor activity and tie it to sales lead information in its Salesforce.com customer relationship management (CRM) system. Identifying sales prospects that visit the Web site regularly and alerting sales reps when those prospects are visiting the site helps the sales team select which prospects to contact by telephone and when to call them.

Zimbra initially used marketing automation software from Eloqua, which had a large number of features but was too complicated for both marketing and sales staff to use. For example, the Eloqua system required salespeople to code conditional logic for any data field containing data they wanted to collect. Though doable, this task was a poor usage of Zimbra's sales staff time. Eloqua only worked with the Internet Explorer Web browser, while two-thirds of Zimbra's sales department used Mozilla Firefox. And Eloqua was expensive. Zimbra could only afford its entry-level package, which provided access to only five salespeople and one marketing person.

Zimbra did not need many of Eloqua's features, but it did need a more streamlined solution that focused on the core areas of its marketing strategy: lead generation, e-mail marketing, and Web analytics. The new marketing automation system had to be easy to install and maintain. Many available options required several well-trained administrators, and Zimbra could not afford to allocate even one employee for this purpose.

After examining several software products, Zimbra choose OneView, an on-demand marketing automation solution from LoopFuse, a Georgia-based software company that specializes in sales and marketing automation. OneView was more highly targeted than the Eloqua software. Not only that, but much of OneView consists of automated processes that allowed Zimbra to quickly implement the solution and to maintain it without dedicating someone to the task full-time. The core functions of OneView include Web site visitor tracking, automated marketing program communication, customer activity alerts, and CRM integration.

Zimbra was also pleased with LoopFuse's convenient pricing options, including its "unlimited seating" and "pay-per-use" options, which allowed Zimbra to pay for only the services it needed for as many users as it required. Because of these options, Zimbra was able to deploy LoopFuse across almost its entire 30-person sales force.

Other benefits of OneView include easy integration with Salesforce.com, Zimbra's preferred CRM solution, simplified reporting processes, and the ability to manage a larger number of leads thanks to having more salespeople and time to devote to demand generation. OneView works with multiple Web browsers, including Firefox. The old solution offered so many ways to handle and organize data that generating data reports could take a long time. With OneView's simplified reporting processes, the sales staff can generate reports in a fraction of the time.

Has OneView improved Zimbra's bottom line? OneView reduced the amount of time Zimbra spent using and maintaining its marketing system by 50 percent. Zimbra reports that since changing vendors, it has witnessed a jump in its close rate on qualified sales leads from 10 to 15 percent, a huge increase. The answer appears to be a resounding "yes."

Sources: Jessica Tsai, "Less is More," *Customer Relationship Management*, August 2009, www.destinationCRM.com; and "LoopFuse OneView helps Zimbra Raise Sales and Marketing Efficiency by 50 Percent," www.loopfuse.com, May 2009.

CASE STUDY QUESTIONS

1. Describe the steps in Zimbra's sales process. How well did its old marketing automation system support that process? What problems did it create? What was the business impact of these problems?

2. List and describe Zimbra's requirements for a new marketing software package. If you were preparing the RFP for Zimbra's new system, what questions would you ask?

3. How did the new marketing system change the way Zimbra ran its business? How successful was it?

MIS IN ACTION

Visit the LoopFuse Web site and then answer the following questions:

1. List and describe each of the major features of LoopFuse OneView.

2. Select two of these features and describe how they would help Zimbra's sales team.

the project, including its requirements, method of implementation, source of expected benefits, cost components, and metrics for measuring performance.

Many firms underestimate costs for identifying and evaluating vendors of information technology services, for transitioning to a new vendor, for improving internal software development methods to match those of outsourcing vendors, and for monitoring vendors to make sure they are fulfilling their contractual obligations. Outsourcing offshore incurs additional costs for coping with cultural differences that drain productivity and dealing with human resources issues, such as terminating or relocating domestic employees. These hidden costs undercut some of the anticipated benefits from outsourcing. Firms should be especially cautious when using an outsourcer to develop or to operate applications that give it some type of competitive advantage.

Figure 11-5 shows best- and worst-case scenarios for the total cost of an offshore outsourcing project. It shows how much hidden costs affect the total project cost. The best case reflects the lowest estimates for additional costs, and the worst case reflects the highest estimates for these costs. As you can see, hidden costs increase the total cost of an offshore outsourcing project by an extra 15 to 57 percent. Even with these extra costs, many firms will benefit from offshore outsourcing if they manage the work well.

RAPID APPLICATION DEVELOPMENT FOR E-BUSINESS

Technologies and business conditions are changing so rapidly that agility and scalability have become critical elements of system solutions. Companies are adopting shorter, more informal development processes for many of their e-commerce and e-business applications, processes that provide fast solutions that do not disrupt their core transaction processing systems and organizational databases. In addition to using software packages, application service providers, and other outsourcing services, they are relying more heavily on fast-cycle techniques, such as joint application design (JAD), prototypes, and reusable standardized software components that can be assembled into a complete set of services for e-commerce and e-business.

The term **rapid application development (RAD)** refers to the process of creating workable systems in a very short period of time. RAD includes the use of visual program-

TOTAL COST OF OFFSHORE OUTSOURCING				
Cost of outsourcing contract			$10,000,000	
Hidden Costs	Best Case	Additional Cost ($)	Worst Case	Additional Cost ($)
1. Vendor selection	0.2%	20,000	2%	200,000
2. Transition costs	2%	200,000	3%	300,000
3. Layoffs & retention	3%	300,000	5%	500,000
4. Lost productivity/cultural issues	3%	300,000	27%	2,700,000
5. Improving development processes	1%	100,000	10%	1,000,000
6. Managing the contract	6%	600,000	10%	1,000,000
Total additional costs		1,520,000		5,700,000
	Outstanding Contract ($)	Additional Cost ($)	Total Cost ($)	Additional Cost
Total cost of outsourcing (TCO) best case	10,000,000	1,520,000	11,520,000	15.2%
Total cost of outsourcing (TCO) worst case	10,000,000	5,700,000	15,700,000	57.0%

Figure 11-5
Total Cost of Offshore Outsourcing
If a firm spends $10 million on offshore outsourcing contracts, that company will actually spend 15.2 percent in extra costs even under the best-case scenario. In the worst-case scenario, where there is a dramatic drop in productivity along with exceptionally high transition and layoff costs, a firm can expect to pay up to 57 percent in extra costs on top of the $10 million outlay for an offshore contract.

ming and other tools for building graphical user interfaces, iterative prototyping of key system elements, the automation of program code generation, and close teamwork among end users and information systems specialists. Simple systems often can be assembled from prebuilt components (see Section 11.3). The process does not have to be sequential, and key parts of development can occur simultaneously.

Sometimes a technique called **joint application design (JAD)** will be used to accelerate the generation of information requirements and to develop the initial systems design. JAD brings end users and information systems specialists together in an interactive session to discuss the system's design. Properly prepared and facilitated, JAD sessions can significantly speed up the design phase and involve users at an intense level.

11.3 Modeling and Designing Systems

We have just described alternative methods for building systems. There are also alternative methodologies for modeling and designing systems. The two most prominent are structured methodologies and object-oriented development.

STRUCTURED METHODOLOGIES

Structured methodologies have been used to document, analyze, and design information systems since the 1970s. **Structured** refers to the fact that the techniques are step by step, with each step building on the previous one. Structured methodologies are top-down, progressing from the highest, most abstract level to the lowest level of detail—from the general to the specific.

Structured development methods are process-oriented, focusing primarily on modeling the processes, or actions, that capture, store, manipulate, and distribute data as the data flow through a system. These methods separate data from processes. A separate programming procedure must be written every time someone wants to take an action on a particular piece of data. The procedures act on data that the program passes to them.

The primary tool for representing a system's component processes and the flow of data between them is the **data flow diagram (DFD)**. The data flow diagram offers a logical graphic model of information flow, partitioning a system into modules that show manageable levels of detail. It rigorously specifies the processes or transformations that occur within each module and the interfaces that exist between them.

Figure 11-6 shows a simple data flow diagram for a mail-in university course registration system. The rounded boxes represent processes, which portray the transformation of data. The square box represents an external entity, which is an originator or receiver of

Figure 11-6
Data Flow Diagram for Mail-in University Registration System
The system has three processes: Verify availability (1.0), Enroll student (2.0), and Confirm registration (3.0). The name and content of each of the data flows appear adjacent to each arrow. There is one external entity in this system: the student. There are two data stores: the student master file and the course file.

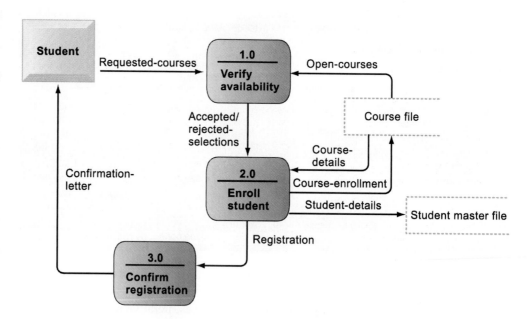

information located outside the boundaries of the system being modeled. The open rectangles represent data stores, which are either manual or automated inventories of data. The arrows represent data flows, which show the movement between processes, external entities, and data stores. They always contain packets of data with the name or content of each data flow listed beside the arrow.

This data flow diagram shows that students submit registration forms with their names, identification numbers, and the numbers of the courses they wish to take. In Process 1.0, the system verifies that each course selected is still open by referencing the university's course file. The file distinguishes courses that are open from those that have been canceled or filled. Process 1.0 then determines which of the student's selections can be accepted or rejected. Process 2.0 enrolls the student in the courses for which he or she has been accepted. It updates the university's course file with the student's name and identification number and recalculates the class size. If maximum enrollment has been reached, the course number is flagged as closed. Process 2.0 also updates the university's student master file with information about new students or changes in address. Process 3.0 then sends each student applicant a confirmation-of-registration letter listing the courses for which he or she is registered and noting the course selections that could not be fulfilled.

Through leveled data flow diagrams, a complex process can be broken down into successive levels of detail. An entire system can be divided into subsystems with a high-level data flow diagram. Each subsystem, in turn, can be divided into additional subsystems with lower-level data flow diagrams, and the lower-level subsystems can be broken down again until the lowest level of detail has been reached. **Process specifications** describe the transformation occurring within the lowest level of the data flow diagrams, showing the logic for each process.

In structured methodology, software design is modeled using hierarchical structure charts. The **structure chart** is a top-down chart, showing each level of design, its relationship to other levels, and its place in the overall design structure. The design first considers the main function of a program or system, then breaks this function into subfunctions, and decomposes each subfunction until the lowest level of detail has been reached. Figure 11-7 shows a high-level structure chart for a payroll system. If a design has too many levels to fit onto one structure chart, it can be broken down further on more detailed structure charts. A structure chart may document one program, one system (a set of programs), or part of one program.

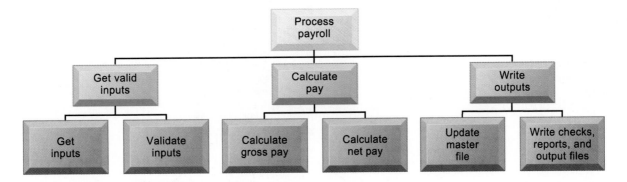

Figure 11-7 High-Level Structure Chart for a Payroll System
This structure chart shows the highest or most abstract level of design for a payroll system, providing an overview of the entire system.

OBJECT-ORIENTED DEVELOPMENT

Structured methods treat data and processes as logically separate entities, whereas in the real world such separation seems unnatural. Different modeling conventions are used for analysis (the data flow diagram) and for design (the structure chart).

Object-oriented development addresses these issues. Object-oriented development uses the object, which we introduced in Chapter 4, as the basic unit of systems analysis and design. An object combines data and the specific processes that operate on those data. Data encapsulated in an object can be accessed and modified only by the operations, or methods, associated with that object. Instead of passing data to procedures, programs send a message for an object to perform an operation that is already embedded in it. The system is modeled as a collection of objects and the relationships among them. Because processing logic resides within objects rather that in separate software programs, objects must collaborate with each other to make the system work.

Object-oriented modeling is based on the concepts of *class* and *inheritance*. Objects belonging to a certain class, or general categories of similar objects, have the features of that class. Classes of objects in turn inherit all the structure and behaviors of a more general class and then add variables and behaviors unique to each object. New classes of objects are created by choosing an existing class and specifying how the new class differs from the existing class, instead of starting from scratch each time.

We can see how class and inheritance work in Figure 11-8, which illustrates the relationships among classes concerning employees and how they are paid. Employee is the common ancestor, or superclass, for the other three classes. Salaried, Hourly, and Temporary are subclasses of Employee. The class name is in the top compartment, the attributes for each class are in the middle portion of each box, and the list of operations is in the bottom portion of each box. The features that are shared by all employees (ID, name, address, date hired, position, and pay) are stored in the Employee superclass, whereas each subclass stores features that are specific to that particular type of employee. Specific to Hourly employees, for example, are their hourly rates and overtime rates. A solid line from the subclass to the superclass is a generalization path showing that the subclasses Salaried, Hourly, and Temporary have common features that can be generalized into the superclass Employee.

Object-oriented development is more iterative and incremental than traditional structured development. During systems analysis, systems builders document the functional requirements of the system, specifying its most important properties and what the proposed system must do. Interactions between the system and its users are analyzed to identify objects, which include both data and processes. The object-oriented design phase describes how the objects will behave and how they will interact with one other. Similar objects are

Figure 11-8
Class and
Inheritance
*This figure illustrates
how classes inherit the
common features of their
superclass.*

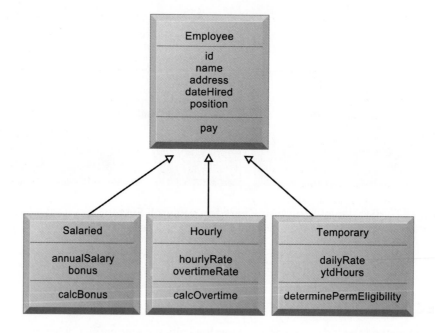

grouped together to form a class, and classes are grouped into hierarchies in which a subclass inherits the attributes and methods from its superclass.

The information system is implemented by translating the design into program code, reusing classes that are already available in a library of reusable software objects and adding new ones created during the object-oriented design phase. Implementation may also involve the creation of an object-oriented database. The resulting system must be thoroughly tested and evaluated.

Because objects are reusable, object-oriented development could potentially reduce the time and cost of writing software if organizations reuse software objects that have already been created as building blocks for other applications. New systems can be created by using some existing objects, changing others, and adding a few new objects.

Component-Based Development, Web Services, and Cloud-Based Development

To further expedite software creation, groups of objects have been assembled into software components for common functions, such as a graphical user interface or online ordering capability, and these components can be combined to create large-scale business applications. This approach to software development is called **component-based development**. Businesses are using component-based development to create their e-commerce applications by combining commercially available components for shopping carts, user authentication, search engines, and catalogs with pieces of software for their own unique business requirements.

Chapter 4 introduced Web services as loosely coupled, reusable software components based on Extensible Markup Language (XML) and other open protocols and standards that enable one application to communicate with another with no custom programming required. In addition to supporting internal and external integration of systems, Web services provide nonproprietary tools for building new information system applications or enhancing existing systems.

Platform as a service, introduced in the Chapter 4 discussion of cloud computing, also holds considerable potential for helping system developers quickly write and test customer- or employee-facing Web applications. These online development environments come from a range of vendors, including Sun, IBM, Salesforce.com (Force.com), and Microsoft (Azure). These platforms automate tasks such as setting up a newly composed application as a Web service or linking to other applications and services. Some also offer a cloud infrastructure service, or links to cloud vendors such as Amazon, so that developers can launch what they build in a cloud infrastructure.

COMPUTER-AIDED SOFTWARE ENGINEERING (CASE)

Computer-aided software engineering (CASE)—sometimes called computer-aided systems engineering—provides software tools to automate the methodologies we have just described to reduce the amount of repetitive work in systems development. CASE tools provide automated graphics facilities for producing charts and diagrams, screen and report generators, data dictionaries, extensive reporting facilities, analysis and checking tools, code generators, and documentation generators. CASE tools also contain features for validating design diagrams and specifications.

CASE tools facilitate clear documentation and coordination of team development efforts. Team members can share their work by accessing each other's files to review or modify what has been done. Modest productivity benefits are achieved if the tools are used properly. Many CASE tools are PC based, with powerful graphical capabilities.

11.4 Project Management

Your company might have developed what appears to be an excellent system solution. Yet when the system is in use, it does not work properly or it doesn't deliver the benefits that were promised. If this occurs, your firm is not alone. There is a very high failure rate among information systems projects because they have not been properly managed. The Standish Group consultancy, which monitors IT project success rates, found that only 29 percent of all technology investments were completed on time, on budget, and with all features and functions originally specified (Levinson, 2006). Firms may have incorrectly assessed the business value of the new system or were unable to manage the organizational change required by the new technology. That's why it's essential to know how to manage information systems projects and the reasons why they succeed or fail.

The Interactive Session on People provides an example of a failed project. Kaiser Permanente, one of the largest health management organizations in the United States, was unable to establish its own center for handling kidney transplants. Kaiser opened its transplant center in 2004, but had to shut down the facility less than two years after it opened. A major factor was the company's mismanagement of information and information systems.

PROJECT MANAGEMENT OBJECTIVES

A **project** is a planned series of related activities for achieving a specific business objective. Information systems projects include the development of new information systems, enhancement of existing systems, or projects for replacement or upgrading of the firm's information technology (IT) infrastructure.

Project management refers to the application of knowledge, skills, tools, and techniques to achieve specific targets within specified budget and time constraints. Project management activities include planning the work, assessing risk, estimating resources required to accomplish the work, organizing the work, acquiring human and material resources, assigning tasks, directing activities, controlling project execution, reporting progress, and analyzing the results. As in other areas of business, project management for information systems must deal with five major variables: scope, time, cost, quality, and risk.

Scope defines what work is or is not included in a project. For example, the scope of a project for a new order processing system might include new modules for inputting orders and transmitting them to production and accounting but not any changes to related accounts receivable, manufacturing, distribution, or inventory control systems. Project management defines all the work required to complete a project successfully, and should ensure that the scope of a project does not expand beyond what was originally intended.

INTERACTIVE SESSION: PEOPLE   Kaiser Permanente Botches Its Kidney Transplant Center Project

Kaiser Permanente is one of the country's foremost health maintenance organizations (HMOs), also referred to as integrated managed care organizations. HMOs provide health care that is fulfilled by hospitals, doctors, and other providers with which the HMO has a contract. While Kaiser is a non-profit organization, the company earned $34.4 billion in revenues in 2007. Kaiser has approximately 170,000 employees, over 13,000 doctors, and serves 8.7 million members in nine states. The company is headquartered in Oakland, CA.

Kaiser is known for pioneering electronic medical records and currently boasts the world's largest electronic medical record storage system. The company also consistently ranks among the top HMOs in customer satisfaction. However, a 2004 attempt by Kaiser to handle kidney transplants on its own by setting up a transplant center was a public relations and information technology disaster. The company forced its members to transfer to its kidney transplant program without having adequately prepared to treat those patients.

In 2004, Kaiser implemented a kidney transplant program in Northern California under which transplants would be performed in-house at a transplant center owned and managed by Kaiser. Previously, the HMO had contracted with nearby university-affiliated California hospitals, such as UC San Francisco and UC Davis. The fledgling transplant center was shut down just two years later because of a litany of mistakes pertaining to paperwork, technology, and procedural planning. Through the duration of the doomed project, twice as many people died waiting for a transplant as received successful transplants. Patients now receive care from local hospitals once again.

Kaiser did very little correctly in its attempt to create its own kidney transplant program. The company lost track of records when transferring them to the new transplant center. More than 1,000 of the 1,500 patient records had incomplete or incorrect data, such as erroneous social security numbers and missing test results. Despite Kaiser's longtime experience with electronic medical records, the new center's records were stored primarily on paper. Kaiser had no comprehensive transplant patient master list or database. Many other transplant programs have multiple IT professionals assigned to maintain the complicated databases required for a transplant program. Kaiser attempted to run such a program without similar resources. Kaiser employees dedicated to processing information on prospective transplant recipients were overworked, logging 10- to 16-

hour days as they tried to keep up with the avalanche of information. The company did not accurately anticipate the personnel requirements of their undertaking.

These were by no means the company's only mistakes, however. There were no specific procedures for transferring data on the initial patients to the United Network for Organ Sharing (UNOS), which oversees national transplant waiting lists. There were no systematic processes for tracking or responding to patient complaints or requests. The Kaiser staff lacked guidance and training regarding their job requirements and uniformly lacked prior experience with transplant programs. And there was no executive governance to identify and correct any of these procedural problems that arose almost immediately after the beginning of the project. Kaiser had seemingly made no attempt to identify and define the processes required to ensure a smooth transition from external transplant programs to an in-house program.

Kaiser also failed to give patients credit for time spent on waiting lists at other hospitals, sometimes dropping patients who had waited the longest down to the bottom of the list. Unlike other companies, IT mismanagement in health care companies can cost individuals their lives, and in Kaiser's case many plaintiffs seeking damages against the company believe the errors surrounding the Kaiser transplant center have done just that.

At the outset of the transition, Kaiser mailed potential kidney recipients consent forms but did not offer specific directions about what to do with the forms. Many patients failed to respond to the letter, unsure of how to handle it, and others returned the forms to the wrong entity. Other patients were unable to correct inaccurate information, and as a result, UNOS was not able to approve those patients for inclusion on Kaiser's repopulated kidney wait list.

Despite all of the IT mishaps, the medical aspect of the transplant program was quite successful. All 56 transplant recipients in the first full year of business were still living one year later, which is considered to be strong evidence of high quality. But as the organizational woes continued to mount, Kaiser was forced to shut the program down in 2006, absorbing heavy losses and incurring what figures to be considerable legal expenses.

Kaiser paid a $2 million fine to be levied by the California Department of Managed Health Care (DMHC) for the various state and federal regulations it failed to adhere to in its attempt to set up a transplant program. Kaiser was also forced to make a $3 million charitable donation.

Many families of people who died waiting for kidneys from Kaiser are suing the company for medical negligence and wrongful death. Other patients, such as Bernard Burks, are going after Kaiser themselves for the same reasons. In March 2008, Burks won the right to have his case heard by a jury in a public courtroom, rather than a private judge or lawyer in arbitration. Most patient disputes with Kaiser are traditionally settled behind closed doors, presumably to minimize the damage to the company's reputation and increase the likelihood of winning their cases. Burks was the first of over 100 patients on Kaiser's kidney transplant waiting list to win the right to a jury trial.

Sources: Marie-Anne Hogarth, "Kidney Patient Beats Kaiser Arbitration Rule," *East Bay Business Times*, March 21, 2008 and Kim S. Nash, "We Really Did Screw Up," *Baseline Magazine*, May, 2007.

CASE STUDY QUESTIONS

1. Classify and describe the problems Kaiser faced in setting up the transplant center. What was the role of information systems and information management in these problems?

2. What were the people, organization, and technology factors responsible for those problems?

3. What steps would you have taken to increase the project's chances for success?

4. Were there any ethical problems created by this failed project? Explain your answer.

MIS IN ACTION

Explore the Web site for TeleResults (www.teleresults.com), a provider of state-of-the-art electronic medical record (EMR) solutions and transplant software, then answer the following question:

1. How could this company's products have helped Kaiser Permanente manage transplant information?

Time is the amount of time required to complete the project. Project management typically establishes the amount of time required to complete major components of a project. Each of these components is further broken down into activities and tasks. Project management tries to determine the time required to complete each task and establish a schedule for completing the work.

Cost is based on the time to complete a project multiplied by the daily cost of human resources required to complete the project. Information systems project costs also include the cost of hardware, software, and work space. Project management develops a budget for the project and monitors ongoing project expenses.

Quality is an indicator of how well the end result of a project satisfies the objectives specified by management. The quality of information systems projects usually boils down to improved organizational performance and decision making. Quality also considers the accuracy and timeliness of information produced by the new system and ease of use.

Risk refers to potential problems that would threaten the success of a project. These potential problems might prevent a project from achieving its objectives by increasing time and cost, lowering the quality of project outputs, or preventing the project from being completed altogether. We discuss the most important risk factors for information systems projects later in this section.

SELECTING PROJECTS: MAKING THE BUSINESS CASE FOR A NEW SYSTEM

Companies typically are presented with many different projects for solving problems and improving performance. There are far more ideas for systems projects than there are resources. You will need to select the projects that promise the greatest benefit to the business.

Determining Project Costs and Benefits

As we pointed out earlier, the systems analysis includes an assessment of the economic feasibility of each alternative solution—whether each solution represents a good investment for the company. In order to identify the information systems projects that will deliver the most business value, you'll need to identify their costs and benefits and how they relate to the firm's information systems plan.

Table 11.3 lists some of the more common costs and benefits of systems. **Tangible benefits** can be quantified and assigned a monetary value. **Intangible benefits**, such as more efficient customer service or enhanced decision making, cannot be immediately quantified. Yet systems that produce mainly intangible benefits may still be good investments if they produce quantifiable gains in the long run.

To determine the benefits of a particular solution, you'll need to calculate all of its costs and all of its benefits. Obviously, a solution where costs exceed benefits should be rejected. But even if the benefits outweigh the costs, some additional financial analysis is required to determine whether the investment represents a good return on the firm's invested capital. Capital budgeting methods, such as net present value, internal rate of return (IRR), or accounting rate of return on investment (ROI), would typically be employed to evaluate the proposed information system solution as an investment. You can find out more about how these capital budgeting methods are used to justify information system investments in our Learning Tracks.

Some of the tangible benefits obtained by the Girl Scouts were increased productivity and lower operational costs resulting from automating the ordering process and from reducing errors. Intangible benefits included enhanced volunteer job satisfaction and improved operations.

The Information Systems Plan

An **information systems plan** shows how specific information systems fit into a company's overall business plan and business strategy. Table 11.4 lists the major components of such a

TABLE 11.3

Costs and Benefits of Information Systems

IMPLEMENTATION COSTS
Hardware
Telecommunications
Software
Personnel costs

OPERATIONAL COSTS
Computer processing time
Maintenance
Operating staff
User time
Ongoing training costs
Facility costs

TANGIBLE BENEFITS
Increased productivity
Lower operational costs
Reduced workforce
Lower computer expenses
Lower outside vendor costs
Lower clerical and professional costs
Reduced rate of growth in expenses
Reduced facility costs
Increased sales

INTANGIBLE BENEFITS
Improved asset utilization
Improved resource control
Improved organizational planning
Increased organizational flexibility
More timely information
More information
Increased organizational learning
Legal requirements attained
Enhanced employee goodwill
Increased job satisfaction
Improved decision making
Improved operations
Higher client satisfaction
Better corporate image

TABLE 11.4

Information Systems Plan

1. **Purpose of the Plan**
   Overview of plan contents
   Current business organization and future organization
   Key business processes
   Management strategy

2. **Strategic Business Plan Rationale**
   Current situation
   Current business organization
   Changing environments
   Major goals of the business plan
   Firm's strategic plan

3. **Current Systems**
   Major systems supporting business functions and processes
   Current infrastructure capabilities
   - Hardware
   - Software
   - Database
   - Telecommunications and the Internet
   Difficulties meeting business requirements
   Anticipated future demands

4. **New Developments**
   New system projects
   - Project descriptions
   - Business rationale
   - Applications' role in strategy
   New infrastructure capabilities required
   - Hardware
   - Software
   - Database
   - Telecommunications and the Internet

5. **Management Strategy**
   Acquisition plans
   Milestones and timing
   Organizational realignment
   Internal reorganization
   Management controls
   Major training initiatives
   Personnel strategy

6. **Implementation of the Plan**
   Anticipated difficulties in implementation
   Progress reports

7. **Budget Requirements**
   Requirements
   Potential savings
   Financing
   Acquisition cycle

plan. The plan contains a statement of corporate goals and specifies how information technology will help the business attain these goals. The report shows how general goals will be achieved by specific systems projects. It identifies specific target dates and milestones that can be used later to evaluate the plan's progress in terms of how many objectives were actually attained in the time frame specified in the plan. The plan indicates the key management decisions concerning hardware acquisition; telecommunications; centralization/decentralization of authority, data, and hardware; and required organizational change.

The plan should describe organizational changes, including management and employee training requirements, changes in business processes, and changes in authority, structure, or management practice. When you are making the business case for a new information system project, you show how the proposed system fits into that plan.

Portfolio Analysis

Once you have determined the overall direction of systems development, **portfolio analysis** will help you evaluate alternative system projects. Portfolio analysis inventories all of the firm's information systems projects and assets, including infrastructure, outsourcing contracts, and licenses. This portfolio of information systems investments can be described as having a certain profile of risk and benefit to the firm (see Figure 11-9), similar to a financial portfolio. Each information systems project carries its own set of risks and benefits. Firms try to improve the return on their information system portfolios by balancing the risk and return from their systems investments.

Obviously, you begin first by focusing on systems of high benefit and low risk. These promise early returns and low risks. Second, high-benefit, high-risk systems should be examined; low-benefit, high-risk systems should be totally avoided; and low-benefit, low-risk systems should be reexamined for the possibility of rebuilding and replacing them with more desirable systems having higher benefits. By using portfolio analysis, management can determine the optimal mix of investment risk and reward for their firms, balancing riskier, high-reward projects with safer, lower-reward ones.

The U.S. Army's Office of the CIO/G-6, which oversees an annual IT budget of more than $7 billion and manages over 1,500 systems and programs, uses portfolio analysis to inventory, evaluate, and rank its IT investments. Portfolio analysis helped the Office identify redundant systems and ensure that its IT investments provide needed capabilities.

Another method for evaluating alternative system solutions is a **scoring model**. Scoring models give alternative systems a single score based on the extent to which they meet selected objectives. Table 11.5 shows part of a simple scoring model that could have been used by the Girl Scouts in evaluating their alternative systems. The first column lists the criteria that decision makers use to evaluate the systems. Table 11.5 shows that the Girl Scouts attach the most importance to capabilities for sales order processing, ease of use, ability to support users in many different locations, and low cost. The second column in Table 11.5 lists the weights that decision makers attached to the decision criteria. Columns 3 and 5 show the percentage of requirements for each function that each alternative system

Figure 11-9
A System Portfolio
Companies should examine their portfolio of projects in terms of potential benefits and likely risks. Certain kinds of projects should be avoided altogether and others developed rapidly. There is no ideal mix. Companies in different industries have different information systems needs.

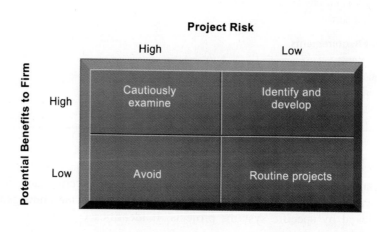

Example of a Scoring Model for the Girl Scouts Cookie System

Criteria	Weight	Microsoft Access System (%)	Microsoft Access System Score	QuickBase System (%)	QuickBase System Score
1.0 Order processing					
1.1 Online order entry	5	67	335	83	415
1.2 Order tracking by troop	5	81	405	87	435
1.3 Order tracking by individual Girl Scout	5	72	360	80	400
1.4 Reserving warehouse pickups	3	66	198	79	237
Total order processing			1,298		1,487
2.0 Ease of use					
2.1 Web access from multiple locations	5	55	275	92	460
2.2 Short training time	4	79	316	85	340
2.3 User-friendly screens and data entry forms	4	65	260	87	348
Total ease of use			851		1,148
3.0 Costs					
3.1 Software costs	3	51	153	65	195
3.2 Hardware (server) costs	4	57	228	90	360
3.3 Maintenance and support costs	4	42	168	89	356
Total costs			549		911
Grand Total			2,698		3,546

meets. Each alternative's score is calculated by multiplying the percentage of requirements met for each function by the weight attached to that function. The QuickBase solution has the highest total score.

MANAGING PROJECT RISK AND SYSTEM-RELATED CHANGE

Some systems development projects are more likely to run into problems or to suffer delays because they carry a much higher level of risk than others. The level of project risk is influenced by project size, project structure, and the level of technical expertise of the information systems staff and project team. The larger the project—as indicated by the dollars spent, project team size, and how many parts of the organization will be affected by the new system—the greater the risk. Very large-scale systems projects have a failure rate that is 50 to 75 percent higher than that for other projects because such projects are complex and difficult to control. Risks are also higher for systems where information requirements are not clear and straightforward or the project team must master new technology.

Implementation and Change Management

Dealing with these project risks requires an understanding of the implementation process and change management. A broader definition of **implementation** refers to all the organizational activities working toward the adoption and management of an innovation, such as a new information system. Successful implementation requires a high level of user involvement in a project and management support.

If users are heavily involved in the development of a system, they have more opportunities to mold the system according to their priorities and business requirements, and more opportunities to control the outcome. They also are more likely to react positively to the completed system because they have been active participants in the change process. Incorporating user knowledge and expertise leads to better solutions.

The relationship between end users and information systems specialists has traditionally been a problem area for information systems implementation efforts because of differing backgrounds, interests, and priorities. These differences create a **user-designer communications gap**. Information systems specialists often have a highly technical orientation to problem solving, focusing on technical solutions in which hardware and software efficiency is optimized at the expense of ease of use or organizational effectiveness. End users prefer systems that are oriented toward solving business problems or facilitating organizational tasks. Often the orientations of both groups are so at odds that they appear to speak in different tongues.

These differences are illustrated in Table 11.6, which depicts the typical concerns of end users and technical specialists (information systems designers) regarding the development of a new information system. Communication problems between end users and designers are a major reason why user requirements are not properly incorporated into information systems and why users are driven out of the implementation process.

If an information systems project has the backing and commitment of management at various levels, it is more likely to receive higher priority from both users and the technical information systems staff. Management backing also ensures that a systems project receives sufficient funding and resources to be successful. Furthermore, to be enforced effectively, all the changes in work habits and procedures and any organizational realignments associated with a new system depend on management backing.

Controlling Risk Factors

There are strategies you can follow to deal with project risk and increase the chances of a successful system solution. If the new system involves challenging and complex technology, you can recruit project leaders with strong technical and administrative experience. Outsourcing or using external consultants are options if your firm does not have staff with the required technical skills or expertise.

TABLE 11.6

The User-Designer Communications Gap

User Concerns	Designer Concerns
Will the system deliver the information I need for my work?	How much disk storage space will the master file consume?
How quickly can I access the data?	How many lines of program code will it take to perform this function?
How easily can I retrieve the data?	How can we cut down on CPU time when we run the system?
How much clerical support will I need to enter data into the system?	What is the most efficient way of storing the data?
How will the operation of the system fit into my daily business schedule?	What database management system should we use?

Large projects benefit from appropriate use of **formal planning and tools** for documenting and monitoring project plans. The two most commonly used methods for documenting project plans are Gantt charts and PERT charts. A **Gantt chart** lists project activities and their corresponding start and completion dates. The Gantt chart visually represents the timing and duration of different tasks in a development project as well as their human resource requirements (see Figure 11-10). It shows each task as a horizontal bar whose length is proportional to the time required to complete it.

Although Gantt charts show when project activities begin and end, they don't depict task dependencies, how one task is affected if another is behind schedule, or how tasks should be ordered. That is where **PERT charts** are useful. PERT stands for Program Evaluation and Review Technique, a methodology developed by the U.S. Navy during the 1950s to manage the Polaris submarine missile program. A PERT chart graphically depicts project tasks and their interrelationships. The PERT chart lists the specific activities that make up a project and the activities that must be completed before a specific activity can start, as illustrated in Figure 11-11.

The PERT chart portrays a project as a network diagram consisting of numbered nodes (either circles or rectangles) representing project tasks. Each node is numbered and shows the task, its duration, the starting date, and the completion date. The direction of the arrows on the lines indicates the sequence of tasks and shows which activities must be completed before the commencement of another activity. In Figure 11-11, the tasks in nodes 2, 3, and 4 are not dependent on each other and can be undertaken simultaneously, but each is dependent on completion of the first task.

Project Management Software Commercial software tools are available to automate the creation of Gantt and PERT charts and to facilitate the project management process. Project management software typically features capabilities for defining and ordering tasks, assigning resources to tasks, establishing starting and ending dates for tasks, tracking progress, and facilitating modifications to tasks and resources. The most widely used project management tool today is Microsoft Office Project.

Overcoming User Resistance

You can overcome user resistance by promoting user participation (to elicit commitment as well as to improve design), by making user education and training easily available, and by providing better incentives for users who cooperate. End users can become active members of the project team, take on leadership roles, and take charge of system installation and training.

You should pay special attention to areas where users interface with the system, with sensitivity to ergonomics issues. **Ergonomics** refers to the interaction of people and machines in the work environment. It considers the design of jobs, health issues, and the end-user interface of information systems. For instance, if a system has a series of complicated online data entry screens that are extremely difficult or time-consuming to work with, users will reject the system if it increases their work load or level of job stress.

Users will be more cooperative if organizational problems are solved prior to introducing the new system. In addition to procedural changes, transformations in job functions, organizational structure, power relationships, and behavior should be identified during systems analysis using an **organizational impact analysis**.

MANAGING PROJECTS ON A GLOBAL SCALE

As globalization proceeds, companies will be building many more new systems that are global in scale, spanning many different units in many different countries. The project management challenges for global systems are similar to those for domestic systems, but they are complicated by the international environment. User information requirements, business processes, and work cultures differ from country to country. It is difficult to convince local managers anywhere in the world to change their business processes and ways of working to align with units in other countries, especially if this might interfere with their local performance.

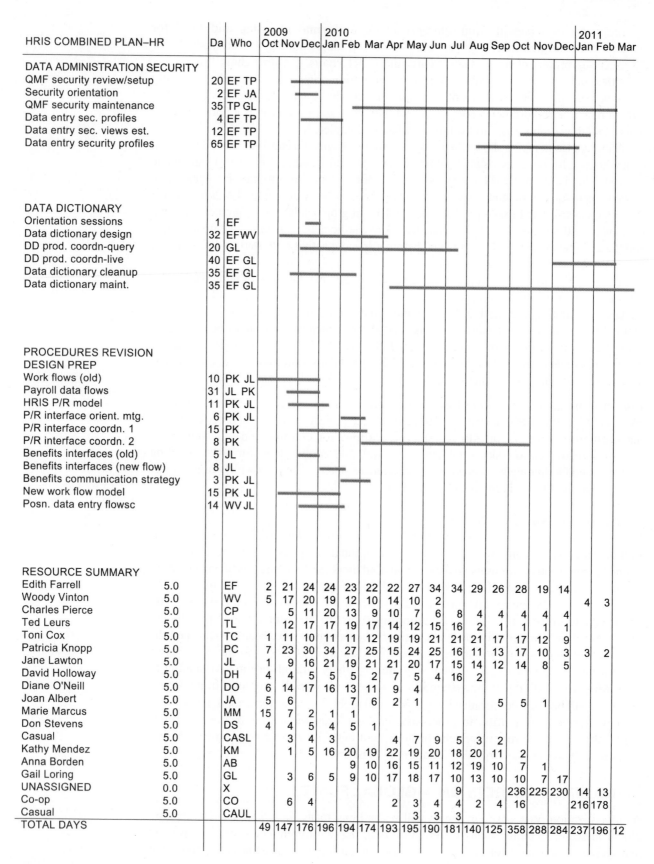

HRIS COMBINED PLAN–HR

Task	Da	Who
DATA ADMINISTRATION SECURITY		
QMF security review/setup	20	EF TP
Security orientation	2	EF JA
QMF security maintenance	35	TP GL
Data entry sec. profiles	4	EF TP
Data entry sec. views est.	12	EF TP
Data entry security profiles	65	EF TP
DATA DICTIONARY		
Orientation sessions	1	EF
Data dictionary design	32	EFWV
DD prod. coordn-query	20	GL
DD prod. coordn-live	40	EF GL
Data dictionary cleanup	35	EF GL
Data dictionary maint.	35	EF GL
PROCEDURES REVISION / DESIGN PREP		
Work flows (old)	10	PK JL
Payroll data flows	31	JL PK
HRIS P/R model	11	PK JL
P/R interface orient. mtg.	6	PK JL
P/R interface coordn. 1	15	PK
P/R interface coordn. 2	8	PK
Benefits interfaces (old)	5	JL
Benefits interfaces (new flow)	8	JL
Benefits communication strategy	3	PK JL
New work flow model	15	PK JL
Posn. data entry flowsc	14	WV JL

RESOURCE SUMMARY

Name	Rate		2009 Oct	Nov	Dec	2010 Jan	Feb	Mar	Apr	May	Jun	Jul	Aug	Sep	Oct	Nov	Dec	2011 Jan	Feb	Mar
Edith Farrell	5.0	EF	2	21	24	24	23	22	22	27	34	34	29	26	28	19	14			
Woody Vinton	5.0	WV	5	17	20	19	12	10	14	10	2							4	3	
Charles Pierce	5.0	CP		5	11	20	13	9	10	7	6	8	4	4	4	4	4			
Ted Leurs	5.0	TL		12	17	17	17	19	17	14	12	15	16	2	1	1	1			
Toni Cox	5.0	TC	1	11	10	11	11	12	19	19	21	21	17	17	12	9				
Patricia Knopp	5.0	PC	7	23	30	34	27	25	15	24	25	16	11	13	17	10	3	3	2	
Jane Lawton	5.0	JL	1	9	16	21	19	21	21	20	17	15	14	12	14	8	5			
David Holloway	5.0	DH	4	4	5	5	5	2	7	5	4	16	2							
Diane O'Neill	5.0	DO	6	14	17	16	13	11	9	4										
Joan Albert	5.0	JA	5	6			7	6	2	1				5	5	1				
Marie Marcus	5.0	MM	15	7	2	1	1													
Don Stevens	5.0	DS	4	4	5	4	5	1												
Casual	5.0	CASL		3	4	3			4	7	9	5	3	2						
Kathy Mendez	5.0	KM		1	5	16	20	19	22	19	20	18	20	11	2					
Anna Borden	5.0	AB					9	10	16	15	11	12	19	10	7	1				
Gail Loring	5.0	GL		3	6	5	9	10	17	18	17	10	13	10	10	7	17			
UNASSIGNED	0.0	X												9	236	225	230	14	13	
Co-op	5.0	CO	6	4					2	3	4	4	2	4	16			216	178	
Casual	5.0	CAUL									3	3	3							
TOTAL DAYS			49	147	176	196	194	174	193	195	190	181	140	125	358	288	284	237	196	12

Figure 11-10
A Gantt Chart

The Gantt chart in this figure shows the task, person-days, and initials of each responsible person, as well as the start and finish dates for each task. The resource summary provides a good manager with the total person-days for each month and for each person working on the project to manage the project successfully. The project described here is a data administration project.

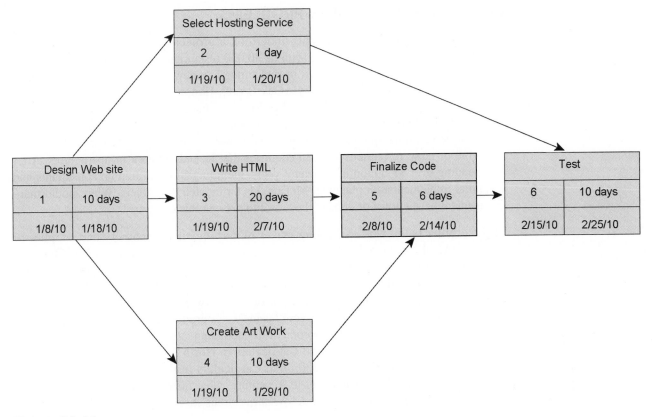

Figure 11-11
A PERT Chart
This is a simplified PERT chart for creating a small Web site. It shows the ordering of project tasks and the relationship of a task with preceding and succeeding tasks.

Involving people in change, and assuring them that change is in the best interests of the company and their local units, is a key tactic for convincing users to adopt global systems and standards. Information systems projects should involve users in the design process without giving up control over the project to parochial interests.

One tactic is to permit each country unit in a global corporation to develop one transnational application first in its home territory, and then throughout the world. In this manner, each major country systems group is given a piece of the action in developing a transnational system, and local units feel a sense of ownership in the transnational effort. On the downside, this assumes the ability to develop high-quality systems is widely distributed, and that, a German team, for example, can successfully implement systems in France and Italy. This will not always be the case.

A second tactic is to develop new transnational centers of excellence, or a single center of excellence. These centers draw heavily from local national units, are based on multinational teams, and must report to worldwide management. Centers of excellence perform the business and systems analysis and accomplish all design and testing. Implementation, however, and pilot testing are rolled out to other parts of the globe. Recruiting a wide range of local groups to transnational centers of excellence helps send the message that all significant groups are involved in the design and will have an influence.

11.5 Hands-On MIS Projects

The projects in this section give you hands-on experience evaluating information systems projects, designing and building a customer system for auto sales, and analyzing Web site information requirements.

MANAGEMENT DECISION PROBLEMS

1. In 2001, McDonald's Restaurants undertook a project called Innovate to create an intranet connecting headquarters with its 30,000 restaurants in 120 countries to provide detailed operational information in real time. The new system would, for instance, inform a manager at the company's Oak Brook, Illinois, headquarters immediately if sales were slowing at a franchise in London, or if the grill temperature in a Rochester, Minnesota, restaurant wasn't hot enough. The idea was to create a global enterprise resource planning application touching the workings of every McDonald's restaurant. Some of these restaurants were in countries that lacked network infrastructures. After spending over $1 billion over several years, including $170 million on consultants and initial implementation planning, McDonalds terminated the project. What should management have known or done at the outset to prevent this outcome?

2. Caterpillar is the world's leading maker of earthmoving machinery and supplier of agricultural equipment. Caterpillar wants to end its support for its Dealer Business System (DBS), which it licenses to its dealers to help them run their businesses. The software in this system is becoming outdated, and senior management wants to transfer support for the hosted version of the software to Accenture Consultants so Caterpillar can concentrate on its core business. Caterpillar never required its dealers to use DBS, but the system had become a de-facto standard for doing business with the company. The majority of the 50 Cat dealers in North America use some version of DBS, as do about half of the 200 or so Cat dealers in the rest of the world. Before Caterpillar turns the product over to Accenture, what factors and issues should it consider? What questions should it ask? What questions should its dealers ask?

IMPROVING DECISION MAKING: USING DATABASE SOFTWARE TO DESIGN A CUSTOMER SYSTEM FOR AUTO SALES

Software skills: Database design, querying, reporting, and forms
Business skills: Sales lead and customer analysis

This project requires you to perform a systems analysis and then design a system solution using database software.

Ace Auto Dealers specializes in selling new vehicles from Subaru. The company advertises in local newspapers and also is listed as an authorized dealer on the Subaru Web site and other major Web sites for auto buyers. The company benefits from a good local word-of-mouth reputation and name recognition and is a leading source of information for Subaru vehicles in the Portland, Oregon, area.

When a prospective customer enters the showroom, he or she is greeted by an Ace sales representative. The sales representative manually fills out a form with information such as the prospective customer's name, address, telephone number, date of visit, and make and model of the vehicle in which the customer is interested. The representative also asks where the prospect heard about Ace—whether it was from a newspaper ad, the Web, or word of mouth—and this information is noted on the form also. If the customer decides to purchase an auto, the dealer fills out a bill of sale form.

Ace does not believe it has enough information about its customers. It cannot easily determine which prospects have made auto purchases, nor can it identify which customer touch points have produced the greatest number of sales leads or actual sales so it can focus advertising and marketing more on the channels that generate the most revenue. Are purchasers discovering Ace from newspaper ads, from word of mouth, or from the Web?

Prepare a systems analysis report detailing Ace's problem and a system solution that can be implemented using PC database management software. Then use database software to develop a simple system solution. Your systems analysis report should include the following:

- Description of the problem and its organizational and business impact.
- Proposed solution, solution objectives, and solution feasibility.
- Costs and benefits of the solution you have selected. The company has a PC with Internet access and the full suite of Microsoft Office desktop productivity tools.
- Information requirements to be addressed by the solution.
- People, organization, and technology issues to be addressed by the solution, including changes in business processes.

On the basis of the requirements you have identified, design the database and populate it with at least 10 records per table. Consider whether you can use or modify the existing customer database in your design. Print out the database design. Then use the system you have created to generate queries and reports that would be of most interest to management. Create several prototype data input forms for the system and review them with your instructor. Then revise the prototypes.

ACHIEVING OPERATIONAL EXCELLENCE: ANALYZING WEB SITE DESIGN AND INFORMATION REQUIREMENTS

Software skills: Web browser software
Business skills: Information requirements analysis, Web site design

Visit the Web site of your choice and explore it thoroughly. Prepare a report analyzing the various functions provided by that Web site and its information requirements. Your report should answer these questions: What functions does the Web site perform? What data does it use? What are its inputs, outputs, and processes? What are some of its other design specifications? Does the Web site link to any internal systems or systems of other organizations? What value does this Web site provide the firm?

LEARNING TRACKS

The following Learning Tracks provide content relevant to topics covered in this chapter:

1. Capital Budgeting Methods for Information System Investments
2. Enterprise Analysis (Business Systems Planning) and Critical Success Factors (CSFs)
3. Unified Modeling Language (UML)
4. IT Investments and Productivity

Review Summary

1 **What are the core problem-solving steps for developing new information systems?** The core problem-solving steps for developing new information systems are: (1) define and understand the problem, (2) develop alternative solutions, (3) evaluate and choose the solution, and (4) implement the solution. The third step includes an assessment of the technical, financial, and organizational feasibility of each alternative. The fourth step entails finalizing design specifications, acquiring hardware and software, testing, providing training and documentation, conversion, and evaluating the system solution once it is in production.

2 **What are the alternative methods for building information systems?** The systems lifecycle requires that information systems be developed in formal stages. The stages must proceed sequentially and have defined outputs; each requires formal approval before the next stage can commence. The system lifecycle is rigid and costly but nevertheless useful for large projects.

Prototyping consists of building an experimental system rapidly and inexpensively for end users to interact with and evaluate. The prototype is refined and enhanced until users are satisfied that it includes all of their requirements and can be used as a template to create the final system. End-user-developed systems can be created rapidly and informally using fourth-generation software tools. End-user development can improve requirements determination and reduce application backlog.

Application software packages eliminate the need for writing software programs when developing an information system. Application software packages are helpful if a firm does not have the internal information systems staff or financial resources to custom-develop a system.

Outsourcing consists of using an external vendor to build (or operate) a firm's information systems. If it is properly managed, outsourcing can save application development costs or enable firms to develop applications without an internal information systems staff.

Rapid application design, joint application design (JAD), cloud-based platforms, and reusable software components (including Web services) can be used to speed up the systems development process.

3 **What are the principal methodologies for modeling and designing systems?** The two principal methodologies for modeling and designing information systems are structured methodologies and object-oriented development. Structured methodologies focus on modeling processes and data separately. The data flow diagram is the principal tool for structured analysis, and the structure chart is the principal tool for representing structured software design. Object-oriented development models a system as a collection of objects that combine processes and data.

4 **How should information systems projects be selected and evaluated?** To determine whether an information system project is a good investment, one must calculate its costs and benefits. Tangible benefits are quantifiable, and intangible benefits cannot be immediately quantified but may provide quantifiable benefits in the future. Benefits that exceed costs should then be analyzed using capital budgeting methods to make sure they represent a good return on the firm's invested capital.

Organizations should develop information systems plans that describe how information technology supports the company's overall business plan and strategy. Portfolio analysis and scoring models can be used to evaluate alternative information systems projects.

5 **How should information systems projects be managed?** Information systems projects and the entire implementation process should be managed as planned organizational change using an organizational impact analysis. Management support and control of the implementation process are essential, as are mechanisms for dealing with the level of risk in each new systems project. Project risks are influenced by project size, project structure, and the level of technical expertise of the information systems staff and project team. Formal planning and control tools (including Gantt and PERT charts) track the resource allocations and specific project activities. Users can be encouraged to take active roles in systems development and become involved in installation and training. Global information systems projects should involve local units in the creation of the design without giving up control of the project to parochial interests.

Key Terms

Acceptance testing, 384
Component-based
    development, 396
Computer-aided software
    engineering (CASE), 397
Conversion, 386
Customization, 390
Data flow diagram
    (DFD), 393
Direct cutover strategy, 386
Documentation, 384
End-user development, 389
Ergonomics, 405
Feasibility study, 383
Formal planning and
    tools, 405
Gantt chart, 405
Implementation, 404
Information
    requirements, 382

Information systems
    plan, 400
Intangible benefits, 400
Joint application design
    (JAD), 393
Maintenance, 386
Object-oriented
    development, 395
Organizational impact
    analysis, 405
Parallel strategy, 386
PERT charts, 405
Phased approach, 386
Portfolio analysis, 402
Process specifications, 394
Production, 386
Project, 397
Project management, 397
Prototyping, 388

Rapid application
    development (RAD), 392
Request for Proposal
    (RFP), 389
Scope, 397
Scoring model, 402
Structure chart, 394
Structured, 393
System testing, 384
Systems analysis, 382
Systems design, 383
Systems development
    lifecycle (SDLC), 387
Tangible benefits, 400
Test plan, 384
Testing, 384
Unit testing, 384
User-designer communica-
    tions gap, 404

Review Questions

1. What are the core problem-solving steps for developing new information systems?
   - List and describe the problem-solving steps for building a new system.
   - Define information requirements and explain why they are important for developing a system solution.
   - List the various types of design specifications required for a new information system.
   - Explain why the testing stage of systems development is so important. Name and describe the three stages of testing for an information system.
   - Describe the roles of documentation, conversion, production, and maintenance in systems development.

2. What are the alternative methods for building information systems?
   - Define the traditional systems lifecycle and describe its advantages and disadvantages for systems building.
   - Define information system prototyping and describe its benefits and limitations. List and describe the steps in the prototyping process.
   - Define end-user development and explain its advantages and disadvantages.
   - Describe the advantages and disadvantages of developing information systems based on application software packages.
   - Define outsourcing. Describe the circumstances in which it should be used for building information systems. List and describe the hidden costs of offshore software outsourcing.
   - Explain how businesses can rapidly develop e-business applications.

3. What are the principal methodologies for modeling and designing systems?
   - Compare object-oriented and traditional structured approaches for modeling and designing systems.

4. How should information systems projects be selected and evaluated?
   - Explain the difference between tangible and intangible benefits.
   - List six tangible benefits and six intangible benefits.

- List and describe the major components of an information systems plan.
- Describe how portfolio analysis and scoring models can be used to establish the worth of systems.

5. How should information systems projects be managed?
- Explain the importance of implementation for managing the organizational change surrounding a new information system.
- Define the user-designer communications gap and explain the kinds of implementation problems it creates.
- List and describe the factors that influence project risk and describe strategies for minimizing project risks.
- Describe tactics for managing global projects.

Discussion Questions

1. Discuss the role of business end users and information system professionals in developing a system solution. How do both roles differ when the solution is developed using prototyping or end-user development?

2. It has been said that systems fail when systems builders ignore "people" problems. Why might this be so?

Video Cases

Video Cases and Instructional Videos illustrating some of the concepts in this chapter are available. Contact your instructor to access these videos.

Collaboration and Teamwork

Preparing Web Site Design Specifications

With three or four of your classmates, select a system described in this text that uses the Web. Review the Web site for the system you select. Use what you have learned from the Web site and the description in this book to prepare a report describing some of the design specifications for the system you select. If possible, use Google Sites to post links to Web pages, team communication announcements, and work assignments; to brainstorm; and to work collaboratively on project documents. Try to use Google Docs to develop a presentation of your findings for the class.

BUSINESS PROBLEM-SOLVING CASE

The U.S. Census Bureau Field Data Collection Project: Don't Count On It

The U.S. Census is an enumeration of the American population performed once every 10 years, also called a decennial census. It is the responsibility of the United States Census Bureau and is used to determine allocation of congressional seats, allocation of federal assistance, and realignment of the boundaries of legislative districts within states. Correctly managing the census leads to billions of dollars in savings, improved service to the public, and strengthened confidence and trust in government.

Reports from the U.S. Government Accountability Office (GAO) and other sources suggest that the 2010 census represents a high-risk area that has been misman-aged for years. The bureau botched implementation of the Field Data Collection Automation (FDCA) program, an effort to integrate handheld electronic devices into the census data collection process. The handhelds were intended to replace the millions of paper forms and maps that census workers carried when going door to door to collect household data. Paper-based methods for collect-ing and recording data made gathering census informa-tion time-consuming and difficult to organize.

The FDCA program is intended to assist with the initial step of the process: the collection of respondent information. The goal of the program is to implement handheld devices that make census participation as simple as signing for a package. The result would be reduced costs, improved data quality, and better collection efficiency. In 2006, the bureau contracted with Harris Corporation for $595.7 million to oversee the implementation of these mobile computing devices. Harris develops communications products for government and commercial customers worldwide, including wireless transmission equipment. As of this writing, the handhelds have been far too slow and report data too inconsistently to be used reliably for the 2010 census.

Lack of executive oversight is more common in the federal sector as opposed to the private sector, because there are more incentives in the private sector for execu-tives to perform. Federal projects such as the FDCA pro-ject can suffer from lack of accountability for the same reason. The federal government doesn't use certified pro-gram managers and highly qualified executives for these kinds of projects, and they didn't for the FDCA program.

The FDCA suffered from poor communication and appropriate testing procedures. For example, the project team did not specify the testing process to measure performance of handheld devices. It also did not accurately describe the technical requirements of the

census to Harris Corp. Due to the immaturity of the mobile technology selected and the inexperience of Harris regarding projects of this size and scale, it was important that the bureau give accurate system requirements and scheduling information, which it failed to do. Implementations of mobile technology tend to be very complicated, requiring sound management and careful planning. The systems have a variety of components, carriers, devices, and applications to organize and coordinate.

Census Bureau Director Steve Murdock testified before Congress in April 2008 that the Census Bureau had failed to effectively convey the complexity of census operations or the project's IT requirements to Harris. The initial contract contained 600 requirements for the mobile handheld systems, but the Census Bureau later added 418 more. The constant addition of more require-ments made designing the product unnecessarily difficult. The bureau did not press Harris hard enough to provide continued updates on project progress. Yet Harris also did not present the bureau with an accurate initial estimate to begin with.

The struggles of the FCDA don't threaten the completion of the 2010 census. It will occur as scheduled, but will be far less efficient and cost a great deal more, approximately $3 billion in additional fund-ing over five years. The bureau will do what it can with the mobile devices it has and continue to rely on paper. The mobile handhelds will be used to initially canvas addresses, but won't be able to be used during the second-stage canvassing of people who don't respond to initial census questionnaires. The bureau will consequently be forced to abandon several new initia-tives to ensure accurate coverage of areas that have been traditionally undercounted.

The initial estimate was that rolling out mobile devices and providing complementary systems would cost $3 billion of a total $11.5 billion project cost. The total costs of the 2010 census will approach $14.5 billion, well over the initial budget. The bureau's blunders set census modernization back at least another decade. The bulk of the FDCA "dress rehearsal" was slated to take place during 2008 and 2009 in order to ensure the success of the handheld devices in 2010, but these setbacks forced the rehearsal to be less compre-hensive than was originally planned.

The GAO had reported in March 2006 that the FDCA had not adequately prepared to effectively manage the FDCA program. In that report, the agency cited lack of validated and approved baseline requirements for the project, lack of a risk management process, and ineffective management oversight as factors potentially damaging to the project. The most prominent example of the inadequacy of the project's risk management is that the performance problems with the handhelds had been reported to project management, but were not identified as a risk going forward. In 2007, GAO reported that changes in system requirements made after the fact were the primary cause for scheduling delays and budget overruns. GAO's 2008 report reiterated its earlier recommendations and emphasized the importance of quickly implementing them in time for the 2010 census, if possible.

The most crucial area in which the bureau fell short with the FDCA program were in its risk management activities. During testing in 2007, field operatives had reported the mobile devices' slow speeds in processing addresses in large assignment areas, their tendency to fail while transmitting data to the central data processing center, and other associated bugs and flaws. However, the bureau had no procedures in place to record those observations as potential risks and handle them accordingly. The risks related to mobile handheld performance were not documented.

Also, the bureau has not yet determined a method of measuring the handhelds' performance. The FDCA contract described a "control panel" application that would easily record and display the performance of handhelds on the Web, accessible via any computer with Internet connectivity. That application has not been developed. Without the ability to accurately measure device performance, it is impossible for the FDCA to verify that the devices are ready for the 2010 census. The large variation in performance specifications submitted to the contract or upon initiation of the contract and the additional specifications added after the fact also attest to the lack of a process for measuring adequate handheld performance. The report also notes that there were no processes for sharing risks and suggesting appropriate solutions to bureau executives.

While the bureau agreed with the majority of the report's recommendations, it often argued that the contractor was to blame for a portion of the failings of the project thus far. For example, it claimed that Harris

was responsible for the risks associated with the handhelds, and that its initial contract estimate was inaccurate. Regardless, the bureau admits that it committed many crucial management errors with the FDCA project.

Despite Harris's role in mismanaging the project, the company was not penalized for its performance. A March 2009 report by the U.S. Department of Commerce Office of the Inspector General noted that "award fees were excessive and not supported by technical assessments of Harris's performance." The project had not adequately defined criteria for good performance or established any measurable goals that could be used to reward excellent performance. Harris received 93 percent ($3.2 million) and 91 percent ($11 million) of available fees during the early phases of the project, despite serious performance problems noted by the Census Bureau's technical reviewers.

Taxpayers will now bear the brunt of the FDCA's mismanagement, and the bureau will need to wait another 10 years for the 2020 census for another opportunity to revamp the way the U.S. Census is done.

Sources: U.S. Department of Commerce, Office of Audit and Evaluation, "Census 2010: Revised Field Data Collection Automation Contract Incorporated OIG Recommendations, But Concerns Remain Over Fee Awarded During Negotiations," Field Report No. CAR 18702, March 2009; Jean Thilmany, "Don't Count on It," *CIO Insight*, May 2008; and U.S. Government Accountability Office, "Significant Problems of Critical Automation Contribute to Risks Facing 2010 Census," March 5, 2008.

Case Study Questions

1. How important is the FDCA project for the U.S. Census Bureau? How does it impact decision making and operational activities?

2. Evaluate the risks of the FDCA project and key risk factors.

3. Classify and describe the problems the Census Bureau faced in implementing its new wireless data collection system. What people, organization, and technology factors caused these problems?

4. Describe the steps you would have taken to control the risk in this project.

5. If you were in charge of managing this project, what else would you have done differently to increase chances for success?

Ethical and Social Issues in Information Systems

CHAPTER 12

STUDENT LEARNING OBJECTIVES

After completing this chapter, you will be able to answer the following questions:

1. What ethical, social, and political issues are raised by information systems?

2. What specific principles for conduct can be used to guide ethical decisions?

3. Why do contemporary information systems technology and the Internet pose challenges to the protection of individual privacy and intellectual property?

4. How have information systems affected everyday life?

CHAPTER OUTLINE

Chapter-Opening Case: *Behavioral Targeting and Your Privacy: You're the Target*

12.1 Understanding Ethical and Social Issues Related to Systems

12.2 Ethics in an Information Society

12.3 The Moral Dimensions of Information Systems

12.4 Hands-on MIS Projects

Business Problem-Solving Case: *Google, Microsoft, and IBM: The Health of Your Medical Records' Privacy*

Chapter 12 is located online at
www.pearsonhighered.com/laudon.

Glossary

3G networks High-speed cellular networks based on packet-switched technology, enabling users to transmit video, graphics, and other rich media, in addition to voice.

4G networks The next evolution in wireless communication is entirely packet switched and capable of providing between 1 Mbps and 1 Gbps speeds; up to ten times faster than 3G networks. Not widely deployed in 2010.

acceptable use policy (AUP) Defines acceptable uses of the firm's information resources and computing equipment, including desktop and laptop computers, wireless devices, telephones, and the Internet, and specifies consequences for noncompliance.

acceptance testing Provides the final certification that the system is ready to be used in a production setting.

access control Policies and procedures a company uses to prevent improper access to systems by unauthorized insiders and outsiders.

accountability The mechanisms for assessing responsibility for decisions made and actions taken.

accumulated balance digital payment systems Systems enabling users to make micropayments and purchases on the Web, accumulating a debit balance on their credit card or telephone bills.

affiliate revenue model an e-commerce revenue model in which Web sites are paid as "affiliates" for sending their visitors to other sites in return for a referral fee.

agile development Rapid delivery of working software by breaking a large project into a series of small sub-projects that are completed in short periods of time using iteration and continuous feedback.

Ajax Technology for creating interactive Web applications capable of updating the user interface without reloading the entire browser page.

analytical CRM Customer relationship management applications dealing with the analysis of customer data to provide information for improving business performance.

antivirus software Software designed to detect, and often eliminate, computer viruses from an information system.

applet Miniature program designed to reside on centralized network servers.

application controls Specific controls unique to each computerized application that ensure that only authorized data are completely and accurately processed by that application.

application proxy filtering Firewall screening technology that uses a proxy server to inspect and transmit data packets flowing into and out of the organization so that all the organization's internal applications communicate with the outside using a proxy application.

application server Software that handles all application operations between browser-based computers and a company's back-end business applications or databases.

application software Programs written for a specific application to perform functions specified by end users.

artificial intelligence (AI) The effort to develop computer-based systems that can behave like humans, with the ability to learn languages, accomplish physical tasks, use a perceptual apparatus, and emulate human expertise and decision making.

attributes Pieces of information describing a particular entity.

audio input Voice input devices such as microphones that convert spoken words into digital form for processing by the computer.

audio output Voice output devices that convert digital output data back into intelligible speech.

authentication The ability of each party in a transaction to ascertain the identity of the other party.

authorization management systems Systems for allowing each user access only to those portions of a system or the Web that person is permitted to enter, based on information established by a set of access rules.

authorization policies Determine differing levels of access to information assets for different levels of users in an organization.

autonomic computing Effort to develop systems that can manage themselves without user intervention.

backbone Part of a network handling the major traffic and providing the primary path for traffic flowing to or from other networks.

balanced scorecard method Framework for operationalizing a firm's strategic plan by focusing on measurable financial, business process, customer, and learning and growth outcomes of firm performance.

bandwidth The capacity of a communications channel as measured by the difference between the highest and lowest frequencies that can be transmitted by that channel.

banner ad A graphic display on a Web page used for advertising. The banner is linked to the advertiser's Web site so that a person clicking on it will be transported to the advertiser's Web site.

batch processing A method of collecting and processing data in which transactions are accumulated and stored until a specified time when it is convenient or necessary to process them as a group.

behavioral targeting Tracking the click-streams (history of clicking behavior) of individuals across multiple Web sites for the purpose of understanding their interests and intentions, and exposing them to advertisements which are uniquely suited to their interests.

benchmarking Setting strict standards for products, services, or activities and measuring organizational performance against those standards.

best practices The most successful solutions or problem-solving methods that have been developed by a specific organization or industry.

biometric authentication Technology for authenticating system users that compares a person's unique characteristics such as fingerprints, face, or retinal image, against a stored set profile of these characteristics.

bit A binary digit representing the smallest unit of data in a computer system. It can only have one of two states, representing 0 or 1.

blog Popular term for Weblog, designating an informal yet structured Web site where individuals can publish stories, opinions, and links to other Web sites of interest.

blogosphere The totality of blog-related Web sites.

Bluetooth Standard for wireless personal area networks that can transmit up to 722 Kbps within a 10-meter area.

botnet A group of computers that have been infected with bot malware without users' knowledge, enabling a hacker to use the amassed resources of the computers to launch distributed denial-of-service attacks, phishing campaigns or spam.

broadband High-speed transmission technology. Also designates a single communications medium that can transmit multiple channels of data simultaneously.

bugs Software program code defects.

bullwhip effect Distortion of information about the demand for a product as it passes from one entity to the next across the supply chain.

bundling Cross-selling in which a combination of products is sold as a bundle at a price lower than the total cost of the individual products.

bus networks Network topology linking a number of computers by a single circuit with all messages broadcast to the entire network.

business A formal organization whose aim is to produce products or provide services for a profit.

business continuity planning Planning that focuses on how the company can restore business operations after a disaster strikes.

business intelligence (BI) Applications and technologies to help users make better business decisions.

business model An abstraction of what an enterprise is and how the enterprise delivers a product or service, showing how the enterprise creates wealth.

business process reengineering (BPR) The radical redesign of business processes, combining steps to cut waste and eliminating repetitive, paper-intensive tasks in order to improve cost, quality, and service, and to maximize the benefits of information technology.

business processes The unique ways in which organizations coordinate and organize work activities, information, and knowledge to produce a product or service.

business process management Business process management (BPM) is an approach to business which aims to continuously improve and manage business processes.

business strategy Set of activities and decisions that determine the products and services the firm produces, the industries in which the firm competes, firm competitors, suppliers, and customers, and the firm's long-term goals.

business-to-business (B2B) electronic commerce Electronic sales of goods and services among businesses.

business-to-consumer (B2C) electronic commerce Electronic retailing of products and services directly to individual consumers.

C A powerful programming language with tight control and efficiency of execution; is portable across different microprocessors and is used primarily with PCs.

cable Internet connections Use digital cable coaxial lines to deliver high-speed Internet access to homes and businesses.

call center An organizational department responsible for handling customer service issues by telephone and other channels.

campus area network (CAN) An interconnected set of local area networks in a limited geographical area such as a college or corporate campus.

capacity planning The process of predicting when a computer hardware system becomes saturated to ensure that adequate computing resources are available for work of different priorities and that the firm has enough computing power for its current and future needs.

carpal tunnel syndrome (CTS) Type of RSI in which pressure on the median nerve through the wrist's bony carpal tunnel structure produces pain.

case-based reasoning (CBR) Artificial intelligence technology that represents knowledge as a database of cases and solutions.

cathode ray tube (CRT) Electronic gun that shoots a beam of electrons illuminating pixels on a display screen.

CD-ROM (compact disk read-only memory) Read-only optical disk storage used for imaging, reference, and database applications with massive amounts of unchanging data and for multimedia.

CD-RW (CD-ReWritable) Optical disk storage that can be rewritten many times by users.

cellular telephones (cell phones) A device that transmits voice or data, using radio waves to communicate with radio antennas placed within adjacent geographic areas called cells.

central processing unit (CPU) Area of the computer system that manipulates symbols, numbers, and letters, and controls the other parts of the computer system.

centralized processing Processing that is accomplished by one large central computer.

change agent In the context of implementation, the individual acting as the catalyst during the change process to ensure successful organizational adaptation to a new system or innovation.

change management Giving proper consideration to the impact of organizational change associated with a new system or alteration of an existing system.

chat Live, interactive conversations over a public network.

chief information officer (CIO) Senior manager in charge of the information systems function in the firm.

chief knowledge officer (CKO) Responsible for the firm's knowledge management program.

chief privacy officer (CPO) Responsible for ensuring the company complies with existing data privacy laws.

chief security officer (CSO) Heads a formal security function for the organization and is responsible for enforcing the firm's security policy.

choice Simon's third stage of decision making, when the individual selects among the various solution alternatives.

Chrome OS Google's lightweight computer operating system for users who do most of their computing on the Internet; runs on computers ranging from netbooks to desktop computers.

churn rate Measurement of the number of customers who stop using or purchasing products or services from a company. Used as an indicator of the growth or decline of a firm's customer base.

clickstream tracking Tracking data about customer activities at Web sites and storing them in a log.

client The user point-of-entry for the required function in client/server computing. Normally a desktop computer, workstation, or laptop computer.

client/server computing A model for computing that splits processing between clients and servers on a network, assigning functions to the machine most able to perform the function.

cloud computing Web-based applications that are stored on remote servers and accessed via the "cloud" of the Internet using a standard Web browser.

coaxial cable A transmission medium consisting of thickly insulated copper wire; can transmit large volumes of data quickly.

COBOL (Common Business Oriented Language) Major programming language for business applications because it can process large data files with alphanumeric characters.

collaboration Working with others to achieve shared and explicit goals.

collaborative filtering Tracking users' movements on a Web site, comparing the information gleaned about a user's behavior against data about other customers with similar interests to predict what the user would like to see next.

co-location a kind of Web site hosting in which firm purchase or rent a physical server computer at a hosting company's location in order to operate a Web site.

community provider a Web site business model that creates a digital online environment where people with similar interests can transact (buy and sell goods); share interests, photos, videos; communicate with like-minded people; receive interest-related information; and even play out fantasies by adopting online personalities called avatars.

competitive forces model Model used to describe the interaction of external influences, specifically threats and opportunities, that affect an organization's strategy and ability to compete.

component-based development Building large software systems by combining pre-existing software components.

computer Physical device that takes data as an input, transforms the data by executing stored instructions, and outputs information to a number of devices.

computer abuse The commission of acts involving a computer that may not be illegal but are considered unethical.

computer crime The commission of illegal acts through the use of a computer or against a computer system.

computer forensics The scientific collection, examination, authentication, preservation, and analysis of data held on or retrieved from computer storage media in such a way that the information can be used as evidence in a court of law.

computer hardware Physical equipment used for input, processing, and output activities in an information system.

computer literacy Knowledge about information technology, focusing on understanding of how computer-based technologies work.

computer software Detailed, preprogrammed instructions that control and coordinate the work of computer hardware components in an information system.

computer virus Rogue software program that attaches itself to other software programs or data files in order to be executed, often causing hardware and software malfunctions.

computer vision syndrome (CVS) Eyestrain condition related to computer display screen use; symptoms include headaches, blurred vision, and dry and irritated eyes.

computer-aided design (CAD) system Information system that automates the creation and revision of designs using sophisticated graphics software.

computer-aided software engineering (CASE) Automation of step-by-step methodologies for software and systems development to reduce the amounts of repetitive work the developer needs to do.

consumer-to-consumer (C2C) electronic commerce electronic commerce Consumers selling goods and services electronically to other consumers.

controls All of the methods, policies, and procedures that ensure protection of the organization's assets, accuracy and reliability of its records, and operational adherence to management standards.

conversion The process of changing from the old system to the new system.

cookies Tiny file deposited on a computer hard drive when an individual visits certain Web sites. Used to identify the visitor and track visits to the Web site.

copyright A statutory grant that protects creators of intellectual property against copying by others for any purpose during the life of the author plus an additional 70 years after the author's death.

core competency Activity at which a firm excels as a world-class leader.

cost-benefit ratio A method for calculating the returns from a capital expenditure by dividing total benefits by total costs.

cost transparency The ability of consumers to discover the actual costs merchants pay for products.

cracker A hacker with criminal intent.

critical thinking Sustained suspension of judgment with an awareness of multiple perspectives and alternatives.

cross-selling Marketing complementary products to customers.

crowdsourcing Using large Internet audiences for advice, market feedback, new ideas and solutions to business problems. Related to the 'wisdom of crowds' theory.

culture Fundamental set of assumptions, values, and ways of doing things that has been accepted by most members of an organization.

customer decision-support systems (CDSS) Systems to support the decision-making process of an existing or potential customer.

customer lifetime value (CLTV) Difference between revenues produced by a specific customer and the expenses for acquiring and servicing that customer minus the cost of promotional marketing over the lifetime of the customer relationship, expressed in today's dollars.

customer relationship management (CRM) systems Information systems that track all the ways in which a company interacts with its customers and analyze these interactions to optimize revenue, profitability, customer satisfaction, and customer retention.

customization The modification of a software package to meet an organization's unique requirements without destroying the package software's integrity.

cybervandalism Intentional disruption, defacement, or even destruction of a Web site or corporate information system.

cycle time The total elapsed time from the beginning of a process to its end.

data Streams of raw facts representing events occurring in organizations or the physical environment before they have been organized and arranged into a form that people can understand and use.

data administration A special organizational function for managing the organization's data resources, concerned with information policy, data planning, maintenance of data dictionaries, and data quality standards.

data cleansing Activities for detecting and correcting data in a database or file that are incorrect, incomplete, improperly formatted, or redundant. Also known as data scrubbing.

data definition Specifies the structure of the content of a database.

data dictionary An automated or manual tool for storing and organizing information about the data maintained in a database.

data flow diagram (DFD) Primary tool for structured analysis that graphically illustrates a system's component process and the flow of data between them.

data management software Software used for creating and manipulating lists, creating files and databases to store data, and combining information for reports.

data management technology The software that governs the organization of data on physical storage media.

data manipulation language A language associated with a database management system that end users and programmers use to manipulate data in the database.

data mart A small data warehouse containing only a portion of the organization's data for a specified function or population of users.

data mining Analysis of large pools of data to find patterns and rules that can be used to guide decision making and predict future behavior.

data quality audit A survey and/or sample of files to determine accuracy and completeness of data in an information system.

data visualization Technology for helping users see patterns and relationships in large amounts of data by presenting the data in graphical form.

data warehouse A database, with reporting and query tools, that stores current and historical data extracted from various operational systems and consolidated for management reporting and analysis.

data workers People such as secretaries or bookkeepers who process the organization's paperwork.

database A group of related files.

database administration Refers to the more technical and operational aspects of managing data, including physical database design and maintenance.

database management system (DBMS) Special software to create and maintain a database and enable individual business applications to extract the data they need without having to create separate files or data definitions in their computer programs.

database server A computer in a client/server environment that is responsible for running a DBMS to process SQL statements and perform database management tasks.

decision-support systems (DSS) Information systems at the organization's management level that combine data and sophisticated analytical models or data analysis tools to support semistructured and unstructured decision making.

deep packet inspection (DPI) Technology for managing network traffic by examining data packets, sorting out low-priority data from higher priority business-critical data, and sending packets in order of priority.

demand planning Determining how much product a business needs to make to satisfy all its customers' demands.

denial of service (DoS) attack Flooding a network server or Web server with false communications or requests for services in order to crash the network.

Descartes' rule of change A principle that states that if an action cannot be taken repeatedly, then it is not right to be taken at any time.

design Simon's second stage of decision making, when the individual conceives of possible alternative solutions to a problem.

digital asset management systems Classify, store, and distribute digital objects such as photographs, graphic images, video, and audio content.

digital certificates Attachments to an electronic message to verify the identity of the sender and to provide the receiver with the means to encode a reply.

digital checking Systems that extend the functionality of existing checking accounts so they can be used for online shopping payments.

digital dashboard Displays all of a firm's key performance indicators as graphs and charts on a single screen to provide one-page overview of all the critical measurements necessary to make key executive decisions

digital divide Large disparities in access to computers and the Internet among different social groups and different locations.

digital goods Goods that can be delivered over a digital network.

digital market A marketplace that is created by computer and communication technologies that link many buyers and sellers.

Digital Millennium Copyright Act (DMCA) Adjusts copyright laws to the Internet Age by making it illegal to make, distribute, or use devices that circumvent technology-based protections of copy-righted materials.

digital signature A digital code that can be attached to an electronically transmitted message to uniquely identify its contents and the sender.

digital subscriber line (DSL) A group of technologies providing high-capacity transmission over existing copper telephone lines.

digital video disk (DVD) High-capacity optical storage medium that can store full-length videos and large amounts of data.

digital wallet Software that stores credit card, electronic cash, owner identification, and address information and provides this data automatically during electronic commerce purchase transactions.

direct cutover A risky conversion approach where the new system completely replaces the old one on an appointed day.

disaster recovery planning Planning for the restoration of computing and communications services after they have been disrupted.

disintermediation The removal of organizations or business process layers responsible for certain intermediary steps in a value chain.

disruptive technologies Technologies with disruptive impact on industries and businesses, rendering existing products, services and business models obsolete.

distributed denial-of-service (DDoS) attack Uses numerous computers to inundate and overwhelm a network from numerous launch points.

distributed processing The distribution of computer processing work among multiple computers linked by a communications network.

documentation Descriptions of how an information system works from either a technical or end-user standpoint.

domain name English-like name that corresponds to the unique 32-bit numeric Internet Protocol (IP) address for each computer connected to the Internet.

Domain Name System (DNS) A hierarchical system of servers maintaining a database enabling the conversion of domain names to their numeric IP addresses.

domestic exporter Form of business organization characterized by heavy centralization of corporate activities in the home county of origin.

downtime Period of time in which an information system is not operational.

drill down The ability to move from summary data to lower and lower levels of detail.

DSS database A collection of current or historical data from a number of applications or groups. Can be a small PC database or a massive data warehouse.

DSS software system Collection of software tools that are used for data analysis, such as OLAP tools, datamining tools, or a collection of mathematical and analytical models.

due process A process in which laws are well-known and understood and there is an ability to appeal to higher authorities to ensure that laws are applied correctly.

dynamic pricing Pricing of items based on real-time interactions between buyers and sellers that determine what a item is worth at any particular moment.

e-government Use of the Internet and related technologies to digitally enable government and public sector agencies' relationships with citizens, businesses, and other arms of government.

electronic billing presentment and payment systems Systems used for paying routine monthly bills that allow users to view their bills electronically and pay them through electronic funds transfers from banks or credit card accounts.

electronic business (e-business) The use of the Internet and digital technology to execute all the business processes in the enterprise. Includes e-commerce as well as processes for the internal management of the firm and for coordination with suppliers and other business partners.

electronic commerce (e-commerce) The process of buying and selling goods and services electronically involving transactions using the Internet, networks, and other digital technologies.

electronic data interchange (EDI) The direct computer-to-computer exchange between two organizations of standard business transactions, such as orders, shipment instructions, or payments.

electronic mail (e-mail) The computer-to-computer exchange of messages.

electronic records management (ERM) Policies, procedures, and tools for managing the retention, destruction, and storage of electronic records.

employee relationship management (ERM) Software dealing with employee issues that are closely related to CRM, such as setting objectives, employee performance management, performance-based compensation, and employee training.

encryption The coding and scrambling of messages to prevent their being read or accessed without authorization.

end users Representatives of departments outside the information systems group for whom applications are developed.

end-user development The development of information systems by end users with little or no formal assistance from technical specialists.

end-user interface The part of an information system through which the end user interacts with the system, such as on-line screens and commands.

enterprise applications Systems that can coordinate activities, decisions, and knowledge across many different functions, levels, and business units in a firm. Include enterprise systems, supply chain management systems, customer relationship management systems, and knowledge management systems.

enterprise content management systems Help organizations manage structured and semistructured knowledge, providing corporate repositories of documents, reports, presentations, and best practices and capabilities for collecting and organizing e-mail and graphic objects.

enterprise software Set of integrated modules for applications such as sales and distribution, financial accounting, materials management, production planning, and human resources that allow data to be used by multiple functions and business processes.

enterprise systems Integrated enterprise-wide information systems that coordinate key internal processes of the firm. Also known as enterprise resource planning (ERP).

enterprise-wide knowledge management systems General-purpose, firmwide systems that collect, store, distribute, and apply digital content and knowledge.

entity A person, place, thing, or event about which information must be kept.

entity-relationship diagram A methodology for documenting databases illustrating the relationship between various entities in the database.

ergonomics The interaction of people and machines in the work environment, including the design of jobs, health issues, and the end-user interface of information systems.

e-tailer Online retail stores from the giant Amazon to tiny local stores that have Web sites where retail goods are sold.

Ethernet The dominant LAN standard at the physical network level, specifying the physical medium to carry signals between computers; access control rules; and a standardized set of bits to carry data over the system.

ethical "no free lunch" rule Assumption that all tangible and intangible objects are owned by someone else, unless there is a specific declaration otherwise, and that the creator wants compensation for this work.

ethics Principles of right and wrong that can be used by individuals acting as free moral agents to make choices to guide their behavior.

evil twins Wireless networks that pretend to be legitimate Wi-Fi networks to entice participants to log on and reveal passwords or credit card numbers.

exchanges Third-party Net marketplaces that are primarily transaction oriented and that connects many buyers and suppliers for spot purchasing.

executive support systems (ESS) Information systems at the organization's strategic level designed to address unstructured decision making through advanced graphics and communications.

expert systems Knowledge-intensive computer programs that capture the expertise of a human in limited domains of knowledge.

Extensible Markup Language (XML) A more powerful and flexible markup language than hypertext markup language (HTML) for Web pages.

extranets Private intranets that are accessible to authorized outsiders.

Fair Information Practices (FIP) A set of principles originally set forth in 1973 that governs the collection and use of information about individuals and forms the basis of most U.S. and European privacy laws.

fault-tolerant computer systems Systems that contain extra hardware, software, and power supply components that can back a system up and keep it running to prevent system failure.

feasibility study As part of the systems analysis process, the way to determine whether the solution is achievable, given the organization's resources and constraints.

feedback Output that is returned to the appropriate members of the organization to help them evaluate or correct input.

fiber-optic cable A fast, light, and durable transmission medium consisting of thin strands of clear glass fiber bound into cables. Data are transmitted as light pulses.

field A grouping of characters into a word, a group of words, or a complete number, such as a person's name or age.

file transfer protocol (FTP) Tool for retrieving and transferring files from a remote computer.

finance and accounting information systems Systems keep track of the firm's financial assets and fund flows.

firewalls Hardware and software placed between an organization's internal network and an external network to prevent outsiders from invading private networks.

FLOPS Stands for floating point operations per second and is a measure of computer processing speed.

folksonomies User-created taxonomies for classifying and sharing information.

foreign key Field in a database table that enables users to find related information in another database table.

formal planning and control tools Improve project management by listing the specific activities that make up a project, their duration, and the sequence and timing of tasks.

fourth-generation languages Programming languages that can be employed directly by end users or less-skilled programmers to develop computer applications more rapidly than conventional programming languages.

franchiser Form of business organization in which a product is created, designed, financed, and initially produced in the home country, but for product-specific reasons relies heavily on foreign personnel for further production, marketing, and human resources.

free/fremium revenue model an e-commerce revenue model in which a firm offers basic services or content for free, while charging a premium for advanced or high value features.

fuzzy logic Rule-based AI that tolerates imprecision by using nonspecific terms called membership functions to solve problems.

Gantt chart Visually represents the timing, duration, and human resource requirements of project tasks, with each task represented as a horizontal bar whose length is proportional to the time required to complete it.

general controls Overall control environment governing the design, security, and use of computer programs and the security of data files in general throughout the organization's information technology infrastructure.

genetic algorithms Problem-solving methods that promote the evolution of solutions to specified problems using the model of living organisms adapting to their environment.

geographic information systems (GIS) Systems with software that can analyze and display data using digitized maps to enhance planning and decision-making.

gigabyte Approximately one billion bytes.

Gramm-Leach-Bliley Act Requires financial institutions to ensure the security and confidentiality of customer data.

graphical user interface (GUI) The part of an operating system users interact with that uses graphic icons and the computer mouse to issue commands and make selections.

grid computing Applying the resources of many computers in a network to a single problem.

group decision-support system (GDSS) An interactive computer-based system to facilitate the solution to unstructured problems by a set of decision makers working together as a group.

hacker A person who gains unauthorized access to a computer network for profit, criminal mischief, or personal pleasure.

hertz Measure of frequency of electrical impulses per second, with 1 Hertz equivalent to 1 cycle per second.

high-availability computing Tools and technologies ,including backup hardware resources, to enable a system to recover quickly from a crash.

HIPAA Law outlining medical security and privacy rules and procedures for simplifying the administration of healthcare billing and automating the transfer of healthcare data between healthcare providers, payers, and plans.

home page A World Wide Web text and graphical screen display that welcomes the user and explains the organization that has established the page.

hotspots Specific geographic locations in which an access point provides public Wi-Fi network service.

hubs Very simple devices that connect network components, sending a packet of data to all other connected devices.

human resources information systems Systems that maintain employee records, track employee skills, job performance and training, and support planning for employee compensation and career development.

hypertext markup language (HTML) Page description language for creating Web pages and other hypermedia documents.

hypertext transport protocol (HTTP) The communications standard used to transfer pages on the Web. Defines how messages are formatted and transmitted.

identity theft Theft of key pieces of personal information, such as credit card or Social Security numbers, in order to obtain merchandise and services in the name of the victim or to obtain false credentials.

Immanuel Kant's Categorical Imperative A principle that states that if an action is not right for everyone to take it is not right for anyone.

implementation Simon's final stage of decision-making, when the individual puts the decision into effect and reports on the progress of the solution.

inference engine The strategy used to search through the rule base in an expert system; can be forward or backward chaining.

information Data that have been shaped into a form that is meaningful and useful to human beings.

information appliance Device that has been customized to perform a few specialized computing tasks well with minimal user effort.

information asymmetry Situation where the relative bargaining power of two parties in a transaction is determined by one party in the transaction possessing more information essential to the transaction than the other party.

information density The total amount and quality of information available to all market participants, consumers, and merchants

information policy Formal rules governing the maintenance, distribution, and use of information in an organization.

information requirements A detailed statement of the information needs that a new system must satisfy; identifies who needs what information, and when, where, and how the information is needed.

information rights The rights that individuals and organizations have with respect to information that pertains to themselves.

information system Interrelated components working together to collect, process, store, and disseminate information to support decision making, coordination, control, analysis, and visualization in an organization.

information systems department The formal organizational unit that is responsible for the information systems function in the organization.

information systems literacy Broad-based understanding of information systems that includes behavioral knowledge about organizations and individuals using information systems as well as technical knowledge about computers.

information systems managers Leaders of the various specialists in the information systems department.

information systems plan A road map indicating the direction of systems development the rationale, the current situation, the management strategy, the implementation plan, and the budget.

information technology (IT) All the hardware and software technologies that a firm needs to use in order to achieve its business objectives.

information technology (IT) infrastructure Computer hardware, software, data, storage technology, and networks providing a portfolio of shared IT resources for the organization.

informed consent Consent given with knowledge of all the facts needed to make a rational decision.

input The capture or collection of raw data from within the organization or from its external environment for processing in an information system.

input devices Device which gathers data and converts them into electronic form for use by the computer.

instant messaging Chat service that allows participants to create their own private chat channels so that a person can be alerted whenever someone on his or her private list is on-line to initiate a chat session with that particular individual.

intangible benefits Benefits that are not easily quantified; they include more efficient customer service or enhanced decision making.

intellectual property Intangible property created by individuals or corporations that is subject to protections under trade secret, copyright, and patent law.

intelligence The first of Simon's four stages of decision making, when the individual collects information to identify problems occurring in the organization.

intelligent agents Software programs that use a built-in or learned knowledge base to carry out specific, repetitive, and predictable tasks for an individual user, business process, or software application.

intelligent techniques Technologies that aid decision makers by capturing individual and collective knowledge, discovering patterns and behaviors in very large quantities of data, and generating solutions to problems that are too large and complex for human beings to solve on their own.

Internet global network of networks using univeral standards to connect millions of different networks.

Internet Protocol (IP) address Four-part numeric address indicating a unique computer location on the Internet.

Internet service provider (ISP) A commercial organization with a permanent connection to the Internet that sells temporary connections to subscribers.

Internet telephony Technologies that use the Internet Protocol's packet-switched connections for voice service.

Internet2 Research network with new protocols and transmission speeds that provides an infrastructure for supporting high-bandwidth Internet applications.

internetworking The linking of separate networks, each of which retains its own identity, into an interconnected network.

interorganizational system Information systems that automate the flow of information across organizational boundaries and link a company to its customers, distributors, or suppliers.

intranets Internal networks based on Internet and World Wide Web technology and standards.

intrusion detection systems Tools to monitor the most vulnerable points in a network to detect and deter unauthorized intruders.

investment workstations Powerful desktop computers for financial specialists, which are optimized to access and manipulate massive amounts of financial data.

IT governance Strategy and policies for using information technology within an organization, specifying the decision rights and accountabilities to ensure that information technology supports the organization's strategies and objectives.

Java An operating system-independent, processor-independent, object-oriented programming language that has become a leading interactive programming environment for the Web.

Joint application design (JAD) Process to accelerate the generation of information requirements by having end users and information systems specialists work together in intensive interactive design sessions.

just-in-time Scheduling system for minimizing inventory by having components arrive exactly at the moment they are needed and finished goods shipped as soon as they leave the assembly line.

key field A field in a record that uniquely identifies instances of that record so that it can be retrieved, updated, or sorted.

key loggers Spyware that records every keystroke made on a computer.

key performance indicators Measures proposed by senior management for understanding how well the firm is performing along specified dimensions.

knowledge base Model of human knowledge that is used by expert systems.

knowledge management The set of processes developed in an organization to create, gather, store, maintain, and disseminate the firm's knowledge.

knowledge management systems (KMS) Systems that support the creation, capture, storage, and dissemination of firm expertise and knowledge.

knowledge network systems Online directory for locating corporate experts in well-defined knowledge domains.

knowledge work systems Information systems that aid knowledge workers in the creation and integration of new knowledge in the organization.

knowledge workers People such as engineers or architects who design products or services and create knowledge for the organization.

learning management system (LMS) Tools for the management, delivery, tracking, and assessment of various types of employee learning.

legacy systems System that have been in existence for a long time and that continue to be used to avoid the high cost of replacing or redesigning them.

liability The existence of laws that permit individuals to recover the damages done to them by other actors, systems, or organizations.

Linux Reliable and compactly designed operating system that is an open-source offshoot of UNIX and that can run on many different hardware platforms and is available free or at very low cost.

local area network (LAN) A telecommunications network that requires its own dedicated channels and that encompasses a limited distance, usually one building or several buildings in close proximity.

long tail marketing Refers to the ability of firms to profitably market goods to very small online audiences, largely because of the lower costs of reaching very small market segements (people who fall into the long tail ends of a Bell curve).

magnetic disk A secondary storage medium in which data are stored by means of magnetized spots on a hard or floppy disk.

magnetic tape Inexpensive, older secondary-storage medium in which large volumes of information are stored sequentially by means of magnetized and nonmagnetized spots on tape.

mainframe Largest category of computer, used for major business processing.

maintenance Changes in hardware, software, documentation, or procedures to a production system to correct errors, meet new requirements, or improve processing efficiency.

malware Malicious software programs such as computer viruses, worms, and Trojan horses.

managed security service providers (MSSPs) Companies that provide security management services for subscribing clients.

management information systems (MIS) The study of information systems focusing on their use in business and management..

manufacturing and production information systems Systems that deal with the planning, development, and production of products and services and with controlling the flow of production.

market creator An e-commerce business model in which firms provide a digital online environment where buyers and sellers can meet, search for products, and engage in transactions.

market entry costs The cost merchants must pay simply to bring their goods to market.

marketspace A marketplace extended beyond traditional boundaries and removed from a temporal and geographic location.

mashups Composite software applications that depend on high-speed networks, universal communication standards, and open source code and are intended to be greater than the sum of their parts.

mass customization The capacity to offer individually tailored products or services on a large scale.

menu prices Merchants' costs of changing prices.

metropolitan area network (MAN) Network that spans a metropolitan area, usually a city and its major suburbs. Its geographic scope falls between a WAN and a LAN.

microbrowser Web browser software with a small file size that can work with low-memory constraints, tiny screens of handheld wireless devices, and low bandwidth of wireless networks.

micropayment Payment for a very small sum of money, often less than $10.

microprocessor Very large scale integrated circuit technology that integrates the computer's memory, logic, and control on a single chip.

microwave A high-volume, long-distance, point-to-point transmission in which high-frequency radio signals are transmitted through the atmosphere from one terrestrial transmission station to another.

middle management People in the middle of the organizational hierarchy who are responsible for carrying out the plans and goals of senior management.

middleware Software that connects two disparate applications, allowing them to communicate with each other and to exchange data.

midrange computers Middle-size computers that are capable of supporting the computing needs of smaller organizations or of managing networks of other computers.

minicomputers Middle-range computers used in systems for universities, factories, or research laboratories.

MIS audit Identifies all the controls that govern individual information systems and assesses their effectiveness.

mobile commerce (m-commerce) The use of wireless devices, such as cell phones or handheld digital information appliances, to conduct both business-to-consumer and business-to-business e-commerce transactions over the Internet.

model An abstract representation that illustrates the components or relationships of a phenomenon.

modem A device for translating a computer's digital signals into analog form for transmission over ordinary telephone lines, or for translating analog signals back into digital form for reception by a computer.

mouse Handheld input device with point-and-click capabilities that is usually connected to the computer by a cable.

MP3 (MPEG3) Standard for compressing audio files for transfer over the Internet.

multicore processor Integrated circuit to which two or more processors have been attached for enhanced performance, reduced power consumption and more efficient simultaneous processing of multiple tasks.

multinational Form of business organization that concentrates financial management and control out of a central home base while decentralizing production, sales, and marketing operations to units in other countries.

nanotechnology Technology that builds structures and processes based on the manipulation of individual atoms and molecules.

natural languages Nonprocedural languages that enable users to communicate with the computer using conversational commands resembling human speech.

net marketplaces Digital marketplaces based on Internet technology linking many buyers to many sellers.

netbook Small low-cost lightweight subnotebooks optimized for wireless communication and Internet access.

network The linking of two or more computers to share data or resources, such as a printer.

network address translation (NAT) Conceals the IP addresses of the organization's internal host computer(s) to prevent sniffer programs outside the firewall from ascertaining them and using that information to penetrate internal systems.

network economics Model of strategic systems at the industry level based on the concept of a network where adding another participant entails zero marginal costs but can create much larger marginal gains.

network interface card (NIC) Expansion card inserted into a computer to enable it to connect to a network.

network operating system (NOS) Special software that routes and manages communications on the network and coordinates network resources.

networking and telecommunications technology Physical devices and software that link various pieces of hardware and transfer data from one physical location to another.

neural networks Hardware or software that attempts to emulate the processing patterns of the biological brain.

nonobvious relationship awareness (NORA) Technology that can find obscure hidden connections between people or other entities by analyzing information from many different sources to correlate relationships.

normalization The process of creating small stable data structures from complex groups of data when designing a relational database.

n-tier client/server architecture Client/server arrangement which balances the work of the entire network over multiple levels of servers.

object Software building block that combines data and the procedures acting on the data.

object-oriented DBMS An approach to data management that stores both data and the procedures acting on the data as objects that can be automatically retrieved and shared; the objects can contain multimedia.

object-oriented development Approach to systems development that uses the object as the basic unit of systems analysis and design. The system is modeled as a collection o objects and the relationship between them.

object-relational DBMS A database management system that combines the capabilities of a relational DBMS for storing traditional information and the capabilities of an object-oriented DBMS for storing graphics and multimedia.

Office 2007 Microsoft desktop software suite with capabilities for supporting collaborative work on the Web or incorporating information from the Web into documents.

Office 2010 The latest version of Microsoft desktop software suite with capabilities for supporting collaborative work on the Web or incorporating information from the Web into documents.

offshore software outsourcing Outsourcing systems development work or maintenance of existing systems to external vendors in another country.

on-demand computing Firms off-loading peak demand for computing power to remote, large-scale data processing centers, investing just enough to handle average processing loads and paying for only as much additional computing power as they need. Also called utility computing.

online analytical processing (OLAP) Capability for manipulating and analyzing large volumes of data from multiple perspectives.

online processing A method of collecting and processing data in which transactions are entered directly into the computer system and processed immediately.

online transaction processing Transaction processing mode in which transactions entered on-line are immediately processed by the computer.

open source software Software that provides free access to its program code, allowing users to modify the program code to make improvements or fix errors.

operating system The system software that manages and controls the activities of the computer.

operational CRM Customer-facing applications, such as sales force automation, call center and customer service support, and marketing automation.

operational management People who monitor the day-to-day activities of the organization.

opt-in Model of informed consent permitting prohibiting an organization from collecting any personal information unless the individual specifically takes action to approve information collection and use.

opt-out Model of informed consent permitting the collection of personal information until the consumer specifically requests that the data not be collected.

organizational impact analysis Study of the way a proposed system will affect organizational structure, attitudes, decision making, and operations.

output The distribution of processed information to the people who will use it or to the activities for which it will be used.

output devices Device that displays data after they have been processed.

outsourcing The practice of contracting computer center operations, telecommunications networks, or applications development to external vendors.

P3P Industry standard designed to give users more control over personal information gathered on Web sites they visit. Stands for Platform for Privacy Preferences Project.

packet filtering Examines selected fields in the headers of data packets flowing back and forth between the trusted network and the Internet

packet switching Technology that breaks messages into small, fixed bundles of data and routes them in the most economical way through any available communications channel.

parallel processing Type of processing in which more than one instruction can be processed at a time by breaking down a problem into smaller parts and processing them simultaneously with multiple processors.

parallel strategy A safe and conservative conversion approach where both the old system and its potential replacement are run together for a time until everyone is assured that the new one functions correctly.

partner relationship management (PRM) Automation of the firm's relationships with its selling partners using customer data and analytical tools to improve coordination and customer sales.

patches Small pieces of software that repair flaws in programs without disturbing the proper operation of the software.

patent A legal document that grants the owner an exclusive monopoly on the ideas behind an invention for 17 years; designed to ensure that inventors of new machines or methods are rewarded for their labor while making widespread use of their inventions.

peer-to-peer Network architecture that gives equal power to all computers on the network; used primarily in small networks.

people perspective Consideration of the firm's management, as well as employees as individuals and their interrelationships in workgroups.

personal computer (PC) Small desktop or portable computer.

Personal digital assistants (PDA) Small, pen-based, handheld computers with built-in wireless telecommunications capable of entirely digital communications transmission.

personal-area networks (PANs) Computer networks used for communication among digital devices (including telephones and PDAs) that are close to one person.

personalization Ability of merchants to target their marketing messages to specific individuals by adjusting the message to a person's name, interests, and past purchases.

PERT chart Graphically depicts project tasks and their interrelationships, showing the specific activities that must be completed before others can start.

pharming Phishing technique that redirects users to a bogus Web page, even when the individual types the correct Web page address into his or her browser.

phased approach Introduces the new system in stages either by functions or by organizational units.

phishing A form of spoofing involving setting up fake Web sites or sending e-mail messages that look like those of legitimate businesses to ask users for confidential personal data.

pilot study A strategy to introduce the new system to a limited area of the organization until it is proven to be fully functional; only then can the conversion to the new system across the entire organization take place.

pivot table Spreadsheet tool for reorganizing and summarizing two or more dimensions of data in a tabular format.

podcasting Method of publishing audio broadcasts via the Internet, allowing subscribing users to download audio files onto their personal computers or portable music players.

pop-up ads Ads that open automatically and do not disappear until the user clicks on them.

portal Web interface for presenting integrated personalized content from a variety of sources. Also refers to a Web site service that provides an initial point of entry to the Web.

portfolio analysis An analysis of the portfolio of potential applications within a firm to determine the risks and benefits, and to select among alternatives for information systems.

prediction markets An analysis of the portfolio of potential applications within a firm to determine the risks and benefits, and to select among alternatives for information systems.

predictive analysis Use of datamining techniques, historical data, and assumptions about future conditions to predict outcomes of events.

presentation graphics Software to create professional-quality graphics presentations that can incorporate charts, sound, animation, photos, and video clips.

price discrimination Selling the same goods, or nearly the same goods, to different targeted groups at different prices.

price transparency the ease with which consumers can find out the variety of prices in a market.

primary activities Activities most directly related to the production and distribution of a firm's products or services.

primary key Unique identifier for all the information in any row of a database table.

privacy The claim of individuals to be left alone, free from surveillance or interference from other individuals, organizations, or the state.

private exchange Another term for a private industrial network.

private industrial networks Web-enabled networks linking systems of multiple firms in an industry for the coordination of trans-organizational business processes.

process specifications Describe the logic of the processes occurring within the lowest levels of a data flow diagram.

processing The conversion, manipulation, and analysis of raw input into a form that is more meaningful to humans.

procurement Sourcing goods and materials, negotiating with suppliers, paying for goods, and making delivery arrangements.

product differentiation Competitive strategy for creating brand loyalty by developing new and unique products and services that are not easily duplicated by competitors.

production The stage after the new system is installed and the conversion is complete; during this time the system is reviewed by users and technical specialists to determine how well it has met its original goals.

production or service workers People who actually produce the products or services of the organization.

profiling The use of computers to combine data from multiple sources and create electronic dossiers of detailed information on individuals.

program Series of instructions for the computer.

programmers Highly trained technical specialists who write computer software instructions.

programming The process of translating the system specifications prepared during the design stage into program code.

project A planned series of related activities for achieving a specific business objective.

project management Application of knowledge, skills, tools and techniques to achieve specific targets within specified budget and time constraints.

protocol A set of rules and procedures that govern transmission between the components in a network.

prototyping The process of building an experimental system quickly and inexpensively for demonstration and evaluation so that users can better determine information requirements.

public key encryption Uses two keys one shared (or public) and one private.

public key infrastructure (PKI) System for creating public and private keys using a certificate authority (CA) and digital certificates for authentication.

pull-based model Supply chain driven by actual customer orders or purchases so that members of the supply chain produce and deliver only what customers have ordered.

pure-play Business models based purely on the Internet.

push-based model Supply chain driven by production master schedules based on forecasts or best guesses of demand for products, and products are "pushed" to customers.

quality Product or service's conformance to specifications and standards.

query languages Software tools that provide immediate online answers to requests for information that are not predefined.

radio frequency identification (RFID) Technology using tiny tags with embedded microchips containing data about an item and its location to transmit short-distance radio signals to special RFID readers that then pass the data on to a computer for processing.

Rapid application development (RAD) Process for developing systems in a very short time period by using prototyping, fourth-generation tools, and close teamwork among users and systems specialists.

rationalization of procedures The streamlining of standard operating procedures, eliminating obvious bottlenecks, so that automation makes operating procedures more efficient.

reach Measurement of how many people a business can connect with and how many products it can offer those people.

records Groups of related fields.

recovery-oriented computing Computer systems designed to recover rapidly when mishaps occur.

referential integrity Rules to ensure that relationships between coupled database tables remain consistent.

relational database A type of logical database model that treats data as if they were stored in two-dimensional tables. It can relate data stored in one table to data in another as long as the two tables share a common data element.

repetitive stress injury (RSI) Occupational disease that occurs when muscle groups are forced through repetitive actions with high-impact loads or thousands of repetitions with low-impact loads.

Request for Proposal (RFP) A detailed list of questions submitted to vendors of software or other services to determine how well the vendor's product can meet the organization's specific requirements.

responsibility Accepting the potential costs, duties, and obligations for the decisions one makes.

revenue model A description of how a firm will earn revenue, generate profits, and produce a return on investment.

richness Measurement of the depth and detail of information that a business can supply to the customer as well as information the business collects about the customer.

ring networks A network topology in which all computers are linked by a closed loop in a manner that passes data in one direction from one computer to another.

ringtones Digitized snippets of music that play on mobile phones when a user receives or places a call.

risk assessment Determining the potential frequency of the occurrence of a problem and the potential damage if the problem were to occur. Used to determine the cost/benefit of a control.

Risk Aversion Principle Principle that one should take the action that produces the least harm or incurs the least cost.

router Specialized communications processor that forwards packets of data from one network to another network.

RSS Technology using aggregator software to pull content from Web sites and feed it automatically to subscribers' computers.

SaaS (Software as a Service) Services for delivering and providing access to software remotely as a Web-based service.

safe harbor Private self-regulating policy and enforcement mechanism that meets the objectives of government regulations but does not involve government regulation or enforcement.

sales and marketing information systems Systems that help the firm identify customers for the firm's products or services, develop products and services to meet their needs, promote these products and services, sell the products and services, and provide ongoing customer support.

Sarbanes-Oxley Act Law passed in 2002 that imposes responsibility on companies and their management to protect investors by safeguarding the accuracy and integrity of financial information that is used internally and released externally.

satellites The transmission of data using orbiting satellites that serve as relay stations for transmitting microwave signals over very long distances.

scalability The ability of a computer, product, or system to expand to serve a larger number of users without breaking down.

scope Defines what work is or is not included in a project.

scoring model A quick method for deciding among alternative systems based on a system of ratings for selected objectives.

search costs The time and money spent locating a suitable product and determining the best price for that product.

search engine marketing Use of search engines to deliver sponsored links, for which advertisers have paid, in search engine results.

search engine optimization (SEO) the process of changing a Web site's content, layout, and format in order to increase the ranking of the site on popular search engines, and to generate more site visitors.

search engines Tools for efficiently searching the Internet for information based on user queries (search engine arguments).

secondary storage Relatively long term, nonvolatile storage of data outside the CPU and primary storage.

Secure Hypertext Transfer Protocol (S-HTTP) Protocol used for encrypting data flowing over the Internet; limited to individual messages.

Secure Sockets Layer (SSL) Enables client and server computers to manage encryption and decryption activities as they communicate with each other during a secure Web session.

security Policies, procedures, and technical measures used to prevent unauthorized access, alteration, theft, or physical damage to information systems.

security policy Statements ranking information risks, identifying acceptable security goals, and identifying the mechanisms for achieving these goals.

Semantic web Collaborative effort led by the World Wide Web Consortium to make Web searching more efficient by reducing the amount of human involvement in searching for and processing web information.

semistructured decisions Decisions in which only part of the problem has a clear-cut answer provided by an accepted procedure.

semistructured knowledge Information in the form of less structured objects, such as e-mail, chat room exchanges, videos, graphics, brochures, or bulletin boards.

senior management People occupying the topmost hierarchy in an organization who are responsible for making long-range decisions.

sensitivity analysis Models that ask "what-if" questions repeatedly to determine the impact of changes in one or more factors on the outcomes.

sensors Devices that collect data directly from the environment for input into a computer system.

server Computer specifically optimized to provide software and other resources to other computers over a network.

service level agreement (SLA) Formal contract between customers and their service providers that defines the specific responsibilities of the service provider and the level of service expected by the customer.

service-oriented architecture (SOA) Software architecture of a firm built on a collection of software programs that communicate with each other to perform assigned tasks to create a working software application.

service platform Integration of multiple applications from multiple business functions or business units to deliver a seamless experience for the customer, employee, manager, or business partner.

shopping bots Software with varying levels of built-in intelligence to help electronic commerce shoppers locate and evaluate products or service they might wish to purchase.

six sigma A specific measure of quality, representing 3.4 defects per million opportunities; used to designate a set of methodologies and techniques for improving quality and reducing costs.

smart card A credit-card-size plastic card that stores digital information and that can be used for electronic payments in place of cash.

smartphones Wireless phones with voice, messaging, scheduling, e-mail, and Internet capabilities.

sniffer A type of eavesdropping program that monitors information traveling over a network.

social bookmarking Capability for users to save their bookmarks to Web pages on a public Web site and tag these bookmarks with keywords to organize documents and share information with others.

social engineering Tricking people into revealing their passwords by pretending to be legitimate users or members of a company in need of information.

social networking Online community for expanding users' business or social contacts by making connections through their mutual business or personal connections.

social shopping Use of Web sites featuring user-created Web pages to share knowledge about items of interest to other shoppers.

software package A prewritten, precoded, commercially available set of programs that eliminates the need to write software programs for certain functions.

spam Unsolicited commercial e-mail.

spamming A form of abuse in which thousands and even hundreds of thousands of unsolicited e-mail and electronic messages are sent out, creating a nuisance for both businesses and individual users.

spoofing Misrepresenting one's identity on the Internet or redirecting a Web link to an address different from the intended one, with the site masquerading as the intended destination.

spreadsheet Software displaying data in a grid of columns and rows, with the capability of easily recalculating numerical data.

spyware Technology that aids in gathering information about a person or organization without their knowledge.

SQL injection attack Attacks against a Web site that take advantage of vulnerabilities in poorly coded SQL (a standard and common database software application) applications in order to introduce malicious program code into a company's systems and networks.

star network A network topology in which all computers and other devices are connected to a central host computer. All communications between network devices must pass through the host computer.

stateful inspection Provides additional security by determining whether packets are part of an ongoing dialogue between a sender and a receiver.

Storage area networks (SAN) High-speed networks dedicated to storage that connects different kinds of storage devices, such as tape libraries and disk arrays so they can be shared by multiple servers.

stored value payment systems Systems enabling consumers to make instant on-line payments to merchants and other individuals based on value stored in a digital account.

strategic information system Computer system at any level of the organization that changes goals, operations, products, services, or environmental relationships to help the organization gain a competitive advantage.

strategic transitions A movement from one level of sociotechnical system to another. Often required when adopting strategic systems that demand changes in the social and technical elements of an organization.

structure chart System documentation showing each level of design, the relationship among the levels, and the overall place in the design structure; can document one program, one system, or part of one program.

structured Refers to the fact that techniques are carefully drawn up, step by step, with each step building on a previous one.

structured decisions Decisions that are repetitive, routine, and have a definite procedure for handling them.

structured knowledge Knowledge in the form of structured documents and reports.

structured knowledge systems Systems for organizing structured knowledge in a repository where it can be accessed throughout the organization. Also known as content management systems.

Structured Query Language (SQL) The standard data manipulation language for relational database management systems.

supercomputer Highly sophisticated and powerful computer that can perform very complex computations extremely rapidly.

supply chain Network of organizations and business processes for procuring materials, transforming raw materials into intermediate and finished products, and distributing the finished products to customers.

supply chain execution systems Systems to manage the flow of products through distribution centers and warehouses to ensure that products are delivered to the right locations in the most efficient manner.

supply chain management (SCM) systems Information systems that automate the flow of information between a firm and its suppliers in order to optimize the planning, sourcing, manufacturing, and delivery of products and services.

supply chain planning systems Systems that enable a firm to generate demand forecasts for a product and to develop sourcing and manufacturing plans for that product.

support activities Activities that make the delivery of a firm's primary activities possible. Consist of the organization's infrastructure, human resources, technology, and procurement.

switch Device to connect network components that has more intelligence than a hub and can filter and forward data to a specified destination.

switching costs The expense a customer or company incurs in lost time and expenditure of resources when changing from one supplier or system to a competing supplier or system.

syndicators Business aggregating content or applications from multiple sources, packaging them for distribution, and reselling them to third-party Web sites.

system software Generalized programs that manage the computer's resources, such as the central processor, communications links, and peripheral devices.

system testing Tests the functioning of the information system as a whole in order to determine if discrete modules will function together as planned.

systems analysis The analysis of a problem that the organization will try to solve with an information system.

systems analysts Specialists who translate business problems and requirements into information requirements and systems, acting as liaison between the information systems department and the rest of the organization.

systems design Details how a system will meet the information requirements as determined by the systems analysis.

systems development The activities that go into producing an information systems solution to an organizational problem or opportunity.

systems development life cycle (SDLC) A traditional methodology for developing an information system that partitions the systems development process into formal stages that must be completed sequentially with a very formal division of labor between end users and information systems specialists.

systems integration Ensuring that a new infrastructure works with a firm's older, so-called legacy systems and that the new elements of the infrastructure work with one another.

T lines High-speed data lines leased from communications providers, such as T-1 lines (with a transmission capacity of 1.544 Mbps).

tacit knowledge Expertise and experience of organizational members that has not been formally documented.

tangible benefits Benefits that can be quantified and assigned a monetary value; they include lower operational costs and increased cash flows.

taxonomy Method of classifying things according to a predetermined system.

technostress Stress induced by computer use; symptoms include aggravation, hostility toward humans, impatience, and enervation.

teams Teams are formal groups whose members collaborate to achieve specific goals.

telepresence Telepresence is a technology that allows a person to give the appearance of being present at a location other than his or her true physical location.

terabyte Approximately one trillion bytes.

test plan Prepared by the development team in conjunction with the users; it includes all of the preparations for the series of tests to be performed on the system.

testing The exhaustive and thorough process that determines whether the system produces the desired results under known conditions.

text mining Discovery of patterns and relationships from large sets of unstructured data.

token Physical device, similar to an identification card, that is designed to prove the identity of a single user.

topology The way in which the components of a network are connected.

Total cost of ownership (TCO) Designates the total cost of owning technology resources, including initial purchase costs, the cost of hardware and software upgrades, maintenance, technical support, and training.

Total quality management (TQM) A concept that makes quality control a responsibility to be shared by all people in an organization.

touch point Method of firm interaction with a customer, such as telephone, e-mail, customer service desk, conventional mail, or point-of-purchase.

touch screen Device that allows users to enter limited amounts of data by touching the surface of a sensitized video display monitor with a finger or a pointer.

trade secret Any intellectual work or product used for a business purpose that can be classified as belonging to that business, provided it is not based on information in the public domain.

transaction fee revenue model An online e-commerce revenue model where the firm receives a fee for enabling or executing transactions.

transaction processing systems (TPS) Computerized systems that perform and record the daily routine transactions necessary to conduct the business; they serve the organization's operational level.

Transmission Control Protocol/Internet Protocol (TCP/IP) Dominant model for achieving connectivity among different networks. Provides a universally agreed-on method for breaking up digital messages into packets, routing them to the proper addresses, and then reassembling them into coherent messages.

transnational Truly global form of business organization where value-added activities are managed from a global perspective without reference to national borders, optimizing sources of supply and demand and local competitive advantage.

Trojan horse A software program that appears legitimate but contains a second hidden function that may cause damage.

tuples Rows or records in a relational database.

twisted wire A transmission medium consisting of pairs of twisted copper wires; used to transmit analog phone conversations but can be used for data transmission.

unified communications Integrates disparate channels for voice communications, data communications, instant messaging, e-mail, and electronic conferencing into a single experience where users can seamlessly switch back and forth between different communication modes.

unified threat management (UTM) Comprehensive security management tool that combines multiple security tools, including firewalls, virtual private networks, intrusion detection systems, and Web content filtering and anti-spam software.

Uniform Resource Locator (URL) The address of a specific resource on the Internet.

unit testing The process of testing each program separately in the system. Sometimes called program testing.

UNIX Operating system for all types of computers, which is machine independent and supports multiuser processing, multitasking, and networking. Used in high-end workstations and servers.

unstructured decisions Nonroutine decisions in which the decision maker must provide judgment, evaluation, and insights into the problem definition; there is no agreed-upon procedure for making such decisions.

up-selling Marketing higher-value products or services to new or existing customers.

user interface The part of the information system through which the end user interacts with the system; type of hardware and the series of on-screen commands and responses required for a user to work with the system.

user-designer communications gap The difference in backgrounds, interests, and priorities that impede communication and problem solving among end users and information systems specialists.

Utilitarian Principle Principle that assumes one can put values in rank order and understand the consequences of various courses of action.

utility computing Model of computing in which companies pay only for the information technology resources they actually use during a specified time period. Also called on-demand computing or usage-based pricing.

value chain model Model that highlights the primary or support activities that add a margin of value to a firm's products or services where information systems can best be applied to achieve a competitive advantage.

value web Customer-driven network of independent firms who use information technology to coordinate their value chains to collectively produce a product or service for a market.

virtual company Uses networks to link people, assets, and ideas, enabling it to ally with other companies to create and distribute products and services without being limited by traditional organizational boundaries or physical locations.

Virtual private network (VPN) A secure connection between two points across the Internet to transmit corporate data. Provides a low-cost alternative to a private network.

Virtual Reality Modeling Language (VRML) A set of specifications for interactive three-dimensional modeling on the World Wide Web.

virtual reality systems Interactive graphics software and hardware that create computer-generated simulations that provide sensations that emulate real-world activities.

virtual world Computer-based simulated environment intended for its users to inhabit and interact via graphical representations called avatars.

virtualization Presenting a set of computing resources so that they can all be accessed in ways that are not restricted by physical configuration or geographic location.

visual programming language Allows users to manipulate graphic or iconic elements to create programs.

Voice over IP (VoIP) Facilities for managing the delivery of voice information using the Internet Protocol (IP).

voice portals Capability for accepting voice commands for accessing Web content, e-mail, and other electronic applications from a cell phone or standard telephone and for translating responses to user requests for information back into speech for the customer.

war driving An eavesdropping technique in which eavesdroppers drive by buildings or park outside and try to intercept wireless network traffic.

Web 2.0 Second-generation, interactive Internet-based services that enable people to collaborate, share information, and create new services online, including mashups, blogs, RSS, and wikis.

Web 3.0 Future vision of the Web where all digital information is woven together with intelligent search capabilities.

Web browsers Easy-to-use software tool for accessing the World Wide Web and the Internet.

Web bugs Tiny graphic files embedded in e-mail messages and Web pages that are designed to monitor online Internet user behavior.

Web hosting service Company with large Web server computers to maintain the Web sites of fee-paying subscribers.

Web mining Discovery and analysis of useful patterns and information from the World Wide Web.

Web server Software that manages requests for Web pages on the computer where they are stored and that delivers the page to the user's computer.

Web services Set of universal standards using Internet technology for integrating different applications from different sources without time-consuming custom coding. Used for linking systems of different organizations or for linking disparate systems within the same organization.

Web site All of the World Wide Web pages maintained by an organization or an individual.

Webmaster The person in charge of an organization's Web site.

Wide area networks (WANs) Telecommunications networks that span a large geographical distance. May consist of a variety of cable, satellite, and microwave technologies.

widget Small software program that can be added to a Web page or placed on the desktop to provide additional functionality.

Wi-Fi Standards for Wireless Fidelity and refers to the 802.11 family of wireless networking standards.

wiki Collaborative Web site where visitors can add, delete, or modify content on the site, including the work of previous authors.

WiMax Popular term for IEEE Standard 802.16 for wireless networking over a range of up to 31 miles with a data transfer rate of up to 75 Mbps. Stands for Worldwide Interoperability for Microwave Access.

Windows 7 The successor to Microsoft Windows Vista operating system released in 2009.

Windows Server 2003 Most recent Windows operating system for servers.

Windows Vista Microsoft Windows operating system featuring improved security; diagnostics; parental controls; usability; desktop searching, synchronization with mobile devices, cameras, and Internet services; and better support for video and TV.

Windows XP Powerful Windows operating system that provides reliability, robustness, and ease of use for both corporate and home PC users.

wireless portals Portals with content and services optimized for mobile devices to steer users to the information they are most likely to need.

wireless sensor networks (WSNs) Networks of interconnected wireless devices with built-in processing, storage, and radio frequency sensors and antennas that are embedded into the physical environment to provide measurements of many points over large spaces.

wisdom of crowds The belief that large numbers of people can make better decisions about a wide range of topics or products than a single person or even a small committee of experts (first proposed in a book by James Surowiecki).

Word processing software Software for electronically creating, editing, formatting, and printing documents.

workflow management The process of streamlining business procedures so that documents can be moved easily and efficiently from one location to another.

workstation Desktop computer with powerful graphics and mathematical capabilities and the ability to perform several complicated tasks at once.

World Wide Web A system with universally accepted standards for storing, retrieving, formatting, and displaying information in a networked environment.

worms Independent software programs that propagate themselves to disrupt the operation of computer networks or destroy data and other programs.

References

CHAPTER 1

Belson, Ken. "Technology Lets High-End Hotels Anticipate Guests' Whims." *The New York Times* (November 16, 2005).

Brynjolfsson, Erik. "VII Pillars of IT Productivity." *Optimize* (May 2005).

Bureau of Economic Analysis. *National Income and Product Accounts*, 2007. Table 5.3.5. Private Fixed Investment by Type (A) (Q).

Campbell, Don. "10 Red Hot BI Trends." Information Management Special Report (June 23, 2009).

Carr, Nicholas. "IT Doesn't Matter." *Harvard Business Review* (May 2003).

Dutta, Amitava, and Rahul Roy. "Offshore Outsourcing: A Dynamic Causal Model of Counteracting Forces." *Journal of Management Information Systems* 22, no. 2 (Fall 2005).

Emarketer. "U.S. Advertising Spending: the New Reality" (April 2009).

FedEx Corporation. "SEC Form 10-K For the Fiscal Year Ended 2008."

Friedman, Thomas. *The World is Flat*. New York: Farrar, Straus, and Giroux (2006).

Garretson, Rob. "IT Still Matters." *CIO Insight* 81 (May 2007).

Greenspan Alan. "The Revolution in Information Technology." Boston College Conference on the New Economy (March 6, 2000).

Gurbaxani, Vijay, and Phillippe Jorion. "The Value of Information Systems Outsourcing Arrangements: An Event Study Analysis." Center for Research on IT and Organizations, University of California, Irvine, Draft (April 2005).

Ives, Blake, Joseph S. Valacich, Richard T. Watson, and Robert W. Zmud. "What Every Business Student Needs to Know about Information Systems." *CAIS* 9, Article 30 (December 2002).

Pew Internet and American Life Project. "Daily Internet Activities." (January 6, 2009.)

The Radicati Group. "Instant Messaging Market, 2008-2012." Reuters.com (January 7, 2009).

Tuomi, Ilkka. "Data Is More Than Knowledge. *Journal of Management Information Systems* 16, no. 3 (Winter 1999-2000).

U.S. Bureau of Labor Statistics. Occupational Outlook Handbook, 2008-2009 Edition. Washington D.C.: Bureau of Labor Statistics (2009).

U.S. Department of Commerce, Bureau of the Census. Statistical Abstract of the United States, 2009. Washington D.C. (2009).

Weill, Peter and Jeanne Ross. IT Savvy: What Top Executives Must Know to Go from Pain to Gain. Boston: Harvard Business School Press (2009).

CHAPTER 2

Alter, Allan. "Unlocking the Power of Teams." CIO Insight (March 2008).

Aral, Sinan; Erik Brynjolfsson; and Marshall Van Alstyne, "Productivity Effects of Information Diffusion in Networks," MIT Center for Digital Business (July 2007).

Basu, Amit and Chip Jarnagin. "How to Tap IT's Hidden Potential." The Wall Street Journal (March 10, 2008).

Bernoff, Josh and Charlene Li."Harnessing the Power of Social Applications." MIT Sloan Management Review (Spring 2008).

Broadbent, Marianne and Ellen Kitzis. The New CIO Leader. Boston, MA: Harvard Business Press (2004).

Cash, James I. Jr., Michael J. Earl, and Robert Morison. "Teaming Up to Crack Innovation and Enterprise Integration." Harvard Business Review (November 2008).

Choi, Soon-Yong, and Andrew B. Whinston. "Communities of Collaboration." IQ Magazine. (July/August 2001).eMarketer. "Wireless Subscribers: North America." (March, 2007).

Easley, Robert F., Sarv Devaraj, and J. Michael Crant."Relating Collaborative Technology Use to Teamwork Quality and Performance: An Empirical Analysis." Journal of Management Information Systems 19, no. 4 (Spring 2003)

Ferdows, Kasra, Michael A. Lewis, and Jose A. D. Machuca. "Rapid-Fire Fulfillment." Harvard Business Review (November 2004).

Frost and Sullivan. "Meetings around the World: The Impact of Collaboration on Business Performance." (2007).

Gupta, Amar. "Expanding the 24-Hour Workplace." The New York Times (September 15, 2007).

Johnson, Bradfor, James Manyika, and Lareina Yee. "The Next Revolution in Interactions," McKinsey Quarterly No. 4 (2005).

Kalakota, Ravi, and Marcia Robinson. e-Business2.0: Roadmap for Success. Reading, MA: Addison-Wesley (2001).

Lardi-Nadarajan, Kamales. "Doing Business in Virtual Worlds." CIO Insight (March 2008).

Malone, Thomas M., Kevin Crowston, Jintae Lee, and Brian Pentland. "Tools for Inventing Organizations: Toward a Handbook of Organizational Processes." Management Science 45, no. 3 (March 1999).

McAfee, Andrew P. "Shattering the Myths About Enterprise 2.0." Harvard Business Review (November 2009).

McDougall, Paul. "Google Shows Next-Gen Messaging Platform." Information Week (June1, 2009).

Nolan, Richard, and F. Warren McFarland. "Information Technology and the Board of Directors." Harvard Business Review (October 1, 2005).

Radicatti Group. "Taming the Growth of E-Mail: An ROI Analysis." (July, 2007).

Raghupathi, W. "RP". "Corporate Governance of IT: A Framework for Development." Communications of the ACM 50, No. 8 (August 2007).

Reinig, Bruce A. "Toward an Understanding of Satisfaction with the Process and Outcomes of Teamwork." Journal of Management Information Systems 19, no. 4 (Spring 2003)

Shirky, Clay. "Social Media Changes the Enterprise." CIO Insight (May 2008).

Siebdrat, Frank, Martin Hoegl, and Holger Ernst. "How to Manage Virtual Teams." MIT Sloan Management Review 50, No. 4 (Summer 2009).

Soat, John. "Tomorrow's CIO." Information Week (June 16, 2008).

Tapscott, Don and Anthony D. Williams. "The Global Plant Floor." Business Week (March 20, 2007).

"The Radicati Group Releases 'Instant Messaging Market, 2008-2012.'" Reuters.com (January 7, 2009).

Vance, Ashlee. "Microsoft's SharePoint Thrives in the Recession." The New York Times (August 7, 2009).

Vara, Vauhini. "Wikis at Work." The Wall Street Journal (June 18, 2007).

Weill, Peter and Jeanne W. Ross. IT Governance. Boston: Harvard Business School Press (2004).

Weill, Peter, and Jeanne Ross. "A Matrixed Approach to Designing IT Governance." MIT Sloan Management Review 46, no. 2 (Winter 2005).

CHAPTER 3

Bhatt, Ganesh D., and Varun Grover. "Types of Information Technology Capabilities and Their Role in Competitive Advantage." Journal of Management Information Systems 22, no.2 (Fall 2005).

Bughin, Jacques, Michael Chui, and Brad Johnson. "The Next Step in Open Innovation." The McKinsey Quarterly (June 2008).

Champy, James. Outsmart: How to Do What Your Competitors Can't. Upper Saddle River, NJ: FT Press (2008).

Champy, James A. X-Engineering the Corporation: Reinventing Your Business in the Digital Age. New York: Warner Books (2002).

Chen, Pei-Yu (Sharon), and Lorin M. Hitt. "Measuring Switching Costs and the Determinants of Customer Retention in Internet-Enabled Businesses: A Study of the Online Brokerage Industry." Information Systems Research 13, no.3 (September 2002).

Christensen, Clayton. "The Past and Future of Competitive Advantage." Sloan Management Review 42, no. 2 (Winter 2001).

Christensen, Clayton, Jeanne G. Harris, and Ajay K. Kohli. "How Do They Know Their Customers So Well?" Sloan Management Review 42, no. 2 (Winter 2001).

Copeland, Michael V. "The Mighty Micro-Multinational." Business 2.0 (July 28, 2006).

Davenport, Thomas H. and Jeanne G. Harris. Competing on Analytics: The New Science of Winning. Boston: Harvard Business School Press (2007). _____

Eisenhardt, Kathleen M. "Has Strategy Changed?" Sloan Management Review 43, no.2 (Winter 2002).

El Sawy, Omar A. Redesigning Enterprise Processes for E-Business. New York: McGraw-Hill (2001).

Engardio, Pete. " Mom-and-Pop Multinationals." Business Week (July 3, 2008).

Ferguson, Glover, Sanjay Mathur, and Baiju Shah. "Evolving from Information to Insight." MIT Sloan Management Review 46, no. 2 (Winter 2005).

Fine, Charles H., Roger Vardan, Robert Pethick, and Jamal E-Hout. "Rapid-Response Capability in Value-Chain Design." Sloan Management Review 43, no.2 (Winter 2002).

Garretson, Rob. "IS IT Still Strategic?" CIO Insight (May 7, 2007).

Gilbert, Clark and Joseph L. Bower, "Disruptive Change." Harvard Business Review (May 2002),

Hagel, John, III, and John Seeley Brown. "The Shifting Industrial Landscape." Optimize (April 2005).

Hammer, Michael, and James Champy. Reengineering the Corporation. New York: HarperCollins (1993).

Hammer, Michael. "Process Management and the Future of Six Sigma." Sloan Management Review 43, no.2 (Winter 2002).

Iansiti, Marco, and Roy Levien. "Strategy as Ecology." Harvard Business Review (March 2004).

IBM. "Catia Enables Nikon to Speed Through the Design Process." www.ibm.com (January 6, 2009).

Kauffman, Robert J., and Yu-Ming Wang. "The Network Externalities Hypothesis and Competitive Network Growth." Journal of Organizational Computing and Electronic Commerce 12, no. 1 (2002).

Kouloupoulos, Thomas, and James Champy. "Building Digital Value Chains." Optimize (September 2005).

Krishnan, M.S. "Moving Beyond Alignment: IT Grabs the Baton."Optimize Magazine (April 2007).

Lohr, Steve. "Who Says Innovation Belongs to the Small? " The New York Times (May 24, 2009)

Luftman, Jerry. Competing in the Information Age: Align in the Sand,. Oxford University Press , USA; 2 edition (August 6, 2003).

Massie, Roy"Process Management: The Ideal Meeting Place for Business and IT." KM World (January 2008).

McAfee, Andrew and Erik Brynjolfsson. "Investing in the IT That Makes a Competitive Difference." Harvard Business Review (July/August 2008).

Piccoli, Gabriele, and Blake Ives. "Review: IT-Dependent Strategic Initiatives and Sustained Competitive Advantage: A Review and Synthesis of the Literature." MIS Quarterly 29, no. 4 (December 2005).

Porter, Michael. Competitive Advantage. New York: Free Press (1985).

Porter, Michael. "Strategy and the Internet." Harvard Business Review (March 2001).

Porter, Michael. "The Five Competitive Forces that Shape Strategy." Harvard Business Review (January 2008).

Porter, Michael E., and Scott Stern. "Location Matters." Sloan Management Review 42, no. 4 (Summer 2001).

Prahalad, C.K.and M.S.Krishnan. The New Age of Innovation. Driving Cocreated Value Through Global Networks. New York: McGraw Hill (2008).

Rowsell-Jones, Andrew, and Mark McDonald. "Giving Global Strategies Local Flavor." Optimize (April 2005).

Shapiro, Carl, and Hal R. Varian. Information Rules. Boston: Harvard Business School Press (1999).

Shpilberg, David, Steve Berez, Rudy Puryear, and Sachin Shah. "Avoiding the Alignment Trap in Information Technology." MIT Sloan Management Review 49, no. 1 (Fall 2007).

Watson, Brian P. "Is Strategic Alignment Still a Priority?" CIO Insight (October 2007).

CHAPTER 4

Babcock, Charles. "Linux No Longer the Cool New Kid on the Block. Now What?" Information Week (April 14, 2008).

Barry, Douglas K. Web Services and Service-Oriented Architectures: The Savvy Manager's Guide. New York: Morgan Kaufman (2003).

Carr, David F. "Scaling Up or Scaling Out?" Baseline (January 2008).

Carr, Nicholas. The Big Switch. New York: Norton (2008).

Chickowski, Ericka."How Good Are Your Service-Level Agreements?" Baseline (January 2008).

Cole, Arthur. "Mainframes They Are A'Changin," ITBusinessEdge.com, January 20, 2009.

Cone, Edward. "The Grid Wins." CIO Insight (January 2008).

David, Julie Smith, David Schuff, and Robert St. Louis. "Managing Your IT Total Cost of Ownership." Communications of the ACM 45, no. 1 (January 2002).

Dubey, Abhijit and Dilip Wagle. "Delivering Software as a Service." McKinsey Quarterly (June 2007).

Erickson, Jonathan. "Dr. Dobb's Report: Mobile Platforms." Information Week (March 30, 2009).

Fitzgerald, Brian. "The Transformation of Open Source Software." MIS Quarterly 30, No. 3 (September 2006).

Foley, John. "IBM Cloud Shapes Up." Information Week (June 22, 2009).

Fox, Armando, and David Patterson. "Self-Repairing Computers." Scientific American (May 2003.).

Ganek, A. G., and T. A. Corbi. "The Dawning of the Autonomic Computing Era." IBM Systems Journal 42, no 1, (2003).

Hagel, John, III, and John Seeley Brown. "Your Next IT Strategy." Harvard Business Review (October 2001).

Helft, Miguel and Ashlee Vance. "Google Plans a PC Operating System." The New York Times (July 8, 2009).

Helft, Miguel. "Reaching for the Cloud." The New York Times (July 12, 2009).

Hoover, J. Nicholas and Richard Martin. "Demystifying the Cloud." Information Week (June 23, 2008).

IBM. "Gridlines: The Intersection of Technology and Business." http://www-1.ibm.com/grid/gridlines/January2004/feature/teamwork .shtml, accessed July 2004.

IBM. "IBM Launches New Autonomic Offerings for Self-Managing IT Systems." IBM Media Relations (June 30, 2005).

King, Rachael. "How Cloud Computing is Changing the World." Business Week (August 4, 2008).

Kontzer, Tony. "The Cloud's the Limit: Anything as A Service." Baseline (June 2009).

Lawton, Christopher and Don Clark. "'Virtualization' is Pumping Up Servers." The Wall Street Journal (March 6, 2007).

Lohr, Steve. "I.B.M. to Help Clients Fight Cost and Complexity." The New York Times (June 15, 2009).

Markoff, John. "After the Transistor, a Leap into the Microcosm." The New York Times, August 31, 2009

McAfee, Andrew. "Will Web Services Really Transform Collaboration?" MIT Sloan Management Review 46, no. 2 (Winter 2005).

Mearian, Lucas. "A Zettabyte by 2010: Corporate Data Grows Fiftyfold in Three Years." Computerworld (March 6, 2007).

Millard, Elizabeth. "The State of Mobile Applications." Baseline (August 20, 2008).

Patel, Samir, and Suneel Saigal. "When Computers Learn to Talk: A Web Services Primer." McKinsey Quarterly no. 1 (2002).

Rapoza, Jim. "Browsers Battle for Enterprise Dominance." EWeek (June 15, 2009).

Reisinger, Don. "Can Google Android Beat Windows 7 in the Netbook Market?" eWeek (June 5, 2009).

Rogow, Rruce."Tracking Core Assets." Optimize Magazine (April 2006).

Sandler, Kathy. "The Future of Touch." The Wall Street Journal (June 2, 2009).

SunGard Availability Services. "Sungard Availability Services' Responsible Computing Project Powers Worldwide Volunteer Research." (August 31, 2009).

Toigo, Jon. "Storage in the Cloud." Information Week (May 11, 2009).

Vance, Ashlee and Matt Richtel. "Light and Cheap, Netbooks Are Poised to Reshape PC Industry." The New York Times (April 2, 2009)

Vance, Ashlee. "Microsoft Office 2010 Starts Ascension to the Cloud." The New York Times (July 13, 2009).

Vance, Ashlee. "PC Touch Screens Move Ahead." The New York Times (June 2, 2009).

Vascellaro, Jessica. "Google Strives to Help Online Software Catch Up." The Wall Street Journal (July 15, 2009).

Walsh, Lawrence. "Outsourcing: A Means of Business Enablement." Baseline (May 2008).

Weier, Mary Hayes. "Business Gone Mobile." Information Week (March 30, 2009).

Weill, Peter, Mani Subramani, and Marianne Broadbent. "Building IT Infrastructure for Strategic Agility." Sloan Management Review 44, no. 1 (Fall 2002).

Williams, Mark. "The Digital Utility." Technology Review (March/April 2008).

CHAPTER 5

Cappiello, Cinzia, Chiara Francalanci, and Barbara Pernici. "Time-Related Factors of Data Quality in Multichannel Information Systems." Journal of Management Information Systems 20, no. 3 (Winter 2004).

Chen, Andrew N. K., Paulo B. Goes, and James R. Marsden. "A Query-Driven Approach to the Design and Management of Flexible Database Systems." Journal of Management Information Systems 19, no. 3 (Winter 2002-2003).

Clifford, James, Albert Croker, and Alex Tuzhilin. "On Data Representation and Use in a Temporal Relational DBMS." Information Systems Research 7, no. 3 (September 1996).

Eckerson, Wayne W. "Data Quality and the Bottom Line." The Data Warehousing Institute (2002).

Fayyad, Usama, Ramasamy Ramakrishnan, and Ramakrisnan Srikant. "Evolving Data Mining into Solutions for Insights." Communications of the ACM 45, no.8 (August 2002).

Foshay, Neil, Avinandan Mukherjee and Andrew Taylor. "Does Data Warehouse End-User Metadata Add Value? Communications of the ACM 50, no. 11 (November 2007).

Gartner Inc. "'Dirty Data' is a Business Problem, not an IT Problem, Says Gartner." Sydney, Australia (March 2, 2007).

Henschen, Doug. "The Data Warehouse Revised." Information Week (May 26, 2008).

Hoffer, Jeffrey A., Mary Prescott, and Heikki Toppi. Modern Database Management, 9th ed. Upper Saddle River, NJ: Prentice-Hall (2009)

Kim, Yong Jin, Rajiv Kishore, and G. Lawrence Sanders. "From DQ to EQ: Understanding Data Quality in the Context of E-Business Systems. "Communications of the ACM 48, no. 10 (October 2005).

Klau, Rick. "Data Quality and CRM." Line56.com, accessed March 4, 2003.

Kroenke, David M. and David Auer. Database Processing 11e. Upper Saddle River, NJ: Prentice-Hall (2010).

Lee, Yang W., and Diane M. Strong. "Knowing-Why about Data Processes and Data Quality." Journal of Management Information Systems 20, no. 3 (Winter 2004).

Loveman, Gary. "Diamonds in the Datamine." Harvard Business Review (May 2003).

McKnight, William. "Seven Sources of Poor Data Quality." Information Management (April 2009).

Pierce, Elizabeth M. "Assessing Data Quality with Control Matrices." Communications of the ACM 47, no. 2 (February 2004).

Redman, Thomas. Data Driven: Profiting from Your Most Important Business Asset. Boston: Harvard Business Press (2008).

Scanlon, Robert J. "A New Route to Performance Management." Baseline Magazine. (January/February 2009).

Weier, Mary Hayes. "In Depth: Business Intelligence." Information Week (April 14, 2008).

CHAPTER 6

Borland, John. "A Smarter Web." Technology Review (March/April 2007).

Brooks, Jason. "WiMax Back on the Map." eWeek (April 7, 2008).

Chopra, Sunil and Manmohan S. Sodhi. "In Search of RFID's Sweet Spot." The Wall Street Journal (March 3, 2007).

Dekleva, Sasha, J.P. Shim, Upkar Varshney, and Geoffrey Knoerzer. "Evolution and Emerging Issues in Mobile Wireless Networks." Communications of the ACM 50, No. 6 (June 2007).

Fish, Lynn A. and Wayne C. Forrest. "A Worldwide Look at RFID." Supply Chain Management Review (April 1, 2007).

Ginevan, Sean. "Will WiMax Go the Distance?" Information Week (March 17, 2008).

Greenemeier, Larry. "RFID Tags Are on the Menu." Information Week (February 5, 2007).

Helft, Miguel. "Google Makes a Case That It Isn't So Big." The New York Times (June 29, 2009)

Hoover, J. Nicholas. "Enterprise 2.0." Information Week (February 26, 2007).

Housel, Tom, and Eric Skopec. Global Telecommunication Revolution: The Business Perspective. New York: McGraw-Hill (2001).

Jesdanun, Anick. "Researchers Explore Scrapping Internet."Associated Press (April 13, 2007).

Kocas, Cenk. "Evolution of Prices in Electronic Markets under Diffusion of Price-Comparison Shopping." Journal of Management Information Systems 19, no. 3 (Winter 2002-2003).

Lager, Marshall. "The Second Coming of 2.0." Customer Relationship Management (June 2008).

McCafferty, Dennis. "All for One-Platform." Baseline (May 2009).

McGee, Marianne Kolbasuk. "Track This." Information Week (February 11, 2008).

Nicopolitidis, Petros, Georgios Papademitriou, Mohammad S. Obaidat, and Adreas S. Pomportsis. "The Economics of Wireless Networks." Communications of the ACM 47, no. 4 (April 2004).

Panko, Raymond. Business Data Networks and Telecommunications 7e. Upper Saddle River, NJ: Prentice-Hall (2009).

Papazoglou, Mike P. "Agent-Oriented Technology in Support of E-Business." Communications of the ACM 44, no. 4 (April 2001).

Pottie, G. J., and W.J Kaiser. "Wireless Integrated Network Sensors." Communications of the ACM 43, no. 5 (May 2000).

Talbot, David. "The Internet Is Broken." Technology Review (December 2005/January 2006).

Varshney, Upkar, Andy Snow, Matt McGivern, and Christi Howard. "Voice Over IP." Communications of the ACM 45, no. 1 (January 2002).

Vascellaro, Jessica E. "Coming Soon to a Phone Near You." The Wall Street Journal (March 31, 2008).

Weiser, Mark. "What Ever Happened to the Next-Generation Internet?" Communications of the ACM 44, no. 9 (September 2001).

Wingfield, Nick and Suzanne Vranica. "Microsoft's 'Bing' to Take on Google." The Wall Street Journal (May 12, 2009).

Xiao, Bo and Izak Benbasat. "E-Commerce Product Recommendation Agents: Use, Characteristics, and Impact." MIS Quarterly 31, no. 1 (March 2007).

CHAPTER 7

Acohido, Byron. "Cybercrooks Descend on Twitter with Spam, Attacks." USA Today (July 6, 2009).

Austin, Robert D., and Christopher A. R. Darby. "The Myth of Secure Computing." Harvard Business Review (June 2003).

Baldor, Lolita C."White House Among Targets of Sweeping Cyber Attack." Associated Press (July 8, 2009).

Bernstein, Corinne. "The Cost of Data Breaches." Baseline (April 2009)

Bowley, Graham. "Ex-Worker Said to Steal Goldman Code." The New York Times (July 7, 2009).

Brenner, Susan W. "U.S. Cygbercrime Law: Defining Offenses." Information Systems Frontiers 6, no. 2 (June 2004).

Carvajal, Doreen. "High-Tech Crime is an Online Bubble that Hasn't Burst." The New York Times (April 7, 2008).

Cavusoglu, Huseyin, Birendra Mishra, and Srinivasan Raghunathan. "A Model for Evaluating IT Security Investments." Communications of the ACM 47, no. 7 (July 2004).

Checkler, Joseph. "Programmer Suspended Following His Arrest." The Wall Street Journal (July 8, 2009).

Chickowski, Ericka. "Is Your Information Really Safe?" Baseline (April 2009).

Choe Sang-Hun, "Cyberattacks Hit U.S. and South Korean Web Sites," The New York Times, July 9, 2009

Consumer Reports. "State of the Net 2009." (June 2009).

D'Arcy, John and Anat Hovav. "Deterring Internal Information Systems Use." Communications of the ACM 50, no. 10 (October 2007).

Dreger, Richard and Grant Moerschel. "Inside Smartphone Security." Information Week (October 6, 2008).

Epstein, Keith. Defenseless on the Net." Business Week (April 16, 2008).

Erickson, Jonathan. "Dr. Dobb's Report: Information Security." Information Week (June 22, 2009).

Feretic, Eileen. "Is Security a Myth?" Baseline (April 2009).

Fernandez, Manny. "Computer Error Caused Rent Troubles for Public Housing Tenants." The New York Times (August 5, 2009).

Foley, John. "P2P Peril." Information Week (March 17, 2008).

Fratto, Mike. "What's Your Appetite for Risk?" Information Week (June 22, 2009).

Fratto, Mike. "Precision Security." Information Week (June 30/July 7, 2008).

Gaur, Nalneesh and Bob Kiep. "Managing Mobile Menaces." Optimize Magazine (May 2007).

Giordano, Scott M. "Electronic Evidence and the Law." Information Systems Frontiers 6, no. 2 (June 2004).

Gorman, Siobhan. "Electricity Grid in U.S. Penetrated by Spies." The Wall Street Journal (April 8, 2009).

Grow, Brian, Keith Epstein, and Chi-Chu Tschang. "The New E-spionage Threat." Business Week (April 10, 2008).

Hoover, J. Nicholas. "Cybersecurity Balancing Act." Information Week (April 27, 2009).

Housley, Russ, and William Arbaugh. "Security Problems in 802.11b Networks." Communications of the ACM 46, no. 5 (May 2003).

Ives, Blake, Kenneth R. Walsh, and Helmut Schneider. "The Domino Effect of Password Reuse." Communications of the ACM 47, no.4 (April 2004).

Jagatic, Tom, Nathaniel Johnson, Markus Jakobsson, and Filippo Menczer. "Social Phishing." Communications of the ACM 50, no. 10 (October 2007).

Javelin Research. "2009 Identity Fraud Survey Report." (February 9, 2009.)

Kirk, Jeremy. "MySpace Users Struggle to Overcome Cybervandalism." PC World (June 30, 2008).

Markoff, John and Thom Shanker. "Panel Advises Clarifying U.S. Plans on Cyberwar." The New York Times (April 30, 2009).

Markoff, John. "Tracking Cyberspies Through the Web Wilderness." The New York Times (May 12, 2009).

Markoff, John. "Vast Spy System Loots Computers in 103 Countries." The New York Times (March 29, 2009).

McDougall, Paul. "High Cost of Data Loss." Information Week (March 20,2006).

Meckbach, Greg. "MasterCard's Robust Data Centre: Priceless." Computerworld Canada (March 26, 2008).

Mercuri, Rebeca T. "Analyzing Security Costs." Communications of the ACM 46, no. 6 (June 2003).

Mike Fratto, "Cloud Control," Information Week (January 26, 2009).

Mills, Elinor. "Facebook Disables Rogue Data-Stealing, Spamming Apps." CNET News (August 20, 2009).

Mitchell, Dan. "It's Here: It's There; It's Spyware." The New York Times (May 20, 2006).

Naraine, Ryan and Brian Prince. "Data Breaches Cause Concern." eWeek, April 7, 2008.

Naraine, Ryan. "Inside a Modern Malware System." EWeek (January 7, 2008).

Null, Christopher. "WPA Cracked in 1 Minute." Yahoo! Tech (August 27, 2009).

Panko, Raymond R. Corporate Computer and Network Security 2e. Upper Saddle River, NJ: Pearson Prentice Hall (2010).

Pasztor, Andy and Daniel Michaels, "Computer Failures Are Probed in Jet Crash," The Wall Street Journal, June 27, 2009

Perez, Juan Carlos. "Facebook Stamps Out Malware Attack." PC World (August 8, 2008).

Perez, Sarah. "The Facebook Virus Spreads: No Social Network Is Safe." The New York Times (December11, 2008).

Prince, Brian. "The Growing E-Mail Security Challenge." eWeek (April 21, 2008).

Richardson, Robert. "2008 CSI Computer Crime and Security Survey." Computer Security Institute (2008).

Robertson, Jordan. "Hackers: Social Networking Sites Flawed." Associated Press (August 3, 2007).

Roche, Edward M., and George Van Nostrand. Information Systems, Computer Crime and Criminal Justice. New York: Barraclough Ltd. (2004).

Russ Banham, "The Strategic Advantages of Managing Risk," The Wall Street Journal, June 5, 2007-Ess8 file.

Ryan Naraine, "ActiveX Under Siege," eWeek (February 11, 2008).

Sample, Char and Diana Kelley. "Cloud Computing Security: Infrastructure Issues." Security Curve June 23, 2009).

Sanger, David E. and Thom Shanker, "Pentagon Plans New Arm to Wage Wars in Cyberspace." The New York Times (May 29, 2009).

Schmidt, Howard. "Cyber Anxiety." Optimize Magazine (May 2007).

Schwerha, Joseph J., IV. "Cybercrime: Legal Standards Governing the Collection of Digital Evidence." Information Systems Frontiers 6, no. 2 (June 2004).

Shanker Thom. and David E. Sanger, "Privacy May Be a Victim in Cyberdefense Plan," The New York Times, Jun3 13, 2009.

Shanker, Thom. "New Military Command for Cyberspace," The New York Times, June 24, 2009.

Shields, Greg. "Modern Malware Threats and Countermeasures." Sunbelt Software (2008).

Siobhan Gorman and Evan Ramstad, "Cyber Blitz Hits U.S., Korea." The Wall Street Journal (July 9, 2009).

Siobhan Gorman, "FAA's Air-Traffic Networks Breached by Hackers." The Wall Street Journal (May 7, 2009).

Siobhan Gorman, August Cole, and Yochi Dreazen, "Computer Spies Breach Fighter-Jet Project," The Wall Street Journal, April 21, 2009;

Software World. "U.S. Consumers Losing Billions in Cyber Attacks." (September 1, 2006).

Sophos Plc. "Security Threat Report: 2009" (2008).

Steel, Emily. "Web Ad Sales Open Door to Viruses." The Wall Street Journal (June 15, 2009).

Steele, Betty K. "Due Diligence." Baseline, March 2009.

Symantec Corporation. "Symantec Internet Threat Security Report." (2009).

Vaas,Lisa. "The Final 'Final'Nail in WEP's Coffin?" EWeek (April 5, 2007).

Volonino, Linda., Reynaldo Anzaldua, and Jana Godwin: Computer Forensics: Principles and Practices. Upper Saddle River, NJ: Prentice Hall (2007).

Wang, Huaiqing, and Chen Wang. "Taxonomy of Security Considerations and Software Quality." Communications of the ACM 46, no. 6 (June 2003).

Warkentin, Merrill, Xin Luo, and Gary F. Templeton. "A Framework for Spyware Assessement." Communications of the ACM 48, no. 8 (August 2005).

Westerman, George. IT Risk: Turning Business Threats into Competitive Advantage. Harvard Business School Publishing (2007)

Wiens, Jordan. "With Security, More Is Better." Information Week (March 10, 2008).

CHAPTER 8

Barrett, Joe. "Whirlpool Cleans Up Its Delivery Act." The Wall Street Journal (September 24, 2009).

Chickowski, Ericka. "5 ERP Disasters Explained."www.Baselinemag.com, accessed October 8, 2009.

D'Avanzo, Robert, Hans von Lewinski, and Luk N. Van Wassenhove. "The Link between Supply Chain and Financial Performance." Supply Chain Management Review (November 1, 2003).

Davenport, Thomas H. Mission Critical: Realizing the Promise of Enterprise Systems. Boston: Harvard Business School Press (2000).

Day, George S. "Creating a Superior Customer-Relating Capability." MIT Sloan Management Review 44, no. 3 (Spring 2003).

Dvorak, Phred. "Clarity is Missing Link in Supply Chain." The Wall Street Journal (May 18, 2009).

Evans, Bob. "Global CIO: LG Transforms Global Operations with Oracle ERP," Information Week (August 24, 2009).

Ferrer, Jaume, Johan Karlberg, and Jamie Hintlian."Integration: The Key to Global Success." Supply Chain Management Review (March 1, 2007).

Fleisch, Elgar, Hubert Oesterle, and Stephen Powell. "Rapid Implementation of Enterprise Resource Planning Systems." Journal of Organizational Computing and Electronic Commerce 14, no. 2 (2004).

Garber, Randy and Suman Sarkar. "Want a More Flexible Supply Chain?" Supply Chain Management Review (January 1, 2007).

Goodhue, Dale L., Barbara H. Wixom, and Hugh J. Watson. "Realizing Business Benefits through CRM: Hitting the Right Target in the Right Way." MIS Quarterly Executive 1, no. 2 (June 2002).

Greenbaum, Joshiua. "Is ERP Dead? Or Has It Just Gone Underground?" SAP NetWeaver Magazine 3 (2007).

Guinipero, Larry, Robert B. Handfield, and Douglas L. Johansen. "Beyond Buying." The Wall Street Journal (March 10, 2008).

Handfield, Robert B. and Ernest L. Nichols. Supply Chain Redesign: Transforming Supply Chains into Integrated Value Systems. Financial Times Press (2002).

Hitt, Lorin, D. J. Wu, and Xiaoge Zhou. "Investment in Enterprise Resource Planning: Business Impact and Productivity Measures." Journal of Management Information Systems 19, no. 1 (Summer 2002).

Kalakota, Ravi, and Marcia Robinson. E-Business 2.0. Boston: Addison-Wesley (2001).

_____. Services Blueprint: Roadmap for Execution. Boston: Addison-Wesley (2003).

Kanakamedala, Kishore, Glenn Ramsdell, and Vats Srivatsan. "Getting Supply Chain Software Right." McKinsey Quarterly no. 1 (2003).

Klein, Richard and Arun Rai. "Interfirm Strategic Information Flows in Logistics Supply Chain Relationships. MIS Quarterly 33, No. 4 (December 2009).

Kopczak, Laura Rock, and M. Eric Johnson. "The Supply-Chain Management Effect." MIT Sloan Management Review 44, no. 3 (Spring 2003).

Lee, Hau, L., V. Padmanabhan, and Seugin Whang. "The Bullwhip Effect in Supply Chains." Sloan Management Review (Spring 1997).

Lee, Hau. "The Triple-A Supply Chain." Harvard Business Review (October 2004).

Liang, Huigang, Nilesh Sharaf, Quing Hu, and Yajiong Xue. "Assimilation of Enterprise Systems: The Effect of Institutional Pressures and the Mediating Role of Top Management." MIS Quarterly 31, no. 1 (March 2007).

Malhotra, Arvind, Sanjay Gosain, and Omar A. El Sawy. "Absorptive Capacity Configurations in Supply Chains: Gearing for Partner-Enabled Market Knowledge Creation." MIS Quarterly 29, no. 1 (March 2005).

Maylett, Tracy and Kate Vitasek. "For Closer Collaboration, Try Education." Supply Chain Management Review (January 1, 2007).

McKay, Lauren. "CRM and the iPhone." Customer Relationship Management (March 2009).

_____. "Everything's Social Now." Customer Relationship Management (June 2009).

Oracle Corporation. "Alcoa Implements Oracle Solution 20% below Projected Cost, Eliminates 43 Legacy Systems." www.oracle.com, accessed August 21, 2005.

Rai, Arun, Ravi Patnayakuni, and Nainika Seth. "Firm Performance Impacts of Digitally Enabled Supply Chain Integration Capabilities." MIS Quarterly 30 No. 2 (June 2006).

Ranganathan, C. and Carol V. Brown. "ERP Iinvestments and the Market Value of Firms: Toward an Understanding of Influential ERP Project Variables." Information Systems Research 17, No. 2 (June 2006).

Robey, Daniel, Jeanne W. Ross, and Marie-Claude Boudreau. "Learning to Implement Enterprise Systems: An Exploratory Study of the Dialectics of Change." Journal of Management Information Systems 19, no. 1 (Summer 2002).

Schwartz, Ephraim. "Does ERP Matter-Industry Stalwarts Speak Out." InfoWorld (April 10, 2007).

Scott, Judy E., and Iris Vessey. "Managing Risks in Enterprise Systems Implementations." Communications of the ACM 45, no. 4 (April 2002).

Slone, Reuben E. "Leading a Supply Chain Turnaround." Harvard Business Review (October 2004)

Sullivan, Laurie. "ERPZilla." Information Week (July 11, 2005).

Violino, Bob. "The Next-Generation ERP." CIO Insight (May 2008).

Whiting, Rick."You Look Marvelous!" Information Week (July 24, 2006).

CHAPTER 9

Adomavicius, Gediminas and Alexander Tuzhilin. "Personalization Technologies: A Process-Oriented Perspective." Communications of the ACM 48, no. 10 (October 2005).

Baker, Stephen. "Learning, and Profiting, from Online Friendships," Business Week, May 21, 2009.

Baker, Stephen. "Mapping a New, Mobile Internet." Business Week, February 26, 2009

Bakos, Yannis. "The Emerging Role of Electronic Marketplaces and the Internet." Communications of the ACM 41, no. 8 (August 1998).

Bernoff, Josh and Charlene Li. "Harnessing the Power of Social Applications." MIT Sloan Management Review (February 14, 2008).

Bo, Xiao and Izak Benbasat. "E-Commerce Product Recommendation Agents: Use, Characteristics, and Impact." MIS Quarterly 31, no. 1 (March 2007).

Boehret, Katherine. "Tracking Friends the Google Way." The Wall Street Journal (February 4, 2009).

Brynjolfsson, Erik,Yu Hu, and Michael D. Smith."Consumer Surpus in the Digital Economy: Estimating the Value of Increased Product Variety at Online Booksellers." Management Science 49, no. 11 (November 2003).

Clifford, Stephanie. "Put Ad on Web, Count Clicks, Revise." The New York Times (May 31, 2009).

eMarketer, "Broadband: Household Penetration in the U.S." eMarketer Report (July 2009).

eMarketer. "Retail E-commerce Forecast." eMarketer Report (June 2009).

eMarketer. "Mobile Phone Sucscribers Wordwide." eMarketer Quickstats (August 3, 2009).

eMarketer. "Subscription and Down Media Store Revenues, 2009." (eMarketer, 2009).

eMarketer. "US Advertising Spending." (April 2009).

eMarketer. "US Retail E-commerce: Slower But Steady Growth." (May 2008).

eMarketer. "Mobile Spending: US Non-Voice Services." September 2007).

Evans, Philip and Thomas S. Wurster. Blown to Bits: How the New Economics of Information Transforms Strategy. Boston, MA: Harvard Business School Press (2000).

Gartner Group. "Technology Barriers to Mobile Commerce are Coming Down." (February, 2008).

"Google: A Shopper's Best Friend." The Wall Street Journal (May 8, 2009).

Hallerman, David. "US Advertising Spending: The New Reality." EMarketer (April 2009a).

Helft, Miguel. "Data, Not Design, Is King in the Age of Google." The New York Times (May 10, 2009).

Howe, Heff. Crowdsourcing: Why the Power of the Crowd Is Driving the Future of Business. New York: Random House (2008).

Kane, Yukari Iwatani. "IPhone Gets Bigger as Ad Medium." The Wall Street Journal (May 12, 2009).

Kaplan, Steven and Mohanbir Sawhney. "E-Hubs: the New B2B Marketplaces." Harvard Business Review (May-June 2000).

Kauffman, Robert J. and Bin Wang. "New Buyers' Arrival Under Dynamic Pricing Market Microstructure: The Case of Group-Buying Discounts on the Internet, Journal of Management Information Systems 18, no. 2 (Fall 2001).

Kolbasuk-McGee, Marianne."Track This." Information Week (February 11, 2008).

Laseter, Timothy M., Elliott Rabinovich, Kenneth K. Boyer, and M. Johnny Rungtusanatham. "Critical Issues in Internet Retailing." MIT Sloan Management Review 48, no. 3 (Spring 2007).

Laudon, Kenneth C. and Carol Guercio Traver. E-Commerce: Business, Technology, Society, 6th edition. Upper Saddle River, NJ: Prentice-Hall (2010).

Leimeister, Jan Marco, Michael Huber, Ulrich Bretschneider, and Helmut Krcmar." Leveraging Crowdsourcing: Activation-Supporting Components for IT-Based Ideas Competition." Journal of Management Information Systems 26, No. 1 (Summer 2009).

Magretta, Joan. "Why Business Models Matter." Harvard Business Review (May 2002).

Markoff, John. "The Cellphone, Navigating Our Lives." The New York Times (February 17, 2009).

Miller, Claire Cain. "Ad Revenue on the Web? No Sure Bet." The New York Times (May 25, 2009).

Pavlou, Paul A., Huigang Liang, and Yajiong Xue. "Understanding and Mitigating Uncertainty in Online Exchange Relationships: A Principal-Agent Perspective." MIS Quarterly 31, no. 1 (March 2007).

Philips, Jeremy. "To Rake It In, Give It Away." The Wall Street Journal (July 8, 2009).

Rayport, Jeffrey. "Demand-Side Innovation: Where IT Meets Marketing." Optimize Magazine (February 2007).

Roger Cheng, "On the Road," The Wall Street Journal, April 20, 2009;

Sartain, Julie. "Opinion: Using MySpace and Facebook as Business Tools." Computerworld (May 23, 2008).

Schultze, Ulrike and Wanda J. Orlikowski. "A Practice Perspective on Technology-Mediated Network Relations: The Use of Internet-Based Self-Serve Technologies." Information Systems Research 15, no. 1 (March 2004).

Smith, Michael D., Joseph Bailey and Erik Brynjolfsson."Understanding Digital Markets: Review and Assessment" in Erik Brynjolfsson and Brian Kahin, ed. Understanding the Digital Economy. Cambridge, MA: MIT Press (1999).

Michael D. Smith and Rahul Telang. "Competing with Free: The Impact of Movie Broadcasts on DVD Sales and Internet Piracy." MIS Quarterly 33, No. 2 (June 2009).

Stellin, Susan. "Bank Will Let Customers Deposit Checks by iPhone." The New York Times (August 9, 2009).

Story, Louise. "To Aim Ads, Web Is Keeping Closer Eye on You. " The New York Times (March 10, 2008).

Stross, Randall. "Just Browsing? A Web Store May Follow You Out the Door." The New York Times (May 17, 2009).

Surowiecki, James. The Wisdom of Crowds: Why the Many Are Smarter Than the Few and How Collective Wisdom Shapes Business, Economies, Societies and Nations. Boston: Little, Brown (2004).

Tsai, Jessica. "Shopping on the Go." CRM Magazine (May 2009).

Tsai, Jessica. "Social Media: The Five-Year Forecast." destinationcrm.com (April 27, 2009).

Tsai, Jessica. "The Moving Target." Customer Relationship Management (May 2008).

United States Census Bureau. "Advance Monthly Sales For Retail Trade." (September 15, 2009).

Vascellaro, Jessica E. "Google Maps Go Social." The Wall Street Journal (February 4, 2009).

Weier, Mary Hayes. "IPhone a Hit with Consumer Companies." Information Week (August 5, 2009).

Worthen, Ben. "Branching Out: Mobile Banking Finds New Users." The Wall Street Journal (February 3, 2009).

CHAPTER 10

Alavi, Maryam and Dorothy Leidner. "Knowledge Management and Knowledge Management Systems: Conceptual Foundations and Research Issues," MIS Quarterly 25, No. 1 (March 2001).

Alavi, Maryam, Timothy R. Kayworth, and Dorothy E. Leidner. "An Empirical Investigation of the Influence of Organizational Culture on Knowledge Management Practices." Journal of Management Information Systems 22, No.3 (Winter 2006).

Anson, Rob and Bjorn Erik Munkvold. "Beyond Face-to-Face: A Field Study of Electronic Meetings in Different Time and Place Modes." Journal of Organizational Computing and Electronic Commerce 14, no. 2 (2004).

Anthes, Gary H. "Agents Change."Computerworld (January 27, 2003).

Bazerman, Max H. and Dolly Chugh. "Decisions Without Blinders." Harvard Business Review (January 2006).

Booth, Corey and Shashi Buluswar. "The Return of Artificial Intelligence," The McKinsey Quarterly No. 2 (2002).

Burtka, Michael. "Generic Algorithms." The Stern Information Systems Review 1, no. 1 (Spring 1993).

Clark, Thomas D., Jr., Mary C. Jones, and Curtis P. Armstrong. "The Dynamic Structure of Management Support Systems: Theory Development, Research Focus, and Direction." MIS Quarterly 31, no. 3 (September 2007).

Cross, Rob and Lloyd Baird."Technology is Not Enough: Improving Performance by Building Organizational Memory." Sloan Management Review 41, no. 3 (Spring 2000).

Davenport, Thomas H., and Lawrence Prusak. Working Knowledge: How Organizations Manage What They Know. Boston, MA: Harvard Business School Press (1997).

Davenport, Thomas H., Laurence Prusak, and Bruce Strong. "Putting Ideas to Work." The Wall Street Journal (March 10, 2008).

Davenport, Thomas H., Robert J. Thomas and Susan Cantrell. "The Mysterious Art and Science of Knowledge-Worker Performance." MIT Sloan Management Review 44, no. 1 (Fall 2002).

Davis, Gordon B. "Anytime/ Anyplace Computing and the Future of Knowledge Work." Communications of the ACM 42, no.12 (December 2002).

Dennis, Alan R., Jay E. Aronson, William G. Henriger, and Edward D. Walker III. "Structuring Time and Task in Electronic Brainstorming." MIS Quarterly 23, no. 1 (March 1999).

DeSanctis, Geraldine, and R. Brent Gallupe. "A Foundation for the Study of Group Decision Support Systems." Management Science 33, no. 5 (May 1987).

Dhar, Vasant, and Roger Stein. Intelligent Decision Support Methods: The Science of Knowledge Work. Upper Saddle River, NJ: Prentice Hall (1997).

Earl, Michael. "Knowledge Management Strategies: Toward a Taxonomy." Journal of Management Information Systems 18, no. 1 (Summer 2001).

Franchesi, Katherine, Ronald M. Lee, Stelios H. Zanakis, and David Hinds. "Engaging Group E-Learning in Virtual Worlds." Journal of Management Information Systems 26, No. 1 (Summer 2009).

Frangos, Alex." New Dimensions in Design." The Wall Street Journal (July 7, 2004).

Griffith, Terri L., John E. Sawyer, and Margaret A Neale. "Virtualness and Knowledge in Teams: Managing the Love Triangle of Organizations, Individuals, and Information Technology." MIS Quarterly 27, no. 2 (June 2003).

Grover, Varun and Thomas H. Davenport. "General Perspectives on Knowledge Management: Fostering a Research Agenda." Journal of Management Information Systems 18, no. 1 (Summer 2001).

Henschen, Doug. "In a Down Economy, Companies Turn to Real-Time Analytics to Track Demand," Information Week (February 28, 2009).

Henschen, Doug. "Next-Gen BI Is Here." Information Week (August 31. 2009).

Holland, John H. "Genetic Algorithms." Scientific American (July 1992).

Housel Tom and Arthur A. Bell. Measuring and Managing Knowledge. New York: McGraw-Hill (2001).

Jander, Mary. "The Web 2.0 Balancing Act." Information Week (February 16, 2009).

Jarvenpaa, Sirkka L. and D. Sandy Staples. "Exploring Perceptions of Organizational Ownership of Information and Expertise."Journal of Management Information Systems 18, no. 1 (Summer 2001).

Jones, Quentin, Gilad Ravid, and Sheizaf Rafaeli. "Information Overload and the Message Dynamics of Online Interaction Spaces: A Theoretical Model and Empirical Exploration." Information Systems Research 15, no. 2 (June 2004).

Kankanhalli, Atreyi, Frasiska Tanudidjaja, Juliana Sutanto, and Bernard C.Y Tan."The Role of IT in Successful Knowledge Management Initiatives." Communications of the ACM 46, no. 9 (September 2003).

King, William R., Peter V. Marks, Jr. and Scott McCoy. "The Most Important Issues in Knowledge Management." Communications of the ACM 45, no.9 (September 2002).

Kuo, R.J., K. Chang, and S.Y.Chien."Integration and Self-Organizing Feature Maps and Genetic-Algorithm-Based Clustering Method for Market Segmentation." Journal of Organizational Computing and Electronic Commerce 14, no. 1 (2004).

Kwok, Ron Chi-Wai, Jian Ma, and Douglas R. Vogel."Effects of Group Support Systems and Content Facilitation on Knowledge Acquisition." Journal of Management Information Systems 19, no. 3 (Winter 2002-3).

Leidner, Dorothy E., and Joyce Elam. "The Impact of Executive Information Systems on Organizational Design, Intelligence, and Decision Making." Organization Science 6, no. 6 (November-December 1995).

Leonard-Barton, Dorothy and Walter Swap. "Deep Smarts.' Harvard Business Review (September 1, 2004).

Lev, Baruch. "Sharpening the Intangibles Edge." Harvard Business Review (June 1, 2004).

Markoff, John. "The Coming Superbrain." The New York Times (May 24, 2009).

Markus, M. Lynne. "Toward a Theory of Knowledge Reuse: Types of Knowledge Reuse Situations and Factors in Reuse Success." Journal of Management Information Systems 18, no. 1 (Summer 2001).

Maryam Alavi and Dorothy E. Leidner. "Knowledge Management and Knowledge Management Systems." MIS Quarterly 25, no. 1 (March 2001).

McKay, Lauren. "Decisions, Decisions." Customer Relationship Management (May 2009).

Nunamaker, Jay, Robert O. Briggs, Daniel D. Mittleman, Douglas R. Vogel, and Pierre A. Balthazard. "Lessons from a Dozen Years of Group Support Systems Research: A Discussion of Lab and Field Findings." Journal of Management Information Systems 13, no. 3 (Winter 1997).

Orlikowski, Wanda J. "Knowing in Practice: Enacting a Collective Capability in Distributed Organizing." Organization Science 13, no. 3 (May-June 2002).

Sadeh, Norman, David W. Hildum, and Dag Kjenstad."Agent-Based E-Supply Chain Decision Support." Journal of Organizational Computing and Electronic Commerce 13, no. 3 & 4 (2003)

Samuelson, Douglas A. and Charles M. Macal. "Agent-Based Simulation." OR/MS Today (August 2006).

Schultze, Ulrike and Dorothy Leidner."Studying Knowledge Management in Information Systems Research: Discourses and Theoretical Assumptions." MIS Quarterly 26, no. 3 (September 2002).

Schwabe, Gerhard. "Providing for Organizational Memory in Computer-Supported Meetings." Journal of Organizational Computing and Electronic Commerce 9, no. 2 and 3 (1999).

Simon, H. A. The New Science of Management Decision. New York: Harper & Row (1960).

Softscape. " Dtac Selects Softscape's Learning Management Platform to Drive Employee Engagement." (October 20, 2009).

Steel, Emily. "Modeling Tools Stretch Ad Dollars." The Wall Street Journal (May 18, 2009).

Tiwana, Amrit. The Knowledge Management Toolkit: Orchestrating IT, Strategy, and Knowledge Management Platforms 2e. Upper Saddle River NJ: Prentice-Hall (2003).

Tsai, Jessica. "Intelligence in the Cloud." Customer Relationship Management (August 2009).

Turban, Efraim, Ramesh Sharda, Jay E. Aronson, and David King. Business Intelligence. Upper Saddle River, NJ: Prentice Hall (2008).

Wakefield, Julie. "Complexity's Business Model." Scientific American (January 2001).

Walczak, Stephen."An Emprical Analysis of Data Requirements for Financial Forecasting with Neural Networks." Journal of Management Information Systems 17, no. 4 (Spring 2001).

Wang, Huaiqing, John Mylopoulos, and Stephen Liao. "Intelligent Agents and Financial Risk Monitoring Systems." Communications of the ACM 45, no. 3 (March 2002).

Zack, Michael H "Rethinking the Knowledge-Based Organization." MIS Sloan Management Review 44, no. 4 (Summer 2003).

Zadeh, Lotfi A. "The Calculus of Fuzzy If/Then Rules." AI Expert (March 1992).

CHAPTER 11

Alter, Allan E. "I.T. Outsourcing: Expect the Unexpected." CIO Insight (March 7, 2007).

Andres, Howard P., and Robert W. Zmud. "A Contingency Approach to Software Project Coordination." Journal of Management Information Systems 18, no. 3 (Winter 2001-2002).

Armstrong, Deborah J. and Bill C. Hardgrove. "Understanding Mindshift Learning: The Transition to Object-Oriented Development." MIS Quarterly 31, no. 3 (September 2007).

Aron, Ravi, Eric K.Clemons, and Sashi Reddi. "Just Right Outsourcing: Understanding and Managing Risk." *Journal of Management Information Systems* 22, no. 1 (Summer 2005).

Ashrafi Noushin and Hessam Ashrafi. Object-Oriented Systems Analysis and Design. Upper Saddle River, NY: Prentice-Hall (2009).

Avison, David E., and Guy Fitzgerald. "Where Now for Development Methodologies?" *Communications of the ACM* 41, no. 1 (January 2003).

Babcock, Charles. "Platform as a Service: What Vendors Offer." Information Week (October 3, 2009).

Biehl, Markus. "Success Factors For Implementing Global Information Systems." *Communications of the ACM* 50, No. 1 (January 2007).

Brewer, Jeffrey and Kevin Dittman. Methods of IT Project Management. Upper Saddle River, NJ: Prentice-Hall (2010).

Chickowski, Ericka. "Projects Gone Wrong." Baseline (May 15, 2009).

Delone, William H., and Ephraim R. McLean. "The Delone and McLean Model of Information Systems Success: A Ten-Year Update. *Journal of Management Information Systems* 19, no. 4 (Spring 2003).

Dibbern, Jess, Jessica Winkler, and Armin Heinzl. "Explaining Variations in Client Extra Costs between Software Projects Offshored to India." MIS Quarterly 32, no. 2 (June 2008).

Erickson, Jonathan. "Dr Dobb's Report: Agile Development." Information Week (April 27, 2009).

Feeny, David, Mary Lacity, and Leslie P. Willcocks. "Taking the Measure of Outsourcing Providers." MIT Sloan Management Review 46, no. 3 (Spring 2005).

Gefen, David and Erarn Carmel. "Is the World Really Flat? A Look at Offshoring in an Online Programming Marketplace." MIS Quarterly 32, no. 2 (June 2008).

Goo, Jahyun, Rajive Kishore, H. R. Rao, and Kichan Nam. The Role of Service Level Agreements in Relational Management of Information Technology Outsourcing: An Empirical Study." MIS Quarterly 33, No. 1 (March 2009).

Hahn, Eugene D., Jonathan P. Doh, and Kraiwinee Bunyaratavej. "The Evolution of Risk in Information Systems Offshoring: The Impact of Home Country Risk, Firm Learning, and Competitive Dynamics. MIS Quarterly 33, No. 3 (September 2009).

Hickey, Ann M., and Alan M. Davis. "A Unified Model of Requirements Elicitation." *Journal of Management Information Systems* 20, no. 4 (Spring 2004).

Hoffer, Jeffrey, Joey George, and Joseph Valacich. *Modern Systems Analysis and Design*, 5th ed. Upper Saddle River, NJ: Prentice Hall (2008).

Information Builders."Elie Tahari Ltd. Unveils New End-User Reporting Framework." www.informationbuilders.com, accessed October 21, 2007.

Jeffrey, Mark, and Ingmar Leliveld. "Best Practices in IT Portfolio Management." *MIT Sloan Management Review* 45, no. 3 (Spring 2004).

Kendall, Kenneth E., and Julie E. Kendall. *Systems Analysis and Design*, 8th ed. Upper Saddle River, NJ: Prentice Hall (2008).

Kettinger, William J., and Choong C. Lee. "Understanding the IS-User Divide in IT Innovation." *Communications of the ACM* 45, no.2 (February 2002).

Kim, Hee Woo and Atreyi Kankanhalli. "Investigating User Resistance to Information Systems Implementation: A Status Quo Bias Perspective." MIS Quarterly 33, No. 3 (September 2009).

Kirsch, Laurie J. "Deploying Common Systems Globally: The Dynamic of Control." Information Systems Research 15, no. 4 (December 2004).

Koh, Christine, Song Ang, and Detmar W. Straub. "IT Outsourcing Success: A Psychological Contract Perspective." *Information Systems Research* 15 no. 4 (December 2004).

Lapointe, Liette, and Suzanne Rivard. "A Multilevel Model of Resistance to Information Technology Implementation." *MIS Quarterly* 29, no. 3 (September2005).

Levina, Natalia, and Jeanne W. Ross. "From the Vendor's Perspective: Exploring the Value Proposition in Information Technology Outsourcing." MIS QuarterlyMIS Quarterly 27, no. 3 (September 2003).

Liang, Huigang, Nilesh Sharaf, Qing Hu, and Yajiong Xue. "Assimilation of Enterprise Systems: The Effect of Institutional Pressures and the Mediating Role of Top Management." MIS Quarterly 31, no 1 (March 2007).

Limayem, Moez, Mohamed Khalifa, and Wynne W. Chin. "Case Tools Usage and Impact on System Development Performance." *Journal of Organizational Computing and Electronic Commerce* 14, no. 3 (2004).

Majchrzak, Ann, Cynthia M. Beath, and Ricardo A. Lim. "Managing Client Dialogues during Information Systems Design to Facilitate Client Learning." MIS QuarterlyMIS Quarterly 29, no. 4 (December 2005).

Murphy, Chris."A Different Way to See Development." Information Week (January 19, 2009).

Nelson, H. James, Deborah J. Armstrong, and Kay M. Nelson. Patterns of Transition: The Shift from Traditional to Object-Oriented Development." Journal of Management Information Systems 25, No. 4 (Spring 2009).

Overby, Stephanie. "The Hidden Costs of Offshore Outsourcing," *CIO Magazine* (September 1, 2003).

Palmer, Jonathan W. "Web Site Usability, Design and Performance Metrics." *Information Systems Research* 13, no.3 (September 2002).

Rai, Arun, Sandra S. Lang, and Robert B. Welker. "Assessing the Validity of IS Success Models: An Empirical Test and Theoretical Analysis." *Information Systems Research* 13, no. 1 (March 2002).

Rapoza, Jim. "Next-Gen Project Management." eWeek (March 3, 2008).

Ravichandran, T., and Marcus A. Rothenberger. "Software Reuse Strategies and Component Markets." *Communications of the ACM* 46, no. 8 (August 2003).

Robey, Daniel, Jeanne W. Ross, and Marie-Claude Boudreau. "Learning to Implement Enterprise Systems: An Exploratory Study of the Dialectics of Change." *Journal of Management Information Systems* 19, no. 1 (Summer 2002).

Ryan, Sherry D., David A. Harrison, and Lawrence L Schkade. "Information Technology Investment Decisions: When Do Cost and Benefits in the Social Subsystem Matter?" *Journal of Management Information Systems* 19, no. 2 (Fall 2002).

Sakthivel, S. "Managing Risk in Offshore Systems Development." *Communications of the ACM* 50, No. 4 (April 2007).

Sauer, Chris, Andrew Gemino, and Blaize Horner Reich. "The Impact of Size and Volatility on IT Project Performance. "*Communications of the ACM* 50, no. 11 (November 2007).

Sharma, Rajeev and Philip Yetton. "The Contingent Effects of Training, Technical Complexity, and Task Interdependence on Successful Information Systems Implementation." *MIS Quarterly* 31, no. 2 (June 2007).

Silva, Leiser and Rudy Hirschheim. "Fighting Against Windmills: Strategic Information Systems and Organizational Deep Structures." *MIS Quarterly* 31, no. 2 (June 2007).

Sircar, Sumit, Sridhar P. Nerur, and Radhakanta Mahapatra. "Revolution or Evolution? A Comparison of Object-Oriented and Structured Systems Development Methods." *MIS Quarterly* 25, no. 4 (December 2001).

Smith, H. Jeff, Mark Keil, and Gordon Depledge. "Keeping Mum as the Project Goes Under." *Journal of Management Information Systems* 18, no. 2 (Fall 2001).

Schwalbe, Kathy. *Information Technology Project Management, 6/e.* Course Technology (2010).

Swanson, E. Burton, and Enrique Dans. "System Life Expectancy and the Maintenance Effort: Exploring Their Equilibration." *MIS Quarterly* 24, no. 2 (June 2000).

Turetken, Ozgur, David Schuff, Ramesh Sharda, and Terence T. Ow. "Supporting Systems Analysis and Design through Fisheye Views." *Communications of the ACM* 47, no. 9 (September 2004).

Venkatesh, Viswanath, Michael G. Morris, Gordon B Davis, and Fred D. Davis. "User Acceptance of Information Technology: Toward a Unified View." *MIS Quarterly* 27, no. 3 (September 2003).

Wang, Eric T.G., Gary Klein, and James J. Jiang. "ERP Misfit: Country of Origin and Organizational Factors." *Journal of Management Information Systems* 23, No. 1 (Summer 2006).

Wipro Technologies. "Case Studies: Pinacle West."www.wipro.com, accessed October 21, 2007.

Wulf, Volker, and Matthias Jarke. "The Economics of End-User Development." *Communications of the ACM* 47, no. 9 (September 2004).

Xia, Weidong, and Gwanhoo Lee. "Complexity of Information Systems Development Projects." *Journal of Management Information Systems* 22, no. 1 (Summer 2005).

"Winning the IT Portfolio Battle," Projects@Work (September 6, 2007).

Zhu, Kevin, Kenneth L. Kraemer, Sean Xu, and Jason Dedrick. "Information Technology Payoff in E-Business Environments: An International Perspective on Value Creation of E-business in the Financial Services Industry." *Journal of Management Information Systems* 21, no. 1 (Summer 2004).

CHAPTER 12

Angst, Corey M. and Ritu Agarwal. "Adoption of Electronic Health Records in the Presence of Privacy Concerns: The Elaboration Likelihood Model and Individual Persuasion." MIS Quarterly 33, No. 2 (June 2009).

Baumstein, Avi. "New Tools Close Holes in Cam-Spam." Information Week (February 23, 2009).

Bhattacharjee, Sudip, Ram D. Gopal, and G. Lawrence Sanders. "Digital Music and Online Sharing: Software Piracy 2.0?" Communications of the ACM 46, no.7 (July 2003).

Borland, John, "The Technology That Toppled Eliot Spitzer," Technology Review (March 19, 2008).

Bowen, Jonathan. "The Ethics of Safety-Critical Systems."Communications of the ACM 43, no. 3 (April 2000).

Brown Bag Software vs. Symantec Corp. 960 F2D 1465 (Ninth Circuit, 1992).

Business Software Alliance. "Fifth Annual BSA and IDC Global Software Piracy Study." (May 2008).

Chellappa, Ramnath K. and Shivendu Shivendu. "An Economic Model of Privacy: A Property Rights Approach to Regulatory Choices for Online Personalization." Journal of Management Information Systems 24, no. 3 (Winter 2008).

Culnan, Mary J. and Cynthia Clark Williams. "How Ethics Can Enhance Organizational Privacy." MIS Quarterly 33, No. 4 (December 2009).

Downes, Larry. "Avoiding Web Rocks and Shoals." CIO Insight (May 2008).

Farmer, Dan and Charles C. Mann. "Surveillance Nation." Part I Technology Review (April 2003) and Part II (Technology Review (May 2003).

Federal Trade Commission. "FTC Staff Revises Online Behavioral Advertising Principles." February 12, 2009.

Foley, John. "P2P Peril." Information Week (March 17, 2008).

Goodman, Joshua, Gordon V. Cormack, and David Heckerman. "Spam and the Ongoing Battle for the Inbox." Communications of the ACM 50, No. 2 (February 2007).

Gorman, Siobhan. "NSA's Domestic Spying Grows As Agency Sweeps Up Data." The Wall Street Journal (March 10, 2008).

Grimes, Galen A. "Compliance with the CAN-SPAM Act of 2003." Communications of the ACM 50, No. 2 (February 2007).

Holmes, Allan. The Profits in Privacy. CIO Magazine (March 15, 2006).

Hsieh, J.J. Po-An, Arun Rai, and Mark Keil. "Understanding Digital Inequality: Comparing Continued Use Behavioral Models of the Socio-Economically Advantaged and Disadvantaged." MIS Quarterly 32, no. 1 (March 2008).

Jackson, Linda A., Alexander von Eye, Gretchen Barbatsis, Frank Biocca, Hiram E. Fitzgerald, and Yong Zhao. "The Impact of Internet Use on

the Other Side of the Digital Divide." Communications of the ACM 47, no. 7 (July 2004).

Jackson, Thomas W., Ray Dawson, and Darren Wilson. "Understanding Email Interaction Increases Organizational Productivity." Communications of the ACM 46, no. 8 (August 2003).

Laudon, Kenneth C. and Carol Guercio Traver. E-Commerce: Business, Technology, Society 6th Edition. Upper Saddle River, NJ: Prentice-Hall (2010).

Laudon, Kenneth C. Dossier Society: Value Choices in the Design of National Information Systems. New York: Columbia University Press (1986b).

Lee, Jintae. "An End-User Perspective on File-Sharing Systems," Communications of the ACM 46, no. 2 (February 2003).

Mann, Catherine L. "What Global Sourcing Means for U.S. I.T. Workers and for the U.S. Economy." Communications of the ACM 47, no. 7 (July 2004).

Martin, Jr. David M., Richard M. Smith, Michael Brittain, Ivan Fetch, and Hailin Wu."The Privacy Practices of Web Browser Extensions." Communications of the ACM 44, no. 2 (February 2001).

Nord, G. Daryl, Tipton F. McCubbins, and Jeretta Horn Nord. "E-Monitoring in the Workplace: Privacy, Legislation, and Surveillance Software. Communications of the ACM 49, No. 8 (August 2006).

Okerson, Ann. "Who Owns Digital Works?" Scientific American (July 1996).

Payton, Fay Cobb."Rethinking the Digital Divide." Communications of the ACM 46, no. 6 (June 2003)

Rapoza, Jim. "Web Bug Alert." EWeek (June 15, 2009).

Risen, James and Eric Lichtblau. "E-Mail Surveillance Renews Concerns in Congress." The New York Times (June 17, 2009).

Rifkin, Jeremy. "Watch Out for Trickle-Down Technology." The New York Times (March 16, 1993).

Rigdon, Joan E. "Frequent Glitches in New Software Bug Users." The Wall Street Journal (January 18, 1995).

Sipior, Janice C. "Unintended Invitation: Organizational Wi-Fi Use by External Roaming Users." Communications of the ACM 50, no.8 (August 2007).

Smith, H. Jeff, and John Hasnas. "Ethics and Information Systems: The Corporate Domain." MIS Quarterly 23, no. 1 (March 1999).

Smith, H. Jeff. "The Shareholders vs. Stakeholders Debate." MIS Sloan Management Review 44, no. 4 (Summer 2003).

Sophos Plc. "Security Threat Report//Q1 08." (2008).

Steel, Emily and Vishesh Kumar. "Targeted Ads Raise Privacy Concerns." The Wall Street Journal (July 8, 2008)

Story, Louise. "To Aim Ads, Web Is Keeping Closer Eye on You." The New York Times (March 10, 2008).

Thomas, Jennifer. "'Cell Phone Elbow'-a New Ill for the Wired Age." Yahoo! News (6/2/09).

Tuttle, Brad, Adrian Harrell, and Paul Harrison. "Moral Hazard, Ethical Considerations, and the Decision to Implement an Information System." Journal of Management Information Systems 13, no. 4 (Spring 1997).

United States Department of Health, Education, and Welfare. Records, Computers, and the Rights of Citizens. Cambridge: MIT Press (1973).

Urbaczewski, Andrew and Leonard M. Jessup. "Does Electronic Monitoring of Employee Internet Usage Work?" Communications of the ACM 45, no. 1 (January 2002).

Vara, Vauhini."New Sites Make It Easier to Spy on Your Friends." The Wall Street Journal (June 4, 2008).

Vijayan, Jaikumar. "TD Bank Struggles to Fix Computer Glitch." Computerworld, October 2, 2009.

Index

Subject Index

Photo and Screen Shot Credits

BUSINESS CASES AND INTERACTIVE SESSIONS

Here are the cases and Interactive Sessions you'll find in the ninth edition of *Essentials of Management Information Systems*. These cases and Interactive Sessions cover new developments in information systems and real-world company applications of systems.

Chapter 1: Business Information Systems in Your Career

The New Yankee Stadium Looks to the Future
MIS in Your Pocket
UPS Competes Globally with Information Technology
What's the Buzz on Smart Grids?

Chapter 2: Global E-Business and Collaboration

The Tata Nano Makes History Using Digital Manufacturing
"Fresh, Hot, Fast"—Can Information Systems Help Johnny's Lunch Go National?
Virtual Meetings: Smart Management
Collaboration at Coca-Cola: It's the Real Thing

Chapter 3: Achieving Competitive Advantage with Information Systems

Verizon or AT&T: Which Company Has the Best Digital Strategy?
What Do Credit Card Companies Know About You?
Will TV Succumb to the Internet?
EBay Fine-Tunes Its Strategy

Chapter 4: IT Infrastructure: Hardware and Software

Cars.Com's IT Infrastructure Drives Rapid Business Growth
Is Green Computing Good for Business?
New to the Touch
Salesforce.com: Cloud Software Services Go Mainstream

Chapter 5: Foundations of Business Intelligence: Databases and Information Management

R.R. Donnelley Tries to Master Its Data
The IRS Uncovers Tax Fraud with a Data Warehouse
Credit Bureau Errors—Big People Problems
Trouble with the Terrorist Watch-List Database

Chapter 6: Telecommunications, the Internet, and Wireless Technology

Los Angeles International Airport Soars with New Networking Technology
Should Network Neutrality Continue?
Monitoring Employees on Networks: Unethical or Good Business?
Google Versus Microsoft: Clash of the Technology Titans